The
Oxford Book
of American Prose

Chosen & Edited by
Mark van Doren

London & New York
Oxford University Press
1932

COPYRIGHT 1932
BY OXFORD UNIVERSITY PRESS
NEW YORK, INC.

PRINTED IN THE UNITED STATES OF AMERICA

PREFACE

IF there are only seventy-three pieces of prose in this book, as against the six hundred in Sir Arthur Quiller-Couch's *Oxford Book of English Prose*, the reason is not merely — or indeed at all — that I considered English prose by so much the richer thing. It is richer; but the ratio, I imagine, is not eight to one. In the matter of quantity there is no man who could say with the certainty of experience which literature surpassed the other. The older one, we might guess; yet American prose is three hundred years old, and at least in the latter half of that life it has become vastly voluminous. So in the matter of quality would it be difficult to make a safe comparison. The prose of England has its glories. What prose has more? Ours has not so many. Yet we have Roger Williams, Cotton Mather, and Jonathan Edwards; we have Emerson, Hawthorne, Melville, and Thoreau; we have Lincoln and Mark Twain and Mencken; we have Henry Adams, Henry James, and Santayana. It is better, perhaps, that no comparison be made; and I have made none.

It is more to the point to say that from the beginning I have worked on a different scale and plan from that which Sir Arthur adopted. Believing with him that the power of prose makes itself chiefly felt in the long passage, in the complete effort, I have gone farther than he has gone in the demonstration of this faith. Almost everywhere, that is to say, I have restricted myself to pieces which have length and completeness. Whenever it was possible, and usually it was, I refused to abridge an essay, a chapter, or a tale. I avoided, in short, the purple patch.

The purple patch, as Sir Arthur very nobly proves, has its ancient sanctions and uses, and I am so far from denying this as to have included as many as I could. But I resisted the temptation to represent an author by strings of them torn out of their surroundings. I preferred to leave them in the places where they were born and where they still, I am convinced, are most at home and most effective. This procedure limited their number. Emerson and Thoreau, for instance, could have been given a hundred glittering paragraphs between them instead of the four extended pieces which here come under their names. But it seemed better so. The final paragraph of Emerson's *Illusions* is capable of standing magnificently alone; yet from the plateau of the preceding pages it rises to a height which would never be expected by one who had not walked all the way from the plain of the first sentence. Prose is first and last a spacious thing, an experience which takes time, and the power of such a paragraph as I have mentioned is something for which one had better be prepared. There are paragraphs of the same sort in the *Personal Narrative* of Jonathan Edwards. For intensity of feeling and perfection of phrase they have few rivals in all of English prose, and one would know this if one met them without a context. One knows it still better, however, when they appear in their proper place — imbedded in a discourse every syllable of which is impassioned, and all the syllables of which conspire to increase not only the meaning but the music of the stretches in question. The context itself, incidentally, has beauty and strength — is true blue even if it is not purple. I must hasten to say that I have nowhere, so far as I was aware, printed bad prose merely because it led to prose which was better. And I must add the confession that in a few cases after all I have represented an author by the briefest of compositions — Lincoln, for example, who excelled in the writing of single paragraphs, and whose "House Divided" speech I have cut to its famous exordium. So, naturally, with E. W. Howe, since he is at his best in the aphorism or the newspaper paragraph; with Frank Moore Colby, who was as short-winded as he was wicked; and with William Bartram, whose passages on the wonderful fauna of East Florida I have extracted from the long chapters containing them precisely as Coleridge extracted them when his

PREFACE

imagination was preparing to produce *The Ancient Mariner* and *Kubla Khan*.

Committed as I was to the extended passage, I was forced to be especially rigorous in the selection of authors to be represented. Now at the end there are forty-eight. In the beginning there were hundreds, and I do not doubt that in the process of elimination I have been guilty of injustices which I could never explain to readers who will miss their favorites. I can only say that I sought everywhere the qualities of grace, intelligence, sinew, sonorousness, and skill. If any writer had possessed all of these virtues, as no one quite did, he would of course have been admitted without challenge. The remaining question was always this: What writer possesses any of them in a high and pure degree? Or it might take another form: What writer, no matter how famous or interesting generally, has failed nevertheless to produce a piece of prose which will serve the purposes of the volume — stand independently here, have immediate meaning, and exhibit one or more of the qualities necessary to good prose? This question, or rather the answers to it, eliminated a number of scientists, philosophers, theologians, and writers on society or law. It eliminated, too, a great many novelists, as it did nearly all of the literary critics. Frequently a novel was discovered to be, so to speak, all context; and the trouble with literary criticism was that it took its departure from other writing which the reader would not have before him. It was derivative, and one of my prejudices operated against anything which did not contain all of its meaning within itself. Theodore Dreiser, whom I consider with Cooper to have displayed the largest amount of talent in American fiction to date, I tried very hard to include. But I could find no portion of him that was good enough as prose. He is one of the greatest American writers of prose; his is not by any means, however, good prose. The same thing can almost be said of Cooper, yet I did decide that the last chapter of *The Prairie* merited sequestration. I should add that I never to my knowledge read any special meaning into the word American. Any prose written in America I took to be American prose, and I judged it merely as prose. I was not patriotic.

At the same time I could not help being interested in the subject matter of a selection, and when other things were equal I was not above choosing something for the reason — always among a variety of others — that it was native. I made no point of this, and frequently in the later sections I was drawn to pieces which were critical of America — a native thing to be, as it happens. Uppermost, however, was the desire to make the book in itself good reading. I hope that it can be read straight through — or, failing this, that it can be opened anywhere and followed with the simplest kind of interest.

It would be hoping too much to hope that the volume, microscopic as it is in comparison with the imaginary volume which would hold all American prose so far written, is also microcosmic with respect to that prose. Yet I have kept the matter ever in mind. And now that I read the contents again it seems to me that in some measure they do represent or express the larger body out of which they were taken.

In the first place, to commence with something negative, there is very little stuff here in the grand style. This is proper, since American writers have usually avoided the grand style — possibly to their loss. Possibly to their loss; yet in doing so they have spoken truly for a nation which is both susceptible to eloquence and suspicious of it, so that any American is likely to be a master in the art of burlesque, in the science of understatement. Lincoln is our best orator because he is so far from being an orator at all in the popular sense of the term. He seems to be interested in nothing save the necessity of making himself clear. Not that this alone would have made him an artist, as W. C. Brownell might say (see No. 52). No, he had a voice, too, and he kept it miraculously tuned, and it uttered sentences which, whatever their plainness, we cannot forget. But one of the pleasures of reading him is the pleasure of not hearing him say certain

PREFACE

things in certain ways. The address at Gettysburg and the close of the second inaugural address are no more beautiful than the opening of the "House Divided" speech, or the letter to Greeley, or for that matter any of the letters and telegrams.

There is an important line of American writers whose business it has been to grin at all big things and to grimace in the presence of grandeur, whether of style or of pretensions. I have represented this line as fully as I could, since it has the distinction of striking the characteristic note in American humor and since it has given us some of our best writers by any test if the test of splendor be excluded. It runs all the way from Nathaniel Ward to Ring Lardner, and the seventy-first selection here, by Van Wyck Brooks, is in part a commentary upon it. Nathaniel Ward, setting off firecrackers beneath the noses of those graver seventeenth-century persons who argued in organ tones about liberty and authority; Benjamin Franklin, discoursing thinly and coolly as the unbothered man of the eighteenth-century world that he was; David Crockett, impudently and ungrammatically loquacious about his life (if it was Crockett himself who wrote his *Autobiography;* but it does not matter, for some American did); Lincoln, as I have said; Artemus Ward, who trimmed every intellectual or emotional excess of his day with a clean, almost invisible blade of parody; Mark Twain, who was himself an ocean of eloquence but whose wit managed always to ride the waves; E. W. Howe, whose laconic sentences scatter constant salt from Kansas; Frank Moore Colby, who never missed an absurdity; George Ade, almost epic in the scope of his satire; H. L. Mencken, as sensible as he is satanic; Ring Lardner, solvent for meanness that has grown pretentious — these men are of inestimable importance, not only to our prose but to our life. It is to such as they that we ultimately pay our respect, for we are aware that pompousness lies always in wait for us, we know our weakness for it, and we are grateful to these wits who save us from it.

PREFACE

Even Emerson, exalted as he is, borrows from the line and takes his final flavor from it; and Thoreau is indebted to it for the seasoning which makes him almost the best of all Americans who have written prose. Elsewhere it simply gives our prose that speed which is its predominant characteristic — speed, and directness, and a clarity both sensible and nervous. If thinness goes along with this, and a lack of color, and an almost complete absence of aroma, then so be it. The blame, perhaps, can be placed upon the climate of North America. I would not place it there; nor would I speak of blame.

Not that we are altogether without writers of prose who play upon intricate instruments of deep and mysterious sound. There is always Melville, for instance, who is represented here by three chapters from *Moby Dick* — chapters, however, which have the speed I have spoken of, along with a color and a complexity rarely to be found elsewhere in American literature. Even Melville goes like the wind, as Emerson does, however choppy his sentences and however many-hued his mind. These two mystics, with Edwards before them and Henry Adams after them — desiccated though the latter be — and with Santayana experiencing his rational visions slightly to one side, contribute a note which it would be fatal if we did not hear. Melville, to return to the man of all these who is most in vogue at the moment, might have been represented in addition by a chapter from *Pierre* or by the whole of *Billy Budd,* the masterpiece which he wrote during his last year. But the prose of *Pierre* is so little controlled as to be the best illustration, page after page, of Melville's besetting vice, blank verse. And *Billy Budd* is a narrative too organic in all its parts to admit abridgement.

Whenever I came to narrative I was forced either to find a tale which could be reproduced in its entirety, as in the cases of Poe's *William Wilson* and of Lardner's *I Can't Breathe,* or to look through some longer work for a section which, perhaps because it came at a pause in the story, or because for any reason it was expository and independent, stood alone.

PREFACE

I am not speaking of the numerous writers of biography, autobiography, and history who are here — Mather, Edwards, Woolman, Byrd, Irving, Prescott, Parkman, Adams, Crockett, Mark Twain, Ludwig Lewisohn, and Carl Van Doren — but rather of those who professedly were writing fiction. In the case of Stephen Crane it seemed to me that the chapters from the *Red Badge of Courage* which describe the hero's flight from battle had an integrity of their own; and in the case of Willa Cather I took for my purpose a portion of *The Song of the Lark* which I had always remembered quite independently of the narrative in which it is, to be sure, an incident. Hawthorne and Henry James I chose to represent on their discursive side alone, and Sherwood Anderson by the tale which he attributes to another in his autobiography.

I have said that literary criticism is slighted in the book. Yet there do appear the names of W. C. Brownell, Paul Elmer More, Stuart Sherman, T. S. Eliot, and Joseph Wood Krutch; and James Branch Cabell introduces himself in the guise of one who discusses literature rather than writes it. Mr. Cabell's discussion is general, which makes it proper for this volume; and so for the most part is all the criticism I have included. The essays of Sherman on Anatole France and of More on Thoreau are more general than might at first appear.

The line of writers about nature which runs here from William Bartram to John Muir is clearly a distinguished one. The gentle enthusiasms of Bartram gave way in another century to the ferocious zeal of Audubon, who with his long black hair streaming behind him plunged through the forests or crossed the mighty rivers of the Middle West in search of birds and quadrupeds. Soon, in a more northern corner of the country, Thoreau was to invite his cool soul among the trees and weeds of Concord; and Lowell was to emulate one of his favorite English authors, Gilbert White of Selborne, in the task of observing the creatures who came day by day to his study garden. There have been nature-writers galore in later days. But with the exception of John Muir, whose passionate attachments to the wild life of Wisconsin, Florida, and the Far West made him, since he also was an artist in letters, one of the most moving of American prose writers, these inheritors of a tradition have failed wholly to live up to it. John Burroughs almost did, but not quite; his essays, while pleasant, somehow miss the excitement of those older works. For all of Bartram's gentleness there was fire enough in him to take him like a comet into the mind of young Coleridge at the end of the eighteenth century. Audubon is noteworthy not merely for the fidelity with which he describes the wild turkey and the passenger pigeon but for the worshipful posture he struck before an America that seemed to him a golden place in a golden age. He burned with an utterly uncritical love of it, as in less degree another Frenchman, Crèvecoeur, had glowed in the previous century. As for Thoreau, he still is a flame at which the mind may brighten itself. But Thoreau was more than a writer about nature, best in that kind as he is. He was a philosopher and a moralist, too; and in his essay on civil disobedience he produced as scriptural a piece of anarchism as America is likely to see. I thought it important to reprint that essay along with a chapter from *Walden,* since neither by itself would have given the whole man. And the whole man is especially important to American prose.

The nature-writers, the novelists, the mystics, the humorists, the literary critics — these as they stand here divide the nineteenth century between them. Much of the century is left out of such an account. Politics is ignored, and economics, and science, and law, and society. But if my principles of selection were proper the fault lies not with me. And it would have been folly of the poorest sort, I still believe, to admit into the canon of this prose a piece of writing for the mere reason that it hailed from a significant field of intellectual activity.

The eighteenth century shines in these pages through a small but to me brilliant constellation of personalities. No portion of American time is more interesting, no aspect of the

PREFACE

American literary scene more varied. There were thirteen colonies, but the number of cultures surviving and competing within them was even greater. The spectacle then is one of individuals rising here and there to speak for their respective worlds — small worlds, if we think in terms of geography and of population, but very considerable ones when we remember the thoughts they contained, and when we come into contact with the persons who thus raised their voices. No country at any time is without its profusion and confusion of intellectual strains. This is what makes literary history worth writing. And certainly nineteenth-century America presents a pattern which no casual eye may master. But the very fewness of the elements which composed the eighteenth-century mind, if it is allowable to employ such a phrase, and their clearness, and their distance apart — all of this produces an especially charming picture. Edwards and Woolman, for instance, look something alike in the vicinity of Franklin and Byrd, who are so different from them; yet in the vicinity of each other they become as different as Calvinism is from Quakerism. There was piety in both, and this is all that can be said by way of establishing a similarity. The quietism of Mount Holly has nothing to do with the deep, terrible joy which Edwards records in his *Personal Narrative,* or with the power of brain which was required to compose the theological treatises of his later years. In Woolman there is only the strength, great though it may be, of a stubborn mildness, an unconquerable sweetness. In Edwards there is the mightier and more complex strength of a man who could feel and think with an equal intensity, and who never paused from the labor of doing either.

So with Byrd and Franklin, who resemble each other only in that they are worldly men as Edwards and Woolman are not. Left together they separate — Franklin going in the direction of cities and shops and the trading class, Byrd going in the direction of a landed estate where books arrive periodically from England and where upon occasion there come other landed aristocrats with whom conversation may be had. The cynicism of the one has nothing to do with that of the other, just as their gallantries are the very different gallantries of a gentleman and a philosopher. Likewise the American enthusiasm of one foreigner, Tom Paine, departs at many points from that of another foreigner, Crèvecoeur. The first man is doctrinaire, abstract; the second man is all feeling and refined observation. And meanwhile Jefferson is preparing his vision of an agrarian civilization which shall be — but it has never been — at the same time democratic and dignified.

The seventeenth century was more prolific than can be indicated by the four relatively brief selections from its prose which I have given. It argued at great length about a number of things political and ecclesiastical; it wrote a voluminous record of exploration, settlement, and Indian captivity; it preached many sermons and distributed many tracts. I have treated it so sparely because for the most part it wrote a heavy prose which ornaments could not relieve, and because much of what it said cannot be counted on any more to attract the literary visitor. But I trust that there is enough life in the theme of liberty to carry any reader through the pages on which Nathaniel Ward shakes his fantastic Elizabethan pen at those who are so idiotic as to love this harlot tolerance, on which John Winthrop distinguishes classically, suavely between two kinds of liberty, on which Roger Williams hurls his thunderous imprecations against the authors of the Bloody Tenent, and on which Cotton Mather recounts the conviction of a witch. These four men are as various in their prose as they are excellent. This fact may do something to make up for the exclusion of such contemporaries as William Bradford, Thomas Morton, Thomas Shepard, William Penn, Mary Rowlandson, and Increase Mather.

A reader of the volume is more likely to exclaim, however, against the exclusion of writers contemporary with himself. That there are many so excluded I am in a particularly good position to know. And I am well aware that a dozen, perhaps, should be here who are absent. I can only plead the immemorial fact — for I take it to be a fact — that no man can know his own age as any succeeding age will know it. He may know it better for the purpose of living in it, but he cannot prophesy what it is that future men will wish they had been alive then to see — what authors, for instance, they would have liked to be present to appreciate. I am not doubtful, naturally, about anyone I have included. My doubts about the others were long debated in my mind, on grounds that in no case were simple or at any rate wholly personal. Sometimes there was the difficulty of finding a single piece of prose in which its author had disentangled himself sufficiently from the threads of transient controversy. At the moment his article or his essay had done its work perfectly; now at this distance, however, it suffered from having been so well subdued to the circumstances which produced it. In other cases I discovered that the charm or the force of something I once had read was no longer to be felt in it — another instance, shall we say, of art that serves its own hour better that it will ever serve another. This whole question, of course, is complex. For it seems certain that an artist who sets out to please posterity will please no-body — not even his own generation. He must be true or beautiful in the eyes of men like himself before he can be valuable to mankind. The generations are very much like one another; but no artist should know this too well. So, far from looking elsewhere than at the literature of con-troversy, I have looked chiefly there; or, to employ a broader term, I have concentrated my attention upon that literature which is marked by a strict contemporaneity. Edwards, Franklin, Emerson were contemporary to their readers — and they are to us also; but they should not be our contem-poraries now had they not been so in the beginning.

Of writers born since 1900 there is not one whose admirers will find him represented here by a story or a critical article, a hymn or a diatribe or a manifesto. This is not because I fail to find recent American literature interesting. It is

PREFACE

rather for the opposite reason — that choice became so difficult as almost to prescribe injustice and embarrassment. Also, there was the minor difficulty of deciding whether a given piece of new prose would or would not retain its meaning long enough to justify its presence between these covers. That much of the prose in question was good prose I am as far as possible from denying.

What good prose is must be very hard to say, since it has never been said. I make no attempt at definition, though I am willing to confess myself guided by certain convictions in the matter — convictions which may sound like instincts. In the first place I cannot give the name of good prose to prose whose subject matter does not interest me. In the second place I must find the mind of the writer engaging — not necessarily in agreement with my own on any point, but simply engaging, so that I shall feel sure of a willingness to hear this man talking about anything whatever, and at his own length. He must have a voice, a writing voice; one sign of which, if he has it, will be that there is never any doubt as to which words in his discourse are the emphatic ones. All of his words, for that matter, will have their importance; no man writes good prose if he makes it possible for the reader to overlook a single syllable or not to hear it. His words will come in rhythm, too. But the rhythm of prose is so subtle a thing that the most we can demand of it is a fitness with the thing being said and the man saying it. What the thing said was before it was said we may not know. We must have no doubt, however, that it has been said; and that we could not have said it ourselves.

MARK VAN DOREN

NEW YORK
1932

xvi

ACKNOWLEDGMENTS

For permission to include copyright passages in this volume, thanks are due to the following:

Horace Liveright, Inc., New York, for *The American Scene* from *Upstream* by Ludwig Lewisohn; Messrs. D. Appleton and Company, New York, for *The Flight* from *The Red Badge of Courage* by Stephen Crane; The Century Company, New York, for five letters by Abraham Lincoln (*to Horace Greeley, to Miss Fanny McCullough, to General Joseph Hooker* and two letters *to General Grant*) from the *Collected Works* by Abraham Lincoln, edited by Nicolay and Hay, and for *The Water-Ouzel* from *The Mountains of California* by John Muir; Messrs. Henry Holt and Company, New York, for *The Scepticism of Anatole France* from *On Contemporary Literature* by Stuart P. Sherman; B. W. Huebsch, Inc., for *"Highbrow" and "Lowbrow"* from *America's Coming-of-Age* by Van Wyck Brooks, published by The Viking Press, New York (1915); B. W. Huebsch, Inc., New York, and Jonathan Cape, Ltd., London, for *The Story Teller* from *A Story Teller's Story* by Sherwood Anderson, published by The Viking Press, New York (1924); B. W. Huebsch, Inc., and Martin Secker, Ltd., London, for *Conjured Spirit* from *Swift* by Carl Van Doren, published by The Viking Press, New York (1930); The Houghton Mifflin Company, Boston, for *The Ancient People* from *The Song of the Lark, Part IV, Chapters 2–4,* by Willa Sibert Cather, for *A Hermit's Note on Thoreau* from *Shelburne Essays, Volume I, Chapter I,* by Paul Elmer More, for *The Custom House* from *Introduction to the Scarlet Letter* by Nathaniel Hawthorne, for *Illusions* and *Henry David Thoreau* by Ralph Waldo Emerson, for *My Garden Acquaintance* by James Russell Lowell, and for *Civil Disobedience* and *Solitude* from *Walden, Chapter V,* by Henry David Thoreau; Messrs. Charles Scribner's Sons, New York, and Messrs.

ACKNOWLEDGMENTS

Constable and Company, London, for *Love* from *Little Essays* by George Santayana; Messrs. Charles Scribner's Sons, New York, for *The Art of Prose* from *The Genius of Style* by William Crary Brownell, for *I Can't Breathe* from *Round-Up, Chapter 2*, by Ring Lardner, and for *American Character* from *A History of the United States, Book IX, Chapter X*, by Henry Adams; Messrs. Harcourt, Brace and Company, New York, and Jonathan Cape, Ltd., London, for *The Death of Man* from *The Modern Temper, Chapter VIII*, by Joseph Wood Krutch; Messrs. Robert M. McBride and Company, New York, and John Lane, The Bodley Head, Ltd., London, for *The Demiurge* from *Beyond Life, Chapter II*, by James Branch Cabell; Messrs. Harper and Brothers, New York, for *The Pony Express, Snow in Nevada* and *Learning the Mississippi* from *Roughing It* and *Life on the Mississippi* by Mark Twain, for *A Potted Flower, Writers on Peril* and *Some of the Difficulties of Frolicking* from *The Colby Essays* by Frank Moore Colby, for *The Fable of the Misdirected Sympathy* and *The Fable of the Old Fox and the Young Fox* from *True Bills* by George Ade; Messrs. Harper and Brothers, New York, and Messrs. James B. Pinker and Son, Ltd., London, for *Charleston* from *The American Scene, Chapter XIII*, by Henry James; Alfred A. Knopf, Inc., New York, for *Aphorisms* from *Ventures in Common Sense* by Edgar Watson Howe and for *The Feminine Mind* and *In Memoriam: W. J. B.* from *Prejudices* and *In Defense of Women* by Henry Louis Mencken; Alfred A. Knopf, Inc., New York, and Messrs. Methuen and Company, Ltd., London, for *Tradition and the Individual Talent* from *The Sacred Wood* by Thomas Stearns Eliot.

CONTENTS

CONTENTS

CONTENTS

CONTENTS

NATHANIEL WARD

1578–1652

I   *Toleration*

EITHER I am in an apoplexy, or that man is in a lethargy, who doth not now sensibly feel God shaking the heavens over his head and the earth under his feet: The heavens so, as the sun begins to turn into darkness, the moon into blood, the stars to fall down to the ground; So that little light of comfort or counsel is left to the sons of men: The earth so, as the foundations are failing, the righteous scarce know where to find rest, the inhabitants stagger like drunken men: it is in a manner dissolved both in religions and relations: And no marvel; for they have defiled it by transgressing the laws, changing the ordinances, and breaking the Everlasting Covenant. The truths of God are the pillars of the world, whereon states and churches may stand quiet if they will; if they will not, He can easily shake them off into delusions and distractions enough.

Satan is now in his passions, he feels his passion approaching; he loves to fish in roiled waters. Though that dragon cannot sting the vitals of the elect mortally, yet that Beelzebub can fly-blow their intellectuals miserably: The finer religion grows, the finer he spins his cobwebs, he will hold pace with Christ so long as his wits will serve him. He sees himself beaten out of gross idolatries, heresies, ceremonies, where the light breaks forth with power; he will therefore bestir him to prevaricate Evangelical truths and ordinances, that if they will needs be walking, yet they shall *laborare varicibus,* and not keep their path, he will put them out of time and place; assassinating for his engineers, men of Paracelsian parts; well complexioned for honesty; for such are fittest to mountebank his chimistry into sick churches and weak judgements.

Nor shall he need to stretch his strength overmuch in this work: Too many men having not laid their foundations sure, nor ballasted their spirits deep with humility and fear, are pressed enough of themselves to evaporate their own apprehensions. Those that are acquainted with story know, it hath ever been so in new editions of churches: Such as are least able, are most busy to pudder in the rubbish and to raise dust in the eye of more steady repairers. Civil commotions make room for uncivil practices: Religious mutations for irreligious opinions: Change of air discovers corrupt bodies; Reformation of religion, unsound minds. He that hath any well-faced phansy in his crown, and doth not vent it now, fears the pride of his own heart will dub him dunce forever. Such a one will trouble the whole Israel of God with his most untimely births, though he makes the bones of his vanity stick up to the view and grief of all that are godly wise. The devil desires no better sport than to see light heads handle their heels and fetch their careers in a time when the roof of liberty stands open.

The next perplexed question with pious and ponderous men will be: What should be done for the healing of these comfortless exulcerations. I am the unablest adviser of a thousand, the unworthiest of ten thousand; yet I hope I may presume to assert what follows without just offense.

First, such as have given or taken any unfriendly reports of us New-English should do well to recollect themselves. We have been reputed a colluvies of wild opinionists, swarmed into a remote wilderness to find elbow-room for our fanatic doctrines and practices: I trust our diligence past, and constant sedulity against such persons and courses, will plead better things for us. I dare take upon me to be the herald of New-England so far as to proclaim to the world, in the name of our colony, that all Familists, Antinomians, Anabaptists, and other Enthusiasts shall have free liberty to keep away from us, and such as will come to be gone as fast as they can, the sooner the better.

Secondly, I dare aver that God doth nowhere in his word tolerate Christian states to give toleration to such adversaries of his truth if they have power in their hands to suppress them.

NATHANIEL WARD

Here is lately brought us an extract of a Magna Charta, so called, compiled between the sub-planters of a West-Indian island; whereof the first article of constipulation firmly provides free stable-room and litter for all kind of consciences, be they never so dirty or jadish; making it actionable, yea, treasonable, to disturb any man in his religion, or to discommend it, whatever it be. We are very sorry to see such professed profaneness in English professors as industriously to lay their religious foundations on the ruin of true religion; which strictly binds every conscience to contend earnestly for the truth: to preserve unity of spirit, faith and ordinances, to be all like-minded, of one accord; every man to take his brother into his Christian care: to stand fast with one spirit, with one mind, striving together for the faith of the Gospel, and by no means to permit heresies or erroneous opinions: But God abhorring such loathsome beverages, hath in his righteous judgment blasted that enterprise, which might otherwise have prospered well for ought I know; I presume their case is generally known ere this.

If the devil might have his free option, I believe he would ask nothing else but liberty to enfranchise all false religions and to embondage the true; nor should he need: It is much to be feared that lax tolerations upon state-pretences and planting necessities will be the next subtle stratagem he will spread to distate the truth of God and supplant the peace of the churches. Tolerations in things tolerable, exquisitely drawn out by the lines of the Scripture and pencil of the spirit, are the sacred favors of truth, the due latitudes of love, the fair compartments of Christian fraternity: but irregular dispensations, dealt forth by the facilities of men, are the frontiers of error, the redoubts of schism, the perilous irritaments of carnal and spiritual enmity.

My heart hath naturally detested four things: The standing of the Apocrypha in the Bible; Foreigners dwelling in my country, to crowd out native subjects into the corners of the earth; Alchymized coins; Tolerations of divers religions, or of one religion in segregant shapes. He that willingly assents

3

to the last, if he examines his heart by daylight, his conscience will tell him, he is either an atheist, or an heretic, or an hypocrite, or at best a captive to some lust. Poly-piety is the greatest impiety in the world. True religion is *Ignis probationis,* which doth *congregare homogenea et segregare heterogenea.*

Not to tolerate things merely indifferent to weak consciences argues a conscience too strong: pressed uniformity in these causes much disunity: To tolerate more than indifference is not to deal indifferently with God: He that doth it takes his scepter out of his hand and bids him stand by. Who hath to do to institute religion but God. The power of all religion and ordinances lies in their purity: their purity in their simplicity: then are mixtures pernicious. I lived in a city where a Papist preached in one church, a Lutheran in another, a Calvinist in a third; a Lutheran one part of the day, a Calvinist the other, in the same pulpit: the religion of that place was but motley and meagre, their affections leopard-like.

If the whole creature should conspire to do the Creator a mischief, or offer him an insolency, it would be in nothing more than in erecting untruths against his truth, or by sophisticating his truths with human medleys: the removing of some one iota in Scripture may draw out all the life and traverse all the truth of the whole Bible: but to authorize an untruth by a toleration of state is to build a sconce against the walls of heaven to batter God out of his chair: To tell a practical lie is a great sin, but yet transient; but to set up a theorical untruth is to warrant every lie that lies from its root to the top of every branch it hath, which are not a few.

I would willingly hope that no Member of the Parliament hath skillfully ingratiated himself into the hearts of the House, that he might watch a time to midwife out some ungracious toleration for his own turn, and for the sake of that, some other; I would also hope that a word of general caution should not be particularly misapplied. I am the freer

4

to suggest it because I know not one man of that mind, my aim is general, and I desire may be so accepted. Yet, good gentlemen, look well about you, and remember how Tiberius play'd the fox with the Senate of Rome, and how Fabius Maximus cropt his ears for his cunning.

That State is wise that will improve all pains and patience rather to compose than tolerate differences in religion. There is no divine truth but hath much celestial fire in it from the spirit of truth: nor no irreligious untruth without its proportion of antifire from the spirit of error to contradict it: the zeal of the one, the virulency of the other, must necessarily kindle combustions. Fiery diseases, seated in the spirit, embroil the whole frame of the body: others more external and cool are less dangerous. They which divide in religion, divide in God; they who divide in him, divide beyond *Genus Generalissimum,* where there is no reconciliation without atonement; that is, without uniting in him who is One, and in his truth, which is also one.

Wise are those men who will be persuaded rather to live within the pale of truth where they may be quiet than in the purlieus where they are sure to be haunted ever and anon, do authority what it can. Every singular opinion hath a singular opinion of itself; and he that holds it a singular opinion of himself, and a simple opinion of all contra-sentients: he that confutes them must confute at three at once, or else he does nothing; which will not be done without more stir than the peace of the state or church can endure.

And prudent are those Christians that will rather give what may be given than hazard all by yielding nothing. To sell all peace of country to buy some peace of conscience unseasonably is more avarice than thrift, imprudence than patience: they deal not equally that set any truth of God at such a rate; but they deal wisely that will stay till the market is fallen.

My prognostics deceive me not a little, if once within three seven years peace prove not such a penny-worth at most marts in Christendom, that he that would not lay down his money, his lust, his opinion, his will, I had almost said the best flower of his crown for it, while he might have had it, will tell his own heart he played the very ill husband.

Concerning tolerations I may further assert.

That persecution of true religion and toleration of false are the Jannes and Jambres to the Kingdom of Christ, whereof the last is far the worst. Augustine's tongue had not owed his mouth one penny-rent though he had never spake word more in it but this, *Nullum malum pejus libertate errandi*.

Frederick Duke of Saxon spake not one foot beyond the mark when he said: He had rather the earth should swallow him up quick, than he should give a toleration to any opinion against any truth of God.

He that is willing to tolerate any religion, or discrepant way of religion, besides his own, unless it be in matters merely indifferent, either doubts of his own or is not sincere in it.

He that is willing to tolerate any unsound opinion, that his own may also be tolerated, though never so sound, will for a need hang God's Bible at the Devil's girdle.

Every toleration of false religions or opinions hath as many errors and sins in it as all the false religions and opinions it tolerates, and one sound one more.

That state that will give liberty of conscience in matters of religion must give liberty of conscience and conversation in their moral laws, or else the fiddle will be out of tune, and some of the strings crack.

He that will rather make an irreligious quarrel with other religions than try the truth of his own by valuable arguments and peaceable sufferings; either his religion or himself is irreligious.

Experience will teach churches and Christians that it is far better to live in a state united, though a little corrupt, than in a state whereof some part is incorrupt and all the rest divided.

I am not altogether ignorant of the eight rules given by

orthodox divines about giving tolerations, yet with their favor I dare affirm,

That there is no rule given by God for any state to give an affirmative toleration to any false religion or opinion whatsoever; they must connive in some cases, but may not concede in any.

That the state of England (so far as my intelligence serves) might in time have prevented with ease and may yet without any great difficulty deny both toleration and irregular connivances *salva Republica*.

That if the state of England shall either willingly tolerate or weakly connive at such courses, the church of that kingdom will sooner become the devil's dancing-school than God's temple: The civil state a bear-garden than an exchange: The whole realm a Pais base than an England. And what pity it is that that country which hath been the staple of truth to all Christendom should now become the aviary of errors to the whole world, let every fearing heart judge.

I take liberty of conscience to be nothing but a freedom from sin and error. *Conscientia in tantum libera in quantum ab errore liberata.* And liberty of error nothing but a prison for conscience. Then small will be the kindness of a state to build such prisons for their subjects.

The Scripture saith, there is nothing makes free but truth, and truth saith, there is no truth but one: if the states of the world would make it their sumoperous care to preserve this one truth in its purity and authority it would ease you of all other political cares. I am sure Satan makes it his grand, if not only task, to adulterate truth; Falsehood is his sole scepter whereby he first ruffled and ever since ruined the World.

If truth be but one, methinks all the opinionists in England should not be all in that one truth, some of them I doubt are out. He that can extract an unity out of such a disparity, or contract such a disparity into an unity; had need be a better artist than ever was Drebell.

If two centers (as we may suppose) be in one circle, and

lines drawn from both to all the points of the compass, they will certainly cross one another, and probably cut through the centers themselves.

There is talk of an universal toleration; I would talk as loud as I could against it, did I know what more apt and reasonable sacrifice England could offer to God for his late performing all his heavenly truths than an universal toleration of all hellish errors, or how they shall make an universal reformation, but by making Christ's academy the Devil's university, where any man may commence heretic *per saltum;* where he that is *filius Diabolicus,* or *simpliciter pessimus,* may have his grace to go to Hell *cum Publico Privilegio;* and carry as many after him as he can. . . .

It is said, though a man have light enough himself to see in the truth, yet if he hath not enough to enlighten others he is bound to tolerate them. I will engage myself that all the devils in Britanie shall sell themselves to their shirts to purchase a lease of this position for three of their lives, under the seal of the Parliament.

It is said that men ought to have liberty of their conscience, and that it is persecution to debar them of it: I can rather stand amazed than reply to this: it is an astonishment to think that the brains of men should be parboiled in such impious ignorance. Let all the wits under the heavens lay their heads together and find an assertion worse than this (one excepted) I will petition to be chosen the universal idiot of the world.

It is said that civil magistrates ought not to meddle with ecclesiastical matters.

I would answer to this so well as I could, did I not know that some papers lately brought out of New England are going to the press, wherein the opinions of the elders there in a late synod, concerning this point are manifested, which I suppose will give clearer satisfaction than I can.

The true English of all this their false Latin is nothing but a general toleration of all opinions: which motion if it be like to take, it were very requisite that the city would repair

Paul's with all the speed they can for an English Pantheon, and bestow it upon the sectaries, freely to assemble in, then there may be some hope that London will be quiet in time.

JOHN WINTHROP

1588–1649

2   *A Little Speech on Liberty*

. . . THEN was the deputy governor desired by the court to go up and take his place again upon the bench, which he did accordingly, and the court being about to arise, he desired leave for a little speech, which was to this effect.

I suppose something may be expected from me, upon this charge that is befallen me, which moves me to speak now to you; yet I intend not to intermeddle in the proceedings of the court, or with any of the persons concerned therein. Only I bless God, that I see an issue of this troublesome business. I also acknowledge the justice of the court, and, for mine own part, I am well satisfied, I was publicly charged, and I am publicly and legally acquitted, which is all I did expect or desire. And though this be sufficient for my justification before men, yet not so before the God, who hath seen so much amiss in my dispensations (and even in this affair) as calls me to be humble. For to be publicly and criminally charged in this court, is matter of humiliation (and I desire to make a right use of it), notwithstanding I be thus acquitted. If her father had spit in her face (saith the Lord concerning Miriam), should she not have been ashamed seven days? Shame had lien upon her, whatever the occasion had been. I am unwilling to stay you from your urgent affairs, yet give me leave (upon this special occasion) to speak a little more to this assembly.

It may be of some good use, to inform and rectify the judgments of some of the people, and may prevent such distempers as have arisen amongst us. The great questions that have troubled the country, are about the authority of the magistrates and the liberty of the people. It is yourselves who have called us to this office, and being called by you, we have our authority from God, in way of an ordinance, such as hath the image of God eminently stamped upon it, the contempt and violation whereof hath been vindicated with examples of divine vengeance. I entreat you to consider, that when you choose magistrates, you take them from among yourselves, men subject to like passions as you are. Therefore when you see infirmities in us, you should reflect upon your own, and that would make you bear the more with us, and not be severe censurers of the failings of your magistrates, when you have continual experience of the infirmities in yourselves and others. We account him a good servant, who breaks not his covenant. The covenant between you and us is the oath you have taken of us, which is to this purpose, that we shall govern you and judge your causes by the rules of God's laws and our own, according to our best skill. When you agree with a workman to build you a ship or house, etc., he undertakes as well for his skill as for his faithfulness, for it is his profession, and you pay him for both. But when you call one to be a magistrate, he doth not profess nor undertake to have sufficient skill for that office, nor can you furnish him with gifts, etc., therefore you must run the hazard of his skill and ability. But if he fail in faithfulness, which by his oath he is bound unto, that he must answer for. If it fall out that the case be clear to common apprehension, and the rule clear also, if he transgress here, the error is not in the skill, but in the evil of the will: it must be required of him. But if the case be doubtful, or the rule doubtful, to men of such understanding and parts as your magistrates are, if your magistrates should err here, yourselves must bear it.

For the other point concerning liberty, I observe a great mistake in the country about that. There is a twofold liberty, natural (I mean as our nature is now corrupt) and civil or federal. The first is common to man with beasts and other creatures. By this, man, as he stands in relation to man simply, hath liberty to do what he lists; it is a liberty to evil as well as to good. This liberty is incompatible and inconsistent with authority, and cannot endure the least restraint of the most just authority. The exercise and maintaining of this liberty makes men grow more evil, and in time to be worse than brute beasts: omnes sumus licentia deteriores. This is that great enemy of truth and peace, that wild beast, which all the ordinances of God are bent against, to restrain and subdue it. The other kind of liberty I call civil or federal, it may also be termed moral, in reference to the covenant between God and man, in the moral law, and the politic covenants and constitutions, amongst men themselves. This liberty is the proper end and object of authority, and cannot subsist without it; and it is a liberty to that only which is good, just, and honest. This liberty you are to stand for, with the hazard (not only of your goods, but) of your lives, if need be. Whatsoever crosseth this, is not authority, but a distemper thereof. This liberty is maintained and exercised in a way of subjection to authority; it is of the same kind of liberty wherewith Christ hath made us free. The woman's own choice makes such a man her husband; yet being so chosen, he is her lord, and she is to be subject to him, yet in a way of liberty, not of bondage; and a true wife accounts her subjection her honor and freedom, and would not think her condition safe and free, but in her subjection to her husband's authority. Such is the liberty of the church under authority of Christ, her king and husband; his yoke is so easy and sweet to her as a bride's ornaments; and if through frowardness or wantonness, etc., she shake it off, at any time, she is at no rest in her spirit, until she take it up again; and whether her lord smiles upon her, and embraceth her in his arms, or whether he frowns, or rebukes, or smites her, she apprehends the sweetness of his love in all, and is refreshed, supported, and instructed by every such dispensation of his authority over her. On the other side, ye know who they are that complain of this yoke and say, let us break their bands, etc., we will not have this man to rule over us. Even so, brethren, it will be between you and your magistrates. If you stand for your natural corrupt liberties, and will do what is good in your own eyes, you will not endure the least weight of authority, but will murmur, and oppose, and be always striving to shake off that yoke; but if you will be satisfied to enjoy such civil and lawful liberties, such as Christ allows you, then will you quietly and cheerfully submit unto that authority which is set over you, in all the administrations of it, for your good. Wherein, if we fail at any time, we hope we shall be willing (by God's assistance) to hearken to good advice from any of you, or in any other way of God; so shall your liberties be preserved, in upholding the honor and power of authority amongst you.

ROGER WILLIAMS
1604–1684

3   *A Bloody Tenent*

A TENENT of high blasphemy against the God of Peace, the God of Order, who hath of one blood made all mankind to dwell upon the face of the earth, now all confounded and destroyed in their civil beings and subsistences by mutual flames of war from their several religions and consciences.

A tenent warring against the Prince of Peace, Christ Jesus, denying his appearance and coming in the flesh, to put an end to and abolish the shadows of that ceremonial and typical Land of Canaan.

A tenent fighting against the sweet end of his coming, which was not to destroy men's lives for their religions, but to save them by the meek and peaceful invitations and persuasions of his peaceable wisdom's maidens.

A tenent foully charging his wisdom, faithfulness and love in so poorly providing such magistrates and civil powers all the world over as might effect so great a charge pretended to be committed to them.

A tenent lamentably guilty of his most precious blood, shed in the blood of so many hundred thousands of his poor servants by the civil powers of the world, pretending to suppress blasphemies, heresies, idolatries, superstition, etc.

A tenent fighting with the spirit of love, holiness, and meekness, by kindling fiery spirits of false zeal and fury when yet such spirits know not of what Spirit they are.

A tenent fighting with those mighty angels who stand up for the peace of the Saints against Persia, Greece, etc., and so consequently all other nations, who fighting for their several religions, and against the truth, leave no room for such as fear and love the Lord of the Earth.

A tenent against which the blessed souls under the altar cry loud for vengeance, this tenent having cut their throats, torn out their hearts, and poured forth their blood in all ages, as the only heretics and blasphemers in the world.

A tenent which no uncleanness, no adultery, incest, sodomy, or bestiality can equal, this ravishing and forcing (explicitly or implicitly) the very souls and consciences of all the nations and inhabitants of the world.

A tenent that puts out the very eye of all true faith, which cannot but be as free and voluntary as any virgin in the world in refusing or embracing any spiritual offer or object.

A tenent loathsome and ugly (in the eyes of the God of Heaven, and serious sons of men), I say, loathsome with the palpable filths of gross dissimulations and hypocrisy: Thousands of peoples and whole nations compelled by this tenent to put on the foul vizard of religious hypocrisy for fear of laws, losses and punishments, and for the keeping and hoping for of favor, liberty, worldly commodity, etc.

A tenent woefully guilty of hardening all false and deluded consciences (of whatsoever sect, faction, heresy, or idolatry, though never so horrid and blasphemous) by cruelties and violences practiced against them: all false teachers and their followers (ordinarily) contracting a brawny and steely hardness from their sufferings for their consciences.

A tenent that shuts and bars out the gracious prophecies and promises and discoveries of the most glorious Sun of Righteousness, Christ Jesus, that burns up the holy Scriptures and forbids them (upon the point) to be read in English, or that any trial or search or (truly) free disquisition be made by them: when the most able, diligent and conscionable readers must pluck forth their own eyes and be forced to read by the (whichsoever predominant) clergy's spectacles.

A tenent that seals up the spiritual graves of all men, Jews and Gentiles (and consequently stands guilty of the damnation of all men), since no preachers nor trumpets of Christ himself may call them out, but such as the several and respective nations of the world themselves allow of.

A tenent that fights against the common principles of all civility, and the very civil being and combinations of men in nations, cities, etc., by commixing (explicitly or implicitly) a spiritual and civil state together, and so confounding and overthrowing the purity and strength of both.

A tenent that kindles the devouring flames of combustions and wars in most nations of the world, and (if God were not infinitely gracious) had almost ruined the English, French, the Scotch and Irish, and many other nations, German, Polonian, Hungarian, Bohemian, etc.

A tenent that bows down the backs and necks of all civil states and magistrates, kings, and emperors under the proud feet of that man and monster of sin and pride the Pope, and all popish and proud clergymen rendering such laics and seculars (as they call them) but slavish executioners (upon the point) of their most imperious synodical decrees and sentences.

A tenent that renders the highest civil magistrates and ministers of justice (the fathers and Gods of their countries) either odious or lamentably grievous unto the very best subjects by either clapping or keeping on the iron yokes of cruellest oppression. No yoke or bondage comparably so grievous as that upon the soul's neck of men's religion and consciences.

A tenent all besprinkled with the bloody murders, stabs, poisonings, pistolings, powder-plots, etc., against many famous kings, princes, and states, either actually performed or attempted, in France, England, Scotland, Low Countries, and other Nations.

A tenent all red and bloody with those most barbarous and tiger-like massacres of so many thousands and ten thousands formerly in France, and other parts, and so lately and horribly in Ireland: of which, whatever causes be assigned, this chiefly will be found the true, and while this continues (to wit, violence against conscience), this bloody issue sooner or later must break forth again (except God wonderfully stop it) in Ireland and other places too.

A tenent that stunts the growth and flourishing of the most likely and hopefulest commonweals and countries, while consciences the best, and the best deserving subjects are forced to fly (by enforced or voluntary banishment) from their native countries; the lamentable proof whereof England hath felt in the flight of so many worthy English into the Low Countries and New England, and from New England into old again and other foreign parts.

A tenent whose gross partiality denies the principles of common justice, while men weigh out to the consciences of all others that which they judge not fit nor right to be weighed out to their own: Since the persecutor's rule is, to take and persecute all consciences, only, himself must not be touched.

A tenent that is but Machiavellianism, and makes a religion but a cloak or stalking horse to policy and private ends of Jereboam's crown, and the priest's benefice, etc.

A tenent that corrupts and spoils the very civil honesty and natural conscience of a nation. Since conscience to God, violated, proves (without repentance) ever after a very jade, a drug, loose and unconscionable in all converse with men.

Lastly, a tenent in England most unseasonable, as pouring

oil upon those flames which the high wisdom of the Parliament (by easing the yokes on men's consciences) had begun to quench.

COTTON MATHER

1663–1728

4 *The Trial of George Burroughs*

Held in Salem. 1692

GLAD should I have been if I had never known the name of this man; or never had this occasion to mention so much as the first letters of his name. But the Government requiring some account of his trial to be inserted in this book, it becomes me with all obedience to submit unto the order.

I. This *G. B.* was indicted for *witchcraft;* and in the prosecution of the charge against him, he was accused by five or six of the bewitched as the author of their miseries; he was accused by eight of the confessing witches, as being an head actor at some of their hellish rendezvouzes, and one who had the promise of being a king in Satan's kingdom, now going to be erected; he was accused by nine persons for extraordinary lifting, and such feats of strength as could not be done without a diabolical assistance. And for other such things he was accused, until about thirty testimonies were brought in against him; nor were these judg'd the half of what might have been considered for his conviction: however, they were enough to fix the character of a *witch* upon him, according to the rules of reasoning by the judicious *Gaule,* in that case directed.

II. The Court being sensible that the testimonies of the parties bewitched use to have a room among the suspicions, or presumptions, brought in against one indicted for witchcraft; there were now heard the testimonies of several persons who were most notoriously bewitched, and every day tortured by invisible hands, and these now all charged the specters of *G. B.* to have a share in their torments. At the examination of this *G. B.* the bewitched people were grievously harassed with preternatural mischiefs which could not possibly be dissembled; and they still ascribed it unto the endeavors of *G. B.* to kill them. And now upon his trial, one of the bewitched persons testify'd that in her agonies, a little black-hair'd man came to her, saying his name was *B.* and bidding her set her hand unto a Book which he show'd unto her; and bragging that he was a conjurer above the ordinary rank of witches; that he often persecuted her, with the offer of that Book, saying, *She should be well, and need fear no body, if she would but sign it;* but he inflicted cruel pains and hurts upon her, because of her denying so to do. The testimonies of the other sufferers concurred with these; and it was remarkable that whereas biting was one of the ways which the witches used for the vexing of the sufferers, when they cry'd out of *G. B.* biting them, the print of the teeth would be seen on the flesh of the complainers; and just such a set of teeth as *G. B.'s* would then appear upon them, which could be distinguished from those of some other men. Others of them testify'd that in their torments *G. B.* tempted them to go unto a sacrament, unto which they perceived him with a sound of trumpet summoning of other witches; who quickly after the sound would come from all quarters unto the rendezvous. One of them falling into a kind of trance, afterwards affirmed that *G. B.* had carried her into a very high mountain, where he show'd her mighty and glorious kingdoms, and said, *He would give them all to her, if she would write in his Book;* but she told him, *They were none of his to give;* and refused the motions; enduring of much misery for that refusal.

It cost the Court a wonderful deal of trouble to hear the testimonies of the sufferers; for when they were going to give in their depositions, they would for a long while be taken with fits, that made them uncapable of saying anything. The Chief Judge asked the prisoner, who he thought hindered these witnesses from giving their testimonies? and he answered, *He supposed it was the Divel.* That Honorable person then reply'd, *How comes the Divel so loath to have any testimony born against you?* Which cast him into very great confusion.

III. It has been a frequent thing for the bewitched people to be entertained with apparitions of ghosts of murdered people, at the same time that the specters of the witches trouble them. These ghosts do always affright the beholders more than all the other spectral representations; and when they exhibit themselves, they cry out of being murdered by the witchcrafts or other violences of the persons who are then in specter present. It is further considerable, that once or twice these apparitions have been seen by others at the very same time they have shown themselves to the bewitched; and seldom have there been these apparitions but when something unusual and suspected had attended the death of the party thus appearing. Some that have been accused by these apparitions, accosting of the bewitched people, who had never heard a word of any such persons ever being in the world, have upon a fair examination freely and fully confessed the murders of those very persons, altho' these also did not know how the apparitions had complained of them. Accordingly several of the bewitched had given in their testimony that they had been troubled with the apparitions of two women, who said that they were *G. B.'s* two wives; and that he had been the death of them; and that the magistrates must be told of it, before whom if *B.* upon his trial deny'd it, they did not know but that they should appear again in court. Now *G. B.* had been infamous for the barbarous usage of his two successive wives, all the country over. Moreover, it was testifi'd, the specter of *G. B.* threatening of the sufferers told them he had killed (besides others) Mrs. Lawson and her daughter Ann. And it was noted that these were the virtuous wife and daughter of one at whom this *G. B.* might have a prejudice for his being serviceable at Salem Village, from whence himself had in ill terms removed some years before: and that when they died, which was long since, there were some odd circumstances about them, which made some of the attendants there suspect something of witchcraft, tho' none imagined from what quarter it should come.

Well, *G. B.* being now upon his trial, one of the bewitched persons was cast into horror at the Ghosts of *B's* two deceased wives, then appearing before him, and crying for vengeance against him. Hereupon several of the bewitched persons were successively called in, who all not knowing what the former had seen and said, concurred in their horror of the apparition, which they affirmed that he had before him. But he, tho' much appalled, utterly deny'd that he discerned any thing of it; nor was it any part of his conviction.

IV. Judicious writers have assigned it a great place in the conviction of witches, when persons are impeached by other notorious witches to be as ill as themselves; especially, if the persons have been much noted for neglecting the worship of God. Now, as there might have been testimonies enough of *G. B.'s* antipathy to prayer and the other ordinances of God, tho' by his profession singularly obliged thereunto; so, there now came in against the prisoner the testimonies of several persons who confessed their own having been horrible witches, and ever since their confessions had been themselves terribly tortured by the devils and other witches, even like the other sufferers; and therein undergone the pains of many deaths for their confessions.

These now testify'd that *G. B.* had been at witch-meetings with them; and that he was the person who had seduced and compelled them into the snares of witchcraft: That he promised them fine clothes for doing it; that he brought poppets to them, and thorns to stick into those poppets, for the afflicting of other people: and that he exhorted them, with the rest of the crew, to bewitch all Salem Village, but be sure to do it gradually if they would prevail in what they did.

When the Lancashire witches were condemn'd, I don't remember that there was any considerable further evidence than that of the bewitched, and then that of some that confessed. We see so much already against *G. B.* But this being indeed not enough, there were other things to render what had been already produced credible.

V. A famous Divine recites this among the convictions of a witch; *The testimony of the party bewitched, whether pining or dying; together with the joint oaths of sufficient persons that have seen certain prodigious pranks or feats wrought by the party accused.* Now God had been pleased so to leave this *G. B.* that he had ensnared himself by several instances which he had formerly given of a preternatural strength, and which were now produced against him. He was a very puny man; yet he had often done things beyond the strength of a giant. A gun of about seven foot barrel, and so heavy that strong men could not steadily hold it out with both hands; there were several testimonies, given in by persons of credit and honor, that he made nothing of taking up such a gun behind the lock with but one hand, and holding it out like a pistol at arm's-end. *G. B.* in his vindication was so foolish as to say, *That an Indian was there, and held it out at the same time:* Whereas, none of the Spectators ever saw any such Indian; but they suppos'd the Black Man (as the witches call the Devil; and they generally say he resembles an Indian) might give him that assistance. There was evidence likewise brought in that he made nothing of taking up whole barrels fill'd with molasses, or cider, in very disadvantageous postures, and carrying of them through the difficultest places, out of a canoe to the shore.

Yea, there were two testimonies that *G. B.* with only putting the fore-finger of his right hand into the muzzle of an heavy gun, a fowling-piece of about six or seven foot barrel, did lift up the gun and hold it out at arm's-end; a gun which the deponents, though strong men, could not with both hands lift up and hold out at the butt end, as is usual. Indeed, one of these witnesses was over-persuaded by some persons to be out of the way upon *G. B.'s* Trial; but he came afterwards, with sorrow for his withdraw, and gave in his testimony: Nor were either of these witnesses made use of as evidences in the trial.

VI. There came in several testimonies relating to the domestic affairs of *G. B.* which had a very hard aspect upon him; and not only prov'd him a very ill man; but also confirmed the belief of the character which had been already fastened on him.

T'was testified, that keeping his two successive wives in a strange kind of slavery, he would when he came home from abroad pretend to tell the talk which any had with them. That he has brought them to the point of death by his harsh dealings with his wives, and then made the people about him to promise that in case death should happen, they would say nothing of it. That he used all means to make his wives write, sign, seal, and swear a covenant, never to reveal any of his secrets. That his wives had privately complained unto the neighbors about frightful apparitions of evil spirits with which their house was sometimes infested; and that many such things have been whispered among the neighborhood. There were also some other testimonies relating to the death of people, whereby the consciences of an impartial jury were convinced that *G. B.* had bewitched the persons mentioned in the complaints. But I am forced to omit several passages in this as well as in all the succeeding trials, because the scribes who took notice of them have not supplied me.

VII. One Mr. Ruck, brother in law to this *G. B.*, testifi'd, that *G. B.* and he himself, and his sister who was *G. B.'s* wife, going out for two or three miles to gather strawberries, Ruck, with his sister the wife of *G. B.* rode home very softly, with *G. B.* on foot in their company. *G. B.* stept aside a little into the bushes; whereupon they halted and halloo'd for him. He not answering, they went away homewards, with a quickened pace; without any expectation of seeing him in a considerable while: and yet when they were got near home, to their astonishment they found him on foot with them, having a basket of strawberries. *G. B.* immediately then fell to chiding his wife on the account of what she had been speaking to her brother of him on the road: which when they wondered at, he said, *He knew their thoughts.* Ruck being startled at that, made some reply, intimating that the devil himself did not know so far; but *G. B.* answered, *My God makes known your thoughts unto me.* The prisoner now at the bar had nothing to answer, unto what was thus witnessed against him, that was worth considering. Only he said, *Ruck and his wife left a man with him, when they left him.* Which Ruck now affirm'd to be false; and when the court asked *G. B. What the man's name was?* his countenance was much altered; nor could he say who 'twas. But the court began to think that he then step'd aside, only that by the assistance of the Black Man he might put on his invisibility, and in that fascinating mist gratify his own jealous humor, to hear what they said of him. Which trick of rendering themselves invisible our witches do in their confessions pretend that they sometimes are masters of; and it is the more credible, because there is demonstration that they often render many other things utterly invisible.

VIII. Faltering, faulty, unconstant, and contrary answers upon judicial and deliberate examination, are counted some unlucky symptoms of guilt, in all crimes; especially in witchcrafts. Now there never was a prisoner more eminent for them than *G. B.* both at his examination and on his trial. His tergiversations, contradictions, and falsehoods were very sensible: he had little to say but that he had heard some things that he could not prove, reflecting upon the reputation of some of the witnesses. Only he gave in a paper to the jury; wherein, altho' he had many times before granted, not only that there are witches, but also that the present sufferings of the country are the effect of horrible witchcrafts, yet he now goes to evince it, *That there neither are, nor ever were, witches that having made a compact with the Divel can send a Divel to torment other people at a distance.* This paper was transcribed out of Ady; which the court presently knew, as soon as they heard it. But he said, he had taken none of it out of any book; for which his evasion afterwards was, that a gentleman gave him the discourse in a manuscript, from whence he transcribed it.

IX. The jury brought him in *guilty;* But when he came to die, he utterly deny'd the fact whereof he had been thus convicted.

5   *A General Introduction*

I WRITE the wonders of the Christian religion, flying from the depravations of Europe to the American strand: and, assisted by the Holy Author of that religion, I do, with all conscience of truth required therein by him, who is the truth itself, report the wonderful displays of his infinite power, wisdom, goodness, and faithfulness, wherewith his Divine Providence hath irradiated an Indian wilderness.

I relate the considerable matters that produced and attended the first settlement of colonies, which have been renowned for the degree of reformation professed and attained by evangelical churches erected in those ends of the earth: and a field being thus prepared, I proceed unto a relation of the considerable matters which have been acted thereupon.

I first introduce the actors that have, in a more exemplary manner, served those colonies; and give remarkable occurrences in the exemplary lives of many magistrates, and of more ministers, who so lived as to leave unto posterity examples worthy of everlasting remembrance.

I add hereunto the notables of the only Protestant university that ever shone in that hemisphere of the New World; with particular instances of Criolians, in our biography, provoking the whole world with virtuous objects of emulation.

I introduce, then, the actions of a more eminent importance that have signalized those colonies: whether the establishments, directed by their synods, with a rich variety of synodical and ecclesiastical determinations; or the disturbances with which they have been from all sorts of temptations and enemies tempestuated; and the methods by which they have still weathered out each horrible tempest.

And into the midst of these actions, I interpose an entire book, wherein there is, with all possible veracity, a collection made of memorable occurrences; and amazing judgments and mercies, befalling many particular persons among the people of New England.

Let my readers expect all that I have promised them in this bill of fare; and it may be that they will find themselves entertained with yet many other passages, above and beyond their expectations, deserving likewise a room in history: in all which there will be nothing but the author's too mean way of preparing so great entertainments, to reproach the invitation.

WILLIAM BYRD

1674–1744

6   A Visit to Colonel Spotswood

I RODE eight miles together over a stony road, and had on either side continual poisoned fields, with nothing but saplings growing on them. Then I came into the main county road, that leads from Fredericksburg to Germanna, which last place I reached in ten miles more. This famous town consists of Col. Spotswood's enchanted castle on one side of the street, and a baker's dozen of ruinous tenements on the other, where so many German families had dwelt some years ago; but are now removed ten miles higher, in the fork of Rappahannock, to land of their own. There had also been a chapel about a bow-shot from the colonel's house, at the end of an avenue of cherry trees, but some pious people had lately burnt it down, with intent to get another built nearer to their own homes. Here I arrived about three o'clock, and found only Mrs. Spotswood at home, who received her old acquaintance with many a gracious smile. I was carried into a room elegantly set off with pier glasses, the largest of which came soon after to an odd misfortune. Amongst other favorite animals that cheered this lady's solitude, a brace of tame deer ran familiarly about the house, and one of them came to stare at me as a stranger. But unluckily spying his own figure in the glass, he made a spring over the tea table that stood under it, and shattered the glass to pieces, and falling back upon the tea table, made a terrible fracas among the china. This exploit was so sudden, and accompanied with such a noise, that it surprised me, and perfectly frightened Mrs. Spotswood. But it was worth all the damage, to show the moderation and good humor with which she bore this disaster. In the evening the noble colonel came home from his mines, who saluted me very civilly, and Mrs. Spotswood's sister, Miss Theky, who had been to meet him *en cavalier,* was so kind too as to bid me welcome. We talked over a legend of old stories, supped about nine, and then prattled with the ladies, till it was time for a traveler to retire. In the meantime I observed my old friend to be very uxorious, and exceedingly fond of his children. This was so opposite to the maxims he used to preach up before he was married, that I could not forbear rubbing up the memory of them. But he gave a very good-natured turn to his change of sentiments, by alleging that whoever brings a poor gentlewoman into so solitary a place, from all her friends and acquaintance, would be ungrateful not to use her and all that belongs to her with all possible tenderness.

28th. We all kept snug in our several apartments till nine, except Miss Theky, who was the housewife of the family. At that hour we met over a pot of coffee, which was not quite strong enough to give us the palsy. After breakfast the colonel and I left the ladies to their domestic affairs, and took a turn in the garden, which has nothing beautiful but three terrace walks that fall in slopes one below another. I let him understand, that besides the pleasure of paying him a visit, I came to be instructed by so great a master in the mystery of making iron, wherein he had led the way, and was the Tubal Cain of Virginia. He corrected me a little there, by assuring me he was not only the first in this country, but the first in North America, who had erected a regular furnace. That they ran altogether upon bloomeries in New England and Pennsylvania, till his example had made them attempt greater works. But in this last colony, they have so few ships to carry their iron to Great Britain, that they must be content to make it only for their own use, and must be obliged to manufacture it when they have done. That he hoped he had done the country very great service by setting so good an example. That the four furnaces now at work in Virginia circulated a great sum of money for provisions and all other necessaries in the adjacent counties. That they took off a great number of hands from planting tobacco, and employed them in works that produced a large sum of money in England to the persons concerned, whereby the country is so much the richer. That they are besides a considerable advantage to Great Britain, because it lessens the quantity of bar iron imported from Spain, Holland, Sweden, Denmark and Muscovy, which used to be no less than twenty thousand tons yearly, though at the same time no sow iron is imported thither from any country but only from the plantations. For most of this bar iron they do not only pay silver, but our friends in the Baltic are so nice, they even expect to be paid all in crown pieces. On the contrary, all the iron they receive from the plantations, they pay for it in their own manufactures, and send for it in their own shipping. Then I inquired after his own mines, and hoped, as he was the first that engaged in this great undertaking, that he had brought them to the most perfection. He told me he had iron in several parts of his great tract of land, consisting of forty-five thousand acres. But that the mine he was at work upon was thirteen miles below Germanna. That his ore (which was very rich) he raised a mile from his furnace, and was obliged to cart the iron, when it was made, fifteen miles to Massaponux, a plantation he had upon Rappahannock river; but that the road was exceeding good, gently declining all the way, and had no more than one hill to go up in the whole journey. For this reason his loaded carts went it in a day without difficulty. He said it was true his works were of the oldest standing: but that his long absence in England, and the wretched management of Mr. Greame, whom he had entrusted with his affairs, had put him back very much. That what with neglect and severity, above eighty of his slaves were lost while he was in England, and most of his cattle starved. That his furnace stood still great part of the time, and all his plantations ran to ruin. That indeed he was rightly served for committing his affairs to the care of a mathematician, whose thoughts were always among the stars. That nevertheless, since his return, he had applied himself to rectify his steward's mistakes, and bring his business again into order. That now he had contrived to do everything with his own people, except raising the mine and running the iron, by which he had contracted his expense very much. Nay, he believed that by his directions he could bring sensible negroes to perform those parts of the work tolerably well. But at the same time he gave me to understand, that his furnace had done no great feats lately, because he had been taken up in building an air furnace at Massaponux, which he had now brought to perfection, and should be thereby able to furnish the whole country with all sorts of cast iron, as cheap and as good as ever came from England. I told him he must do one thing more to have a full vent for those commodities, he must keep a shallop running into all the rivers, to carry his wares home to people's own doors. And if he would do that I would set a good example, and take off a whole ton of them. Our conversation on this subject continued till dinner, which was both elegant and plentiful. The afternoon was devoted to the ladies, who showed me one of their most beautiful walks. They conducted me through a shady lane to the landing, and by the way made me drink some very fine water that issued from a marble fountain, and ran incessantly. Just behind it was a covered bench, where Miss Theky often sat and bewailed her virginity. Then we proceeded to the river, which is the south branch of Rappahannock, about fifty yards wide, and so rapid that the ferry boat is drawn over by a chain, and therefore called the Rapidan. At night we drank prosperity to all the colonel's projects in a bowl of rack punch, and then retired to our devotions.

29th. Having employed about two hours in retirement, I

sallied out at the first summons to breakfast, where our conversation with the ladies, like whip sillabub, was very pretty, but had nothing in it. This it seems was Miss Theky's birthday, upon which I made her my compliments, and wished she might live twice as long a married woman as she had lived a maid. I did not presume to pry into the secret of her age, nor was she forward to disclose it, for this humble reason, lest I should think her wisdom fell short of her years. She contrived to make this day of her birth a day of mourning, for having nothing better at present to set her affections upon, she had a dog that was a great favorite. It happened that very morning the poor cur had done something very uncleanly upon the colonel's bed, for which he was condemned to die. However, upon her entreaty, she got him a reprieve; but was so concerned that so much severity should be intended on her birthday, that she was not to be comforted; and lest such another accident might oust the poor cur of his clergy, she protested she would board out her dog at a neighbor's house, where she hoped he would be more kindly treated. Then the colonel and I took another turn in the garden, to discourse farther on the subject of iron. . . .

We had a Michaelmas goose for dinner, of Miss Theky's own raising, who was now good-natured enough to forget the jeopardy of her dog. In the afternoon we walked in a meadow by the river side, which winds in the form of a horseshoe about Germanna, making it a peninsula, containing about four hundred acres. Rappahannock forks about fourteen miles below this place, the northern branch being the larger, and consequently must be the river that bounds my lord Fairfax's grant of the Northern Neck.

30th. The sun rose clear this morning, and so did I, and finished all my little affairs by breakfast. It was then resolved to wait on the ladies on horseback, since the bright sun, the fine air, and the wholesome exercise, all invited us to it. We forded the river a little above the ferry, and rode six miles up the neck to a fine level piece of rich land, where we found about twenty plants of ginseng, with the scarlet berries growing on the top of the middle stalk. The root of this is of wonderful virtue in many cases, particularly to raise the spirits and promote perspiration, which makes it a specific in colds and coughs. The colonel complimented me with all we found, in return for my telling him the virtues of it. We were all pleased to find so much of this king of plants so near the colonel's habitation, and growing too upon his own land; but were, however, surprised to find it upon level ground, after we had been told it grew only upon the north side of stony mountains. I carried home this treasure, with as much joy, as if every root had been a graft of the tree of life, and washed and dried it carefully. This airing made us as hungry as so many hawks, so that between appetite and a very good dinner, it was difficult to eat like a philosopher. In the afternoon the ladies walked me about amongst all their little animals, with which they amuse themselves, and furnish the table; the worst of it is, they are so tender-hearted, they shed a silent tear every time any of them are killed. At night the colonel and I quitted the threadbare subject of iron, and changed the scene of politics. He told me the ministry had receded from their demand upon New England, to raise a standing salary for all succeeding governors, for fear some curious members of the house of commons should inquire how the money was disposed of, that had been raised in the other American colonies for the support of their governors. And particularly what becomes of the four and a half per cent, paid in the sugar colonies for that purpose. That duty produces near twenty thousand pounds a year, but being remitted into the exchequer, not one of the West India governors is paid out of it; but they, like falcons, are let loose upon the people, who are complaisant enough to settle other revenues upon them, to the great impoverishing of these colonies. In the meantime, it is certain the money raised by the four and a half per cent molders away between the minister's fingers, nobody knows how, like the quitrents of Virginia. And it is for this reason that the instructions, forbidding all governors to accept of any presents from their assemblies, are dispensed with in the sugar islands, while it is strictly insisted upon everywhere else, where the assemblies were so wise as to keep their revenues among themselves. He said further, that if the assembly in New England would stand bluff, he did not see how they could be forced to raise money against their will, for if they should direct it to be done by act of parliament, which they have threatened to do, (though it be against the right of Englishmen to be taxed but by their representatives), yet they would find it no easy matter to put such an act in execution. Then the colonel read me a lecture upon tar, affirming that it cannot be made in this warm climate, after the manner they make it in Sweden and Muscovy, by barking the tree two yards from the ground, whereby the turpentine descends all into the stump in a year's time, which is then split in pieces in order for the kiln. But here the sun fries out the turpentine in the branches of the tree, when the leaves are dried, and hinders it from descending. But, on the contrary, those who burn tar of lightwood in the common way, and are careful about it, make as good as that which comes from the east country, nor will it burn the cordage more than that does. Then we entered upon the subject of hemp, which the colonel told me he never could raise here from foreign seed, but at last sowed the seed of wild hemp (which is very common in the upper parts of the country), and that came up very thick. That he sent about five hundred pounds of it to England, and that the commissioners of the navy, after a full trial of it, reported to the lords of the admiralty, that it was equal in goodness to the best that comes from Riga. I told him if our hemp were never so good, it would not be worth the making here, even though they should continue the bounty. And my reason was, because labor is not more than two pence a day in the east country where they produce hemp, and here we cannot compute it at less than ten pence, which being five times as much as their labor, and considering besides, that our freight is three times as dear as theirs, the price that will make them rich will ruin us, as I have found by woeful experience. Besides, if the king, who must have the refusal, buys our hemp, the navy is so long in paying both the price and the bounty, that we who live from hand to mouth cannot afford to wait so long for it. And then our good friends, the merchants, load it with so many charges, that they run away with great part of the profit themselves. Just like the bald eagle, which after the fishing hawk has been at great pains to catch a fish, pounces upon and takes it from him. Our conversation was interrupted by a summons to supper, for the ladies, to show their power, had by this time brought us tamely to go to bed with our bellies full, though we both at first declared positively against it. So very pliable a thing is frail man, when women have the bending of him.

October 1st. Our ladies overslept themselves this morning, so that we did not break our fast till ten. We drank tea made of the leaves of ginseng, which has the virtues of the root in a weaker degree, and is not disagreeable. So soon as we could force our inclinations to quit the ladies, we took a turn on the terrace walk, and discoursed upon quite a new subject. The colonel explained to me the difference betwixt the galleons and the flota, which very few people know. The galleons, it seems, are the ships which bring the treasure and other rich merchandise to Carthagena from Portobel, to which place it is brought over land, from Panama and Peru. And the flota is the squadron that brings the treasure, &c., from Mexico and New Spain, which make up at La Vera Cruz. Both these squadrons rendezvous at the Havanna, from hence they shoot the gulf of Florida, in their return to Old Spain. That this important port of the Havanna is very poorly fortified, and worse garrisoned and provided, for which reason it may be easily taken. Besides, both the galleons and flota, being confined to sail through the gulf, might be intercepted by our stationing a squadron of men of war at the most convenient of the Bahama islands. And that those islands are of vast consequence for that purpose. He told me also that the azogue ships are they that carry quicksilver to Portobello and La Vera Cruz, to refine the silver, and that, in Spanish, azogue signifies quicksilver. Then my friend unriddled to me the great mystery, why we have endured all the late insolences of the Spaniards so tamely. The asiento contract, and the liberty of sending a ship every year to the Spanish West Indies, make it very necessary for the South Sea Company to have effects of great value in that part of the world. Now these being always in the power of the Spaniards, make the directors of that company very fearful of a breach, and consequently very generous in their offers to the ministry to prevent it. For fear these worthy gentlemen should suffer, the English squadron, under Admiral Hosier, lay idle at the Bastimentos, till the ships' bottoms were eaten out by the worm, and the officers and men, to the number of five thousand, died like rotten sheep, without being suffered, by the strictest orders, to strike one stroke, though they might have taken both the flota and galleons, and made themselves masters of the Havanna into the bargain, if they had not been chained up from doing it. All this moderation, our peaceable ministry showed even at a time when the Spaniards were furiously attacking Gibraltar, and taking all the English ships they could, both in Europe and America, to the great and everlasting reproach of the British nation. That some of the ministry, being tired out with the clamors of the merchants, declared their opinion for war, and while they entertained those sentiments they pitched upon him, Col. Spotswood, to be governor of Jamaica, that by his skill and experience in the art military, they might be the better able to execute their design of taking the Havanna. But the courage of these worthy patriots soon cooled, and the arguments used by the South Sea directors, persuaded them once again into more pacific measures. When the scheme was dropped, his government of Jamaica was dropped at the same time, and then General Hunter was judged fit enough to rule that island in time of peace. After this the colonel endeavored to convince me that he came fairly by his place of postmaster-general, notwithstanding the report of some evil disposed persons to the contrary. The case was this, Mr. Hamilton, of

New Jersey, who had formerly had that post, wrote to Col. Spotswood, in England, to favor him with his interest to get it restored to him. But the colonel, considering wisely that charity began at home, instead of getting the place for Hamilton, secured it for a better friend: though, as he tells the story, that gentleman was absolutely refused, before he spoke the least good word for himself.

2d. This being the day appointed for my departure from hence, I packed up my effects in good time; but the ladies, whose dear companies we were to have to the mines, were a little tedious in their equipment. However, we made a shift to get into the coach by ten o'clock; but little master, who is under no government, would by all means go on horseback. Before we set out I gave Mr. Russel the trouble of distributing a pistole among the servants of which I fancy the nurse had a pretty good share, being no small favorite.

JONATHAN EDWARDS

1703–1758

7 *Personal Narrative*

I HAD a variety of concerns and exercises about my soul from my childhood; but had two more remarkable seasons of awakening, before I met with that change by which I was brought to those new dispositions, and that new sense of things, that I have since had. The first time was when I was a boy, some years before I went to college, at a time of remarkable awakening in my father's congregation. I was then very much affected for many months, and concerned about the things of religion, and my soul's salvation; and was abundant in duties. I used to pray five times a day in secret, and to spend much time in religious talk with other boys, and used to meet with them to pray together. I experienced I know not what kind of delight in religion. My mind was much engaged in it, and had much self-righteous pleasure; and it was my delight to abound in religious duties. I with some of my schoolmates joined together, and built a booth in a swamp, in a very retired spot, for a place of prayer. And besides, I had particular secret places of my own in the woods, where I used to retire by myself; and was from time to time much affected. My affections seemed to be lively and easily moved, and I seemed to be in my element when engaged in religious duties. And I am ready to think, many are deceived with such affections, and such a kind of delight as I then had in religion, and mistake it for grace.

But in process of time, my convictions and affections wore off; and I entirely lost all those affections and delights and left off secret prayer, at least as to any constant performance of it; and returned like a dog to his vomit, and went on in the ways of sin. Indeed I was at times very uneasy, especially towards the latter part of my time at college; when it pleased God, to seize me with the pleurisy; in which he brought me nigh to the grave, and shook me over the pit of hell. And yet, it was not long after my recovery, before I fell again into my old ways of sin. But God would not suffer me to go on with my quietness; I had great and violent inward struggles, till, after many conflicts, with wicked inclinations, repeated resolutions, and bonds that I laid myself under by a kind of vows to God, I was brought wholly to break off all former wicked ways, and all ways of known outward sin; and to apply myself to seek salvation, and practice many religious duties; but without that kind of affection and delight which I had formerly experienced. My concern now wrought more by inward struggles and conflicts, and self-reflections. I made seeking my salvation the main business of my life. But yet, it seems to me, I sought after a miserable manner; which has made me sometimes since to question, whether ever it issued in that which was saving; being ready to doubt, whether such miserable seeking ever succeeded. I was indeed brought to seek salvation in a manner that I never was before; I felt a spirit to part with all things in the world, for an interest in Christ. — My concern continued and prevailed, with many exercising thoughts and inward struggles; but yet it never seemed to be proper to express that concern by the name of terror.

From my childhood up, my mind had been full of objections against the doctrine of God's sovereignty, in choosing whom he would to eternal life, and rejecting whom he pleased; leaving them eternally to perish, and be everlastingly tormented in hell. It used to appear like a horrible doctrine to me. But I remember the time very well, when I seemed to be convinced, and fully satisfied, as to the sovereignty of God, and his justice in thus eternally disposing of men, according to his sovereign pleasure. But never could give an account, how, or by what means, I was thus convinced, not in the least imagining at the time, nor a long time after, that there was any extraordinary influence of God's Spirit in it; but only that now I saw further, and my reason apprehended the justice and reasonableness of it. However, my mind rested in it; and it put an end to all those cavils and objections. And there has been a wonderful alteration in my mind, with respect to the doctrine of God's sovereignty, from that day to this; so that I scarce ever have found so much as the rising of an objection against it, in the most absolute sense, in God's showing mercy to whom he will show mercy, and hardening whom he will. God's absolute sovereignty and justice, with respect to salvation and damnation, is what my mind seems to rest assured of, as much as of any thing that I see with my eyes; at least it is so at times. But I have often, since that first conviction, had quite another kind of sense of God's sovereignty than I had then. I have often since had not only a conviction, but a delightful conviction. The doctrine has very often appeared exceeding pleasant, bright, and sweet.

Absolute sovereignty is what I love to ascribe to God. But my first conviction was not so.

The first instance that I remember of that sort of inward, sweet delight in God and divine things that I have lived much in since, was on reading those words, 1 Tim. i: 17. *Now unto the King eternal, immortal, invisible, the only wise God, be honor and glory forever and ever, Amen.* As I read the words, there came into my soul, and was as it were diffused through it, a sense of the glory of the Divine Being; a new sense, quite different from any thing I ever experienced before. Never any words of scripture seemed to me as these words did. I thought within myself, how excellent a being that was, and how happy I should be, if I might enjoy that God, and be wrapt up in heaven, and be as it were swallowed up in him forever! I kept saying, and as it were singing over these words of scripture to myself; and went to pray to God that I might enjoy him, and prayed in a manner quite different from what I used to do; with a new sort of affection. But it never came into my thought, that there was any thing spiritual, or of a saving nature in this.

From about that time, I began to have a new kind of apprehensions and ideas of Christ, and the work of redemption, and the glorious way of salvation by him. An inward, sweet sense of these things, at times, came into my heart; and my soul was led away in pleasant views and contemplations of them. And my mind was greatly engaged to spend my time in reading and meditating on Christ, on the beauty and excellency of his person, and the lovely way of salvation by free grace in him. I found no books so delightful to me, as those that treated of these subjects. Those words, Cant. ii: 1, used to be abundantly with me, *I am the Rose of Sharon, and the Lily of the valleys.* The words seemed to me, sweetly to represent the loveliness and beauty of Jesus Christ. The whole book of Canticles used to be pleasant to me, and I used to be much in reading it, about that time; and found, from time to time, an inward sweetness, that would carry me away, in my contemplations. This I know not how to express otherwise, than by a calm, sweet abstraction of soul from all the concerns of this world; and sometimes a kind of vision, or fixed ideas and imaginations, of being alone in the mountains, or some solitary wilderness, far from all mankind, sweetly conversing with Christ, and wrapt and swallowed up in God. The sense I had of divine things, would often of a sudden kindle up, as it were, a sweet burning in my heart; an ardor of soul, that I know not how to express.

Not long after I began to experience these things, I gave an account to my father of some things that had passed in my mind. I was pretty much affected by the discourse we had together; and when the discourse was ended, I walked abroad alone, in a solitary place in my father's pasture for contemplation. And as I was walking there and looking up on the sky and clouds, there came into my mind so sweet a sense of the glorious *majesty* and *grace* of God, that I know not how to express. I seemed to see them both in a sweet conjunction; majesty and meekness joined together; it was a gentle, and holy majesty; and also a majestic meekness; a high, great, and holy gentleness.

After this my sense of divine things gradually increased, and became more and more lively, and had more of that inward sweetness. The appearance of every thing was altered; there seemed to be, as it were, a calm, sweet cast, or appearance of divine glory, in almost every thing. God's excellency, his wisdom, his purity and love, seemed to appear in every thing; in the sun, moon, and stars; in the clouds, and blue sky; in the grass, flowers, trees; in the water, and all nature; which used greatly to fix my mind. I often used to sit and view the moon for continuance; and in the day, spent much time in viewing the clouds and sky to behold the sweet glory of God in these things; in the mean time, singing forth, with a low voice, my contemplations of the Creator and Redeemer. And scarce any thing, among all the works of nature, was so delightful to me as thunder and lightning; formerly, nothing had been so terrible to me. Before, I used to be uncommonly terrified with thunder, and to be struck with terror when I saw a thunder storm rising; but now, on the contrary, it rejoiced me. I felt God, so to speak, at the first appearance of a thunder storm; and used to take the opportunity, at such times, to fix myself in order to view the clouds, and see the lightnings play, and hear the majestic and awful voice of God's thunder, which oftentimes was exceedingly entertaining, leading me to sweet contemplations of my great and glorious God. While thus engaged, it always seemed natural to me to sing, or chant for my meditations; or, to speak my thoughts in soliloquies with a singing voice.

I felt then great satisfaction, as to my good state; but that did not content me. I had vehement longings of soul after God and Christ, and after more holiness, wherewith my heart seemed to be full, and ready to break; which often brought to my mind the words of the Psalmist, Psal. cxix: 28: *My soul breaketh for the longing it hath.* I often felt a mourning and lamenting in my heart, that I had not turned to God sooner, that I might have had more time to grow in grace. My mind was greatly fixed on divine things; almost perpetually in the contemplation of them. I spent most of my time in thinking of divine things, year after year; often walking alone in the woods, and solitary places, for meditation, soliloquy, and prayer, and converse with God; and it was always my manner, at such times, to sing forth my contemplations. I was almost constantly in ejaculatory prayer, wherever I was. Prayer seemed to be natural to me, as the breath by which the inward burnings of my heart had vent. The delights which I now felt in the things of religion, were of an exceedingly different kind from those before mentioned, that I had when a boy; and what I then had no more notion of, than one born blind has of pleasant and beautiful colors. They were of a more inward, pure, soul-animating and refreshing nature. Those former delights never reached the heart; and did not arise from any sight of the divine excellency of the things of God; or any taste of the soul-satisfying and life-giving good there is in them.

My sense of divine things seemed gradually to increase, until I went to preach at New York, which was about a year and a half after they began; and while I was there, I felt them, very sensibly, in a higher degree than I had done before. My longings after God and holiness, were much increased. Pure and humble, holy and heavenly Christianity, appeared exceedingly amiable to me. I felt a burning desire to be in every thing a complete Christian; and conform to the blessed image of Christ; and that I might live, in all things, according to the pure and blessed rules of the gospel. I had an eager thirsting after progress in these things; which put me upon pursuing and pressing after them. It was my continual strife day and night, and constant inquiry, how I should *be* more holy, and *live* more holily, and more becoming a child of God, and a disciple of Christ. I now sought an increase of grace and holiness, and a holy life, with much more earnestness, than ever I sought grace before I had it. I used to be continually examining myself, and studying and contriving for likely ways and means, how I should live holily, with far greater diligence and earnestness, than ever I pursued any thing in my life; but yet with too great a dependence on my own strength; which afterwards proved a great damage to me. My experience had not then taught me, as it has done since, my extreme feebleness and impotence, every manner of way; and the bottomless depths of secret corruption and deceit there was in my heart. However, I went on with my eager pursuit after more holiness, and conformity to Christ.

The heaven I desired was a heaven of holiness; to be with God, and to spend my eternity in divine love, and holy communion with Christ. My mind was very much taken up with contemplations on heaven, and the enjoyments there; and living there in perfect holiness, humility and love. And it used at that time to appear a great part of the happiness of heaven, that there the saints could express their love to Christ. It appeared to me a great clog and burden, that what I felt within, I could not express as I desired. The inward ardor of my soul seemed to be hindered and pent up, and could not freely flame out as it would. I used often to think, how in heaven this principle should freely and fully vent and express itself. Heaven appeared exceedingly delightful, as a world of love; and that all happiness consisted in living in pure, humble, heavenly, divine love.

I remember the thoughts I used then to have of holiness; and said sometimes to myself, " I do certainly know that I love holiness, such as the gospel prescribes." It appeared to me, that there was nothing in it but what was ravishingly lovely; the highest beauty and amiableness — a *divine* beauty; far purer than any thing here upon earth; and that every thing else was like mire and defilement, in comparison of it.

Holiness, as I then wrote down some of my contemplations on it, appeared to me to be of a sweet, pleasant, charming, serene, calm nature; which brought an inexpressible purity, brightness, peacefulness and ravishment to the soul. In other words, that it made the soul like a field or garden of God, with all manner of pleasant flowers; all pleasant, delightful, and undisturbed; enjoying a sweet calm, and the gently vivifying beams of the sun. The soul of a true Christian, as I then wrote my meditations, appeared like such a little white flower as we see in the spring of the year; low and humble on the ground, opening its bosom to receive the pleasant beams of the sun's glory; rejoicing as it were in a calm rapture; diffusing around a sweet fragrancy; standing peacefully and lovingly, in the midst of other flowers round about; all in like manner opening their bosoms, to drink in the light of the sun. There was no part of creature holiness, that I had so great a sense of its loveliness, as humility, brokenness of heart and poverty of spirit; and there was nothing that I so earnestly longed for. My heart panted after this, to lie low before God, as in the dust; that I might be nothing, and that God might be ALL, that I might become as a little child.

While at New York, I was sometimes much affected with reflections on my past life, considering how late it was before I began to be truly religious; and how wickedly I had lived till then; and once so as to weep abundantly, and for a considerable time together.

On January 12, 1723, I made a solemn dedication of myself to God, and wrote it down; giving up myself, and all that I had to God; to be for the future in no respect my own; to act as one that had no right to himself, in any respect. And solemnly vowed to take God for my whole portion and felicity; looking on nothing else as any part of my happiness, nor acting as if it were; and his law for the constant rule of my obedience; engaging to fight with all my might, against the world, the flesh and the devil, to the end of my life. But I have reason to be infinitely humbled, when I consider how much I have failed of answering my obligation.

I had then abundance of sweet religious conversation in the family where I lived, with Mr. John Smith and his pious mother. My heart was knit in affection to those in whom were appearances of true piety; and I could bear the thoughts of no other companions, but such as were holy, and the disciples of the blessed Jesus. I had great longings for the advancement of Christ's kingdom in the world; and my secret prayer used to be, in great part, taken up in praying for it. If I heard the least hint of any thing that happened, in any part of the world, that appeared, in some respect or other, to have a favorable aspect on the interest of Christ's kingdom, my soul eagerly catched at it; and it would much animate and refresh me. I used to be eager to read public news letters, mainly for that end; to see if I could not find some news favorable to the interest of religion in the world.

I very frequently used to retire into a solitary place, on the banks of Hudson's river, at some distance from the city, for contemplation on divine things, and secret converse with God; and had many sweet hours there. Sometimes Mr. Smith and I walked there together, to converse on the things of God; and our conversation used to turn much on the advancement of Christ's kingdom in the world, and the glorious things that God would accomplish for his church in the latter days. I had then, and at other times the greatest delight in the holy scriptures, of any book whatsoever. Oftentimes in reading it, every word seemed to touch my heart. I felt a harmony between something in my heart, and those sweet and powerful words. I seemed often to see so much light exhibited by every sentence, and such a refreshing food communicated, that I could not get along in reading; often dwelling long on one sentence, to see the wonders contained in it; and yet almost every sentence seemed to be full of wonders.

I came away from New York in the month of April, 1723, and had a most bitter parting with Madam Smith and her son. My heart seemed to sink within me at leaving the family and city, where I had enjoyed so many sweet and pleasant days. I went from New York to Weathersfield by water, and as I sailed away, I kept sight of the city as long as I could. However, that night, after this sorrowful parting, I was greatly comforted in God at Westchester, where we went ashore to lodge; and had a pleasant time of it all the voyage to Saybrook. It was sweet to me to think of meeting dear Christians in heaven, where we should never part more. At Saybrook we went ashore to lodge, on Saturday, and there kept the Sabbath; where I had a sweet and refreshing season, walking alone in the fields.

After I came home to Windsor, I remained much in a like frame of mind, as when at New York; only sometimes I felt my heart ready to sink with the thoughts of my friends at New York. My support was in contemplations on the heavenly state; as I find in my Diary of May 1, 1723. It was a comfort to think of that state, where there is fulness of joy; where reigns heavenly, calm, and delightful love, without alloy; where there are continually the dearest expressions of this love; where is the enjoyment of the persons loved, without ever parting; where those persons who appear so lovely in this world, will really be inexpressibly more lovely and full of love to us. And how sweetly will the mutual lovers join together to sing the praises of God and the Lamb! How will it fill us with joy to think, that this enjoyment, these sweet exercises will never cease, but will last to all eternity! I continued much in the same frame, in the general, as when at New York, till I went to New Haven as tutor to the college; particularly once at Bolton, on a journey from Boston, while walking out alone in the fields. After I went to New Haven I sunk in religion; my mind being diverted from my eager pursuits after holiness, by some affairs that greatly perplexed and distracted my thoughts.

In September, 1725, I was taken ill at New Haven, and

while endeavoring to go home to Windsor, was so ill at the North Village, that I could go no further; where I lay sick for about a quarter of a year. In this sickness God was pleased to visit me again with the sweet influences of his Spirit. My mind was greatly engaged there in divine, pleasant contemplations, and longings of soul. I observed that those who watched with me, would often be looking out wishfully for the morning; which brought to my mind those words of the Psalmist, and which my soul with delight made its own language, *My soul waiteth for the Lord, more than they that watch for the morning, I say, more than they that watch for the morning;* and when the light of day came in at the windows, it refreshed my soul from one morning to another. It seemed to be some image of the light of God's glory.

I remember, about that time, I used greatly to long for the conversion of some that I was concerned with; I could gladly honor them, and with delight be a servant to them, and lie at their feet, if they were but truly holy. But, some time after this, I was again greatly diverted in my mind with some temporal concerns that exceedingly took up my thoughts, greatly to the wounding of my soul; and went on through various exercises, that it would be tedious to relate, which gave me much more experience of my own heart, than ever I had before.

Since I came to this town [Northampton], I have often had sweet complacency in God, in views of his glorious perfections and the excellency of Jesus Christ. God has appeared to me a glorious and lovely being, chiefly on the account of his holiness. The holiness of God has always appeared to me the most lovely of all his attributes. The doctrines of God's absolute sovereignty, and free grace, in showing mercy to whom he would show mercy; and man's absolute dependence on the operations of God's Holy Spirit, have very often appeared to me as sweet and glorious doctrines. These doctrines have been much my delight. God's sovereignty has ever appeared to me, great part of his glory. It has often been my delight to approach God, and adore him as a sovereign God, and ask sovereign mercy of him.

I have loved the doctrines of the gospel; they have been to my soul like green pastures. The gospel has seemed to me the richest treasure; the treasure that I have most desired, and longed that it might dwell richly in me. The way of salvation by Christ has appeared, in a general way, glorious and excellent, most pleasant and most beautiful. It has often seemed to me, that it would in a great measure spoil heaven, to receive it in any other way. That text has often been affecting and delightful to me. Isa. xxxii: 2. *A man shall be an hiding place from the wind, and a covert from the tempest,* &c.

It has often appeared to me delightful, to be united to Christ; to have him for my head, and to be a member of his body; also to have Christ for my teacher and prophet. I very often think with sweetness, and longings, and pantings of soul, of being a little child, taking hold of Christ, to be led by him through the wilderness of this world. That text, Matth. xviii: 3, has often been sweet to me, *except ye be converted and become as little children,* &c. I love to think of coming to Christ, to receive salvation of him, poor in spirit, and quite empty of self, humbly exalting him alone; cut off entirely from my own root, in order to grow into, and out of Christ; to have God in Christ to be all in all; and to live by faith on the Son of God, a life of humble unfeigned confidence in him. That scripture has often been sweet to me, Psal. cxx: 1. *Not unto us, O Lord, not unto us, but to thy name give glory, for thy mercy and for thy truth's sake.* And those words of Christ, Luke x: 21. *In that hour Jesus rejoiced in spirit, and said, I thank thee, O Father, Lord of heaven and earth, that thou hast hid these things from the wise and prudent, and hast revealed them unto babes; even so, Father, for so it seemed good in thy sight.* That sovereignty of God which Christ rejoiced in, seemed to me worthy of such joy; and that rejoicing seemed to show the excellency of Christ, and of what spirit he was.

Sometimes, only mentioning a single word caused my heart to burn within me; or only seeing the name of Christ, or the name of some attribute of God. And God has appeared glorious to me, on account of the Trinity. It has made me have exalting thoughts of God, that he subsists in three persons; Father, Son and Holy Ghost. The sweetest joys and delights I have experienced, have not been those that have arisen from a hope of my own good estate; but in a direct view of the glorious things of the gospel. When I enjoy this sweetness, it seems to carry me above the thoughts of my own estate; it seems at such times a loss that I cannot bear, to take off my eye from the glorious pleasant object I behold without me, to turn my eye in upon myself, and my own good estate.

My heart has been much on the advancement of Christ's kingdom in the world. The histories of the past advancement of Christ's kingdom have been sweet to me. When I have read histories of past ages, the pleasantest thing in all my reading has been, to read of the kingdom of Christ being promoted. And when I have expected, in my reading, to come to any such thing, I have rejoiced in the prospect, all the way as I read. And my mind has been much entertained and delighted with the scripture promises and prophecies, which relate to the future glorious advancement of Christ's kingdom upon earth.

I have sometimes had a sense of the excellent fulness of Christ, and his meetness and suitableness as a Saviour; whereby he has appeared to me, far above all, the chief of ten thousands. His blood and atonement have appeared sweet, and his righteousness sweet; which was always accompanied with ardency of spirit; and inward strugglings and breathings, and groanings that cannot be uttered, to be emptied of myself, and swallowed up in Christ.

Once as I rode out into the woods for my health, in 1737, having alighted from my horse in a retired place, as my manner commonly has been, to walk for divine contemplation and prayer, I had a view that for me was extraordinary, of the glory of the Son of God, as Mediator between God and man, and his wonderful, great, full, pure and sweet grace and love, and meek and gentle condescension. This grace that appeared so calm and sweet, appeared also great above the heavens. The person of Christ appeared ineffably excellent with an excellency great enough to swallow up all thought and conception — which continued as near as I can judge, about an hour; which kept me the greater part of the time in a flood of tears, and weeping aloud. I felt an ardency of soul to be, what I know not otherwise how to express, emptied and annihilated; to lie in the dust, and to be full of Christ alone; to love him with a holy and pure love; to trust in him; to live upon him; to serve and follow him; and to be perfectly sanctified and made pure, with a divine and heavenly purity. I have, several other times, had views very much of the same nature, and which have had the same effects.

I have many times had a sense of the glory of the third person in the Trinity, in his office of Sanctifier; in his holy operations, communicating divine light and life to the soul. God, in the communications of his Holy Spirit, has appeared as an infinite fountain of divine glory and sweetness; being full, and sufficient to fill and satisfy the soul; pouring forth itself in sweet communications; like the sun in its glory, sweetly and pleasantly diffusing light and life. And I have sometimes had an affecting sense of the excellency of the word of God, as a word of life; as the light of life; a sweet, excellent, life-giving word; accompanied with a thirsting after that word, that it might dwell richly in my heart.

Often, since I lived in this town, I have had very affecting views of my own sinfulness and vileness; very frequently to such a degree as to hold me in a kind of loud weeping, sometimes for a considerable time together; so that I have often been forced to shut myself up. I have had a vastly greater sense of my own wickedness, and the badness of my own heart, than ever I had before my conversion. It has often appeared to me, that if God should mark iniquity against me, I should appear the very worst of all mankind; of all that have been, since the beginning of the world to this time; and that I should have by far the lowest place in hell. When others, that have come to talk with me about their soul concerns, have expressed the sense they have had of their own wickedness, by saying that it seemed to them, that they were as bad as the devil himself; I thought their expression seemed exceedingly faint and feeble, to represent my wickedness.

My wickedness, as I am in myself, has long appeared to me perfectly ineffable, and swallowing up all thought and imagination; like an infinite deluge, or mountains over my head. I know not how to express better what my sins appear to me to be, than by heaping infinite upon infinite, and multiplying infinite by infinite. Very often, for these many years, these expressions are in my mind, and in my mouth, " Infinite upon infinite — Infinite upon infinite ! " When I look into my heart, and take a view of my wickedness, it looks like an abyss infinitely deeper than hell. And it appears to me, that were it not for free grace, exalted and raised up to the infinite height of all the fulness and glory of the great Jehovah, and the arm of his power and grace stretched forth in all the majesty of his power, and in all the glory of his sovereignty, I should appear sunk down in my sins below hell itself; far beyond the sight of everything, but the eye of sovereign grace, that can pierce even down to such a depth. And yet, it seems to me, that my conviction of sin is exceedingly small, and faint; it is enough to amaze me, that I have no more sense of my sin. I know certainly, that I have very little sense of my sinfulness. When I have had turns of weeping and crying for my sins, I thought I knew at the time, that my repentance was nothing to my sin.

I have greatly longed of late, for a broken heart, and to lie low before God; and, when I ask for humility, I cannot bear the thoughts of being no more humble than other Christians. It seems to me, that though their degrees of humility may be suitable for them, yet it would be a vile self-exaltation to me, not to be the lowest in humility of all mankind. Others speak of their longing to be " humbled to the dust; " that may be a proper expression for them, but I always think of myself, that

I ought, and it is an expression that has long been natural for me to use in prayer, "to lie infinitely low before God." And it is affecting to think, how ignorant I was, when a young Christian, of the bottomless, infinite depths of wickedness, pride, hypocrisy and deceit, left in my heart.

I have a much greater sense of my universal, exceeding dependence on God's grace and strength, and mere good pleasure, of late, than I used formerly to have; and have experienced more of an abhorrence of my own righteousness. The very thought of any joy arising in me, on any consideration of my own amiableness, performances, or experiences, or any goodness of heart or life, is nauseous and detestable to me. And yet I am greatly afflicted with a proud and self-righteous spirit, much more sensibly than I used to be formerly. I see that serpent rising and putting forth its head continually, everywhere, all around me.

Though it seems to me, that, in some respects, I was a far better Christian, for two or three years after my first conversion, than I am now; and lived in a more constant delight and pleasure; yet, of late years, I have had a more full and constant sense of the absolute sovereignty of God, and a delight in that sovereignty; and have had more of a sense of the glory of Christ, as a Mediator revealed in the gospel. On one Saturday night, in particular, I had such a discovery of the excellency of the gospel above all other doctrines, that I could not but say to myself, "This is my chosen light, my chosen doctrine;" and of Christ, "This is my chosen Prophet." It appeared sweet, beyond all expression, to follow Christ, and to be taught, and enlightened, and instructed by him; to learn of him, and live to him. Another Saturday night (January, 1739), I had such a sense, how sweet and blessed a thing it was to walk in the way of duty; to do that which was right and meet to be done, and agreeable to the holy mind of God; that it caused me to break forth into a kind of loud weeping, which held me some time, so that I was forced to shut myself up, and fasten the doors. I could not but, as it were, cry out, "How happy are they which do that which is right in the sight of God! They are blessed indeed, they are the happy ones!" I had, at the same time, a very affecting sense, how meet and suitable it was that God should govern the world, and order all things according to his own pleasure; and I rejoiced in it, that God reigned, and that his will was done.

BENJAMIN FRANKLIN

1706–1790

8   *The Way to Wealth*

COURTEOUS READER:

I have heard that nothing gives an author so great pleasure as to find his works respectfully quoted by other learned authors. This pleasure I have seldom enjoyed, for, though I have been, if I may say it without vanity, an eminent author (of almanacs) annually now a full quarter of a century, my brother authors in the same way, for what reason I know not, have ever been very sparing in their applauses and no other author has taken the least notice of me, so that, did not my writings produce me some solid pudding, the great deficiency of praise would have quite discouraged me.

I concluded at length that the people were the best judges of my merit, for they buy my works; and, besides, in my rambles where I am not personally known, I have frequently heard one or other of my adages repeated with "As Poor Richard says" at the end on 't; this gave me some satisfaction, as it showed not only that my instructions were regarded, but discovered likewise some respect for my authority; and I own that, to encourage the practice of remembering and repeating those wise sentences, I have sometimes *quoted myself* with great gravity.

Judge then how much I must have been gratified by an incident I am going to relate to you. I stopped my horse lately where a great number of people were collected at a vendue of merchant goods. The hour of sale not being come, they were conversing on the badness of the times, and one of the company called to a plain, clean old man with white locks, "Pray, Father Abraham, what think you of the times? Won't these heavy taxes quite ruin the country? How shall we be ever able to pay them? What would you advise us to do?" Father Abraham stood up and replied, "If you'd have my advice, I'll give it to you in short; for A word to the wise is enough, and Many words won't fill a bushel, as Poor Richard says." They joined in desiring him to speak his mind, and gathering round him, he proceeded as follows:

"Friends," says he, "and neighbors, the taxes are indeed very heavy, and if those laid on by the government were the only ones we had to pay, we might more easily discharge them; but we have many others, and much more grievous to some of us. We are taxed twice as much by our idleness, three times as much by our pride, and four times as much by our folly; and from these taxes the commissioners cannot ease or deliver us by allowing an abatement. However, let us hearken to good advice, and something may be done for us; God helps them that help themselves, as Poor Richard says in his almanac of 1733.

"It would be thought a hard government that should tax its people one tenth part of their time, to be employed in its service; but idleness taxes many of us much more if we reckon all that is spent in absolute sloth, or doing of nothing, with that which is spent in idle employments or amusements, that amount to nothing. Sloth, by bringing on diseases, absolutely shortens life. Sloth, like rust, consumes faster than labor wears, while the used key is always bright, as Poor Richard says. But dost thou love life? Then do not squander time, for that's the stuff life is made of, as Poor Richard says. How much more than is necessary do we spend in sleep, forgetting that The sleeping fox catches no poultry, and that There will be sleeping enough in the grave, as Poor Richard says. If time be of all things the most precious, wasting time must be, as Poor Richard says, the greatest prodigality; since, as he elsewhere tells us, Lost time is never found again, and what we call time enough always proves little enough. Let us, then, up and be doing, and doing to the purpose; so by diligence shall we do more with less perplexity. Sloth makes all things difficult, but industry, all things easy, as Poor Richard says; and, He that riseth late must trot all day and shall scarce overtake his business at night; while Laziness travels so slowly that Poverty soon overtakes him, as we read in Poor Richard, who adds, Drive thy business, let not that drive thee; and, Early to bed, and early to rise, makes a man healthy, wealthy and wise.

"So what signifies wishing and hoping for better times? We may make these times better if we bestir ourselves. Industry need not wish, as Poor Richard says, and he that lives upon hope will die fasting. There are no gains without pains; then help, hands, for I have no lands; or if I have, they are smartly taxed. And as Poor Richard likewise observes, He that hath a trade hath an estate; and he that hath a calling, hath an office of profit and honor; but then the trade must be worked at and the calling well followed, or neither the estate nor the office will enable us to pay our taxes. If we are industrious, we shall never starve; for, as Poor Richard says, At the workingman's house hunger looks in, but dares not enter. Nor will the bailiff or the constable enter; for Industry pays debts, while despair increaseth them, says Poor Richard. — What though you have found no treasure, nor has any rich relation left you a legacy; Diligence is the mother of good luck, as Poor Richard says, and God gives all things to Industry. Then plow deep while sluggards sleep, and you shall have corn to sell and to keep, says Poor Dick. Work while it is called to-day, or you know not how much you may be hindered to-morrow, which makes Poor Richard say, One to-day is worth two to-morrows; and farther, Have you somewhat to do to-morrow, do it to-day. If you were a servant, would you not be ashamed that a good master should catch you idle? Are you, then, your own master? Be ashamed to catch yourself idle, as Poor Dick says. When there is so much to be done for yourself, your family, your country, and your gracious King, be up by peep of day. Let not the sun look down and say, Inglorious here he lies. Handle your tools without mittens; remember that The cat in gloves catches no mice, as Poor Richard says. It is true there is much to be done, and perhaps you are weak-handed; but stick to it steadily, and you will see great effects; for, Constant dropping wears away stones; and, By diligence and patience the mouse ate in two the cable; and Little strokes fell great oaks, as Poor Richard says in his almanac, the year I cannot just now remember.

"Methinks I hear some of you say, Must a man afford himself no leisure? I will tell thee, my friend, what Poor Richard says: Employ thy time well, if thou meanest to gain leisure; and since thou art not sure of a minute, throw not away an hour. Leisure is time for doing something useful; this leisure the diligent man will obtain, but the lazy man never; so that, as Poor Richard says, A life of leisure and a life of laziness are two things. Do you imagine that sloth will afford you more comfort than labor? No, for as Poor Richard says, Trouble springs from idleness, and grievous toil from needless ease. Many, without labor, would live by their wits only, but they break for want of stock. Whereas industry gives comfort and plenty and respect. Fly pleasures and they'll follow you. The diligent spinner has a large shift; and now I have a sheep and a cow everybody bids me good morrow. All which is well said by Poor Richard.

"But with our industry we must likewise be steady, settled, and careful, and oversee our own affairs with our own eyes, and not trust too much to others; for, as Poor Richard says:

> I never saw an oft-removed tree,
> Nor yet an oft-removed family,
> That throve so well as those that settled be.

And again, Three removes is as bad as a fire; and again, Keep thy shop, and thy shop will keep thee; and again, If you would have your business done, go; if not, send. And again,

BENJAMIN FRANKLIN

> He that by the plow would thrive,
> Himself must either hold or drive.

And again, The eye of a master will do more work than both his hands; and again, Want of care does us more damage than want of knowledge; and again, Not to oversee workmen is to leave them your purse open. Trusting too much to others' care is the ruin of many; for, as the *Almanac* says, In the affairs of this world men are saved, not by faith, but by the want of it. But a man's own care is profitable; for saith Poor Dick, Learning is to the studious, and riches to the careful, as well as power to the bold, and heaven to the virtuous. And, farther, If you would have a faithful servant and one that you like, serve yourself. And again, he adviseth to circumspection and care, even in the smallest matters, because sometimes, A little neglect may breed great mischief; adding, For want of a nail the shoe was lost, for want of a shoe the horse was lost, and for want of a horse the rider was lost, being overtaken and slain by the enemy; all for want of care about a horseshoe nail.

"So much for industry, my friends, and attention to one's own business; but to these we must add frugality, if we would make our industry more certainly successful. A man may, if he knows not how to save as he gets, keep his nose all his life to the grindstone, and die not worth a groat at last. A fat kitchen makes a lean will, as Poor Richard says; and

> Many estates are spent in the getting,
> Since women for tea forsook spinning and knitting,
> And men for punch forsook hewing and splitting.

If you would be wealthy, says he, in another *Almanac*, Think of saving as well as of getting. The Indies have not made Spain rich, because her outgoes are greater than her incomes.

"Away, then, with your expensive follies, and you will not then have so much cause to complain of hard times, heavy taxes, and chargeable families; for, as Poor Dick says,

BENJAMIN FRANKLIN

Women and wine, game and deceit,
Make the wealth small, and the wants great.

And farther, What maintains one vice would bring up two
children. You may think, perhaps, that a *little* tea or a *little*
punch now and then, diet a *little* more costly, clothes a *little*
finer, and a *little* entertainment now and then, can be no *great*
matter: but remember what Poor Richard says, Many a little makes a mickle; and farther, Beware of little expenses;
A small leak will sink a great ship; and again, Who dainties
love shall beggars prove; and moreover, Fools make feasts
and wise men eat them.

"Here you are all got together at this vendue of fineries
and knick knacks. You call them goods; but, if you do not
take care, they will prove evils to some of you. You expect
they will be sold cheap, and perhaps they may for less than
they cost; but, if you have no occasion for them, they must be
dear to you. Remember what Poor Richard says; Buy what
thou hast no need of, and ere long thou shalt sell thy necessaries. And again, At a great pennyworth pause awhile. He
means that perhaps the cheapness is *apparent* only, and not
real; or, the bargain, by straitening thee in thy business, may
do thee more harm than good. For in another place he says,
Many have been ruined by buying good pennyworths. Again,
Poor Richard says, 'Tis foolish to lay out money in a purchase of repentance; and yet this folly is practised every day
at vendues for want of minding the *Almanac.* Wise men, as
Poor Dick says, learn by others' harms, fools scarcely by
their own; but *Felix quem facirent aliena pericula cautum.*
Many a one, for the sake of finery on the back have gone with
a hungry belly, and half-starved their families. Silks and
satins, scarlet and velvets, as Poor Richard says, put out the
kitchen fire.

"These are not the necessaries of life; they can scarcely be
called the conveniences; and yet, only because they look
pretty, how many want to have them. The artificial wants of
mankind thus become more numerous than the natural; and
as Poor Dick says, For one poor person there are an hundred

indigent. By these and other extravagances the genteel are reduced to poverty, and forced to borrow of those whom they formerly despised, but who, through industry and frugality, have maintained their standing; in which case it appears plainly that, A plowman on his legs is higher than a gentleman on his knees, as Poor Richard says. Perhaps they have had a small estate left them which they knew not the getting of; they think, 'Tis day and will never be night; that a little to be spent out of so much is not worth minding; a child and a fool, as Poor Richard says, imagine twenty shilling and twenty years can never be spent, but, Always take out of the meal tub and never putting in, soon comes to the bottom; then as Poor Dick says, When the well's dry they know the worth of water. But this they might have known before, if they had taken his advice. If you would know the value of money, go and try to borrow some; for he that goes a borrowing goes a sorrowing; and, indeed, so does he that lends to such people, when he goes to get it in again. Poor Dick farther advises and says:

> Fond pride of dress is sure a very curse;
> Ere fancy you consult, consult your purse.

And again, Pride is as loud a beggar as want, and a great deal more saucy. When you have bought one fine thing, you must buy ten more, that your appearance may be all of a piece; but Poor Dick says, 'Tis easier to suppress the first desire than to satisfy all that follow it. And 'tis as truly folly for the poor to ape the rich, as for the frog to swell in order to equal the ox.

> Great estates may venture more,
> But little boats should keep near shore.

'Tis, however, a folly soon punished; for, Pride that dines on vanity sups on contempt, as Poor Richard says. And in another place, Pride breakfasted with Plenty, dined with Poverty, and supped with Infamy. And, after all, of what use is this pride of appearance, for which so much is risked, so much is suffered? It cannot promote health or ease pain; it makes no increase of merit in the person, it creates envy, it hastens misfortune.

> What is a butterfly? At best
> He's but a caterpillar dressed.
> The gaudy fop's his picture just,

as Poor Richard says.

"But what madness must it be to run in debt for these superfluities! We are offered by the terms of this vendue six month's credit; and that, perhaps, has induced some of us to attend it, because we cannot spare the ready money, and hope now to be fine without it. But ah, think what you do when you run in debt; you give to another power over your liberty. If you cannot pay at the time, you will be ashamed to see your creditor; you will be in fear when you speak to him; you will make poor, pitiful, sneaking excuses, and by degrees come to lose your veracity, and sink into base, downright lying; for, as Poor Richard says, The second vice is lying, the first is running in debt. And again to the same purpose, Lying rides upon debt's back; whereas a free-born Englishman ought not to be ashamed or afraid to see or speak to any man living. But poverty often deprives a man of all spirit and virtue. 'Tis hard for an empty bag to stand upright, as Poor Richard truly says.

"What would you think of that prince, or that government, who should issue an edict forbidding you to dress like a gentleman or a gentlewoman, on pain of imprisonment or servitude? Would you not say that you are free, have a right to dress as you please, and that such an edict would be a breach of your privileges and such a government tyrannical? And yet you are about to put yourself under that tyranny, when you run in debt for such dress. Your creditor has authority, at his pleasure, to deprive you of your liberty by confining you in jail for life, or to sell you for a servant, if you should not be able to pay him. When you have got your bargain, you may, perhaps, think little of payment! But, Creditors,

Poor Richard tells us, have better memories than debtors; and in another place says, Creditors are a superstitious sect, great observers of set days and times. The day comes round before you are aware, and the demand is made before you are prepared to satisfy it; or, if you bear your debt in mind, the term, which at first seemed so long, will, as it lessens, appear extremely short. Time will seem to have added wings to his heels as well as shoulders. Those have a short Lent, saith Poor Richard, who owe money to be paid at Easter. Then, since as he says, The borrower is slave to the lender, and the debtor to the creditor, disdain the chain, preserve your freedom; and maintain your independency; be industrious and free; be frugal and free. At present, perhaps you may think yourself in thriving circumstances, and that you can bear a little extravagance without injury; but

> For age and want save while you may;
> No morning sun lasts a whole day,

as Poor Richard says. Gain may be temporary and uncertain, but ever, while you live, expense is constant and certain; and, 'Tis easier to build two chimneys than to keep one in fuel, as Poor Richard says. So Rather go to bed supperless than rise in debt.

> Get what you can, and what you get, hold;
> 'Tis the stone that will turn all your lead into gold,

as Poor Richard says. And when you have got the philosopher's stone, sure you will no longer complain of bad times or the difficulty of paying taxes.

"This doctrine, my friends, is reason and wisdom; but, after all do not depend too much upon your own industry and frugality and prudence, though excellent things; for they may all be blasted, without the blessing of Heaven; and, therefore, ask that blessing humbly, and be not uncharitable to those that at present seem to want it, but comfort and help them. Remember Job suffered, and was afterward prosperous.

"And now, to conclude, Experience keeps a dear school, but fools will learn in no other, and scarce in that; for, it is true, We may give advice, but we cannot give conduct, as Poor Richard says. However, remember this: They that won't be counseled can't be helped, as Poor Richard says; and farther that, If you will not hear Reason, she'll surely rap your knuckles."

Thus the old gentleman ended his harangue. The people heard it, and approved the doctrine, and immediately practised the contrary, just as if it had been a common sermon; for the vendue opened and they began to buy extravagantly notwithstanding his cautions, and their own fear of taxes. I found the good man had thoroughly studied my almanacs, and digested all I had dropped on these topics during the course of five-and-twenty years. The frequent mention he made of me must have tired anyone else; but my vanity was wonderfully delighted with it, though I was conscious that not a tenth part of the wisdom was my own which he ascribed to me, but rather the gleanings I had made of the sense of all ages and nations. However, I resolved to be the better for the echo of it; and, though I had at first determined to buy stuff for a new coat, I went away resolved to wear my old one a little longer. Reader, if thou wilt do the same, thy profit will be as great as mine. I am, as ever, thine to serve thee,

Richard Saunders

9   *An Economical Project*

TO THE AUTHORS OF THE JOURNAL OF PARIS

MESSIEURS,
   You often entertain us with accounts of new discoveries. Permit me to communicate to the public, through your paper, one that has lately been made by myself, and which I conceive may be of great utility.

I was the other evening in a grand company, where the new lamp of Messrs. Quinquet and Lange was introduced, and much admired for its splendor; but a general inquiry was made, whether the oil it consumed was not in proportion to the light it afforded, in which case there would be no saving in the use of it. No one present could satisfy us in that point, which all agreed ought to be known, it being a very desirable thing to lessen, if possible, the expense of lighting our apartments, when every other article of family expense was so much augmented.

I was pleased to see this general concern for economy, for I love economy exceedingly.

I went home, and to bed, three or four hours after midnight, with my head full of the subject. An accidental sudden noise waked me about six in the morning, when I was surprised to find my room filled with light; and I imagined at first, that a number of those lamps had been brought into it; but, rubbing my eyes, I perceived the light came in at the windows. I got up and looked out to see what might be the occasion of it, when I saw the sun just rising above the horizon, from whence he poured his rays plentifully into my chamber, my domestic having negligently omitted, the preceding evening, to close the shutters.

I looked at my watch, which goes very well, and found that it was but six o'clock; and still thinking it something extraordinary that the sun should rise so early, I looked into the almanac, where I found it to be the hour given for his rising on that day. I looked forward, too, and found he was to rise still earlier every day till towards the end of June; and that at no time in the year he retarded his rising so long as till eight o'clock. Your readers, who with me have never seen any signs of sunshine before noon, and seldom regard the astronomical part of the almanac, will be as much astonished as I was, when they hear of his rising so early; and especially when I assure them, *that he gives light as soon as he rises*. I am convinced of this. I am certain of my fact. One cannot be more certain of any fact. I saw it with my own eyes. And, having repeated this observation the three following mornings, I found always precisely the same result.

Yet it so happens, that when I speak of this discovery to others, I can easily perceive by their countenances, though they forbear expressing it in words, that they do not quite believe me. One, indeed, who is a learned natural philosopher, has assured me that I must certainly be mistaken as to the circumstance of the light coming into my room; for it being well known, as he says, that there could be no light abroad at that hour, it follows that none could enter from without; and that of consequence, my windows being accidentally left open, instead of letting in the light, had only served to let out the darkness; and he used many ingenious arguments to show me how I might, by that means, have been deceived. I owned that he puzzled me a little, but he did not satisfy me; and the subsequent observations I made, as above mentioned, confirmed me in my first opinion.

This event has given rise in my mind to several serious and important reflections. I considered that, if I had not been awakened so early in the morning, I should have slept six hours longer by the light of the sun, and in exchange have lived six hours the following night by candle-light; and, the latter being a much more expensive light than the former, my love of economy induced me to muster up what little arithmetic I was master of, and to make some calculations, which I shall give you, after observing that utility is, in my opinion the test of value in matters of invention, and that a discovery which can be applied to no use, or is not good for something, is good for nothing.

I took for the basis of my calculation the supposition that there are one hundred thousand families in Paris, and that these families consume in the night half a pound of bougies, or candles, per hour. I think this is a moderate allowance, taking one family with another; for though I believe some consume less, I know that many consume a great deal more.

Then estimating seven hours per day as a medium quantity between the time of the sun's rising and ours, he rising during the six following months from six to eight hours before noon, and there being seven hours of course per night in which we burn candles, the account will stand thus; —

In the six months between the 20th of March and the 20th of September, there are

Nights	183
Hours of each night in which we burn candles	7
Multiplication gives for the total number of hours	1,281
These 1,281 hours multiplied by 100,000, the number of inhabitants, give	128,100,000
One hundred twenty-eight millions and one hundred thousand hours, spent at Paris by candle-light, which, at half a pound of wax and tallow per hour, gives the weight of .	64,050,000
Sixty-four millions and fifty thousand of pounds, which, estimating the whole at the medium price of thirty sols the pound, makes the sum of ninety-six millions and seventy-five thousand livres tournois . .	96,075,000

An immense sum! that the city of Paris might save every year, by the economy of using sunshine instead of candles.

If it should be said, that people are apt to be obstinately attached to old customs, and that it will be difficult to induce them to rise before noon, consequently my discovery can be of little use; I answer, *Nil desperandum.* I believe all who have common sense, as soon as they have learnt from this paper that it is daylight when the sun rises, will contrive to rise with him; and, to compel the rest, I would propose the following regulations;

First. Let a tax be laid of a louis per window, on every window that is provided with shutters to keep out the light of the sun.

Second. Let the same salutary operation of police be made use of, to prevent our burning candles, that inclined us last winter to be more economical in burning wood; that is, let guards be placed in the shops of the wax and tallow chandlers, and no family be permitted to be supplied with more than one pound of candles per week.

Third. Let guards also be posted to stop all the coaches, &c. that would pass the streets after sunset, except those of physicians, surgeons, and midwives.

Fourth. Every morning, as soon as the sun rises, let all the bells in every church be set ringing; and if that is not sufficient, let cannon be fired in every street, to wake the sluggards effectually, and make them open their eyes to see their true interest.

All the difficulty will be in the first two or three days; after which the reformation will be as natural and easy as the present irregularity; for, *ce n'est que le premier pas qui coûte.* Oblige a man to rise at four in the morning, and it is more than probable he will go willingly to bed at eight in the evening; and, having had eight hours sleep, he will rise more willingly at four in the morning following. But this sum of ninety-six millions and seventy-five thousand livres is not the whole of what may be saved by my economical project. You may observe, that I have calculated upon only one half of the year, and much may be saved in the other, though the days are shorter. Besides, the immense stock of wax and tallow left unconsumed during the summer, will probably make candles much cheaper for the ensuing winter, and continue them cheaper as long as the proposed reformation shall be supported.

For the great benefit of this discovery, thus freely communicated and bestowed by me on the public, I demand neither place, pension, exclusive privilege, nor any other reward whatever. I expect only to have the honor of it. And yet I know there are little, envious minds, who will, as usual, deny me this, and say, that my invention was known to the ancients, and perhaps they may bring passages out of the old books in proof of it. I will not dispute with these people, that the ancients knew not the sun would rise at certain hours; they possibly had, as we have, almanacs that predicted it; but it does not follow thence, that they knew *he gave light as soon as he rose.* This is what I claim as my discovery. If the ancients knew it, it might have been long since forgotten; for it certainly was unknown to the moderns, at least to the Parisians, which to prove, I need use but one plain simple argument. They are as well instructed, judicious, and prudent a people as exist anywhere in the world, all professing, like myself, to be lovers of economy; and, from the many heavy taxes required from them by the necessities of the state, have surely an abundant reason to be economical. I say it is impossible that so sensible a people, under such circumstances, should have lived so long by the smoky, unwholesome, and enormously expensive light of candles, if they had really known, that they might have had as much pure light of the sun for nothing. I am, &c.

A Subscriber

JOHN WOOLMAN

1720–1772

10   The Inward Life

I WAS born in Northampton, in Burlington County, West-Jersey, in the year 1720; and before I was seven years old I began to be acquainted with the operations of divine love. Through the care of my parents, I was taught to read nearly as soon as I was capable of it; and, as I went from school one seventh day, I remember, while my companions went to play by the way, I went forward out of sight, and, sitting down, I read the 22d Chapter of the Revelations: "He shewed me a pure river of water of life, clear as crystal, proceeding out of the throne of God and of the Lamb, *etc.*" and, in reading it, my mind was drawn to seek after that pure habitation, which, I then believed, God had prepared for his servants. The place where I sat, and the sweetness that attended my mind, remain fresh in my memory.

This, and the like gracious visitations, had that effect upon me, that when boys used ill language it troubled me; and, through the continued mercies of God, I was preserved from it.

The pious instructions of my parents were often fresh in my mind when I happened to be among wicked children, and were of use to me. My parents, having a large family of children, used frequently, on first days after meeting, to put us to read in the holy Scriptures, or some religious books, one after another, the rest sitting by without much conversation; which, I have since often thought, was a good practice. From what I had read and heard, I believed there had been, in past ages, people who walked in uprightness before God, in a degree exceeding any that I knew, or heard of, now living: And the apprehension of there being less steadiness and firmness, amongst people in this age than in past ages, often troubled me while I was a child.

A thing remarkable in my childhood was, that once, going to a neighbor's house, I saw, on the way, a robin sitting on her nest, and as I came near she went off, but, having young ones, flew about, and with many cries expressed her concern for them; I stood and threw stones at her, till, one striking her, she fell down dead: At first I was pleased with the exploit, but after a few minutes was seized with horror, as having, in a sportive way, killed an innocent creature while she was careful for her young: I beheld her lying dead, and thought these young ones, for which she was so careful, must now perish for want of their dam to nourish them; and, after some painful considerations on the subject, I climbed up the tree, took all the young birds, and killed them; supposing that better than to leave them to pine away and die miserably: And believed, in this case, that Scripture-proverb was fulfilled, "The tender mercies of the wicked are cruel." I then went on my errand, but, for some hours, could think of little else but the cruelties I had committed, and was much troubled. Thus he, whose tender mercies are over all his works, hath placed a principle in the human mind, which incites to exercise goodness towards every living creature; and this being singly attended to, people become tender hearted and sympathizing; but being frequently and totally rejected, the mind becomes shut up in a contrary disposition.

About the twelfth year of my age, my father being abroad, my mother reproved me for some misconduct, to which I made an undutiful reply; and, the next first day, as I was with my father returning from meeting, he told me he understood I had behaved amiss to my mother, and advised me to be more careful in future. I knew myself blameable, and in shame and confusion remained silent. Being thus awakened to a sense of my wickedness, I felt remorse in my mind, and, getting home, I retired and prayed to the Lord to forgive me; and do not remember that I ever, after that, spoke unhandsomely to either of my parents, however foolish in some other things.

Having attained the age of sixteen years, I began to love wanton company; and though I was preserved from profane language, or scandalous conduct, still I perceived a plant in me which produced much wild grapes; yet my merciful Father forsook me not utterly, but, at times, through his grace, I was brought seriously to consider my ways; and the sight of my backslidings affected me with sorrow; but, for want of rightly attending to the reproofs of instruction, vanity was added to vanity, and repentance to repentance: Upon the whole, my mind was more and more alienated from the truth, and I hastened toward destruction. While I meditate on the gulph towards which I traveled, and reflect on my youthful disobedience, for these things I weep, mine eyes run down with water.

Advancing in age, the number of my acquaintances increased, and thereby my way grew more difficult; though I had found comfort in reading the holy Scriptures, and thinking on heavenly things, I was now estranged therefrom: I knew I was going from the flock of Christ, and had no resolution to return; hence serious reflections were uneasy to me, and youthful vanities and diversions my greatest pleasure. Running in this road I found many like myself; and we associated in that which is the reverse of true friendship.

But in this swift race it pleased God to visit me with sickness, so that I doubted of recovering; and then did darkness, horror, and amazement, with full force, seize me, even when my pain and distress of body was very great. I thought it would have been better for me never to have had a being, than to see the day which I now saw. I was filled with confusion; and in great affliction, both of mind and body, I lay and bewailed myself. I had not confidence to lift up my cries to God, whom I had thus offended; but, in a deep sense of my great folly, I was humbled before him; and, at length, that Word which is as a fire and a hammer, broke and dissolved my rebellious heart, and then my cries were put up in contrition; and in the multitude of his mercies I found inward relief, and felt a close engagement, that, if he was pleased to restore my health, I might walk humbly before him.

After my recovery, this exercise remained with me a considerable time; but, by degrees, giving way to youthful vanities, they gained strength, and, getting with wanton young people I lost ground. The Lord had been very gracious, and spoke peace to me in the time of my distress; and I now most ungratefully turned again to folly; on which account, at times, I felt sharp reproof. I was not so hardy as to commit things scandalous; but to exceed in vanity, and promote mirth, was my chief study. Still I retained a love for pious people, and their company brought an awe upon me. My dear parents, several times, admonished me in the fear of the Lord, and their admonition entered into my heart, and had a good effect for a season; but, not getting deep enough to pray rightly, the Tempter, when he came, found entrance. I remember once, having spent a part of the day in wantonness, as I went to bed at night, there lay in a window, near my bed, a Bible, which I opened, and first cast my eye on this text, "We lie down in our shame, and our confusion covers us:" This I knew to be my case; and, meeting with so unexpected a reproof, I was somewhat affected with it, and went to bed under remorse of conscience; which I soon cast off again.

Thus time passed on: My heart was replenished with mirth and wantonness, and pleasing scenes of vanity were presented to my imagination, till I attained the age of eighteen years; near which time I felt the judgments of God, in my soul, like a consuming fire; and, looking over my past life, the prospect was moving. — I was often sad, and longed to be delivered from those vanities; then again, my heart was strongly inclined to them, and there was in me a sore conflict: At times I turned to folly, and then again, sorrow and confusion took hold of me. In a while, I resolved totally to leave off some of my vanities; but there was a secret reserve, in my heart, of the more refined part of them, and I was not low enough to find true peace. Thus, for some months, I had great troubles; there remaining in me an unsubjected will, which rendered my labors fruitless, till at length, through the merciful continuance of heavenly visitations, I was made to bow down in spirit before the Lord. I remember one evening I had spent some time in reading a pious author; and walking out alone, I humbly prayed to the Lord for his help, that I might be delivered from all those vanities which so ensnared me. Thus, being brought low, he helped me; and, as I learned to bear the Cross, I felt refreshment to come from his presence; but, not keeping in that strength which gave victory, I lost ground again; the sense of which greatly affected me; and I sought deserts and lonely places, and there, with tears, did confess my sins to God, and humbly craved help of him. And I may say with reverence, he was near to me in my troubles, and in those times of humiliation opened my ear to discipline. I was now led to look seriously at the means by which I was drawn from the pure truth, and learned this, that, if I would live in the life which the faithful servants of God lived in, I must not go into company as heretofore in my own will; but all the cravings of sense must be governed by a divine principle. In times of sorrow and abasement these instructions were sealed upon me, and I felt the power of Christ prevail over selfish desires, so that I was preserved in a good degree of steadiness; and, being young, and believing at that time that a single life was best for me, I was strengthened to keep from such company as had often been a snare to me.

I kept steadily to meetings; spent first-day afternoons chiefly in reading the Scriptures and other good books; and was early convinced in mind, that true religion consisted in an inward life, wherein the heart doth love and reverence God the Creator, and learns to exercise true justice and goodness, not only toward all men, but also toward the brute creatures. — That as the mind was moved, by an inward principle, to love God as an invisible incomprehensible Being, by the same principle it was moved to love him in all his manifestations in the visible world. — That, as by his breath the flame of life was kindled in all animal sensible creatures, to say we love God, and, at the same time exercise cruelty toward the least creature, is a contradiction in itself.

I found no narrowness respecting sects and opinions; but believed, that sincere upright-hearted people, in every society, who truly love God, were accepted of him.

As I lived under the Cross, and simply followed the openings of truth, my mind, from day to day, was more enlightened; my former acquaintance were left to judge of me as they would, for I found it safest for me to live in private, and keep these things sealed up in my own breast. While I silently ponder on that change wrought in me, I find no language equal to it, nor any means to convey to another a clear idea of it. I looked on the works of God in this visible creation, and an awfulness covered me; my heart was tender and often contrite, and universal love to my fellow-creatures increased in me: This will be understood by such as have trodden the same path. Some glances of real beauty may be seen in their faces, who dwell in true meekness. There is a harmony in the sound of that voice to which divine love gives utterance, and some appearance of right order in their temper and conduct, whose passions are regulated; yet all these do not fully show forth that inward life to such as have not felt it: But this white stone and new name is known rightly to such only as have it.

Though I had been thus strengthened to bear the Cross, I still found myself in great danger, having many weaknesses attending me, and strong temptations to wrestle with; in the feeling whereof I frequently withdrew into private places, and often with tears besought the Lord to help me, whose gracious ear was open to my cry.

All this time I lived with my parents, and wrought on the plantation; and, having had schooling pretty well for a planter, I used to improve it in winter evenings, and other leisure times; and, being now in the twenty-first year of my age, a man, in much business at shop-keeping and baking, asked me, if I would hire with him to tend shop and keep books. I acquainted my father with the proposal; and, after some deliberation, it was agreed for me to go.

At home I had lived retired; and now, having a prospect of being much in the way of company, I felt frequent and fervent cries in my heart to God, the Father of Mercies, that he would preserve me from all corruption; that in this public employment, I might serve him, my gracious Redeemer, in that humility and self-denial, with which I had been, in a small degree, exercised in a more private life. The man, who employed me, furnished a shop in Mount-Holly, about five miles from my father's house, and six from his own; and there I lived alone, and tended his shop. Shortly after my settlement here I was visited by several young people, my former acquaintance, who knew not but vanities would be as agreeable to me now as ever; and, at these times, I cried to the Lord in secret, for wisdom and strength; for I felt myself encompassed with difficulties, and had fresh occasion to bewail the follies of time past, in contracting a familiarity with libertine people; and, as I had now left my father's house outwardly, I found my heavenly Father to be merciful to me beyond what I can express.

By day I was much amongst people, and had many trials to go through; but, in the evenings, I was mostly alone, and may with thankfulness acknowledge, that, in those times, the spirit of supplication was often poured upon me; under which I was frequently exercised, and felt my strength renewed.

In a few months after I came here, my master bought several Scotchmen, servants, from on-board a vessel, and brought them to Mount-Holly to sell; one of which was taken sick, and died.

In the latter part of his sickness, he, being delirious, used to curse and swear most sorrowfully; and, the next night after his burial, I was left to sleep alone in the same chamber where he died; I perceived in me a timorousness; I knew, however, I had not injured the man, but assisted in taking care of him according to my capacity; and was not free to ask any one, on that occasion, to sleep with me: Nature was feeble; but every trial was a fresh incitement to give myself up wholly to the service of God, for I found no helper like him in times of trouble.

After a while, my former acquaintance gave over expecting me as one of their company; and I began to be known to some whose conversation was helpful to me: And now, as I had experienced the love of God, through Jesus Christ, to redeem me from many pollutions, and to be a succor to me through a sea of conflicts, with which no person was fully acquainted; and as my heart was often enlarged in this heavenly principle, I felt a tender compassion for the youth, who remained entangled in snares, like those which had entangled me from one time to another: This love and tenderness increased; and my mind was more strongly engaged for the good of my fellow-creatures. I went to meetings in an awful frame of mind, and endeavored to be inwardly acquainted with the language of the true Shepherd; and, one day, being under a strong exercise of spirit, I stood up, and said some words in a meeting; but, not keeping close to the divine opening, I said more than was required of me; and being soon sensible of my error, I was afflicted in mind some weeks, without any light or comfort, even to that degree that I could not take satisfaction in any thing: I remembered God, and was troubled, and, in the depth of my distress, he had pity upon me, and sent the Comforter: I then felt forgiveness for my offense, and my mind became calm and quiet, being truly thankful to my gracious Redeemer for his mercies; and, after this, feeling the spring of divine love opened, and a concern to speak, I said a few words in a meeting, in which I found peace; this, I believe, was about six weeks from the first time: And, as I was thus humbled and disciplined under the Cross, my understanding became more strengthened to distinguish the pure spirit which inwardly moves upon the heart, and taught me to wait in silence sometimes many weeks together, until I felt that rise which prepares the creature.

From an inward purifying, and stedfast abiding under it, springs a lively operative desire for the good of others: All the faithful are not called to the public ministry; but whoever are, are called to minister of that which they have tasted and handled spiritually. The outward modes of worship are various; but, wherever any are true ministers of Jesus Christ, it is from the operation of his spirit upon their hearts, first purifying them, and thus giving them a just sense of the conditions of others.

This truth was clearly fixed in my mind; and I was taught to watch the pure opening, and to take heed, lest, while I was standing to speak, my own will should get uppermost, and cause me to utter words from godly wisdom, and depart from the channel of the true Gospel ministry.

In the management of my outward affairs, I may say, with thankfulness, I found truth to be my support; and I was respected in my master's family, who came to live in Mount-Holly within two years after my going there.

About the twenty-third year of my age, I had many fresh and heavenly openings, in respect to the care and providence of the Almighty over his creatures in general, and over man as the most noble amongst those which are visible. And being clearly convinced in my judgment, that to place my whole trust in God was best for me, I felt renewed engagements, that in all things I might act on an inward principle of virtue, and pursue worldly business no farther, than as truth opened my way therein.

About the time called Christmas, I observed many people from the country, and dwellers in town, who, resorting to public-houses, spent their time in drinking and vain sports, tending to corrupt one another; on which account I was much troubled. At one house, in particular, there was much disorder; and I believed it was a duty incumbent on me to go and speak to the master of that house. I considered I was young, and that several elderly Friends in town had opportunity to see these things; but though I would gladly have been excused, yet I could not feel my mind clear.

The exercise was heavy; and as I was reading what the Almighty said to Ezekiel, respecting his duty as a watchman, the matter was set home more clearly; and then, with prayers and tears, I besought the Lord for his assistance, who, in loving-kindness, gave me a resigned heart: Then, at a suitable opportunity, I went to the public-house, and, seeing the man amongst much company, I went to him, and told him, I wanted to speak with him; so we went aside, and there, in the fear of the Almighty, I expressed to him what rested on my mind; which he took kindly, and afterward showed more regard to me than before. In a few years afterwards he died, middle-aged; and I often thought that, had I neglected my duty in that case, it would have given me great trouble; and I was humbly thankful to my gracious Father, who had supported me herein.

My employer having a Negro woman, sold her, and desired me to write a bill of sale, the man being waiting who bought her: The thing was sudden; and, though the thoughts of writing an instrument of slavery for one of my fellow-creatures felt uneasy, yet I remembered I was hired by the year, that it was my master who directed me to do it, and that it was an elderly man, a member of our Society, who bought her; so, through weakness, I gave way, and wrote; but, at the executing it, I was so afflicted in my mind, that I said, before my master and the friend, that I believed slave-keeping to be a practice inconsistent with the Christian religion: This in some degree abated my uneasiness; yet, as often as I reflected seriously upon it, I thought I should have been clearer, if I had desired to have been excused from it, as a thing against my conscience; for such it was. And, some time after this, a young man, of our Society, spoke to me to write a conveyance of a slave to him, he having lately taken a Negro into his house: I told him I was not easy to write it; for, though many of our meeting and in other places kept slaves, I still believed the practice was not right, and desired to be excused from the writing. I spoke to him in good-will; and he told me that keeping slaves was not altogether agreeable to his mind; but that the slave being a gift to his wife, he had accepted of her.

HECTOR ST. JOHN DE CRÈVECOEUR
1735–1813

11 *On the Situation, Feelings, and Pleasures of an American Farmer*

AS you are the first enlightened European I have ever had the pleasure of being acquainted with, you will not be surprised that I should, according to your earnest desire

HECTOR ST. JOHN DE CRÈVECOEUR

and my promise, appear anxious of preserving your friendship and correspondence. By your accounts, I observe a material difference subsists between your husbandry, modes, and customs, and ours; everything is local; could we enjoy the advantages of the English farmer, we should be much happier, indeed, but this wish, like many others, implies a contradiction; and could the English farmer have some of those privileges we possess, they would be the first of their class in the world. Good and evil I see is to be found in all societies, and it is in vain to seek for any spot where those ingredients are not mixed. I therefore rest satisfied, and thank God that my lot is to be an American farmer, instead of a Russian boor, or an Hungarian peasant. I thank you kindly for the idea, however dreadful, which you have given me of their lot and condition; your observations have confirmed me in the justness of my ideas, and I am happier now than I thought myself before. It is strange that misery, when viewed in others, should become to us a sort of real good, though I am far from rejoicing to hear that there are in the world men so thoroughly wretched; they are no doubt as harmless, industrious, and willing to work as we are. Hard is their fate to be thus condemned to a slavery worse than that of our negroes. Yet when young I entertained some thoughts of selling my farm. I thought it afforded but a dull repetition of the same labors and pleasures. I thought the former tedious and heavy, the latter few and insipid; but when I came to consider myself as divested of my farm, I then found the world so wide, and every place so full, that I began to fear lest there would be no room for me. My farm, my house, my barn, presented to my imagination objects from which I adduced quite new ideas; they were more forcible than before. Why should not I find myself happy, said I, where my father was before? He left me no good books it is true, he gave me no other education than the art of reading and writing; but he left me a good farm, and his experience; he left me free from debts, and no kind of difficulties to struggle with.—I married, and this perfectly

74

reconciled me to my situation; my wife rendered my house all at once cheerful and pleasing; it no longer appeared gloomy and solitary as before; when I went to work in my fields I worked with more alacrity and sprightliness; I felt that I did not work for myself alone, and this encouraged me much. My wife would often come with her knitting in her hand, and sit under the shady trees, praising the straightness of my furrows, and the docility of my horses; this swelled my heart and made everything light and pleasant, and I regretted that I had not married before.

I felt myself happy in my new situation, and where is that station which can confer a more substantial system of felicity than that of an American farmer, possessing freedom of action, freedom of thoughts, ruled by a mode of government which requires but little from us? I owe nothing, but a pepper corn to my country, a small tribute to my king, with loyalty and due respect; I know no other landlord than the lord of all land, to whom I owe the most sincere gratitude. My father left me three hundred and seventy-one acres of land, forty-seven of which are good timothy meadow, an excellent orchard, a good house, and a substantial barn. It is my duty to think how happy I am that he lived to build and to pay for all these improvements; what are the labors which I have to undergo, what are my fatigues when compared to his, who had everything to do, from the first tree he felled to the finishing of his house? Every year I kill from 1500 to 2000 weight of pork, 1200 of beef, half a dozen of good wethers in harvest: of fowls my wife has always a great stock: what can I wish more? My negroes are tolerably faithful and healthy; by a long series of industry and honest dealings, my father left behind him the name of a good man; I have but to tread his paths to be happy and a good man like him. I know enough of the law to regulate my little concerns with propriety, nor do I dread its power; these are the grand outlines of my situation, but as I can feel much more than I am able to express, I hardly know how to proceed.

HECTOR ST. JOHN DE CRÈVECOEUR

When my first son was born, the whole train of my ideas were suddenly altered; never was there a charm that acted so quickly and powerfully; I ceased to ramble in imagination through the wide world; my excursions since have not exceeded the bounds of my farm, and all my principal pleasures are now centered within its scanty limits: but at the same time there is not an operation belonging to it in which I do not find some food for useful reflections. This is the reason, I suppose, that when you was here, you used, in your refined style, to denominate me the farmer of feelings; how rude must those feelings be in him who daily holds the ax or the plow, how much more refined on the contrary those of the European, whose mind is improved by education, example, books, and by every acquired advantage! Those feelings, however, I will delineate as well as I can, agreeably to your earnest request.

When I contemplate my wife, by my fireside, while she either spins, knits, darns, or suckles our child, I cannot describe the various emotions of love, of gratitude, of conscious pride, which thrill in my heart and often overflow in involuntary tears. I feel the necessity, the sweet pleasure of acting my part, the part of an husband and father, with an attention and propriety which may entitle me to my good fortune. It is true these pleasing images vanish with the smoke of my pipe, but though they disappear from my mind, the impression they have made on my heart is indelible. When I play with the infant, my warm imagination runs forward, and eagerly anticipates his future temper and constitution. I would willingly open the book of fate, and know in which page his destiny is delineated; alas! where is the father who in those moments of paternal ecstasy can delineate one half of the thoughts which dilate his heart? I am sure I cannot; then again I fear the health of those who are become so dear to me, and in their sicknesses I severely pay for the joys I experienced while they were well. Whenever I go abroad it is always involuntary. I never return home without feeling some pleasing emotion, which I often suppress as useless and foolish. The instant I enter on my own land, the bright idea of property, of exclusive right, of independence exalt my mind. Precious soil, I say to myself, by what singular custom of law is it that thou wast made to constitute the riches of the freeholder? What should we American farmers be without the distinct possession of that soil? It feeds, it clothes us, from it we draw even a great exuberancy, our best meat, our richest drink, the very honey of our bees comes from this privileged spot. No wonder we should thus cherish its possession, no wonder that so many Europeans who have never been able to say that such portion of land was theirs, cross the Atlantic to realize that happiness. This formerly rude soil has been converted by my father into a pleasant farm, and in return it has established all our rights; on it is founded our rank, our freedom, our power as citizens, our importance as inhabitants of such a district. These images I must confess I always behold with pleasure, and extend them as far as my imagination can reach: for this is what may be called the true and the only philosophy of an American farmer.

Pray do not laugh in thus seeing an artless countryman tracing himself through the simple modifications of his life; remember that you have required it, therefore with candor, though with diffidence, I endeavor to follow the thread of my feelings, but I cannot tell you all. Often when I plow my low ground, I place my little boy on a chair which screws to the beam of the plough — its motion and that of the horses please him, he is perfectly happy and begins to chat. As I lean over the handle, various are the thoughts which crowd into my mind. I am now doing for him, I say, what my father formerly did for me, may God enable him to live that he may perform the same operations for the same purposes when I am worn out and old! I relieve his mother of some trouble while I have him with me, the odoriferous furrow exhilarates his spirits, and seems to do the child a great deal of good, for he looks more blooming since I have adopted that practice; can more pleasure, more dignity be added to that primary occupation? The father thus plowing with his child, and to feed his family, is inferior only to the emperor of China plowing as an example to his kingdom. In the evening when I return home through my low grounds, I am astonished at the myriads of insects which I perceive dancing in the beams of the setting sun. I was before scarcely acquainted with their existence, they are so small that it is difficult to distinguish them; they are carefully improving this short evening space, not daring to expose themselves to the blaze of our meridian sun. I never see an egg brought on my table but I feel penetrated with the wonderful change it would have undergone but for my gluttony; it might have been a gentle useful hen leading her chickens with a care and vigilance which speaks shame to many women. A cock perhaps, arrayed with the most majestic plumes, tender to its mate, bold, courageous, endowed with an astonishing instinct, with thoughts, with memory, and every distinguishing characteristic of the reason of man. I never see my trees drop their leaves and their fruit in the autumn, and bud again in the spring, without wonder; the sagacity of those animals which have long been the tenants of my farm astonish me: some of them seem to surpass even men in memory and sagacity. I could tell you singular instances of that kind. What then is this instinct which we so debase, and of which we are taught to entertain so diminutive an idea? My bees, above any other tenants of my farm, attract my attention and respect; I am astonished to see that nothing exists but what has its enemy, one species pursue and live upon the other: unfortunately our kingbirds are the destroyers of those industrious insects; but on the other hand, these birds preserve our fields from the depredation of crows which they pursue on the wing with great vigilance and astonishing dexterity.

Thus divided by two interested motives, I have long resisted the desire I had to kill them, until last year, when I thought they increased too much, and my indulgence had been carried too far; it was at the time of swarming when they all came and fixed themselves on the neighboring trees, from whence they catched those that returned loaded from the fields. This made me resolve to kill as many as I could, and I was just ready to fire, when a bunch of bees as big as my fist, issued from one of the hives, rushed on one of the birds, and probably stung him, for he instantly screamed, and flew, not as before, in an irregular manner, but in a direct line. He was followed by the same bold phalanx, at a considerable distance, which unfortunately becoming too sure of victory, quitted their military array and disbanded themselves. By this inconsiderate step they lost all that aggregate of force which had made the bird fly off. Perceiving their disorder he immediately returned and snapped as many as he wanted; nay, he had even the impudence to alight on the very twig from which the bees had drove him. I killed him and immediately opened his craw, from which I took 171 bees; I laid them all on a blanket in the sun, and to my great surprise 54 returned to life, licked themselves clean, and joyfully went back to the hive; where they probably informed their companions of such an adventure and escape, as I believe had never happened before to American bees! I draw a great fund of pleasure from the quails which inhabit my farm; they abundantly repay me, by their various notes and peculiar tameness, for the inviolable hospitality I constantly show them in the winter. Instead of perfidiously taking advantage of their great and affecting distress, when nature offers nothing but a barren universal bed of snow, when irresistible necessity forces them to my barn doors, I permit them to feed unmolested; and it is not the least agreeable spectacle which that dreary season presents, when I see those beautiful birds, tamed by hunger, intermingling with all my cattle and sheep, seeking in security for the poor scanty grain which but for them would be useless and lost. Often in the angles of the fences where the motion of the wind prevents the snow from settling, I carry them both chaff

HECTOR ST. JOHN DE CRÈVECOEUR

and grain; the one to feed them, the other to prevent their tender feet from freezing fast to the earth as I have frequently observed them to do.

I do not know an instance in which the singular barbarity of man is so strongly delineated, as in the catching and murthering those harmless birds, at that cruel season of the year. Mr. ——, one of the most famous and extraordinary farmers that has ever done honor to the province of Connecticut, by his timely and humane assistance in a hard winter, saved this species from being entirely destroyed. They perished all over the country, none of their delightful whistlings were heard the next spring, but upon this gentleman's farm; and to his humanity we owe the continuation of their music. When the severities of that season have dispirited all my cattle, no farmer ever attends them with more pleasure than I do; it is one of those duties which is sweetened with the most rational satisfaction. I amuse myself in beholding their different tempers, actions, and the various effects of their instinct now powerfully impelled by the force of hunger. I trace their various inclinations, and the different effects of their passions, which are exactly the same as among men; the law is to us precisely what I am in my barn yard, a bridle and check to prevent the strong and greedy from oppressing the timid and weak. Conscious of superiority, they always strive to encroach on their neighbors; unsatisfied with their portion, they eagerly swallow it in order to have an opportunity of taking what is given to others, except they are prevented. Some I chide, others, unmindful of my admonitions, receive some blows. Could victuals thus be given to men without the assistance of any language, I am sure they would not behave better to one another, nor more philosophically than my cattle do.

The same spirit prevails in the stable; but there I have to do with more generous animals, there my well-known voice has immediate influence, and soon restores peace and tranquillity. Thus by superior knowledge I govern all my cattle as wise men are obliged to govern fools and the ignorant. A variety of other thoughts crowd on my mind at that peculiar instant, but they all vanish by the time I return home. If in a cold night I swiftly travel in my sledge, carried along at the rate of twelve miles an hour, many are the reflections excited by surrounding circumstances. I ask myself what sort of an agent is that which we call frost? Our minister compares it to needles, the points of which enter our pores. What is become of the heat of the summer; in what part of the world is it that the N. W. keeps these grand magazines of nitre? When I see in the morning a river over which I can travel, that in the evening before was liquid, I am astonished indeed! What is become of those millions of insects which played in our summer fields, and in our evening meadows; they were so puny and so delicate, the period of their existence was so short, that one cannot help wondering how they could learn, in that short space, the sublime art to hide themselves and their offspring in so perfect a manner as to baffle the rigor of the season, and preserve that precious embryo of life, that small portion of ethereal heat, which if once destroyed would destroy the species! Whence that irresistible propensity to sleep so common in all those who are severely attacked by the frost. Dreary as this season appears, yet it has like all others its miracles, it presents to man a variety of problems which he can never resolve; among the rest, we have here a set of small birds which never appear until the snow falls; contrary to all others, they dwell and appear to delight in that element.

It is my bees, however, which afford me the most pleasing and extensive themes; let me look at them when I will, their government, their industry, their quarrels, their passions, always present me with something new; for which reason, when weary with labor, my common place of rest is under my locust-tree, close by my bee-house. By their movements I can predict the weather, and can tell the day of their swarming; but the most difficult point is, when on the wing, to know whether they want to go to the woods or not. If they have previously pitched in some hollow trees, it is not the allurements of salt and water, of fennel, hickory leaves, etc., nor the finest box, that can induce them to stay; they will prefer those rude, rough habitations to the best polished mahogany hive. When that is the case with mine, I seldom thwart their inclinations; it is in freedom that they work: were I to confine them, they would dwindle away and quit their labor. In such excursions we only part for a while; I am generally sure to find them again the following fall. This elopement of theirs only adds to my recreations; I know how to deceive even their superlative instinct; nor do I fear losing them, though eighteen miles from my house, and lodged in the most lofty trees, in the most impervious of our forests. I once took you along with me in one of these rambles, and yet you insist on my repeating the detail of our operations: it brings back into my mind many of the useful and entertaining reflections with which you so happily beguiled our tedious hours.

After I have done sowing, by way of recreation, I prepare for a week's jaunt in the woods, not to hunt either the deer or the bears, as my neighbors do, but to catch the more harmless bees. I cannot boast that this chase is so noble, or so famous among men, but I find it less fatiguing, and full as profitable; and the last consideration is the only one that moves me. I take with me my dog, as a companion, for he is useless as to this game; my gun, for no man you know ought to enter the woods without one; my blanket, some provisions, some wax, vermilion, honey, and a small pocket compass. With these implements I proceed to such woods as are at a considerable distance from any settlements. I carefully examine whether they abound with large trees, if so, I make a small fire on some flat stones, in a convenient place; on the fire I put some wax; close by this fire, on another stone, I drop honey in distinct drops, which I surround with small quantities of vermilion, laid on the stone; and then I retire carefully to watch whether any bees appear. If there are any in that neighborhood, I rest assured that the smell of the burnt wax will unavoidably attract them;

they will soon find out the honey, for they are fond of preying on that which is not their own; and in their approach they will necessarily tinge themselves with some particles of vermilion, which will adhere long to their bodies. I next fix my compass, to find out their course, which they keep invariably straight, when they are returning home loaded. By the assistance of my watch, I observe how long those are returning which are marked with vermilion. Thus possessed of the course, and, in some measure, of the distance, which I can easily guess at, I follow the first, and seldom fail of coming to the tree where those republics are lodged. I then mark it; and thus, with patience, I have found out sometimes eleven swarms in a season; and it is inconceivable what a quantity of honey these trees will sometimes afford. It entirely depends on the size of the hollow, as the bees never rest nor swarm till it is all replenished; for like men, it is only the want of room that induces them to quit the maternal hive. Next I proceed to some of the nearest settlements, where I procure proper assistance to cut down the trees, get all my prey secured, and then return home with my prize. The first bees I ever procured were thus found in the woods, by mere accident; for at that time I had no kind of skill in this method of tracing them. The body of the tree being perfectly sound, they had lodged themselves in the hollow of one of its principal limbs, which I carefully sawed off and with a good deal of labor and industry brought it home, where I fixed it up again in the same position in which I found it growing. This was in April; I had five swarms that year, and they have been ever since very prosperous. This business generally takes up a week of my time every fall, and to me it is a week of solitary ease and relaxation.

The seed is by that time committed to the ground; there is nothing very material to do at home, and this additional quantity of honey enables me to be more generous to my home bees, and my wife to make a due quantity of mead. The reason, Sir, that you found mine better than that of others is, that she puts two gallons of brandy in each barrel, which ripens it, and takes off that sweet, luscious taste, which it is apt to retain a long time. If we find anywhere in the woods (no matter on whose land) what is called a bee-tree, we must mark it; in the fall of the year when we propose to cut it down, our duty is to inform the proprietor of the land, who is entitled to half the contents; if this is not complied with we are exposed to an action of trespass, as well as he who should go and cut down a bee-tree which he had neither found out nor marked.

We have twice a year the pleasure of catching pigeons, whose numbers are sometimes so astonishing as to obscure the sun in their flight. Where is it that they hatch? For such multitudes must require an immense quantity of food. I fancy they breed toward the plains of Ohio, and those about lake Michigan, which abound in wild oats; though I have never killed any that had that grain in their craws. In one of them, last year, I found some undigested rice. Now the nearest rice fields from where I live must be at least 560 miles; and either their digestion must be suspended while they are flying, or else they must fly with the celerity of the wind. We catch them with a net extended on the ground, to which they are allured by what we call *tame wild pigeons,* made blind, and fastened to a long string; his short flights, and his repeated calls, never fail to bring them down. The greatest number I ever catched was fourteen dozen, though much larger quantities have often been trapped. I have frequently seen them at the market so cheap, that for a penny you might have as many as you could carry away; and yet from the extreme cheapness you must not conclude, that they are but an ordinary food; on the contrary, I think they are excellent. Every farmer has a tame wild pigeon in a cage at his door all the year round, in order to be ready whenever the season comes for catching them.

The pleasure I receive from the warblings of the birds in the spring, is superior to my poor description, as the continual succession of their tuneful notes is for ever new to me. I generally rise from bed about that indistinct interval, which, properly speaking, is neither night nor day; for this is the moment of the most universal vocal choir. Who can listen unmoved to the sweet love tales of our robins, told from tree to tree? or to the shrill cat birds? The sublime accents of the thrush from on high always retard my steps that I may listen to the delicious music. The variegated appearances of the dew drops, as they hang to the different objects, must present even to a clownish imagination, the most voluptuous ideas. The astonishing art which all birds display in the construction of their nests, ill provided as we may suppose them with proper tools, their neatness, their convenience, always make me ashamed of the slovenliness of our houses; their love to their dame, their incessant careful attention, and the peculiar songs they address to her while she tediously incubates their eggs, remind me of my duty could I ever forget it. Their affection to their helpless little ones, is a lively precept; and in short, the whole economy of what we proudly call the brute creation, is admirable in every circumstance; and vain man, though adorned with the additional gift of reason, might learn from the perfection of instinct, how to regulate the follies, and how to temper the errors which this second gift often makes him commit. This is a subject, on which I have often bestowed the most serious thoughts; I have often blushed within myself, and been greatly astonished, when I have compared the unerring path they all follow, all just, all proper, all wise, up to the necessary degree of perfection, with the coarse, the imperfect systems of men, not merely as governors and kings, but as masters, as husbands, as fathers, as citizens. But this is a sanctuary in which an ignorant farmer must not presume to enter.

If ever man was permitted to receive and enjoy some blessings that might alleviate the many sorrows to which he is exposed, it is certainly in the country, when he attentively considers those ravishing scenes with which he is everywhere surrounded. This is the only time of the year in which I am avaricious of every moment, I therefore lose none that can add to this simple and inoffensive happiness. I roam early throughout all my fields; not the least operation do I perform, which is not accompanied with the most pleasing observations; were I to extend them as far as I have carried them, I should become tedious; you would think me guilty of affectation, and I should perhaps represent many things as pleasurable from which you might not perhaps receive the least agreeable emotions. But, believe me, what I write is all true and real.

Some time ago, as I sat smoking a contemplative pipe in my piazza, I saw with amazement a remarkable instance of selfishness displayed in a very small bird, which I had hitherto respected for its inoffensiveness. Three nests were placed almost contiguous to each other in my piazza: that of a swallow was affixed in the corner next to the house, that of a phebe in the other, a wren possessed a little box which I had made on purpose, and hung between. Be not surprised at their tameness, all my family had long been taught to respect them as well as myself. The wren had shown before signs of dislike to the box which I had given it, but I knew not on what account; at last it resolved, small as it was, to drive the swallow from its own habitation, and to my very great surprise it succeeded. Impudence often gets the better of modesty, and this exploit was no sooner performed, than it removed every material to its own box with the most admirable dexterity; the signs of triumph appeared very visible, it fluttered its wings with uncommon velocity, an universal joy was perceivable in all its movements. Where did this little bird learn that spirit of injustice? It was not endowed with what we term reason! Here then is a proof that both those gifts border very near on one another; for we see the perfection of the one mixing with the errors of the other! The peaceable swallow, like the passive Quaker, meekly sat at a small distance and never offered the least resistance; but no sooner was the plunder carried away, than the injured bird went to work with unabated ardor, and in a few days the depredations were repaired. To prevent however a repetition of the same violence, I removed the wren's box to another part of the house.

In the middle of my new parlor I have, you may remember, a curious republic of industrious hornets; their nest hangs to the ceiling, by the same twig on which it was so admirably built and contrived in the woods. Its removal did not displease them, for they find in my house plenty of food; and I have left a hole open in one of the panes of the window, which answers all their purposes. By this kind usage they are become quite harmless; they live on the flies, which are very troublesome to us throughout the summer; they are constantly busy in catching them, even on the eyelids of my children. It is surprising how quickly they smear them with a sort of glue, lest they might escape, and when thus prepared, they carry them to their nests, as food for their young ones. These globular nests are most ingeniously divided into many stories, all provided with cells, and proper communications. The materials with which this fabric is built, they procure from the cottony furze, with which our oak rails are covered; this substance tempered with glue, produces a sort of pasteboard, which is very strong, and resists all the inclemencies of the weather. By their assistance, I am but little troubled with flies. All my family are so accustomed to their strong buzzing, that no one takes any notice of them; and though they are fierce and vindictive, yet kindness and hospitality has made them useful and harmless.

We have a great variety of wasps; most of them build their nests in mud, which they fix against the shingles of our roofs, as nigh the pitch as they can. These aggregates represent nothing, at first view, but coarse and irregular lumps, but if you break them, you will observe, that the inside of them contains a great number of oblong cells, in which they deposit their eggs, and in which they bury themselves in the fall of the year. Thus immured they securely pass through the severity of that season, and on the return of the sun are enabled to perforate their cells, and to open themselves a passage from these recesses into the sunshine. The yellow wasps, which build under ground, in our meadows, are much more to be dreaded, for when the mower unwittingly passes his scythe over their holes they immediately sally forth with a fury and velocity superior even to the strength of man. They make the boldest fly, and the only remedy is to lie down and cover our heads with hay, for it is only at the head they aim their blows; nor is there any possibility of finishing that part of the work until, by means of fire and brimstone, they are all silenced. But though I have been obliged to execute this dreadful sentence in my own defence, I have often thought it a great pity, for the sake of a little hay, to lay waste so ingenious a subterranean town, furnished with every conveniency, and built with a most surprising mechanism.

I never should have done were I to recount the many objects which involuntarily strike my imagination in the midst of my work, and spontaneously afford me the most pleasing relief. These appear insignificant trifles to a person who has traveled through Europe and America, and is acquainted with books and with many sciences; but such simple objects of contemplation suffice me, who have no time to bestow on more extensive observations. Happily these require no study, they are obvious, they gild the moments I dedicate to them, and enliven the severe labors which I perform. At home my happiness springs from very different objects; the gradual unfolding of my children's reason, the study of their dawning tempers attract all my paternal attention. I have to contrive little punishments for their little faults, small encouragements for their good actions, and a variety of other expedients dictated by various occasions. But these are themes unworthy your perusal, and which ought not to be carried beyond the walls of my house, being domestic mysteries adapted only to the locality of the small sanctuary wherein my family resides. Sometimes I delight in inventing and executing machines, which simplify my wife's labor. I have been tolerably successful that way; and these, Sir, are the narrow circles within which I constantly revolve, and what can I wish for beyond them? I bless God for all the good he has given me; I envy no man's prosperity, and with no other portion of happiness than that I may live to teach the same philosophy to my children; and give each of them a farm, show them how to cultivate it, and be like their father, good substantial independent American farmers — an appellation which will be the most fortunate one a man of my class can possess, so long as our civil government continues to shed blessings on our husbandry. Adieu.

THOMAS PAINE

1737–1809

12   *The Crisis*

THESE are the times that try men's souls. The summer soldier and the sunshine patriot will, in this crisis, shrink from the service of their country; but he that stands it *now*, deserves the love and thanks of man and woman. Tyranny, like hell, is not easily conquered; yet we have this consolation with us, that the harder the conflict, the more glorious the triumph. What we obtain too cheap, we esteem too lightly: it is dearness only that gives everything its value. Heaven knows how to put a proper price upon its goods; and it would be strange indeed, if so celestial an article as FREEDOM should not be highly rated. Britain, with an army to enforce her tyranny, has declared that she has a right (*not only to* TAX) but " to BIND *us in* ALL CASES WHATSOVER," and if being *bound in that manner,* is not slavery, then is there not such a thing as slavery upon earth. Even the expression is impious; for so unlimited a power can belong only to God.

Whether the independence of the continent was declared too soon, or delayed too long, I will not now enter into as an argument; my own simple opinion is, that had it been eight months earlier, it would have been much better. We did not make a proper use of last winter, neither could we, while we were in a dependent state. However, the fault, if it were one, was all our own; we have none to blame but ourselves. But no great deal is lost yet. All that Howe has been doing for this month past, is rather a ravage than a conquest, which the spirit of the Jerseys, a year ago, would have quickly repulsed, and which time and a little resolution will soon recover.

I have as little superstition in me as any man living, but my secret opinion has ever been, and still is, that God Almighty will not give up a people to military destruction, or leave them unsupportedly to perish, who have so earnestly and so repeatedly sought to avoid the calamities of war, by every decent method which wisdom could invent. Neither have I so much of the infidel in me, as to suppose that He has relinquished the government of the world, and given us up to the care of devils; and as I do not, I cannot see on what grounds the king of Britain can look up to heaven for help against us: a common murderer, a highwayman, or a housebreaker, has as good a pretence as he.

'Tis surprising to see how rapidly a panic will sometimes run through a country. All nations and ages have been subject to them: Britain has trembled like an ague at the report of a French fleet of flat bottomed boats; and in the fourteenth century the whole English army, after ravaging the kingdom of France, was driven back like men petrified with fear; and this brave exploit was performed by a few broken forces collected and headed by a woman, Joan of Arc. Would that heaven might inspire some Jersey maid to spirit up her countrymen, and save her fair fellow sufferers from ravage and ravishment! Yet panics, in some cases, have their uses; they produce as much good as hurt. Their duration is always short; the mind soon grows through them, and acquires a firmer habit than before. But their peculiar advantage is, that they are the touchstones of sincerity and hypocrisy, and bring things and men to light, which might otherwise have lain forever undiscovered. In fact, they have the same effect on secret traitors, which an imaginary apparition would have upon a private murderer. They sift out the hidden thoughts of man, and hold them up in public to the world. Many a disguised tory has lately shown his head, that shall penitentially solemnize with curses the day on which Howe arrived upon the Delaware.

As I was with the troops at Fort Lee, and marched with them to the edge of Pennsylvania, I am well acquainted with many circumstances, which those who live at a distance know but little or nothing of. Our situation there was exceedingly cramped, the place being a narrow neck of land between the North River and the Hackensack. Our force was inconsiderable, being not one fourth so great as Howe could bring against us. We had no army at hand to have relieved the garrison, had we shut ourselves up and stood on our defense. Our ammunition, light artillery, and the best part of our stores, had been removed, on the apprehension that Howe would endeavor to penetrate the Jerseys, in which case Fort Lee could be of no use to us; for it must occur to every thinking man, whether in the army or not, that these kind of field forts are only for temporary purposes, and last in use no longer than the enemy directs his force against the particular object, which such forts are raised to defend. Such was our situation and condition at Fort Lee on the morning of the 20th of November, when an officer arrived with information that the enemy with 200 boats had landed about seven miles above: Major General Green, who commanded the garrison, immediately ordered them under arms, and sent express to General Washington at the town of Hackensack, distant by the way of the ferry, six miles. Our first object was to secure the bridge over the Hackensack, which laid up the river between the enemy and us, about six miles from us, and three from them. General Washington arrived in about three quarters of an hour, and marched at the head of the troops towards the bridge, which place I expected we should have a brush for; however, they did not choose to dispute it with us, and the greatest part of our troops went over the bridge, the rest over the ferry, except some which passed at a mill on a small creek, between the bridge and the ferry, and made their way through some marshy grounds up to the town of Hackensack, and there passed the river. We brought off as much baggage as the wagons could contain, the rest was lost. The simple object was to bring off the garrison, and march them on till they could be strengthened by the Jersey or Pennsylvania militia, so as to be enabled to make a stand. We stayed four days at Newark, collected our outposts with some of the Jersey militia, and marched out twice to meet the enemy, on being informed that they were advancing, though our numbers were greatly inferior to theirs. Howe, in my little opinion, committed a great error in generalship in not throwing a body of forces off from Staten Island through Amboy, by which means he might have seized all our stores at Brunswick, and intercepted our march into Pennsylvania; but if we believe the power of hell to be limited, we must likewise believe that their agents are under some providential control.

I shall not now attempt to give all the particulars of our retreat to the Delaware; suffice it for the present to say, that both officers and men, though greatly harassed and fatigued, frequently without rest, covering, or provision, the inevitable consequences of a long retreat, bore it with a manly and martial spirit. All their wishes centered in one, which was, that the country would turn out and help them to drive the enemy back. Voltaire has remarked that King William never appeared to full advantage but in difficulties and in action; the same remark may be made on General Washington, for the character fits him. There is a natural firmness in some minds which cannot be unlocked by trifles, but which, when unlocked, discovers a cabinet of fortitude; and I reckon it among those kind of public blessings, which we do not immediately see, that God hath blessed him with uninterrupted health, and given him a mind that can even flourish upon care.

I shall conclude this paper with some miscellaneous remarks on the state of our affairs; and shall begin with asking the following question, Why is it that the enemy have left the

New-England provinces, and made these middle ones the seat of war? The answer is easy: New-England is not infested with tories, and we are. I have been tender in raising the cry against these men, and used numberless arguments to show them their danger, but it will not do to sacrifice a world either to their folly or their baseness. The period is now arrived, in which either they or we must change our sentiments, or one or both must fall. And what is a tory? Good God! what is he? I should not be afraid to go with a hundred whigs against a thousand tories, were they to attempt to get into arms. Every tory is a coward; for servile, slavish, self-interested fear is the foundation of toryism; and a man under such influence, though he may be cruel, never can be brave.

But, before the line of irrecoverable separation be drawn between us, let us reason the matter together: Your conduct is an invitation to the enemy, yet not one in a thousand of you has heart enough to join him. Howe is as much deceived by you as the American cause is injured by you. He expects you will all take up arms, and flock to his standard, with muskets on your shoulders. Your opinions are of no use to him, unless you support him personally, for 'tis soldiers, and not tories, that he wants.

I once felt all that kind of anger, which a man ought to feel, against the mean principles that are held by the tories: a noted one, who kept a tavern at Amboy, was standing at his door, with as pretty a child in his hand, about eight or nine years old, as I ever saw, and after speaking his mind as freely as he thought was prudent, finished with this unfatherly expression, " *Well! give me peace in my day.*" Not a man lives on the continent but fully believes that a separation must some time or other finally take place, and a generous parent should have said, *" If there must be trouble, let it be in my day, that my child may have peace;"* and this single reflection, well applied, is sufficient to awaken every man to duty. Not a place upon earth might be so happy as America. Her situation is remote from all the wrangling world, and she has nothing to do but to trade with them. A man can distinguish himself between temper and principle, and I am as confident, as I am that God governs the world, that America will never be happy till she gets clear of foreign dominion. Wars, without ceasing, will break out till that period arrives, and the continent must in the end be conqueror; for though the flame of liberty may sometimes cease to shine, the coal can never expire.

America did not, nor does not want force; but she wanted a proper application of that force. Wisdom is not the purchase of a day, and it is no wonder that we should err at the first setting off. From an excess of tenderness, we were unwilling to raise an army, and trusted our cause to the temporary defense of a well-meaning militia. A summer's experience has now taught us better; yet with those troops, while they were collected, we were able to set bounds to the progress of the enemy, and, thank God! they are again assembling. I always considered militia as the best troops in the world for a sudden exertion, but they will not do for a long campaign. Howe, it is probable, will make an attempt on this city; should he fail on this side the Delaware, he is ruined: if he succeeds, our cause is not ruined. He stakes all on his side against a part on ours; admitting he succeeds, the consequence will be, that armies from both ends of the continent will march to assist their suffering friends in the middle states; for he cannot go everywhere, it is impossible. I consider Howe as the greatest enemy the tories have; he is bringing a war into their country, which, had it not been for him and partly for themselves, they had been clear of. Should he now be expelled, I wish with all the devotion of a Christian, that the names of whig and tory may never more be mentioned; but should the tories give him encouragement to come, or assistance if he come, I as sincerely wish that our next year's arms may expel them from the continent, and the congress appropriate their possessions to the relief of those who have suffered in well-doing. A single successful battle next year will settle the whole. America could carry on a two years' war by the confiscation of the property of disaffected persons, and be made happy by their expulsion. Say not that this is revenge, call it rather the soft resentment of a suffering people, who, having no object in view but the *good* of *all,* have staked their *own all* upon a seemingly doubtful event. Yet it is folly to argue against determined hardness; eloquence may strike the ear, and the language of sorrow draw forth the tear of compassion, but nothing can reach the heart that is steeled with prejudice.

Quitting this class of men, I turn with the warm ardor of a friend to those who have nobly stood, and are yet determined to stand the matter out: I call not upon a few, but upon all: not on *this* state or *that* state, but on *every* state; up and help us; lay your shoulders to the wheel; better have too much force than too little, when so great an object is at stake. Let it be told to the future world, that in the depth of winter, when nothing but hope and virtue could survive, that the city and the country, alarmed at one common danger, came forth to meet and to repulse it. Say not that thousands are gone, turn out your tens of thousands; throw not the burden of the day upon Providence, but *" show your faith by your works,"* that God may bless you. It matters not where you live, or what rank of life you hold, the evil or the blessing will reach you all. The far and the near, the home counties and the back, the rich and the poor, will suffer or rejoice alike. The heart that feels not now, is dead: the blood of his children will curse his cowardice, who shrinks back at a time when a little might have saved the whole, and made *them* happy. I love the man that can smile in trouble, that can gather strength from distress, and grow brave by reflection. 'Tis the business of little minds to shrink; but he whose heart is firm, and whose conscience approves his conduct, will pursue his principles unto death. My own line of reasoning is to myself as straight and clear as a ray of light. Not all the treasures of the world, so far as I believe, could have induced me to support an offensive war, for I think it murder; but if a thief breaks into my house, burns and destroys my property, and kills me or threatens to kill me, or those that are in it, and to *" bind me in all cases whatsover,"* to his absolute will, am I to suffer it? What signifies it to me, whether he who does it is a king or a common man; my countryman or not my countryman; whether it be done by an individual villain, or an army of them? If we reason to the root of things we shall find no difference; neither can any just cause be assigned why we should punish in the one case and pardon in the other. Let them call me rebel, and welcome, I feel no concern from it; but I should suffer the misery of devils, were I to make a whore of my soul by swearing allegiance to one whose character is that of a sottish, stupid, stubborn, worthless, brutish man. I conceive likewise a horrid idea in receiving mercy from a being, who at the last day shall be shrieking to the rocks and mountains to cover him, and fleeing with terror from the orphan, the widow, and the slain of America.

There are cases which cannot be overdone by language, and this is one. There are persons, too, who see not the full extent of the evil which threatens them; they solace themselves with hopes that the enemy, if he succeed, will be merciful. It is the madness of folly, to expect mercy from those who have refused to do justice; and even mercy, where conquest is the object, is only a trick of war; the cunning of the fox is as murderous as the violence of the wolf, and we ought to guard equally against both. Howe's first object is, partly by threats and partly by promises, to terrify or seduce the people to deliver up their arms and receive mercy. The ministry recommended the same plan to Gage, and this is what the tories call making their peace, *" a peace which passeth all understanding"* indeed! A peace which would be the immediate forerunner of a worse ruin than any we have yet thought of. Ye men of Pennsylvania, do reason upon these things! Were the back counties to give up their arms, they would fall an easy prey to the Indians, who are all armed: this perhaps is what some tories would not be sorry for. Were the home counties to deliver up their arms, they would be exposed to the resentment of the back counties, who would then have it in their power to chastise their defection at pleasure. And were any one state to give up its arms, *that* state must be garrisoned by all Howe's army of Britons and Hessians to preserve it from the anger of the rest. Mutual fear is the principal link in the chain of mutual love, and woe be to that state that breaks the compact. Howe is mercifully inviting you to barbarous destruction, and men must be either rogues or fools that will not see it. I dwell not upon the powers of imagination; I bring reason to your ears; and, in language as plain as A, B, C, hold up truth to your eyes.

I thank God, that I fear not. I see no real cause for fear. I know our situation well, and can see the way out of it. While our army was collected, Howe dared not risk a battle; and it is no credit to him that he decamped from the White Plains, and waited a mean opportunity to ravage the defenseless Jerseys; but it is great credit to us, that, with a handful of men, we sustained an orderly retreat for near an hundred miles, brought off our ammunition, all our field pieces, the greatest part of our stores, and had four rivers to pass. None can say that our retreat was precipitate, for we were near three weeks in performing it, that the country might have time to come in. Twice we marched back to meet the enemy, and remained out till dark. The sign of fear was not seen in our camp, and had not some of the cowardly and disaffected inhabitants spread false alarms through the country, the Jerseys had never been ravaged. Once more we are again collected and collecting; our new army at both ends of the continent is recruiting fast, and we shall be able to open the next campaign with sixty thousand men, well armed and clothed. This is our situation, and who will may know it. By perseverance and fortitude we have the prospect of a glorious issue; by cowardice and submission, the sad choice of a variety of evils — a ravaged country — a depopulated city — habitations without safety, and slavery without hope — our homes turned into barracks and bawdy-houses for Hessians, and a future race to provide for, whose fathers we shall doubt of. Look on this picture and weep over it! and if there yet remains one thoughtless wretch who believes it not, let him suffer it unlamented.

Common Sense

December 23, 1776.

13   *Thoughts on the Peace*

THE times that tried men's souls " are over — and the greatest and completest revolution the world ever knew, gloriously and happily accomplished.

But to pass from the extremes of danger to safety — from the tumult of war to the tranquillity of peace, though sweet in contemplation, requires a gradual composure of the senses to receive it. Even calmness has the power of stunning, when it opens too instantly upon us. The long and raging hurricane that should cease in a moment, would leave us in a state rather of wonder than enjoyment; and some moments of recollection must pass, before we could be capable of tasting the felicity of repose. There are but few instances, in which the mind is fitted for sudden transitions: it takes in its pleasures by reflection and comparison and those must have time to act, before the relish for new scenes is complete.

In the present case — the mighty magnitude of the object — the various uncertainties of fate it has undergone — the numerous and complicated dangers we have suffered or escaped — the eminence we now stand on, and the vast prospect before us, must all conspire to impress us with contemplation.

To see it in our power to make a world happy — to teach mankind the art of being so — to exhibit, on the theater of the universe a character hitherto unknown — and to have, as it were, a new creation intrusted to our hands, are honours that command reflection, and can neither be too highly estimated, nor too gratefully received.

In this pause then of recollection — while the storm is ceasing, and the long agitated mind vibrating to a rest, let us look back on the scenes we have passed, and learn from experience what is yet to be done.

Never, I say, had a country so many openings to happiness as this. Her setting out in life, like the rising of a fair morning, was unclouded and promising. Her cause was good. Her principles just and liberal. Her temper serene and firm. Her conduct regulated by the nicest steps, and everything about her wore the mark of honor. It is not every country (perhaps there is not another in the world) that can boast so fair an origin. Even the first settlement of America corresponds with the character of the revolution. Rome, once the proud mistress of the universe, was originally a band of ruffians. Plunder and rapine made her rich, and her oppression of millions made her great. But America need never be ashamed to tell her birth, nor relate the stages by which she rose to empire.

The remembrance, then, of what is past, if it operates rightly, must inspire her with the most laudable of all ambition, that of adding to the fair fame she began with. The world has seen her great in adversity; struggling, without a thought of yielding, beneath accumulated difficulties, bravely, nay proudly, encountering distress, and rising in resolution as the storm increased. All this is justly due to her, for her fortitude has merited the character. Let, then, the world see that she can bear prosperity: and that her honest virtue in time of peace, is equal to the bravest virtue in time of war.

She is now descending to the scenes of quiet and domestic life. Not beneath the cypress shade of disappointment, but to enjoy in her own land, and under her own vine, the sweet of her labors, and the reward of her toil. — In this situation, may she never forget that a fair national reputation is of as much importance as independence. That it possesses a charm that wins upon the world, and makes even enemies civil. That it gives a dignity which is often superior to power, and commands reverence where pomp and splendor fail.

It would be a circumstance ever to be lamented and never to be forgotten, were a single blot, from any cause whatever, suffered to fall on a revolution, which to the end of time must be an honor to the age that accomplished it: and which has contributed more to enlighten the world, and diffuse a spirit of freedom and liberality among mankind, than any human event (if this may be called one) that ever preceded it.

It is not among the least of the calamities of a long continued war, that it unhinges the mind from those nice sensations which at other times appear so amiable. The continual spectacle of woe blunts the finer feelings, and the necessity of bearing with the sight, renders it familiar. In like manner, are many of the moral obligations of society weakened, till the custom of acting by necessity becomes an apology, where it is truly a crime. Yet let but a nation conceive rightly of its character, and it will be chastely just in protecting it. None ever began with a fairer than America and none can be under a greater obligation to preserve it.

The debt which America has contracted, compared with the cause she has gained, and the advantages to flow from it, ought scarcely to be mentioned. She has it in her choice to do, and to live as happily as she pleases. The world is in her hands. She has no foreign power to monopolize her commerce, perplex her legislation, or control her prosperity. The struggle is over, which must one day have happened, and, perhaps, never could have happened at a better time. And instead of a domineering master, she has gained an *ally* whose exemplary greatness, and universal liberality, have extorted a confession even from her enemies.

With the blessings of peace, independence, and an universal commerce, the states, individually and collectively, will have leisure and opportunity to regulate and establish their domestic concerns, and to put it beyond the power of calumny to throw the least reflection on their honor. Character is much easier kept than recovered, and that man, if any such there be, who, from sinister views, or littleness of soul, lends unseen his hand to injure it, contrives a wound it will never be in his power to heal.

As we have established an inheritance for posterity, let that inheritance descend, with every mark of an honorable conveyance. The little it will cost, compared with the worth of the states, the greatness of the object, and the value of the national character, will be a profitable exchange.

But that which must more forcibly strike a thoughtful, penetrating mind, and which includes and renders easy all inferior concerns, is the UNION OF THE STATES. On this our great national character depends. It is this which must give us importance abroad and security at home. It is through this only that we are, or can be, nationally known in the world; it is the flag of the United States which renders our ships and commerce safe on the seas, or in a foreign port. Our Mediterranean passes must be obtained under the same style. All our treaties, whether of alliance, peace, or commerce, are formed under the sovereignty of the United States, and Europe knows us by no other name or title.

The division of the empire into states is for our own convenience, but abroad this distinction ceases. The affairs of each state are local. They can go no further than to itself. And were the whole worth of even the richest of them expended in revenue, it would not be sufficient to support sovereignty against a foreign attack. In short, we have no other national sovereignty than as United States. It would even be fatal for us if we had — too expensive to be maintained, and impossible to be supported. Individuals, or individual states, may call themselves what they please; but the world, and especially the world of enemies, is not to be held in awe by the whistling of a name. Sovereignty must have power to protect all the parts that compose and constitute it: and as UNITED STATES we are equal to the importance of the title, but otherwise we are not. Our union, well and wisely regulated and cemented, is the cheapest way of being great — the easiest way of being powerful, and the happiest invention in government which the circumstances of America can admit of. — Because it collects from each state, that which, by being inadequate, can be of no use to it, and forms an aggregate that serves for all.

The states of Holland are an unfortunate instance of the effects of individual sovereignty. Their disjointed condition exposes them to numerous intrigues, losses, calamities, and enemies; and the almost impossibility of bringing their measures to a decision, and that decision into execution, is to them, and would be to us, a source of endless misfortune.

It is with confederated states as with individuals in society; something must be yielded up to make the whole secure. In this view of things we gain by what we give, and draw an annual interest greater than the capital. — I ever feel myself hurt when I hear the union, that great palladium of our liberty and safety, the least irreverently spoken of. It is the most sacred thing in the constitution of America, and that which every man should be most proud and tender of. Our citizenship in the United States is our national character. Our citizenship in any particular state is only our local distinction. By the latter we are known at home, by the former to the world. Our great title is AMERICANS — our inferior one varies with the place.

So far as my endeavors could go, they have all been directed to conciliate the affections, unite the interests, and draw and keep the mind of the country together; and the better to assist in this foundation work of the revolution, I have avoided all places of profit or office, either in the state I live in, or in the United States; kept myself at a distance from all parties and party connections, and even disregarded all private and inferior concerns: and when we take into view the great work which we have gone through, and feel, as we ought to feel, the just importance of it, we shall then see, that the little wranglings and indecent contentions of personal parley, are as dishonorable to our characters, as they are injurious to our repose.

It was the cause of America that made me an author. The force with which it struck my mind, and the dangerous condition the country appeared to me in, by courting an impossible and an unnatural reconciliation with those who were determined to reduce her, instead of striking out into the only line that could cement and save her, A DECLARATION OF INDEPENDENCE, made it impossible for me, feeling as I did, to be silent: and if, in the course of more than seven years, I have rendered her any service, I have likewise added something to the reputation of literature, by freely and disinterestedly employing it in the great cause of mankind, and showing that there may be genius without prostitution.

Independence always appeared to me practicable and probable, provided the sentiment of the country could be formed and held to the object: and there is no instance in the world, where a people so extended, and wedded to former habits of thinking, and under such a variety of circumstances, were so instantly and effectually pervaded, by a turn in politics, as in the case of independence; and who supported their opinion, undiminished, through such a succession of good and ill fortune, till they crowned it with success.

But as the scenes of war are closed, and every man preparing for home and happier times, I therefore take my leave of the subject. I have most sincerely followed it from beginning to end, and through all its turns and windings: and whatever country I may hereafter be in, I shall always feel an honest pride at the part I have taken and acted, and a gratitude to nature and providence for putting it in my power to be of some use to mankind.

Common Sense

Philadelphia, April 19, 1783.

WILLIAM BARTRAM

1739–1823

14 *The Alligators of East Florida*

THE noise of the crocodiles kept me awake the greater part of the night; but when I arose in the morning, contrary to my expectations, there was perfect peace; very few of them to be seen, and those were asleep on the shore. Yet I was not able to suppress my fears and apprehensions of being attacked by them in future; and indeed yesterday's combat with them, notwithstanding I came off in a manner victorious, or at least made a safe retreat, had left sufficient impression on my mind to damp my courage; and it seemed too much for one of my strength, being alone in a very small boat, to encounter such collected danger. To pursue my voyage up the river, and be obliged every evening to pass such dangerous defiles, appeared to me as perilous as running the gauntlet betwixt two rows of Indians armed with knives and firebrands. I however resolved to continue my voyage one day longer, if I possibly could with safety, and then return down the river, should I find the like difficulties to oppose. Accordingly I got everything on board, charged my gun, and set sail, cautiously, along shore. As I passed by Battle lagoon, I began to tremble and keep a good look-out; when suddenly a huge alligator rushed out of the reeds, and with a tremendous roar came up, and darted as swift as an arrow under my boat, emerging upright on my lee quarter, with open jaws, and belching water and smoke that fell upon me like rain in a hurricane. I laid soundly about his head with my club, and beat him off; and after plunging and darting about my boat, he went off on a straight line through the water, seemingly with the rapidity of lightning, and entered the cape of the lagoon. I now employed my time to the very best advantage in paddling close along ashore, but could not forbear looking now and then behind me, and presently perceived one of them coming up again. The water of the river hereabouts was shoal and very clear; the monster came up with the usual roar and menaces, and passed close by the side of my boat, when I could distinctly see a young brood of alligators, to the number of one hundred or more, following after her in a long train. They kept close together in a column, without straggling off to the one side or the other; the young appeared to be of an equal size, about fifteen inches in length, almost black, with pale yellow transverse waved clouds or blotches, much like rattlesnakes in color. I now lost sight of my enemy again.

Still keeping close along shore, on turning a point or projection of the river bank, at once I beheld a great number of hillocks or small pyramids, resembling hay-cocks, ranged like an encampment along the banks. They stood fifteen or twenty yards distant from the water, on a high marsh, about four feet perpendicular above the water. I knew them to be the nests of the crocodile, having had a description of them before; and now expected a furious and general attack, as I saw several large crocodiles swimming abreast of these buildings. These nests being so great a curiosity to me, I was determined at all events immediately to land and examine them. Accordingly, I ran my bark on shore at one of their landing-places, which was a sort of nick or little dock, from which ascended a sloping path or road up to the edge of the meadow, where their nests were; most of them were deserted, and the great thick whitish egg-shells lay broken and scattered upon the ground round about them.

The nests or hillocks are of the form of an obtuse cone, four feet high and four or five feet in diameter at their bases; they are constructed with mud, grass and herbage. At first they lay a floor of this kind of tempered mortar on the ground, upon which they deposit a layer of eggs, and upon this a stratum of mortar, seven or eight inches in thickness, and then another layer of eggs; and in this manner one stratum upon another, nearly to the top. I believe they commonly lay from one to two hundred eggs in a nest: these are hatched, I suppose, by the heat of the sun; and perhaps the vegetable substances mixed with the earth, being acted upon by the sun, may cause a small degree of fermentation, and so increase the heat in those hillocks. The ground for several acres about these nests showed evident marks of a continual resort of alligators; the grass was everywhere beaten down, hardly a blade or straw was left standing; whereas, all about, at a distance, it was five or six feet high, and as thick as it could grow together. The female, as I imagine, carefully watches her own nest of eggs until they are all hatched; or perhaps while she is attending her own brood, she takes under her care and protection as many as she can get at one time, either from her own particular nest or others; but certain it is, that the young are not left to shift for themselves; for I have had frequent opportunities of seeing the female alligator leading about the shores her train of young ones, just as a hen does her brood of chickens; and she is equally assiduous and courageous in defending the young, which are under her care, and providing for their subsistence; and when she is basking upon the warm banks, with her brood around her, you may hear the young ones continually whining and barking like young puppies. I believe but few of a brood live to the years of full growth and magnitude, as the old feed on the young as long as they can make prey of them.

The alligator when full grown is a very large and terrible creature, and of prodigious strength, activity and swiftness in the water. I have seen them twenty feet in length, and some are supposed to be twenty-two or twenty-three feet. Their body is as large as that of a horse; their shape exactly resembles that of a lizard, except their tail, which is flat or cuneiform, being compressed on each side, and gradually diminishing from the abdomen to the extremity, which, with the whole body is covered with horny plates or squamæ, impenetrable when on the body of the live animal, even to a rifle ball, except about their head and just behind their fore-legs or arms, where it is said they are only vulnerable. The head of a full grown one is about three feet, and the mouth opens nearly the same length; their eyes are small in proportion, and seem sunk deep in the head, by means of the prominency of the brows; the nostrils are large, inflated and prominent on the top, so that the head in the water resembles, at a distance, a great chunk of wood floating about. Only the upper jaw moves, which they raise almost perpendicular, so as to form a right angle with the lower one. In the fore-part of the upper jaw, on each side, just under the nostrils, are two very large, thick, strong teeth or tusks, not very sharp, but rather the shape of a cone: these are as white as the finest polished ivory, and are not covered by any skin or lips, and always in sight, which gives the creature a frightful appearance: in the lower jaw are holes opposite to these teeth, to receive them: when they clap their jaws together it causes a surprising noise, like that which is made by forcing a heavy plank with violence upon the ground, and may be heard at a great distance.

But what is yet more surprising to a stranger, is the incredible loud and terrifying roar, which they are capable of making, especially in the spring season, their breeding time. It most resembles very heavy distant thunder, not only shaking the air and waters, but causing the earth to tremble; and when hundreds and thousands are roaring at the same time, you can scarcely be persuaded, but that the whole globe is violently and dangerously agitated.

An old champion, who is perhaps absolute sovereign of a little lake or lagoon (when fifty less than himself are obliged to content themselves with swelling and roaring in little coves round about) darts forth from the reedy coverts all at once, on the surface of the waters, in a right line; at first seemingly as rapid as lightning, but gradually more slowly until he arrives at the center of the lake, when he stops. He now swells himself by drawing in wind and water through his mouth, which causes a loud sonorous rattling in the throat for near a minute, but it is immediately forced out again through his mouth and nostrils, with a loud noise, brandishing his tail in the air, and the vapor ascending from his nostrils like smoke. At other times, when swollen to an extent ready to burst, his head and tail lifted up, he spins or twirls round on the surface of the water. He acts his part like an Indian chief when rehearsing his feats of war; and then retiring, the exhibition is continued by others who dare to step forth, and strive to excel each other, to gain the attention of the favorite female.

15   *A Paradise of Fish*

I NOW directed my steps towards my encampment, in a different direction. I seated myself upon a swelling green knoll, at the head of the crystal basin. Near me, on the left, was a point or projection of an entire grove of the aromatic

Illicium Floridanum; on my right, and all around behind me, was a fruitful Orange grove, with Palms and Magnolias interspersed; in front, just under my feet, was the enchanting and amazing crystal fountain, which incessantly threw up, from dark, rocky caverns below, tons of water every minute, forming a basin, capacious enough for large shallops to ride in, and a creek of four or five feet depth of water, and near twenty yards over, which meanders six miles through green meadows, pouring its limpid waters into the great Lake George, where they seem to remain pure and unmixed. About twenty yards from the upper edge of the basin, and directly opposite to the mouth or outlet of the creek, is a continual and amazing ebullition, where the waters are thrown up in such abundance and amazing force, as to jet and swell up two or three feet above the common surface: white sand and small particles of shells are thrown up with the waters, near to the top, when they diverge from the center, subside with the expanding flood, and gently sink again, forming a large rim or funnel round about the aperture or mouth of the fountain, which is a vast perforation through a bed of rocks, the ragged points of which are projected out on every side. Thus far I know to be matter of real fact, and I have related it as near as I could conceive or express myself. But there are yet remaining scenes inexpressibly admirable and pleasing.

Behold, for instance, a vast circular expanse before you, the waters of which are so extremely clear as to be absolutely diaphanous or transparent as the ether; the margin of the basin ornamented with a great variety of fruitful and floriferous trees, shrubs, and plants, the pendent golden Orange dancing on the surface of the pellucid waters, the balmy air vibrating with the melody of the merry birds, tenants of the encircling aromatic grove.

At the same instant innumerable bands of fish are seen, some clothed in the most brilliant colors; the voracious crocodile stretched along at full length, as the great trunk of a tree in size; the devouring garfish, inimical trout, and all the varieties of gilded painted bream; the barbed catfish, dreaded sting-ray, skate, and flounder, spotted bass, sheepshead and ominous drum; all in their separate bands and communities, with free and unsuspicious intercourse performing their evolutions: there are no signs of enmity, no attempt to devour each other; the different bands seem peaceably and complaisantly to move a little aside, as it were to make room for others to pass by.

But behold yet something far more admirable, see whole armies descending into an abyss, into the mouth of the bubbling fountain: they disappear! are they gone forever? I raise my eyes with terror and astonishment; I look down again to the fountain with anxiety, when behold them as it were emerging from the blue ether of another world, apparently at a vast distance; at their first appearance, no bigger than flies or minnows; now gradually enlarging, their brilliant colors begin to paint the fluid.

Now they come forward rapidly, and instantly emerge, with the elastic expanding column of crystalline waters, into the circular basin or funnel: see now how gently they rise, some upright, others obliquely, or seem to lie as it were on their sides, suffering themselves to be gently lifted or borne up by the expanding fluid towards the surface, sailing or floating like butterflies in the cerulean ether: then again they as gently descend, diverge and move off; when they rally, form again, and rejoin their kindred tribes.

This amazing and delightful scene, though real, appears at first but as a piece of excellent painting; there seems no medium; you imagine the picture to be within a few inches of your eyes, and that you may without the least difficulty touch any one of the fish, or put your finger upon the crocodile's eye, when it really is twenty or thirty feet under water.

And although this paradise of fish may seem to exhibit a just representation of the peaceable and happy state of nature which existed before the fall, yet in reality it is a mere representation: for the nature of the fish is the same as if they were in Lake George or the river; but here the water or element in which they live and move, is so perfectly clear and transparent, it places them all on an equality with regard to their ability to injure or escape from one another (as all river fish of prey, or such as feed upon each other, as well as the unwieldy crocodile, take their prey by surprise; secreting themselves under covert or in ambush, until an opportunity offers, when they rush suddenly upon them): but here is no covert, no ambush; here the trout freely passes by the very nose of the alligator, and laughs in his face, and the bream by the trout.

But what is really surprising is, that the consciousness of each other's safety, or some other latent cause, should so absolutely alter their conduct, for here is not the least attempt made to injure or disturb one another.

16   *The Alligator-Hole*

NEXT day early in the morning we left the town and the river, in order to fix our encampment in the forests about twelve miles from the river; our companions with the packhorses went ahead to the place of rendezvous, and our chief conducted me another way to show me a very curious place, called the Alligator-Hole, which was lately formed by an extraordinary eruption or jet of water. It is one of those vast circular sinks which we beheld almost everywhere about us as we traversed these forests, after we left the Alachua savanna. This remarkable one is on the verge of a spacious meadow, the surface of the ground round about uneven by means of gentle rising knolls: some detached groups of rocks and large spreading live oaks shade it on every side: it is about sixty yards over, and the surface of the water six or seven feet below the rim of the funnel or basin: the water is transparent, cool, and pleasant to drink, and well stored with fish; a very large alligator at present is lord or chief; many have been killed here, but the throne is never long vacant, the vast neighboring ponds so abound with them.

The account that this gentleman, who was an eye-witness of

the last eruption, gave me of its first appearance, being very wonderful, I proceed to relate what he told me whilst we were in town, which was confirmed by the Indians, and one or more of our companions, who also saw its progress, as well as by my own observations after I came to the ground.

This trader being near the place (before it had any visible existence in its present appearance), about three years ago, as he was looking for some horses which he expected to find in these parts, on a sudden was astonished by an inexpressible rushing noise, like a mighty hurricane or thunder storm; and looking round, he saw the earth overflowed by torrents of water, which came, wave after wave, rushing down a vale or plain very near him, which it filled with water, and soon began to overwhelm the higher ground, attended with a terrific noise and tremor of the earth. Recovering from his first surprise, he immediately resolved to proceed for the place from whence the noise seemed to come; and soon came in sight of the incomparable fountain, and saw, with amazement, the floods rushing upwards many feet high, and the expanding waters, which prevailed every way, spreading themselves far and near. He at length concluded (he said) that the fountains of the deep were again broken up, and that an universal deluge had commenced; and instantly turned about and fled to alarm the town, about nine miles distance: but before he could reach it, he met several of the inhabitants, who, already alarmed by the unusual noise, were hurrying on towards the place; upon which he returned with the Indians, taking their stand on an eminence to watch its progress and the event. It continued to jet and flow in this manner for several days, forming a large, rapid creek or river, descending and following the various courses and windings of the valley, for the distance of seven or eight miles, emptying itself into a vast savanna, where was a lake and sink which received and gave vent to its waters.

The fountain, however, gradually ceased to overflow, and finally withdrew itself beneath the common surface of the earth, leaving this capacious basin of waters, which, though continually near full, hath never since overflowed. There yet remains, and will, I suppose, remain for ages, the dry bed of the river or canal, generally four, five, and six feet below the natural surface of the land; the perpendicular, ragged banks of which, on each side, show the different strata of the earth; and at places, where ridges or a swelling bank crossed and opposed its course and fury, are vast heaps of fragments of rocks, white chalk, stones, and pebbles, which were collected and thrown into the lateral valleys, until the main stream prevailed over and forced them aside, overflowing the levels and meadows, for some miles distance from the principal stream, on either side. We continued down the great vale, along its banks, quite to the savanna and lake where it vented itself, while its ancient subterranean channel was gradually opening, which, I imagine, from some hidden event or cause had been choked up, and which, we may suppose, was the immediate cause of the eruption.

THOMAS JEFFERSON

1743–1826

17 *Conversations with Washington*

FEBRUARY the 28th, 1792. I was to have been with him long enough before three o'clock (which was the hour and day he received visits), to have opened to him a proposition for doubling the velocity of the post riders, who now travel about fifty miles a day, and might, without difficulty, go one hundred, and for taking measures (by way bills) to know where the delay is, when there is any. I was delayed by business, so as to have scarcely time to give him the outlines. I run over them rapidly, and observed afterwards, that I had hitherto never spoken to him on the subject of the post office, not knowing whether it was considered as a revenue law, or a law for the general accommodation of the citizens: that the law just passed seemed to have removed the doubt, by declaring that the whole profits of the office should be applied to extending the posts, and that even the past profits should be refunded by the treasury for the same purpose: that I therefore conceived it was now in the department of the Secretary of State: that I thought it would be advantageous so to declare it for another reason, to wit: that the department of the Treasury possessed already such an influence as to swallow up the whole executive powers, and that even the future Presidents (not supported by the weight of character which himself possessed), would not be able to make head against this department. That in urging this measure I had certainly no personal interest, since, if I was supposed to have any appetite for power, yet as my career would certainly be exactly as short as his own, the intervening time was too short to be an object. My real wish was to avail the public of every occasion, during the residue of the President's period, to place things on a safe footing. He was now called on to attend his company, and he desired me to come and breakfast with him the next morning.

February the 29th. I did so; and after breakfast we retired to his room, and I unfolded my plan for the post office, and after such an approbation of it as he usually permitted himself on the first presentment of any idea, and desiring me to commit it to writing, he, during that pause of conversation which follows a business closed, said in an affectionate tone, that he had felt much concern at an expression which dropped from me yesterday, and which marked my intention of retiring when he should. That as to himself, many motives obliged him to it. He had, through the whole course of the war, and most particularly at the close of it, uniformly declared his resolution to retire from public affairs, and never to act in any public office; that he had retired under that firm resolution: that the government, however, which had been formed, being found evidently too inefficacious, and it being supposed that his aid was of some consequence towards bringing the people to consent to one of sufficient efficacy for their own good, he consented to come into the convention, and on the same motive, after much pressing, to take a part in the new government, and get it under way. That were he to continue longer, it might give room to say, that having tasted the sweets of office, he could not do without them: that he really felt himself growing old, his bodily health less firm, his memory, always bad, becoming worse, and perhaps the other faculties of his mind showing a decay to others of which he was insensible himself; that this apprehension particularly oppressed him: that he found, moreover, his activity lessened, business therefore more irksome, and tranquillity and retirement become an irresistible passion. That however he felt himself obliged, for these reasons, to retire from the government, yet he should consider it as unfortunate, if that should bring on the retirement of the great officers of the government, and that this might produce a shock on the public mind of dangerous consequence.

I told him that no man had ever had less desire of entering into public offices than myself; that the circumstance of a perilous war, which brought everything into danger, and called for all the services which every citizen could render, had induced me to undertake the administration of the government of Virginia; that I had both before and after refused repeated appointments of Congress to go abroad in that sort of office, which, if I had consulted my own gratification, would almost have been the most agreeable to me; that at the end of two years, I resigned the government of Virginia, and retired with a firm resolution never more to appear in public life; that a domestic loss, however, happened, and made me fancy that absence and a change of scene for a time might be expedient for me; that I therefore accepted a foreign appointment, limited to two years; that at the close of that, Doctor Franklin having left France, I was appointed to supply his place, which I had accepted, and though I continued in it three or four years, it was under the constant idea of remaining only a year or two longer; that the revolution in France coming on, I had so interested myself in the event of that, that when obliged to bring my family home, I had still an idea of returning and awaiting the close of that, to fix the era of my final retirement; that on my arrival here I found he had appointed me to my present office; that he knew I had not come into it without some reluctance; that it was, on my part, a sacrifice of inclination to the opinion that I might be more serviceable here than in France, and with a firm resolution in my mind, to indulge my constant wish for retirement at no very distant day; that when, therefore, I had received his letter, written from Mount Vernon, on his way to Carolina and Georgia (April the 1st, 1791), and discovered, from an expression in that, that he meant to retire from the government ere long, and as to the precise epoch there could be no doubt, my mind was immediately made up, to make that the epoch of my own retirement from those labors of which I was heartily tired. That, however, I did not believe there was any idea in any of my brethren in the administration of retiring; that on the contrary, I had perceived at a late meeting of the trustees of the sinking fund, that the Secretary of the Treasury had developed the plan he intended to pursue, and that it embraced years in its view.

He said, that he considered the Treasury department as a much more limited one, going only to the single object of revenue, while that of the Secretary of State, embracing nearly all the objects of administration, was much more important, and the retirement of the officer therefore, would be more noticed: that though the government had set out with a pretty general good will of the public, yet that symptoms of dissatisfaction had lately shown themselves far beyond what he could have expected, and to what height these might arise, in case of too great a change in the administration, could not be foreseen.

I told him, that in my opinion, there was only a single source of these discontents. Though they had indeed appeared to spread themselves over the War department also, yet I considered that as an overflowing only from their real channel, which would never have taken place, if they had not first been generated in another department, to wit, the Treasury. That a system had there been contrived, for deluging the States with paper money instead of gold and silver, for withdrawing our citizens from the pursuits of commerce, manufactures, buildings, and other branches of useful industry, to occupy themselves and their capitals in a species of gambling, destructive of morality, and which had introduced its poison into the government itself. That it was a fact, as certainly known as that he and I were then conversing, that particular members of the legislature, while those laws were on the carpet, had feathered their nests with paper, had then voted for the laws, and constantly since lent all the energy of their talents, and instrumentality of their offices, to the establishment and enlargement of this system; that they had chained it about our necks for a great length of time, and in order to keep the game in their hands had, from time to time, aided in making such legislative constructions of the constitution, as made it a very different thing from what the people thought they had submitted to; that they had now brought forward a proposition far beyond any one ever yet advanced, and to which the eyes of many were turned, as the decision which was to let us know, whether we lived under a limited or an unlimited government. He asked me to what proposition I alluded? I answered, to that in the report on manufactures, which, under color of giving *bounties* for the encouragement of particular manufactures, meant to establish the doctrine, that the power given by the constitution to collect taxes to provide for the *general welfare* of the United States, permitted Congress to take everything under their management which *they* should deem for the *public welfare*, and which is susceptible of the application of money; consequently, that the subsequent enumeration of their powers was not the description to which resort must be had, and did not at all constitute the limits of their authority; that this was a very different question from that of the bank, which was thought an incident to an enumerated power; that, therefore, this decision was expected with great anxiety; that, indeed, I hoped the proposition would be rejected, believing there was a majority in both Houses against it, and that if it should be, it would be considered as a proof that things were returning into their true channel; and that, at any rate, I looked forward to the broad representation which would shortly take place, for keeping the general constitution on its true ground; and that this would remove a great deal of the discontent which had shown itself. The conversation ended with this last topic. It is here stated nearly as much at length as it really was; the expressions preserved where I could recollect them, and their substance always faithfully stated. March 1, 1792.

Bladensburg, October the 1st, 1792. This morning, at Mount Vernon, I had the following conversation with the President. He opened it by expressing his regret at the resolution in which I appeared so fixed, in the letter I had written him, of retiring from public affairs. He said, that he should be extremely sorry that I should do it, as long as he was in office, and that he could not see where he should find another character to fill my office. That, as yet, he was quite undecided whether to retire in March or not. His inclinations led him strongly to do it. Nobody disliked more the ceremonies of his office, and he had not the least taste or gratification in the execution of its functions. That he was happy at home alone, and that his presence there was now peculiarly called for by the situation of Major Washington, whom he thought irrecoverable, and should he get well, he would remove into another part of the country, which might better agree with him. That he did not believe his presence necessary; that there were other characters who would do the business as well or better. Still, however, if his aid was thought necessary to save the cause to which he had devoted his life principally, he would make the sacrifice of a longer continuance. That he therefore reserved himself for future decision, as his declaration would be in time if made a month before the day of election. He had desired Mr. Lear to find out from conversation, without appearing to make the inquiry, whether any other person would be desired by anybody. He had informed him, he judged from conversations that it was the universal desire he should continue, and he believed that those who expressed a doubt of his continuance, did it in the language of apprehension, and not of desire. But this, says he, is only from the north; it may be very different in the south. I thought this meant as an opening to me to say what was the sentiment in the south, from which quarter I came. I told him, that as far as I knew, there was but one voice there, which was for his continuance. That as to myself, I had ever preferred the pursuits of the private life to those of public, which had nothing in them agreeable to me. I explained to him the circumstances of the war which had first called me into public life, and those following the war, which had called me from a retirement on which I had determined. That I had constantly kept my eye on my own home, and could no longer refrain from returning to it. As to himself, his presence was important; that he was the only man in the United States who possessed the confidence of the whole; that government was founded in opinion and confidence, and that the longer he remained, the stronger would become the habits of the people in submitting to the government, and in thinking it a thing to be maintained; that there was no other person who would be thought anything more than the head of a party. He then expressed his concern at the difference which he found to subsist between the Secretary of the Treasury and myself, of which he said he had not been aware. He knew, indeed, that there was a marked difference in our political sentiments, but he had never suspected it had gone so far in producing personal difference, and he wished he could be the mediator to put an end to it. That he thought it important to preserve the check of my opinions in the administration, in order to keep things in their proper channel, and prevent them from going too far. That as to the idea of transforming this government into a monarchy, he did not believe there were ten men in the United States whose opinions were worth attention, who entertained such a thought. I told him there were many more than he imagined. I recalled to his memory a dispute at his own table, a little before we left Philadelphia, between General Schuyler on one side and Pinckney and myself on the other, wherein the former maintained the position, that hereditary descent was as likely to produce good magistrates as election. I told him, that though the people were sound, there were a numerous sect who had monarchy in contemplation; that the Secretary of the Treasury was one of these. That I had heard him say that this constitution was a shilly shally thing, of mere milk and water, which could not last, and was only good as a step to something better. That when we reflected, that he had endeavored in the convention, to make an English constitution of it, and when failing in that, we saw all his measures tending to bring it to the same thing, it was natural for us to be jealous; and particularly, when we saw that these measures had established corruption in the legislature, where there was a squadron devoted to the nod of the Treasury, doing whatever he had directed, and ready to do what he should direct. That if the equilibrium of the three great bodies, legislative, executive and judiciary, could be preserved, if the legislature could be kept independent, I should never fear the result of such a government; but that I could not but be uneasy, when I saw that the executive had swallowed up the legislative branch. He said, that as to that interested spirit in the legislature, it was what could not be avoided in any government, unless we were to exclude particular descriptions of men, such as the holders of the funds, from all office. I told him, there was great difference between the little accidental schemes of self-interest, which would take place in every body of men, and influence their votes, and a regular system for forming a corps of interested persons, who should be steadily at the orders of the Treasury. He touched on the merits of the funding system, observed there was a difference of opinion about it, some thinking it very bad, others very good; that experience was the only criterion of right which he knew, and this alone would decide which opinion was right. That for himself, he had seen our affairs desperate and our credit lost, and that this was in a sudden and extraordinary degree raised to the highest pitch. I told him, all that was ever necessary to establish our credit, was an efficient government and an honest one, declaring it would sacredly pay our debts, laying taxes for this purpose, and applying them to it. I avoided going further into the subject. He finished by another exhortation to me not to decide too positively on retirement, and here we were called to breakfast.

August the 6th, 1793. The President calls on me at my house in the country, and introduces my letter of July the 31st, announcing that I should resign at the close of the next month. He again expressed his repentance at not having resigned himself, and how much it was increased by seeing that he was to be deserted by those on whose aid he had counted; that he did not know where he should look to find characters to fill up the offices; that mere talents did not suffice for the department of State, but it required a person conversant in foreign affairs, perhaps acquainted with foreign courts; that without this, the best talents would be awkward and at a loss. He told me that Colonel Hamilton had three or four weeks ago written to him, informing him that private as well as public reasons had brought him to the determination to retire, and that he should do it towards the close of the next session. He said he had often before intimated dispositions to resign, but never as decisively before; that he supposed he had fixed on the latter part of next session, to give an opportunity to Congress to examine into his conduct; that our going out at times so different, increased his difficulty; for if he had both places to fill at once, he might consult both the particular talents and geographical situation of our successors. He expressed great apprehensions at the fermentation which seemed to be working in the mind of the public; that many descriptions of persons, actuated by different causes, appeared to be uniting; what it would end in he knew not; a new Congress was to assemble, more numerous, perhaps of a different spirit; the first expressions of their sentiments would be important; if

I would only stay to the end of that, it would relieve him considerably.

I expressed to him my excessive repugnance to public life, that particular uneasiness of my situation in this place, where the laws of society oblige me always to move exactly in the circle which I know to bear me peculiar hatred; that is to say, the wealthy aristocrats, the merchants connected closely with England, the new created paper fortunes; that thus surrounded, my words were caught, multiplied, misconstrued, and even fabricated and spread abroad to my injury; that he saw also, that there was such an opposition of views between myself and another part of the administration, as to render it peculiarly unpleasing, and to destroy the necessary harmony. Without knowing the views of what is called the republican party here, or having any communication with them, I could undertake to assure him, from my intimacy with that party in the late Congress, that there was not a view in the republican party as spread over the United States, which went to the frame of the government; that I believed the next Congress would attempt nothing material, but to render their own body independent; that that party were firm in their dispositions to support the government; that the maneuvers of Mr. Genet might produce some little embarrassment, but that he would be abandoned by the republicans the moment they knew the nature of his conduct; and on the whole, no crisis existed which threatened anything.

He said he believed the views of the republican party were perfectly pure, but when men put a machine into motion, it is impossible for them to stop it exactly where they would choose, or to say where it will stop. That the constitution we have is an excellent one, if we can keep it where it is; that it was, indeed, supposed there was a party disposed to change it into a monarchical form, but that he could conscientiously declare there was not a man in the United States who would set his face more decidedly against it than himself. Here I interrupted him, by saying, "No rational man in the United States suspects you of any other disposition; but there does not pass a week, in which we cannot prove declarations dropping from the monarchical party that our government is good for nothing, is a milk and water thing which cannot support itself, we must knock it down, and set up something of more energy." He said if that was the case, he thought it a proof of their insanity, for that the republican spirit of the Union was so manifest and so solid, that it was astonishing how any one could expect to move it.

He returned to the difficulty of naming my successor; he said Mr. Madison would be his first choice, but that he had always expressed to him such a decision against public office, that he could not expect he would undertake it. Mr. Jay would prefer his present office. He said that Mr. Jay had a great opinion of the talents of Mr. King; that there was also Mr. Smith of South Carolina, and E. Rutledge; but he observed, that name whom he would, some objections would be made, some would be called speculators, some one thing, some another; and he asked me to mention any characters occurring to me. I asked him if Governor Johnson of Maryland had occurred to him? He said he had; that he was a man of great good sense, an honest man, and he believed, clear of speculations; but his, says he, is an instance of what I was observing; with all these qualifications, Governor Johnson, from a want of familiarity with foreign affairs, would be in them like a fish out of water; everything would be new to him, and he awkward in everything. I confessed to him that I had considered Johnson rather as fit for the Treasury Department. Yes, says he, for that he would be the fittest appointment that could be made; he is a man acquainted with figures, and having as good a knowledge of the resources of this country as any man. I asked him if Chancellor Livingston had occurred to him? He said yes; but he was from New York, and to appoint him while Hamilton was in, and before it should be known he was going out, would excite a newspaper conflagration, as the ultimate arrangement would not be known. He said McLurg had occurred to him as a man of first-rate abilities, but it is said that he is a speculator. He asked me what sort of a man Wolcott was. I told him I knew nothing of him, myself; I had heard him characterized as a cunning man. I asked him whether some person could not take my office *par interim,* till he should make an appointment, as Mr. Randolph, for instance. Yes, says he, but there you would raise the expectation of keeping it, and I do not know that he is fit for it, nor what is thought of Mr. Randolph. I avoided noticing the last observation, and he put the question to me directly. I then told him, I went into society so little as to be unable to answer it: I knew that the embarrassments in his private affairs had obliged him to use expedients, which had injured him with the merchants and shop-keepers, and affected his character of independence; that these embarrassments were serious, and not likely to cease soon. He said if I would only stay in till the end of another quarter (the last of December) it would get us through the difficulties of this year, and he was satisfied that the affairs of Europe would be settled with this campaign; for that either France would be overwhelmed by it, or the confederacy would give up the contest. By that time, too, Congress will have manifested its character and view. I told him that I had set my private affairs in motion in a line which had powerfully called for my presence the last spring, and that they had suffered immensely from my not going home; that I had now calculated them to my return in the fall, and to fail in going then, would be the loss of another year, and prejudicial beyond measure. I asked him whether he could not name Governor Johnson to my office, under an express arrangement that at the close of the session he should take that of the Treasury. He said that men never chose to descend; that being once in a higher department, he would not like to go into a lower one. He asked me whether I could not arrange my affairs by going home. I told him I did not think the public business would admit of it; that there never was a day now in which the absence of the Secretary of State would not be inconvenient to the public. And he concluded by desiring that I would take two or three days to consider whether I could not stay in till the end of another quarter, for that like a man going to the gallows, he was willing to put it off as long as he could; but if I persisted, he must then look about him and make up his mind to do the best he could; and so he took leave.

JOHN JAMES AUDUBON

1780–1851

18   *The Passenger Pigeon*

THE multitudes of wild pigeons in our woods are astonishing. Indeed, after having viewed them so often, and under so many circumstances, I even now feel inclined to pause, and assure myself that what I am going to relate is fact. Yet I have seen it all, and that, too, in the company of persons who, like myself, were struck with amazement.

In the autumn of 1813 I left my house at Henderson, on the banks of the Ohio, on my way to Louisville. In passing over the Barrens, a few miles beyond Hardensburg, I observed the pigeons flying from northeast to southwest, in greater numbers than I thought I had ever seen them before, and feeling an inclination to count the flocks that might pass within reach of my eye in one hour, I dismounted, seated myself on an eminence, and began to mark with my pencil, making a dot for every flock that passed. In a short time, finding the task which I had undertaken impracticable, as the birds poured in in countless multitudes, I rose, and counting the dots then put down found that one hundred and sixty-three had been made in twenty-one minutes. I traveled on, and still met more the farther I proceeded. The air was literally filled with pigeons; the light of noonday was obscured as by an eclipse; the dung fell in spots not unlike melting flakes of snow; and the continued buzz of wings had a tendency to lull my senses to repose.

Whilst waiting for dinner at Young's Inn, at the confluence of Salt River with the Ohio, I saw, at my leisure, immense legions still going by, with a front reaching far beyond the Ohio on the west, and the beech wood forests directly on the east of me. Not a single bird alighted, for not a nut or acorn was that year to be seen in the neighborhood. They consequently flew so high, that different trials to reach them with a capital rifle proved ineffectual; nor did the reports disturb them in the least. I cannot describe to you the extreme beauty of their aerial evolutions, when a hawk chanced to press upon the rear of a flock. At once, like a torrent, and with a noise like thunder, they rushed into a compact mass, pressing upon each other towards the center. In these almost solid masses, they darted forward in undulating and angular lines, descended and swept close over the earth with inconceivable velocity, mounted perpendicularly so as to resemble a vast column, and, when high, were seen whirling and twisting within their continued lines, which then resembled the coils of a gigantic serpent.

Before sunset I reached Louisville, distant from Hardensburg fifty-five miles. The pigeons were still passing in undiminished numbers and continued to do so for three days in succession. The people were all in arms. The banks of the Ohio were crowded with men and boys, incessantly shooting at the pilgrims, which there flew lower, as they passed the river. Multitudes were thus destroyed. For a week or more, the population fed on no other flesh than that of pigeons, and talked of nothing but pigeons. The atmosphere, during this time, was strongly impregnated with the peculiar odor which emanates from the species.

As soon as the pigeons discover a sufficiency of food to entice them to alight, they fly round in circles, reviewing the country below. During their evolutions, on such occasions, the dense mass which they form exhibits a beautiful appearance, as it changes its direction, now displaying a glistening sheet of azure, when the backs of the birds come simultaneously into view, and anon suddenly presenting a mass of rich, deep purple. Then they pass lower, over the woods, and for a moment are lost among the foliage, but again emerge, and are seen gliding aloft. They now alight; but the next moment, as if suddenly alarmed, they take to wing, producing by the flappings of their wings a noise like the roar of distant thunder, and sweep through the forests to see if danger is near. Hunger, however, soon brings them to the ground. When alighted, they are seen industriously throwing up the withered leaves in quest of the fallen mast. The rear ranks are continually rising, passing over the main body, and alighting in front, in such rapid succession, that the whole flock seems still on the wing. The quantity of ground thus swept is astonishing; and so completely has it been cleared, that the gleaner who might follow in their rear would find his labor completely lost. Whilst feeding, their avidity is at times so great, that in attempting to swallow a large acorn or nut, they are seen gasping for a long while, as if in the agonies of suffocation.

On such occasions, when the woods are filled with these pigeons, they are killed in immense numbers, although no apparent diminution ensues. About the middle of the day, after their repast is finished, they settle on the trees, to enjoy rest and digest their food. On the ground they walk with ease, as well as on the branches, frequently jerking their beautiful tails, and moving their necks backward and forward in the most graceful manner. As the sun begins to sink beneath the horizon, they depart *en masse* for the roosting-place, which not unfrequently is hundreds of miles distant, as has been ascertained by persons who have kept an account of their arrivals and departures.

Let us now inspect their place of nightly rendezvous. One of these curious roosting-places, on the banks of the Green River, in Kentucky, I repeatedly visited. It was, as is always the case, in a portion of the forest where the trees were of great magnitude, and where there was little underwood. I rode through it upwards of forty miles, and, crossing it in different parts, found its average breadth to be rather more than three miles. My first view of it was about a fortnight subsequent to the period when they had made choice of it, and I arrived there nearly two hours before sunset. Few pigeons were then to be seen, but a great number of persons, with horses and wagons, guns and ammunition, had already established encampments on the borders. Two farmers from the vicinity of Russelsville, distant more than a hundred miles, had driven upwards of three hundred hogs to be fattened on the pigeons which were to be slaughtered. Here and there the people employed in plucking and salting what had already been procured were seen sitting in the midst of large piles of these birds. The dung lay several inches deep, covering the whole extent of the roosting-place, like a bed of snow. Many trees two feet in diameter, I observed, were broken off at no great distance from the ground; and the branches of many of the largest and tallest had given way, as if the forest had been swept by a tornado. Everything proved to me that the number of birds resorting to this part of the forest must be immense beyond conception. As the period of their arrival approached, their foes anxiously prepared to receive them. Some were furnished with iron pots containing sulphur, others with torches of pine knots, many with poles, and the rest with guns. The sun was lost to our view, yet not a pigeon had arrived. Everything was ready, and all eyes were gazing on the clear sky, which appeared in glimpses amidst the tall trees. Suddenly there burst forth a general cry of, "Here they come!" The noise which they made, though yet distant, reminded me of a hard gale at sea passing through the rigging of a close-reefed vessel. As the birds arrived and passed over me, I felt a current of air that surprised me. Thousands were soon knocked down by the pole-men. The birds continued to pour in. The fires were lighted, and a magnificent, as well as wonderful and almost terrifying, sight presented itself. The pigeons, arriving by thousands, alighted everywhere, one above another, until solid masses, as large as hogsheads, were formed on the branches all around. Here and there the perches gave way under the weight with a crash, and falling to the ground, destroyed hundreds of the birds beneath, forcing down the dense groups with which every stick was loaded. It was a scene of uproar and confusion. I found it quite useless to speak, or even to shout, to those persons who were nearest to me. Even the reports of the guns were seldom heard, and I was made aware of the firing only by seeing the shooters reloading.

No one dared venture within the line of devastation. The hogs had been penned up in due time, the picking up of the dead and wounded being left for the next morning's employment. The pigeons were constantly coming, and it was past midnight before I perceived a decrease in the number of those that arrived. The uproar continued the whole night; and as I was anxious to know to what distance the sound reached, I sent off a man, accustomed to perambulate the forest, who, returning two hours afterward, informed me he had heard it distinctly when three miles distant from the spot. Towards the approach of day, the noise in some measure subsided, long before objects were distinguishable, the pigeons began to move off in a direction quite different from that in which they had arrived the evening before, and at sunrise all that were able to fly had disappeared. The howlings of the wolves now reached our ears, and the foxes, lynxes, cougars, bears, raccoons, opossums, and polecats were seen sneaking off, whilst eagles, and hawks of different species, accompanied by a crowd of vultures, came to supplant them, and enjoy their share of the spoil.

WASHINGTON IRVING

1783-1859

19 *The Golden Reign of Wouter Van Twiller*

THE renowned WOUTER (or Walter) VAN TWILLER was descended from a long line of dutch burgomasters, who had successively dozed away their lives and grown fat upon the bench of magistracy in Rotterdam; and who had comported themselves with such singular wisdom and propriety, that they were never either heard or talked of — which, next to being universally applauded, should be the object of ambition of all sage magistrates and rulers.

His surname of Twiller is said to be a corruption of the original *Twijfler,* which in English means *doubter;* a name admirably descriptive of his deliberative habits. For though he was a man, shut up within himself like an oyster, and of such a profoundly reflective turn, that he scarcely ever spoke except in monosyllables, yet did he never make up his mind on any doubtful point. This was clearly accounted for by his adherents, who affirmed that he always conceived every object on so comprehensive a scale, that he had not room in his head, to turn it over and examine both sides of it, so that he always remained in doubt, merely in consequence of the astonishing magnitude of his ideas!

There are two opposite ways by which some men get into notice — one by talking a vast deal and thinking a little, and the other by holding their tongues and not thinking at all. By the first many a vaporing, superficial pretender acquires the reputation of a man of quick parts — by the other many a vacant dunderpate, like the owl, the stupidest of birds, comes to be complimented, by a discerning world, with all the attributes of wisdom. This, by the way, is a mere casual remark, which I would not for the universe have it thought, I apply to Governor Van Twiller. On the contrary he was a very wise dutchman, for he never said a foolish thing — and of such invincible gravity, that he was never known to laugh, or even to smile, through the course of a long and prosperous life. Certain however it is, there never was a matter proposed, however simple, and on which your common narrow minded mortals would rashly determine at the first glance, but what the renowned Wouter put on a mighty mysterious, vacant kind of look, shook his capacious head, and having smoked for five minutes with redoubled earnestness, sagely observed, that " he had his doubts about the matter " — which in process of time gained him the character of a man slow of belief, and not easily imposed on.

The person of this illustrious old gentleman was as regularly formed and nobly proportioned, as though it had been molded by the hands of some cunning dutch statuary, as a model of majesty and lordly grandeur. He was exactly five feet six inches in height, and six feet five inches in circumference. His head was a perfect sphere, far excelling in magnitude that of the great Pericles (who was thence waggishly called *Schenocephalus,* or onion head) — indeed, of such stupendous dimensions was it, that dame nature herself, with all her sex's ingenuity, would have been puzzled to construct a neck capable of supporting it; wherefore she wisely declined the attempt, and settled it firmly on the top of his back bone, just between the shoulders; where it remained as snugly bedded as a ship of war in the mud of the Potowmac. His body was of an oblong form, particularly capacious at bottom; which was wisely ordered by providence, seeing that he was a man of sedentary habits, and very averse to the idle labor of walking. His legs, though exceeding short, were sturdy in proportion to the weight they had to sustain; so that when erect, he had not a little the appearance of a robustious beer barrel, standing on skids. His face, that infallible index of the mind, presented a vast expanse perfectly unfurrowed or deformed by any of those lines and angles which disfigure the human countenance with what is termed expression. Two small gray eyes twinkled feebly in the midst, like two stars of lesser magnitude in a hazy firmament; and his full fed cheeks, which seemed to have taken toll of every thing that went into his mouth, were curiously mottled and streaked with dusky red, like a spitzenberg apple.

His habits were as regular as his person. He daily took his four stated meals, appropriating exactly an hour to each; he smoked and doubted eight hours, and he slept the remaining twelve of the four and twenty. Such was the renowned Wouter Van Twiller — a true philosopher, for his mind was either elevated above, or tranquilly settled below, the cares and perplexities of this world. He had lived in it for years, without feeling the least curiosity to know whether the sun revolved round it, or it round the sun; and he had even watched for at least half a century, the smoke curling from his pipe to the ceiling, without once troubling his head with any of those numerous theories, by which a philosopher would have perplexed his brain, in accounting for its rising above the surrounding atmosphere.

In his council he presided with great state and solemnity. He sat in a huge chair of solid oak hewn in the celebrated forest of the Hague, fabricated by an experienced Timmerman of Amsterdam, and curiously carved about the arms and feet, into exact imitations of gigantic eagle's claws. Instead of a scepter he swayed a long turkish pipe, wrought with jasmin and amber, which had been presented to a stadtholder of Holland, at the conclusion of a treaty with one of the petty Barbary powers. — In this stately chair would he sit, and this magnificent pipe would he smoke, shaking his right knee with a constant motion, and fixing his eye for hours together upon a little print of Amsterdam, which hung in a black frame, against the opposite wall of the council chamber. Nay, it has ever been said, that when any deliberation of extraordinary length and intricacy was on the carpet, the renowned Wouter would absolutely shut his eyes for full two hours at a time, that he might not be disturbed by external objects — and at such times the internal commotion of his mind was evinced by certain regular guttural sounds, which his admirers declared were merely the noise of conflict, made by his contending doubts and opinions.

It is with infinite difficulty I have been enabled to collect these biographical anecdotes of the great man under consideration. The facts respecting him were so scattered and vague, and divers of them so questionable in point of authenticity, that I have had to give up the search after many, and decline the admission of still more, which would have tended to heighten the colouring of his portrait.

I have been the more anxious to delineate fully the person and habits of the renowned Van Twiller, from the consideration that he was not only the first, but also the best governor that ever presided over this ancient and respectable province; and so tranquil and benevolent was his reign, that I do not find throughout the whole of it a single instance of any offender being brought to punishment: — a most indubitable sign of a merciful governor, and a case unparalleled, excepting in the reign of the illustrious King Log, from whom, it is hinted, the renowned Van Twiller was a lineal descendant.

The very outset of the career of this excellent magistrate, like that of Solomon, or to speak more appropriately, like that of the illustrious governor of Barataria, was distinguished by an example of legal acumen that gave flattering presage of a wise and equitable administration. The very morning after he had been solemnly installed in office, and at the moment that he was making his breakfast from a prodigious earthen dish, filled with milk and Indian pudding, he was suddenly interrupted by the appearance of one Wandle Schoonhoven, a very important old burgher of New Amsterdam, who complained bitterly of one Barent Bleecker, inasmuch as he fraudulently refused to come to a settlement of accounts, seeing that there was a heavy balance in favor of the said Wandle. Governor Van Twiller, as I have already observed, was a man of few words, he was likewise a mortal enemy to multiplying writings — or being disturbed at his breakfast. Having therefore listened attentively to the statement of Wandle Schoonhoven, giving an occasional grunt as he shoveled a mighty spoonful of Indian pudding into his mouth — either as a sign that he relished the dish, or comprehended the story — he called unto him his constable, and pulling out of his breeches pocket a huge jack-knife, dispatched it after the defendant as a summons, accompanied by his tobacco box as a warrant.

This summary process was as effectual in those simple days, as was the seal ring of the great Haroun Alraschid among the true believers — the two parties, being confronted before him, each produced a book of accounts, written in a language and character that would have puzzled any but a High Dutch commentator, or a learned decipherer of Egyptian obelisks, to understand. The sage Wouter took them one after the other, and having poised them in his hands, and attentively counted over the number of leaves, fell straightway into a very great doubt, and smoked for half an hour without saying a word; at length, laying his finger beside his nose, and shutting his eyes for a moment, with the air of a man who has just caught a subtle idea by the tail, he slowly took his pipe from his mouth, puffed forth a column of to-bacco smoke, and with marvelous gravity and solemnity pro-nounced — that having carefully counted over the leaves and weighed the books, it was found, that one was just as thick and as heavy as the other — therefore it was the final opinion of the court that the accounts were equally balanced — there-fore Wandle should give Barent a receipt, and Barent should give Wandle a receipt — and the constable should pay the costs.

This decision being straightway made known, diffused gen-eral joy throughout New Amsterdam, for the people immedi-ately perceived that they had a very wise and equitable magistrate to rule over them. But its happiest effect was, that not another law suit took place throughout the whole of his administration — and the office of constable fell into such decay, that there was not one of those losel scouts known in the province for many years. I am the more particular in dwelling on this transaction, not only because I deem it one of the most sage and righteous judgments on record, and well worthy the attention of modern magistrates, but because it was a miraculous event in the history of the renowned Wouter — being the only time he was ever known to come to a decision, in the whole course of his life.

In those good days of simplicity and sunshine, a passion for cleanliness was the grand desideratum in domestic econ-omy and the universal test of an able housewife — a char-acter which formed the utmost ambition of our unenlightened grandmothers. The front door was never opened except on marriages, funerals, new year's days, the festival of St. Nicho-las, or some such great occasion. — It was ornamented with a gorgeous brass knocker, curiously wrought, sometimes into the device of a dog, and sometimes of a lion's head, and was daily burnished with such religious zeal, that it was ofttimes worn out, by the very precautions taken for its preservation. The whole house was constantly in a state of inundation, under the discipline of mops and brooms and scrubbing brushes; and the good housewives of those days were a kind of amphibious animal, delighting exceedingly to be dabbling in water — insomuch that an historian of the day gravely tells us, that many of his townswomen grew to have webbed fingers like unto a duck; and some of them, he had little doubt, could the matter be examined into, would be found to have the tails of mermaids — but this I look upon to be a mere sport of fancy, or what is worse, a wilful misrepresentation.

The grand parlor was the sanctum sanctorum, where the passion for cleaning was indulged without control. In this sacred apartment no one was permitted to enter, excepting the mistress and her confidential maid, who visited it once a week, for the purpose of giving it a thorough cleaning, and putting things to rights — always taking the precaution of leaving their shoes at the door and entering devoutly, on their stocking feet. After scrubbing the floor, sprinkling it with fine white sand, which was curiously stroked into angles, and curves, and rhomboids, with a broom — after washing the windows, rubbing and polishing the furniture, and putting a new bunch of evergreens in the fireplace — the window shutters were again closed to keep out the flies, and the room carefully locked up until the revolution of time brought round the weekly cleaning day.

As to the family, they always entered in at the gate, and most generally lived in the kitchen. To have seen a numerous household assembled around the fire, one would have imagined that he was transported back to those happy days of primeval simplicity which float before our imaginations like golden visions. The fireplaces were of a truly patriarchal magnitude, where the whole family, old and young, master and servant, black and white, nay even the very cat and dog, enjoyed a community of privilege, and had each a prescriptive right to a corner. Here the old burgher would sit in perfect silence, puffing his pipe, looking in the fire with half shut eyes, and thinking of nothing for hours together; the goede vrouw on the opposite side would employ herself diligently in spinning her yarn, or knitting stockings. The young folks would crowd around the hearth, listening with breathless attention to some old crone of a negro, who was the oracle of the family, — and who, perched like a raven in a corner of the chimney, would croak forth for a long winter afternoon, a string of incredible stories about New England witches — grisly ghosts — horses without heads — and hairbreadth scapes and bloody encounters among the Indians.

In those happy days a well regulated family always rose with the dawn, dined at eleven, and went to bed at sundown. Dinner was invariably a private meal, and the fat old burghers showed incontestable symptoms of disapprobation and uneasiness at being surprised by a visit from a neighbor on such occasions. But though our worthy ancestors were thus singularly averse to giving dinners, yet they kept up the social bands of intimacy by occasional banquetings, called tea parties.

As this is the first introduction of those delectable orgies which have since become so fashionable in this city, I am conscious my fair readers will be very curious to receive information on the subject. Sorry am I, that there will be but little in my description calculated to excite their admiration. I can neither delight them with accounts of suffocating crowds, nor brilliant drawing rooms, nor towering feathers, nor sparkling diamonds, nor immeasurable trains. I can detail no choice anecdotes of scandal, for in those primitive times the simple folk were either too stupid, or too good natured to pull each other's characters to pieces — nor can I furnish any whimsical anecdotes of brag — how one lady cheated, or another bounced into a passion; for as yet there was no junto of dulcet old dowagers, who met to win each other's money, and lose their own tempers at a card table.

These fashionable parties were generally confined to the higher classes, or noblesse, that is to say, such as kept their own cows, and drove their own wagons. The company commonly assembled at three o'clock, and went away about six, unless it was in winter time, when the fashionable hours were a little earlier, that the ladies might get home before dark. I do not find that they ever treated their company to iced creams, jellies or syllabubs; or regaled them with musty almonds, moldy raisins, or sour oranges, as is often done in the present age of refinement. — Our ancestors were fond of more sturdy, substantial fare. The tea table was crowned with a huge earthen dish, well stored with slices of fat pork, fried brown, cut up into mouthfuls, and swimming in doup or gravy. The company being seated around the genial board, and each furnished with a fork, evinced their dexterity in launching at the fattest pieces in this mighty dish — in much the same manner as sailors harpoon porpoises at sea, or our Indians spear salmon in the lakes. Sometimes the table was graced with immense apple pies, or saucers full of preserved peaches and pears; but it was always sure to boast an enormous dish of balls of sweetened dough, fried in hog's fat, and called dough nuts, or oly koeks — a delicious kind of cake, at present scarce known in this city, excepting in genuine dutch families; but which retains its preëminent station at the tea tables in Albany.

The tea was served out of a majestic delft tea-pot ornamented with paintings of fat little dutch shepherds and shepherdesses, tending pigs — with boats sailing in the air, and houses built in the clouds, and sundry other ingenious dutch fantasies. The beaux distinguished themselves by their adroitness in replenishing this pot, from a huge copper tea kettle, which would have made the pigmy macaronies of these degenerate days sweat merely to look at it. To sweeten the beverage, a lump of sugar was laid beside each cup — and the company alternately nibbled and sipped with great decorum, until an improvement was introduced by a shrewd and economic old lady, which was to suspend a large lump directly over the tea table, by a string from the ceiling, so that it could be swung from mouth to mouth — an ingenious expedient, which is still kept up by some families in Albany; but which prevails without exception in Communipaw, Bergen, Flat-Bush, and all our uncontaminated dutch villages.

At these primitive tea parties the utmost propriety and dignity of deportment prevailed. No flirting nor coquetting — no gambling of old ladies nor hoyden chattering and romping of young ones — no self satisfied struttings of wealthy gentlemen with their brains in their pockets — nor amusing conceits, and monkey divertisements of smart young gentlemen, with no brains at all. On the contrary, the young ladies seated themselves demurely in their rush-bottomed chairs, and knit their own woollen stockings; nor ever opened their lips, excepting to say, *yah Mynher,* or *yah, ya Vrouw,* to any question that was asked them; behaving in all things, like decent, well educated damsels. As to the gentlemen, each of them tranquilly smoked his pipe, and seemed lost in contemplation of the blue and white tiles with which the fireplaces were decorated; wherein sundry passages of scripture were piously portrayed — Tobit and his dog figured to great advantage; Haman swung conspicuously on his gibbet, and Jonah appeared most manfully bouncing out of the whale, like Harlequin through a barrel of fire.

The parties broke up without noise and without confusion — for, strange as it may seem, the ladies and gentlemen were content to take their own cloaks and shawls and hats; not dreaming, simple souls! of the ingenious system of exchange established in modern days; by which those who first leave a party are authorized to choose the best shawl or hat they can find — a custom which has doubtless arisen in consequence of our commercial habits. They were carried home by their own carriages, that is to say, by the vehicles nature had provided them, excepting such of the wealthy, as could afford to keep a wagon. The gentlemen gallantly attended their fair ones to their respective abodes, and took leave of them with a hearty smack at the door: which as it was an established piece of etiquette, done in perfect simplicity and honesty of heart, occasioned no scandal at that time, nor should it at the present — if our great-grandfathers approved of the custom, it would argue a great want of reverence in their descendants to say a word against it.

In this dulcet period of my history, when the beauteous island of Mannahata presented a scene, the very counterpart of those glowing pictures drawn by old Hesiod of the golden reign of Saturn, there was a happy ignorance, an honest simplicity prevalent among its inhabitants, which were I even able to depict, would be but little understood by the degenerate age for which I am doomed to write. Even the female sex, those arch innovators upon the tranquillity, the honesty, and graybeard customs of society, seemed for a while to conduct themselves with incredible sobriety and comeliness, and indeed behaved almost as if they had not been sent into the world to bother mankind, baffle philosophy, and confound the universe.

Their hair, untortured by the abominations of art, was scrupulously pomatomed back from their foreheads with a candle, and covered with a little cap of quilted calico, which fitted exactly to their heads. Their petticoats of linsey woolsey were striped with a variety of gorgeous dyes, rivaling the many colored robes of Iris — though I must confess these gallant garments were rather short, scarce reaching below the knee; but then they made up in the number, which generally equaled that of the gentlemen's small-clothes; and what is still more praiseworthy, they were all of their own manufacture — of which circumstance, as may well be supposed, they were not a little vain.

These were the honest days, in which every woman stayed at home, read the bible and wore pockets — aye, and that too of a goodly size, fashioned with patchwork into many curious devices, and ostentatiously worn on the outside. These, in fact, were convenient receptacles, where all good housewives carefully stowed away such things as they wished to have at hand; by which means they often came to be incredibly crammed — and I remember there was a story current when

I was a boy, that the lady of Wouter Van Twiller, having occasion to empty her right pocket in search of a wooden ladle, the contents filled three corn baskets, and the utensil was at length discovered lying among some rubbish in one corner — but we must not give too much faith to all these stories, the anecdotes of these remote periods being very subject to exaggeration.

Beside these notable pockets, they likewise wore scissors and pincushions suspended from their girdles by red ribbands, or among the more opulent and showy classes, by brass and even silver chains — indubitable tokens of thrifty housewives and industrious spinsters. I cannot say much in vindication of the shortness of the petticoats; it doubtless was introduced for the purpose of giving the stockings a chance to be seen, which were generally of blue worsted with magnificent red clocks — or perhaps to display a well turned ankle, and a neat, though serviceable foot; set off by a high-heeled leathern shoe, with a large and splendid silver buckle. Thus we find that the gentle sex in all ages have shown the same disposition to infringe a little upon the laws of decorum, in order to betray a lurking beauty, or gratify an innocent love of finery.

From the sketch here given it will be seen that our good grandmothers differed considerably in their ideas of a fine figure, from their scantily dressed descendants of the present day. A fine lady, in those times, waddled under more clothes, even on a fair summer's day, than would have clad the whole bevy of a modern ball room. Nor were they the less admired by the gentlemen in consequence thereof. On the contrary, the greatness of a lover's passion seemed to increase in proportion to the magnitude of its object — and a voluminous damsel, arrayed in a dozen of petticoats, was declared by a low-dutch sonneteer of the province, to be radiant as a sunflower, and luxuriant as a full blown cabbage. Certain it is, that in those days, the heart of a lover could not contain more than one lady at a time; whereas the heart of a modern gallant has often room enough to accommodate half a dozen — The reason of which I conclude to be, that either the hearts of the gentlemen have grown larger, or the persons of the ladies smaller — this however is a question for physiologists to determine.

But there was a secret charm in these petticoats, which no doubt entered into the consideration of the prudent gallant. The wardrobe of a lady was in those days her only fortune; and she who had a good stock of petticoats and stockings was as absolutely an heiress as is a Kamschatka damsel with a store of bearskins, or a Lapland belle with a plenty of reindeer. The ladies, therefore, were very anxious to display these powerful attractions to the greatest advantage; and the best rooms in the house instead of being adorned with caricatures of dame nature, in water colors and needlework, were always hung round with abundance of home-spun garments; the manufacture and property of the females — a piece of laudable ostentation that still prevails among the heiresses of our dutch villages. Such were the beauteous belles of the ancient city of New Amsterdam, rivaling in primeval simplicity of manners the renowned and courtly dames so loftily sung by Dan Homer — who tells us that the princess Nausicaa washed the family linen, and the fair Penelope wove her own petticoats.

The gentlemen, in fact, who figured in the circles of the gay world in these ancient times, corresponded in more particulars with the beauteous damsels whose smiles they were ambitious to deserve. True it is, their merits would make but a very inconsiderable impression upon the heart of a modern fair; they neither drove in their curricles nor sported their tandems, for as yet these gaudy vehicles were not even dreamt of — neither did they distinguish themselves by their brilliance at the table, and their consequent rencountres with watchmen, for our forefathers were of too pacific a disposition to need those guardians of the night, every soul throughout the town being in full snore before nine o'clock. Neither did they establish their claims by gentility at the expense of their taylors — for as yet those offenders against the pockets of society, and the tranquillity of all aspiring young gentlemen, were unknown in New Amsterdam; every good housewife made the clothes of her husband and family, and even the goede vrouw of Van Twiller himself thought it no disparagement to cut out her husband's linsey woolsey galligaskins.

Not but what there were some two or three youngsters who manifested the first dawnings of what is called fire and spirit. Who held all labor in contempt; skulked about docks and market places; loitered in the sunshine; squandered what little money they could procure at hustle cap and chuck farthing, swore, boxed, fought cocks, and raced their neighbors' horses — in short who promised to be the wonder, the talk and abomination of the town, had not their stylish career been unfortunately cut short by an affair of honor with a whipping post.

Far other, however, was the truly fashionable gentleman of those days — his dress, which served for both morning and evening, street and drawing room, was a linsey woolsey coat, made perhaps by the fair hands of the mistress of his affections, and gallantly bedecked with abundance of large brass buttons. — Half a score of breeches heightened the proportions of his figure — his shoes were decorated by enormous copper buckles — a low crowned broad brimmed hat overshadowed his burly visage, and his hair dangled down his back, in a prodigious queue of eel skin.

Thus equipped, he would manfully sally forth with pipe in mouth to besiege some fair damsel's obdurate heart — not such a pipe, good reader, as that which Acis did sweetly tune in praise of his Galatea, but one of true delft manufacture and furnished with a charge of fragrant Cow-pen tobacco. With this would he resolutely set himself down before the fortress, and rarely failed in the process of time to smoke the fair enemy into a surrender, upon honorable terms.

Such was the happy reign of Wouter Van Twiller, celebrated in many a long forgotten song as the real golden age, the rest being nothing but counterfeit copper-washed coin. In that delightful period, a sweet and holy calm reigned over the whole province. The Burgomaster smoked his pipe in peace — the substantial solace of his domestic house, his well petticoated *yffrouw,* after her daily cares were done, sat soberly at her door, with arms crossed over her apron of snowy white, without being insulted by ribald street walkers or vagabond boys — those unlucky urchins, who do so infest our streets, displaying under the roses of youth, the thorns and briars of iniquity. Then it was that the lover with ten breeches and the damsel with petticoats of half a score indulged in all the innocent endearments of virtuous love, without fear and without reproach — for what had that virtue to fear, which was defended by a shield of good linsey woolseys, equal at least to the seven bull hides of the invincible Ajax.

Thrice happy, and never to be forgotten age! when every thing was better than it has ever been since, or ever will be again — when Buttermilk channel was quite dry at low water — when the shad in the Hudson were all salmon, and when the moon shone with a pure and resplendent whiteness, instead of that melancholy yellow light which is the consequence of her sickening at the abominations she every night witnesses in this degenerate city!

DAVID CROCKETT

1786–1836

20   *His Courtship*

I NEXT went to the house of an honest old Quaker, by the name of John Kennedy, who had removed from North Carolina, and proposed to hire myself to him, at two shillings a day. He agreed to take me a week on trial; at the end of which he appeared pleased with my work, and informed me that he held a note on my father for forty dollars, and that he would give me that note if I worked for him six months. I was certain enough that I should never get any part of the note; but then I remembered it was my father that owed it, and I concluded it was my duty as a child to help him along, and ease his lot as much as I could. I told the Quaker I would take him up at his offer, and immediately went to work. I never visited my father's house during the whole time of this engagement, though he lived only fifteen miles off. But when it was finished, and I had got the note, I borrowed one of my employer's horses, and, on a Sunday evening, went to pay my parents a visit. Some time after I got there, I pulled out the note and handed it to my father, who supposed Mr. Kennedy had sent it for collection. The old man looked mighty sorry, and said to me he had not the money to pay it, and didn't know what he should do. I then told him I had paid it for him, and it was then his own; that it was not presented for collection, but as a present from me. At this, he shed a heap of tears; and as soon as he got a little over it, he said he was sorry he couldn't give me anything, but he was not able, he was too poor.

The next day, I went back to my old friend, the Quaker, and set in to work for him for some clothes; for I had now worked a year without getting any money at all, and my clothes were nearly all worn out, and what few I had left were mighty indifferent. I worked in this way for about two months; and in that time a young woman from North Carolina, who was the Quaker's niece, came on a visit to his house. And now I am just getting on a part of my history that I know I never can forget. For though I have heard people talk about hard loving, yet I reckon no poor devil in this world was ever cursed with such hard love as mine has always been, when it came on me. I soon found myself head over heels in love with this girl, whose name the public could make no use of; and I thought that if all the hills about there were pure chink, and all belonged to me, I would give them if I could just talk to her as I wanted to; but I was afraid to begin, for when I would think of saying anything to her, my heart would begin to flutter like a duck in a puddle; and if I tried to outdo it and speak, would get right smack up in my throat, and choak me like a cold potato. It bore on my mind in this way, till at last I concluded I must die if I didn't broach the subject; and so I determined to begin and hang on a trying to speak, till my heart would get out of my throat one way or t'other. And so one day at it I went, and after several trials I could say a little. I told her how well I loved her; that she was the darling object of my soul and body; and I must have her, or else I should pine down to nothing, and just die away with the consumption.

I found my talk was not disagreeable to her; but she was an honest girl, and didn't want to deceive nobody. She told me she was engaged to her cousin, a son of the old Quaker. This news was worse to me than war, pestilence, or famine; but still I knowed I could not help myself. I saw quick enough my cake was dough, and I tried to cool off as fast as possible; but I had hardly safety pipes enough, as my love was so hot as mighty nigh to burst my boilers. But I didn't press my claims any more, seeing there was no chance to do anything.

I began now to think, that all my misfortunes growed out of my want of learning. I had never been to school but four days, as the reader has already seen, and did not yet know a letter.

I thought I would try to go to school some; and as the Quaker had a married son, who was living about a mile and a half from him, and keeping a school, I proposed to him that I would go to school four days in the week, and work for him the other two, to pay my board and schooling. He agreed I might come on those terms; and so at it I went, learning and working back and forwards, until I had been with him nigh on to six months. In this time I learned to read a little in my primer, to write my own name, and to cipher some in the three first rules in figures. And this was all the schooling I ever had in my life, up to this day. I should have continued longer, if it hadn't been that I concluded I couldn't do any longer without a wife; and so I cut out to hunt me one.

I found a family of very pretty little girls that I had known when very young. They had lived in the same neighborhood with me, and I had thought very well of them. I made an offer to one of them, whose name is nobody's business, no more than the Quaker girl's was, and I found she took it very well. I still continued paying my respects to her, until I got to love her as bad as I had the Quaker's niece; and I would have agreed to fight a whole regiment of wild cats if she would only have said she would have me. Several months passed in this way, during all of which time she continued very kind and friendly. At last, the son of the old Quaker and my first girl had concluded to bring their matter to a close, and my own little queen and myself were called on to wait on them. We went on the day, and performed our duty as attendants. This made me worse than ever; and after it was over, I pressed my claim very hard on her, but she would still give me a sort of evasive answer. However, I gave her mighty little peace, till she told me at last she would have me. I thought this was glorification enough, even without spectacles. I was then about eighteen years old. We fixed the time to be married; and I thought if that day come, I should be the happiest man in the created world, or in the moon, or anywhere else.

I had by this time got to be mighty fond of the rifle, and had bought a capital one. I most generally carried her with me wherever I went, and though I had got back to the old Quaker's to live, who was a very particular man, I would sometimes slip out and attend the shooting matches, where they shot for beef; I always tried, though, to keep it a secret from him. He had at the same time a bound boy living with him, who I had gotten into almost as great a notion of the girls as myself. He was about my own age, and was deeply smitten with the sister to my intended wife. I know'd it was in vain to try to get the leave of the old man for my young associate to go with me on any of my courting frolics; but I thought I could fix a plan to have him along, which would not injure the Quaker, as we had no notion that he should ever know it. We commonly slept upstairs, and at the gable end of the house there was a window. So one Sunday, when the old man and his family were all gone to meeting, we went out and cut a long pole, and, taking it to the house, we set it up on one end in the corner, reaching up the chimney as high as the window. After this we would go upstairs to bed, and then putting on our Sunday clothes, would go out at the window, and climb down the pole, take a horse apiece, and ride about ten miles to where his sweetheart lived, and the girl I claimed as my wife. I was always mighty careful to be back before day, so as to escape being found out; and in this way I continued my attentions very closely until a few days before I was to be married, or at least thought I was, for I had no fear that anything was about to go wrong.

Just now I heard of a shooting-match in the neighborhood, right between where I lived and my girl's house; and I determined to kill two birds with one stone, — to go to the shooting-match first, and then to see her. I therefore made the Quaker believe I was going to hunt for deer, as they were pretty plenty about in those parts; but, instead of hunting them, I went straight on to the shooting-match, where I joined in with a partner, and we put in several shots for the beef. I was mighty lucky, and when the match was over I had won the whole beef. This was on a Saturday, and my success had put me in the finest humor in the world. So I sold my part of the beef for five dollars in the real grit, for I believe that was before bank-notes were invented; at least I had never heard of any. I now started on to ask for my wife; for, though the next Thursday was our wedding day, I had never said a word to her parents about it. I had always dreaded the undertaking so bad, that I had put the evil hour off as long as possible; and, indeed, I calculated they knowed me so well, they wouldn't raise any objections to having me for their son-in-law. I had a great deal better opinion of myself, I found, than other people had of me; but I moved on with a light heart, and my five dollars jingling in my pocket, thinking all the time there was but few greater men in the world than myself.

In this flow of good humor I went ahead, till I got within about two miles of the place, when I concluded I would stop awhile at the house of the girl's uncle; where I might inquire about the family, and so forth, and so on. I was indeed just about ready to consider her uncle, my uncle; and her affairs, my affairs. When I went in, tho', I found her sister there. I asked how all was at home? In a minute I found from her countenance something was wrong. She looked mortified, and didn't answer as quick as I thought she ought, being it was her *brother-in-law* talking to her. However, I asked her again. She then burst into tears, and told me her sister was going to deceive me; and that she was to be married to another man the next day. This was as sudden to me as a clap of thunder of a bright sunshiny day. It was the cap-stone of all the afflictions I had ever met with; and it seemed to me, that it was more than any human creature could en-dure. It struck me perfectly speechless for some time, and made me feel so weak, that I thought I should sink down. I however recovered from my shock after a little, and rose and started without any ceremony, or even bidding anybody good-bye. The young woman followed me out to the gate, and entreated me to go on to her father's, and said she would go with me. She said the young man, who was going to marry her sister, had got his license, and had asked for her; but she assured me her father and mother both preferred me to him; and that she had no doubt but that, if I would go on, I could break off the match. But I found I could go no further. My heart was bruised, and my spirits were broken down; so I bid her farewell, and turned my lonesome and miserable steps back again homeward, concluding that I was only born for hardships, misery, and disappointment. I now began to think, that in making me, it was entirely forgotten to make my mate; that I was born odd, and should always remain so, and that nobody would have me.

But all these reflections did not satisfy my mind, for I had no peace day nor night for several weeks. My appetite failed me, and I grew daily worse and worse. They all thought I was sick; and so I was. And it was the worse kind of sick-ness, — a sickness of the heart, and all the tender parts, pro-duced by disappointed love.

I continued in this down-spirited situation for a good long time, until one day I took my rifle and started hunting. While out, I made a call at the house of a Dutch widow, who had a daughter that was well enough as to smartness, but she was as ugly as a stone fence. She was, however, quite talkative, and soon began to laugh at me about my disappointment.

She seemed disposed, though, to comfort me as much as she could; and, for that purpose, told me to keep in good-heart, that " there was as good fish in the sea as had ever been caught out of it." I doubted this very much; but whether or not, I was certain that she was not one of them, for she was so homely that it almost give me a pain in the eyes to look at her.

But I couldn't help thinking, that she had intended what she had said as a banter for me to court her! ! ! — the last thing in creation I could have thought of doing. I felt little inclined to talk on the subject, it is true; but, to pass off the time, I told her I thought I was born odd, and that no fellow to me could be found. She protested against this, and said if I would come to their reaping, which was not far off, she would show me one of the prettiest little girls there I had ever seen. She added that the one who had deceived me was nothing to be compared with her. I didn't believe a word of all this, for I had thought that such a piece of flesh and blood as she was had never been manufactured, and never would again. I agreed with her, though, that the little varment had treated me so bad, that I ought to forget her, and yet I couldn't do it. I concluded the best way to accomplish it was to cut out again, and see if I could find any other that would answer me; and so I told the Dutch girl I would be at the reaping, and would bring as many as I could with me.

I employed my time pretty generally in giving information of it, as far as I could, until the day came; and I then offered to work for my old friend, the Quaker, two days, if he would let his bound boy go with me one to the reaping. He refused, and reproved me pretty considerable roughly for my proposition; and said, if he was in my place he wouldn't go; that there would be a great deal of bad company there; and that I had been so good a boy, he would be sorry for me to get a bad name. But I knowed my promise to the Dutch girl, and I was resolved to fulfil it; so I shouldered my rifle, and started by myself. When I got to the place, I found a large company of men and women, and among them an old Irish woman, who had a great deal to say. I soon found out from my Dutch girl, that this old lady was the mother of the little girl she had promised me, though I had not yet seen her. She was in an outhouse with some other youngsters, and had not yet made her appearance. Her mamma, however, was no way bashful. She came up to me, and began to praise my red cheeks, and said she had a sweetheart for me. I had no doubt she had been told what I come for, and all about it. In the evening I was introduced to her daughter, and I must confess, I was plaguy well pleased with her from the word go. She had a good countenance, and was very pretty, and I was full bent on making up an acquaintance with her.

It was not long before the dancing commenced, and I asked her to join me in a reel. She very readily consented to do so; and after we had finished our dance, I took a seat alongside of her, and entered into a talk. I found her very interesting; while I was setting by her, making as good a use of my time as I could, her mother came to us, and very jocularly called me her son-in-law. This rather confused me, but I looked on it as a joke of the old lady, and tried to turn it off as well as I could; but I took care to pay as much attention to her through the evening as I could. I went on the old saying, of salting the cow to catch the calf. I soon become so much pleased with this little girl, that I began to think the Dutch girl had told me the truth, when she said there was still good fish in the sea.

We continued our frolic till near day, when we joined in some plays, calculated to amuse youngsters. I had not often spent a more agreeable night. In the morning, however, we all had to part; and I found my mind had become much better reconciled than it had been for a long time. I went home to the Quaker's, and made a bargain to work with his son for a low-priced horse. He was the first one I had ever owned, and I was to work six months for him. I had been engaged very closely five or six weeks, when this little girl run in my mind so, that I concluded I must go and see her, and find out what sort of people they were at home. I mounted my horse and away I went to where she lived, and when I got there I found her father a very clever old man, and the old woman as talkative as ever. She wanted badly to find out all about me, and as I thought to see how I would do for her girl. I had not yet seen her about, and I began to feel some anxiety to know where she was.

In a short time, however, my impatience was relieved, as she arrived at home from a meeting to which she had been. There was a young man with her, who I soon found was disposed to set up claim to her, as he was so attentive to her that I could hardly get to slip in a word edgeways. I began to think I was barking up the wrong tree again; but I was determined to stand up to my rack, fodder or no fodder. And so, to know her mind a little on the subject, I began to talk about starting, as I knowed she would then show some sign, from which I could understand which way the wind blowed. It was then near night, and my distance was fifteen miles home. At this my little girl soon began to indicate to the other gentleman that his room would be the better part of his company. At length she left him, and came to me, and insisted mighty hard that I should not go that evening; and, indeed, from all her actions and the attempts she made to get rid of him, I saw that she preferred me all holler. But it wasn't long before I found trouble enough in another quarter. Her mother was deeply enlisted for my rival, and I had to fight against her influence as well as his. But the girl herself was the prize I was fighting for; and as she welcomed me, I was determined to lay siege to her, let what would happen. I commenced a close courtship, having cornered her from her old beau; while he set off, looking on, like a poor man at a country frolic, and all the time almost gritting his teeth with pure disappointment. But he didn't dare to attempt anything more, for now I had gotten a start, and I looked at him every once in a while as fierce as a wild-cat. I stayed with her until Monday morning, and then I put out for home.

It was about two weeks after this that I was sent for to engage in a wolf hunt, where a great number of men were to meet, with their dogs and guns, and where the best sort of sport was expected. I went as large as life, but I had to hunt in strange woods, and in a part of the country which was very thinly inhabited. While I was out it clouded up, and I began to get scared; and in a little while I was so much so, that I didn't know which way home was, nor anything about it. I set out the way I thought it was, but it turned out with me, as it always does with a lost man, I was wrong, and took exactly the contrary direction from the right one. And for the information of young hunters, I will just say, in this place, that whenever a fellow gets bad lost, the way home is just the way he don't think it is. This rule will hit nine times out of ten. I went ahead, though, about six or seven miles, when I found night was coming on fast; but at this distressing time I saw a little woman streaking it along through the woods like all wrath, and so I cut on too, for I was determined I wouldn't lose sight of her that night any more. I run on till she saw me, and she stopped; for she was as glad to see me as I was to see her, as she was lost as well as me. When I came up to her, who should she be but my little girl, that I had been paying my respects to. She had been out hunting her father's horses, and had missed her way, and had no knowledge where she was, or how far it was to any house, or what way would take us there. She had been traveling all day, and was mighty tired; and I would have taken her up, and toted her, if it hadn't been that I wanted her just where I could see her all the time, for I thought she looked sweeter than sugar; and by this time I loved her almost well enough to eat her.

As last I came to a path, that I know'd must go somewhere, and so we followed it, till we came to a house, at about dark. Here we stayed all night. I set up all night courting; and in the morning we parted. She went to her home, from which we were distant about seven miles, and I to mine, which was ten miles off.

I now turned in to work again; and it was about four weeks before I went back to see her. I continued to go occasionally, until I had worked long enough to pay for my horse, by putting in my gun with my work, to the man I had purchased from; and then I began to count whether I was to be deceived again or not. At our next meeting we set the day for our wedding; and I went to my father's and made arrangements for an infair, and returned to ask her parents for her. When I got there, the old lady appeared to be mighty wrathy; and when I broached the subject, she looked at me as savage as a meat axe. The old man appeared quite willing, and treated me very clever. But I hadn't been there long, before the old woman as good as ordered me out of her house. I thought I would put her in mind of old times, and see how that would go with her. I told her she had called me her son-in-law before I had attempted to call her my mother-in-law, and I thought she ought to cool off. But her Irish was up too high to do anything with her, and so I quit trying. All I cared for was, to have her daughter on my side, which I knowed was the case then; but how soon some other fellow might knock my nose out of joint again, I couldn't tell. I however felt rather insulted at the old lady, and I thought I wouldn't get married in her house. And so I told her girl, that I would come the next Thursday, and bring a horse, a bridle, and saddle for her, and she must be ready to go. Her mother declared I shouldn't have her; but I know'd I should, if somebody else didn't get her before Thursday. I then started, bidding them good day, and went by the house of a justice of the peace, who lived on the way to my father's, and made a bargain with him to marry me.

When Thursday came, all necessary arrangements were

made at my father's to receive my wife; and so I took my eldest brother and his wife, and another brother, and a single sister that I had, and two other young men with me, and cut out to her father's house to get her. We went on, until we got within two miles of the place, where we met a large company that had heard of the wedding, and were waiting. Some of that company went on with my brother and sister, and the young man I had picked out to wait on me. When they got there, they found the old lady as wrathy as ever. However the old man filled their bottle, and the young men returned in a hurry. I then went on with my company, and when I arrived I never pretended to dismount from my horse, but rode up to the door, and asked the girl if she was ready; and she said she was. I then told her to light on the horse I was leading; and she did so. Her father, though, had gone out to the gate, and when I started he commenced persuading me to stay and marry there; that he was entirely willing to the match, and that his wife, like most women, had entirely too much tongue; but that I oughtn't to mind her. I told him if she would ask me to stay and marry at her house, I would do so. With that he sent for her, and after they had talked for some time out by themselves, she came to me and looked at me mighty good, and asked my pardon for what she had said, and invited me stay. She said it was the first child she had ever had to marry; and she couldn't bear to see her go off in that way; that if I would light, she would do the best she could for us. I couldn't stand everything, and so I agreed, and we got down, and went in. I sent off then for my parson, and got married in a short time; for I was afraid to wait long, for fear of another defeat. We had as good treatment as could be expected; and that night all went on well. The next day we cut out for my father's, where we met a large company of people, that had been waiting a day and a night for our arrival. We passed the time quite merrily, until the company broke up; and having gotten my wife, I thought I was completely made up, and needed nothing more in the whole world. But I soon found this was all a mistake — for now having a wife, I wanted everything else; and, worse than all, I had nothing to give for it.

I remained a few days at my father's, and then went back to my new father-in-law's; where, to my surprise, I found my old Irish mother in the finest humor in the world.

She gave us two likely cows and calves, which though it was a small marriage-portion, was still better than I had expected, and indeed, it was about all I ever got. I rented a small farm and cabin, and went to work; but I had much trouble to find out a plan to get anything to put in my house. At this time, my good friend the Quaker came forward to my assistance, and gave me an order to a store for fifteen dollars' worth of such things as my little wife might choose. With this, we fixed up pretty grand, as we thought, and allowed to get on very well. My wife had a good wheel, and knew exactly how to use it. She was also a good weaver, as most of the Irish are, whether men or women; and being very industrious with her wheel, she had, in little or no time, a fine web of cloth, ready to make up; and she was good at that too, and at almost anything else that a woman could do.

We worked on for some years, renting ground, and paying high rent, until I found it wan't the thing it was cracked up to be; and that I couldn't make a fortune at it just at all. So I concluded to quit it, and cut out for some new country. In this time we had two sons, and I found I was better at increasing my family than my fortune. It was therefore the more necessary that I should hunt some better place to get along; and as I knowed I would have to move at some time, I thought it was better to do it before my family got too large, that I might have less to carry.

The Duck and Elk river country was just beginning to settle, and I determined to try that. I had now one old horse, and a couple of two year old colts. They were both broke to the halter, and my father-in-law proposed, that, if I went, he would go with me, and take one horse to help me move. So we all fixed up, and I packed my two colts with as many of my things as they could bear; and away we went across the mountains. We got on well enough, and arrived safely in Lincoln county, on the head of the Mulberry fork of Elk river. I found this a very rich country, and so new, that game, of different sorts, was very plenty. It was here that I began to distinguish myself as a hunter, and to lay the foundation for all my future greatness; but mighty little did I know of what sort it was going to be. Of deer and smaller game I killed an abundance; but the bear had been much hunted in those parts before, and were not so plenty as I could have wished. I lived here in the years 1809 and '10, to the best of my recollection, and then I moved to Franklin county, and settled on Bean creek, where I remained till after the close of the last war.

JAMES FENIMORE COOPER
1789–1851

21   *The Death of Leather-Stocking*

THE local importance Middleton had acquired, by his union with the daughter of so affluent a proprietor as Don Augustin, united to his personal merit, attracted the attention of the government. He was soon employed in various situations of responsibility and confidence, which both served to elevate his character in the public estimation, and to afford the means of patronage. The bee-hunter was among the first of those to whom he saw fit to extend his favor. It was far from difficult to find situations suited to the abilities of Paul, in the state of society that existed three-and-twenty years ago in those regions. The efforts of Middleton and Inez, in behalf of her husband, were warmly and sagaciously seconded by Ellen, and they succeeded, in process of time, in working a great and beneficial change in his character. He soon became a landholder, then a prosperous cultivator of the soil, and shortly after a town-officer. By that progressive change in fortune, which in the republic is often seen to be so singularly accompanied by a corresponding improvement in knowledge and self-respect, he went on, from step to step, until his wife enjoyed the maternal delight of seeing her children placed far beyond the danger of returning to that state from which both their parents had issued. Paul is actually at this moment a member of the lower branch of the legislature of the State where he has long resided; and he is even notorious for making speeches that have a tendency to put that deliberative body in good humor, and which, as they are based on great practical knowledge suited to the condition of the country, possess a merit that is much wanted in many more subtle and fine-spun theories, that are daily heard in similar assemblies, to issue from the lips of certain instinctive politicians. But all these happy fruits were the results of much care, and of a long period of time. Middleton, who fills, with a credit better suited to the difference in their educations, a seat in a far higher branch of legislative authority, is the source from which we have derived most of the intelligence necessary to compose our legend. In addition to what he has related of Paul, and of his own continued happiness, he has added a short narrative of what took place in a subsequent visit to the prairies, with which, as we conceive it a suitable termination to what has gone before, we shall judge it wise to conclude our labors.

In the autumn of the year that succeeded the season in which the preceding events occurred, the young man, still in the military service, found himself on the waters of the Missouri, at a point not far remote from the Pawnee towns. Released from any immediate calls of duty, and strongly urged to the measure by Paul, who was in his company, he determined to take horse and cross the country to visit the partisan, and to inquire into the fate of his friend the trapper. As his train was suited to his functions and rank, the journey was effected with the privations and hardships that are the accompaniments of all traveling in a wild, but without any of those dangers and alarms that marked his former passage through the same regions. When within a proper distance, he dispatched an Indian runner, belonging to a friendly tribe, to announce the approach of himself and party, continuing his route at a deliberate pace, in order that the intelligence might, as was customary, precede his arrival. To the surprise of the travelers their message was unanswered. Hour succeeded hour, and mile after mile was passed, without bringing either the signs of an honorable reception, or the more simple assurances of a friendly welcome. At length the cavalcade, at whose head rode Middleton and Paul, descended from the elevated plain, on which they had long been journeying, to a luxuriant bottom, that brought them to the level of the village of the Loups. The sun was beginning to fall, and a sheet of golden light was spread over the placid plain, lending to its even surface those glorious tints and hues, that, the human imagination is apt to conceive, forms the embellishment of still more imposing scenes. The verdure of the year yet remained, and herds of horses and mules were grazing peacefully in the vast natural pasture, under the keeping of vigilant Pawnee boys. Paul pointed out among them the well-known form of Asinus, sleek, fat, and luxuriating in the fulness of content, as he stood with reclining ears and closed eye-lids, seemingly musing on the exquisite nature of his present indolent enjoyment.

The route of the party led them at no great distance from one of those watchful youths, who was charged with a trust heavy as the principal wealth of his tribe. He heard the trampling of the horses, and cast his eye aside, but instead of manifesting curiosity or alarm, his look instantly returned whence it had been withdrawn, to the spot where the village was known to stand.

"There is something remarkable in all this," muttered Middleton, half offended at what he conceived to be not only a slight to his rank, but offensive to himself personally; "yonder boy has heard of our approach, or he would not fail to notify his tribe; and yet he scarcely deigns to favor us with a glance. Look to your arms, men; it may be necessary to let these savages feel our strength."

"Therein, Captain, I think you're in an error," returned

Paul: "if honesty is to be met on the prairies at all, you will find it in our old friend Hard-Heart; neither is an Indian to be judged of by the rules of a white. See! we are not altogether slighted, for here comes a party at last to meet us, though it is a little pitiful as to show and numbers."

Paul was right in both particulars. A group of horsemen were at length seen wheeling round a little copse, and advancing across the plain directly towards them. The advance of this party was slow and dignified. As it drew nigh, the partisan of the Loups was seen at its head, followed by a dozen younger warriors of his tribe. They were all unarmed, nor did they even wear any of those ornaments or feathers which are considered testimonials of respect to the guest an Indian receives, as well as evidence of his own importance.

The meeting was friendly, though a little restrained on both sides. Middleton, jealous of his own consideration no less than of the authority of his government, suspected some undue influence on the part of the agents of the Canadas; and, as he was determined to maintain the authority of which he was the representative, he felt himself constrained to manifest a hauteur that he was far from feeling. It was not so easy to penetrate the motives of the Pawnees. Calm, dignified, and yet far from repulsive, they set an example of courtesy, blended with reserve, that many a diplomatist of the most polished court might have strove in vain to imitate.

In this manner the two parties continued their course to the town. Middleton had time, during the remainder of the ride, to revolve in his mind all the probable reasons which his ingenuity could suggest for this strange reception. Although he was accompanied by a regular interpreter, the chiefs made their salutations in a manner that dispensed with his services. Twenty times the Captain turned his glance on his former friend, endeavoring to read the expression of his rigid features. But every effort and all conjectures proved equally futile. The eye of Hard-Heart was fixed, composed, and a little anxious; but as to every other emotion, impenetrable.

He neither spoke himself, nor seemed willing to invite discourse in his visitors; it was therefore necessary for Middleton to adopt the patient manners of his companions, and to await the issue for the explanation.

When they entered the town, its inhabitants were seen collected in an open space, where they were arranged with the customary deference to age and rank. The whole formed a large circle, in the center of which were perhaps a dozen of the principal chiefs. Hard-Heart waved his hand as he approached, and, as the mass of bodies opened, he rode through, followed by his companions. Here they dismounted; and as the beasts were led apart, the strangers found themselves environed by a thousand grave, composed, but solicitous faces.

Middleton gazed about him, in growing concern, for no cry, no song, no shout welcomed him among a people from whom he had so lately parted with regret. His uneasiness, not to say apprehensions, was shared by all his followers. Determination and stern resolution began to assume the place of anxiety in every eye, as each man silently felt for his arms, and assured himself, that his several weapons were in a state for service. But there was no answering symptom of hostility on the part of their hosts. Hard-Heart beckoned for Middleton and Paul to follow, leading the way towards the cluster of forms that occupied the center of the circle. Here the visitors found a solution of all the movements which had given them so much reason for apprehension.

The trapper was placed on a rude seat, which had been made, with studied care, to support his frame in an upright and easy attitude. The first glance of the eye told his former friends that the old man was at length called upon to pay the last tribute of nature. His eye was glazed, and apparently as devoid of sight as of expression. His features were a little more sunken and strongly marked than formerly; but there, all change, so far as exterior was concerned, might be said to have ceased. His approaching end was not to be ascribed to any positive disease, but had been a gradual and mild decay of the physical powers. Life, it is true, still lingered in his system; but it was as if at times entirely ready to depart, and then it would appear to re-animate the sinking form, reluctant to give up the possession of a tenement that had never been corrupted by vice, or undermined by disease. It would have been no violent fancy to have imagined that the spirit fluttered about the placid lips of the old woodsman, reluctant to depart from a shell that had so long given it an honest and an honorable shelter.

His body was placed so as to let the light of the setting sun fall full upon the solemn features. His head was bare, the long, thin, locks of gray fluttering lightly in the evening breeze. His rifle lay upon his knee, and the other accouterments of the chase were placed at his side, within reach of his hand. Between his feet lay the figure of a hound, with its head crouching to the earth as if it slumbered; and so perfectly easy and natural was its position, that a second glance was necessary to tell Middleton, he saw only the skin of Hector, stuffed by Indian tenderness and ingenuity in a manner to represent the living animal. His own dog was playing at a distance, with the child of Tachechana and Mahtoree. The mother herself stood at hand, holding in her arms a second offspring, that might boast of a parentage no less honorable than that which belonged to the son of Hard-Heart. Le Balafré was seated nigh the dying trapper, with every mark about his person that the hour of his own departure was not far distant. The rest of those immediately in the center were aged men, who had apparently drawn near in order to observe the manner in which a just and fearless warrior would depart on the greatest of his journeys.

The old man was reaping the rewards of a life remarkable for temperance and activity, in a tranquil and placid death. His vigor in a manner endured to the very last. Decay, when it did occur, was rapid, but free from pain. He had hunted with the tribe in the spring, and even throughout most of the summer, when his limbs suddenly refused to perform their customary offices. A sympathizing weakness took possession of all his faculties; and the Pawnees believed, that they were going to lose, in this unexpected manner, a sage and counselor whom they had begun both to love and respect. But as we have already said, the immortal occupant seemed unwilling to desert its tenement. The lamp of life flickered without becoming extinguished. On the morning of the day on which Middleton arrived, there was a general reviving of the powers of the whole man. His tongue was again heard in wholesome maxims, and his eye from time to time recognized the persons of his friends. It merely proved to be a brief and final intercourse with the world on the part of one who had already been considered, as to mental communion, to have taken his leave of it forever.

When he had placed his guests in front of the dying man, Hard-Heart, after a pause that proceeded as much from sorrow as decorum, leaned a little forward and demanded —

"Does my father hear the words of his son?"

"Speak," returned the trapper, in tones that issued from his chest, but which were rendered awfully distinct by the stillness that reigned in the place. "I am about to depart from the village of the Loups, and shortly shall be beyond the reach of your voice."

"Let the wise chief have no cares for his journey," continued Hard-Heart with an earnest solicitude that led him to forget, for the moment, that others were waiting to address his adopted parent; "a hundred Loups shall clear his path from briars."

"Pawnee, I die as I have lived, a Christian man," resumed the trapper with a force of voice that had the same startling effect upon his hearers as is produced by the trumpet, when its blast rises suddenly and freely on the air, after its obstructed sounds have been heard struggling in the distance: "as I came into life so will I leave it. Horses and arms are not needed to stand in the presence of the Great Spirit of my people. He knows my color, and according to my gifts will he judge my deeds."

"My father will tell my young men how many Mingoes he

has struck, and what acts of valor and justice he has done, that they may know how to imitate him."

"A boastful tongue is not heard in the heaven of a white man!" solemnly returned the old man. "What I have done, He has seen. His eyes are always open. That, which has been well done, will he remember; wherein I have been wrong will he not forget to chastise, though he will do the same in mercy. No, my son; a Pale-face may not sing his own praises, and hope to have them acceptable before his God!"

A little disappointed, the young partisan stepped modestly back, making way for the recent comers to approach. Middleton took one of the meager hands of the trapper, and struggling to command his voice, he succeeded in announcing his presence. The old man listened like one whose thoughts were dwelling on a very different subject, but when the other had succeeded in making him understand that he was present, an expression of joyful recognition passed over his faded features —

"I hope you have not so soon forgotten those whom you so materially served!" Middleton concluded. "It would pain me to think my hold on your memory was so light."

"Little that I have ever seen is forgotten," returned the trapper: "I am at the close of many weary days, but there is not one among them all that I could wish to overlook. I remember you with the whole of your company; ay, and your gran'ther, that went before you. I am glad that you have come back upon these plains, for I had need of one who speaks the English, since little faith can be put in the traders of these regions. Will you do a favor to an old and dying man?"

"Name it," said Middleton; "it shall be done."

"It is a far journey to send such trifles," resumed the old man, who spoke at short intervals, as strength and breath permitted; "a far and weary journey is the same; but kindnesses and friendships are things not to be forgotten. There is a settlement among the Otsego hills —"

"I know the place," interrupted Middleton, observing that

he spoke with increasing difficulty; "proceed to tell me, what you would have done."

"Take this rifle, and pouch, and horn, and send them to the person, whose name is graven on the plates of the stock, — a trader cut the letters with his knife, — for it is long that I have intended to send him such a token of my love."

"It shall be so. Is there more that you could wish?"

"Little else have I to bestow. My traps I give to my Indian son; for honestly and kindly has he kept his faith. Let him stand before me."

Middleton explained to the chief what the trapper had said, and relinquished his own place to the other.

"Pawnee," continued the old man, always changing his language to suit the person he addressed, and not unfrequently according to the ideas he expressed, "it is a custom of my people for the father to leave his blessing with the son, before he shuts his eyes forever. This blessing I give to you; take it, for the prayers of a Christian man will never make the path of a just warrior, to the blessed prairies, either longer, or more tangled. May the God of a white man look on your deeds with friendly eyes, and may you never commit an act, that shall cause him to darken his face. I know not whether we shall ever meet again. There are many traditions concerning the place of Good Spirits. It is not for one like me, old and experienced though I am, to set up my opinions against a nation's. You believe in the blessed prairies, and I have faith in the sayings of my fathers. If both are true, our parting will be final; but if it should prove, that the same meaning is hid under different words, we shall yet stand together, Pawnee, before the face of your Wahcondah, who will then be no other than my God. There is much to be said in favor of both religions, for each seems suited to its own people, and no doubt it was so intended. I fear, I have not altogether followed the gifts of my color, inasmuch as I find it a little painful to give up forever the use of the rifle, and the comforts of the chase. But then the fault has been my own, seeing that it could not have been His. Ay, Hector," he continued, leaning forward a little, and feeling for the ears of the hound, "our parting has come at last, dog, and it will be a long hunt. You have been an honest, and a bold, and a faithful hound. Pawnee, you cannot slay the pup on my grave, for where a Christian dog falls, there he lies forever; but you can be kind to him, after I am gone, for the love you bear his master."

"The words of my father are in my ears," returned the young partisan, making a grave and respectful gesture of assent.

"Do you hear, what the chief has promised, dog?" demanded the trapper, making an effort to attract the notice of the insensible effigy of his hound. Receiving no answering look, nor hearing any friendly whine, the old man felt for the mouth and endeavored to force his hand between the cold lips. The truth then flashed upon him, although he was far from perceiving the whole extent of the deception. Falling back in his seat, he hung his head, like one who felt a severe and unexpected shock. Profiting by this momentary forgetfulness, two young Indians removed the skin with the same delicacy of feeling, that had induced them to attempt the pious fraud.

"The dog is dead!" muttered the trapper, after a pause of many minutes; "a hound has his time as well as a man; and well has he filled his days! Captain," he added, making an effort to wave his hand for Middleton, "I am glad you have come; for though kind, and well meaning according to the gifts of their color, these Indians are not the men, to lay the head of a white man in his grave. I have been thinking too, of this dog at my feet; it will not do to set forth the opinion, that a Christian can expect to meet his hound again; still there can be little harm in placing what is left of so faithful a servant nigh the bones of his master."

"It shall be as you desire."

"I'm glad you think with me in this matter. In order then to save labor, lay the pup at my feet, or for that matter put him side by side. A hunter need never be ashamed to be found in company with his dog!"

"I charge myself with your wish."

The old man made a long, and apparently a musing pause. At times he raised his eyes wistfully, as if he would again address Middleton, but some innate feeling appeared always to suppress his words. The other, who observed his hesitation, inquired in a way most likely to encourage him to proceed, whether there was aught else that he could wish to have done.

"I am without kith or kin in the wide world!" the trapper answered: "when I am gone, there will be an end of my race. We have never been chiefs; but honest and useful in our way, I hope it cannot be denied, we have always proved ourselves. My father lies buried near the sea, and the bones of his son will whiten on the prairies —"

"Name the spot, and your remains shall be placed by the side of your father," interrupted Middleton.

"Not so, not so, Captain. Let me sleep, where I have lived, beyond the din of the settlements! Still I see no need, why the grave of an honest man should be hid, like a Redskin in his ambushment. I paid a man in the settlements to make and put a graven stone at the head of my father's resting place. It was of the value of twelve beaver-skins, and cunningly and curiously was it carved! Then it told to all comers that the body of such a Christian lay beneath; and it spoke of his manner of life, of his years, and of his honesty. When we had done with the Frenchers in the old war, I made a journey to the spot, in order to see that all was rightly performed, and glad I am to say, the workman had not forgotten his faith."

"And such a stone you would have at your grave?"

"I! no, no, I have no son but Hard-Heart, and it is little that an Indian knows of White fashions and usages. Besides I am his debtor already, seeing it is so little I have done since I have lived in his tribe. The rifle might bring the value of such a thing — but then I know, it will give the boy pleasure to hang the piece in his hall, for many is the deer and the bird that he has seen it destroy. No, no, the gun must be sent to him whose name is graven on the lock!"

"But there is one who would gladly prove his affection in the way you wish; he, who owes you not only his own deliverance from so many dangers, but who inherits a heavy debt of gratitude from his ancestors. The stone shall be put at the head of your grave."

The old man extended his emaciated hand, and gave the other a squeeze of thanks.

"I thought you might be willing to do it, but I was backward in asking the favor," he said, "seeing that you are not of my kin. Put no boastful words on the same, but just the name, the age, and the time of the death, with something from the holy book; no more, no more. My name will then not be altogether lost on 'arth; I need no more."

Middleton intimated his assent, and then followed a pause, that was only broken by distant and broken sentences from the dying man. He appeared now to have closed his accounts with the world, and to await merely for the final summons to quit it. Middleton and Hard-Heart placed themselves on the opposite sides of his seat, and watched with melancholy solicitude the variations of his countenance. For two hours there was no very sensible alteration. The expression of his faded and time-worn features was that of a calm and dignified repose. From time to time he spoke, uttering some brief sentence in the way of advice, or asking some simple questions concerning those in whose fortunes he still took a friendly interest. During the whole of that solemn and anxious period each individual of the tribe kept his place in the most self-restrained patience. When the old man spoke, all bent their heads to listen; and when his words were uttered, they seemed to ponder on their wisdom and usefulness.

As the flame drew nigher to the socket, his voice was hushed, and there were moments when his attendants doubted whether he still belonged to the living. Middleton who watched each wavering expression of his weather-beaten visage with the interest of a keen observer of human nature, softened by the tenderness of personal regard, fancied he could read the workings of the old man's soul in the strong lineaments of his countenance. Perhaps what the enlightened soldier took for the delusion of mistaken opinion did actually occur, for who has returned from that unknown world to explain by what forms, and in what manner, he was introduced into its awful precincts? Without pretending to explain what must ever be a mystery to the quick, we shall simply relate facts as they occurred.

The trapper had remained nearly motionless for an hour. His eyes, alone, had occasionally opened and shut. When opened, his gaze seemed fastened on the clouds, which hung around the western horizon, reflecting the bright colors, and giving form and loveliness to the glorious tints of an American sunset. The hour — the calm beauty of the season — the occasion, all conspired to fill the spectators with solemn awe. Suddenly, while musing on the remarkable position in which he was placed, Middleton felt the hand, which he held, grasp his own with incredible power, and the old man, supported on either side by his friends, rose upright to his feet. For a moment he looked about him, as if to invite all in presence to listen (the lingering remnant of human frailty), and then, with a fine military elevation of the head, and with a voice that might be heard in every part of that numerous assembly, he pronounced the word —

" Here! "

A movement so entirely unexpected, and the air of grandeur and humility which were so remarkably united in the mien of the trapper, together with the clear and uncommon force of his utterance, produced a short period of confusion in the faculties of all present. When Middleton and Hard-Heart, each of whom had involuntarily extended a hand to support the form of the old man, turned to him again, they found that the subject of their interest was removed forever beyond the necessity of their care. They mournfully placed the body in its seat, and Le Balafré arose to announce the termination of the scene, to the tribe. The voice of the old Indian seemed a sort of echo from that invisible world to which the meek spirit of the trapper had just departed.

"A valiant, a just, and a wise warrior has gone on the path which will lead him to the blessed grounds of his people!" he said. "When the voice of the Wahcondah called him, he was ready to answer. Go, my children; remember the just chief of the Pale-faces, and clear your own tracks from briars!"

The grave was made beneath the shade of some noble oaks. It has been carefully watched to the present hour by the Pawnees of the Loup, and is often shown to the traveler and the trader as a spot where a just Whiteman sleeps. In due time the stone was placed at its head, with the simple inscription which the trapper had himself requested. The only liberty, taken by Middleton, was to add — "*May no wanton hand ever disturb his remains!*"

WILLIAM HICKLING PRESCOTT

1796–1859

22   *The March on Mexico*

EVERYTHING being now restored to quiet in Cholula, the allied army of Spaniards and Tlascalans set forward in high spirits, and resumed the march on Mexico. The road lay through the beautiful savannas and luxuriant plantations that spread out for several leagues in every direction. On the march they were met occasionally by embassies from the neighboring places, anxious to claim the protection of the white men, and to propitiate them by gifts, especially of gold, for which their appetite was generally known throughout the country.

Some of these places were allies of the Tlascalans, and all showed much discontent with the oppressive rule of Montezuma. The natives cautioned the Spaniards against putting themselves in his power by entering his capital; and they stated, as evidence of his hostile disposition, that he had caused the direct road to it to be blocked up, that the strangers might be compelled to choose another, which, from its narrow passes and strong positions, would enable him to take them at great disadvantage.

The information was not lost on Cortés, who kept a strict eye on the movements of the Mexican envoys, and redoubled his own precautions against surprise. Cheerful and active, he was ever where his presence was needed, sometimes in the van, at others in the rear, encouraging the weak, stimulating the sluggish, and striving to kindle in the breasts of others the same courageous spirit which glowed in his own. At night he never omitted to go the rounds, to see that every man was at his post. On one occasion his vigilance had well nigh proved fatal to him. He approached so near a sentinel that the man, unable to distinguish his person in the dark, leveled his cross-bow at him, when, fortunately, an exclamation of the general, who gave the watchword of the night, arrested a movement which might else have brought the campaign to a close, and given a respite for some time longer to the empire of Montezuma.

The army came at length to the place mentioned by the friendly Indians, where the road forked, and one arm of it was found, as they had foretold, obstructed with large trunks of trees and huge stones which had been strewn across it. Cortés inquired the meaning of this from the Mexican ambassadors. They said it was done by the emperor's orders, to prevent their taking a route which, after some distance, they would find nearly impracticable for the cavalry. They acknowledged, however, that it was the most direct road; and Cortés, declaring that this was enough to decide him in favor of it, as the Spaniards made no account of obstacles, commanded the rubbish to be cleared away. Some of the timber might still be seen by the roadside, as Bernal Diaz tells us, many years after. The event left little doubt in the general's mind of the meditated treachery of the Mexicans. But he was too politic to betray his suspicions.

They were now leaving the pleasant champaign country, as the road wound up the bold sierra which separates the great plateaus of Mexico and Puebla. The air, as they ascended, became keen and piercing; and the blasts, sweeping down the frozen sides of the mountains, made the soldiers shiver in their thick harness of cotton, and benumbed the limbs of both men and horses.

They were passing between two of the highest mountains on the North American continent, Popocatepetl, "the hill that smokes," and Iztaccihuatl, or "white woman," — a name suggested, doubtless, by the bright robe of snow spread over its broad and broken surface. A puerile superstition of the Indians regarded these celebrated mountains as gods, and Iztaccihuatl as the wife of her more formidable neighbor. A tradition of a higher character described the northern volcano as the abode of the departed spirits of wicked rulers, whose fiery agonies in their prison-house caused the fearful bellowings and convulsions in times of eruption. It was the classic fable of Antiquity. These superstitious legends had invested the mountain with a mysterious horror that made the natives shrink from attempting its ascent, which indeed was, from natural causes, a work of incredible difficulty.

The great *volcan,* as Popocatepetl was called, rose to the enormous height of 17,852 feet above the level of the sea; more than 2000 feet above the "monarch of mountains," — the highest elevation in Europe. During the present century, it has rarely given evidence of its volcanic origin, and "the hill that smokes" has almost forfeited its claim to the appellation. But at the time of the Conquest it was frequently in a state of activity, and raged with uncommon fury while the Spaniards were at Tlascala; an evil omen, it was thought, for the natives of Anahuac. Its head, gathered into a regular cone by the deposit of successive eruptions, wore the usual form of volcanic mountains, when not disturbed by the falling in of the crater. Soaring towards the skies, with its silver sheet of everlasting snow, it was seen far and wide over the broad plains of Mexico and Puebla, the first object which the morning sun greeted in his rising, the last where his evening rays were seen to linger, shedding a glorious effulgence over its head, that contrasted strikingly with the ruinous waste of sand and lava immediately below, and the deep fringe of funereal pines that shrouded its base.

The mysterious terrors which hung over the spot, and the wild love of adventure, made some of the Spanish cavaliers desirous to attempt the ascent, which the natives declared no man could accomplish and live. Cortés encouraged them in the enterprise, willing to show the Indians that no achievement was above the dauntless daring of his followers. One of his captains, accordingly, Diego Ordaz, with nine Spaniards, and several Tlascalans, encouraged by their example, undertook the ascent. It was attended with more difficulty than had been anticipated.

The lower region was clothed with a dense forest, so thickly matted that in some places it was scarcely possible to penetrate it. It grew thinner, however, as they advanced, dwindling by degrees into a straggling, stunted vegetation, till at the height of somewhat more than thirteen thousand feet it faded away altogether. The Indians who had held on thus far, intimidated by the strange subterraneous sounds of the volcano, even then in a state of combustion, now left them. The track opened on a black surface of glazed volcanic sand and of lava, the broken fragments of which, arrested in its boiling progress in a thousand fantastic forms, opposed continual impediments to their advance. Amidst these, one huge rock, the *Pico del Fraile,* a conspicuous object from below, rose to the perpendicular height of a hundred and fifty feet, compelling them to take a wide circuit. They soon came to the limits of perpetual snow, where new difficulties presented themselves, as the treacherous ice gave an imperfect footing, and a false step might precipitate them into the frozen chasms that yawned around. To increase their distress, respiration in these aërial regions became so difficult that every effort was attended with sharp pains in the head and limbs. Still they pressed on till, drawing nearer the crater, such volumes of smoke, sparks, and cinders were belched forth from its burning entrails, and driven down the sides of the mountain, as nearly suffocated and blinded them. It was too much even for their hardy frames to endure, and, however reluctantly, they were compelled to abandon the attempt on the eve of its completion. They brought back some huge icicles, — a curious sight in these tropical regions, — as a trophy of their achievement, which, however imperfect, was sufficient to strike the minds of the natives with wonder, by showing that with the Spaniards the most appalling and mysterious perils were only as pastimes. . . .

The army held on its march through the intricate gorges of the sierra. The route was nearly the same as that pursued at the present day by the courier from the capital to Puebla, by the way of Mecameca. It was not that usually taken by travelers from Vera Cruz, who follow the more circuitous road round the northern base of Iztaccihuatl, as less fatiguing than the other, though inferior in picturesque scenery and romantic points of view. The icy winds, that now swept down the sides of the mountains, brought with them a tempest of arrowy sleet and snow, from which the Christians suffered even more than the Tlascalans, reared from infancy among the wild solitudes of their own native hills. As night came on, their sufferings would have been intolerable, but they luckily found a shelter in the commodious stone buildings which the Mexican government had placed at stated intervals along the roads for the accommodation of the traveler and their own couriers. It little dreamed it was providing a protection for its enemies.

The troops, refreshed by a night's rest, succeeded, early on the following day, in gaining the crest of the sierra of Ahualco, which stretches like a curtain between the two great mountains on the north and south. Their progress was now comparatively easy, and they marched forward with a buoyant step, as they felt they were treading the soil of Montezuma.

They had not advanced far, when, turning an angle of the sierra, they suddenly came on a view which more than compensated the toils of the preceding day. It was that of the Valley of Mexico, or Tenochtitlan, as more commonly called by the natives; which, with its picturesque assemblage of water, woodland, and cultivated plains, its shining cities and shadowy hills, was spread out like some gay and gorgeous panorama before them. In the highly rarefied atmosphere of these upper regions, even remote objects have a brilliancy of coloring and a distinctness of outline which seem to annihilate distance. Stretching far away at their feet were seen noble forests of oak, sycamore, and cedar, and beyond, yellow fields of maize and the towering maguey, intermingled with orchards and blooming gardens; for flowers, in such demand for their religious festivals, were even more abundant in this populous valley than in other parts of Anahuac. In the center of the great basin were beheld the lakes, occupying then a much larger portion of its surface than at present; their borders thickly studded with towns and hamlets, and, in the midst, — like some Indian empress with her coronal of pearls, — the fair city of Mexico, with her white towers and pyramidal temples, reposing, as it were, on the bosom of the waters, — the far-famed "Venice of the Aztecs." High over all rose the royal hill of Chapultepec, the residence of the Mexican monarchs, crowned with the same grove of gigantic cypresses which at this day fling their broad shadows over the land. In the distance beyond the blue waters of the lake, and nearly screened by intervening foliage, was seen a shining speck, the rival capital of Tezcuco, and, still further on, the dark belt of porphyry, girding the Valley around, like a rich setting which Nature had devised for the fairest of her jewels.

Such was the beautiful vision which broke on the eyes of the conquerors. And even now, when so sad a change has come over the scene; when the stately forests have been laid low, and the soil, unsheltered from the fierce radiance of a tropical sun, is in many places abandoned to sterility; when the waters have retired, leaving a broad and ghastly margin white with the incrustation of salts, while the cities and hamlets on their borders have moldered into ruins; — even now that desolation broods over the landscape, so indestructible are the lines of beauty which Nature has traced on its features, that no traveler, however cold, can gaze on them with any other emotions than those of astonishment and rapture.

What, then, must have been the emotions of the Spaniards, when, after working their toilsome way into the upper air, the cloudy tabernacle parted before their eyes, and they beheld these fair scenes in all their pristine magnificence and beauty! It was like the spectacle which greeted the eyes of Moses from the summit of Pisgah, and, in the warm glow of their feelings, they cried out, "It is the promised land!"

But these feelings of admiration were soon followed by others of a very different complexion; as they saw in all this the evidences of a civilization and power far superior to anything they had yet encountered. The more timid, disheartened by the prospect, shrunk from a contest so unequal, and demanded, as they had done on some former occasions, to be led back again to Vera Cruz. Such was not the effect produced on the sanguine spirit of the general. His avarice was sharpened by the display of the dazzling spoil at his feet; and, if he felt a natural anxiety at the formidable odds, his confidence was renewed, as he gazed on the lines of his veterans, whose weather-beaten visages and battered armor told of battles won and difficulties surmounted, while his bold barbarians, with appetites whetted by the view of their enemy's country, seemed like eagles on the mountains, ready to pounce upon their prey. By argument, entreaty, and menace, he endeavored to restore the faltering courage of the soldiers, urging them not to think of retreat, now that they had reached the goal for which they had panted, and the golden gates were open to receive them. In these efforts he was well seconded by the brave cavaliers, who held honor as dear to them as fortune; until the dullest spirits caught somewhat of the enthusiasm of their leaders, and the general had the satisfaction to see his hesitating columns, with their usual buoyant step, once more on their march down the slopes of the sierra.

With every step of their progress, the woods became thinner; patches of cultivated land more frequent; and hamlets were seen in the green and sheltered nooks, the inhabitants of which, coming out to meet them, gave the troops a kind reception. Everywhere they heard complaints of Montezuma, especially of the unfeeling manner in which he carried off their young men to recruit his armies, and their maidens for his harem. These symptoms of discontent were noticed with satisfaction by Cortés, who saw that Montezuma's "mountain throne," as it was called, was indeed seated on a volcano, with the elements of combustion so active within, that it seemed as if any hour might witness an explosion. He encouraged the disaffected natives to rely on his protection, as he had come to redress their wrongs. He took advantage, moreover, of their favorable dispositions to scatter among them such gleams of spiritual light as time and the preaching of Father Olmedo could afford.

He advanced by easy stages, somewhat retarded by the crowd of curious inhabitants gathered on the highways to see the strangers, and halting at every spot of interest or importance. On the road he was met by another embassy from the capital. It consisted of several Aztec lords, freighted, as usual, with a rich largess of gold, and robes of delicate furs and feathers. The message of the emperor was couched in the same deprecatory terms as before. He even condescended to bribe the return of the Spaniards, by promising, in that event, four loads of gold to the general, and one to each of the captains, with a yearly tribute to their sovereign. So effectually had the lofty and naturally courageous spirit of the barbarian monarch been subdued by the influence of superstition!

But the man whom the hostile array of armies could not daunt, was not to be turned from his purpose by a woman's prayers. He received the embassy with his usual courtesy, declaring, as before, that he could not answer it to his own sovereign, if he were now to return without visiting the emperor in his capital. It would be much easier to arrange matters by a personal interview than by distant negotiation. The Spaniards came in the spirit of peace. Montezuma would so find it, but, should their presence prove burdensome to him, it would be easy for them to relieve him of it.

The Aztec monarch, meanwhile, was a prey to the most dismal apprehensions. It was intended that the embassy above noticed should reach the Spaniards before they crossed the mountains. When he learned that this was accomplished, and that the dread strangers were on their march across the valley, the very threshold of his capital, the last spark of hope died away in his bosom. Like one who suddenly finds himself on the brink of some dark and yawning gulf, he was too much bewildered to be able to rally his thoughts, or even to comprehend his situation. He was the victim of an absolute destiny, against which no foresight or precautions could have availed. It was as if the strange beings, who had thus invaded his shores, had dropped from some distant planet, so different were they from all he had ever seen, in appearance and manners; so superior — though a mere handful in numbers — to the banded nations of Anahuac in strength and science, and all the fearful accompaniments of war! They were now in the valley. The huge mountain-screen, which nature had so kindly drawn around it for its defense, had been overleaped. The golden visions of security and repose, in which he had so long indulged, the lordly sway descended from his ancestors, his broad imperial domain, were all to pass away. It seemed like some terrible dream, — from which he was now, alas! to awake to a still more terrible reality.

In a paroxysm of despair he shut himself up in his palace, refused food, and sought relief in prayer and in sacrifice. But the oracles were dumb. He then adopted the more sensible expedient of calling a council of his principal and oldest nobles. Here was the same division of opinion which had before prevailed. Cacama, the young King of Tezcuco, his nephew, counseled him to receive the Spaniards courteously, as ambassadors, so styled by themselves, of a foreign prince. Cuitlahua, Montezuma's more warlike brother, urged him to muster his forces on the instant, and drive back the invaders from his capital, or die in its defense. But the monarch found it difficult to rally his spirits for this final struggle. With downcast eye and dejected mien he exclaimed, "Of what avail is resistance when the gods have declared themselves against us! Yet I mourn most for the old and infirm, the women and children, too feeble to fight or to fly. For myself and the brave men around me, we must bare our breasts to the storm, and meet it as we may!" Such are the sorrowful and sympathetic tones in which the Aztec emperor is said to have uttered the bitterness of his grief. He would have acted a more glorious part had he put his capital in a posture of defense, and prepared, like the last of the Palæologi, to bury himself under its ruins.

He straightway prepared to send a last embassy to the Spaniards, with his nephew, the lord of Tezcuco, at its head, to welcome them to Mexico.

The Christian army, meanwhile, had advanced as far as Amaquemecan, a well-built town of several thousand inhabitants. They were kindly received by the cacique, lodged in large commodious stone buildings, and at their departure presented, among other things, with gold to the amount of three thousand *castellanos*. Having halted there a couple of days, they descended among flourishing plantations of maize and of maguey, the latter which might be called the Aztec vineyards, towards the lake of Chalco. Their first resting-place was Ajotzinco, a town of considerable size, with a great part of it then standing on piles in the water. It was the first specimen which the Spaniards had seen of this maritime architecture. The canals, which intersected the city instead of streets, presented an animated scene from the number of barks which glided up and down, freighted with provisions and other articles for the inhabitants. The Spaniards were particularly struck with the style and commodious structure of the houses, built chiefly of stone, and with the general aspect of wealth, and even elegance which prevailed there.

Though received with the greatest show of hospitality, Cortés found some occasion for distrust in the eagerness manifested by the people to see and approach the Spaniards. Not content with gazing at them in the roads, some even made their way stealthily into their quarters, and fifteen or twenty unhappy Indians were shot down by the sentinels as spies. Yet there appears, as well as we can judge at this distance of time, to have been no real ground for such suspicion. The undisguised jealousy of the court, and the cautions he had received from his allies, while they very properly put the general on his guard, seem to have given an unnatural acuteness, at least in the present instance, to his perceptions of danger.

Early on the following morning, as the army was preparing to leave the place, a courier came, requesting the general to postpone his departure till after the arrival of the King of Tezcuco, who was advancing to meet him. It was not long before he appeared, borne in a palanquin or litter, richly decorated with plates of gold and precious stones, having pillars curiously wrought, supporting a canopy of green plumes, a favorite color with the Aztec princes. He was accompanied by a numerous suite of nobles and inferior attendants. As he came into the presence of Cortés, the lord of Tezcuco descended from his palanquin, and the obsequious officers swept the ground before him as he advanced. He appeared to be a young man of about twenty-five years of age, with a comely presence, erect and stately in his deportment. He made the Mexican salutation usually addressed to persons of high rank, touching the earth with his right hand, and raising it to his head. Cortés embraced him as he rose, when the young prince informed him that he came as the representative of Montezuma, to bid the Spaniards welcome to his capital. He then presented the general with three pearls of uncommon size and luster. Cortés, in return, threw over Cacama's neck a chain of cut glass, which, where glass was as rare as diamonds, might be admitted to have a value as real as the latter. After this interchange of courtesies, and the most friendly and respectful assurances on the part of Cortés, the Indian prince withdrew, leaving the Spaniards strongly impressed with the superiority of his state and bearing over anything they had hitherto seen in the country.

Resuming its march, the army kept along the southern borders of the lake of Chalco, overshadowed at that time by noble woods, and by orchards glowing with autumnal fruits, of unknown names, but rich and tempting hues. More frequently it passed through cultivated fields waving with the yellow harvest, and irrigated by canals introduced from the neighboring lake; the whole showing a careful and economical husbandry, essential to the maintenance of a crowded population.

Leaving the main land, the Spaniards came on the great dike or causeway, which stretches some four or five miles in length, and divides lake Chalco from Xochicalco on the west. It was a lance in breadth in the narrowest part, and in some places wide enough for eight horsemen to ride abreast. It was a solid structure of stone and lime, running directly through the lake, and struck the Spaniards as one of the most remarkable works which they had seen in the country.

As they passed along, they beheld the gay spectacle of multitudes of Indians darting up and down in their light pirogues, eager to catch a glimpse of the strangers, or bearing the products of the country to the neighboring cities. They were amazed, also, by the sight of the *chinampas,* or floating gardens,—those wandering islands of verdure, to which we shall have occasion to return hereafter,—teeming with flowers and vegetables, and moving like rafts over the waters. All round the margin, and occasionally far in the lake, they beheld little towns and villages, which, half concealed by the foliage, and gathered in white clusters round the shore, looked in the distance like companies of wild swans riding quietly on the waves. A scene so new and wonderful filled their rude hearts with amazement. It seemed like enchantment; and they could find nothing to compare it with, but the magical pictures in the *Amadis de Gaula*. Few pictures, indeed, in that or any other legend of chivalry, could surpass the realities of their own experience. The life of the adventurer in the New World was romance put into action. What wonder, then, if the Spaniard of that day, feeding his imagination with dreams of enchantment at home, and with its realities abroad, should have displayed a Quixotic enthusiasm, — a romantic exaltation of character, not to be comprehended by the colder spirits of other lands!

Midway across the lake the army halted at the town of Cuitlahuac, a place of moderate size, but distinguished by the beauty of the buildings, — the most beautiful, according to Cortés, that he had yet seen in the country. After taking some refreshment at this place, they continued their march along the dike. Though broader in this northern section, the troops found themselves much embarrassed by the throng of Indians, who, not content with gazing on them from the boats, climbed up the causeway, and lined the sides of the roads. The general, afraid that his ranks might be disordered, and that too great familiarity might diminish a salutary awe in the natives, was obliged to resort not merely to command but menace, to clear a passage. He now found, as he advanced, a considerable change in the feelings shown towards the government. He heard only of the pomp and magnificence, nothing of the oppressions of Montezuma. Contrary to the usual fact, it seemed that the respect for the court was greatest in its immediate neighborhood.

From the causeway, the army descended on that narrow point of land which divides the waters of the Chalco from the Tezcucan lake, but which in those days was overflowed for many a mile, now laid bare. Traversing this peninsula, they entered the royal residence of Iztapalapan, a place containing twelve or fifteen thousand houses, according to Cortés. It was governed by Cuitlahua, the emperor's brother, who, to do greater honor to the general, had invited the lords of some neighboring cities, of the royal house of Mexico, like himself, to be present at the interview. This was conducted with much ceremony, and, after the usual presents of gold and delicate stuffs, a collation was served to the Spaniards in one of the great halls of the palace. The excellence of the architecture here, also, excited the admiration of the general, who does not hesitate, in the glow of his enthusiasm, to pronounce some of the buildings equal to the best in Spain. They were of stone, and the spacious apartments had roofs of odorous cedar-wood, while the walls were tapestried with fine cottons stained with brilliant colors.

But the pride of Iztapalapan, on which its lord had freely lavished his care and his revenues, was its celebrated gardens. They covered an immense tract of land; were laid out in regular squares, and the paths intersecting them were bordered with trellises, supporting creepers and aromatic shrubs, that loaded the air with their perfumes. The gardens were stocked with fruit-trees, imported from distant places, and with the gaudy family of flowers which belong to the Mexican flora, scientifically arranged, and growing luxuriant in the equable temperature of the table-land. The natural dryness of the atmosphere was counteracted by means of aqueducts and canals, that carried water into all parts of the grounds.

In one quarter was an aviary, filled with numerous kinds of birds, remarkable in this region both for brilliancy of plumage and of song. The gardens were intersected by a canal communicating with the lake of Tezcuco, and of sufficient size for barges to enter from the latter. But the most elaborate piece of work was a huge reservoir of stone, filled to a considerable height with water, well supplied with different sorts of fish. This basin was sixteen hundred paces in circumference, and was surrounded by a walk, made also of stone, wide enough for four persons to go abreast. The sides were curiously sculptured, and a flight of steps led to the water below, which fed the aqueducts above noticed, or, collected into fountains, diffused a perpetual moisture.

Such are the accounts transmitted of these celebrated gardens, at a period when similar horticultural establishments were unknown in Europe; and we might well doubt their existence in this semi-civilized land, were it not a matter of such notoriety at the time, and so explicitly attested by the invaders. But a generation had scarcely passed after the Conquest before a sad change came over these scenes so beautiful. The town itself was deserted, and the shore of the lake was strewed with the wreck of buildings which once were its ornament and its glory. The gardens shared the fate of the city. The retreating waters withdrew the means of nourishment, converting the flourishing plains into a foul and unsightly morass, the haunt of loathsome reptiles; and the water-fowl built her nest in what had once been the palaces of princes!

In the city of Iztapalapan, Cortés took up his quarters for the night. We may imagine what a crowd of ideas must have pressed on the mind of the Conqueror, as, surrounded by these evidences of civilization, he prepared, with his handful of followers, to enter the capital of a monarch, who, as he had abundant reason to know, regarded him with distrust and aversion. This capital was now but a few miles distant, distinctly visible from Iztapalapan. And as its long lines of glittering edifices, struck by the rays of the evening sun, trembled on the dark blue waters of the lake, it looked like a thing of fairy creation, rather than the work of mortal hands. Into this city of enchantment Cortés prepared to make his entry on the following morning.

RALPH WALDO EMERSON

1803–1882

23　　*Illusions*

SOME years ago, in company with an agreeable party, I spent a long summer day in exploring the Mammoth Cave in Kentucky. We traversed, through spacious galleries affording a solid masonry foundation for the town and county overhead, the six or eight black miles from the mouth of the cavern to the innermost recess which tourists visit, — a niche or grotto made of one seamless stalactite and called, I believe, Serena's Bower. I lost the light of one day. I saw high domes, and bottomless pits; heard the voice of unseen waterfalls; paddled three quarters of a mile in the deep Echo River, whose waters are peopled with the blind fish; crossed the streams "Lethe" and "Styx"; plied with music and guns the echoes in these alarming galleries; saw every form of stalagmite and stalactite in the sculptured and fretted chambers, — icicle, orange-flower, acanthus, grapes, and snowball. We shot Bengal lights into the vaults and groins of the sparry cathedrals, and examined all the masterpieces which the four combined engineers, water, limestone, gravitation, and time, could make in the dark.

The mysteries and scenery of the cave had the same dignity that belongs to all natural objects, and which shames the fine things to which we foppishly compare them. I remarked, especially, the mimetic habit, with which Nature, on new instruments, hums her old tunes, making night to mimic day, and chemistry to ape vegetation. But I then took notice, and still chiefly remember, that the best thing which the cave had to offer was an illusion. On arriving at what is called the "Star Chamber," our lamps were taken from us by the guide, and extinguished or put aside, and, on looking upwards, I saw or seemed to see the night heaven thick with stars glimmering more or less brightly over our heads, and even what seemed a comet flaming among them. All the party were touched with astonishment and pleasure. Our musical friends sung with much feeling a pretty song, "The stars are in the quiet sky," etc., and I sat down on the rocky floor to enjoy the serene picture. Some crystal specks in the black ceiling high overhead, reflecting the light of a half-hid lamp, yielded this magnificent effect.

I own, I did not like the cave so well for eking out its sublimities with this theatrical trick. But I have had many experiences like it, before and since; and we must be content to be pleased without too curiously analyzing the occasions. Our conversation with Nature is not just what it seems. The cloud-rack, the sunrise and sunset glories, rainbows, and northern lights, are not quite so spheral as our childhood thought them; and the part our organization plays in them is too large. The senses interfere everywhere, and mix their own structure with all they report of. Once, we fancied the earth a plane, and stationary. In admiring the sunset, we do not yet deduct the rounding, coördinating, pictorial powers of the eye.

The same interference from our organization creates the most of our pleasure and pain. Our first mistake is the belief that the circumstance gives the joy which we give to the circumstance. Life is an ecstasy. Life is sweet as nitrous oxide; and the fisherman dripping all day over a cold pond, the switchman at the railway intersection, the farmer in the field, the negro in the rice-swamp, the fop in the street, the hunter in the woods, the barrister with the jury, the belle at the ball, all ascribe a certain pleasure to their employment, which they themselves give it. Health and appetite impart the sweetness to sugar, bread, and meat. We fancy that our civilization has got on far, but we still come back to our primers.

We live by our imaginations, by our admirations, by our sentiments. The child walks amid heaps of illusions, which he does not like to have disturbed. The boy, how sweet to him is his fancy! how dear the story of barons and battles! What a hero he is, whilst he feeds on his heroes! What a debt is his to imaginative books! He has no better friend or influence than Scott, Shakespeare, Plutarch, and Homer. The man lives to other objects, but who dare affirm that they are more real? Even the prose of the streets is full of refractions. In the life of the dreariest alderman, fancy enters into all details, and colors them with rosy hue. He imitates the air and actions of people whom he admires, and is raised in his own eyes. He pays a debt quicker to a rich man than to a poor man. He wishes the bow and compliment of some leader in the state, or in society; weighs what he says; perhaps he never comes nearer to him for that, but dies at last better contented for this amusement of his eyes and his fancy.

The world rolls, the din of life is never hushed. In London, in Paris, in Boston, in San Francisco, the carnival, the masquerade is at its height. Nobody drops his domino. The unities, the fictions of the piece, it would be an impertinence to break. The chapter of fascinations is very long. Great is paint; nay God is the painter; and we rightly accuse the critic who destroys too many illusions. Society does not love its unmaskers. It was wittily, if somewhat bitterly, said by D'Alembert, *" qu'un état de vapeur était un état très fâcheux, parcequ'il nous faisait voir les choses comme elles sont."* I find men victims of illusion in all parts of life. Children, youths, adults, and old men, all are led by one bauble or another. Yoganidra, the goddess of illusion, Proteus, or Momus, or Gylfi's Mocking, — for the Power has many names, — is stronger than the Titans, stronger than Apollo. Few have overheard the gods, or surprised their secret. Life is a succession of lessons which must be lived to be understood. All is riddle, and the key to a riddle is another riddle. There are as many pillows of illusion as flakes in a snowstorm. We wake from one dream into another dream. The toys, to be sure, are various, and are graduated in refinement to the quality of the dupe. The intellectual man requires a fine bait; the sots are easily amused. But everybody is drugged with his own frenzy, and the pageant marches at all hours, with music and banner and badge.

Amid the joyous troop who give in to the charivari, comes now and then a sad-eyed boy, whose eyes lack the requisite refractions to clothe the show in due glory, and who is afflicted with a tendency to trace home the glittering miscellany of fruits and flowers to one root. Science is a search after identity, and the scientific whim is lurking in all corners. At the State Fair, a friend of mine complained that all the varieties of fancy pears in our orchards seem to have been selected by somebody who had a whim for a particular kind of pear, and only cultivated such as had that perfume; they were all alike. And I remember the quarrel of another youth with the confectioners, that, when he racked his wit to choose the best comfits in the shops, in all the endless varieties of sweetmeat he could only find three flavors, or two. What then? Pears and cakes are good for something; and because you, unluckily, have an eye or nose too keen, why need you spoil the comfort which the rest of us find in them? I knew a humorist who, in a good deal of rattle, had a grain or two of sense. He shocked the company by maintaining that the attributes of God were two, — power and risibility; and that it was the duty of every pious man to keep up the comedy. And I have known gentlemen of great stake in the community, but whose sympathies were cold, — presidents of colleges, and governors, and senators, — who held themselves bound to sign every temperance pledge, and act with Bible societies, and missions, and peacemakers, and cry *Hist-a-boy!* to every good dog. We must not carry comity too far, but we all have kind impulses in this direction. When the boys come into my yard for leave to gather horse-chestnuts, I own I enter into Nature's game, and affect to grant the permission reluctantly, fearing that any moment they will find out the imposture of that showy chaff. But this tenderness is quite unnecessary; the enchantments are laid on very thick. Their young life is thatched with them. Bare and grim to tears is the lot of the children in the hovel I saw yesterday; yet not the less they hung it round with frippery romance, like the children of the happiest fortune, and talked of "the dear cottage where so many joyful hours had flown." Well, this thatching of hovels is the custom of the country. Women, more than all, are the element and kingdom of illusion. Being fascinated, they fascinate. They see through Claude-Lorraines. And how dare anyone, if he could, pluck away the *coulisses,* stage effects, and ceremonies, by which they live? Too pathetic, too pitiable, is the region of affection, and its atmosphere always liable to mirage.

We are not very much to blame for our bad marriages. We live amid hallucinations; and this especial trap is laid to trip up our feet with, and all are tripped up first or last. But the mighty Mother who had been so sly with us, as if she felt that she owed us some indemnity, insinuates into the Pandora-box of marriage some deep and serious benefits, and some great joys. We find a delight in the beauty and happiness of children, that makes the heart too big for the body. In the worst-assorted connections there is ever some mixture of true marriage. Teague and his jade get some just relations of mutual respect, kindly observation, and fostering of each other, learn something, and would carry themselves wiselier, if they were now to begin.

'Tis fine for us to point at one or another fine madman, as if there were any exempts. The scholar in his library is none. I, who have all my life heard any number of orations and debates, read poems and miscellaneous books, conversed with many geniuses, am still the victim of any new page; and if Marmaduke, or Hugh, or Moosehead or any other, invent a new style or mythology, I fancy that the world will be all brave and right if dressed in these colors, which I had not thought of. Then at once I will daub with this new paint: but it will not stick. 'Tis like the cement which the peddler sells at the door; he makes broken crockery hold with it, but you can never buy of him a bit of the cement which will make it hold when he is gone.

Men who make themselves felt in the world avail themselves of a certain fate in their constitution, which they know how to use. But they never deeply interest us, unless they lift a corner of the curtain, or betray never so slightly their penetration of what is behind it. 'Tis the charm of practical men, that outside of their practicality are a certain poetry and play, as if they led the good horse Power by the bridle, and preferred to walk, though they can ride so fiercely. Bonaparte is intellectual, as well as Cæsar; and the best soldiers, sea captains, and railway men have a gentleness, when off duty; a good natured admission that there are illusions, and who shall say that he is not their sport? We stigmatize the cast-iron fellows, who cannot so detach themselves, as "dragon-ridden," "thunder-stricken," and fools of fate, with whatever powers endowed.

Since our tuition is through emblems and indirections, 'tis well to know that there is method in it, a fixed scale, and rank above rank in the phantasms. We begin low with coarse masks, and rise to the most subtle and beautiful. The red men told Columbus, "they had an herb which took away fatigue"; but he found the illusion of "arriving from the east at the Indies" more composing to his lofty spirit than any tobacco. Is not our faith in the impenetrability of matter more sedative than narcotics? You play with jack-straws, balls, bowls, horse and gun, estates and politics; but there are finer games before you. Is not time a pretty toy? Life will show you masks that are worth all your carnivals. Yonder mountain must migrate into your mind. The fine star-dust and nebulous blur in Orion, "the portentous year of Mizar and Alcor," must come down and be dealt with in your household thought. What if you shall come to discern that the play and playground of all this pompous history are radiations from yourself, and that the sun borrows his beams? What terrible questions we are learning to ask! The former men believed in magic, by which temples, cities, and men were swallowed up and all trace of them gone. We are coming on the secret of a magic which sweeps out of men's minds all vestige of theism and beliefs which they and their fathers held and were framed upon.

There are deceptions of the senses, deceptions of the passions, and the structural, beneficent illusions of sentiment and of the intellect. There is the illusion of love, which attributes to the beloved person all which that person shares with his or her family, sex, age, or condition, nay, with the human mind itself. 'Tis these which the lover loves, and Anna Matilda gets the credit of them. As if one shut up always in a tower, with one window, through which the face of heaven and earth could be seen, should fancy that all the marvels he beheld belonged to that window. There is the illusion of time, which is very deep; who has disposed of it? or come to the conviction that what seems the *succession* of thought is only the distribution of wholes into causal series? The intellect sees that every atom carries the whole of Nature; that the mind opens to omnipotence; that, in the endless striving and ascents, the metamorphosis is entire, so that the soul doth not know itself in its own act, when that act is perfected. There is illusion that shall deceive even the elect. There is illusion that shall deceive even the performer of the miracle. Though he make his body, he denies that he makes it. Though the world exist from thought, thought is daunted in presence of the world. One after the other we accept the mental laws, still resisting those which follow, which however must be accepted. But all our concessions only compel us to new profusion. And what avails it that science has come to treat space and time as simply forms of thought, and the material world as hypothetical, and withal our pretension of *property* and even of self-hood are fading with the rest, if, at last, even our thoughts are not finalities; but the incessant flowing and ascension reach these also, and each thought which yesterday was a finality, today is yielding to a larger generalization?

With such volatile elements to work in, 'tis no wonder if our estimates are loose and floating. We must work and affirm, but we have no guess of the value of what we say or do. The cloud is now as big as your hand, and now it covers a county. That story of Thor, who was set to drain the drinking-horn in Asgard, and to wrestle with the old woman, and to run with the runner Lok, and presently found that he had been drinking up the sea, and wrestling with Time, and racing with Thought, describes us who are contending, amid these seeming trifles, with the supreme energies of Nature. We fancy we have fallen into bad company and squalid condition, low debts, shoe-bills, broken glass to pay for, pots to buy, butcher's meat, sugar, milk, and coal. "Set me some great task, ye gods! and I will show my spirit." "Not so," says the good Heaven; "plod and plow, vamp your old coats and hats, weave a shoestring; great affairs and the best wine by-and-by." Well, 'tis all phantasm; and if we weave a yard of tape in all humility, and as well as we can, long hereafter we shall see it was no cotton tape at all, but some galaxy which we braided, and that the threads were Time and Nature.

We cannot write the order of the variable winds. How can we penetrate the law of our shifting moods and susceptibility? Yet they differ as all and nothing. Instead of the firmament of yesterday, which our eyes require, it is today an eggshell which coops us in; we cannot even see what or where our stars of destiny are. From day to day, the capital facts of human life are hidden from our eyes. Suddenly the mist rolls up, and reveals them, and we think how much good time is gone, that might have been saved had any hint of these things been shown. A sudden rise in the road shows us the system of mountains, and all the summits, which have been just as near us all the year, but quite out of mind. But these alternations are not without their order, and we are parties to our various fortune. If life seem a succession of dreams, yet poetic justice is done in dreams also. The visions of good men are good; it is the undisciplined will that is whipped with bad thoughts and bad fortunes. When we break the laws, we lose our hold on the central reality. Like sick men in hospitals, we change only from bed to bed, from one folly to another; and it cannot signify much what becomes of such castaways, — wailing, stupid, comatose creatures, — lifted from bed to bed, from the nothing of life to the nothing of death.

In this kingdom of illusions we grope eagerly for stays and foundations. There is none but a strict and faithful dealing at home, and a severe barring out of all duplicity or illusion there. Whatever games are played with us, we must play no games with ourselves, but deal in our privacy with the last honesty and truth. I look upon the simple and childish virtues of veracity and honesty as the root of all that is sublime in character. Speak as you think, be what you are, pay your debts of all kinds. I prefer to be owned as sound and solvent, and my word as good as my bond, and to be what cannot be skipped, or dissipated, or undermined, to all the *éclat* in the universe. This reality is the foundation of friendship, religion, poetry, and art. At the top or at the bottom of all illusions, I set the cheat which still leads us to work and live for appearances, in spite of our conviction, in all sane hours, that it is what we really are that avails with friends, with strangers, and with fate or fortune.

One would think from the talk of men, that riches and poverty were a great matter; and our civilization mainly respects it. But the Indians say, that they do not think the white man with his brow of care, always toiling, afraid of heat and cold, and keeping within doors, has any advantage of them. The permanent interest of every man is, never to be in a false position, but to have the weight of Nature to back him in all that he does. Riches and poverty are a thick or thin costume; and our life — the life of all of us — identical. For we transcend the circumstance continually, and taste the real quality of existence; as in our employments, which only differ in the manipulations, but express the same laws; or in our thoughts, which wear no silks and taste no ice-creams. We see God face to face every hour, and know the savor of Nature.

The early Greek philosophers Heraclitus and Xenophanes measured their force on this problem of identity. Diogenes of Apollonia said, that unless the atoms were made of one stuff, they could never blend and act with one another. But the Hindus, in their sacred writings, express the liveliest feeling, both of the essential identity, and of that illusion which they conceive variety to be. "The notions, '*I am*,' and '*This is mine*,' which influence mankind, are but delusions of the mother of the world. Dispel, O Lord of all creatures! the conceit of knowledge which proceeds from ignorance." And the beatitude of man they hold to lie in being freed from fascination.

The intellect is stimulated by the statement of truth in a trope, and the will by clothing the laws of life in illusions. But the unities of Truth and of Right are not broken by the disguise. There need never be any confusion in these. In a crowded life of many parts and performers, on a stage of nations, or in the obscurest hamlet in Maine or California, the same elements offer the same choices to each new comer, and, according to his election, he fixes his fortune in absolute nature. It would be hard to put more mental and moral philosophy than the Persians have thrown into a sentence: —

> "Fooled thou must be, though wisest of the wise:
> Then be the fool of virtue, not of vice."

There is no chance, and no anarchy, in the universe. All is system and gradation. Every god is there sitting in his sphere. The young mortal enters the hall of the firmament: there is he alone with them alone, they pouring on him benedictions and gifts, and beckoning him up to their thrones. On the instant, and incessantly, fall snowstorms of illusions. He fancies himself in a vast crowd which sways this way and that, and whose movement and doings he must obey: he fancies himself poor, orphaned, insignificant. The mad crowd drives hither and thither, now furiously commanding this thing to be done, now that. What is he that he should resist their will, and think or act for himself? Every moment, new changes, and new showers of deceptions, to baffle and distract him. And when, by-and-by, for an instant, the air clears, and the cloud lifts a little, there are the gods still sitting around him on their thrones, — they alone with him alone.

HENRY DAVID THOREAU was the last male descendant of a French ancestor who came to this country from the Isle of Guernsey. His character exhibited occasional traits drawn from this blood, in singular combination with a very strong Saxon genius.

He was born in Concord, Massachusetts, on the 12th of July, 1817. He was graduated at Harvard College in 1837, but without any literary distinction. An iconoclast in literature, he seldom thanked colleges for their service to him, holding them in small esteem, whilst yet his debt to them was important. After leaving the University, he joined his brother in teaching a private school, which he soon renounced. His father was a manufacturer of lead-pencils, and Henry applied himself for a time to this craft, believing he could make a better pencil than was then in use. After completing his experiments, he exhibited his work to chemists and artists in Boston, and having obtained their certificates to its excellence and to its equality with the best London manufacture, he returned home contented. His friends congratulated him that he had now opened his way to fortune. But he replied, that he should never make another pencil. "Why should I? I would not do again what I have done once." He resumed his endless walks and miscellaneous studies, making every day some new acquaintance with Nature, though as yet never speaking of zoölogy or botany, since, though very studious of natural facts, he was incurious of technical and textual science.

At this time, a strong, healthy youth, fresh from college, whilst all his companions were choosing their profession, or eager to begin some lucrative employment, it was inevitable that his thoughts should be exercised on the same question, and it required rare decision to refuse all the accustomed paths and keep his solitary freedom at the cost of disappointing the natural expectations of his family and friends: all the more difficult that he had a perfect probity, was exact in securing his own independence, and in holding every man to the like duty. But Thoreau never faltered. He was a born protestant. He declined to give up his large ambition of knowledge and action for any narrow craft or profession, aiming at a much more comprehensive calling, the art of living well. If he slighted and defied the opinions of others, it was only that he was more intent to reconcile his practice with his own belief. Never idle or self-indulgent, he preferred, when he wanted money, earning it by some piece of manual labor agreeable to him, as building a boat or a fence, planting, grafting, surveying, or other short work, to any long engagements. With his hardy habits and few wants, his skill in wood-craft, and his powerful arithmetic, he was very competent to live in any part of the world. It would cost him less time to supply his wants than another. He was therefore secure of his leisure.

A natural skill for mensuration, growing out of his mathematical knowledge and his habit of ascertaining the measures and distances of objects which interested him, the size of trees, the depth and extent of ponds and rivers, the height of mountains, and the air-line distance of his favorite summits, — this, and his intimate knowledge of the territory about Concord, made him drift into the profession of land-surveyor. It had the advantage for him that it led him continually into new and secluded grounds, and helped his studies of Nature. His accuracy and skill in this work were readily appreciated, and he found all the employment he wanted.

He could easily solve the problems of the surveyor, but he was daily beset with graver questions, which he manfully confronted. He interrogated every custom, and wished to settle all his practice on an ideal foundation. He was a protestant à l'outrance, and few lives contain so many renunciations. He was bred to no profession; he never married; he lived alone; he never went to church; he never voted; he refused to pay a tax to the State; he ate no flesh, he drank no wine, he never knew the use of tobacco; and, though a naturalist, he used neither trap nor gun. He chose, wisely, no doubt, for himself, to be the bachelor of thought and Nature. He had no talent for wealth, and knew how to be poor without the least hint of squalor or inelegance. Perhaps he fell into his way of living without forecasting it much, but approved it with later wisdom. "I am often reminded," he wrote in his journal, "that, if I had bestowed on me the wealth of Crœsus, my aims must be still the same, and my means essentially the same." He had no temptations to fight against, — no appetites, no passions, no taste for elegant trifles. A fine house, dress, the manners and talk of highly cultivated people were all thrown away on him. He much preferred a good Indian, and considered these refinements as impediments to conversation, wishing to meet his companion on the simplest terms. He declined invitations to dinner-parties, because there each was in everyone's way, and he could not meet the individuals to any purpose. "They make their pride," he said, "in making their dinner cost much; I make my pride in making my dinner cost little." When asked at table what dish he preferred, he answered, "The nearest." He did not like the taste of wine, and never had a vice in his life. He said, — "I have a faint recollection of pleasure derived from smoking dried lily-stems, before I was a man. I had commonly a supply of these. I have never smoked anything more noxious."

He chose to be rich by making his wants few, and supplying them himself. In his travels, he used the railroad only to get over so much country as was unimportant to the present purpose, walking hundreds of miles, avoiding taverns, buying a lodging in farmers' and fishermen's houses, as cheaper, and more agreeable to him, and because there he could better find the men and the information he wanted.

There was somewhat military in his nature, not to be subdued, always manly and able, but rarely tender, as if he did not feel himself except in opposition. He wanted a fallacy to expose, a blunder to pillory, I may say required a little sense of victory, a roll of the drum, to call his powers into full exercise. It cost him nothing to say No; indeed, he found it much easier than to say Yes. It seemed as if his first instinct on hearing a proposition was to controvert it, so impatient was he of the limitations of our daily thought. This habit, of course, is a little chilling to the social affections; and though the companion would in the end acquit him of any malice or untruth, yet it mars conversation. Hence, no equal companion stood in affectionate relations with one so pure and guileless. "I love Henry," said one of his friends, "but I cannot like him; and as for taking his arm, I should as soon think of taking the arm of an elm-tree."

Yet, hermit and stoic as he was, he was really fond of sympathy, and threw himself heartily and childlike into the company of young people whom he loved, and whom he delighted to entertain, as he only could, with the varied and endless anecdotes of his experiences by field and river. And he was always ready to lead a huckleberry-party or a search for chestnuts or grapes. Talking, one day, of a public discourse, Henry remarked, that whatever succeeded with the audience was bad. I said, "Who would not like to write something which all can read, like *Robinson Crusoe?* and who does not see with regret that his page is not solid with a right materialistic treatment, which delights everybody?" Henry objected, of course, and vaunted the better lectures which reached only a few persons. But, at supper, a young girl, understanding that he was to lecture at the Lyceum, sharply asked him, "whether his lecture would be a nice, interesting story, such as she wished to hear, or whether it was one of those old philosophical things that she did not care about." Henry turned to her, and bethought himself, and, I saw, was trying to believe that he had matter that might fit her and her brother, who were to sit up and go to the lecture, if it was a good one for them.

He was a speaker and actor of the truth,—born such,— and was ever running into dramatic situations from this cause. In any circumstance, it interested all bystanders to know what part Henry would take, and what he would say; and he did not disappoint expectation, but used an original judgment on each emergency. In 1845 he built himself a small framed house on the shores of Walden Pond, and lived there two years alone, a life of labor and study. This action was quite native and fit for him. No one who knew him would tax him with affectation. He was more unlike his neighbors in his thought than in his action. As soon as he had exhausted the advantages of that solitude, he abandoned it. In 1847, not approving some uses to which the public expenditure was applied, he refused to pay his town tax, and was put in jail. A friend paid the tax for him, and he was released. The like annoyance was threatened the next year. But, as his friends paid the tax, notwithstanding his protest, I believe he ceased to resist. No opposition or ridicule had any weight with him. He coldly and fully stated his opinion of the company. It was of no consequence, if everyone present held the opposite opinion. On one occasion he went to the University Library to procure some books. The librarian refused to lend them. Mr. Thoreau repaired to the President, who stated to him the rules and usages, which permitted the loan of books to resident graduates, to clergymen who were alumni, and to some others resident within a circle of ten miles' radius from the College. Mr. Thoreau explained to the President that the railroad had destroyed the old scale of distances, — that the library was useless, yes, and President and College useless, on the terms of his rules, — that the one benefit he owed to the College was its library, — that, at this moment, not only his want of books was imperative, but he wanted a large number of books, and assured him that he, Thoreau, and not the librarian, was the proper custodian of these. In short, the President found the petitioner so formidable, and the rules getting to look so ridiculous, that he ended by giving him a privilege which in his hands proved unlimited thereafter.

No truer American existed than Thoreau. His preference of his country and condition was genuine, and his aversation from English and European manners and tastes almost reached contempt. He listened impatiently to news or *bon mots* gleaned from London circles; and though he tried to be civil, these anecdotes fatigued him. The men were all imitating each other, and on a small mold. Why can they not live as far apart as possible, and each be a man by himself? What he sought was the most energetic nature; and he wished to go to Oregon, not to London. "In every part of Great Britain," he wrote in his diary, "are discovered traces of the Romans, their funeral urns, their camps, their roads, their dwellings. But New England, at least, is not based on any Roman ruins. We have not to lay the foundations of our houses on the ashes of a former civilization."

But idealist as he was, standing for abolition of slavery, abolition of tariffs, almost for abolition of government, it is needless to say he found himself not only unrepresented in actual politics, but almost equally opposed to every class of reformers. Yet he paid the tribute of his uniform respect to the Anti-Slavery party. One man, whose personal acquaintance he had formed, he honored with exceptional regard. Before the first friendly word had been spoken for Captain John Brown, he sent notices to most houses in Concord, that he would speak in a public hall on the condition and character of John Brown, on Sunday evening, and invited all people to come. The Republican Committee, the Abolitionist Committee, sent him word that it was premature and not advisable. He replied, — "I did not send to you for advice, but to announce that I am to speak." The hall was filled at an early hour by people of all parties, and his earnest eulogy of the hero was heard by all respectfully, by many with a sympathy that surprised themselves.

It was said of Plotinus that he was ashamed of his body, and 'tis very likely he had good reason for it, — that his body was a bad servant, and he had not skill in dealing with the material world, as happens often to men of abstract intellect. But Mr. Thoreau was equipped with a most adapted and serviceable body. He was of short stature, firmly built, of light complexion, with strong, serious blue eyes, and a grave aspect, — his face covered in the late years with a becoming beard. His senses were acute, his frame well-knit and hardy, his hands strong and skillful in the use of tools. And there was a wonderful fitness of body and mind. He could pace sixteen rods more accurately than another man could measure them with rod and chain. He could find his path in the woods at night, he said, better by his feet than his eyes. He could estimate the measure of a tree very well by his eye; he could estimate the weight of a calf or a pig, like a dealer. From a box containing a bushel or more of loose pencils, he could take up with his hands fast enough just a dozen pencils at every grasp. He was a good swimmer, runner, skater, boatman, and would probably outwalk most countrymen in a day's journey. And the relation of body to mind was still finer than we have indicated. He said he wanted every stride his legs made. The length of his walk uniformly made the length of his writing. If shut up in the house, he did not write at all.

He had a strong common sense, like that which Rose Flammock, the weaver's daughter, in Scott's romance, commends in her father, as resembling a yardstick, which, whilst it measures dowlas and diaper, can equally well measure tapestry and cloth of gold. He had always a new resource. When I was planting forest trees, and had procured half a peck of acorns, he said that only a small portion of them would be sound, and proceeded to examine them, and select the sound ones. But finding this took time, he said, "I think if you put them all into water the good ones will sink;" which experiment we tried with success. He could plan a garden, or a house, or a barn; would have been competent to lead a "Pacific Exploring Expedition;" could give judicious counsel in the gravest private or public affairs.

He lived for the day, not cumbered and mortified by his memory. If he brought you yesterday a new proposition, he would bring you today another not less revolutionary. A very industrious man, and setting, like all highly organized men, a high value on his time, he seemed the only man of leisure in town, always ready for any excursion that promised well, or for conversation prolonged into late hours. His trenchant sense was never stopped by his rules of daily prudence, but was always up to the new occasion. He liked and used the simplest food, yet, when some one urged a vegetable diet, Thoreau thought all diets a very small matter, saying that "the man who shoots the buffalo lives better than the man who boards at the Graham House." He said, — "You can sleep near the railroad, and never be disturbed: Nature knows very well what sounds are worth attending to, and has made up her mind not to hear the railroad-whistle. But things respect the devout mind, and a mental ecstasy was never interrupted." He noted, what repeatedly befell him, that, after receiving from a distance a rare plant, he would presently find the same in his own haunts. And those pieces of luck which happen only to good players happened to him. One day, walking with a stranger, who inquired where Indian arrow-heads could be found, he replied, "Everywhere," and, stooping forward, picked one on the instant from the ground. At Mount Washington, in Tucker-man's Ravine, Thoreau had a bad fall, and sprained his foot. As he was in the act of getting up from his fall, he saw for the first time the leaves of the *Arnica mollis*.

His robust common sense, armed with stout hands, keen perceptions, and strong will, cannot yet account for the superiority which shone in his simple and hidden life. I must add the cardinal fact, that there was an excellent wisdom in him, proper to a rare class of men, which showed him the material world as a means and symbol. This discovery, which sometimes yields to poets a certain casual and interrupted light, serving for the ornament of their writing, was in him an unsleeping insight; and whatever faults or obstructions of temperament might cloud it, he was not disobedient to the heavenly vision. In his youth, he said, one day, "The other world is all my art; my pencils will draw no other; my jack-knife will cut nothing else; I do not use it as a means."

RALPH WALDO EMERSON

This was the muse and genius that ruled his opinions, conversation, studies, work, and course of life. This made him a searching judge of men. At first glance he measured his companion, and, though insensible to some fine traits of culture, could very well report his weight and calibre. And this made the impression of genius which his conversation sometimes gave.

He understood the matter in hand at a glance, and saw the limitations and poverty of those he talked with, so that nothing seemed concealed from such terrible eyes. I have repeatedly known young men of sensibility converted in a moment to the belief that this was the man they were in search of, the man of men, who could tell them all they should do. His own dealing with them was never affectionate, but superior, didactic, — scorning their petty ways, — very slowly conceding, or not conceding at all, the promise of his society at their houses, or even at his own. "Would he not walk with them?" "He did not know. There was nothing so important to him as his walk; he had no walks to throw away on company." Visits were offered him from respectful parties, but he declined them. Admiring friends offered to carry him at their own cost to the Yellow-Stone River, — to the West Indies, — to South America. But though nothing could be more grave or considered than his refusals, they remind one in quite new relations of that fop Brummel's reply to the gentleman who offered him his carriage in a shower, "But where will *you* ride, then?" — and what accusing silences, and what searching and irresistible speeches, battering down all defenses, his companions can remember!

Mr. Thoreau dedicated his genius with such entire love to the fields, hills, and waters of his native town, that he made them known and interesting to all reading Americans, and to people over the sea. The river on whose banks he was born and died he knew from its springs to its confluence with the Merrimack. He had made summer and winter observations on it for many years, and at every hour of the day and night. The result of the recent survey of the Water Commissioners appointed by the State of Massachusetts he had reached by his private experiments, several years earlier. Every fact which occurs in the bed, on the banks, or in the air over it; the fishes, and their spawning and nests, their manners, their food; the shad-flies which fill the air on a certain evening once a year, and which are snapped at by the fishes so ravenously that many of these die of repletion; the conical heaps of small stones on the river-shallows, one of which heaps will sometimes overfill a cart — these heaps the huge nests of small fishes; the birds which frequent the stream, heron, duck, sheldrake, loon, osprey; the snake, muskrat, otter, woodchuck, and fox, on the banks; the turtle, frog, hyla, and cricket, which make the banks vocal, — were all known to him, and, as it were, townsmen and fellow-creatures; so that he felt an absurdity or violence in any narrative of one of these by itself apart, and still more of its dimensions on an inch-rule, or in the exhibition of its skeleton, or the specimen of a squirrel or a bird in brandy. He liked to speak of the manners of the river, as itself a lawful creature, yet with exactness, and always to an observed fact. As he knew the river, so the ponds of this region.

One of the weapons he used, more important to him than microscope or alcohol-receiver to other investigators, was a whim which grew on him by indulgence, yet appeared in gravest statement, namely, of extolling his own town and neighborhood as the most favored center for natural observation. He remarked that the flora of Massachusetts embraced almost all the important plants of America, — most of the oaks, most of the willows, the best pines, the ash, the maple, the beech, the nuts. He returned Kane's *Arctic Voyage* to a friend of whom he had borrowed it, with the remark, that "most of the phenomena noted might be observed in Concord." He seemed a little envious of the Pole, for the coincident sunrise and sunset, or five minutes' day after six months: a splendid fact, which Annursnuc had never afforded him. He found red snow in one of his walks, and told me that he expected to find yet the *Victoria regia* in Concord. He was the attorney of the indigenous plants, and owned to a preference of the weeds to the imported plants as of the Indian to the civilized man, — and noticed, with pleasure, that the willow bean-poles of his neighbor had grown more than his beans. "See these weeds," he said, "which have been hoed at by a million farmers all spring and summer, and yet have prevailed, and just now come out triumphant over all lanes, pastures, fields, and gardens, such is their vigor. We have insulted them with low names, too, — as Pigweed, Wormwood, Chickweed, Shad-Blossom." He says, "They have brave names, too, — Ambrosia, Stellaria, Amelanchier, Amaranth, etc."

I think his fancy for referring everything to the meridian of Concord did not grow out of any ignorance or depreciation of other longitudes or latitudes, but was rather a playful expression of his conviction of the indifference of all places, and that the best place for each is where he stands. He expressed it once in this wise: — "I think nothing is to be hoped from you, if this bit of mold under your feet is not sweeter to you to eat than any other in this world, or in any world."

The other weapon with which he conquered all obstacles in science was patience. He knew how to sit immovable, a part of the rock he rested on, until the bird, the reptile, the fish, which had retired from him, should come back and resume its habits, nay, moved by curiosity, should come to him and watch him.

It was a pleasure and a privilege to walk with him. He knew the country like a fox or a bird, and passed through it as freely by paths of his own. He knew every track in the snow or on the ground, and what creature had taken this path before him. One must submit abjectly to such a guide, and the reward was great. Under his arm he carried an old music-book to press plants; in his pocket, his diary and pencil, a spy-glass for birds, microscope, jack-knife, and twine. He wore a straw hat, stout shoes, strong gray trousers, to brave shrub-oaks and smilax, and to climb a tree for a hawk's or a squirrel's nest. He waded into the pool for the water-plants, and his strong legs were no insignificant part of his armor. On the day I speak of he looked for the Menyanthes, detected it across the wide pool, and, on examination of the florets, decided that it had been in flower five days. He drew out of his breast-pocket his diary, and read the names of all the plants that should bloom on this day, whereof he kept account as a banker when his notes fall due. The Cypripedium not due till to-morrow. He thought, that, if waked up from a trance, in this swamp, he could tell by the plants what time of the year it was within two days. The redstart was flying about, and presently the fine grosbeaks, whose brilliant scarlet makes the rash gazer wipe his eye, and whose fine clear note Thoreau compared to that of a tanager which has got rid of its hoarseness. Presently he heard a note which he called that of the night-warbler, a bird he had never identified, had been in search of twelve years, which always, when he saw it, was in the act of diving down into a tree or bush, and which it was vain to seek; the only bird which sings indifferently by night and by day. I told him he must beware of finding and booking it, lest life should have nothing more to show him. He said, "What you seek in vain for, half your life, one day you come full upon, all the family at dinner. You seek it like a dream, and as soon as you find it you become its prey."

His interest in the flower or the bird lay very deep in his mind, was connected with Nature, — and the meaning of Nature was never attempted to be defined by him. He would not offer a memoir of his observations to the Natural History Society. "Why should I? To detach the description from its connections in my mind would make it no longer true or valuable to me: and they do not wish what belongs to it." His power of observation seemed to indicate additional senses. He saw as with microscope, heard as with ear-trumpet, and his memory was a photographic register of all he saw and heard. And yet none knew better than he that it is not the fact that imports, but the impression or effect of the fact on your mind. Every fact lay in glory in his mind, a type of the order and beauty of the whole.

His determination on Natural History was organic. He confessed that he sometimes felt like a hound or a panther, and, if born among Indians, would have been a fell hunter. But, restrained by his Massachusetts culture, he played out the game in this mild form of botany and ichthyology. His intimacy with animals suggested what Thomas Fuller records of Butler the apiologist, that "either he had told the bees things or the bees had told him." Snakes coiled round his leg; the fishes swam into his hand, and he took them out of the water; he pulled the woodchuck out of its hole by the tail and took the foxes under his protection from the hunters. Our naturalist had perfect magnanimity; he had no secrets: he would carry you to the heron's haunt, or even to his most prized botanical swamp, — possibly knowing that you could never find it again, yet willing to take his risks.

No college ever offered him a diploma, or a professor's chair; no academy made him its corresponding secretary, its discoverer, or even its member. Perhaps these learned bodies feared the satire of his presence. Yet so much knowledge of Nature's secret and genius few others possessed, none in a more large and religious synthesis. For not a particle of respect had he to the opinions of any man or body of men, but homage solely to the truth itself; and as he discovered everywhere among doctors some leaning of courtesy, it discredited them. He grew to be revered and admired by his townsmen, who had at first known him only as an oddity. The farmers who employed him as a surveyor soon discovered his rare accuracy and skill, his knowledge of their lands, of trees, of birds, of Indian remains, and the like, which enabled him to tell every farmer more than he knew before of his own farm; so that he began to feel a little as if Mr. Thoreau had better rights in his land than he. They felt, too, the superiority of character which addressed all men with a native authority.

RALPH WALDO EMERSON

Indian relics abound in Concord,—arrow-heads, stone chisels, pestles, and fragments of pottery; and on the river-bank, large heaps of clam-shells and ashes mark spots which the savages frequented. These, and every circumstance touching the Indian, were important in his eyes. His visits to Maine were chiefly for love of the Indian. He had the satisfaction of seeing the manufacture of the bark-canoe, as well as of trying his hand in its management on the rapids. He was inquisitive about the making of the stone arrow-head, and in his last days charged a youth setting out for the Rocky Mountains to find an Indian who could tell him that: "It was well worth a visit to California to learn it." Occasionally, a small party of Penobscot Indians would visit Concord, and pitch their tents for a few weeks in summer on the river-bank. He failed not to make acquaintance with the best of them; though he well knew that asking questions of Indians is like catechizing beavers and rabbits. In his last visit to Maine he had great satisfaction from Joseph Polis, an intelligent Indian of Oldtown, who was his guide for some weeks.

He was equally interested in every natural fact. The depth of his perception found likeness of law throughout Nature, and I know not any genius who so swiftly inferred universal law from the single fact. He was no pedant of a department. His eye was open to beauty, and his ear to music. He found these, not in rare conditions, but wheresoever he went. He thought the best of music was in single strains; and he found poetic suggestion in the humming of the telegraph-wire.

His poetry might be bad or good; he no doubt wanted a lyric facility and technical skill, but he had the source of poetry in his spiritual perception. He was a good reader and critic, and his judgment on poetry was to the ground of it. He could not be deceived as to the presence or absence of the poetic element in any composition, and his thirst for this made him negligent and perhaps scornful of superficial graces. He would pass by many delicate rhythms, but he would have detected every live stanza or line in a volume, and knew very well where to find an equal poetic charm in prose. He was so enamored of the spiritual beauty that he held all actual written poems in very light esteem in the comparison. He admired Æschylus and Pindar; but, when some one was commending them, he said that Æschylus and the Greeks, in describing Apollo and Orpheus, had given no song, or no good one. "They ought not to have moved trees, but to have chanted to the gods such a hymn as would have sung all their old ideas out of their heads, and new ones in." His own verses are often rude and defective. The gold does not yet run pure, is drossy and crude. The thyme and marjoram are not yet honey. But if he want lyric fineness and technical merits, if he have not the poetic temperament, he never lacks the causal thought, showing that his genius was better than his talent. He knew the worth of the Imagination for the uplifting and consolation of human life, and liked to throw every thought into a symbol. The fact you tell is of no value, but only the impression. For this reason his presence was poetic, always piqued the curiosity to know more deeply the secrets of his mind. He had many reserves, an unwillingness to exhibit to profane eyes what was still sacred in his own, and knew well how to throw a poetic veil over his experience. All readers of *Walden* will remember his mythical record of his disappointments: —

"I long ago lost a hound, a bay horse, and a turtle-dove, and am still on their trail. Many are the travelers I have spoken concerning them, describing their tracks, and what calls they answered to. I have met one or two who had heard the hound, and the tramp of the horse, and even seen the dove disappear behind a cloud; and they seemed as anxious to recover them as if they had lost them themselves."

His riddles were worth the reading, and I confide, that, if at any time I do not understand the expression, it is yet just. Such was the wealth of his truth that it was not worth his while to use words in vain. His poem entitled "Sympathy" reveals the tenderness under that triple steel of stoicism, and the intellectual subtility it could animate. His classic poem on "Smoke" suggests Simonides, but is better than any poem of Simonides. His biography is in his verses. His habitual thought makes all his poetry a hymn to the Cause of causes, the Spirit which vivifies and controls his own: —

> " I hearing get, who had but ears,
>   And sight, who had but eyes before;
> I moments live, who lived but years,
>   And truth discern, who knew but learning's lore."

And still more in these religious lines: —

> " Now chiefly is my natal hour,
>   And only now my prime of life;
> I will not doubt the love untold,
> Which not my worth or want hath bought,
> Which wooed me young, and woos me old,
>   And to this evening hath me brought."

Whilst he used in his writings a certain petulance of remark in reference to churches or churchmen, he was a person of a rare, tender, and absolute religion, a person incapable of any profanation, by act or by thought. Of course, the same isolation which belonged to his original thinking and living detached him from the social religious forms. This is neither to be censured nor regretted. Aristotle long ago explained it, when he said, "One who surpasses his fellow-citizens in virtue is no longer a part of the city. Their law is not for him, since he is a law to himself."

Thoreau was sincerity itself, and might fortify the convictions of prophets in the ethical laws by his holy living. It was an affirmative experience which refused to be set aside. A truth-speaker he, capable of the most deep and strict conversation; a physician to the wounds of any soul; a friend, knowing not only the secret of friendship, but almost worshiped by those few persons who resorted to him as their confessor and prophet, and knew the deep value of his mind and great heart. He thought that without religion or devotion of some kind nothing great was ever accomplished: and he thought that the bigoted sectarian had better bear this in mind.

His virtues, of course, sometimes ran into extremes. It was easy to trace to the inexorable demand on all for exact truth that austerity which made this willing hermit more solitary even than he wished. Himself of a perfect probity, he required not less of others. He had a disgust at crime, and no worldly success would cover it. He detected paltering as readily in dignified and prosperous persons as in beggars, and with equal scorn. Such dangerous frankness was in his dealing that his admirers called him "that terrible Thoreau," as if he spoke when silent, and was still present when he had departed. I think the severity of his ideal interfered to deprive him of a healthy sufficiency of human society.

The habit of a realist to find things the reverse of their appearance inclined him to put every statement in a paradox. A certain habit of antagonism defaced his earlier writings, — a trick of rhetoric not quite outgrown in his later, of substituting for the obvious word and thought its diametrical opposite. He praised wild mountains and winter forests for their domestic air, in snow and ice he would find sultriness, and commended the wilderness for resembling Rome and Paris. "It was so dry, that you might call it wet."

The tendency to magnify the moment, to read all the laws of Nature in the one object or one combination under your eye, is of course comic to those who do not share the philsopher's perception of identity. To him there was no such thing as size. The pond was a small ocean; the Atlantic, a large Walden Pond. He referred every minute fact to cosmical laws. Though he meant to be just, he seemed haunted by a certain chronic assumption that the science of the day pretended completeness, and he had just found out that the *savans* had neglected to discriminate a particular botanical variety, had failed to describe the seeds or count the sepals. "That is to say," we replied, "the blockheads were not born in Concord; but who said they were? It was their unspeakable misfortune to be born in London, or Paris, or Rome; but, poor fellows, they did what they could, considering that they never saw Bateman's Pond, or Nine-Acre Corner, or Becky Stow's Swamp; besides, what were you sent into the world for, but to add this observation?"

Had this genius been only contemplative, he had been fitted to his life, but with his energy and practical ability he seemed born for great enterprise and for command; and I so much regret the loss of his rare powers of action, that I cannot help counting it a fault in him that he had no ambition. Wanting this, instead of engineering for all America, he was the captain of a huckleberry-party. Pounding beans is good to the end of pounding empires one of these days; but if, at the end of years, it is still only beans!

But these foibles, real or apparent, were fast vanishing in the incessant growth of a spirit so robust and wise, and which effaced its defeats with new triumphs. His study of Nature was a perpetual ornament to him, and inspired his friends with curiosity to see the world through his eyes, and to hear his adventures. They possessed every kind of interest.

He had many elegancies of his own, whilst he scoffed at conventional elegance. Thus, he could not bear to hear the sound of his own steps, the grit of gravel; and therefore never willingly walked in the road, but in the grass, on mountains and in woods. His senses were acute, and he remarked that by night every dwelling-house gives out bad air, like a slaughter-house. He liked the pure fragrance of melilot. He honored certain plants with special regard, and, over all, the pond-lily, — then, the gentian, and the *Mikania scandens,* and "life-everlasting," and a bass-tree which he visited every year when it bloomed, in the middle of July. He thought the scent a more oracular inquisition than the sight, — more oracular and trustworthy. The scent, of course, reveals what is concealed from the other senses. By it he detected earthiness. He delighted in echoes, and said they were almost the only kind of kindred voices that he heard. He loved Nature so well, was so happy in her solitude, that he became very jealous of cities and the sad work which their refinements and artifices made with man and his dwelling.

RALPH WALDO EMERSON

The ax was always destroying his forest. "Thank God," he said, "they cannot cut down the clouds!" "All kinds of figures are drawn on the blue ground with this fibrous white paint."

I subjoin a few sentences taken from his unpublished manuscripts, not only as records of his thought and feeling, but for their power of description and literary excellence.

"Some circumstantial evidence is very strong, as when you find a trout in the milk."

"The chub is a soft fish, and tastes like boiled brown paper salted."

"The youth gets together his materials to build a bridge to the moon, or, perchance, a palace or temple on the earth, and, at length the middle-aged man concludes to build a wood-shed with them."

"The locust z-ing."

"Devil's-needles zigzagging along the Nut-Meadow brook."

"Sugar is not so sweet to the palate as sound to the healthy ear."

"I put on some hemlock-boughs, and the rich salt crackling of their leaves was like mustard to the ear, the crackling of uncountable regiments. Dead trees love the fire."

"The bluebird carries the sky on his back."

"The tanager flies through the green foliage as if it would ignite the leaves."

"If I wish for a horse-hair for my compass-sight I must go to the stable; but the hair-bird, with her sharp eyes, goes to the road."

"Immortal water, alive even to the superficies."

"Fire is the most tolerable third party."

"Nature made ferns for pure leaves, to show what she could do in that line."

"No tree has so fair a bole and so handsome an instep as the beech."

"How did these beautiful rainbow-tints get into the shell

of the fresh-water clam, buried in the mud at the bottom of our dark river?"

"Hard are the times when the infant's shoes are second-foot."

"We are strictly confined to our men to whom we give liberty."

"Nothing is so much to be feared as fear. Atheism may comparatively be popular with God himself."

"Of what significance the things you can forget? A little thought is sexton to all the world."

"How can we expect a harvest of thought who have not had a seed-time of character?"

"Only he can be trusted with gifts who can present a face of bronze to expectations."

"I ask to be melted. You can only ask of the metals that they be tender to the fire that melts them. To nought else can they be tender."

There is a flower known to botanists, one of the same genus with our summer plant called "Life-Everlasting," a *Gnaphalium* like that, which grows on the most inaccessible cliffs of the Tyrolese mountains, where the chamois dare hardly venture, and which the hunter, tempted by its beauty, and by his love (for it is immensely valued by the Swiss maidens), climbs the cliffs to gather, and is sometimes found dead at the foot, with the flower in his hand. It is called by botanists the *Gnaphalium leontopodium,* but by the Swiss *Edelweiss,* which signifies *Noble Purity.* Thoreau seemed to me living in the hope to gather this plant, which belonged to him of right. The scale on which his studies proceeded was so large as to require longevity, and we were the less prepared for his sudden disappearance. The country knows not yet, or in the least part, how great a son it has lost. It seems an injury that he should leave in the midst his broken task, which none else can finish, — a kind of indignity to so noble a soul that he should depart out of Nature before yet he has been really shown to his peers for what he is. But he, at least, is content. His soul was made for the noblest society; he had in a short life exhausted the capabilities of this world; wherever there is knowledge, wherever there is virtue, wherever there is beauty, he will find a home.

NATHANIEL HAWTHORNE

1804–1864

25 *The Custom House*

IN my native town of Salem, at the head of what, half a century ago, in the days of old King Derby, was a bustling wharf, — but which is now burdened with decayed wooden warehouses, and exhibits few or no symptoms of commercial life; except, perhaps, a bark or brig, half-way down its melancholy length, discharging hides; or, nearer at hand, a Nova Scotia schooner, pitching out her cargo of firewood, — at the head, I say, of this dilapidated wharf, which the tide often overflows, and along which, at the base and in the rear of the row of buildings, the track of many languid years is seen in a border of unthrifty grass, — here, with a view from its front windows adown this not very enlivening prospect, and thence across the harbor, stands a spacious edifice of brick. From the loftiest point of its roof, during precisely three and a half hours of each forenoon, floats or droops, in breeze or calm, the banner of the republic; but with the thirteen stripes turned vertically, instead of horizontally, and thus indicating that a civil, and not a military post of Uncle Sam's government is here established. Its front is ornamented with a portico of half a dozen wooden pillars, supporting a balcony, beneath which a flight of wide granite steps descends towards the street. Over the entrance hovers an enormous specimen of the American eagle, with outspread wings, a shield before her breast, and, if I recollect aright, a bunch of intermingled thunderbolts and barbed arrows in each claw. With the customary infirmity of temper that characterizes this unhappy fowl, she appears, by the fierceness of her beak and eye, and the general truculency of her attitude, to threaten mischief to the inoffensive community; and especially to warn all citizens, careful of their safety, against intruding on the premises which she overshadows with her wings. Nevertheless, vixenly as she looks, many people are seeking, at this very moment, to shelter themselves under the wing of the federal eagle; imagining, I presume, that her bosom has all the softness and snugness of an eider-down pillow. But she has no great tenderness, even in her best of moods, and, sooner or later, — oftener soon than late, — is apt to fling off her nestlings, with a scratch of her claw, a dab of her beak, or a rankling wound from her barbed arrows.

The pavement round about the above-described edifice — which we may as well name at once as the Custom House of the port — has grass enough growing in its chinks to show that it has not, of late days, been worn by any multitudinous resort of business. In some months of the year, however, there often chances a forenoon when affairs move onward with a livelier tread. Such occasions might remind the elderly citizen of that period before the last war with England, when Salem was a port by itself; not scorned, as she is now, by her own merchants and ship-owners, who permit her wharves to crumble to ruin, while their ventures go to swell, needlessly and imperceptibly, the mighty flood of commerce at New York or Boston. On some such morning, when three or four vessels happen to have arrived at once, — usually from Africa or South America, — or to be on the verge of their departure thitherward, there is a sound of frequent feet, passing briskly up and down the granite steps. Here, before his own wife has greeted him, you may greet the sea-flushed shipmaster, just in port, with his vessel's papers under his arm, in a tarnished tin box. Here, too, comes his owner, cheerful or somber, gracious or in the sulks, accordingly as his scheme of the now accomplished voyage has been realized in merchandise that will readily be turned to gold, or has buried him under a bulk of incommodities, such as nobody will care to rid him of. Here, likewise, — the germ of the wrinkle-browed, grizzly-bearded, care-worn merchant, — we have the smart young clerk, who gets the taste of traffic as a wolf-cub does of blood, and already sends adventures in his master's ships, when he had better be sailing mimic-boats upon a mill-pond. Another figure in the scene is the outward-bound sailor in quest of a protection; or the recently arrived one, pale and feeble, seeking a passport to the hospital. Nor must we forget the captains of the rusty little schooners that bring firewood from the British provinces; a rough-looking set of tarpaulins, without the alertness of the Yankee aspect, but contributing an item of no slight importance to our decaying trade.

Cluster all these individuals together, as they sometimes were, with other miscellaneous ones to diversify the group, and, for the time being, it made the Custom House a stirring scene. More frequently, however, on ascending the steps, you would discern — in the entry, if it were summer time, or in their appropriate rooms, if wintry or inclement weather — a row of venerable figures, sitting in old-fashioned chairs, which were tipped on their hind legs back against the wall. Oftentimes they were asleep, but occasionally might be heard talking together, in voices between speech and a snore, and with that lack of energy that distinguishes the occupants of almshouses, and all other human beings who depend for subsistence on charity, on monopolized labor, or anything else, but their own independent exertions. These old gentlemen — seated, like Matthew, at the receipt of customs, but not very liable to be summoned thence, like him, for apostolic errands — were Custom House officers.

Furthermore, on the left hand as you enter the front door, is a certain room or office, about fifteen feet square, and of a lofty height; with two of its arched windows commanding a view of the aforesaid dilapidated wharf, and the third looking across a narrow lane, and along a portion of Derby Street. All three give glimpses of the shops of grocers, blockmakers, slop-sellers, and ship-chandlers; around the doors of which are generally to be seen, laughing and gossiping, clusters of old salts, and such other wharf-rats as haunt the

Wapping of a seaport. The room itself is cobwebbed, and dingy with old paint; its floor is strewn with gray sand, in a fashion that has elsewhere fallen into long disuse; and it is easy to conclude, from the general slovenliness of the place, that this is a sanctuary into which womankind, with her tools of magic, the broom and mop, has very infrequent access. In the way of furniture, there is a stove with a voluminous funnel; an old pine desk, with a three-legged stool beside it; two or three wooden-bottom chairs, exceedingly decrepit and infirm; and — not to forget the library — on some shelves, a score or two of volumes of the Acts of Congress, and a bulky Digest of the Revenue Laws. A tin pipe ascends through the ceiling, and forms a medium of vocal communication with other parts of the edifice. And here, some six months ago, — pacing from corner to corner, or lounging on the long-legged stool, with his elbow on the desk, and his eyes wandering up and down the columns of the morning newspaper, — you might have recognized, honored reader, the same individual who welcomed you into his cheery little study, where the sunshine glimmered so pleasantly through the willow branches, on the western side of the Old Manse. But now, should you go thither to seek him, you would inquire in vain for the Locofoco Surveyor. The besom of reform has swept him out of office; and a worthier successor wears his dignity, and pockets his emoluments.

This old town of Salem — my native place, though I have dwelt much away from it, both in boyhood and maturer years — possesses, or did possess, a hold on my affections, the force of which I have never realized during my seasons of actual residence here. Indeed, so far as its physical aspect is concerned, with its flat, unvaried surface, covered chiefly with wooden houses, few or none of which pretend to architectural beauty, — its irregularity, which is neither picturesque nor quaint, but only tame, — its long and lazy street lounging wearisomely through the whole extent of the peninsula, with Gallows Hill and New Guinea at one end, and a view of the almshouse at the other, — such being the features of my native town, it would be quite as reasonable to form a sentimental attachment to a disarranged checker-board. And yet, though invariably happiest elsewhere, there is within me a feeling for old Salem, which, in lack of a better phrase, I must be content to call affection. The sentiment is probably assignable to the deep and aged roots which my family has struck into the soil. It is now nearly two centuries and a quarter since the original Briton, the earliest emigrant of my name, made his appearance in the wild and forest-bordered settlement, which has since become a city. And here his descendants have been born and died, and have mingled their earthly substance with the soil, until no small portion of it must necessarily be akin to the mortal frame wherewith, for a little while, I walk the streets. In part, therefore, the attachment which I speak of is the mere sensuous sympathy of dust for dust. Few of my countrymen can know what it is; nor, as frequent transplantation is perhaps better for the stock, need they consider it desirable to know.

But the sentiment has likewise its moral quality. The figure of that first ancestor, invested by family tradition with a dim and dusky grandeur, was present to my boyish imagination, as far back as I can remember. It still haunts me, and induces a sort of home-feeling with the past, which I scarcely claim in reference to the present phase of the town. I seem to have a stronger claim to a residence here on account of this grave, bearded, sabled-cloaked and steeple-crowned progenitor, — who came so early, with his Bible and his sword, and trode the unworn street with such a stately port, and made so large a figure, as a man of war and peace, — a stronger claim than for myself, whose name is seldom heard and my face hardly known. He was a soldier, legislator, judge; he was a ruler in the Church; he had all the Puritanic traits, both good and evil. He was likewise a bitter persecutor, as witness the Quakers, who have remembered him in their histories, and relate an incident of his hard severity towards a woman of their sect, which will last longer, it is to be feared, than any record of his better deeds, although these were many. His son, too, inherited the persecuting spirit, and made himself so conspicuous in the martyrdom of the witches, that their blood may fairly be said to have left a stain upon him. So deep a stain, indeed, that his old dry bones, in the Charter Street burial-ground, must still retain it, if they have not crumbled utterly to dust! I know not whether these ancestors of mine bethought themselves to repent, and ask pardon of Heaven for their cruelties; or whether they are now groaning under the heavy consequences of them, in another state of being. At all events, I, the present writer, as their representative, hereby take shame upon myself for their sakes, and pray that any curse incurred by them — as I have heard, and as the dreary and unprosperous condition of the race, for many a long year back, would argue to exist — may be now and henceforth removed.

Doubtless, however, either of these stern and black-browed Puritans would have thought it quite a sufficient retribution for his sins, that, after so long a lapse of years, the old trunk of the family tree, with so much venerable moss upon it, should have borne, as its topmost bough, an idler like myself. No aim, that I have ever cherished, would they recognize as laudable; no success of mine — if my life, beyond its domestic scope, had ever been brightened by success — would they deem otherwise than worthless, if not positively disgraceful. "What is he?" murmurs one gray shadow of my forefathers to the other. "A writer of story-books! What kind of a business in life, — what mode of glorifying God, or being serviceable to mankind in his day and generation, — may that be? Why, the degenerate fellow might as well have been a fiddler!" Such are the compliments bandied between my great-grandsires and myself, across the gulf of time! And yet, let them scorn me as they will, strong traits of their nature have intertwined themselves with mine.

Planted deep, in the town's earliest infancy and childhood, by these two earnest and energetic men, the race has ever since subsisted here; always, too, in respectability; never, so far as I have known, disgraced by a single unworthy member; but seldom or never, on the other hand, after the first two generations, performing any memorable deed, or so much as putting forward a claim to public notice. Gradually, they have sunk almost out of sight; as old houses, here and there about the streets, get covered half-way to the eaves by the accumulation of new soil. From father to son, for above a hundred years, they followed the sea; a gray-headed shipmaster, in each generation, retiring from the quarter-deck to the homestead, while a boy of fourteen took the hereditary place before the mast, confronting the salt spray and the gale, which had blustered against his sire and grandsire. The boy, also, in due time, passed from the forecastle to the cabin, spent a tempestuous manhood, and returned from his world-wanderings, to grow old, and die, and mingle his dust with the natal earth. This long connection of a family with one spot, as its place of birth and burial, creates a kindred between the human being and the locality, quite independent of any charm in the scenery or moral circumstances that surround him. It is not love, but instinct. The new inhabitant — who came himself from a foreign land, or whose father or grandfather came — has little claim to be called a Salemite; he has no conception of the oyster-like tenacity with which an old settler, over whom his third century is creeping, clings to the spot where his successive generations have been imbedded. It is no matter that the place is joyless for him; that he is weary of the old wooden houses, the mud and dust, the dead level of site and sentiment, the chill east wind, and the chillest of social atmospheres, — all these, and whatever faults besides he may see or imagine, are nothing to the purpose. The spell survives, and just as powerfully as if the natal spot were an earthly paradise. So has it been in my case. I felt it almost as a destiny to make Salem my home; so that the mold of features and cast of character which had all along been familiar here, — ever, as one representative of the race lay down in his grave, another assuming, as it were, his sentry-march along the main street, — might still in my little day be seen and recognized in the old town. Nevertheless, this very sentiment is an evidence that the connection, which has become an unhealthy one, should at last be severed. Human nature will not flourish, any more than a potato, if it be planted and replanted, for too long a series of generations, in the same worn-out soil. My children have had other birthplaces, and, so far as their fortunes may be within my control, shall strike their roots into unaccustomed earth.

On emerging from the Old Manse, it was chiefly this strange, indolent, unjoyous attachment for my native town, that brought me to fill a place in Uncle Sam's brick edifice, when I might as well, or better, have gone somewhere else. My doom was on me. It was not the first time, nor the second, that I had gone away, — as it seemed, permanently, — but yet returned, like the bad half-penny; or as if Salem were for me the inevitable center of the universe. So, one fine morning, I ascended the flight of granite steps, with the President's commission in my pocket, and was introduced to the corps of gentlemen who were to aid me in my weighty responsibility, as chief executive officer of the Custom House.

I doubt greatly — or, rather, I do not doubt at all — whether any public functionary of the United States, either in the civil or military line, has ever had such a patriarchal body of veterans under his orders as myself. The whereabouts of the Oldest Inhabitant was at once settled, when I looked at them. For upwards of twenty years before this epoch, the independent position of the Collector had kept the Salem Custom House out of the whirlpool of political vicissitude, which makes the tenure of office generally so fragile. A soldier, — New England's most distinguished soldier, — he stood firmly on the pedestal of his gallant services; and, himself secure in the wise liberality of the successive administrations through which he had held office, he had been the safety of his subordinates in many an hour of danger and heartquake. General Miller was radically conservative; a man over whose kindly nature habit had no slight influence;

attaching himself strongly to familiar faces, and with difficulty moved to change, even when change might have brought unquestionable improvement. Thus, on taking charge of my department, I found few but aged men. They were ancient sea-captains, for the most part, who, after being tossed on every sea, and standing up sturdily against life's tempestuous blast, had finally drifted into this quiet nook; where, with little to disturb them, except the periodical terrors of a presidential election, they one and all acquired a new lease of existence. Though by no means less liable than their fellow-men to age and infirmity, they had evidently some talisman or other that kept death at bay. Two or three of their number, as I was assured, being gouty and rheumatic, or perhaps bedridden, never dreamed of making their appearance at the Custom House during a large part of the year; but, after a torpid winter, would creep out into the warm sunshine of May or June, go lazily about what they termed duty, and, at their own leisure and convenience, betake themselves to bed again. I must plead guilty to the charge of abbreviating the official breath of more than one of these venerable servants of the republic. They were allowed, on my representation, to rest from their arduous labors, and soon afterwards — as if their sole principle of life had been zeal for their country's service, as I verily believe it was — withdrew to a better world. It is a pious consolation to me, that, through my interference, a sufficient space was allowed them for repentance of the evil and corrupt practices into which, as a matter of course, every Custom House officer must be supposed to fall. Neither the front nor the back entrance of the Custom House opens on the road to Paradise.

The greater part of my officers were Whigs. It was well for their venerable brotherhood that the new Surveyor was not a politician, and though a faithful Democrat in principle, neither received nor held his office with any reference to political services. Had it been otherwise, — had an active politician been put into this influential post, to assume the easy task of making head against a Whig Collector, whose infirmities withheld him from the personal administration of his office, — hardly a man of the old corps would have drawn the breath of official life, within a month after the exterminating angel had come up the Custom House steps. According to the received code in such matters, it would have been nothing short of duty, in a politician, to bring every one of those white heads under the ax of the guillotine. It was plain enough to discern that the old fellows dreaded some such discourtesy at my hands. It pained, and at the same time amused me, to behold the terrors that attended my advent; to see a furrowed cheek, weather-beaten by half a century of storm, turn ashy pale at the glance of so harmless an individual as myself; to detect, as one or another addressed me, the tremor of a voice, which, in long-past days, had been wont to bellow through a speaking-trumpet hoarsely enough to frighten Boreas himself to silence. They knew, these excellent old persons, that, by all established rule, — and, as regarded some of them, weighed by their own lack of efficiency for business, — they ought to have given place to younger men, more orthodox in politics, and altogether fitter than themselves to serve our common Uncle. I knew it too, but could never quite find in my heart to act upon the knowledge. Much and deservedly to my own discredit, therefore, and considerably to the detriment of my official conscience, they continued, during my incumbency, to creep about the wharves, and loiter up and down the Custom House steps. They spent a good deal of time, also, asleep in their accustomed corners, with their chairs tilted back against the wall; awaking, however, once or twice in a forenoon, to bore one another with the several thousandth repetition of old sea-stories, and moldy jokes, that had grown to be passwords and countersigns among them.

The discovery was soon made, I imagine, that the new Surveyor had no great harm in him. So, with lightsome hearts, and the happy consciousness of being usefully employed, — in their own behalf, at least, if not for our beloved country, — these good old gentlemen went through the various formalities of office. Sagaciously, under their spectacles, did they peep into the holds of vessels! Mighty was their fuss about little matters, and marvelous, sometimes, the obtuseness that allowed greater ones to slip between their fingers! Whenever such a mischance occurred, — when a wagon-load of valuable merchandise had been smuggled ashore, at noonday, perhaps, and directly beneath their unsuspicious noses, — nothing could exceed the vigilance and alacrity with which they proceeded to lock, and double-lock, and secure with tape and sealing wax, all the avenues of the delinquent vessel. Instead of a reprimand for their previous negligence, the case seemed rather to require an eulogium on their praiseworthy caution, after the mischief had happened; a grateful recognition of the promptitude of their zeal, the moment that there was no longer any remedy.

Unless people are more than commonly disagreeable, it is my foolish habit to contract a kindness for them. The better part of my companion's character, if it have a better part, is that which usually comes uppermost in my regard, and forms the type whereby I recognize the man. As most of these old Custom House officers had good traits, and as my position in reference to them, being paternal and protective, was favorable to the growth of friendly sentiments, I soon grew to like them all. It was pleasant, in the summer forenoons, — when the fervent heat, that almost liquefied the rest of the human family, merely communicated a genial warmth to their half-torpid systems, — it was pleasant to hear them chatting in the back entry, a row of them all tipped against the wall, as usual; while the frozen witticisms of past generations were thawed out, and came bubbling with laughter from their lips. Externally, the jollity of aged men has much in common with the mirth of children; the intellect, any more than a deep sense of humor, has little to do with the matter; it is, with both, a gleam that plays upon the surface, and imparts a sunny and cheery aspect alike to the green branch, and gray, moldering trunk. In one case, however, it is real sunshine; in the other, it more resembles the phosphorescent glow of decaying wood.

It would be sad injustice, the reader must understand, to represent all my excellent old friends as in their dotage. In the first place, my coadjutors were not invariably old; there were men among them in their strength and prime, of marked ability and energy, and altogether superior to the sluggish and dependent mode of life on which their evil stars had cast them. Then, moreover, the white locks of age were sometimes found to be the thatch of an intellectual tenement in good repair. But, as respects the majority of my corps of veterans, there will be no wrong done, if I characterize them generally as a set of wearisome old souls, who had gathered nothing worth preservation from their varied experience of life. They seemed to have flung away all the golden grain of practical wisdom, which they had enjoyed so many opportunities of harvesting, and most carefully to have stored their memories with the husks. They spoke with far more interest and unction of their morning's breakfast, or yesterday's, today's, or to-morrow's dinner, than of the shipwreck of forty or fifty years ago, and all the world's wonders which they had witnessed with their youthful eyes.

The father of the Custom House — the patriarch, not only of this little squad of officials, but, I am bold to say, of the respectable body of tide-waiters all over the United States — was a certain permanent Inspector. He might truly be termed a legitimate son of the revenue system, dyed in the wool, or, rather, born in the purple; since his sire, a Revolutionary colonel, and formerly collector of the port, had created an office for him, and appointed him to fill it, at a period of the early ages which few living men can now remember. This Inspector, when I first knew him, was a man of fourscore years, or thereabouts, and certainly one of the most wonderful specimens of wintergreen that you would be likely to discover in a lifetime's search. With his florid cheek, his compact figure, smartly arrayed in a bright-buttoned blue coat, his brisk and vigorous step, and his hale and hearty aspect, altogether he seemed — not young, indeed — but a kind of new contrivance of Mother Nature in the shape of man, whom age and infirmity had no business to touch. His voice and laugh, which perpetually reëchoed through the Custom House, had nothing of the tremulous quaver and cackle of an old man's utterance; they came strutting out of his lungs, like the crow of a cock, or the blast of a clarion. Looking at him merely as an animal, — and there was very little else to look at, — he was a most satisfactory object, from the thorough healthfulness and wholesomeness of his system, and his capacity, at that extreme age, to enjoy all, or nearly all, the delights which he had ever aimed at, or conceived of. The careless security of his life in the Custom House, on a regular income, and with but slight and infrequent apprehensions of removal, had no doubt contributed to make time pass lightly over him. The original and more potent causes, however, lay in the rare perfection of his animal nature, the moderate proportion of intellect, and the very trifling admixture of moral and spiritual ingredients; these latter qualities, indeed, being in barely enough measure to keep the old gentleman from walking on all-fours. He possessed no power of thought, no depth of feeling, no troublesome sensibilities; nothing, in short, but a few commonplace instincts, which, aided by the cheerful temper that grew inevitably out of his physical well-being, did duty very respectably, and to general acceptance, in lieu of a heart. He had been the husband of three wives, all long since dead; the father of twenty children, most of whom, at every age of childhood or maturity, had likewise returned to dust. Here, one would suppose, might have been sorrow enough to imbue the sunniest disposition, through and through, with a sable tinge. Not so with our old Inspector! One brief sigh sufficed to carry off the entire burden of these dismal reminiscences. The next moment, he was as ready for sport as any unbreeched infant; far readier than the Collector's junior clerk, who, at nineteen years, was much the elder and graver man of the two.

I used to watch and study this patriarchal personage with, I think, livelier curiosity, than any other form of humanity there presented to my notice. He was, in truth, a rare phenomenon; so perfect, in one point of view; so shallow, so delusive, so impalpable, such an absolute nonentity, in every other. My conclusion was that he had no soul, no heart, no mind; nothing, as I have already said, but instincts; and yet, withal, so cunningly had the few materials of his character been put together, that there was no painful perception of deficiency, but, on my part, an entire contentment with what I found in him. It might be difficult — and it was so — to conceive how he should exist hereafter, so earthly and sensuous did he seem; but surely his existence here, admitting that it was to terminate with his last breath, had been not unkindly given; with no higher moral responsibilities than the beasts of the field, but with a larger scope of enjoyment than theirs, and with all their blessed immunity from the dreariness and duskiness of age.

One point, in which he had vastly the advantage over his four-footed brethren, was his ability to recollect the good dinners which it had made no small portion of the happiness of his life to eat. His gourmandism was a highly agreeable trait; and to hear him talk of roast meat was as appetizing as a pickle or an oyster. As he possessed no higher attribute, and neither sacrificed nor vitiated any spiritual endowment by devoting all his energies and ingenuities to subserve the delight and profit of his maw, it always pleased and satisfied me to hear him expatiate on fish, poultry, and butcher's meat, and the most eligible methods of preparing them for the table. His reminiscences of good cheer, however ancient the date of the actual banquet, seemed to bring the savor of pig or turkey under one's very nostrils. There were flavors on his palate, that had lingered there not less than sixty or seventy years, and were still apparently as fresh as that of the mutton-chop which he had just devoured for his breakfast. I have heard him smack his lips over dinners, every guest at which, except himself, had long been food for worms.

It was marvelous to observe how the ghosts of bygone meals were continually rising up before him; not in anger or retribution, but as if grateful for his former appreciation and seeking to reduplicate an endless series of enjoyment, at once shadowy and sensual. A tenderloin of beef, a hindquarter of veal, a sparerib of pork, a particular chicken, or a remarkably praiseworthy turkey, which had perhaps adorned his board in the days of the elder Adams, would be remembered; while all the subsequent experience of our race, and all the events that brightened or darkened his individual career, had gone over him with as little permanent effect as the passing breeze. The chief tragic event of the old man's life, so far as I could judge, was his mishap with a certain goose which lived and died some twenty or forty years ago; a goose of most promising figure, but which, at table, proved so inveterately tough that the carving-knife would make no impression on its carcass, and it could only be divided with an ax and handsaw.

But it is time to quit this sketch; on which, however, I should be glad to dwell at considerably more length, because, of all men whom I have ever known, this individual was fittest to be a Custom House officer. Most persons, owing to causes which I may not have space to hint at, suffer moral detriment from this peculiar mode of life. The old Inspector was incapable of it, and, were he to continue in office to the end of time, would be just as good as he was then, and sit down to dinner with just as good an appetite.

There is one likeness, without which my gallery of Custom House portraits would be strangely incomplete; but which my comparatively few opportunities for observation enable me to sketch only in the merest outline. It is that of the Collector, our gallant old General, who, after his brilliant military service, subsequently to which he had ruled over a wild Western territory, had come hither, twenty years before, to spend the decline of his varied and honorable life. The brave soldier had already numbered, nearly or quite, his threescore years and ten, and was pursuing the remainder of his earthly march, burdened with infirmities which even the martial music of his own spirit-stirring recollections could do little towards lightening. The step was palsied now that had been foremost in the charge. It was only with the assistance of a servant, and by leaning his hand heavily on the iron balustrade, that he could slowly and painfully ascend the Custom House steps, and, with a toilsome progress across the floor, attain his customary chair beside the fireplace. There he used to sit, gazing with a somewhat dim serenity of aspect at the figures that came and went; amid the rustle of papers, the administering of oaths, the discussion of business, and the casual talk of the office; all which sounds and circumstances seemed but indistinctly to impress his senses, and hardly to make their way into his inner sphere of contemplation. His countenance, in this repose, was mild and kindly. If his notice was sought, an expression of courtesy and interest gleamed out upon his features; proving that there was light within him, and that it was only the outward medium of the intellectual lamp that obstructed the rays in their passage. The closer you penetrated to the substance of his mind, the sounder it appeared. When no longer called upon to speak, or listen, either of which operations cost him an evident effort, his face would briefly subside into its former not uncheerful quietude. It was not painful to behold this look; for, though dim, it had not the imbecility of decaying age. The framework of his nature, originally strong and massive, was not yet crumbled into ruin.

To observe and define his character, however, under such disadvantages, was as difficult a task as to trace out and build up anew, in imagination, an old fortress, like Ticonderoga, from a view of its gray and broken ruins. Here and there, perchance, the walls may remain almost complete, but elsewhere may be only a shapeless mound, cumbrous with its very strength, and overgrown, through long years of peace and neglect, with grass and alien weeds.

Nevertheless, looking at the old warrior with affection, —

for, slight as was the communication between us, my feeling towards him, like that of all bipeds and quadrupeds who knew him, might not improperly be termed so, — I could discern the main points of his portrait. It was marked with the noble and heroic qualities which showed it to be not by a mere accident, but of good right, that he had won a distinguished name. His spirit could never, I conceive, have been characterized by an uneasy activity; it must, at any period of his life, have required an impulse to set him in motion; but, once stirred up, with obstacles to overcome, and an adequate object to be attained, it was not in the man to give out or fail. The heat that had formerly pervaded his nature, and which was not yet extinct, was never of the kind that flashes and flickers in a blaze; but, rather, a deep, red glow, as of iron in a furnace. Weight, solidity, firmness; this was the expression of his repose, even in such decay as had crept untimely over him, at the period of which I speak. But I could imagine, even then, that under some excitement which should go deeply into his consciousness, — roused by a trumpet-peal loud enough to awaken all his energies that were not dead, but only slumbering, — he was yet capable of flinging off his infirmities like a sick man's gown, dropping the staff of age to seize a battle-sword, and starting up once more a warrior. And, in so intense a moment, his demeanor would have still been calm. Such an exhibition, however, was but to be pictured in fancy; not to be anticipated, nor desired. What I saw in him — as evidently as the indestructible ramparts of Old Ticonderoga already cited as the most appropriate simile — were the features of stubborn and ponderous endurance, which might well have amounted to obstinacy in his earlier days; of integrity, that, like most of his other endowments, lay in a somewhat heavy mass, and was just as unmalleable and unmanageable as a ton of iron ore; and of benevolence, which, fiercely as he led the bayonets on at Chippewa or Fort Erie, I take to be of quite as genuine a stamp as what actuates any or all the polemical philanthropists of the age. He had slain men with his own hand for aught I know, — certainly they had fallen, like blades of grass at the sweep of the scythe, before the charge to which his spirit imparted its triumphant energy; but, be that as it might, there was never in his heart so much cruelty as would have brushed the down off a butterfly's wing. I have not known the man, to whose innate kindliness I would more confidently make an appeal.

Many characteristics — and those, too, which contribute not the least forcibly to impart resemblance in a sketch — must have vanished, or been obscured, before I met the General. All merely graceful attributes are usually the most evanescent; nor does Nature adorn the human ruin with blossoms of new beauty that have their roots and proper nutriment only in the chinks and crevices of decay, as she sows wall-flowers over the ruined fortress of Ticonderoga. Still, even in respect of grace and beauty, there were points well worth noting. A ray of humor, now and then, would make its way through the veil of dim obstruction, and glimmer pleasantly upon our faces. A trait of native elegance, seldom seen in the masculine character after childhood or early youth, was shown in the General's fondness for the sight and fragrance of flowers. An old soldier might be supposed to prize only the bloody laurel on his brow; but here was one who seemed to have a young girl's appreciation of the floral tribe.

There, beside the fireplace, the brave old General used to sit; while the Surveyor — though seldom, when it could be avoided, taking upon himself the difficult task of engaging him in conversation — was fond of standing at a distance, and watching his quiet and almost slumberous countenance. He seemed away from us, although we saw him but a few yards off; remote, though we passed close beside his chair; unattainable, though we might have stretched forth our hands and touched his own. It might be that he lived a more real life within his thoughts than amid the unappropriate environment of the Collector's office. The evolutions of the parade; the tumult of the battle; the flourish of old, heroic music, heard thirty years before, — such scenes and sounds, perhaps, were all alive before his intellectual sense. Meanwhile, the merchants and shipmasters, the spruce clerks and uncouth sailors, entered and departed; the bustle of this commercial and Custom House life kept up its little murmur round about him; and neither with the men nor their affairs did the General appear to sustain the most distant relation. He was as much out of place as an old sword — now rusty, but which had flashed once in the battle's front, and showed still a bright gleam along its blade — would have been, among the inkstands, paper-folders, and mahogany rulers, on the Deputy Collector's desk.

There was one thing that much aided me in renewing and re-creating the stalwart soldier of the Niagara frontier, — the man of true and simple energy. It was the recollection of those memorable words of his, — "I'll try, Sir!" — spoken on the very verge of a desperate and heroic enterprise, and breathing the soul and spirit of New England hardihood, comprehending all perils, and encountering all. If, in our country, valor were rewarded by heraldic honor, this phrase — which it seems so easy to speak, but which only he, with such a task of danger and glory before him, has ever spoken — would be the best and fittest of all mottoes for the General's shield of arms.

It contributes greatly towards a man's moral and intellectual health, to be brought into habits of companionship with individuals unlike himself, who care little for his pursuits, and whose sphere and abilities he must go out of himself to appreciate. The accidents of my life have often afforded me this advantage, but never with more fullness and variety than during my continuance in office. There was one man, especially, the observation of whose character gave me a new idea of talent. His gifts were emphatically those of a man of business; prompt, acute, clear-minded; with an eye that saw through all perplexities, and a faculty of arrangement that made them vanish, as by the waving of an enchanter's wand. Bred up from boyhood in the Custom

House, it was his proper field of activity; and the many intricacies of business, so harassing to the interloper, presented themselves before him with the regularity of a perfectly comprehended system. In my contemplation, he stood as the ideal of his class. He was, indeed, the Custom House in himself, or, at all events, the mainspring that kept its variously revolving wheels in motion; for, in an institution like this, where its officers are appointed to subserve their own profit and convenience, and seldom with a leading reference to their fitness for the duty to be performed, they must perforce seek elsewhere the dexterity which is not in them. Thus, by an inevitable necessity, as a magnet attracts steel-filings, so did our man of business draw to himself the difficulties which everybody met with. With an easy condescension, and kind forbearance towards our stupidity, — which, to his order of mind, must have seemed little short of crime, — would he forthwith, by the merest touch of his finger, make the incomprehensible as clear as daylight. The merchants valued him not less than we, his esoteric friends. His integrity was perfect: it was a law of nature with him, rather than a choice or a principle; nor can it be otherwise than the main condition of an intellect so remarkably clear and accurate as his, to be honest and regular in the administration of affairs. A stain on his conscience, as to anything that came within the range of his vocation, would trouble such a man very much in the same way, though to a far greater degree, than an error in the balance of an account, or an ink-blot on the fair page of a book of record. Here, in a word, — and it is a rare instance in my life, — I had met with a person thoroughly adapted to the situation which he held.

Such were some of the people with whom I now found myself connected. I took it in good part, at the hands of Providence, that I was thrown into a position so little akin to my past habits, and set myself seriously to gather from it whatever profit was to be had. After my fellowship of toil and impracticable schemes with the dreamy brethren of

Brook Farm; after living for three years within the subtile influence of an intellect like Emerson's; after those wild, free days on the Assabeth, indulging fantastic speculations, beside our fire of fallen boughs, with Ellery Channing; after talking with Thoreau about pine-trees and Indian relics, in his hermitage at Walden; after growing fastidious by sympathy with the classic refinement of Hillard's culture; after becoming imbued with poetic sentiment at Longfellow's hearth-stone, — it was time, at length, that I should exercise other faculties of my nature, and nourish myself with food for which I had hitherto had little appetite. Even the old Inspector was desirable, as a change of diet, to a man who had known Alcott. I look upon it as an evidence, in some measure, of a system naturally well balanced, and lacking no essential part of a thorough organization, that, with such associates to remember, I could mingle at once with men of altogether different qualities, and never murmur at the change.

EDGAR ALLAN POE

1809–1849

26 *William Wilson*

What say of it? what says CONSCIENCE grim,
That spectre in my path?
W. Chamberlayne's Pharonnida

LET me call myself for the present, William Wilson. The fair page now lying before me need not be sullied with my real appellation. This has been already too much an object for the scorn, for the horror, for the detestation of my race. To the uttermost regions of the globe have not the indignant winds bruited its unparalleled infamy? Oh, outcast of all outcasts most abandoned! to the earth art thou not forever dead? to its honors, to its flowers, to its golden aspirations? — and a cloud, dense, dismal, and limitless, does it not hang eternally between thy hopes and heaven?

I would not, if I could, here or to-day, embody a record of my later years of unspeakable misery, and unpardonable crime. This epoch — these later years — took unto themselves a sudden elevation in turpitude, whose origin alone it is my present purpose to assign. Men usually grow base by degrees. From me in an instant all virtue dropped bodily as a mantle. From comparatively trivial wickedness I passed, with the stride of a giant, into more than the enormities of an Elagabalus. What chance — what one event brought this evil thing to pass, bear with me while I relate. Death approaches; and the shadow which foreruns him has thrown a softening influence over my spirit. I long, in passing through the dim valley, for the sympathy, — I had nearly said for the pity, — of my fellow-men. I would fain have them believe that I have been in some measure the slave of circumstances beyond human control. I would wish them to seek out for me, in the details I am about to give, some little oasis of *fatality* amid a wilderness of error. I would have them allow — what they cannot refrain from allowing — that although temptation may have erewhile existed as great, man was never *thus,* at least, tempted before, certainly never *thus* fell. And is it therefore that he has never thus suffered? Have I not indeed been living in a dream? And am I not now dying a victim to the horror and the mystery of the wildest of all sublunary visions?

I am the descendant of a race whose imaginative and easily excitable temperament has at all times rendered them remarkable; and in my earliest infancy I gave evidence of having fully inherited the family character. As I advanced in years it was more strongly developed, becoming for many reasons a cause of serious disquietude to my friends, and of positive injury to myself. I grew self-willed, addicted to the wildest caprices, and a prey to the most ungovernable passions. Weak-minded, and beset with constitutional infirmities akin to my own, my parents could do but little to check the evil propensities which distinguished me. Some feeble and ill-directed efforts resulted in complete failure on their part, and of course in total triumph on mine. Thenceforward my voice was a household law; and at an age when few children have abandoned their leading-strings, I was left to the guidance of my own will, and became in all but name the master of my own actions.

My earliest recollections of a school-life are connected with a large rambling Elizabethan house, in a misty-looking village of England, where were a vast number of gigantic and gnarled trees, and where all the houses were excessively ancient. In truth, it was a dream-like and spirit-soothing place, that venerable old town. At this moment, in fancy, I feel the refreshing chilliness of its deeply-shadowed avenues, inhale the fragrance of its thousand shrubberies, and thrill anew with indefinable delight at the deep hollow note of the church-bell, breaking each hour with sullen and sudden roar upon the stillness of the dusky atmosphere in which the fretted Gothic steeple lay imbedded and asleep.

It gives me perhaps as much of pleasure as I can now in any manner experience to dwell upon minute recollections of the school and its concerns. Steeped in misery as I am — misery, alas! only too real — I shall be pardoned for seeking relief, however slight and temporary, in the weakness of a few rambling details. These, moreover, utterly trivial, and even ridiculous in themselves, assume to my fancy adventitious importance, as connected with a period and a locality when and where I recognize the first ambiguous monitions of the destiny which afterwards so fully overshadowed me. Let me then remember.

The house, I have said, was old and irregular. The grounds were extensive, and a high and solid brick wall, topped with a bed of mortar and broken glass, encompassed the whole. This prison-like rampart formed the limit of our domain: beyond it we saw but thrice a week, — once every Saturday afternoon, when, attended by two ushers, we were permitted to take brief walks in a body through some of the neighboring fields; and twice during Sunday, when we were paraded in the same formal manner to the morning and evening service in the one church of the village. Of this church the principal of our school was pastor. With how deep a spirit of wonder and perplexity was I wont to regard him from our remote pew in the gallery, as with step solemn and slow he ascended the pulpit! This reverend man, with countenance so demurely benign, with robes so glossy and so clerically flowing, with wig so minutely powdered, so rigid and so vast — could this be he who, of late, with sour visage, and in snuffy habiliments, administered, ferule in hand, the Draconian laws of the academy? Oh, gigantic paradox, too utterly monstrous for solution!

At an angle of the ponderous wall frowned a more ponderous gate. It was riveted and studded with iron bolts, and surmounted with jagged iron spikes. What impressions of deep awe did it inspire! It was never opened save for the three periodical egressions and ingressions already mentioned; then in every creak of its mighty hinges we found a plenitude of mystery, a world of matter for solemn remark, or for more solemn meditation.

The extensive enclosure was irregular in form, having many capacious recesses. Of these, three or four of the largest constituted the play-ground. It was level, and covered with fine hard gravel. I well remembered it had no trees nor benches, nor anything similar within it. Of course it was in the rear of the house. In front lay a small parterre, planted with box and other shrubs; but through this sacred division we passed only upon rare occasions indeed — such as a first advent to school or final departure thence, or perhaps, when a parent or friend having called for us, we joyfully took our way home for the Christmas or Midsummer holidays.

But the house! — how quaint an old building was this! to me how veritably a palace of enchantment! There was really no end to its windings — to its incomprehensible subdivisions. It was difficult, at any given time, to say with certainty upon which of its two stories one happened to be. From each room to every other there were sure to be found three or four steps either in ascent or descent. Then the lateral branches were innumerable, inconceivable, and so returning in upon themselves that our most exact ideas in regard to the whole mansion were not very far different from those with which we pondered upon infinity. During the five years of my residence here I was never able to ascertain with precision in what remote locality lay the little apartment assigned to myself and some eighteen or twenty other scholars.

The school-room was the largest in the house — I could not help thinking, in the world. It was very long, narrow, and dismally low, with pointed Gothic windows and a ceiling of oak. In a remote and terror-inspiring angle was a square enclosure of eight or ten feet, comprising the *sanctum,* "during hours," of our principal, the Reverend Dr. Bransby. It was a solid structure, with massy door, sooner than open which in the absence of the "dominie" we would all have willingly perished by the *peine forte et dure*. In other angles were two other similar boxes, far less reverenced, indeed, but still greatly matters of awe. One of these was the pulpit of the "classical" usher, one of the "English and mathematical." Interspersed about the room, crossing and recrossing in endless irregularity, were innumerable benches and desks, black, ancient, and time-worn, piled desperately with much-bethumbed books, and so beseamed with initial letters, names at full length, grotesque figures, and other multiplied efforts of the knife, as to have entirely lost what little of original form might have been their portion in days long departed. A huge bucket with water stood at one extremity of the room, and a clock of stupendous dimensions at the other.

Encompassed by the massy walls of this venerable academy, I passed, yet not in a tedium or disgust, the years of the third lustrum of my life. The teeming brain of childhood requires no external world of incident to occupy or amuse it; and the apparently dismal monotony of a school was replete with more intense excitement than my riper youth has derived from luxury, or my full manhood from crime. Yet I must believe that my first mental development had in it much of the uncommon — even much of the *outré*. Upon mankind at large the events of very early existence rarely leave in mature age any definite impression. All is gray shadow — a weak and irregular remembrance — an indistinct regathering of feeble pleasures and phantasmagoric pains. With me this is not so. In childhood I must have felt with the energy of a man what I now find stamped upon memory in lines as vivid, as deep, and as durable as the *exergues* of the Carthaginian medals.

Yet in fact — in the fact of the world's view — how little was there to remember! The morning's awakening, the nightly summons to bed; the connings, the recitations; the periodical half-holidays, and perambulations; the playground, with its broils, its pastimes, its intrigues; — these, by a mental sorcery long forgotten, were made to involve a wilderness of sensation, a world of rich incident, an universe of varied emotion, of excitement the most passionate and spirit-stirring. *"O le bon temps, que ce siècle de fer!"*

In truth, the ardor, the enthusiasm, and the imperiousness of my disposition, soon rendered me a marked character among my schoolmates, and by slow but natural gradations gave me an ascendancy over all not greatly older than myself; — over all with a single exception. This exception was found in the person of a scholar, who, although no relation, bore the same Christian and surname as myself; — a circumstance, in fact, little remarkable; for notwithstanding a noble descent, mine was one of those every-day appellations which seem, by prescriptive right, to have been, time out of mind, the common property of the mob. In this narrative I have therefore designated myself as William Wilson — a fictitious title not very dissimilar to the real. My namesake alone of those who in school phraseology constituted "our set," presumed to compete with me in the studies of the class — in the sports and broils of the playground — to refuse implicit belief in my assertions, and submission to my will—indeed, to interfere with my arbitrary dictation in any respect whatsoever. If there is on earth a supreme and unqualified despotism, it is the despotism of a master-mind in boyhood over the less energetic spirits of its companions.

Wilson's rebellion was to me a source of the greatest embarrassment: the more so as, in spite of the bravado with which in public I made a point of treating him and his pretensions, I secretly felt that I feared him, and could not help thinking the equality which he maintained so easily with myself a proof of his true superiority, since not to be overcome cost me a perpetual struggle. Yet this superiority —even this equality—was in truth acknowledged by no one but myself; our associates, by some unaccountable blindness, seemed not even to suspect it. Indeed, his competition, his resistance, and especially his impertinent and dogged interference with my purposes were not more pointed than private. He appeared to be destitute alike of the ambition which urged, and of the passionate energy of mind which enabled me to excel. In his rivalry he might have been supposed actuated solely by a whimsical desire to thwart, astonish, or mortify myself; although there were times when I could not help observing, with a feeling made up of wonder, abasement, and pique, that he mingled with his injuries, his insults, or his contradictions, a certain most inappropriate, and assuredly most unwelcome *affectionateness* of manner. I could only conceive this singular behavior to arise from a consummate self-conceit assuming the vulgar airs of patronage and protection.

Perhaps it was this latter trait in Wilson's conduct, conjoined with our identity of name, and the mere accident of our having entered the school upon the same day, which set afloat the notion that we were brothers among the senior classes in the academy. These do not usually inquire with much strictness into the affairs of their juniors. I have before said, or should have said, that Wilson was not, in the most remote degree, connected with my family. But assuredly if we *had* been brothers we must have been twins; for, after leaving Dr. Bransby's, I casually learned that my namesake was born on the nineteenth of January, 1813 — and this is a somewhat remarkable coincidence, for the day is precisely that of my own nativity.

It may seem strange that, in spite of the continual anxiety occasioned me by the rivalry of Wilson, and his intolerable spirit of contradiction, I could not bring myself to hate him altogether. We had, to be sure, nearly every day a quarrel, in which, yielding me publicly the palm of victory, he in some manner contrived to make me feel that it was he who had deserved it, yet a sense of pride on my part and a veritable dignity on his own, kept us always upon what are called "speaking terms," while there were many points of strong congeniality in our tempers, operating to awake in me a sentiment which our position alone, perhaps, prevented from ripening into friendship. It is difficult indeed to define or even to describe my real feelings towards him. They formed a motley and heterogeneous admixture; some petulant animosity, which was not yet hatred, some esteem, more respect, much fear, with a world of uneasy curiosity. To the moralist it will be unnecessary to say in addition that Wilson and myself were the most inseparable of companions.

It was no doubt the anomalous state of affairs existing between us which turned all my attacks upon him (and they were many, either open or covert) into the channel of banter or practical joke (giving pain while assuming the aspect of mere fun), rather than into a more serious and determined hostility. But my endeavors on this head were by no means uniformly successful, even when my plans were the most wittily concocted; for my namesake had much about him in character of that unassuming and quiet austerity which, while enjoying the poignancy of its own jokes, has no heel of Achilles in itself, and absolutely refuses to be laughed at. I could find indeed but one vulnerable point, and that lying in a personal peculiarity, arising perhaps from constitutional disease, would have been spared by any antagonist less at his wit's end than myself; my rival had a weakness in the faucial or guttural organs which precluded him from raising his voice at any time *above a very low whisper*. Of this defect I did not fail to take what poor advantage lay in my power.

Wilson's retaliations in kind were many; and there was one form of his practical wit that disturbed me beyond measure. How his sagacity first discovered at all that so petty a thing would vex me is a question I never could solve, but having discovered, he habitually practised the annoyance. I had always felt aversion to my uncourtly patronymic and its very common, if not plebeian prænomen. The words were venom in my ears; and when, upon the day of my arrival, a second William Wilson came also to the academy, I felt angry with him for bearing the name, and doubly disgusted with the name because a stranger bore it, who would be the cause of its twofold repetition, who would be constantly in my presence, and whose concerns, in the ordinary routine of the school business, must inevitably, on account of the detestable coincidence, be often confounded with my own.

The feeling of vexation thus engendered grew stronger with every circumstance tending to show resemblance, moral or physical, between my rival and myself. I had not then discovered the remarkable fact that we were of the same age; but I saw that we were of the same height, and I perceived that we were even singularly alike in general contour of person and outline of feature. I was galled, too, by the rumor touching a relationship, which had grown current in the upper forms. In a word, nothing could more seriously disturb me (although I scrupulously concealed such disturbance), than any allusion to a similarity of mind, person, or condition existing between us. But, in truth, I had no reason to believe that (with the exception of the matter of relationship, and in the case of Wilson himself) this similarity had ever been made a subject of comment or even observed at all by our schoolfellows. That *he* observed it in all its bearings, and as fixedly as I, was apparent; but that he could discover in such circumstances so fruitful a field of annoyance can only be attributed, as I said before, to his more than ordinary penetration.

His cue, which was to perfect an imitation of myself, lay both in words and in actions, and most admirably did he play his part. My dress it was an easy matter to copy; my gait and general manner were without difficulty appropriated; in spite of his constitutional defect, even my voice did not escape him. My louder tones were of course unattempted, but then the key, it was identical; *and his singular whisper, it grew the very echo of my own.*

How greatly this most exquisite portraiture harassed me (for it could not justly be termed a caricature), I will not now venture to describe. I had but one consolation — in the fact that the imitation, apparently, was noticed by myself alone, and that I had to endure only the knowing and strangely sarcastic smiles of my namesake himself. Satisfied with having produced in my bosom the intended effect he seemed to chuckle in secret over the sting he had inflicted, and was characteristically disregardful of the public applause which the success of his witty endeavors might have so easily elicited. That the school, indeed, did not feel his design, perceive its accomplishment, and participate in his sneer, was for many anxious months a riddle I could not resolve. Perhaps the *gradation* of his copy rendered it not so readily perceptible, or more possibly I owed my security to the masterly air of the copyist, who, disdaining the letter (which in a painting is all the obtuse can see), gave but the full spirit of his original for my individual contemplation and chagrin.

I have already more than once spoken of the disgusting air of patronage which he assumed toward me, and of his frequent officious interference with my will. This interference often took the ungracious character of advice — advice not openly given but hinted or insinuated. I received it with a repugnance which gained strength as I grew in

years. Yet at this distant day, let me do him the simple
justice to acknowledge that I can recall no occasion when
the suggestions of my rival were on the side of those errors
or follies so usual to his immature age and seeming inexperience; that his moral sense, at least, if not his general
talents and worldly wisdom, was far keener than my own;
and that I might to-day have been a better, and thus a
happier man, had I less frequently rejected the counsels
embodied in those meaning whispers which I then but too
cordially hated and too bitterly despised.

As it was, I at length grew restive in the extreme under
his distasteful supervision, and daily resented more and
more openly what I considered his intolerable arrogance. I
have said that in the first years of our connection as schoolmates, my feelings in regard to him might have been easily
ripened into friendship; but, in the latter months of my
residence at the academy, although the intrusion of his
ordinary manner had, beyond doubt, in some measure
abated, my sentiments in nearly similar proportion partook
very much of positive hatred. Upon one occasion he saw
this, I think, and afterwards avoided, or made a show of
avoiding me.

It was about the same period, if I remember aright, that,
in an altercation of violence with him, in which he was
more than usually thrown off his guard, and spoke and
acted with an openness of demeanor rather foreign to his
nature, I discovered, or fancied I discovered, in his accent,
his air, and general appearance, a something which first
startled, and then deeply interested me, by bringing to mind
dim visions of my earliest infancy — wild, confused, and
thronging memories of a time when memory herself was yet
unborn. I cannot better describe the sensation which oppressed me than by saying that I could with difficulty shake
off the belief of my having been acquainted with the being
who stood before me at some epoch very long ago — some
point of the past even infinitely remote. The delusion, however, faded rapidly as it came, and I mention it at all but to

define the day of the last conversation I there held with my singular namesake.

The huge old house, with its countless subdivisions, had several large chambers communicating with each other, where slept the greater number of the students. There were, however (as must necessarily happen in a building so awkwardly planned), many little nooks or recesses, the odds and ends of the structure; and these the economic ingenuity of Dr. Bransby had also fitted up as dormitories; although, being the merest closets, they were capable of accommodating but a single individual. One of these small apartments was occupied by Wilson.

One night, about the close of my fifth year at the school, and immediately after the altercation just mentioned, finding everyone wrapped in sleep, I arose from bed, and, lamp in hand, stole through a wilderness of narrow passages from my own bedroom to that of my rival. I had long been plotting one of those ill-natured pieces of practical wit at his expense in which I had hitherto been so uniformly unsuccessful. It was my intention now to put my scheme in operation, and I resolved to make him feel the whole extent of the malice with which I was imbued. Having reached his closet I noiselessly entered, leaving the lamp, with a shade over it, on the outside. I advanced a step and listened to the sound of his tranquil breathing. Assured of his being asleep, I returned, took the light, and with it again approached the bed. Close curtains were around it, which, in the prosecution of my plan, I slowly and quietly withdrew, when the bright rays fell vividly upon the sleeper, and my eyes, at the same moment, upon his countenance. I looked; — and a numbness, an iciness of feeling, instantly pervaded my frame. My breast heaved, my knees tottered, my whole spirit became possessed with an objectless yet intolerable horror. Gasping for breath I lowered the lamp in still nearer proximity to the face. Were these — *these* the lineaments of William Wilson? I saw, indeed, that they were his, but I shook as if with a fit of the ague in fancying they were not. What *was* there about them to confound me in this manner? I gazed; — while my brain reeled with a multitude of incoherent thoughts. Not thus he appeared — assuredly not *thus* — in the vivacity of his waking hours. The same name! the same contour of person! the same day of arrival at the academy! And then his dogged and meaningless imitation of my gait, my voice, my habits, and my manner! Was it, in truth, within the bounds of human possibility that *what I now saw was* the result merely of the habitual practice of this sarcastic imitation? Awe-stricken, and with a creeping shudder, I extinguished the lamp, passed silently from the chamber, and left at once the halls of that old academy, never to enter them again.

After a lapse of some months, spent at home in mere idleness, I found myself a student at Eton. The brief interval had been sufficient to enfeeble my remembrance of the events at Dr. Bransby's, or at least to effect a material change in the nature of the feelings with which I remembered them. The truth, the tragedy, of the drama was no more. I could now find room to doubt the evidence of my senses, and seldom called up the subject at all but with wonder at the extent of human credulity, and a smile at the vivid force of the imagination which I hereditarily possessed. Neither was this species of skepticism likely to be diminished by the character of the life I led at Eton. The vortex of thoughtless folly into which I there so immediately and so recklessly plunged washed away all but the froth of my past hours, engulfed at once every solid or serious impression, and left to memory only the veriest levities of a former existence.

I do not wish, however, to trace the course of my miserable profligacy here — a profligacy which set at defiance the laws, while it eluded the vigilance of the institution. Three years of folly, passed without profit, had but given me rooted habits of vice, and added, in a somewhat unusual degree, to my bodily stature, when, after a week of soulless dissipation, I invited a small party of the most dissolute students to a secret carousal in my chambers. We met at a late hour of the night, for our debaucheries were to be faithfully protracted until morning. The wine flowed freely, and there were not wanting other and perhaps more dangerous seductions, so that the gray dawn had already faintly appeared in the east, while our delirious extravagance was at its height. Madly flushed with cards and intoxication, I was in the act of insisting upon a toast of more than wanted profanity when my attention was suddenly diverted by the violent, although partial, unclosing of the door of the apartment, and by the eager voice of a servant from without. He said that some person, apparently in great haste, demanded to speak with me in the hall.

Wildly excited with wine, the unexpected interruption rather delighted than surprised me. I staggered forward at once, and a few steps brought me to the vestibule of the building. In this low and small room there hung no lamp, and now no light at all was admitted, save that of the exceedingly feeble dawn which made its way through the semicircular window. As I put my foot over the threshold I became aware of the figure of a youth about my own height, and habited in a white kerseymere morning frock, cut in the novel fashion of the one I myself wore at the moment. This the faint light enabled me to perceive, but the features of his face I could not distinguish. Upon my entering he strode hurriedly up to me, and seizing me by the arm with a gesture of petulant impatience, whispered the words "William Wilson!" in my ear.

I grew perfectly sober in an instant.

There was that in the manner of the stranger, and in the tremulous shake of his uplifted finger, as he held it between my eyes and the light, which filled me with unqualified amazement; but it was not this which had so violently moved me. It was the pregnancy of solemn admonition in the singular, low, hissing utterance, and, above all, it was the character, the tone, *the key,* of those few, simple, and familiar, yet *whispered* syllables, which came with a thousand thronging memories of bygone days and struck upon my soul with the shock of a galvanic battery. Ere I could recover the use of my senses he was gone.

Although this event failed not of a vivid effect upon my disordered imagination, yet was it evanescent as vivid. For some weeks, indeed, I busied myself in earnest inquiry, or was wrapped in a cloud of morbid speculation. I did not pretend to disguise from my perception the identity of the singular individual who thus perseveringly interfered with my affairs, and harassed me with his insinuated counsel. But who and what was this Wilson? — and whence came he? — and what were his purposes? Upon neither of these points could I be satisfied — merely ascertaining in regard to him, that a sudden accident in his family had caused his removal from Dr. Bransby's academy on the afternoon of the day in which I myself had eloped. But in a brief period I ceased to think upon the subject, my attention being all absorbed in a contemplated departure for Oxford. Thither I soon went, the uncalculating vanity of my parents furnishing me with an outfit and annual establishment which would enable me to indulge at will in the luxury already so dear to my heart — to vie in profuseness of expenditure with the haughtiest heirs of the wealthiest earldoms in Great Britain.

Excited by such appliances to vice, my constitutional temperament broke forth with redoubled ardor, and I spurned even the common restraints of decency in the mad infatuation of my revels. But it were absurd to pause in the detail of my extravagance. Let it suffice, that among spendthrifts I out-Heroded Herod, and that giving name to a multitude of novel follies, I added no brief appendix to the long catalogue of vices then usual in the most dissolute university of Europe.

It could hardly be credited, however, that I had, even here, so utterly fallen from the gentlemanly estate as to seek acquaintance with the vilest arts of the gambler by profession, and having become an adept in his despicable science, to practice it habitually as a means of increasing my already enormous income at the expense of the weak-minded among my fellow-collegians. Such, nevertheless, was the fact; and the very enormity of this offense against all manly and honorable sentiment proved, beyond doubt, the main, if not the sole reason of the impunity with which it was committed. Who, indeed, among my most abandoned associates would not rather have disputed the clearest evidence of his senses than have suspected of such courses the gay, the frank, the generous William Wilson — the noblest and most liberal commoner at Oxford — him whose follies (said his parasites) were but the follies of youth and unbridled fancy — whose errors but inimitable whim — whose darkest vice but a careless and dashing extravagance?

I had been now two years successfully busied in this way when there came to the university a young *parvenu* nobleman, Glendinning — rich, said report, as Herodes Atticus — his riches, too, as easily acquired. I soon found him of weak intellect, and of course marked him as a fitting subject for my skill. I frequently engaged him in play, and contrived with the gambler's usual art to let him win considerable sums, the more effectually to entangle him in my snares. At length, my schemes being ripe, I met him (with the full intention that this meeting should be final and decisive) at the chambers of a fellow-commoner (Mr. Preston) equally intimate with both, but who, to do him justice, entertained not even a remote suspicion of my design. To give to this a better coloring I had contrived to have assembled a party of some eight or ten, and was solicitously careful that the introduction of cards should appear accidental, and originate in the proposal of my contemplated dupe himself. To be brief upon a vile topic, none of the low finesse was omitted, so customary upon similar occasions, that it is a just matter for wonder how any are still found so besotted as to fall its victim.

We had protracted our sitting far into the night, and I had at length effected the maneuver of getting Glendinning as my sole antagonist. The game, too, was my favorite *écarté.* The rest of the company, interested in the extent of our play, had abandoned their own cards, and were standing around us as spectators. The *parvenu,* who had been induced by my artifices in the early part of the evening to drink deeply, now shuffled, dealt, or played, with a wild nervousness of manner for which his intoxication I thought might partially but could not altogether account. In a very short period he had become my debtor to a large amount, when, having taken a long draft of port, he did precisely what I had been coolly anticipating — he proposed to double our already extravagant stakes. With a well-feigned show of reluctance, and not until after my repeated refusal had seduced him into some angry words which gave a color of *pique* to my compliance, did I finally comply. The result of course did but prove how entirely the prey was in my toils: in less than an hour he had quadrupled his debt. For some time his countenance had been losing the florid tinge lent it by the wine, but now to my astonishment I perceived that it had grown to a pallor truly fearful. I say to my astonishment. Glendinning had been represented to my eager inquiries as immeasurably wealthy; and the sums which he had as yet lost, although in themselves vast, could not, I supposed, very seriously annoy, much less so violently affect him. That he was overcome by the wine just swallowed was the idea which most readily presented itself; and, rather with a view to the preservation of my own character in the eyes of my associates, than from any less interested motive, I was about to insist peremptorily upon a discontinuance of the play, when some expressions at my elbow from among the company, and an ejaculation evincing utter despair on the part of Glendinning, gave me to understand that I had effected his total ruin under circumstances which, rendering him an object for the pity of all, should have protected him from the ill offices even of a fiend.

What now might have been my conduct it is difficult to say. The pitiable condition of my dupe had thrown an air of embarrassed gloom over all, and for some moments a profound silence was maintained, during which I could not help feeling my cheeks tingle with the many burning glances of scorn or reproach cast upon me by the less abandoned of the party. I will even own that an intolerable weight of anxiety was a brief instant lifted from my bosom by the sudden and extraordinary interruption which ensued. The wide heavy folding doors of the apartment were all at once thrown open to their full extent, with a vigorous and rushing impetuosity that extinguished, as if by magic, every candle in the room. Their light, in dying, enabled us just to perceive that a stranger had entered, about my own height, and closely muffled in a cloak. The darkness, however, was now total, and we could only *feel* that he was standing in our midst. Before any one of us could recover from the extreme astonishment into which this rudeness had thrown all, we heard the voice of the intruder.

"Gentlemen," he said, in a low, distinct, and never-to-be-forgotten *whisper* which thrilled to the very marrow of my bones, "gentlemen, I make no apology for this behavior, because in thus behaving, I am but fulfilling my duty. You are, beyond doubt, uninformed of the true character of the person who has to-night won at *écarté* a large sum of money from Lord Glendinning. I will therefore put you upon an expeditious and decisive plan of obtaining this very necessary information. Please to examine at your leisure the inner linings of the cuff of his left sleeve, and the several little packages which may be found in the somewhat capacious pockets of his embroidered morning wrapper."

While he spoke, so profound was the stillness that one might have heard a pin drop upon the floor. In ceasing, he departed at once, and as abruptly as he had entered. Can I — shall I describe my sensations? Must I say that I felt all the horrors of the damned? Most assuredly I had little time for reflection. Many hands roughly seized me upon the spot, and lights were immediately re-procured. A search ensued. In the lining of my sleeve were found all the court cards essential in *écarté*, and in the pockets of my wrapper a number of packs, facsimiles of those used at our sittings, with the single exception that mine were of the species called, technically, *arrondées;* the honors being slightly convex at the ends, the lower cards slightly convex at the sides. In this disposition, the dupe who cuts, as customary, at the length of the pack, will invariably find that he cuts his antagonist an honor; while the gambler, cutting at the breadth, will as certainly cut nothing for his victim which may count in the records of the game.

Any burst of indignation upon this discovery would have affected me less than the silent contempt, or the sarcastic composure, with which it was received.

"Mr. Wilson," said our host, stooping to remove from beneath his feet an exceedingly luxurious cloak of rare furs, "Mr. Wilson, this is your property." (The weather was cold; and, upon quitting my own room, I had thrown a cloak over my dressing wrapper, putting it off upon reaching the scene of play.) "I presume it is supererogatory to seek here (eying the folds of the garment with a bitter smile) for any further evidence of your skill. Indeed, we have had enough. You will see the necessity, I hope, of quitting Oxford — at all events, of quitting instantly my chambers."

Abased, humbled to the dust as I then was, it is probable that I should have resented this galling language by immediate personal violence, had not my whole attention been at the moment arrested by a fact of the most startling character. The cloak which I had worn was of a rare description of fur; how rare, how extravagantly costly, I shall not venture to say. Its fashion, too, was of my own fantastic invention, for I was fastidious to an absurd degree of coxcombry in matters of this frivolous nature. When, therefore, Mr. Preston reached me that which he had picked up upon the floor, and near the folding doors of the apartment, it was with an astonishment nearly bordering upon terror, that I perceived my own already hanging on my arm (where I had no doubt unwittingly placed it), and that the one presented me was but its exact counterpart in every, in even the minutest possible particular. The singular being who had so disastrously exposed me had been muffled, I remembered, in a cloak, and none had been worn at all by any of the members of our party with the exception of myself. Retaining some presence of mind, I took the one offered me by Preston, placed it unnoticed over my own, left the apartment with a resolute scowl of defiance, and next morning, ere dawn of day, commenced a hurried journey from Oxford to the Continent in a perfect agony of horror and of shame.

I fled in vain. My evil destiny pursued me as if in exultation, and proved indeed that the exercise of its mysterious dominion had as yet only begun. Scarcely had I set foot in Paris ere I had fresh evidence of the detestable interest taken by this Wilson in my concerns. Years flew while I experienced no relief. Villain!— at Rome, with how untimely, yet with how spectral an officiousness, stepped he in between me and my ambition! At Vienna, too — at Berlin — and at Moscow! Where, in truth, had I *not* bitter cause to curse him within my heart? From his inscrutable tyranny did I at length flee, panic-stricken, as from a pestilence; and to the very ends of the earth *I fled in vain.*

And again and again, in secret communion with my own spirit, would I demand the questions " Who is he? — whence came he? — and what are his objects? " But no answer was there found. And now I scrutinized, with a minute scrutiny, the forms, and the methods, and the leading traits of his impertinent supervision. But even here there was very little upon which to base a conjecture. It was noticeable, indeed, that in no one of the multiplied instances in which he had of late crossed my path had he so crossed it except to frustrate those schemes, or to disturb those actions, which, if fully carried out, might have resulted in bitter mischief. Poor justification this, in truth, for an authority so imperiously assumed! Poor indemnity for natural rights of self-agency so pertinaciously, so insultingly denied!

I had also been forced to notice that my tormentor for a

very long period of time (while scrupulously and with miraculous dexterity maintaining his whim of an identity of apparel with myself) had so contrived it, in the execution of his varied interference with my will, that I saw not at any moment the features of his face. Be Wilson what he might, *this* at least was but the veriest of affectation or of folly. Could he for an instant have supposed that in my admonisher at Eton — in the destroyer of my honor at Oxford — in him who thwarted my ambition at Rome, my revenge at Paris, my passionate love at Naples, or what he falsely termed my avarice in Egypt, — that in this, my arch-enemy and evil genius, I could fail to recognize the William Wilson of my school-boy days, — the name-sake, the companion, the rival, — the hated and dreaded rival at Dr. Bransby's? Impossible! — But let me hasten to the last eventful scene of the drama.

Thus far I had succumbed supinely to this imperious domination. The sentiment of deep awe with which I habitually regarded the elevated character, the majestic wisdom, the apparent omnipresence and omnipotence of Wilson, added to a feeling of even terror, with which certain other traits in his nature and assumptions inspired me, had operated hitherto to impress me with an idea of my own utter weakness and helplessness, and to suggest an implicit, although bitterly reluctant submission to his arbitrary will. But of late days I had given myself up entirely to wine, and its maddening influence upon my hereditary temper rendered me more and more impatient of control. I began to murmur, — to hesitate, — to resist. And was it only fancy which induced me to believe that, with the increase of my own firmness, that of my tormentor underwent a proportional diminution? Be this as it may, I now began to feel the inspiration of a burning hope, and at length nurtured in my secret thoughts a stern and desperate resolution that I would submit no longer to be enslaved.

It was at Rome, during the Carnival of 18—, that I attended a masquerade in the palazzo of the Neapolitan

Duke Di Broglio. I had indulged more freely than usual in the excesses of the wine-table, and now the suffocating atmosphere of the crowded rooms irritated me beyond endurance. The difficulty, too, of forcing my way through the mazes of the company contributed not a little to the ruffling of my temper; for I was anxiously seeking (let me not say with what unworthy motive) the young, the gay, the beautiful wife of the aged and doting Di Broglio. With a too unscrupulous confidence she had previously communicated to me the secret of the costume in which she would be habited, and now, having caught a glimpse of her person, I was hurrying to make my way into her presence. At this moment I felt a light hand placed upon my shoulder, and that ever-remembered, low, damnable *whisper* within my ear.

In an absolute frenzy of wrath I turned at once upon him who had thus interrupted me, and seized him violently by the collar. He was attired, as I had expected, in a costume altogether similar to my own; wearing a Spanish cloak of blue velvet, begirt about the waist with a crimson belt sustaining a rapier. A mask of black silk entirely covered his face.

"Scoundrel!" I said, in a voice husky with rage, while every syllable I uttered seemed as new fuel to my fury; "scoundrel! impostor! accursed villain! you shall not — you *shall not* dog me unto death! Follow me, or I stab you where you stand!" — and I broke my way from the ballroom into a small ante-chamber adjoining, dragging him unresistingly with me as I went.

Upon entering, I thrust him furiously from me. He staggered against the wall, while I closed the door with an oath, and commanded him to draw. He hesitated but for an instant; then, with a slight sigh, drew in silence, and put himself upon his defense.

The contest was brief indeed. I was frantic with every species of wild excitement, and felt within my single arm the energy and power of a multitude. In a few seconds I forced him by sheer strength against the wainscoting, and thus, getting him at mercy, plunged my sword, with brute ferocity, repeatedly through and through his bosom.

At that instant some person tried the latch of the door. I hastened to prevent an intrusion, and then immediately returned to my dying antagonist. But what human language can adequately portray *that* astonishment, *that* horror which possessed me at the spectacle then presented to view? The brief moment in which I averted my eyes had been sufficient to produce apparently a material change in the arrangements at the upper or farther end of the room. A large mirror — so at first it seemed to me in my confusion — now stood where none had been perceptible before; and, as I stepped up to it in extremity of terror, mine own image, but with features all pale and dabbled in blood, advanced to meet me with a feeble and tottering gait.

Thus it appeared, I say, but was not. It was my antagonist — it was Wilson who then stood before me in the agonies of his dissolution. His mask and cloak lay where he had thrown them upon the floor. Not a thread in all his raiment — not a line in all the marked and singular lineaments of his face which was not, even in the most absolute identity, *mine own!*

It was Wilson; but he spoke no longer in a whisper, and I could have fancied that I myself was speaking while he said:

"*You have conquered and I yield. Yet, henceforward art thou also dead — dead to the World, to Heaven, and to Hope! In me didst thou exist — and, in my death, see by this image, which is thine own, how utterly thou has murdered thyself.*"

ABRAHAM LINCOLN

27 *To Joshua F. Speed*

February 3, 1842

DEAR SPEED: Your letter of the 25th January came to
hand to-day. You well know that I do not feel my
own sorrows much more keenly than I do yours, when I
know of them; and yet I assure you I was not much hurt
by what you wrote me of your excessively bad feeling at the
time you wrote. Not that I am less capable of sympathizing with you now than ever, not that I am less your friend
than ever, but because I hope and believe that your present
anxiety and distress about her health and her life must and
will forever banish those horrid doubts which I know you
sometimes felt as to the truth of your affection for her. If
they can once and forever be removed (and I almost feel
a presentiment that the Almighty has sent your present
affliction expressly for that object), surely nothing can come
in their stead to fill their immeasurable measure of misery.
The death-scenes of those we love are surely painful enough;
but these we are prepared for and expect to see: they happen
to all, and all know they must happen. Painful as they are,
they are not an unlooked-for sorrow. Should she, as you
fear, be destined to an early grave, it is indeed a great
consolation to know that she is so well prepared to meet it.
Her religion, which you once disliked so much, I will venture you now prize most highly. But I hope your melancholy bodings as to her early death are not well founded.
I even hope that ere this reaches you she will have returned
with improved and still improving health, and that you will
have met her, and forgotten the sorrows of the past in the
enjoyments of the present. I would say more if I could, but
it seems that I have said enough. It really appears to me
that you yourself ought to rejoice, and not sorrow, at this
indubitable evidence of your undying affection for her.

Why, Speed, if you did not love her, although you might not wish her death, you would most certainly be resigned to it. Perhaps this point is no longer a question with you, and my pertinacious dwelling upon it is a rude intrusion upon your feelings. If so, you must pardon me. You know the hell I have suffered on that point, and how tender I am upon it. You know I do not mean wrong. I have been quite clear of "hypo" since you left; even better than I was along in the fall. I have seen —————— but once. She seemed very cheerful, and so I said nothing to her about what we spoke of.

Old Uncle Billy Herndon is dead, and it is said this evening that Uncle Ben Ferguson will not live. This, I believe, is all the news, and enough at that unless it were better. Write me immediately on receipt of this.

February 25, 1842

DEAR SPEED: I received yours of the 12th written the day you went down to William's place, some days since, but delayed answering it till I should receive the promised one of the 16th, which came last night. I opened the letter with intense anxiety and trepidation; so much so, that, although it turned out better than I expected, I have hardly yet, at a distance of ten hours, become calm.

I tell you, Speed, our forebodings (for which you and I are peculiar) are all the worst sort of nonsense. I fancied, from the time I received your letter of Saturday, that the one of Wednesday was never to come, and yet it *did* come, and what is more, it is perfectly clear, both from its tone and handwriting, that you were much happier, or, if you think the term preferable, less miserable, when you wrote it than when you wrote the last one before. You had so obviously improved at the very time I so much fancied you would have grown worse. You say that something indescribably horrible and alarming still haunts you. You will not say that three months from now, I will venture. When your nerves once get steady now, the whole trouble will be over forever. Nor should you become impatient at their being even very slow in becoming steady. Again you say, you much fear that that Elysium of which you have dreamed so much is never to be realized. Well, if it shall not, I dare swear it will not be the fault of her who is now your wife. I now have no doubt that it is the peculiar misfortune of both you and me to dream dreams of Elysium far exceeding all that anything earthly can realize. Far short of your dreams as you may be, no woman could do more to realize them than that same black-eyed Fanny. If you could but contemplate her through my imagination, it would appear ridiculous to you that anyone should for a moment think of being unhappy with her. My old father used to have a saying that "If you make a bad bargain, hug it all the tighter"; and it occurs to me that if the bargain you have just closed can possibly be called a bad one, it is certainly the most pleasant one for applying that maxim to which my fancy can by any effort picture.

I write another letter, inclosing this, which you can show her, if she desires it. I do this because she would think strangely, perhaps, should you tell her that you received no letters from me, or, telling her you do, refuse to let her see them. I close this entertaining the confident hope that every successive letter I shall have from you (which I here pray may not be few, or far between) may show you possessing a more steady hand and cheerful heart than the last preceding it.

July 4, 1842

DEAR SPEED: Yours of the 16th of June was received only a day or two since. It was not mailed at Louisville till the 25th. You speak of the great time that has elapsed since I wrote you. Let me explain that. Your letter reached here a day or two after I had started on the circuit. I was gone five or six weeks, so that I got the letters only a few weeks before Butler started to your country. I thought it scarcely worth while to write you the news which he could and would tell you more in detail. On his return he told me you would write me soon, and so I waited for your letter.

As to my having been displeased with your advice, surely you know better than that. I know you do, and therefore will not labor to convince you. True, that subject is painful to me; but it is not your silence, or the silence of all the world, that can make me forget it. I acknowledge the correctness of your advice too; but before I resolve to do the one thing or the other, I must gain my confidence in my own ability to keep my resolves when they are made. In that ability you know I once prided myself as the only or chief gem of my character; that gem I lost — how and where you know too well. I have not yet regained it; and until I do, I cannot trust myself in any matter of much importance. I believe now that had you understood my case at the time as well as I understood yours afterward, by the aid you would have given me I should have sailed through clear, but that does not now afford me sufficient confidence to begin that or the like of that again.

You make a kind acknowledgment of your obligations to me for your present happiness. I am pleased with that acknowledgment. But a thousand times more am I pleased to know that you enjoy a degree of happiness worthy of an acknowledgment. The truth is, I am not sure that there was any merit with me in the part I took in your difficulty; I was drawn to it by a fate. If I would I could not have done less than I did. I always was superstitious; I believe God made me one of the instruments of bringing your Fanny and you together, which union I have no doubt he had foreordained. Whatever he designs he will do for me yet. " Stand still, and see the salvation of the Lord " is my text just now. If, as you say, you have told Fanny all, I should have no objection to her seeing this letter, but for its reference to our friend here: let her seeing it depend upon whether she has ever known anything of my affairs; and if she has not, do not let her.

I do not think I can come to Kentucky this season. I am

so poor and make so little headway in the world, that I drop back in a month of idleness as much as I gain in a year's sowing. I should like to visit you again. I should like to see that " sis " of yours that was absent when I was there, though I suppose she would run away again if she were to hear I was coming.

28   *A House Divided*

IF we could first know where we are, and whither we are tending, we could better judge what to do, and how to do it. We are now far into the fifth year since a policy was initiated with the avowed object and confident promise of putting an end to slavery agitation. Under the operation of that policy, that agitation has not only not ceased, but has constantly augmented. In my opinion it will not cease until a crisis shall have been reached and passed. " A house divided against itself cannot stand." I believe this government cannot endure permanently, half slave and half free. I do not expect the Union to be dissolved — I do not expect the house to fall — but I do expect it will cease to be divided. It will become all one thing, or all the other. Either the opponents of slavery will arrest the further spread of it, and place it where the public mind shall rest in the belief that it is in the course of ultimate extinction; or its advocates will push it forward till it shall become alike lawful in all the states, old as well as new, North as well as South.

29   *To Horace Greeley*

EXECUTIVE MANSION, WASHINGTON, August 22, 1862

DEAR SIR: I have just read yours of the 19th instant, addressed to myself through the *New York Tribune*. If there be in it any statements or assumptions of fact which I may know to be erroneous, I do not now and here controvert them. If there be in it any inferences which I may believe to be falsely drawn, I do not now and here argue against them. If there be perceptible in it an impatient and dictatorial tone, I waive it, in deference to an old friend whose heart I have always supposed to be right.

As to the policy I " seem to be pursuing," as you say, I have not meant to leave anyone in doubt.

I would save the Union. I would save it in the shortest way under the Constitution. The sooner the national authority can be restored, the nearer the Union will be " the Union as it was." If there be those who would not save the Union unless they could at the same time save slavery, I do not agree with them. If there be those who would not save the Union unless they could at the same time destroy slavery, I do not agree with them. My paramount object in this struggle is to save the Union, and is not either to save or to destroy slavery. If I could save the Union without freeing any slave, I would do it; if I could save it by freeing all the slaves, I would do it; and if I could save it by freeing some and leaving others alone, I would also do that. What I do about slavery and the colored race, I do because I believe it helps to save the Union; and what I forbear, I forbear because I do not believe it would help to save the Union. I shall do less whenever I shall believe that what I am doing hurts the cause; and I shall do more whenever I shall believe doing more will help the cause. I shall try to correct errors when shown to be errors, and I shall adopt new views so fast as they shall appear to be true views.

I have here stated my purpose according to my view of official duty, and I intend no modification of my oft-expressed personal wish that all men everywhere could be free.

Yours,

A. LINCOLN

30   *Meditation on the Will of God*

September, 1862

THE will of God prevails. In great contests each party claims to act in accordance with the will of God. Both may be, and one must be, wrong. God cannot be for and against the same thing at the same time. In the present civil war it is quite possible that God's purpose is something different from the purpose of either party; and yet the human instrumentalities, working just as they do, are of the best adaptation to effect his purpose. I am almost ready to say that this is probably true; that God wills this contest, and wills that it shall not end yet. By his mere great power on the minds of the now contestants, he could have either saved or destroyed the Union without a human contest. Yet the contest began. And, having begun, he could give the final victory to either side any day. Yet the contest proceeds.

31   *To Miss Fanny McCullough*

December 23, 1862

DEAR FANNY: It is with deep regret that I learn of the death of your kind and brave father, and especially that it is affecting your young heart beyond what is common in such cases. In this sad world of ours sorrow comes to all, and to the young it comes with bittered agony because it takes them unawares. The older have learned ever to expect it. I am anxious to afford some alleviation of your present distress. Perfect relief is not possible except with time. You cannot now realize that you will ever feel better. Is not this so? And yet it is a mistake. You are sure to be happy again. To know this, which is certainly true, will make you some less miserable now. I have had experience enough to know what I say, and you need only to believe it to feel better at once. The memory of your dear father, instead of an agony, will yet be a sad, sweet feeling in your heart, of a purer and holier sort than you have known before.

Please present my kind regards to your afflicted mother.

Your sincere friend,

A. LINCOLN

32 *To General Joseph Hooker*

EXECUTIVE MANSION, WASHINGTON, D. C., January 26, 1863

GENERAL: I have placed you at the head of the Army of the Potomac. Of course I have done this upon what appear to me to be sufficient reasons, and yet I think it best for you to know that there are some things in regard to which I am not quite satisfied with you. I believe you to be a brave and skillful soldier, which of course I like. I also believe you do not mix politics with your profession, in which you are right. You have confidence in yourself, which is a valuable if not an indispensable quality. You are ambitious, which, within reasonable bounds, does good rather than harm; but I think that during General Burnside's command of the army you have taken counsel of your ambition and thwarted him as much as you could, in which you did a great wrong to the country and to a most meritorious and honorable brother officer. I have heard, in such a way as to believe it, of your recently saying that both the army and the government needed a dictator. Of course it was not for this, but in spite of it, that I have given you the command. Only those generals who gain successes can set up dictators. What I now ask of you is military success, and I will risk the dictatorship. The government will support you to the utmost of its ability, which is neither more nor less than it has done and will do for all commanders. I much fear that the spirit which you have aided to infuse into the army, of criticizing their commander and withholding confidence from him, will now turn upon you. I shall assist you as far as I can to put it down. Neither you nor Napoleon, if he were alive again, could get any good out of an army while such a spirit prevails in it; and now beware of rashness. Beware of rashness, but with energy and sleepless vigilance go forward and give us victories.

Yours very truly,

A. LINCOLN

33 *To General Grant*

EXECUTIVE MANSION, WASHINGTON, July 13, 1863

MY DEAR GENERAL: I do not remember that you and I ever met personally. I write this now as a grateful acknowledgment for the almost inestimable service you have done the country. I wish to say a word further. When you first reached the vicinity of Vicksburg, I thought you should do what you finally did — march the troops across the neck, run the batteries with the transports, and thus go below; and I never had any faith, except a general hope that you knew better than I, that the Yazoo Pass expedition and the like could succeed. When you got below and took Port Gibson, Grand Gulf, and vicinity, I thought you should go down the river and join General Banks, and when you turned northward, east of the Big Black, I feared it was a mistake. I now wish to make the personal acknowledgment that you were right and I was wrong.

Yours very truly,

A. LINCOLN

34   *Address at Gettysburg*

November 19, 1863

FOUR score and seven years ago our fathers brought forth on this continent, a new nation, conceived in Liberty, and dedicated to the proposition that all men are created equal.

Now we are engaged in a great civil war; testing whether that nation, or any nation so conceived and so dedicated, can long endure. We are met on a great battlefield of that war. We have come to dedicate a portion of that field as a final resting-place for those who here gave their lives that that nation might live. It is altogether fitting and proper that we should do this.

But, in a larger sense, we cannot dedicate — we cannot consecrate — we cannot hallow — this ground. The brave men, living and dead, who struggled here have consecrated it, far above our poor power to add or detract. The world will little note, nor long remember, what we say here, but it can never forget what they did here. It is for us the living, rather, to be dedicated here to the unfinished work which they who fought here have thus far so nobly advanced. It is rather for us to be here dedicated to the great task remaining before us — that from these honored dead we take increased devotion to that cause for which they gave the last full measure of devotion; that we here highly resolve that these dead shall not have died in vain; that this nation, under God, shall have a new birth of freedom; and that government of the people, by the people, for the people, shall not perish from the earth.

35   *To General Grant*

EXECUTIVE MANSION, WASHINGTON, April 30, 1864

LIEUTENANT GENERAL GRANT: Not expecting to see you again before the spring campaign opens, I wish to express in this way my entire satisfaction with what you have done up to this time, so far as I understand it. The particulars of your plans I neither know nor seek to know. You are vigilant and self-reliant; and, pleased with this, I wish not to obtrude any constraints or restraints upon you. While I am very anxious that any great disaster or capture of our men in great numbers shall be avoided, I know these points are less likely to escape your attention than they would be mine. If there is anything wanting which is within my power to give, do not fail to let me know it. And now, with a brave army and a just cause, may God sustain you.

Yours very truly,

A. LINCOLN

36   *Second Inaugural Address*

FELLOW COUNTRYMEN: At this second appearing to take the oath of the presidential office, there is less occasion for an extended address than there was at the first. Then a statement, somewhat in detail, of a course to be pursued, seemed fitting and proper. Now, at the expiration of four years, during which public declarations have been constantly called forth on every point and phase of the great contest which still absorbs the attention and engrosses the energies of the nation, little that is new could be presented. The progress of our arms, upon which all else chiefly depends, is as well known to the public as to myself; and it is, I trust, reasonably satisfactory and encouraging to all. With high hope for the future, no prediction in regard to it is ventured.

ABRAHAM LINCOLN

On the occasion corresponding to this four years ago, all thoughts were anxiously directed to an impending civil war. All dreaded it — all sought to avert it. While the inaugural address was being delivered from this place, devoted altogether to saving the Union without war, insurgent agents were in the city seeking to destroy it without war — seeking to dissolve the Union, and divide effects, by negotiation. Both parties deprecated war; but one of them would make war rather than let the nation survive; and the other would accept war rather than let it perish. And the war came.

One eighth of the whole population were colored slaves, not distributed generally over the Union, but localized in the Southern part of it. These slaves constituted a peculiar and powerful interest. All knew that this interest was, somehow, the cause of the war. To strengthen, perpetuate, and extend this interest was the object for which the insurgents would rend the Union, even by war; while the government claimed no right to do more than to restrict the territorial enlargement of it.

Neither party expected for the war the magnitude or the duration which it has already attained. Neither anticipated that the cause of the conflict might cease with, or even before, the conflict itself should cease. Each looked for an easier triumph, and a result less fundamental and astounding. Both read the same Bible, and pray to the same God; and each invokes his aid against the other. It may seem strange that any men should dare to ask a just God's assistance in wringing their bread from the sweat of other men's faces; but let us judge not, that we be not judged. The prayers of both could not be answered — that of neither has been answered fully.

The Almighty has his own purposes. "Woe unto the world because of offenses! for it must needs be that offenses come; but woe to that man by whom the offense cometh." If we shall suppose that American slavery is one of those offenses which, in the providence of God, must needs come, but which, having continued through his appointed time, he now wills to remove, and that he gives to both North and South this terrible war, as the woe due to those by whom the offense came, shall we discern therein any departure from those divine attributes which the believers in a living God always ascribe to him? Fondly do we hope — fervently do we pray — that this mighty scourge of war may speedily pass away. Yet, if God wills that it continue until all the wealth piled by the bondsman's two hundred and fifty years of unrequited toil shall be sunk, and until every drop of blood drawn with the lash shall be paid by another drawn with the sword, as was said three thousand years ago, so still it must be said, "The judgments of the Lord are true and righteous altogether."

With malice toward none; with charity for all; with firmness in the right, as God gives us to see the right, let us strive on to finish the work we are in; to bind up the nation's wounds; to care for him who shall have borne the battle, and for his widow, and his orphan — to do all which may achieve and cherish a just and lasting peace among ourselves, and with all nations.

HENRY DAVID THOREAU

1817–1862

37   *Civil Disobedience*

I HEARTILY accept the motto, — "That government is best which governs least"; and I should like to see it acted up to more rapidly and systematically. Carried out, it finally amounts to this, which also I believe, — "That government is best which governs not at all"; and when men are prepared for it, that will be the kind of government which they will have. Government is at best but an expedient; but most governments are usually, and all governments are sometimes, inexpedient. The objections which have been brought against a standing army, and they are many and weighty, and deserve to prevail, may also at last be brought against a standing government. The standing army is only an arm of the standing government. The government itself, which is only the mode which the people have chosen to execute their will, is equally liable to be abused and perverted before the people can act through it. Witness the present Mexican war, the work of comparatively a few individuals using the standing government as their tool; for, in the outset, the people would not have consented to this measure.

This American government, — what is it but a tradition, though a recent one, endeavoring to transmit itself unimpaired to posterity, but each instant losing some of its integrity? It has not the vitality and force of a single living man; for a single man can bend it to his will. It is a sort of wooden gun to the people themselves. But it is not the less necessary for this; for the people must have some complicated machinery or other, and hear its din, to satisfy that idea of government which they have. Governments show thus how successfully men can be imposed on, even impose on themselves, for their own advantage. It is excellent, we must all allow. Yet this government never of itself furthered any enterprise, but by the alacrity with which it got out of its way. *It* does not keep the country free. *It* does not settle the West. *It* does not educate. The character inherent in the American people has done all that has been accomplished; and it would have done somewhat more, if the government had not sometimes got in its way. For government is an expedient by which men would fain succeed in letting one another alone; and, as has been said, when it is most expedient, the governed are most let alone by it. Trade and commerce, if they were not made of India-rubber, would never manage to bounce over the obstacles which legislators are continually putting in their way; and, if one were to judge these men wholly by the effects of their actions and not partly by their intentions, they would deserve to be classed and punished with those mischievous persons who put obstructions on the railroads.

But, to speak practically and as a citizen, unlike those who call themselves no-government men, I ask for, not at once no government, but *at once* a better government. Let every man make known what kind of government would command his respect, and that will be one step toward obtaining it.

After all, the practical reason why, when the power is once in the hands of the people, a majority are permitted, and for a long period continue, to rule, is not because they are most likely to be in the right, nor because this seems fairest to the minority, but because they are physically the strongest. But a government in which the majority rule in all cases cannot be based on justice, even as far as men understand it. Can there not be a government in which majorities do not virtually decide right and wrong, but conscience? — in which majorities decide only those questions to which the rule of expediency is applicable? Must the citizen ever for a moment, or in the least degree, resign his conscience to the legislator? Why has every man a conscience, then? I think that we should be men first, and subjects afterward. It is not desirable to cultivate a respect for the law, so much as for the right. The only obligation which I have a right to assume is to do at any time what I think right. It is truly enough said, that a corporation has no conscience; but a corporation of conscientious men is a corporation *with* a conscience. Law never made men a whit more just; and, by means of their respect for it, even the well-disposed are daily made the agents of injustice. A common and natural result of an undue respect for law is that you may see a file of soldiers, colonel, captain, corporal, privates, powder-monkeys, and all, marching in admirable order over hill and dale to the wars, against their wills, ay, against their common sense and consciences, which makes it very steep marching indeed, and produces a palpitation of the heart. They have no doubt that it is a damnable business in which they are concerned; they are all peaceably inclined. Now, what are they? Men at all? or small movable forts and magazines, at the service of some unscrupulous man in power? Visit the Navy-yard, and behold a marine, such a man as an American government can make, or such as it can make a man with its black arts, — a mere shadow and reminiscence of humanity, a man laid out alive and standing, and already, as one may say, buried under arms with funeral accompaniments, though it may be, —

> "Not a drum was heard, not a funeral note,
>   As his corse to the rampart we hurried;
> Not a soldier discharged his farewell shot
>   O'er the grave where our hero we buried."

The mass of men serve the State thus, not as men mainly, but as machines, with their bodies. They are the standing army, and the militia, gaolers, constables, posse comitatus, etc. In most cases there is no free exercise whatever of the judgment or of the moral sense; but they put themselves on a level with wood and earth and stones; and wooden men can perhaps be manufactured that will serve the purpose as well. Such command no more respect than men of straw or a lump of dirt. They have the same sort of worth only as horses and dogs. Yet such as these even are commonly esteemed good citizens. Others, — as most legislators, politicians, lawyers, ministers, and office-holders, — serve the State chiefly with their heads; and, as they rarely make any moral distinctions, they are as likely to serve the devil, without *intending* it, as God. A very few, as heroes, patriots, martyrs, reformers in the great sense, and *men*, serve the State with their consciences also, and so necessarily resist it for the most part; and they are commonly treated as enemies by it. A wise man will only be useful as a man, and will not submit to be "clay," and "stop a hole to keep the wind away," but leave that office to his dust at least: —

> "I am too high-born to be propertied,
>   To be a secondary at control,
> Or useful serving-man and instrument
>   To any sovereign state throughout the world."

He who gives himself entirely to his fellow-men appears to them useless and selfish; but he who gives himself partially to them is pronounced a benefactor and philanthropist.

How does it become a man to behave toward this American government today? I answer, that he cannot without disgrace be associated with it. I cannot for an instant recognize that political organization as *my* government which is the *slave's* government also.

All men recognize the right of revolution; that is, the right to refuse allegiance to, and to resist, the government, when its tyranny or its inefficiency are great and unendurable. But almost all say that such is not the case now. But such was the case, they think, in the Revolution of '75. If one were to tell me that this was a bad government because it taxed certain foreign commodities brought to its ports, it is most probable that I should not make an ado about it, for I can do without them. All machines have their friction; and possibly this does enough good to counterbalance the evil. At any rate, it is a great evil to make a stir about it. But when the friction comes to have its machine, and oppression and robbery are organized, I say, let us not have such a machine any longer. In other words, when a sixth of the population of a nation which has undertaken to be the refuge of liberty are slaves, and a whole country is unjustly overrun and conquered by a foreign army, and subjected to military law, I think that it is not too soon for honest men to rebel and revolutionize. What makes this duty the more urgent is the fact, that the country so overrun is not our own, but ours is the invading army.

Paley, a common authority with many on moral questions, in his chapter on the "Duty of Submission to Civil Government," resolves all civil obligation into expediency; and he proceeds to say, "that so long as the interest of the whole society requires it, that is, so long as the established government cannot be resisted or changed without public inconveniency, it is the will of God that the established government be obeyed, and no longer. . . . This principle being admitted, the justice of every particular case of resistance is reduced to a computation of the quality of the danger and grievance on the one side, and of the probability and expense of redressing it on the other." Of this, he says, every man shall judge for himself. But Paley appears never to have contemplated those cases to which the rule of expediency does not apply, in which a people, as well as an individual, must do justice, cost what it may. If I have unjustly wrested a plank from a drowning man, I must restore it to him though I drown myself. This, according to Paley, would be inconvenient. But he that would save his life, in such a case, shall lose it. This people must cease to hold slaves, and to make war on Mexico, though it cost them their existence as a people.

In their practice, nations agree with Paley; but does any one think that Massachusetts does exactly what is right at the present crisis?

> " A drab of state, a cloth-o'-silver slut,
>   To have her train borne up, and her soul trail in the dirt."

Practically speaking, the opponents to a reform in Massachusetts are not a hundred thousand politicians at the South, but a hundred thousand merchants and farmers here, who are more interested in commerce and agriculture than they are in humanity, and are not prepared to do justice to the slave and to Mexico, *cost what it may.* I quarrel not with far-off foes, but with those who, near at home, coöperate with, and do the bidding of, those far away, and without whom the latter would be harmless. We are accustomed to say, that the mass of men are unprepared; but improvement is slow, because the few are not materially wiser or better than the many. It is not so important that many should be as good as you, as that there be some absolute goodness somewhere, for that will leaven the whole lump. There are thousands who are *in opinion* opposed to slavery and to the war, who yet in effect do nothing to put an end to them; who, esteeming themselves children of Washington and Franklin, sit down with their hands in their pockets, and say that they know not what to do, and do nothing; who even postpone the question of freedom to the question of free-trade, and quietly read the prices-current along with the latest advices from Mexico, after dinner, and, it may be, fall asleep over them both. What is the price-current of an honest man and patriot today? They hesitate, and they regret, and sometimes they petition; but they do nothing in earnest and with effect. They will wait, well disposed, for others to remedy the evil, that they may no longer have it to regret. At most, they give only a cheap vote, and a feeble countenance and God-speed, to the right, as it goes by them. There are nine hundred and ninety-nine patrons of virtue to one virtuous man. But it is easier to deal with the real possessor of a thing than with the temporary guardian of it.

All voting is a sort of gaming, like checkers or backgammon, with a slight moral tinge to it, a playing with right and wrong, with moral questions; and betting naturally accompanies it. The character of the voters is not staked. I cast my vote, perchance, as I think right; but I am not vitally concerned that that right should prevail. I am willing to leave it to the majority. Its obligation, therefore, never exceeds that of expediency. Even voting *for the right* is *doing* nothing for it. It is only expressing to men feebly your desire that it should prevail. A wise man will not leave the right to the mercy of chance, nor wish it to prevail through the power of the majority. There is but little virtue in the action of masses of men. When the majority shall at length vote for the abolition of slavery, it will be because they are indifferent to slavery, or because there is but little slavery left to be abolished by their vote. *They* will then be the only slaves. Only *his* vote can hasten the abolition of slavery who asserts his own freedom by his vote.

I hear of a convention to be held at Baltimore, or elsewhere, for the selection of a candidate for the Presidency, made up chiefly of editors, and men who are politicians by profession; but I think, what is it to any independent, intelligent, and respectable man what decision they may come to? Shall we not have the advantage of his wisdom and honesty, nevertheless? Can we not count upon some independent votes? Are there not many individuals in the country who do not attend conventions? But no: I find that the respectable man, so called, has immediately drifted from his position, and despairs of his country, when his country has more reason to despair of him. He forthwith adopts one of the candidates thus selected as the only *available* one, thus proving that he is himself *available* for any purposes of the demagogue. His vote is of no more worth than that of any unprincipled foreigner or hireling native, who may have been bought. Oh for a man who is a *man*, and, as my neighbor says, has a bone in his back which you cannot pass your hand through! Our statistics are at fault: the population has been returned too large. How many *men* are there to a square thousand miles in this country? Hardly one. Does not America offer any inducement for men to settle here? The American has dwindled into an Odd Fellow, — one who may be known by the development of his organ of gregariousness, and a manifest lack of intellect and cheerful self-reliance; whose first and chief concern, on coming into the world, is to see that the almhouses are in good repair; and, before yet he has lawfully donned the virile garb, to collect a fund for the support of the widows and orphans that may be; who, in short, ventures to live only by the aid of the Mutual Insurance Company, which has promised to bury him decently.

It is not a man's duty, as a matter of course, to devote himself to the eradication of any, even the most enormous wrong; he may still properly have other concerns to engage him; but it is his duty, at least, to wash his hands of it, and, if he gives it no thought longer, not to give it practically his support. If I devote myself to other pursuits and contemplations, I must first see, at least, that I do not pursue them sitting upon another man's shoulders. I must get off him first, that he may pursue his contemplations too. See what gross inconsistency is tolerated. I have heard some of my townsmen say, "I should like to have them order me out to help put down an insurrection of the slaves, or to march to

Mexico; — see if I would go"; and yet these very men have each, directly by their allegiance, and so indirectly, at least, by their money, furnished a substitute. The soldier is applauded who refuses to serve in an unjust war by those who do not refuse to sustain the unjust government which makes the war; is applauded by those whose own act and authority he disregards and sets at naught; as if the State were penitent to that degree that it hired one to scourge it while it sinned, but not to that degree that it left off sinning for a moment. Thus, under the name of Order and Civil Government, we are all made at last to pay homage to and support our own meanness. After the first blush of sin comes its indifference; and from immoral it becomes, as it were, *un*moral, and not quite unnecessary to that life which we have made.

The broadest and most prevalent error requires the most disinterested virtue to sustain it. The slight reproach to which the virtue of patriotism is commonly liable, the noble are most likely to incur. Those who, while they disapprove of the character and measures of a government yield to it their allegiance and support, are undoubtedly its most conscientious supporters, and so frequently the most serious obstacles to reform. Some are petitioning the State to dissolve the Union, to disregard the requisitions of the President. Why do they not dissolve it themselves, — the union between themselves and the State, — and refuse to pay their quota into its treasury? Do not they stand in the same relation to the State, that the State does to the Union? And have not the same reasons prevented the State from resisting the Union, which have prevented them from resisting the State?

How can a man be satisfied to entertain an opinion merely and enjoy *it*? Is there any enjoyment in it, if his opinion is that he is aggrieved? If you are cheated out of a single dollar by your neighbor, you do not rest satisfied with knowing that you are cheated, or with saying that you are cheated, or even with petitioning him to pay you your due; but you take effectual steps at once to obtain the full amount, and see that you are never cheated again. Action from principle, the perception and the performance of right, changes things and relations; it is essentially revolutionary, and does not consist wholly with anything which was. It not only divides states and churches, it divides families; ay, it divides the *individual,* separating the diabolical in him from the divine.

Unjust laws exist: shall we be content to obey them, or shall we endeavor to amend them, and obey them until we have succeeded, or shall we transgress them at once? Men generally, under such a government as this, think that they ought to wait until they have persuaded the majority to alter them. They think that, if they should resist, the remedy would be worse than the evil. But it is the fault of the government itself that the remedy *is* worse than the evil. *It* makes it worse. Why is it not more apt to anticipate and provide for reform? Why does it not cherish its wise minority? Why does it cry and resist before it is hurt? Why does it not encourage its citizens to be on the alert to point out its faults and *do* better than it would have them? Why does it always crucify Christ, and excommunicate Copernicus and Luther, and pronounce Washington and Franklin rebels?

One would think, that a deliberate and practical denial of its authority was the only offense never contemplated by government; else, why has it not assigned its definite, its suitable and proportionate penalty? If a man who has no property refuses but once to earn nine shillings for the State, he is put in prison for a period unlimited by any law that I know, and determined only by the discretion of those who placed him there; but if he should steal ninety times nine shillings from the State, he is soon permitted to go at large again.

If the injustice is part of the necessary friction of the machine of government, let it go, let it go: perchance it will wear smooth, — certainly the machine will wear out. If the injustice has a spring, or a pulley, or a rope, or a crank, exclusively for itself, then perhaps you may consider whether the remedy will not be worse than the evil; but if it is of such a nature that it requires you to be the agent of injustice to another, then, I say, break the law. Let your life be a counter-friction to stop the machine. What I have to do is to see, at any rate, that I do not lend myself to the wrong which I condemn.

As for adopting the ways which the State has provided for remedying the evil, I know not of such ways. They take too much time, and a man's life will be gone. I have other affairs to attend to. I came into this world, not chiefly to make this a good place to live in, but to live in it, be it good or bad. A man has not everything to do, but something; and because he cannot do *everything,* it is not necessary that he should do *something* wrong. It is not my business to be petitioning the Governor or the Legislature any more than it is theirs to petition me; and if they should not hear my petition, what should I do then? But in this case the State has provided no way: its very Constitution is the evil. This may seem to be harsh and stubborn and unconciliatory; but it is to treat with the utmost kindness and consideration the only spirit that can appreciate or deserves it. So is all change for the better, like birth and death, which convulse the body.

I do not hesitate to say, that those who call themselves Abolitionists should at once effectually withdraw their support, both in person and property, from the government of Massachusetts, and not wait till they constitute a majority of one, before they suffer the right to prevail through them. I think that it is enough if they have God on their side, without waiting for that other one. Moreover, any man more right than his neighbors constitutes a majority of one already.

I meet this American government, or its representative, the State government, directly, and face to face, once a year — no more — in the person of its tax-gatherer; this is the only mode in which a man situated as I am necessarily meets it; and it then says distinctly, Recognize me; and the simplest, the most effectual, and, in the present posture of affairs, the indispensablest mode of treating with it on this head, of expressing your little satisfaction with and love for it, is to deny it then. My civil neighbor, the tax-gatherer, is the very man I have to deal with, — for it is, after all, with men and not with parchment that I quarrel, — and he has voluntarily chosen to be an agent of the government. How shall he ever know well what he is and does as an officer of the government, or as a man, until he is obliged to consider whether he shall treat me, his neighbor, for whom he has respect, as a neighbor and well-disposed man, or as a maniac and disturber of the peace, and see if he can get over this obstruction to his neighborliness without a ruder and more impetuous thought or speech corresponding with his action. I know this well, that if one thousand, if one hundred, if ten men whom I could name, — if ten *honest* men only, — ay, if *one* HONEST man, in this state of Massachusetts, *ceasing to hold slaves,* were actually to withdraw from this copartnership, and be locked up in the county jail therefor, it would be the abolition of slavery in America. For it matters not how small the beginning may seem to be: what is once well done is done forever. But we love better to talk about it: that we say is our mission. Reform keeps many scores of newspapers in its service, but not one man. If my esteemed neighbor, the State's ambassador, who will devote his days to the settlement of the question of human rights in the Council Chamber, instead of being threatened with the prisons of Carolina, were to sit down the prisoner of Massachusetts, that State which is so anxious to foist the sin of slavery upon her sister, — though at present she can discover only an act of inhospitality to be the ground of a quarrel with her, — the Legislature would not wholly waive the subject the following winter.

Under a government which imprisons any unjustly, the true place for a just man is also a prison. The proper place to-day, the only place which Massachusetts has provided for her freer and less desponding spirits, is in her prisons, to be put out and locked out of the State by her own act, as they have already put themselves out by their principles. It is there that the fugitive slave, and the Mexican prisoner on parole, and the Indian come to plead the wrongs of his race, should find them; on that separate, but more free and honorable ground, where the State places those who are not *with* her, but *against* her,—the only house in a slave State in which a free man can abide with honor. If any think that their influence would be lost there, and their voices no longer afflict the ear of the State, that they would not be as an enemy within its walls, they do not know by how much truth is stronger than error, nor how much more eloquently and effectively he can combat injustice who has experienced a little in his own person. Cast your whole vote, not a strip of paper merely, but your whole influence. A minority is powerless while it conforms to the majority; it is not even a minority then; but it is irresistible when it clogs by its whole weight. If the alternative is to keep all just men in prison, or give up war and slavery, the State will not hesitate which to choose. If a thousand men were not to pay their tax-bills this year, that would not be a violent and bloody measure, as it would be to pay them, and enable the State to commit violence and shed innocent blood. This is, in fact, the definition of a peaceful revolution, if any such is possible. If the tax-gatherer, or any other public officer, asks me, as one has done, "But what shall I do?" my answer is, "If you really wish to do anything, resign your office." When the subject has refused allegiance, and the officer has resigned his office, then the revolution is accomplished. But even suppose blood should flow. Is there not a sort of bloodshed when the conscience is wounded? Through this wound a man's real manhood and immortality flow out, and he bleeds to an everlasting death. I see this blood flowing now.

I have contemplated the imprisonment of the offender, rather than the seizure of his goods,—though both will serve the same purpose,—because they who assert the purest right, and consequently are most dangerous to a corrupt State, commonly have not spent much time in accumulating property. To such the State renders comparatively small service, and a slight tax is wont to appear exorbitant, particularly if they are obliged to earn it by special labor with their hands. If there were one who lived wholly without the use of money, the State itself would hesitate to demand it of him. But the rich man — not to make any invidious comparison — is always sold to the institution which makes him rich. Absolutely speaking, the more money, the less virtue; for money comes between a man and his objects, and obtains them for him; and it was certainly no great virtue to obtain it. It puts to rest many questions which he would otherwise be taxed to answer; while the only new question which it puts is the hard but superfluous one, how to spend it. Thus his moral ground is taken from under his feet. The opportunities of living are diminished in proportion as what are called the "means" are increased. The best thing a man can do for his culture when he is rich is to endeavor to carry out those schemes which he entertained when he was poor. Christ answered the Herodians according to their condition. "Show me the tribute-money," said he; — and one took a penny out of his pocket; — if you use money which has the image of Cæsar on it, and which he has made current and valuable, that is, *if you are men of the State,* and gladly enjoy the advantages of Cæsar's government, then pay him back some of his own when he demands it; "Render therefore to Cæsar that which is Cæsar's, and to God those things which are God's," — leaving them no wiser than before as to which was which; for they did not wish to know.

When I converse with the freest of my neighbors, I perceive that, whatever they may say about the magnitude and seriousness of the question, and their regard for the public tranquillity, the long and the short of the matter is, that they cannot spare the protection of the existing government, and they dread the consequences to their property and families of disobedience to it. For my own part, I should not like to think that I ever rely on the protection of the State. But, if I deny the authority of the State when it presents its tax-bill, it will soon take and waste all my property, and so harass me and my children without end. This is hard. This makes it impossible for a man to live honestly, and at the same time comfortably, in outward respects. It will not be worth the while to accumulate property; that would be sure to go again. You must hire or squat somewhere, and raise but a small crop, and eat that soon. You must live within yourself, and depend upon yourself, always tucked up and ready for a start, and not have many affairs. A man may grow rich in Turkey even, if he will be in all respects a good subject of the Turkish government. Confucius said: "If a state is governed by the principles of reason, poverty and misery are subjects of shame; if a state is not governed by the principles of reason, riches and honors are the subjects of shame." No: until I want the protection of Massachusetts to be extended to me in some distant Southern port, where my liberty is endangered, or until I am bent solely on building up an estate at home by peaceful enterprise, I can afford to refuse allegiance to Massachusetts, and her right to my property and life. It costs me less in every sense to incur the penalty of disobedience to the State, than it would to obey. I should feel as if I were worth less in that case.

Some years ago, the State met me in behalf of the Church, and commanded me to pay a certain sum toward the support of a clergyman whose preaching my father attended, but never I myself. "Pay," it said, "or be locked up in the jail." I declined to pay. But, unfortunately, another man saw fit to pay it. I did not see why the schoolmaster should be taxed to support the priest, and not the priest the schoolmaster; for I was not the State's schoolmaster, but I supported myself by voluntary subscription. I did not see why the lyceum should not present its tax-bill, and have the State to back its demand, as well as the Church. However, at the request of the selectmen, I condescended to make some such statement as this in writing: — " Know all men by these presents, that I, Henry Thoreau, do not wish to be regarded as a member of any incorporated society which I have not joined." This I gave to the town clerk; and he has it. The

State, having thus learned that I did not wish to be regarded as a member of that Church, has never made a like demand on me since; though it said that it must adhere to its original presumption that time. If I had known how to name them, I should then have signed off in detail from all the societies which I never signed on to; but I do not know where to find a complete list.

I have paid no poll-tax for six years. I was put into a jail once on this account, for one night; and, as I stood considering the walls of solid stone, two or three feet thick, the door of wood and iron, a foot thick, and the iron grating which strained the light, I could not help being struck with the foolishness of that institution which treated me as if I were mere flesh and blood and bones, to be locked up. I wondered that it should have concluded at length that this was the best use it could put me to, and had never thought to avail itself of my services in some way. I saw that, if there was a wall of stone between me and my townsmen, there was a still more difficult one to climb or break through, before they could get to be as free as I was. I did not for a moment feel confined, and the walls seemed a great waste of stone and mortar. I felt as if I alone of all my townsmen had paid my tax. They plainly did not know how to treat me, but behaved like persons who are underbred. In every threat and in every compliment there was a blunder; for they thought that my chief desire was to stand the other side of that stone wall. I could not but smile to see how industriously they locked the door on my meditations, which followed them out again without let or hindrance, and *they* were really all that was dangerous. As they could not reach me, they had resolved to punish my body; just as boys, if they cannot come at some person against whom they have a spite, will abuse his dog. I saw that the State was half-witted, that it was timid as a lone woman with her silver spoons, and that it did not know its friends from its foes, and I lost all my remaining respect for it, and pitied it.

Thus the State never intentionally confronts a man's

sense, intellectual or moral, but only his body, his senses. It is not armed with superior wit or honesty, but with superior physical strength. I was not born to be forced. I will breathe after my own fashion. Let us see who is the strongest. What force has a multitude? They only can force me who obey a higher law than I. They force me to become like themselves. I do not hear of *men* being *forced* to live this way or that by masses of men. What sort of life were that to live? When I meet a government which says to me, "Your money or your life," why should I be in haste to give it my money? It may be in a great strait, and not know what to do: I cannot help that. It must help itself; do as I do. It is not worth the while to snivel about it. I am not responsible for the successful working of the machinery of society. I am not the son of the engineer. I perceive that, when an acorn and a chestnut fall side by side, the one does not remain inert to make way for the other, but both obey their own laws, and spring and grow and flourish as best they can, till one, perchance, overshadows and destroys the other. If a plant cannot live according to its nature, it dies; and so a man.

The night in prison was novel and interesting enough. The prisoners in their shirt-sleeves were enjoying a chat and the evening air in the doorway, when I entered. But the jailer said, "Come, boys, it is time to lock up"; and so they dispersed, and I heard the sound of their steps returning into the hollow apartments. My room-mate was introduced to me by the jailer, as "a first-rate fellow and a clever man." When the door was locked, he showed me where to hang my hat, and how he managed matters there. The rooms were whitewashed once a month; and this one, at least, was the whitest, most simply furnished, and probably the neatest apartment in the town. He naturally wanted to know where I came from, and what brought me there; and, when I had told him, I asked him in my turn how he came there, presuming him to be an honest man, of course; and, as the world goes, I believe he was. "Why," said he, "they accuse me of burning a barn; but I never did it." As near as I could discover, he had probably gone to bed in a barn when drunk, and smoked his pipe there; and so a barn was burnt. He had the reputation of being a clever man, had been there some three months waiting for his trial to come on, and would have to wait as much longer; but he was quite domesticated and contented, since he got his board for nothing, and thought that he was well treated.

He occupied one window, and I the other; and I saw, that, if one stayed there long, his principal business would be to look out the window. I had soon read all the tracts that were left there, and examined where former prisoners had broken out, and where a grate had been sawed off, and heard the history of the various occupants of that room; for I found that even here there was a history and a gossip which never circulated beyond the walls of the jail. Probably this is the only house in the town where verses are composed, which are afterwards printed in a circular form, but not published. I was shown quite a long list of verses which were composed by some young men who had been detected in an attempt to escape, who avenged themselves by singing them.

I pumped my fellow-prisoner as dry as I could, for fear I should never see him again; but at length he showed me which was my bed, and left me to blow out the lamp.

It was like traveling into a far country, such as I had never expected to behold, to lie there for one night. It seemed to me that I never had heard the town-clock strike before, nor the evening sounds of the village; for we slept with the windows open, which were inside the grating. It was to see my native village in the light of the Middle Ages, and our Concord was turned into a Rhine stream, and visions of knights and castles passed before me. They were the voices of old burghers that I heard in the streets. I was an involuntary spectator and auditor of whatever was done and said in the kitchen of the adjacent village-inn, — a wholly new and rare experience to me. It was a closer view of my native town. I was fairly inside of it. I never had seen its institutions before. This is one of its peculiar institutions; for it is a shire town. I began to comprehend what its inhabitants were about.

In the morning, our breakfasts were put through the hole in the door, in small oblong-square tin pans, made to fit, and holding a pint of chocolate, with brown bread, and an iron spoon. When they called for the vessels again, I was green enough to return what bread I had left; but my comrade seized it, and said that I should lay that up for lunch or dinner. Soon after he was let out to work at haying in a neighboring field, whither he went every day, and would not be back till noon; so he bade me good-day, saying that he doubted if he should see me again.

When I came out of prison, — for someone interfered, and paid that tax, — I did not perceive that great changes had taken place on the common, such as he observed who went in a youth, and emerged a tottering and gray-headed man; and yet a change had to my eyes come over the scene, — the town, and State, and country, — greater than any that mere time could effect. I saw yet more distinctly the State in which I lived. I saw to what extent the people among whom I lived could be trusted as good neighbors and friends; that their friendship was for summer weather only; that they did not greatly propose to do right; that they were a distinct race from me by their prejudices and superstitions, as the Chinamen and Malays are; that, in their sacrifices to humanity, they ran no risks, not even to their property; that after all, they were not so noble but they treated the thief as he had treated them, and hoped, by a certain outward observance and a few prayers, and by walking in a particular straight though useless path from time to time, to save their souls. This may be to judge my neighbors harshly; for I believe that many of them are not aware that they have such an institution as the jail in their village.

It was formerly the custom in our village, when a poor

debtor came out of jail, for his acquaintances to salute him, looking through their fingers, which were crossed to represent the grating of a jail window, "How do ye do?" My neighbors did not thus salute me, but first looked at me, and then at one another, as if I had returned from a long journey. I was put into jail as I was going to the shoemaker's to get a shoe which was mended. When I was let out the next morning, I proceeded to finish my errand, and having put on my mended shoe, joined a huckleberry party, who were impatient to put themselves under my conduct; and in half an hour,—for the horse was soon tackled,—was in the midst of a huckleberry field, on one of our highest hills, two miles off, and then the State was nowhere to be seen.

This is the whole history of "My Prisons."

I have never declined paying the highway tax, because I am as desirous of being a good neighbor as I am of being a bad subject; and, as for supporting schools, I am doing my part to educate my fellow-countrymen now. It is for no particular item in the tax-bill that I refuse to pay it. I simply wish to refuse allegiance to the State, to withdraw and stand aloof from it effectually. I do not care to trace the course of my dollar, if I could, till it buys a man or a musket to shoot one with,—the dollar is innocent,—but I am concerned to trace the effects of my allegiance. In fact, I quietly declare war with the State, after my fashion, though I will still make what use and get what advantage of her I can, as is usual in such cases.

If others pay the tax which is demanded of me, from a sympathy with the State, they do but what they have already done in their own case, or rather they abet injustice to a greater extent than the State requires. If they pay the tax from a mistaken interest in the individual taxed, to save his property, or prevent his going to jail, it is because they have not considered wisely how far they let their private feelings interfere with the public good.

This, then, is my position at present. But one cannot

be too much on his guard in such a case, lest his action be biased by obstinacy, or an undue regard for the opinions of men. Let him see that he does only what belongs to himself and to the hour.

I think sometimes, Why, this people mean well; they are only ignorant; they would do better if they knew how: why give your neighbors this pain to treat you as they are not inclined to? But I think again, This is no reason why I should do as they do, or permit others to suffer much greater pain of a different kind. Again, I sometimes say to myself, When many millions of men, without heat, without ill-will, without personal feeling of any kind, demand of you a few shillings only without the possibility, such is their constitution, of retracting or altering their present demand, and without the possibility, on your side, of appeal to any other millions, why expose yourself to this overwhelming brute force? You do not resist cold and hunger, the winds and the waves, thus obstinately; you quietly submit to a thousand similar necessities. You do not put your head into the fire. But just in proportion as I regard this as not wholly a brute force, but partly a human force, and consider that I have relations to those millions as to so many millions of men, and not of mere brute or inanimate things, I see that appeal is possible, first and instantaneously, from them to the Maker of them, and, secondly, from them to themselves. But, if I put my head deliberately into the fire, there is no appeal to fire or to the Maker of fire, and I have only myself to blame. If I could convince myself that I have any right to be satisfied with men as they are, and to treat them accordingly, and not according, in some respects, to my requisitions and expectations of what they and I ought to be, then, like a good Mussulman and fatalist, I should endeavor to be satisfied with things as they are, and say it is the will of God. And, above all, there is this difference between resisting this and a purely brute or natural force, that I can resist this with some effect; but I cannot expect, like Orpheus, to change the nature of the rocks and trees and beasts.

I do not wish to quarrel with any man or nation. I do not wish to split hairs, to make fine distinctions, or set myself up as better than my neighbors. I seek rather, I may say, even an excuse for conforming to the laws of the land. I am but too ready to conform to them. Indeed, I have reason to suspect myself on this head; and each year, as the tax-gatherer comes round, I find myself disposed to review the acts and position of the general and State governments, and the spirit of the people, to discover a pretext for conformity.

> " We must affect our country as our parents,
> And if at any time we alienate
> Our love or industry from doing it honor,
> We must respect effects and teach the soul
> Matter of conscience and religion,
> And not desire of rule or benefit."

I believe that the State will soon be able to take all my work of this sort out of my hands, and then I shall be no better a patriot than my fellow-countrymen. Seen from a lower point of view, the Constitution, with all its faults, is very good; the law and the courts are very respectable; even this State and this American government are, in many respects, very admirable and rare things, to be thankful for, such as a great many have described them; but seen from a point of view a little higher, they are what I have described them; seen from a higher still, and the highest, who shall say what they are, or that they are worth looking at or thinking of at all?

However, the government does not concern me much, and I shall bestow the fewest possible thoughts on it. It is not many moments that I live under a government, even in this world. If a man is thought-free, fancy-free, imagination-free, that which *is not* never for a long time appearing *to be* to him, unwise rulers or reformers cannot fatally interrupt him.

I know that most men think differently from myself; but those whose lives are by profession devoted to the study of these or kindred subjects, content me as little as any. Statesmen and legislators, standing so completely within the institution, never distinctly and nakedly behold it. They speak of moving society, but have no resting-place without it. They may be men of a certain experience and discrimination, and have no doubt invented ingenious and even useful systems, for which we sincerely thank them; but all their wit and usefulness lie within certain not very wide limits. They are wont to forget that the world is not governed by policy and expediency. Webster never goes behind government, and so cannot speak with authority about it. His words are wisdom to those legislators who contemplate no essential reform in the existing government; but for thinkers, and those who legislate for all time, he never once glances at the subject. I know of those whose serene and wise speculations on this theme would soon reveal the limits of his mind's range and hospitality. Yet, compared with the cheap professions of most reformers, and the still cheaper wisdom and eloquence of politicians in general, his are almost the only sensible and valuable words, and we thank Heaven for him. Comparatively, he is always strong, original, and, above all, practical. Still his quality is not wisdom, but prudence. The lawyer's truth is not Truth, but consistency, or a consistent expediency. Truth is always in harmony with herself, and is not concerned chiefly to reveal the justice that may consist with wrong-doing. He well deserves to be called, as he has been called, the Defender of the Constitution. There are really no blows to be given by him but defensive ones. He is not a leader, but a follower. His leaders are the men of '87. "I have never made an effort," he says, "and never propose to make an effort; I have never countenanced an effort, and never mean to countenance an effort, to disturb the arrangement as originally made, by which the various States came into the Union." Still thinking of the sanction which the Constitution gives to slavery, he says, "Because it was a part of the original compact, — let it stand." Notwithstanding his special acuteness and ability, he is unable to take a fact out of its merely political relations, and behold it as it lies absolutely to be disposed of by the intellect, — what, for instance, it behooves a man to do here in America to-day with regard to slavery — but ventures, or is driven, to make some such desperate answer as the following, while professing to speak absolutely, and as a private man, — from which what new and singular code of social duties might be inferred? "The manner," says he, "in which the governments of those States where slavery exists are to regulate it, is for their own consideration, under their responsibility to their constituents, to the general laws of propriety, humanity, and justice, and to God. Associations formed elsewhere, springing from a feeling of humanity, or any other cause, have nothing whatever to do with it. They have never received any encouragement from me, and they never will."

They who know of no purer sources of truth, who have traced up its stream no higher, stand, and wisely stand, by the Bible and the Constitution, and drink at it there with reverence and humility; but they who behold where it comes trickling into this lake or that pool, gird up their loins once more, and continue their pilgrimage toward its fountain-head.

No man with a genius for legislation has appeared in America. They are rare in the history of the world. There are orators, politicians, and eloquent men, by the thousand; but the speaker has not yet opened his mouth to speak, who is capable of settling the much-vexed questions of the day. We love eloquence for its own sake, and not for any truth which it may utter, or any heroism it may inspire. Our legislators have not yet learned the comparative value of free-trade and of freedom, of union, and of rectitude, to a nation. They have no genius or talent for comparatively humble questions of taxation and finance, commerce and manufactures and agriculture. If we were left solely to the wordy wit of legislators in Congress for our guidance, uncorrected by the seasonable experience and the effectual complaints of the people, America would not long retain her rank among the nations. For eighteen hundred years, though perchance I have no right to say it, the New Testament has been written; yet where is the legislator who has wisdom and practical talent enough to avail himself of the light which it sheds on the science of legislation?

The authority of government, even such as I am willing to submit to, — for I will cheerfully obey those who know and can do better than I, and in many things even those who neither know nor can do so well, — is still an impure one: to be strictly just, it must have the sanction and consent of the governed. It can have no pure right over my person and property but what I concede to it. The progress from an absolute to a limited monarchy, from a limited monarchy to a democracy, is a progress toward a true respect for the individual. Even the Chinese philosopher was wise enough to regard the individual as the basis of the empire. Is a democracy, such as we know it, the last improvement possible in government? Is it not possible to take a step further towards recognizing and organizing the rights of man? There will never be a really free and enlightened State, until the State comes to recognize the individual as a higher and independent power, from which all its own power and authority are derived, and treats him accordingly. I please myself with imagining a State at last which can afford to be just to all men, and to treat the individual with respect as a neighbor; which even would not think it inconsistent with its own repose, if a few were to live aloof from it, not meddling with it, nor embraced by it, who fulfilled all the duties of neighbors and fellow-men. A State which bore this kind of fruit, and suffered it to drop off as fast as it ripened, would prepare the way for a still more perfect and glorious State, which also I have imagined, but not yet anywhere seen.

38 *Solitude*

THIS is a delicious evening, when the whole body is one sense, and imbibes delight through every pore. I go and come with a strange liberty in Nature, a part of herself.

HENRY DAVID THOREAU

As I walk along the stony shore of the pond in my shirt-sleeves, though it is cool as well as cloudy and windy, and I see nothing special to attract me, all the elements are unusually congenial to me. The bull-frogs trump to usher in the night, and the note of the whippoorwill is borne on the rippling wind from over the water. Sympathy with the fluttering alder and poplar leaves almost takes away my breath; yet, like the lake, my serenity is rippled but not ruffled. These small waves raised by the evening wind are as remote from storm as the smooth reflecting surface. Though it is now dark, the wind still blows and roars in the wood, the waves still dash, and some creatures lull the rest with their notes. The repose is never complete. The wildest animals do not repose, but seek their prey now; the fox, and skunk, and rabbit, now roam the fields and woods without fear. They are Nature's watchmen, — links which connect the days of animated life.

When I return to my house I find that visitors have been there and left their cards, either a bunch of flowers, or a wreath of evergreen, or a name in pencil on a yellow walnut leaf or a chip. They who come rarely to the woods take some little piece of the forest into their hands to play with by the way, which they leave, either intentionally or accidentally. One has peeled a willow wand, woven it into a ring, and dropped it on my table. I could always tell if visitors had called in my absence, either by the bended twigs or grass, or the print of their shoes, and generally of what sex or age or quality they were by some slight trace left, as a flower dropped, or a bunch of grass plucked and thrown away, even as far off as the railroad, half a mile distant, or by the lingering odor of a cigar or pipe. Nay, I was frequently notified of the passage of a traveler along the highway sixty rods off by the scent of his pipe.

There is commonly sufficient space about us. Our horizon is never quite at our elbows. The thick wood is not just at our door, nor the pond, but somewhat is always clearing, familiar and worn by us, appropriated and fenced in some way, and reclaimed from Nature. For what reason have I this vast range and circuit, some square miles of unfrequented forest, for my privacy, abandoned to me by men? My nearest neighbor is a mile distant, and no house is visible from any place but the hill tops within half a mile of my own. I have my horizon bounded by woods all to myself; a distant view of the railroad where it touches the pond on the one hand, and of the fence which skirts the woodland road on the other. But for the most part it is as solitary where I live as on the prairies. It is as much Asia or Africa as New England. I have, as it were, my own sun and moon and stars, and a little world all to myself. At night there was never a traveler passed my house, or knocked at my door, more than if I were the first or last man; unless it were in the spring, when at long intervals some came from the village to fish for pouts, — they plainly fished much more in the Walden Pond of their own natures, and baited their hooks with darkness, — but they soon retreated, usually with light baskets, and left "the world to darkness and to me," and the black kernel of the night was never profaned by any human neighborhood. I believe that men are generally still a little afraid of the dark, though the witches are all hung, and Christianity and candles have been introduced.

Yet I experienced sometimes that the most sweet and tender, the most innocent and encouraging society may be found in any natural object, even for the poor misanthrope and most melancholy man. There can be no very black melancholy to him who lives in the midst of Nature and has his senses still. There was never yet such a storm but it was Æolian music to a healthy and innocent ear. Nothing can rightly compel a simple and brave man to a vulgar sadness. While I enjoy the friendship of the seasons I trust that nothing can make life a burden to me. The gentle rain which waters my beans and keeps me in the house to-day is not drear and melancholy, but good for me, too. Though it prevents my hoeing them, it is of far more worth than my hoeing. If it should continue so long as to cause the seeds to rot in the ground and destroy the potatoes in the low lands, it would still be good for the grass on the uplands, and, being good for the grass, it would be good for me. Sometimes, when I compare myself with other men, it seems as if I were more favored by the gods than they, beyond any deserts that I am conscious of; as if I had a warrant and surety at their hands which my fellows have not, and were especially guided and guarded. I do not flatter myself, but if it be possible they flatter me. I have never felt lonesome, or in the least oppressed by a sense of solitude, but once, and that was a few weeks after I came to the woods, when, for an hour, I doubted if the near neighborhood of man was not essential to a serene and healthy life. To be alone was something unpleasant. But I was at the same time conscious of a slight insanity in my mood, and seemed to foresee my recovery. In the midst of a gentle rain while these thoughts prevailed, I was suddenly sensible of such sweet and beneficent society in Nature, in the very pattering of the drops, and in every sound and sight around my house, an infinite and unaccountable friendliness all at once like an atmosphere sustaining me, as made the fancied advantages of human neighborhood insignificant, and I have never thought of them since. Every little pine needle expanded and swelled with sympathy and befriended me. I was so distinctly made aware of the presence of something kindred to me, even in scenes which we are accustomed to call wild and dreary, and also that the nearest of blood to me and humanest was not a person nor a villager, that I thought no place could ever be strange to me again. —

> "Mourning untimely consumes the sad;
> Few are their days in the land of the living,
> Beautiful daughter of Toscar."

Some of my pleasantest hours were during the long rain storms in the spring or fall, which confined me to the house for the afternoon as well as the forenoon, soothed by their ceaseless roar and pelting; when an early twilight ushered in a long evening in which many thoughts had time to take root and unfold themselves. In those driving northeast rains which tried the village houses so, when the maids stood ready with mop and pail in front entries to keep the deluge out, I sat behind my door in my little house, which was all entry, and thoroughly enjoyed its protection. In one heavy thunder shower the lightning struck a large pitch-pine across the pond, making a very conspicuous and perfectly regular spiral groove from top to bottom, an inch or more deep, and four or five inches wide, as you would groove a walking-stick. I passed it again the other day, and was struck with awe on looking up and beholding that mark, now more distinct than ever, where a terrific and resistless bolt came down out of the harmless sky eight years ago. Men frequently say to me, "I should think you would feel lonesome down there, and want to be nearer to folks, rainy and snowy days and nights especially." I am tempted to reply to such, — This whole earth which we inhabit is but a point in space. How far apart, think you, dwell the two most distant inhabitants of yonder star, the breadth of whose disk cannot be appreciated by our instruments? Why should I feel lonely? is not our planet in the Milky Way? This which you put seems to me not to be the most important question. What sort of space is that which separates a man from his fellows and makes him solitary? I have found that no exertion of the legs can bring two minds much nearer to one another. What do we want most to dwell near to? Not to many men surely, the depot, the post-office, the bar-room, the meeting-house, the school-house, the grocery, Beacon Hill, or the Five Points, where men most congregate, but to the perennial source of our life whence in all our experience we have found that to issue, as the willow stands near the water and sends out its roots in that direction. This will vary with different natures, but this is the place where a wise man will dig his cellar. . . . I one evening overtook one of my townsmen, who has accumulated what is called "a handsome property," — though I never got a *fair* view of it, — on the Walden road, driving a pair of cattle to market, who inquired of me how I could bring my mind to give up so many of the comforts of life. I answered that I was very sure I liked it passably well; I was not joking. And so I went home to my bed, and left him to pick his way through the darkness and the mud to Brighton, — or Bright-town, — which place he would reach some time in the morning.

Any prospect of awakening or coming to life to a dead man makes indifferent all times and places. The place where that may occur is always the same, and indescribably pleasant to all our senses. For the most part we allow only outlying and transient circumstances to make our occasions. They are, in fact, the cause of our distraction. Nearest to all things is that power which fashions their being. *Next* to us the grandest laws are continually being executed. *Next* to us is not the workman whom we have hired, with whom we love so well to talk, but the workman whose work we are.

"How vast and profound is the influence of the subtle powers of Heaven and of Earth!"

"We seek to perceive them, and we do not see them; we seek to hear them, and we do not hear them; identified with the substance of things, they cannot be separated from them."

"They cause that in all the universe men purify and sanctify their hearts, and clothe themselves in their holiday garments to offer sacrifices and oblations to their ancestors. It is an ocean of subtle intelligences. They are everywhere, above us, on our left, on our right; they environ us on all sides."

We are the subjects of an experiment which is not a little interesting to me. Can we not do without the society of our gossips a little while under these circumstances, — have our own thoughts to cheer us? Confucius says truly, "Virtue does not remain as an abandoned orphan; it must of necessity have neighbors."

With thinking we may be beside ourselves in a sane sense. By a conscious effort of the mind we can stand aloof from actions and their consequences; and all things, good and bad, go by us like a torrent. We are not wholly involved in Nature. I may be either the driftwood in the stream, or Indra in the sky looking down on it. I *may* be affected by a theatrical exhibition; on the other hand, I *may not* be affected by an actual event which appears to concern me much more. I only know myself as a human entity; the scene, so to speak, of thoughts and affections; and am sensible of a certain doubleness by which I can stand as remote from myself as from another. However intense my experience, I am conscious of the presence of and criticism of a part of me, which, as it were, is not a part of me, but spectator, sharing no experience, but taking note of it; and that is no more I than it is you. When the play, it may be the tragedy, of life is over, the spectator goes his way. It was a kind of fiction, a work of the imagination only, so far as he was concerned. This doubleness may easily make us poor neighbors and friends sometimes.

I find it wholesome to be alone the greater part of the time. To be in company, even with the best, is soon wearisome and dissipating. I love to be alone. I never found the companion that was so companionable as solitude. We are for the most part more lonely when we go abroad among men than when we stay in our chambers. A man thinking or working is always alone, let him be where he will. Solitude is not measured by the miles of space that intervene between a man and his fellows. The really diligent student in one of the crowded hives of Cambridge College is as solitary as a dervish in the desert. The farmer can work alone in the field or the woods all day, hoeing or chopping, and not feel lonesome, because he is employed; but when he comes home at night he cannot sit down in a room alone, at the mercy of his thoughts, but must be where he can " see the folks," and recreate, and as he thinks remunerate, himself for his day's solitude; and hence he wonders how the student can sit alone in the house all night and most of the day without ennui and "the blues"; but he does not realize that the student, though in the house, is still at work in *his* field, and chopping in *his* woods, as the farmer in his, and in turn seeks the same recreation and society that the latter does, though it may be a more condensed form of it.

Society is commonly too cheap. We meet at very short intervals, not having had time to acquire any new value for each other. We meet at meals three times a day, and give each other a new taste of that old musty cheese that we are. We have to agree on a certain set of rules, called etiquette and politeness, to make this frequent meeting tolerable and that we need not come to open war. We meet at the post-office, and at the sociable, and about the fireside every night; we live thick and are in each other's way, and stumble over one another, and I think that we thus lose some respect for one another. Certainly less frequency would suffice for all important and hearty communications. Consider the girls in a factory,— never alone, hardly in their dreams. It would be better if there were but one inhabitant to a square mile, as where I live. The value of a man is not in his skin, that we should touch him.

I have heard of a man lost in the woods and dying of famine and exhaustion at the foot of a tree, whose loneliness was relieved by the grotesque visions with which, owing to bodily weakness, his diseased imagination surrounded him, and which he believed to be real. So also, owing to bodily and mental health and strength, we may be continually cheered by a like but more normal and natural society, and come to know that we are never alone.

I have a great deal of company in my house; especially in the morning, when nobody calls. Let me suggest a few comparisons, that some one may convey an idea of my situation. I am no more lonely than the loon in the pond that laughs so loud, or than Walden Pond itself. What company has that lonely lake, I pray? And yet it has not the blue devils, but the blue angels in it, in the azure tint of its waters. The sun is alone, except in thick weather, when there sometimes appear to be two, but one is a mock sun. God is alone, — but the devil, he is far from being alone; he sees a great deal of company; he is legion. I am no more lonely than a single mullein or dandelion in a pasture, or a bean leaf, or sorrel, or a horse-fly, or a humble-bee. I am no more lonely than the Mill Brook, or a weathercock, or the north star, or the south wind, or an April shower, or a January thaw, or the first spider in a new house.

I have occasional visits in the long winter evenings, when the snow falls fast and the wind howls in the wood, from an old settler and original proprietor, who is reported to have dug Walden Pond, and stoned it, and fringed it with pine woods; who tells me stories of old time and of new eternity; and between us we manage to pass a cheerful evening with social mirth and pleasant views of things, even without apples or cider, — a most wise and humorous friend, whom I love much, who keeps himself more secret than ever did Goffe or Whalley; and though he is thought to be dead, none can show where he is buried. An elderly dame, too, dwells in my neighborhood, invisible to most persons, in whose odorous herb garden I love to stroll sometimes, gathering simples and listening to her fables; for she has a genius of unequaled fertility, and her memory runs back farther than mythology, and she can tell me the original of every fable, and on what fact every one is founded, for the incidents occurred when she was young. A ruddy and lusty old dame, who delights in all weathers and seasons, and is likely to outlive all her children yet.

The indescribable innocence and beneficence of Nature, — of sun and wind and rain, of summer and winter, — such health, such cheer, they afford forever! and such sympathy have they ever with our race, that all Nature would be affected, and the sun's brightness fade, and the winds would sigh humanely, and the clouds rain tears, and the woods shed their leaves and put on mourning in midsummer, if any man should ever for a just cause grieve. Shall I not have intelligence with the earth? Am I not partly leaves and vegetable mold myself?

What is the pill which will keep us well, serene, contented? Not my or thy great-grandfather's, but our great-grandmother Nature's universal, vegetable, botanic medicines, by which she has kept herself young always, outlived so many old Parrs in her day, and fed her health with their decaying fatness. For my panacea, instead of one of those quack vials of a mixture dipped from Acheron and the Dead Sea, which come out of those long shallow black-schooner-looking wagons which we sometimes see made to carry bottles, let me have a draft of undiluted morning air. Morning air! If men will not drink of this at the fountain-head of the day, why, then, we must even bottle up some and sell it in the shops, for the benefit of those who have lost their subscription ticket to morning time in this world. But remember, it will not keep quite till noonday even in the coolest cellar, but drive out the stopples long ere that and follow westward the steps of Aurora. I am no worshiper of Hygeia, who was the daughter of that old herb-doctor Æsculapius, and who is represented on monuments holding a serpent in one hand, and in the other a cup out of which the serpent sometimes drinks; but rather of Hebe, cup-bearer to Jupiter, who was the daughter of Juno and wild lettuce, and who had the power of restoring gods and men to the vigor of youth. She was probably the only thoroughly sound-conditioned, healthy, and robust young lady that ever walked the globe, and wherever she came it was spring.

Nantucket

NOTHING more happened on the passage worthy the
mentioning; so, after a fine run, we safely arrived at
Nantucket.

Nantucket! Take out your map and look at it. See what
a real corner of the world it occupies; how it stands there,
away off shore, more lonely than the Eddystone lighthouse.
Look at it — a mere hillock, and elbow of sand; all beach,
without a background. There is more sand there than you
would use in twenty years as a substitute for blotting paper.
Some gamesome wights will tell you that they have to plant
weeds there, they don't grow naturally; that they import
Canada thistles; that they have to send beyond seas for a
spile to stop a leak in an oil cask; that pieces of wood in
Nantucket are carried about like bits of the true cross in
Rome; that people there plant toadstools before their houses,
to get under the shade in summer time; that one blade of
grass makes an oasis, three blades in a day's walk a prairie;
that they wear quicksand shoes, something like Laplander
snow-shoes; that they are so shut up, belted about, every
way inclosed, surrounded, and made an utter island of by
the ocean, that to their very chairs and tables small clams
will sometimes be found adhering, as to the backs of sea
turtles. But these extravaganzas only show that Nantucket
is no Illinois.

Look now at the wondrous traditional story of how this
island was settled by the red-men. Thus goes the legend.
In olden times an eagle swooped down upon the New England coast, and carried off an infant Indian in his talons.
With loud lament the parents saw their child borne out
of sight over the wide waters. They resolved to follow in
the same direction. Setting out in their canoes, after a
perilous passage they discovered the island, and there they

found an empty ivory casket, — the poor little Indian's skeleton.

What wonder, then, that these Nantucketers, born on a beach, should take to the sea for a livelihood! They first caught crabs and quohogs in the sand; grown bolder, they waded out with nets for mackerel; more experienced, they pushed off in boats and captured cod; and at last, launching a navy of great ships on the sea, explored this watery world; put an incessant belt of circumnavigations round it; peeped in at Behring's Straits; and in all seasons and all oceans declared everlasting war with the mightiest animated mass that has survived the flood; most monstrous and most mountainous! That Himmalehan, salt-sea Mastodon, clothed with such portentousness of unconscious power, that his very panics are more to be dreaded than his most fearless and malicious assaults!

And thus have these naked Nantucketers, these sea hermits, issuing from their ant-hill in the sea, overrun and conquered the watery world like so many Alexanders; parceling out among them the Atlantic, Pacific, and Indian oceans, as the three pirate powers did Poland. Let America add Mexico to Texas, and pile Cuba upon Canada; let the English overswarm all India, and hang out their blazing banner from the sun; two thirds of this terraqueous globe are the Nantucketer's. For the sea is his; he owns it, as Emperors own empires; other seamen having but a right of way through it. Merchant ships are but extension bridges; armed ones but floating forts; even pirates and privateers, though following the sea as highwaymen the road, they but plunder other ships, other fragments of the land like themselves, without seeking to draw their living from the bottomless deep itself. The Nantucketer, he alone resides and riots on the sea; he alone, in Bible language, goes down to it in ships; to and fro plowing it as his own special plantation. *There* is his home; *there* lies his business, which a Noah's flood would not interrupt, though it overwhelmed all the millions in China. He lives on the sea, as prairie cocks in the prairie; he hides among the waves, he climbs them as chamois hunters climb the Alps. For years he knows not the land; so that when he comes to it at last, it smells like another world, more strangely than the moon would to an Earthsman. With the landless gull, that at sunset folds her wings and is rocked to sleep between billows; so at nightfall, the Nantucketer, out of sight of land, furls his sails, and lays him to his rest, while under his very pillow rush herds of walruses and whales.

40   *Moby Dick*

I, ISHMAEL, was one of that crew; my shouts had gone up with the rest, my oath had been welded with theirs; and stronger I shouted, and more did I hammer and clinch my oath, because of the dread in my soul. A wild, mystical, sympathetical feeling was in me; Ahab's quenchless feud seemed mine. With greedy ears I learned the history of that murderous monster against whom I and all the others had taken our oaths of violence and revenge.

For some time past, though at intervals only, the unaccompanied, secluded White Whale had haunted those uncivilized seas mostly frequented by the Sperm Whale fishermen. But not all of them knew of his existence; only a few of them, comparatively, had knowingly seen him; while the number who as yet had actually and knowingly given battle to him, was small indeed. For, owing to the large number of whale-cruisers; the disorderly way they were sprinkled over the entire watery circumference, many of them adventurously pushing their quest along solitary latitudes, so as seldom or never for a whole twelvemonth or more on a stretch, to encounter a single news-telling sail of any sort; the inordinate length of each separate voyage; the irregularity of the times of sailing from home; all these, with other circumstances, direct and indirect, long obstructed the spread through the whole world-wide whaling-fleet of the special individualizing tidings concerning Moby Dick. It was hardly to be doubted, that several vessels reported to have encountered, at such or such a time, or on such or such a meridian, a Sperm Whale of uncommon magnitude and malignity, which whale, after doing great mischief to his assailants, had completely escaped them; to some minds it was not an unfair presumption, I say, that the whale in question must have been no other than Moby Dick. Yet as of late the Sperm Whale fishery had been marked by various and not unfrequent instances of great ferocity, cunning, and malice in the monster attacked; therefore it was, that those who by accident ignorantly gave battle to Moby Dick; such hunters, perhaps, for the most part, were content to ascribe the peculiar terror he bred, more, as it were, to the perils of the Sperm Whale fishery at large, than to the individual cause. In that way, mostly, the disastrous encounter between Ahab and the whale had hitherto been popularly regarded.

And as for those who, previously hearing of the White Whale, by chance caught sight of him; in the beginning of the thing they had every one of them, almost, as boldly and fearlessly lowered for him, as for any other whale of that species. But at length, such calamities did ensue in these assaults — not restricted to sprained wrists and ankles, broken limbs, or devouring amputations — but fatal to the last degree of fatality; those repeated disastrous repulses, all accumulating and piling their terrors upon Moby Dick; those things had gone far to shake the fortitude of many brave hunters, to whom the story of the White Whale had eventually come.

Nor did wild rumors of all sorts fail to exaggerate, and still the more horrify the true histories of these deadly encounters. For not only do fabulous rumors naturally grow out of the very body of all surprising terrible events — as the smitten tree gives birth to its fungi; but, in maritime life, far more than in that of terra firma, wild rumors abound, wherever there is any adequate reality for them to cling to. And as the sea surpasses the land in this matter, so the whale fishery surpasses every other sort of maritime life, in the wonderfulness and fearfulness of the rumors which sometimes circulate there. For not only are whalemen as a body unexempt from that ignorance and superstitiousness hereditary to all sailors; but of all sailors, they are by all odds the most directly brought into contact with whatever is appallingly astonishing in the sea; face to face they not only eye its greatest marvels, but, hand to jaw, give battle to them. Alone, in such remotest waters, that though you sailed a thousand miles, and passed a thousand shores, you would not come to any chiseled hearthstone, or aught hospitable beneath that part of the sun; in such latitudes and longitudes, pursuing too such a calling as he does, the whaleman is wrapped by influences all tending to make his fancy pregnant with many a mighty birth.

No wonder, then, that ever gathering volume from the mere transit over the wildest watery spaces, the outblown rumors of the White Whale did in the end incorporate with themselves all manner of morbid hints, and half-formed fœtal suggestions of supernatural agencies, which eventually invested Moby Dick with new terrors unborrowed from anything that visibly appears. So that in many cases such a panic did he finally strike, that few who by those rumors, at least, had heard of the White Whale, few of those hunters were willing to encounter the perils of his jaw.

But there were still other and more vital practical influences at work. Not even at the present day has the original prestige of the Sperm Whale, as fearfully distinguished from all other species of the leviathan, died out of the minds of the whalemen as a body. There are those this day among them, who, though intelligent and courageous enough in offering battle to the Greenland or Right Whale, would perhaps — either from professional inexperience, or incompetency, or timidity — decline a contest with the Sperm Whale; at any rate, there are plenty of whalemen, especially among those whaling nations not sailing under the American flag, who have never hostilely encountered the Sperm Whale, but whose sole knowledge of the leviathan is restricted to the ignoble monster primitively pursued in the North; seated on their hatches, these men will hearken with a childish fire-side interest and awe, to the wild, strange tales of Southern whaling. Nor is the preëminent tremendousness of the great Sperm Whale anywhere more feelingly comprehended, than on board of those prows which stem him.

And as if the now tested reality of his might had in former legendary times thrown its shadow before it; we find some book naturalists — Olassen and Povelson — declaring the Sperm Whale not only to be a consternation to every other creature in the sea, but also to be so incredibly ferocious as continually to be athirst for human blood. Nor even down to so late a time as Cuvier's, were these or almost similar impressions effaced. For in his Natural History, the Baron himself affirms that at sight of the Sperm Whale, all fish (sharks included) are "struck with the most lively terrors," and "often in the precipitancy of their flight dash themselves against the rocks with such violence as to cause instantaneous death." And however the general experiences in the fishery may amend such reports as these; yet in their full terribleness, even to the bloodthirsty item of Povelson, the superstitious belief in them is, in some vicissitudes of their vocation, revived in the minds of the hunters.

So that overawed by the rumors and portents concerning him, not a few of the fishermen recalled, in reference to Moby Dick, the earlier days of the Sperm Whale fishery, when it was oftentimes hard to induce long practiced Right whalemen to embark in the perils of this new and daring warfare; such men protesting that although other leviathans might be hopefully pursued, yet to chase and point lances at such an apparition as the Sperm Whale was not for mortal man. That to attempt it, would be inevitably to be torn into a quick eternity. On this head, there are some remarkable documents that may be consulted.

Nevertheless, some there were, who even in the face of these things were ready to give chase to Moby Dick; and a still greater number who, chancing only to hear of him distantly and vaguely, without the specific details of any certain calamity, and without superstitious accompaniments, were sufficiently hardy not to flee from the battle if offered.

One of the wild suggestings referred to, as at last coming to be linked with the White Whale in the minds of the superstitiously inclined, was the unearthly conceit that Moby Dick was ubiquitous; that he had actually been encountered in opposite latitudes at one and the same instant of time.

Nor, credulous as such minds must have been, was this conceit altogether without some faint show of superstitious probability. For as the secrets of the currents in the seas have never yet been divulged, even to the most erudite research; so the hidden ways of the Sperm Whale when beneath the surface remain, in great part, unaccountable to his pursuers; and from time to time have originated the most curious and contradictory speculations regarding them, especially concerning the mystic modes whereby, after sounding to a great depth, he transports himself with such vast swiftness to the most widely distant points.

It is a thing well known to both American and English whale-ships, and as well a thing placed upon authoritative record years ago by Scoresby, that some whales have been captured far north in the Pacific, in whose bodies have been found barbs of harpoons darted in the Greenland seas. Nor is it to be gainsaid, that in some of these instances it has been declared that the interval of time between the two assaults could not have exceeded very many days. Hence, by inference, it has been believed by some whalemen, that the Nor' West Passage, so long a problem to man, was never a problem to the whale. So that here, in the real living experience of living men, the prodigies related in old times to the inland Strello mountain in Portugal (near whose top there was said to be a lake in which the wrecks of ships floated up to the surface); and that still more wonderful story of the Arethusa fountain near Syracuse (whose waters were believed to have come from the Holy Land by an underground passage); these fabulous narrations are almost fully equaled by the realities of the whaleman.

Forced into familiarity, then, with such prodigies as these; and knowing that after repeated, intrepid assaults, the White Whale had escaped alive; it cannot be much matter of surprise that some whalemen should go still further in their superstitions; declaring Moby Dick not only ubiquitous, but immortal (for immortality is but ubiquity in time); that though groves of spears should be planted in his flanks, he would still swim away unharmed; or if indeed he should ever be made to spout thick blood, such a sight would be but a ghastly deception; for again in unensanguined billows hundreds of leagues away, his unsullied jet would once more be seen.

But even stripped of these supernatural surmisings, there was enough in the earthly make and incontestable character of the monster to strike the imagination with unwonted power. For, it was not so much his uncommon bulk that so much distinguished him from other sperm whales, but, as was elsewhere thrown out — a peculiar snow-white wrinkled forehead, and a high, pyramidical white hump. These were his prominent features; the tokens whereby, even in the limitless, uncharted seas, he revealed his identity at a long distance, to those who knew him.

The rest of his body was so streaked, and spotted, and marbled with the same shrouded hue, that, in the end, he had gained his distinctive appellation of the White Whale; a name, indeed, literally justified by his vivid aspect, when seen gliding at high noon through a dark blue sea, leaving a milky-way wake of creamy foam, all spangled with golden gleamings.

Nor was it his unwonted magnitude, nor his remarkable hue, nor yet his deformed lower jaw, that so much invested the whale with natural terror, as that unexampled, intelligent malignity which, according to specific accounts, he had over and over again evinced in his assaults. More than all, his treacherous retreats struck more of dismay than perhaps aught else. For, when swimming before his exulting pursuers, with every apparent symptom of alarm, he had several times been known to turn round suddenly, and, bearing down upon them, either stave their boats to splinters, or drive them back in consternation to their ship.

Already several fatalities had attended his chase. But though similar disasters, however little bruited ashore, were by no means unusual in the fishery; yet, in most instances, such seemed the White Whale's infernal aforethought of ferocity, that every dismembering or death that he caused, was not wholly regarded as having been inflicted by an unintelligent agent.

Judge, then, to what pitches of inflamed, distracted fury the minds of his more desperate hunters were impelled, when amid the chips of chewed boats, and the sinking limbs of torn comrades, they swam out of the white curds of the whale's direful wrath into the serene, exasperating sunlight, that smiled on, as if at a birth or a bridal.

His three boats stove around him, and oars and men both whirling in the eddies; one captain, seizing the line-knife from his broken prow, had dashed at the whale, as an Arkansas duelist at his foe, blindly seeking with a six-inch blade to reach the fathom-deep life of the whale. That captain was Ahab. And then it was, that suddenly sweeping his sickle-shaped lower jaw beneath him, Moby Dick had reaped away Ahab's leg, as a mower a blade of grass in the field. No turbaned Turk, no hired Venetian or Malay, could have smote him with more seeming malice. Small reason was there to doubt, then, that ever since that almost fatal encounter, Ahab had cherished a wild vindictiveness against the whale, all the more fell for that in his frantic morbidness he at last came to identify with him, not only all his bodily woes, but all his intellectual and spiritual exasperations. The White Whale swam before him as the monomaniac incarnation of all those malicious agencies which some deep men feel eating in them, till they are left living on with half a heart and half a lung. That intangible ma-

lignity which has been from the beginning; to whose dominion even the modern Christians ascribe one-half of the
worlds; which the ancient Ophites of the east reverenced in
their statue devil; — Ahab did not fall down and worship
it like them; but deliriously transferring its idea to the
abhorred white whale, he pitted himself, all mutilated, against
it. All that most maddens and torments; all that stirs up
the lees of things; all truth with malice in it; all that cracks
the sinews and cakes the brain; all the subtle demonisms of
life and thought; all evil, to crazy Ahab, were visibly personified, and made practically assailable in Moby Dick. He
piled upon the whale's white hump the sum of all the general
rage and hate felt by his whole race from Adam down; and
then, as if his chest had been a mortar, he burst his hot
heart's shell upon it.

It is not probable that this monomania in him took its
instant rise at the precise time of his bodily dismemberment.
Then, in darting at the monster, knife in hand, he had but
given loose to a sudden, passionate, corporal animosity; and
when he received the stroke that tore him, he probably but
felt the agonizing bodily laceration, but nothing more. Yet,
when by this collision forced to turn toward home, and for
long months of days and weeks, Ahab and anguish lay
stretched together in one hammock, rounding in midwinter
that dreary, howling Patagonian Cape; then it was, that his
torn body and gashed soul bled into one another; and so
interfusing, made him mad. That it was only then, on the
homeward voyage, after the encounter, that the final monomania seized him, seems all but certain from the fact that, at
intervals during the passage, he was a raving lunatic; and,
though unlimbed of a leg, yet such vital strength yet lurked
in his Egyptian chest, and was moreover intensified by his
delirium, that his mates were forced to lace him fast, even
there, as he sailed, raving in his hammock. In a strait-
jacket, he swung to the mad rockings of the gales. And,
when running into more sufferable latitudes, the ship, with
mild stun'sails spread, floated across the tranquil tropics,

and, to all appearances, the old man's delirium seemed left behind him with the Cape Horn swells, and he came forth from his dark den into the blessed light and air; even then, when he bore that firm, collected front, however pale, and issued his calm orders once again; and his mates thanked God the direful madness was now gone; even then, Ahab, in his hidden self, raved on. Human madness is oftentimes a cunning and most feline thing. When you think it fled, it may have but become transfigured into some still subtler form. Ahab's full lunacy subsided not, but deepeningly contracted; like the unabated Hudson, when that noble Northman flows narrowly, but unfathomably through the Highland gorge. But, as in his narrow-flowing monomania, not one jot of Ahab's broad madness had been left behind; so in that broad madness, not one jot of his great natural intellect had perished. That before living agent, now became the living instrument. If such a furious trope may stand, his special lunacy stormed his general sanity, and carried it, and turned all its concentered cannon upon its own mad mark; so that far from having lost his strength, Ahab to that one end, did now possess a thousand fold more potency than ever he had sanely brought to bear upon any one reasonable object.

This is much; yet Ahab's larger, darker, deeper part remains untinted. But vain to popularize profundities, and all truth is profound. Winding far down from within the very heart of this spiked Hotel de Cluny where we here stand — however grand and wonderful, now quit it; — and take your way, ye nobler, sadder souls, to those vast Roman halls of Thermes; where far beneath the fantastic towers of man's upper earth, his root of grandeur, his whole awful essence sits in bearded state; an antique buried beneath antiquities, and throned on torsos! So with a broken throne, the great gods mock that captive king; so like a Caryatid, he patient sits, upholding on his frozen brow the piled entablatures of ages. Wind ye down there, ye prouder, sadder souls! question that proud, sad king! A family likeness! aye, he did beget ye, ye young exiled royalties; and from your grim sire only will the old State-secret come.

Now, in his heart, Ahab had some glimpse of this, namely: all my means are sane, my motive and my object mad. Yet without power to kill, or change, or shun the fact; he likewise knew that to mankind he did long dissemble; in some sort, did still. But that thing of his dissembling was only subject to his perceptibility, not to his will determinate. Nevertheless, so well did he succeed in that dissembling, that when with ivory leg he stepped ashore at last, no Nantucketer thought him otherwise than but naturally grieved, and that to the quick, with the terrible casualty which had overtaken him.

The report of his undeniable delirium at sea was likewise popularly ascribed to a kindred cause. And so too, all the added moodiness which always afterwards, to the very day of sailing in the Pequod on the present voyage, sat brooding on his brow. Nor is it so very unlikely, that far from distrusting his fitness for another whaling voyage, on account of such dark symptoms, the calculating people of that prudent isle were inclined to harbor the conceit, that for those very reasons he was all the better qualified and set on edge, for a pursuit so full of rage and wildness as the bloody hunt of whales. Gnawed within and scorched without, with the infixed, unrelenting fangs of some incurable idea; such an one, could he be found, would seem the very man to dart his iron and lift his lance against the most appalling of all brutes. Or, if for any reason thought to be corporeally incapacitated for that, yet such an one would seem superlatively competent to cheer and howl on his underlings to the attack. But be all this as it may, certain it is, that with the mad secret of his unabated rage bolted up and keyed in him, Ahab had purposely sailed upon the present voyage with the one only and all-engrossing object of hunting the White Whale. Had any one of his old acquaintances on shore but half dreamed of what was lurking in him then, how soon would their aghast and righteous souls have wrenched the ship from such a fiendish man! They were bent on profitable cruises, the profit to be counted down in dollars from the mint. He was intent on an audacious, immitigable, and supernatural revenge.

Here, then, was this gray-headed, ungodly old man, chasing with curses a Job's whale round the world, at the head of a crew, too, chiefly made up of mongrel renegades, and castaways, and cannibals — morally enfeebled also, by the incompetence of mere unaided virtue or right-mindedness in Starbuck, the invulnerable jollity of indifference and recklessness in Stubb, and the pervading mediocrity in Flask. Such a crew, so officered, seemed specially picked and packed by some infernal fatality to help him to his monomaniac revenge. How it was that they so aboundingly responded to the old man's ire — by what evil magic their souls were possessed, that at times his hate seemed almost theirs; the White Whale as much their insufferable foe as his; how all this came to be — what the White Whale was to them, or how to their unconscious understandings, also, in some dim, unsuspected way, he might have seemed the gliding great demon of the seas of life, — all this to explain, would be to dive deeper than Ishmael can go. The subterranean miner that works in us all, how can one tell whither leads his shaft by the ever shifting, muffled sound of his pick? Who does not feel the irresistible arm drag? What skiff in tow of a seventy-four can stand still? For one, I gave myself up to the abandonment of the time and the place; but while yet all a-rush to encounter the whale, could see naught in that brute but the deadliest ill.

41   *The Whiteness of the Whale*

WHAT the white whale was to Ahab, has been hinted; what, at times, he was to me, as yet remains unsaid. Aside from those more obvious considerations touching Moby Dick, which could not but occasionally awaken in any man's soul some alarm, there was another thought, or rather vague, nameless horror concerning him, which at times by its intensity completely overpowered all the rest; and yet so mystical and well nigh ineffable was it, that I almost despair of putting it in a comprehensible form. It was the whiteness of the whale that above all things appalled me. But how can I hope to explain myself here; and yet, in some dim, random way, explain myself I must, else all these chapters might be naught.

Though in many natural objects, whiteness refiningly enhances beauty, as if imparting some special virtue of its own, as in marbles, japonicas, and pearls; and though various nations have in some way recognized a certain royal preëminence in this hue; even the barbaric, grand old kings of Pegu placing the title "Lord of the White Elephants" above all their other magniloquent ascriptions of dominion; and the modern kings of Siam unfurling the same snow-white quadruped in the royal standard; and the Hanoverian flag bearing the one figure of a snow-white charger; and the great Austrian Empire, Cæsarian, heir to overlording Rome, having for the imperial color the same imperial hue; and though this preëminence in it applies to the human race itself, giving the white man ideal mastership over every dusky tribe; and though, besides all this, whiteness has been even made significant of gladness, for among the Romans a white stone marked a joyful day; and though in other mortal sympathies and symbolizings, this same hue is made the emblem of many touching, noble things — the innocence of brides, the benignity of age; though among the Red Men of America the giving of the white belt of wampum was the deepest pledge of honor; though in many climes, whiteness typifies the majesty of Justice in the ermine of the Judge, and contributes to the daily state of kings and queens drawn by milk-white steeds; though even in the higher mysteries of the most august religions it has been made the symbol of the divine spotlessness and power; by the Persian fire worshipers, the white forked flame being held the holiest on the altar; and in the Greek mythologies, Great Jove himself being made incarnate in a snow-white bull; and though to the noble Iroquois, the midwinter sacrifice of the sacred White Dog was by far the holiest festival of their theology, that spotless, faithful creature being held the purest envoy they could send to the Great Spirit with the annual tidings of their own fidelity; and though directly from the Latin word for white, all Christian priests derive the name of one part of their sacred vesture, the alb or tunic, worn beneath the cassock; and though among the holy pomps of the Romish faith, white is specially employed in the celebration of the Passion of our Lord; though in the Vision of St. John, white robes are given to the redeemed, and the four-and-twenty elders stand clothed in white before the great white throne, and the Holy One that sitteth there white like wool; yet for all these accumulated associations, with whatever is sweet, and honorable, and sublime, there yet lurks an elusive something in the innermost idea of this hue, which strikes more of panic to the soul than that redness which affrights in blood.

This elusive quality it is, which causes the thought of whiteness, when divorced from more kindly associations, and coupled with any object terrible in itself, to heighten that terror to the furthest bounds. Witness the white bear of the poles, and the white shark of the tropics; what but their smooth, flaky whiteness makes them the transcendent horrors they are? That ghastly whiteness it is which imparts such an abhorrent mildness, even more loathsome than terrific, to the dumb gloating of their aspect. So that not the fierce-fanged tiger in his heraldic coat can so stagger courage as the white-shrouded bear or shark.

Bethink thee of the albatross, whence come those clouds of spiritual wonderment and pale dread, in which that white phantom sails in all imaginations? Not Coleridge first threw that spell; but God's great, unflattering laureate, Nature.

Most famous in our Western annals and Indian traditions is that of the White Steed of the Prairies; a magnificent milk-white charger, large-eyed, small-headed, bluff-chested, and with the dignity of a thousand monarchs in his lofty, overscorning carriage. He was the elected Xerxes of vast herds of wild horses, whose pastures in those days were only fenced by the Rocky Mountains and the Alleghanies. At their flaming head he westward trooped it like that chosen star which every evening leads on the hosts of light. The flashing cascade of his mane, the curving comet of his tail, invested him with housings more resplendent than gold and silver-beaters could have furnished him. A most imperial and archangelical apparition of that unfallen, Western world, which to the eyes of the old trappers and hunters revived the glories of those primeval times when Adam walked majestic as a god, bluff-browed and fearless as this mighty steed. Whether marching amid his aides and marshals in the van of countless cohorts that endlessly streamed it over the plains, like an Ohio; or whether with his circumambient subjects browsing all around at the horizon, the White Steed gallopingly reviewed them with warm nostrils reddening through his cool milkiness; in whatever aspect he presented himself, always to the bravest Indians he was the object of trembling reverence and awe. Nor can it be questioned from what stands on legendary record of this noble horse, that it was his spiritual whiteness chiefly, which so clothed him with divineness; and that this divineness had that in it which, though commanding worship, at the same time enforced a certain nameless terror.

But there are other instances where this whiteness loses all that accessory and strange glory which invests it in the White Steed and Albatross.

What is it that in the Albino man so peculiarly repels and often shocks the eye, as that sometimes he is loathed by his own kith and kin! It is that whiteness which invests him, a thing expressed by the name he bears. The Albino is as well made as other men — has no substantive deformity —

and yet this mere aspect of all-pervading whiteness makes him more strangely hideous than the ugliest abortion. Why should this be so?

Nor, in quite other aspects, does Nature in her least palpable but not the less malicious agencies, fail to enlist among her forces this crowning attribute of the terrible. From its snowy aspect, the gauntleted ghost of the Southern Seas has been denominated the White Squall. Nor, in some historic instances, has the art of human malice omitted so potent an auxiliary. How wildly it heightens the effect of that passage in Froissart, when, masked in the snowy symbol of their faction, the desperate White Hoods of Ghent murder their bailiff in the market-place!

Nor, in some things, does the common, hereditary experience of all mankind fail to bear witness to the supernaturalism of this hue. It cannot well be doubted, that the one visible quality in the aspect of the dead which most appals the gazer, is the marble pallor lingering there; as if indeed that pallor were as much like the badge of consternation in the other world, as of mortal trepidation here. And from that pallor of the dead, we borrow the expressive hue of the shroud in which we wrap them. Nor even in our superstitions do we fail to throw the same snowy mantle round our phantoms; all ghosts rising in a milk-white fog — Yea, while these terrors seize us, let us add, that even the king of terrors, when personified by the evangelist, rides on his pallid horse.

Therefore, in his other moods, symbolize whatever grand or gracious thing he will by whiteness, no man can deny that in its profoundest idealized significance it calls up a peculiar apparition to the soul.

But though without dissent this point be fixed, how is mortal man to account for it? To analyze it, would seem impossible. Can we, then, by the citation of some of those instances wherein this thing of whiteness — though for the time either wholly or in great part stripped of all direct associations calculated to impart to it aught fearful, but nevertheless, is found to exert over us the same sorcery, however modified — can we thus hope to light upon some chance clue to conduct us to the hidden cause we seek?

Let us try. But in a matter like this, subtlety appeals to subtlety, and without imagination no man can follow another into these halls. And though, doubtless, some at least of the imaginative impressions about to be presented may have been shared by most men, yet few perhaps were entirely conscious of them at the time, and therefore may not be able to recall them now.

Why to the man of untutored ideality, who happens to be but loosely acquainted with the peculiar character of the day, does the bare mention of Whitsuntide marshal in the fancy such long, dreary, speechless processions of slow-pacing pilgrims, down-cast and hooded with new-fallen snow? Or, to the unread, unsophisticated Protestant of the Middle American States, why does the passing mention of a White Friar or a White Nun evoke such an eyeless statue in the soul?

Or what is there apart from the traditions of dungeoned warriors and kings (which will not wholly account for it) that makes the White Tower of London tell so much more strongly on the imagination of an untraveled American, than those other storied structures, its neighbors — the By-ward Tower, or even the Bloody? And those sublimer towers, the White Mountains of New Hampshire, whence, in peculiar moods, comes that gigantic ghostliness over the soul at the bare mention of that name, while the thought of Virginia's Blue Ridge is full of a soft, dewy, distant dreaminess? Or why, irrespective of all latitudes and longitudes, does the name of the White Sea exert such a spectralness over the fancy, while that of the Yellow Sea lulls us with mortal thoughts of long lacquered mild afternoons on the waves, followed by the gaudiest and yet sleepiest of sunsets? Or, to choose a wholly unsubstantial instance, purely addressed to the fancy, why, in reading the old fairy tales of Central Europe, does "the tall pale man" of the Hartz forests, whose changeless pallor unrustlingly glides through the green of the groves — why is this phantom more terrible than all the whooping imps of the Blocksburg?

Nor is it, altogether, the remembrance of her cathedral-toppling earthquakes; nor the stampedoes of her frantic seas; nor the tearlessness of arid skies that never rain; nor the sight of her wide field of leaning spires, wrenched cope-stones, and crosses all adroop (like canted yards of anchored fleets); and her suburban avenues of house-walls lying over upon each other, as a tossed pack of cards — it is not these things alone which make tearless Lima, the strangest, saddest city thou canst see. For Lima has taken the white veil; and there is a higher horror in this whiteness of her woe. Old as Pizarro, this whiteness keeps her ruins forever new; admits not the cheerful greenness of complete decay; spreads over her broken ramparts the rigid pallor of an apoplexy that fixes its own distortions.

I know that, to the common apprehension, this phenomenon of whiteness is not confessed to be the prime agent in exaggerating the terror of objects otherwise terrible; nor to the unimaginative mind is there aught of terror in those appearances whose awfulness to another mind almost solely consists in this one phenomenon, especially when exhibited under any form at all approaching to muteness or universality. What I mean by these two statements may perhaps be respectively elucidated by the following examples.

First: The mariner, when drawing nigh the coasts of foreign lands, if by night he hear the roar of breakers, starts to vigilance, and feels just enough of trepidation to sharpen all his faculties; but under precisely similar circumstances, let him be called from his hammock to view his ship sailing through a midnight sea of milky whiteness — as if from encircling headlands shoals of combed white bears were swimming round him, then he feels a silent, superstitious dread; the shrouded phantom of the whitened waters is horrible to him as a real ghost; in vain the lead assures him he is still off soundings; heart and helm they both go down;

he never rests till blue water is under him again. Yet where is the mariner who will tell thee, "Sir, it was not so much the fear of striking hidden rocks, as the fear of that hideous whiteness that so stirred me?"

Second: To the native Indian of Peru, the continual sight of the snow-howdahed Andes conveys naught of dread, except, perhaps, in the mere fancying of the eternal frosted desolateness reigning at such vast altitudes, and the natural conceit of what a fearfulness it would be to lose oneself in such inhuman solitude. Much the same is it with the backwoodsman of the West, who with comparative indifference views an unbounded prairie sheeted with driven snow, no shadow of tree or twig to break the fixed trance of whiteness. Not so the sailor, beholding the scenery of the Antarctic seas; where at times, by some infernal trick of legerdemain in the powers of frost and air, he, shivering and half shipwrecked, instead of rainbows speaking hope and solace to his misery, views what seems a boundless church-yard grinning upon him with its lean ice monuments and splintered crosses.

But thou sayest, methinks this white-lead chapter about whiteness is but a white flag hung out from a craven soul; thou surrenderest to a hypo, Ishmael.

Tell me, why this strong young colt, foaled in some peaceful valley of Vermont, far removed from all beasts of prey — why is it that upon the sunniest day, if you but shake a fresh buffalo robe behind him, so that he cannot even see it, but only smells its wild animal muskiness — why will he start, snort, and with bursting eyes paw the ground in frenzies of affright? There is no remembrance in him of any gorings of wild creatures in his green northern home, so that the strange muskiness he smells cannot recall to him anything associated with the experience of former perils; for what knows he, this New England colt, of the black bisons of distant Oregon?

No: but here thou beholdest, even in a dumb brute, the instinct of the knowledge of the demonism in the world.

Though thousands of miles from Oregon, still when he smells that savage musk, the rending, goring bison herds are as present as to the deserted wild foal of the prairies, which this instant they may be trampling into dust.

Thus, then, the muffled rollings of a milky sea; the bleak rustlings of the festooned frosts of mountains; the desolate shiftings of the windrowed snows of prairies; all these, to Ishmael, are as the shaking of that buffalo robe to the frightened colt!

Though neither knows where lie the nameless things of which the mystic sign gives forth such hints; yet with me, as with the colt, somewhere those things must exist. Though in many of its aspects this visible world seems formed in love, the invisible spheres were formed in fright.

But not yet have we solved the incantation of this whiteness, and learned why it appeals with such power to the soul; and more strange and far more portentous — why, as we have seen, it is at once the most meaning symbol of spiritual things, nay, the very veil of the Christian's Deity; and yet should be as it is, the intensifying agent in things the most appalling to mankind.

Is it that by its indefiniteness it shadows forth the heartless voids and immensities of the universe, and thus stabs us from behind with the thought of annihilation, when beholding the white depths of the milky way? Or is it, that as in essence whiteness is not so much a color as the visible absence of color, and at the same time the concrete of all colors; is it for these reasons that there is such a dumb blankness, full of meaning, in a wide landscape of snows — a colorless, all-color of atheism from which we shrink? And when we consider that other theory of the natural philosophers, that all other earthly hues — every stately or lovely emblazoning — the sweet tinges of sunset skies and woods; yea, and the gilded velvets of butterflies, and the butterfly cheeks of young girls; all these are but subtle deceits, not actually inherent in substances, but only laid on from without; so that all deified Nature absolutely paints like the harlot, whose allurements cover nothing but the charnel-house within; and when we proceed further, and consider that the mystical cosmetic which produces every one of her hues, the great principle of light, forever remains white or colorless in itself, and if operating without medium upon matter, would touch all objects, even tulips and roses, with its own blank tinge — pondering all this, the palsied universe lies before us a leper; and like willful travelers in Lapland, who refuse to wear colored and coloring glasses upon their eyes, so the wretched infidel gazes himself blind at the monumental white shroud that wraps all the prospect around him. And of all these things the Albino whale was the symbol. Wonder ye then at the fiery hunt?

JAMES RUSSELL LOWELL

1819–1891

42   *My Garden Acquaintance*

ONE of the most delightful books in my father's library was White's *Natural History of Selborne*. For me it has rather gained in charm with years. I used to read it without knowing the secret of the pleasure I found in it, but as I grow older I begin to detect some of the simple expedients of this natural magic. Open the book where you will, it takes you out of doors. In our broiling July weather one can walk out with this genially garrulous Fellow of Oriel and find refreshment instead of fatigue. You have no trouble in keeping abreast of him as he ambles along on his hobby-horse, now pointing to a pretty view, now stopping to watch the motions of a bird or an insect, or to bag a specimen for the Honorable Daines Barrington or Mr. Pennant. In simplicity of taste and natural refinement he reminds one of Walton; in tenderness toward what he would have called the brute creation, of Cowper. I do not know whether his descriptions of scenery are good or not, but they have made me familiar with his neighborhood.

Since I first read him, I have walked over some of his favorite haunts, but I still see them through his eyes rather than by any recollection of actual and personal vision. The book has also the delightfulness of absolute leisure. Mr. White seems never to have had any harder work to do than to study the habits of his feathered fellow-townsfolk, or to watch the ripening of his peaches on the wall. His volumes are the journal of Adam in Paradise,

> "Annihilating all that's made
> To a green thought in a green shade."

It is positive rest only to look into that garden of his. It is vastly better than to

> "See great Diocletian walk
> In the Salonian garden's noble shade,"

for thither ambassadors intrude to bring with them the noises of Rome, while here the world has no entrance. No rumor of the revolt of the American Colonies seems to have reached him. "The natural term of an hog's life" has more interest for him than that of an empire. Burgoyne may surrender and welcome; of what consequence is *that* compared with the fact that we can explain the odd tumbling of rooks in the air by their turning over "to scratch themselves with one claw"? All the couriers in Europe spurring rowel-deep make no stir in Mr. White's little Chartreuse; but the arrival of the house-martin a day earlier or later than last year is a piece of news worth sending express to all his correspondents.

Another secret charm of this book is its inadvertent humor, so much the more delicious because unsuspected by the author. How pleasant is his innocent vanity in adding to the list of the British, and still more of the Selbornian, *fauna!* I believe he would gladly have consented to be eaten by a tiger or a crocodile, if by that means the occasional presence within the parish limits of either of these anthropophagous brutes could have been established. He brags of no fine society, but is plainly a little elated by

"having considerable acquaintance with a tame brown owl."
Most of us have known our share of owls, but few can boast
of intimacy with a feathered one. The great events of Mr.
White's life, too, have that disproportionate importance
which is always humorous. To think of his hands having
actually been thought worthy (as neither Willoughby's nor
Ray's were) to hold a stilted plover, the *Charadrius hima-
niopus,* with no back toe, and therefore "liable, in speculation, to perpetual vacillations"! I wonder, by the way, if
metaphysicians have no hind toes. In 1770 he makes the
acquaintance in Sussex of "an old family tortoise," which
had then been domesticated for thirty years. It is clear
that he fell in love with it at first sight. We have no means
of tracing the growth of his passion; but in 1780 we find
him eloping with its object in a post-chaise. "The rattle
and hurry of the journey so perfectly roused it that, when
I turned it out in a border, it walked twice down to the
bottom of my garden." It reads like a Court Journal:
"Yesterday morning H. R. H. the Princess Alice took an
airing of half an hour on the terrace of Windsor Castle."
This tortoise might have been a member of the Royal
Society, if he could have condescended to so ignoble an
ambition. It had but just been discovered that a surface
inclined at a certain angle with the plane of the horizon took
more of the sun's rays. The tortoise had always known
this (though he unostentatiously made no parade of it),
and used accordingly to tilt himself up against the garden-
wall in the autumn. He seems to have been more of a
philosopher than even Mr. White himself, caring for nothing
but to get under a cabbage leaf when it rained, or the sun
was too hot, and to bury himself alive before frost, — a
four-footed Diogenes, who carried his tub on his back.

There are moods in which this kind of history is infinitely
refreshing. These creatures whom we affect to look down
upon as the drudges of instinct are members of a common-
wealth whose constitution rests on immovable bases. Never
any need of reconstruction there! *They* never dream of

settling it by vote that eight hours are equal to ten, or that one creature is as clever as another and no more. *They* do not use their poor wits in regulating God's clocks, nor think they cannot go astray so long as they carry their guide-board about with them, — a delusion we often practice upon ourselves with our high and mighty reason, that admirable finger-post which points every way and always right. It is good for us now and then to converse with a world like Mr. White's, where Man is the least important of animals. But one who, like me, has always lived in the country and always on the same spot, is drawn to his book by other occult sympathies. Do we not share his indignation at that stupid Martin who had graduated his thermometer no lower than 4° above zero of Fahrenheit, so that in the coldest weather ever known the mercury basely absconded into the bulb, and left us to see the victory slip through our fingers, just as they were closing upon it? No man, I suspect, ever lived long in the country without being bitten by these meteorological ambitions. He likes to be hotter and colder, to have been more deeply snowed up, to have more trees and larger blow down than his neighbors. With us descendants of the Puritans especially, these weather-competitions supply the abnegated excitement of the race-course. Men learn to value thermometers of the true imaginative temperament, capable of prodigious elations and corresponding dejections. The other day (5th July) I marked 98° in the shade, my high water mark, higher by one degree than I had ever seen it before. I happened to meet a neighbor; as we mopped our brows at each other, he told me that he had just cleared 100°, and I went home a beaten man. I had not felt the heat before, save as a beautiful exaggeration of sunshine; but now it oppressed me with the prosaic vulgarity of an oven. What had been poetic intensity became all at once rhetorical hyperbole. I might suspect his thermometer (as indeed I did, for we Harvard men are apt to think ill of any graduation but our own); but it was a poor consolation. The fact remained that his

herald Mercury, standing a tiptoe, could look down on mine.
I seem to glimpse something of this familiar weakness in
Mr. White. He, too, has shared in these mercurial triumphs
and defeats. Nor do I doubt that he had a true country-
gentleman's interest in the weathercock; that his first question on coming down of a morning was, like Barabas's,

" Into what quarter peers my halcyon's bill? "

It is an innocent and healthful employment of the mind,
distracting one from too continual study of himself, and
leading him to dwell rather upon the indigestions of the
elements than his own. "Did the wind back round, or go
about with the sun?" is a rational question that bears not
remotely on the making of hay and the prosperity of crops.
I have little doubt that the regulated observation of the vane
in many different places, and the interchange of results by
telegraph, would put the weather, as it were, in our power,
by betraying its ambushes before it is ready to give the
assault. At first sight, nothing seems more drolly trivial
than the lives of those whose single achievement is to record
the wind and the temperature three times a day. Yet such
men are doubtless sent into the world for this special end,
and perhaps there is no kind of accurate observation, whatever its object, that has not its final use and value for some
one or other. It is even to be hoped that the speculations
of our newspaper editors and their myriad correspondence
upon the signs of the political atmosphere may also fill their
appointed place in a well-regulated universe, if it be only
that of supplying so many more jack-o'-lanterns to the
future historian. Nay, the observations on finance of an
M. C. whose sole knowledge of the subject has been derived
from a life-long success in getting a living out of the public
without paying any equivalent therefor, will perhaps be of
interest hereafter to some explorer of our *cloaca maxima,*
whenever it is cleansed.

For many years I have been in the habit of noting down
some of the leading events of my embowered solitude, such

as the coming of certain birds and the like,—a kind of *mémoires pour servir,* after the fashion of White, rather than properly digested natural history. I thought it not impossible that a few simple stories of my winged acquaintances might be found entertaining by persons of kindred taste.

There is a common notion that animals are better meteorologists than men, and I have little doubt that in immediate weather-wisdom they have the advantage of our sophisticated senses (though I suspect a sailor or shepherd would be their match), but I have seen nothing that leads me to believe their minds capable of erecting the horoscope of a whole season, and letting us know beforehand whether the winter will be severe or the summer rainless. I more than suspect that the clerk of the weather himself does not always know very long in advance whether he is to draw an order for hot or cold, dry or moist, and the musquash is scarce likely to be wiser. I have noted but two days' difference in the coming of the song-sparrow between a very early and a very backward spring. This very year I saw the linnets at work thatching, just before a snow-storm which covered the ground several inches deep for a number of days. They struck work and left us for a while, no doubt in search of food. Birds frequently perish from sudden changes in our whimsical spring weather of which they had no foreboding. More than thirty years ago, a cherry-tree, then in full bloom, near my window, was covered with humming-birds benumbed by a fall of mingled rain and snow, which probably killed many of them. It should seem that their coming was dated by the height of the sun, which betrays them into unthrifty matrimony;

" So priketh hem Nature in hir corages; "

but their going is another matter. The chimney swallows leave us early, for example, apparently so soon as their latest fledglings are firm enough of wing to attempt the long rowing-match that is before them. On the other hand the wild-geese probably do not leave the North till they are frozen out, for I have heard their bugles sounding southward so late as the middle of December. What may be called local migrations are doubtless dictated by the chances of food. I have once been visited by large flights of cross-bills; and whenever the snow lies long and deep on the ground, a flock of cedar-birds comes in midwinter to eat the berries on my hawthorns. I have never been quite able to fathom the local, or rather geographical partialities of birds. Never before this summer (1870) have the king-birds, handsomest of fly-catchers, built in my orchard; though I always know where to find them within half a mile. The rose-breasted grosbeak has been a familiar bird in Brookline (three miles away), yet I never saw one here till last July, when I found a female busy among my rasp-berries and surprisingly bold. I hope she was *prospecting* with a view to settlement in our garden. She seemed, on the whole, to think well of my fruit, and I would gladly plant another bed if it would help to win over so delightful a neighbor.

The return of the robin is commonly announced by the newspapers, like that of eminent or notorious people to a watering-place, as the first authentic notification of spring. And such his appearance in the orchard and garden un-doubtedly is. But, in spite of his name of migratory thrush, he stays with us all winter, and I have seen him when the thermometer marked 15 degrees below zero of Fahrenheit, armed impregnably within, like Emerson's Titmouse, and as cheerful as he. The robin has a bad reputation among people who do not value themselves less for being fond of cherries. There is, I admit, a spice of vulgarity in him, and his song is rather of the Bloomfield sort, too largely ballasted with prose. His ethics are of the Poor Richard school, and the main chance which calls forth all his energy is altogether of the belly. He never has these fine intervals of lunacy into which his cousins, the catbird and the mavis, are apt to fall. But for a' that and twice as muckle 's a' that, I would not exchange him for all the cherries that ever came out of Asia Minor. With whatever faults, he has not wholly forfeited that superiority which belongs to the children of nature. He has a finer taste in fruit than could be distilled from many successive committees of the Horticultural Society, and he eats with a relishing gulp not inferior to Dr. Johnson's. He feels and freely exercises his right of eminent domain. His is the earliest mess of green peas; his all the mulberries I had fancied mine. But if he get also the lion's share of the raspberries, he is a great planter, and sows those wild ones in the woods that solace the pedestrian, and give a momentary calm even to the jaded victims of the White Hills. He keeps a strict eye over one's fruit, and knows to a shade of purple when your grapes have cooked long enough in the sun. During the severe drought a few years ago the robins wholly vanished from my garden. I neither saw nor heard one for three weeks. Meanwhile a small foreign grape-vine, rather shy of bearing, seemed to find the dusty air congenial, and, dreaming, perhaps of its sweet Argos across the sea, decked itself with a score or so of fair bunches. I watched them from day to day till they should have secreted sugar enough from the sunbeams, and at last made up my mind that I would celebrate my vintage the next morning. But the robins, too, had somehow kept note of them. They must have sent out spies, as did the Jews into the promised land, before I was stirring. When I went with my basket at least a dozen of these winged vintagers bustled out from among the leaves, and alighting on the nearest trees interchanged some shrill remarks about me of a derogatory nature. They had fairly sacked the vine. Not Wellington's veterans made cleaner work of a Spanish town; not Federals or Confederates were ever more impartial in the confiscation of neutral chickens. I was keeping my grapes a secret to surprise the fair Fidele with, but the robins made them a profounder secret to her than I had meant. The tattered remnant of a single bunch was all my harvest-home. How paltry it looked at the bottom of my basket, — as if a humming bird had laid her egg in an eagle's nest! I could not help laughing; and the robins seemed to join heartily in the merriment. There was a native grape-vine close by, blue with its less refined abundance, but my cunning thieves preferred the foreign flavor. Could I tax them with want of taste?

The robins are not good solo singers, but their chorus, as, like primitive fire-worshippers, they hail the return of light and warmth to the world, is unrivaled. There are a hundred singing like one. They are noisy enough then, and sing, as poets should, with no afterthought. But when they come after cherries to the tree near my window, they muffle their voices, and their faint *pip pip pop!* sounds far away at the bottom of the garden, where they know I shall not suspect them of robbing the great black-walnut of its bitter-rinded store. They are feathered Pecksniffs, to be sure, but then how brightly their breasts, that look rather shabby in the sunlight, shine in a rainy day against the dark green of the fringe-tree! After they have pinched and shaken all the life of an earthworm, as Italian cooks pound all the spirit out of a steak, and then gulped him, they stand up in honest self-confidence, expand their red waistcoats with the virtuous air of a lobby member, and outface you with an eye that calmly challenges inquiry. "Do *I* look like a bird that knows the flavor of raw vermin? I throw myself upon a jury of my peers. Ask any robin if he ever ate anything less ascetic than the frugal berry of the juniper, and he will answer that his vow forbids him." Can such an open bosom cover such depravity? Alas, yes! I have no doubt his breast was redder at that very moment with the blood of my raspberries. On the whole, he is a doubtful friend in the garden. He makes his dessert of all kinds of berries, and is not averse from early pears. But when we remember how omnivorous he is, eating his own weight in an incredibly short time, and that Nature seems exhaustless in her invention of new insects hostile to vegetation, perhaps we may reckon that he does more good than harm. For my own part, I would rather have his cheerfulness and kind neighborhood than many berries.

For his cousin, the catbird, I have a still warmer regard. Always a good singer, he sometimes nearly equals the brown thrush, and has the merit of keeping up his music later in the evening than any bird of my familiar acquaintance. Ever since I can remember, a pair of them have built in a gigantic syringa near our front door, and I have known the male to sing almost uninterruptedly during the evenings of early summer till twilight duskened into dark. They differ greatly in vocal talent, but all have a delightful way of crooning over, and, as it were, rehearsing their song in an undertone, which makes their nearness always unobtrusive. Though there is the most trustworthy witness to the imitative propensity of this bird, I have only once, during an intimacy of more than forty years, heard him indulge it. In that case, the imitation was by no means so close as to deceive, but a free reproduction of the notes of some other birds, especially of the oriole, as a kind of variation in his own song. The catbird is as shy as the robin is vulgarly familiar. Only when his nest or his fledglings are approached does he become noisy and almost aggressive. I have known him to station his young in a thick cornel-bush on the edge of the raspberry-bed, after the fruit began to ripen, and feed them there for a week or more. In such cases he shows none of that conscious guilt which makes the robin contemptible. On the contrary, he will maintain his post in the thicket, and sharply scold the intruder who ventures to steal *his* berries. After all, his claim is only for tithes, while the robin will bag your entire crop if he get a chance.

Dr. Watts's statement that "birds in their little nests agree," like too many others intended to form the infant mind, is very far from being true. On the contrary, the most peaceful relation of the different species to each other is that of armed neutrality. They are very jealous of neighbors. A few years ago I was much interested in the housebuilding of a pair of summer yellow-birds. They had chosen a very pretty site near the top of a tall white lilac, within easy eye-shot of a chamber window. A very pleasant thing it was to see their little home growing with mutual help, to watch their industrious skill interrupted only by little flirts and snatches of endearment, frugally cut short by the common-sense of the tiny housewife. They had brought their work nearly to an end, and had already begun to line it with fern-down, the gathering of which demanded more distant journeys and longer absences. But, alas! the syringa, immemorial manor of the catbirds, was not more than twenty feet away, and these "giddy neighbors" had, as it appeared, been all along jealously watchful, though silent, witnesses of what they deemed an intrusion of squatters. No sooner were the pretty mates fairly gone for a new load of lining, than

> "To their unguarded nest these weasel Scots
> Came stealing."

Silently they flew back and forth, each giving a vengeful dab at the nest in passing. They did not fall-to and deliberately destroy it, for they might have been caught at their mischief. As it was, whenever the yellow-birds came back, their enemies were hidden in their own sight-proof bush. Several times their unconscious victims repaired damages, but at length, after counsel taken together, they gave it up. Perhaps, like other unlettered folk, they came to the conclusion that the Devil was in it, and yielded to the invisible persecution of witchcraft.

The robins, by constant attacks and annoyances, have succeeded in driving off the blue-jays who used to build in our pines, their gay colors and quaint, noisy ways making them welcome and amusing neighbors. I once had the chance of doing a kindness to a household of them, which they received with very friendly condescension. I had had my eye for some time upon a nest, and was puzzled by a constant fluttering of what seemed full-grown wings in it whenever I drew nigh. At last I climbed the tree, in spite of angry protests from the old birds against my intrusion. The mystery had a very simple solution. In building the nest, a long piece of packthread had been somewhat loosely woven in. Three of the young had contrived to entangle themselves in it, and had become full-grown without being able to launch themselves upon the air. One was unharmed; another had so tightly twisted the cord about its shank that one foot was curled up and seemed paralyzed; the third, in its struggle to escape, had sawn through the flesh of the thigh and so much harmed itself that I thought it humane to put an end to its misery. When I took out my knife to cut their hempen bonds, the heads of the family seemed to divine my friendly intent. Suddenly ceasing their cries and threats, they perched quietly within reach of my hand, and watched me in my work of manumission. This, owing to the fluttering terror of the prisoners, was an affair of some delicacy; but ere long I was rewarded by seeing one of them fly away to a neighboring tree, while the cripple, making a parachute of his wings, came lightly to the ground, and hopped off as well as he could with one leg, obsequiously waited on by his elders. A week later I had the satisfaction of meeting him in the pine-walk, in good spirits, and already so far recovered as to be able to balance himself with the lame foot. I have no doubt that in his old age he accounted for his lameness by some handsome story of a wound received at the famous Battle of the Pines, when our tribe, overcome by numbers, was driven from its ancient camping-ground. Of late years the jays have visited us only at intervals; and in winter their bright plumage, set off by the snow, and their cheerful cry, are especially welcome. They would have furnished Æsop with a fable, for the feathered crest in which they seem to take so much satisfaction is often their fatal snare. Country boys make a hole with their finger in the snow-crust just large enough to admit the jay's head, and, hollowing it out somewhat beneath, bait it with a few kernels of corn. The crest slips easily into the trap, but refuses to be pulled out again, and he who came to feast remains a prey.

Twice have the crow-blackbirds attempted a settlement in my pines, and twice have the robins, who claim a right of preëmption, so successfully played the part of border-ruffians as to drive them away, — to my great regret, for they are the best substitute we have for rooks. At Shady Hill (now, alas! empty of its so long-loved household) they build by hundreds, and nothing can be more cheery than their creaking clatter (like a convention of old-fashioned tavern-signs) as they gather at evening to debate in mass meeting their windy politics, or to gossip at their tent-doors over the events of the day. Their port is grave, and their stalk across the turf as martial as that of a second-rate ghost in Hamlet. They never meddled with my corn, so far as I could discover.

For a few years I had crows, but their nests are an ir-resistible bait for boys, and their settlement was broken up. They grew so wonted as to throw off a great part of their shyness, and to tolerate my near approach. One very hot day I stood for some time within twenty feet of a mother and three children, who sat on an elm bough over my head gasping in the sultry air, and holding their wings half-spread for coolness. All birds during the pairing season be-come more or less sentimental, and murmur soft nothings in a tone very unlike the grinding-organ repetition and loud-ness of their habitual song. The crow is very comical as a lover, and to hear him trying to soften his croak to the proper Saint Preux standard has something the effect of a Mississippi boatman quoting Tennyson. Yet there are few things to my ear more melodious than his caw of a clear winter morning as it drops to you filtered through five hun-dred fathoms of crisp blue air. The hostility of all smaller birds makes the moral character of the crow, for all his deaconlike demeanor and garb, somewhat questionable. He could never sally forth without insult. The golden robins, especially, would chase him as far as I could follow with my eye, making him duck clumsily to avoid their importunate bills. I do not believe, however, that he robbed any nests hereabouts, for the refuse of the gas-works, which, in our free-and-easy community, is allowed to poison the river, supplied him with dead alewives in abundance. I used to watch him making his periodical visits to the salt-marshes and coming back with a fish in his beak to his young savages, who, no doubt, like it in that condition which makes it savory to the Kanakas and other corvine races of men.

Orioles are in great plenty with me. I have seen seven males flashing about the garden at once. A merry crew of them swing their hammocks from the pendulous boughs. During one of these later years, when the canker-worms stripped our elms as bare as winter, these birds went to the trouble of rebuilding their unroofed nests, and chose for the purpose trees which are safe from those swarming vandals, such as the ash and the button-wood. One year a pair (disturbed, I suppose, elsewhere) built a second nest in an elm within a few yards of the house. My friend, Edward E. Hale, told me once that the oriole rejected from his web all strands of brilliant color, and I thought it a striking example of that instinct of concealment noticeable in many birds, though it should seem in this instance that the nest was amply protected by its position from all marauders but owls and squirrels. Last year, however, I had the fullest proof that Mr. Hale was mistaken. A pair of orioles built on the lowest trailer of a weeping elm, which hung within ten feet of our drawing-room window, and so low that I could reach it from the ground. The nest was wholly woven and felted with ravelings of woolen carpet in which scarlet predominated. Would the same thing have happened in the woods? Or did the nearness of a human dwelling perhaps give the birds a greater feeling of security? They are very bold, by the way, in quest of cordage, and I have often watched them stripping the fibrous bark from a honeysuckle growing over the very door. But, indeed, all my birds look upon me as if I were a mere tenant at will, and they were landlords. With shame I confess it, I have been bullied even by a humming bird. This spring, as I was cleansing a pear-tree of its lichens, one of these little zigzagging blurs came purring toward me, couching his long bill like a lance, his throat sparkling with angry fire, to warn me off from a Missouri-currant whose honey he was sipping. And many a time he has driven me out of a flower-bed. This summer, by the way, a pair of these winged emeralds fastened their mossy acorn-cup upon a bough of the same elm which the orioles had enlivened the year before. We watched all their proceedings from the window through an opera-glass, and saw their two nestlings grow from black needles with a tuft of down at the lower end, till they whirled away on their first short experimental flights. They became strong of wing in a surprisingly short time, and I never saw them or the male bird after, though the female was regular as usual in her visits to our petunias and verbenas. I do not think it ground enough for a generalization, but in the many times when I watched the old birds feeding their young, the mother always alighted, while the father as uniformly remained upon the wing.

The bobolinks are generally chance visitors, tinkling through the garden in blossoming-time, but this year, owing to the long rains early in the season, their favorite meadows were flooded, and they were driven to the upland. So I had a pair of them domiciled in my grass field. The male used to perch in an apple-tree, then in full bloom, and, while I stood perfectly still close by, he would circle away, quivering round the entire field of five acres, with no break in his song, and settle down again among the blossoms, to be hurried away almost immediately by a new rapture of music. He had the volubility of an Italian charlatan at a fair, and, like him, appeared to be proclaiming the merits of some quack remedy. *Opodeldoc-opodeldoc-try-Doctor-Lincoln's-opodeldoc!* he seemed to repeat over and over again, with a rapidity that would have distanced the deftest-tongued Figaro that ever rattled. I remember Count Gurowski saying once, with that easy superiority of knowledge about this country which is the monopoly of foreigners, that we had no singing-birds! Well, well, Mr. Hepworth Dixon has found the typical America in Oneida and Salt Lake City. Of course, an intelligent European is the best judge of these matters. The truth is there are more singing-birds in Europe because there are fewer forests. These songsters love the neighborhood of man because hawks and owls are rarer, while their own food is more abundant. Most people seem to think, the more trees, the more birds. Even Châteaubriand, who first tried the primitive-forest-cure, and whose description of the wilderness in its imaginative effects is unmatched, fancies the "people of the air singing their hymns to him." So far as my own observation goes, the farther one penetrates the somber solitudes of the woods, the more seldom does he hear the voice of any singing-bird. In spite of Châteaubriand's minuteness of detail, in spite of that marvelous reverberation of the decrepit tree falling of its own weight, which he was the first to notice, I cannot help doubting whether he made his way very deep into the wilderness. At any rate, in a letter to Fontanes, written in 1804, he speaks of *mes chevaux paissant à quelque distance*. To be sure Châteaubriand was apt to mount the high horse, and this may have been but an afterthought of the *grand seigneur*, but certainly one would not make much headway on horseback toward the druid fastnesses of the primeval pine.

The bobolinks build in considerable numbers in a meadow within a quarter of a mile of us. A houseless lane passes through the midst of their camp, and in clear westerly weather, at the right season, one may hear a score of them singing at once. When they are breeding, if I chance to pass, one of the male birds always accompanies me like a constable, flitting from post to post of the rail-fence, with a short note of reproof continually repeated, till I am fairly out of the neighborhood. Then he will swing away into the air and run down the wind, gurgling music without stint over the unheeding tussocks of meadow-grass and dark clumps of bulrushes that mark his domain.

We have no bird whose song will match the nightingale's in compass, none whose note is so rich as that of the European blackbird; but for mere rapture I have never heard the bobolink's rival. But his opera-season is a short one. The ground and tree sparrows are our most constant performers. It is now late in August, and one of the latter sings every day and all day long in the garden. Till within a fortnight, a pair of indigo-birds would keep up their lively *duo* for an hour together. While I write, I hear an oriole gay as in June, and the plaintive *may-be* of the goldfinch tells me he is stealing my lettuce-seeds. I know not what the experience of others may have been, but the only bird I have ever heard sing in the night has been the chip-bird. I should say he sang about as often during the darkness as cocks crow. One can hardly help fancying that he sings in his dreams.

> " Father of light, what sunnie seed,
>   What glance of day hast thou confined
>   Into this bird? To all the breed
>   This busie ray thou hast assigned;
>   Their magnetism works all night,
>   And dreams of Paradise and light."

On second thought, I remember to have heard the cuckoo strike the hours nearly all night with the regularity of a Swiss clock.

The dead limbs of our elms, which I spare to that end, bring us the flicker every summer, and almost daily I hear his wild scream and laugh close at hand, himself invisible. He is a shy bird, but a few days ago I had the satisfaction of studying him through the blinds, as he sat on a tree within a few feet of me. Seen so near and at rest, he makes good his claim to the title of pigeon-woodpecker. Lumberers have a notion that he is harmful to timber, digging little holes through the bark to encourage the settlement of insects. The regular rings of such perforations which one may see in almost any apple-orchard seem to give some probability to this theory. Almost every season a solitary quail visits us, and, unseen among the currant bushes, calls *Bob White, Bob*

White, as if he were playing at hide-and-seek with that imaginary being. A rarer visitant is the turtle-dove, whose pleasant coo (something like the muffled crow of a cock from a coop covered with snow) I have sometimes heard, and whom I once had the good luck to see close by me in the mulberry-tree. The wild-pigeon, once numerous, I have not seen for many years. Of savage birds, a hen-hawk now and then quarters himself upon us for a few days, sitting sluggish in a tree after a surfeit of poultry. One of them once offered me a near shot from my study-window one drizzly day for several hours. But it was Sunday, and I gave him the benefit of its gracious truce of God.

Certain birds have disappeared from our neighborhood within my memory. I remember when the whippoorwill could be heard in Sweet Auburn. The night-hawk, once common, is now rare. The brown thrush has moved farther up country. For years I have not seen or heard any of the larger owls, whose hooting was one of my boyish terrors. The cliff-swallow, strange emigrant, that eastward takes his way, has come and gone again in my time. The bank-swallows, wellnigh innumerable during my boyhood, no longer frequent the crumbly cliff of the gravel-pit by the river. The barn-swallows, which once swarmed in our barn, flashing through the dusty sun-streaks of the mow, have been gone these many years. My father would lead me out to see them gather on the roof, and take counsel before their yearly migration, as Mr. White used to see them at Selborne. *Eheu fugaces!* Thank fortune, the swift still glues his nest, and rolls his distant thunders night and day in the wide-throated chimneys, still sprinkles the evening air with his merry twittering. The populous heronry in Fresh Pond meadows has wellnigh broken up, but still a pair or two haunt the old home, as the gypsies of Ellangowan their ruined huts, and every evening fly over us riverwards, clearing their throats with a hoarse hawk as they go, and, in cloudy weather, scarce higher than the tops of the chimneys. Sometimes I have known one to alight in one of our trees, though for what purpose I never could divine. Kingfishers have sometimes puzzled me in the same way, perched at high noon in a pine, springing their watchman's rattle when they flitted away from my curiosity, and seeming to shove their top-heavy heads along as a man does a wheelbarrow.

Some birds have left us, I suppose, because the country is growing less wild. I once found a summer duck's nest within a quarter of a mile of our house, but such a *trouvaille* would be impossible now as Kidd's treasure. And yet the mere taming of the neighborhood does not quite satisfy me as an explanation. Twenty years ago, on my way to bathe in the river, I saw every day a brace of woodcock, on the miry edge of a spring within a few rods of a house, and constantly visited by thirsty cows. There was no growth of any kind to conceal them, and yet these ordinarily shy birds were almost as indifferent to my passing as common poultry would have been. Since bird-nesting has become scientific, and dignified itself as oölogy, that, no doubt, is partly to blame for some of our losses. But some old friends are constant. Wilson's thrush comes every year to remind me of that most poetic of ornithologists. He flits before me through the pine-walk like the very genius of solitude. A pair of pewees have built immemorially on a jutting brick in the arched entrance to the ice-house; always on the same brick, and never more than a single pair, though two broods of five each are raised there every summer. How do they settle their claim to the homestead? By what right of primogeniture? Once the children of a man employed about the place oölogized the nest, and the pewees left us for a year or two. I felt towards those boys as the messmates of the Ancient Mariner did towards him after he had shot the albatross. But the pewees came back at last, and one of them is now on his wonted perch, so near my window that I can hear the click of his bill as he snaps a fly on the wing with the unerring precision a stately Trasteverina shows in the capture of her smaller deer. The pewee is the first bird to pipe up in the morning; and during the early summer he preludes his matutinal ejaculation of *pewee* with a slender whistle, unheard at any other time. He saddens with the season, and, as summer declines, he changes his note to *eheu, pewee!* as if in lamentation. Had he been an Italian bird, Ovid would have had a plaintive tale to tell about him. He is so familiar as often to pursue a fly through the open window into my library.

There is something inexpressibly dear to me in these old friendships of a lifetime. There is scarce a tree of mine but has had, at some time or other, a happy homestead among its boughs, and to which I cannot say,

> " Many light hearts and wings,
> Which now be dead, lodged in thy living bowers."

My walk under the pines would lose half its summer charm were I to miss that shy anchorite, the Wilson's thrush, nor hear in haying-time the metallic ring of his song, that justifies his rustic name of *scythe-whet*. I protect my game as jealously as an English squire. If anybody had oölogized a certain cuckoo's nest I know of (I have a pair in my garden every year), it would have left me a sore place in my mind for weeks. I love to bring these aborigines back to the mansuetude they showed to the early voyagers, and before (forgive the involuntary pun) they had grown accustomed to man and knew his savage ways. And they repay your kindness with a sweet familiarity too delicate ever to breed contempt. I have made a Penn-treaty with them, preferring that to the Puritan way with the natives, which converted them to a little Hebraism and a great deal of Medford rum. If they will not come near enough to me (as most of them will), I bring them close with an opera-glass, — a much better weapon than a gun. I would not, if I could, convert them from their pretty pagan ways. The only one I sometimes have savage doubts about is the red squirrel. I *think* he oölogizes. I *know* he eats cherries (we counted five of them at one time in a single tree, the stones pattering down like the sparse hail that preludes a storm), and that he gnaws off the small end of pears to get at the seeds. He steals the corn from under the noses of my poultry. But what would you have? He will come down upon the limb of the tree I am lying under till he is within a yard of me. He and his mate will scurry up and down the great black-walnut for my diversion, chattering like monkeys. Can I sign his death-warrant who has tolerated me about his grounds so long? Not I. Let them steal, and welcome. I am sure I should, had I had the same bringing up and the same temptation. As for the birds, I do not believe there is one of them but does more good than harm; and of how many featherless bipeds can this be said?

FRANCIS PARKMAN

1823–1893

43 *Iroquois and Algonquin*

FOREMOST in war, foremost in eloquence, foremost in their savage arts of policy, stood the fierce people called by themselves the *Hodenosaunee,* and by the French the *Iroquois,* a name which has since been applied to the entire family of which they formed the dominant member. They extended their conquests and their depredations from Quebec to the Carolinas, and from the western prairies to the forests of Maine. On the south, they forced tribute from the subjugated Delawares, and pierced the mountain fastnesses of the Cherokees with incessant forays. On the north, they uprooted the ancient settlements of the Wyandots; on the west they exterminated the Eries and the Andastes, and spread havoc and dismay among the tribes of the Illinois; and on the east, the Indians of New England fled at the first peal of the Mohawk war-cry. Nor was it the Indian race alone who quailed before their ferocious valor. All Canada shook with the desolating fury of their onset; the people fled to the forts for refuge; the blood-besmeared conquerors roamed like wolves among the burning settlements, and the youthful colony trembled on the brink of ruin.

The Iroquois in some measure owed their triumphs to the position of their country; for they dwelt within the present limits of the State of New York, whence several great rivers and the inland oceans of the northern lakes opened ready thoroughfares to their roving warriors through all the adjacent wilderness. But the true fountain of their success is to be sought in their own inherent energies, wrought to the most effective action under a political fabric well suited to the Indian life; in their mental and moral organization; in their insatiable ambition and restless ferocity.

In their scheme of government, as in their social customs and religious observances, the Iroquois displayed, in full symmetry and matured strength, the same characteristics which in other tribes are found distorted, withered, decayed to the root, or, perhaps, faintly visible in an imperfect germ. They consisted of five tribes or nations — the Mohawks, the Oneidas, the Onondagas, the Cayugas, and the Senecas, to whom a sixth, the Tuscaroras, was afterwards added. To each of these tribes belonged an organization of its own. Each had several sachems, who, with the subordinate chiefs and principal men, regulated all its internal affairs; but, when foreign powers were to be treated with, or matters involving the whole confederacy required deliberation, all the sachems of the several tribes convened in general assembly at the great council-house, in the Valley of Onondaga. Here ambassadors were received, alliances were adjusted, and all subjects of general interest discussed with exemplary harmony. The order of debate was prescribed by time-honored customs, and, in the fiercest heat of controversy, the assembly maintained its iron self-control.

But the mainstay of Iroquois polity was the system of *totemship*. It was this which gave the structure its elastic strength; and but for this, a mere confederacy of jealous and warlike tribes must soon have been rent asunder by shocks from without or discord from within. At some early period, the Iroquois must have formed an individual nation; for the whole people, irrespective of their separation into tribes, consisted of eight totemic clans; and the members of each clan, to what nation soever they belonged, were mutually bound to one another by those close ties of fraternity which mark this singular institution. Thus the five nations of the confederacy were laced together by an eight-fold band; and to this hour their slender remnants cling to one another with invincible tenacity.

It was no small security to the liberties of the Iroquois — liberties which they valued beyond any other possession — that by the Indian custom of descent in the female line, which among them was more rigidly adhered to than elsewhere, the office of the sachem must pass, not to his son, but to his brother, his sister's son, or some yet remoter kinsman. His power was constantly deflected into the collateral branches of his family; and thus one of the strongest temptations of ambition was cut off. The Iroquois had no laws; but they had ancient customs which took the place of laws. Each man, or rather each clan, was the avenger of its own wrongs; but the manner of the retaliation was fixed by established usage. The tribal sachems, and even the great council at Onondaga, had no power to compel the execution of their decrees; yet they were looked up to with a respect which the soldier's bayonet or the sheriff's staff would never have commanded; and it is highly to the honor of the Indian character that they could exert so great an authority where there was nothing to enforce it but the weight of moral power.

The origin of the Iroquois is lost in hopeless obscurity. That they came from the west; that they came from the north; that they sprang from the soil of New York, are the testimonies of three conflicting traditions, all equally worthless as aids to historic inquiry. It is at the era of their confederacy — the event to which the five tribes owed all their greatness and power, and to which we need assign no remoter date than that of a century before the first arrival

of the Dutch in New York — that faint rays of light begin
to pierce the gloom, and the chaotic traditions of the earlier
epoch mold themselves into forms more palpable and
distinct.

Taounyawatha, the God of the Waters — such is the
belief of the Iroquois — descended to the earth to instruct
his favorite people in the arts of savage life; and when he
saw how they were tormented by giants, monsters, and evil
spirits, he urged the divided tribes, for the common defence, to band themselves together in an everlasting
league. While the injunction was as yet unfulfilled, the
sacred messenger was recalled to the Great Spirit; but,
before his departure, he promised that another should appear, empowered to instruct the people in all that per-
tained to their confederation. And accordingly, as a band
of Mohawk warriors was threading the funereal labyrinth
of an ancient pine forest, they heard, amid its blackest
depths, a hoarse voice chanting in measured cadence; and,
following the sound, they saw, seated among the trees,
a monster of so hideous an aspect, that one and all they
stood benumbed with terror. His features were wild and
frightful. He was encompassed by hissing rattlesnakes,
which, Medusa-like, hung writhing from his head; and on
the ground around him were strewn implements of incantation, and magic vessels formed of human skulls. Recovering from their amazement, the warriors could perceive that in the mystic words of the chant, which he still
poured forth, were couched the laws and principles of the
destined confederacy. The tradition further declares that
the monster, being surrounded and captured, was presently transformed to human shape, that he became a chief
of transcendent wisdom and prowess, and to the day of
his death ruled the councils of the now united tribes. To
this hour the presiding sachem of the council at Onondaga
inherits from him the honored name of Atotarho.

The traditional epoch which preceded the auspicious event
of the confederacy, though wrapped in clouds and darkness,

and defying historic scrutiny, has yet a character and meaning of its own. The gloom is peopled thick with phantoms; with monsters and prodigies, shapes of wild enormity, yet offering, in the Teutonic strength of their conception, the evidence of a robustness of mind unparalleled among tribes of a different lineage. In these evil days, the scattered and divided Iroquois were beset with every form of peril and disaster. Giants, cased in armor of stone, descended on them from the mountains of the north. Huge beasts trampled down their forests like fields of grass. Human heads, with streaming hair and glaring eyeballs, shot through the air like meteors, shedding pestilence and death throughout the land. A great horned serpent rose from Lake Ontario; and only the thunderbolts of the skies could stay his ravages, and drive him back to his native deeps. The skeletons of men, victims of some monster of the forest, were seen swimming in the Lake of Teungktoo; and around the Seneca village on the Hill of Genundewah, a two-headed serpent coiled himself, of size so monstrous that the wretched people were unable to ascend his scaly sides, and perished in multitudes by his pestilential breath. Mortally wounded at length by the magic arrow of a child, he rolled down the steep, sweeping away the forest with his writhings, and plunging into the lake below, where he lashed the black waters till they boiled with blood and foam, and at length, exhausted with his agony, sank, and perished at the bottom. Under the falls of Niagara dwelt the Spirit of the Thunder, with his brood of giant sons; and the Iroquois trembled in their villages when, amid the blackening shadows of the storm, they heard his deep shout roll along the firmament.

The energy of fancy, whence these barbarous creations drew their birth, displayed itself, at a later period, in that peculiar eloquence which the wild democracy of the Iroquois tended to call forth, and to which the mountain and the forest, the torrent and the storm, lent their stores of noble imagery. That to this imaginative vigor was joined mental power of a different stamp, is witnessed by the caustic irony of Garangula and Sagoyewatha, and no less by the subtle policy, sagacious as it was treacherous, which marked the dealings of the Iroquois with surrounding tribes.

With all this intellectual superiority, the arts of life among them had not emerged from their primitive rudeness; and their coarse pottery, their spear and arrow heads of stone, were in no way superior to those of many other tribes. Their agriculture deserves a higher praise. In 1696, the invading army of Count Frontenac found the maize fields extending a league and a half or two leagues from their villages; and, in 1779, the troops of General Sullivan were filled with amazement at their abundant stores of corn, beans, and squashes, and at the ancient apple orchards which grew around their settlements.

Their dwellings and works of defense were far from contemptible, either in their dimensions or in their structure; and though by the several attacks of the French, and especially by the invasion of De Nonville, in 1687, and of Frontenac, nine years later, their fortified towns were leveled to the earth, never again to reappear; yet in the works of Champlain and other early writers we find abundant evidence of their pristine condition. Along the banks of the Mohawk, among the hills and hollows of Onondaga, in the forests of Oneida and Cayuga, on the romantic shores of Seneca Lake and the rich borders of the Genesee, surrounded by waving maize fields, and encircled from afar by the green margin of the forest, stood the ancient strongholds of the confederacy. The clustering dwellings were encompassed by palisades, in single, double, or triple rows, pierced with loopholes, furnished with platforms within, for the convenience of the defenders, with magazines of stones to hurl upon the heads of the enemy, and with water conductors to extinguish any fire which might be kindled from without.

The area which these defenses enclosed was often several

acres in extent, and the dwellings, ranged in order within, were sometimes more than a hundred feet in length. Posts, firmly driven into the ground, with an intervening framework of poles, formed the basis of the structure; and its sides and arched roof were closely covered with layers of elm bark. Each of the larger dwellings contained several distinct families, whose separate fires were built along the central space, while compartments on each side, like the stalls of a stable, afforded some degree of privacy. Here, rude couches were prepared, and bear and deer skins spread; while above, the ripened ears of maize, suspended in rows, formed a golden tapestry.

In the long evenings of midwinter, when in the wilderness without the trees cracked with biting cold, and the forest paths were clogged with snow, then, around the lodge-fires of the Iroquois, warriors, squaws, and restless naked children were clustered in social groups, each dark face brightening in the fickle firelight, while, with jest and laugh, the pipe passed round from hand to hand. Perhaps some shriveled old warrior, the story-teller of the tribe, recounted to attentive ears the deeds of ancient heroism, legends of spirits and monsters, or tales of witches and vampires — superstitions not less rife among this all-believing race, than among the nations of the transatlantic world.

The life of the Iroquois, though void of those multiplying phases which vary the routine of civilized existence, was one of sharp excitement and sudden contrast. The chase, the war-path, the dance, the festival, the game of hazard, the race of political ambition, all had their votaries. When the assembled sachems had resolved on war against some foreign tribe, and when, from their great council-house of bark, in the Valley of Onondaga, their messengers had gone forth to invite the warriors to arms, then from east to west, through the farthest bounds of the confederacy, a thousand warlike hearts caught up the summons with glad alacrity. With fasting and praying, and consulting dreams and omens; with invoking the war-god, and dancing the frantic war-dance, the warriors sought to insure the triumph of their arms; and, these strange rites concluded, they began their stealthy progress full of confidence through the devious pathways of the forest. For days and weeks, in anxious expectation, the villagers await the result. And now, as evening closes, a shrill, wild cry, pealing from afar, over the darkening forest, proclaims the return of the victorious warriors. The village is alive with sudden commotion; and snatching sticks and stones, knives and hatchets, men, women, and children, yelling like fiends let loose, swarm out of the narrow portal, to visit upon the miserable captives a foretaste of the deadlier torments in store for them. And now, the black arches of the forest glow with the fires of death; and with brandished torch and firebrand the frenzied multitude close around their victim. The pen shrinks to write, the heart sickens to conceive, the fierceness of his agony; yet still, amid the din of his tormentors, rises his clear voice of scorn and defiance. The work is done; the blackened trunk is flung to the dogs, and, with clamorous shouts and hootings, the murderers seek to drive away the spirit of their victim.

The Iroquois reckoned these barbarities among their most exquisite enjoyments; and yet they had other sources of pleasure, which made up in frequency and in innocence all that they lacked in intensity. Each passing season had its feasts and dances, often mingling religion with social pastime. The young had their frolics and merry-makings; and the old had their no less frequent councils, where conversation and laughter alternated with grave deliberations for the public weal. There were also stated periods marked by the recurrence of momentous ceremonies, in which the whole community took part — the mystic sacrifice of the dogs, the wild orgies of the dream feast, and the loathsome festival of the exhumation of the dead. Yet in the intervals of war and hunting, these multiform occupations would often fail; and, while the women were toiling in the cornfields, the lazy warriors vainly sought relief from the scanty resources of their own minds, and beguiled the hours with smoking or sleeping, with gambling or gallantry.

If we seek for a single trait preëminently characteristic of the Iroquois, we shall find it in that boundless pride which impelled them to style themselves, not inaptly as regards their own race, "the men surpassing all others." "Must I," exclaimed one of their great warriors, as he fell wounded among a crowd of Algonquins, — "must I, who have made the whole earth tremble, now die by the hands of children?" Their power kept pace with their pride. Their war-parties roamed over half America, and their name was a terror from the Atlantic to the Mississippi; but, when we ask the numerical strength of the dreaded confederacy, when we discover that, in the days of their greatest triumphs, their united cantons could not have mustered four thousand warriors, we stand amazed at the folly and dissension which left so vast a region the prey of a handful of bold marauders. Of the cities and villages now so thickly scattered over the lost domain of the Iroquois, a single one might boast a more numerous population than all the five united tribes. . . .

Turning his course northward, traversing Lakes Michigan and Superior, and skirting the western margin of Lake Huron, the voyager would have found the solitudes of the wild waste around him broken by scattered lodges of the Ojibwas, Pottawattamies, and Ottawas. About the bays and rivers west of Lake Michigan, he would have seen the Sacs, the Foxes, and the Menomonies; and penetrating the frozen wilderness of the north, he would have been welcomed by the rude hospitality of the wandering Knisteneaux.

The Ojibwas, with their kindred, the Pottawattamies, and their friends the Ottawas, — the latter of whom were fugitives from the eastward, whence they had fled from the wrath of the Iroquois, — were banded into a sort of confederacy. In blood and language, in manners and character they were closely allied. The Ojibwas, by far the most numerous of the three, occupied the basin of Lake Superior, and extensive adjacent regions. In their boundaries, the career of Iroquois conquest found at length a check. The fugitive Wyandots sought refuge in the Ojibwa hunting-grounds; and tradition relates that, at the outlet of Lake Superior, an Iroquois war-party once encountered a disastrous repulse.

In their mode of life, they were far more rude than the Iroquois, or even the southern Algonquin tribes. The totemic system is found among them in its most imperfect state. The original clans have become broken into fragments, and indefinitely multiplied; and many of the ancient customs of the institution are but loosely regarded. Agriculture is little known, and, through summer and winter, they range the wilderness with restless wandering, now gorged to repletion, and now perishing with want. In the calm days of summer, the Ojibwa fishermen pushes out his birch canoe upon the great inland ocean of the north; and, as he gazes down into the pellucid depths, he seems like one balanced between earth and sky. The watchful fish-hawk circles above his head; and below, farther than his line will reach, he sees the trout glide shadowy and silent over the glimmering pebbles. The little islands on the verge of the horizon seem now starting into spires, now melting from the sight, now shaping themselves into a thousand fantastic forms, with the strange mirage of the waters; and he fancies that the evil spirits of the lake lie basking their serpent forms on those unhallowed shores. Again, he explores the watery labyrinths where the stream sweeps among pine-tufted islands, or runs, black and deep, beneath the shadows of moss-bearded firs; or he lifts his canoe upon the sandy beach, and, while his camp-fire crackles on the grass-plat, reclines beneath the trees, and smokes and laughs away the sultry hours, in a lazy luxury of enjoyment.

But when winter descends upon the north, sealing up the fountains, fettering the streams, and turning the green-robed forests to shivering nakedness, then, bearing their frail dwellings on their backs, the Ojibwa family wander forth into the wilderness, cheered only on their dreary track by the whistling of the north wind, and the hungry howl of wolves. By the banks of some frozen stream, women and children, men and dogs, lie crouched together around the fire. They spread their benumbed fingers over the embers, while the wind shrieks through the fir-trees like the gale through the rigging of a frigate, and the narrow concave of the wigwam sparkles with the frost-work of their congealed breath. In vain they beat the magic drum, and call upon their guardian manitoes; — the wary moose keeps aloof, the bear lies close in his hollow tree, and famine stares them in the face. And now the hunter can fight no more against the nipping cold and blinding sleet. Stiff and stark, with haggard cheek and shriveled lip, he lies among the snowdrifts; till, with tooth and claw, the famished wildcat strives in vain to pierce the frigid marble of his limbs. Such harsh schooling is thrown away on the incorrigible mind of the northern Algonquin. He lives in misery, as his fathers lived before him. Still, in the brief hour of plenty he forgets the season of want; and still the sleet and the snow descend upon his houseless head. . . .

The fireside stories of every primitive people are faithful reflections of the form and coloring of the national mind; and it is no proof of sound philosophy to turn with contempt from the study of a fairy tale. The legendary lore of the Iroquois, black as the midnight forests, awful in its gloomy strength, is but another manifestation of that spirit of mastery which uprooted whole tribes from the earth, and deluged the wilderness with blood. The traditionary tales of the Algonquins wear a different aspect. The credulous circle around an Ojibwa lodge-fire listened to wild recitals of necromancy and witchcraft — men transformed to beasts, and beasts transformed to men, animated trees, and birds who spoke with human tongue. They heard of malignant sorcerers dwelling among the lonely islands of spell-bound lakes; of grisly weendigoes, and bloodless geebi; of evil manitoes lurking in the dens and fastnesses of the woods; of pygmy champions, diminutive in stature, but mighty in soul, who, by the potency of charm and talisman, subdued the direst monsters of the waste; and of heroes, who, not by downright force and open onset, but by subtle strategy, by trick or magic art, achieved marvelous triumphs over the brute force of their assailants. Sometimes the tale will breathe a different spirit, and tell of orphan children abandoned in the heart of a hideous wilderness, beset with fiends and cannibals. Some enamored maiden, scornful of earthly suitors, plights her troth to the graceful manito of the grove; or bright aërial beings, dwellers of the sky, descend to tantalize the gaze of mortals with evanescent forms of loveliness.

The mighty giant, the God of the Thunder, who made his home among the caverns, beneath the cataract of Niagara, was a conception which the deep imagination of the Iroquois might fitly engender. The Algonquins held a simpler faith, and maintained that the thunder was a bird who built his nest on the pinnacle of towering mountains. Two daring boys once scaled the height, and thrust sticks into the eyes of the portentous nestlings; which hereupon flashed forth such wrathful scintillations, that the sticks were shivered to atoms.

The religious belief of the Algonquins — and the remark holds good, not of the Algonquins only, but of all the hunting tribes of America — is a cloudy bewilderment, where we seek in vain for system or coherency. Among a primitive and savage people, there were no poets to vivify its images, no priests to give distinctness and harmony to its rites and symbols. To the Indian mind, all nature was instinct with deity. A spirit was embodied in every mountain, lake, and cataract; every bird, beast, or reptile, every tree, shrub, or grass-blade, was endued with mystic influence; yet this untutored pantheism did not exclude the conception of certain divinities, of incongruous and ever-shifting attributes. The sun, too, was a god, and the moon was a goddess. Conflicting powers of good and evil divided the universe; but if, before the arrival of Europeans, the Indian recognized the existence of a one, almighty, self-existent Being, the Great

Spirit, the Lord of Heaven and Earth, the belief was so vague and dubious as scarcely to deserve the name. His perceptions of moral good and evil were perplexed and shadowy; and the belief in a state of future reward and punishment was by no means of universal prevalence.

Of the Indian character much has been written foolishly, and credulously believed. By the rhapsodies of poets, the cant of sentimentalists, and the extravagance of some who should have known better, a counterfeit image has been tricked out, which might seek in vain for its likeness through every corner of the habitable earth; an image bearing no more resemblance to its original than the monarch of the tragedy and the hero of the epic poem bear to their living prototypes in the palace and the camp. The shadows of his wilderness home, and the darker mantle of his own inscrutable reserve, have made the Indian warrior a wonder and a mystery. Yet to the eye of rational observation there is nothing unintelligible in him. He is full, it is true, of contradiction. He deems himself the center of greatness and renown; his pride is proof against the fiercest torments of fire and steel; and yet the same man would beg for a dram of whisky, or pick up a crust of bread thrown to him like a dog, from the tent door of the traveler. At one moment, he is wary and cautious to the verge of cowardice; at the next, he abandons himself to a very insanity of recklessness; and the habitual self-restraint which throws an impenetrable veil over emotion is joined to the wild, impetuous passions of a beast or a madman.

Such inconsistencies, strange as they seem in our eyes, when viewed under a novel aspect, are but the ordinary incidents of humanity. The qualities of the mind are not uniform in their action through all the relations of life. With different men, and different races of men, pride, valor, prudence, have different forms of manifestation, and where in one instance they lie dormant, in another they are keenly awake. The conjunction of greatness and littleness, meanness and pride, is older than the days of the patriarchs; and such antiquated phenomena, displayed under a new form in the unreflecting, undisciplined mind of a savage, call for no special wonder, but should rather be classed with the other enigmas of the fathomless human heart. The dissecting knife of a Rochefoucault might lay bare matters of no less curious observation in the breast of every man.

Nature has stamped the Indian with a hard and stern physiognomy. Ambition, revenge, envy, jealousy, are his ruling passions; and his cold temperament is little exposed to those effeminate vices which are the bane of milder races. With him revenge is an overpowering instinct; nay, more, it is a point of honor and a duty. His pride sets all language at defiance. He loathes the thought of coercion; and few of his race have ever stooped to discharge a menial office. A wild love of liberty, an utter intolerance of control, lie at the basis of his character, and fire his whole existence. Yet, in spite of this haughty independence, he is a devout hero-worshiper; and high achievement in war or policy touches a chord to which his nature never fails to respond. He looks up with admiring reverence to the sages and heroes of his tribe; and it is this principle, joined to the respect for age, which springs from the patriarchal element in his social system, which, beyond all others, contributes union and harmony to the erratic members of an Indian community. With him the love of glory kindles into a burning passion; and to allay its cravings, he will dare cold and famine, fire, tempest, torture, and death itself.

These generous traits are overcast by much that is dark, cold, and sinister, by sleepless distrust, and rankling jealousy. Treacherous himself, he is always suspicious of treachery in others. Brave as he is, — and few of mankind are braver, — he will vent his passion by a secret stab rather than an open blow. His warfare is full of ambuscade and stratagem; and he never rushes into battle with that joyous self-abandonment, with which the warriors of the Gothic races flung themselves into the ranks of their enemies. In his feasts and his drinking-bouts we find none of that robust and full-toned mirth which reigned at the rude carousals of our barbaric ancestry. He is never jovial in his cups, and maudlin sorrow or maniacal rage is the sole result of his potations.

Over all emotion he throws the veil of an iron self-control, originating in a peculiar form of pride, and fostered by rigorous discipline from childhood upward. He is trained to conceal passion, and not to subdue it. The inscrutable warrior is aptly imaged by the hackneyed figure of a volcano covered with snow; and no man can say when or where the wild-fire will burst forth. This shallow self-mastery serves to give dignity to public deliberation, and harmony to social life. Wrangling and quarrel are strangers to an Indian dwelling; and while an assembly of the ancient Gauls was garrulous as a convocation of magpies, a Roman senate might have taken a lesson from the grave solemnity of an Indian council. In the midst of his family and friends, he hides affections, by nature none of the most tender, under a mask of icy coldness; and in the torturing fires of his enemy, the haughty sufferer maintains to the last his look of grim defiance.

His intellect is as peculiar as his moral organization. Among all savages, the powers of perception preponderate over those of reason and analysis; but this is more especially the case with the Indian. An acute judge of character, at least of such parts of it as his experience enables him to comprehend; keen to a proverb in all exercises of war and the chase, he seldom traces effects to their causes, or follows out actions to their remote results. Though a close observer of external nature, he no sooner attempts to account for her phenomena than he involves himself in the most ridiculous absurdities; and quite content with these puerilities, he has not the least desire to push his inquiries further. His curiosity, abundantly active within its own narrow circle, is dead to all things else; and to attempt rousing it from its torpor is but a bootless task. He seldom takes cognizance of general or abstract ideas; and his language has scarcely the power to express them, except through the medium of figures drawn from the external world, and often highly picturesque and forcible. The absence of reflection makes him grossly improvident, and unfits him for pursuing any complicated scheme of war or policy.

Some races of men seem molded in wax, soft and melting, at once plastic and feeble. Some races, like some metals, combine the greatest flexibility with the greatest strength. But the Indian is hewn out of a rock. You cannot change the form without destruction of the substance. Such, at least, has too often proved the case. Races of inferior energy have possessed a power of expansion and assimilation to which he is a stranger; and it is this fixed and rigid quality which has proved his ruin. He will not learn the arts of civilization, and he and his forest must perish together. The stern, unchanging features of his mind excite our admiration, from their very immutability; and we look with deep interest on the fate of this irreclaimable son of the wilderness, the child who will not be weaned from the breast of his rugged mother. And our interest increases when we discern in the unhappy wanderer, mingled among his vices, the germs of heroic virtues — a hand bountiful to bestow, as it is rapacious to seize, and, even in extremest famine, imparting its last morsel to a fellow-sufferer; a heart which, strong in friendship as in hate, thinks it not too much to lay down life for its chosen comrade; a soul true to its own idea of honor, and burning with an unquenchable thirst for greatness and renown.

The imprisoned lion in the showman's cage differs not more widely from the lord of the desert, than the beggarly frequenter of frontier garrisons and dramshops differs from the proud denizen of the woods. It is in his native wilds alone that the Indian must be seen and studied. Thus to depict him is the aim of the ensuing History; and if, from the shades of rock and forest, the savage features should look too grimly forth, it is because the clouds of a tempestuous war have cast upon the picture their murky shadows and lurid fires.

ARTEMUS WARD (CHARLES FARRAR BROWNE)

1834–1867

44 *One of Mr. Ward's Business Letters*

TO THE EDITOR OF THE ——

SIR: I'm movin along — slowly along — down tords your place. I want you should rite me a letter, sayin how is the show bizniss in your place. My show at present consists of three moral Bares, a Kangaroo (a amoozin little Raskal — t'would make you larf yerself to deth to see the little cuss jump up and squeal) wax figgers of G. Washington Gen. Tayler John Bunyan Capt. Kidd and Dr Webster in the act of killin Dr Parkman, besides several miscellanyus moral wax statoots of celebrated piruts & murderers, &c., ekalled by a few & exceld by none. Now Mr Editor, scratch orf a few lines sayin how is the show bizniss down to your place. I shall hav my hanbills dun at your offiss. Depend upon it. I want you should git my hanbills up in flamin stile. Also git up a tremenjus excitemunt in yr. paper 'bowt my onparaleld Show. We must fetch the public sumhow. We must wurk on their feelins. Cum the moral on 'em strong. If it's a temprance community tell 'em I sined the pledge fifteen minits arter Ise born, but on the contery ef your peple take their tods, say Mister Ward is as Jenial a feller as we ever met, full of conwiviality, & the life an Sole of the Soshul Bored. Take, don't you? If you say anythin abowt my show say my snaiks is as harmliss as the new born Babe. What a interestin study it is to see a zewological animil like a snaik under perfeck subjecshun! My kangaroo is the most larfable little cuss I ever saw. All for 15 cents. I am anxyus to skewer your infloounce. I repeet in regard to them hanbills that I shall git 'em struck orf up to your printin office. My perliteral sentiments agree with yourn exactly. I know thay do, becawz I never saw a man whoos didn't.   Respectively yures,   A. WARD.

P.S. — You scratch my back & Ile scratch your back.

45 *Artemus Ward's Autobiography*

New York, near Fifth Avenoo Hotel,
Org. 31ct.
Editor of PLAY BILL.

DR SIR,— Yrs, into which you ask me to send you
sum leadin incidents in my life so you can write my
Bogfry for the papers, cum dooly to hand. I hav no
doubt that a article onto my life, grammattycally jerked
and properly punktooated, would be a addition to the chois
literatoor of the day.

To the yooth of Ameriky it would be vallyble as showin
how high a pinnykle of fame a man can reach who com-
menst his career with a small canvas tent and a pea-green
ox, which he rubbed it off while scratchin hisself agin the
center pole, causin in Rahway, N. J., a discriminatin mob
to say humbugs would not go down in their village. The ox
resoom'd agricultooral pursoots shortly afterwards.

I next tried my hand at givin Blind-man concerts, ap-
pearin as the poor blind man myself. But the infamous cuss
who I hired to lead me round towns in the day time to excite simpathy drank freely of spiritoous licker unbeknowns
to me one day, & while under their inflooance he led me
into the canal. I had to either tear the green bandige from
my eyes or be drownded. I tho't I'd restore my eyesight.

In writin about these things, Mr Editer, kinder smooth
'em over. Speak of 'em as eccentrissities of gen'us.

My next ventur would hav bin a success if I hadn't tried
to do too much. I got up a series of wax figgers, and among
others one of Socrates. I tho't a wax figger of old Sock.
would be poplar with eddycated peple, but unfortinitly I
put a Brown linen duster and a U. S. Army regulation cap
on him, which peple with classycal eddycations said it was
a farce. This enterprise was onfortnit in other respecks.
At a certin town I advertised a wax figger of the Hon'ble

Amos Perkins, who was a Railroad President, and a great person in them parts. But it appeared I had shown the same figger for a Pirut named Gibbs in that town the previs season, which created a intense toomult, & the audience remarked "shame onto me," & other statements of the same similarness. I tried to mollify 'em. I told 'em that any family possessin children might have my she tiger to play with half a day, & I wouldn't charge 'em a cent, but alars! it was of no avail. I was forced to leave, & I infer from a article in the *Advertiser* of that town, in which the Editer says, "Altho' time has silvered this man's hed with its frosts, he still brazenly wallows in infamy. Still are his snakes stuffed, and his wax works unreliable. We are glad that he has concluded to never revisit our town, altho', incredible as it may appear, the fellow really did contemplate so doing last summer, when, still true to the craven instincts of his black heart, he wrote the hireling knaves of the obscure journal across the street to know what they would charge for 400 small bills, to be done on yellow paper! We shall recur to this matter again."

I say, I infer from this article that a prejudiss still exists agin me in that town.

I will not speak of my once bein in straitend circumstances in a sertin town, and of my endeaverin to accoomulate welth by lettin myself to Sabbath School picnics to sing ballads adapted to the understandins of little children, accompanyin myself on a claironett — which I forgot where I was one day, singin, instid of "Oh, how pleasant to be a little child,"

> "Rip slap — set 'em up again,
> Right in the middle of a three-cent pie."

which mistake, added to the fact that I couldn't play onto the claironett except making it howl dismal, broke up the picnic, and children said, in voices choked with sobs and emotions, where was their home and where was their Pa? and I said, Be quiet, dear children, I am your Pa, which made a young woman with two twins by her side say very angryly, "Good heavens forbid you should ever be the Pa of any of these innocent ones, unless it is much desirable for them to expire igminyusly up onto a murderer's gallus!"

I say I will not speak of this. Let it be Berrid into Oblivyun.

In your article, Mr Editer, please tell him what sort of a man I am.

If you see fit to kriticise my Show, speak your mind freely. I do not object to kriticism. Tell the public, in a candid and graceful article, that my Show abounds in moral and startlin cooriosities, any one of whom is wuth dubble the price of admission.

I hav thus far spoke of myself excloosively as a exhibiter.

I was born in the State of Maine of parents. As a infant I attracted a great deal of attention. The nabers would stand over my cradle for hours and say, "How bright that little face looks! How much it nose!" The young ladies would carry me round in their arms, sayin I was muzzer's bezzy darling and a sweety 'eety 'ittle ting. It was nice, tho' I wasn't old enuff to properly appreciate it. I'm a healthy old darlin now.

I have allers sustained a good moral character. I was never a Railroad director in my life.

Altho' in early life I did not invarably confine myself to truth in my small bills, I have been gradooally growin respectabler and respectabler ev'ry year. I luv my children, and never mistake another man's wife for my own. I'm not a member of any meetin house, but firmly believe in meetin houses, and shouldn't feel safe to take a dose of laudnum and lay down in the street of a village that hadn't any, with a thousand dollars in my vest pockets.

My temperament is billious, altho' I don't owe a dollar in the world.

I am a early riser, but my wife is a Presbyterian. I may add that I am also bald-heded. I keep two cows.

I liv in Baldinsville, Indiany. My next door naber is Old Steve Billins. I'll tell you a little story about Old Steve

that will make you larf. He jined the Church last spring,
and the minister said, "You must go home now, Brother Billins, and erect a family altar in your own house," whereupon
the egrejis old ass went home and built a reg'lar pulpit in his
settin room. He had the jiners in his house over four days.

I am 56 (56) years of age. Time, with its relentless scythe
is ever busy. The Old Sexton gathers them in, he gathers
them in! I keep a pig this year.

I don't think of anything more, Mr Editer.

If you should giv my portrait in connection with my
Bogfry, please have me ingraved in a languishin attitood,
leanin on a marble pillar, leavin my back hair as it is now.

Trooly yours,
<small>Artemus Ward.</small>

MARK TWAIN (Samuel Langhorne Clemens)
<small>1835–1910</small>

46   *The Pony Express*

IN a little while all interest was taken up in stretching our
necks and watching for the "pony-rider"—the fleet
messenger who sped across the continent from St. Joe to
Sacramento, carrying letters nineteen hundred miles in eight
days! Think of that for perishable horse and human flesh
and blood to do! The pony-rider was usually a little bit of
a man, brimful of spirit and endurance. No matter what
time of the day or night his watch came on, and no matter
whether it was winter or summer, raining, snowing, hailing,
or sleeting, or whether his "beat" was a level straight road
or a crazy trail over mountain crags and precipices, or
whether it led through peaceful regions or regions that
swarmed with hostile Indians, he must be always ready to
leap into the saddle and be off like the wind! There was no
idling-time for a pony-rider on duty. He rode fifty miles
without stopping, by daylight, moonlight, starlight, or
through the blackness of darkness—just as it happened.

He rode a splendid horse that was born for a racer and fed and lodged like a gentleman; kept him at his utmost speed for ten miles, and then, as he came crashing up to the station where stood two men holding fast a fresh, impatient steed, the transfer of rider and mail-bag was made in the twinkling of an eye, and away flew the eager pair and were out of sight before the spectator could get hardly the ghost of a look. Both rider and horse went " flying light." The rider's dress was thin, and fitted close; he wore a " roundabout," and a skull-cap, and tucked his pantaloons into his boot-tops like a race-rider. He carried no arms — he carried nothing that was not absolutely necessary, for even the postage on his literary freight was worth *five dollars a letter*. He got but little frivolous correspondence to carry — his bag had business letters in it, mostly. His horse was stripped of all unnecessary weight, too. He wore a little wafer of a racing-saddle, and no visible blanket. He wore light shoes, or none at all. The little flat mail-pockets strapped under the rider's thighs would each hold about the bulk of a child's primer. They held many and many an important business chapter and newspaper letter, but these were written on paper as airy and thin as gold-leaf, nearly, and thus bulk and weight were economized. The stage-coach traveled about a hundred to a hundred and twenty-five miles a day (twenty-four hours), the pony-rider about two hundred and fifty. There were about eighty pony-riders in the saddle all the time, night and day, stretching in a long, scattering procession from Missouri to California, forty flying eastward, and forty toward the west, and among them making four hundred gallant horses earn a stirring livelihood and see a deal of scenery every single day in the year.

We had had a consuming desire, from the beginning, to see a pony-rider, but somehow or other all that passed us and all that met us managed to streak by in the night, and so we heard only a whizz and a hail, and the swift phantom of the desert was gone before we could get our heads out of the windows. But now we were expecting one along every moment, and would see him in broad daylight. Presently the driver exclaims:

" HERE HE COMES ! "

Every neck is stretched further, and every eye strained wider. Away across the endless dead level of the prairie a black speck appears against the sky, and it is plain that it moves. Well, I should think so! In a second or two it becomes a horse and rider, rising and falling, rising and falling — sweeping toward us uearer and nearer — growing more and more distinct, more and more sharply defined — nearer and still nearer, and the flutter of the hoofs comes faintly to the ear — another instant a whoop and a hurrah from our upper deck, a wave of the rider's hand, but no reply, and man and horse burst past our excited faces, and go swinging away like a belated fragment of a storm!

So sudden is it all, and so like a flash of unreal fancy, that but for the flake of white foam left quivering and perishing on a mail-sack after the vision had flashed by and disappeared, we might have doubted whether we had seen any actual horse and man at all, maybe.

47   *Snow in Nevada*

WE seemed to be in a road, but that was no proof. We tested this by walking off in various directions — the regular snow-mounds and the regular avenues between them convinced each man that *he* had found the true road, and that the others had found only false ones. Plainly the situation was desperate. We were cold and stiff and the horses were tired. We decided to build a sage-brush fire and camp out till morning. This was wise, because if we were wandering from the right road and the snow-storm continued another day our case would be the next thing to hopeless if we kept on.

All agreed that a camp-fire was what would come nearest to saving us, now, and so we set about building it. We could find no matches, and so we tried to make shift with the pistols. Not a man in the party had ever tried to do such a thing before, but not a man in the party doubted that it *could* be done, and without any trouble — because every man in the party had read about it in books many a time and had naturally come to believe it, with trusting simplicity, just as he had long ago accepted and believed *that other* common book-fraud about Indians and lost hunters making a fire by rubbing two dry sticks together.

We huddled together on our knees in the deep snow, and the horses put their noses together and bowed their patient heads over us; and while the feathery flakes eddied down and turned us into a group of white statuary, we proceeded with the momentous experiment. We broke twigs from a sage-bush and piled them on a little cleared place in the shelter of our bodies. In the course of ten or fifteen minutes all was ready, and then, while conversation ceased and our pulses beat low with anxious suspense, Ollendorff applied his revolver, pulled the trigger and blew the pile clear out of the county! It was the flattest failure that ever was.

This was distressing, but it paled before a greater horror — the horses were gone! I had been appointed to hold the bridles, but in my absorbing anxiety over the pistol experiment I had unconsciously dropped them and the released animals had walked off in the storm. It was useless to try to follow them, for their footfalls could make no sound, and one could pass within two yards of the creatures and never see them. We gave them up without an effort at recovering them, and cursed the lying books that said horses would stay by their masters for protection and companionship in a distressful time like ours.

We were miserable enough, before; we felt still more forlorn, now. Patiently, but with blighted hope, we broke more sticks and piled them, and once more the Prussian shot them into annihilation. Plainly, to light a fire with a pistol was an art requiring practice and experience, and the middle of a desert at midnight in a snow-storm was not a good place or time for the acquiring of the accomplishment. We gave it up and tried the other. Each man took a couple of sticks and fell to chafing them together. At the end of half an hour we were thoroughly chilled, and so were the sticks. We bitterly execrated the Indians, the hunters, and the books that had betrayed us with the silly device, and wondered dismally what was next to be done. At this critical moment Mr. Ballou fished out four matches from the rubbish of an overlooked pocket. To have found four gold bars would have seemed poor and cheap good luck compared to this. One cannot think how good a match looks under such circumstances — or how lovable and precious, and sacredly beautiful to the eye. This time we gathered sticks with high hopes; and when Mr. Ballou prepared to light the first match, there was an amount of interest centered upon him that pages of writing could not describe. The match burned hopefully a moment, and then went out. It could not have carried more regret with it if it had been a human life. The next match simply flashed and died. The wind puffed the third one out just as it was on the imminent verge of success. We gathered together closer than ever, and developed a solicitude that was rapt and painful, as Mr. Ballou scratched our last hope on his leg. It lit, burned blue and sickly, and then budded into a robust flame. Shading it with his hands, the old gentleman bent gradually down and every heart bent with him — every body, too, for that matter — and blood and breath stood still. The flame touched the sticks at last, took gradual hold upon them — hesitated — took a stronger hold — hesitated again — held its breath five heartbreaking seconds, then gave a sort of human gasp, and went out.

Nobody said a word for several minutes. It was a solemn sort of silence; even the wind put on a stealthy, sinister quiet, and made no more noise than the falling flakes of snow. Finally a sad-voiced conversation began, and it was soon apparent that in each of our hearts lay the conviction that this was our last night with the living. I had so hoped that I was the only one who felt so. When the others calmly acknowledged their conviction, it sounded like the summons itself. Ollendorff said:

"Brothers, let us die together. And let us go without one hard feeling toward each other. Let us forget and forgive bygones. I know that you have felt hard toward me for turning over the canoe, and for knowing too much and leading you round and round in the snow — but I meant well; forgive me. I acknowledge freely that I have had hard feelings against Mr. Ballou for abusing me and calling me a logarithm, which is a thing I do not know what, but no doubt a thing considered disgraceful and unbecoming in America, and it has scarcely been out of my mind and has hurt me a great deal — but let it go; I forgive Mr. Ballou with all my heart, and —"

Poor Ollendorff broke down and the tears came. He was not alone, for I was crying too, and so was Mr. Ballou. Ollendorff got his voice again and forgave me for things I had done and said. Then he got out his bottle of whisky and said that whether he lived or died he would never touch another drop. He said he had given up all hope of life, and although ill-prepared, was ready to submit humbly to his fate; that he wished he could be spared a little longer, not for any selfish reason, but to make a thorough reform in his character, and by devoting himself to helping the poor, nursing the sick, and pleading with the people to guard themselves against the evils of intemperance, make his life a beneficent example to the young, and lay it down at last with the precious reflection that it had not been lived in vain. He ended by saying that his reform should begin at this moment, even here in the presence of death, since no longer time was to be vouchsafed wherein to prosecute it to men's help and benefit — and with that he threw away the bottle of whisky.

Mr. Ballou made remarks of similar purport, and began the reform he could not live to continue, by throwing away the ancient pack of cards that had solaced our captivity during the flood and made it bearable. He said he never gambled, but still was satisfied that the meddling with cards in any way was immoral and injurious, and no man could be wholly pure and blemishless without eschewing them. "And therefore," continued he, "in doing this act I already feel more in sympathy with that spiritual saturnalia necessary to entire and obsolete reform." These rolling syllables touched him as no intelligible eloquence could have done, and the old man sobbed with a mournfulness not unmingled with satisfaction.

My own remarks were of the same tenor as those of my comrades, and I know that the feelings that prompted them were heartfelt and sincere. We were all sincere, and all deeply moved and earnest, for we were in the presence of death and without hope. I threw away my pipe, and in doing it felt that at last I was free of a hated vice and one that had ridden me like a tyrant all my days. While I yet talked, the thought of the good I might have done in the world, and the still greater good I might *now* do, with these new incentives and higher and better aims to guide me if I could only be spared a few years longer, overcame me and the tears came again. We put our arms about each other's necks and awaited the warning drowsiness that precedes death by freezing.

It came stealing over us presently, and then we bade each other a last farewell. A delicious dreaminess wrought its web about my yielding senses, while the snowflakes wove a winding sheet about my conquered body. Oblivion came. The battle of life was done.

I do not know how long I was in a state of forgetfulness, but it seemed an age. A vague consciousness grew upon me by degrees, and then came a gathering anguish of pain in my limbs and through all my body. I shuddered. The thought flitted through my brain, "this is death — this is the hereafter."

Then came a white upheaval at my side, and a voice said, with bitterness:

"Will some gentleman be so good as to kick me behind?"

It was Ballou — at least it was a tousled snow image in a sitting posture, with Ballou's voice.

I rose up, and there in the gray dawn, not fifteen steps from us, were the frame buildings of a stage-station, and under a shed stood our still saddled and bridled horses!

An arched snowdrift broke up, now, and Ollendorff emerged from it, and the three of us sat and stared at the houses without speaking a word. We really had nothing to say. We were like the profane man who could not " do the subject justice," the whole situation was so painfully ridiculous and humiliating that words were tame and we did not know where to commence anyhow.

The joy in our hearts at our deliverance was poisoned; well-nigh dissipated, indeed. We presently began to grow pettish by degrees, and sullen; and then, angry at each other, angry at ourselves, angry at everything in general, we moodily dusted the snow from our clothing and in unsociable single file plowed our way to the horses, unsaddled them, and sought shelter in the station.

I have scarcely exaggerated a detail of this curious and absurd adventure. It occurred almost exactly as I have stated it. We actually went into camp in a snow-drift in a desert, at midnight in a storm, forlorn and hopeless, within fifteen steps of a comfortable inn.

For two hours we sat apart in the station and ruminated in disgust. The mystery was gone, now, and it was plain enough why the horses had deserted us. Without a doubt they were under that shed a quarter of a minute after they had left us, and they must have overheard and enjoyed all our confessions and lamentations.

After breakfast we felt better, and the zest of life soon came back. The world looked bright again, and existence was as dear to us as ever. Presently an uneasiness came

over me — grew upon me — assailed me without ceasing.
Alas, my regeneration was not complete — I wanted to
smoke! I resisted with all my strength, but the flesh was
weak. I wandered away alone and wrestled with myself
an hour. I recalled my promises of reform and preached to
myself persuasively, upbraidingly, exhaustively. But it was
all in vain, I shortly found myself sneaking among the snowdrifts hunting for my pipe. I discovered it after a considerable search, and crept away to hide myself and enjoy it.
I remained behind the barn a good while, asking myself
how I would feel if my braver, stronger, truer comrades
should catch me in my degradation. At last I lit the pipe,
and no human being can feel meaner and baser than I did
then. I was ashamed of being in my own pitiful company.
Still dreading discovery, I felt that perhaps the further side
of the barn would be somewhat safer, and so I turned the
corner. As I turned the one corner, smoking, Ollendorff
turned the other with his bottle to his lips, and between us
sat unconscious Ballou deep in a game of " solitaire " with
the old greasy cards!

Absurdity could go no farther. We shook hands and
agreed to say no more about " reform " and " examples to the
rising generation."

48 *Learning the Mississippi*

I. The Boys' Ambition

WHEN I was a boy, there was but one permanent ambition among my comrades in our village on the west
bank of the Mississippi River. That was, to be a steamboatman. We had transient ambitions of other sorts, but
they were only transient. When a circus came and went, it
left us all burning to become clowns; the first negro minstrel
show that ever came to our section left us all suffering to try
that kind of life; now and then we had a hope that, if we
lived and were good, God would permit us to be pirates.

These ambitions faded out, each in its turn; but the ambition to be a steamboatman always remained.

Once a day a cheap, gaudy packet arrived upward from St. Louis, and another downward from Keokuk. Before these events, the day was glorious with expectancy; after them, the day was a dead and empty thing. Not only the boys, but the whole village, felt this. After all these years I can picture that old time to myself now, just as it was then: the white town drowsing in the sunshine of a summer's morning; the streets empty, or pretty nearly so; one or two clerks sitting in front of the Water Street stores, with their splint-bottomed chairs tilted back against the walls, chins on breasts, hats slouched over their faces, asleep — with shingle-shavings enough around to show what broke them down; a sow and a litter of pigs loafing along the sidewalk, doing a good business in watermelon rinds and seeds; two or three lonely little freight piles scattered about the "levee"; a pile of "skids" on the slope of the stone-paved wharf, and the fragrant town drunkard asleep in the shadow of them; two or three wood flats at the head of the wharf, but nobody to listen to the peaceful lapping of the wavelets against them; the great Mississippi, the majestic, the magnificent Mississippi, rolling its mile-wide tide along, shining in the sun; the dense forest away on the other side; the "point" above the town, and the "point" below, bounding the river-glimpse and turning it into a sort of sea, and withal a very still and brilliant and lonely one. Presently a film of dark smoke appears above one of those remote "points"; instantly a negro drayman, famous for his quick eye and prodigious voice, lifts up the cry, "S-t-e-a-m-boat a-comin' !" and the scene changes! The town drunkard stirs, the clerks wake up, a furious clatter of drays follows, every house and store pours out a human contribution, and all in a twinkling the dead town is alive and moving. Drays, carts, men, boys, all go hurrying from many quarters to a common center, the wharf. Assembled there, the people fasten their eyes upon the coming boat as upon a wonder they are seeing for the first time. And the boat *is* rather a handsome sight, too. She is long and sharp and trim and pretty; she has two tall, fancy-topped chimneys, with a gilded device of some kind swung between them; a fanciful pilot-house, all glass and " gingerbread," perched on top of the " texas " deck behind them; the paddle boxes are gorgeous with a picture or with gilded rays above the boat's name; the boiler-deck, the hurricane-deck, and the texas deck are fenced and ornamented with clean white railings; there is a flag gallantly flying from the jack-staff; the furnace doors are open and the fires glaring bravely; the upper decks are black with passengers; the captain stands by the big bell, calm, imposing, the envy of all; great volumes of the blackest smoke are rolling and tumbling out of the chimneys — a husbanded grandeur created with a bit of pitch-pine just before arriving at a town; the crew are grouped on the forecastle; the broad stage is run far out over the port bow, and an envied deck-hand stands picturesquely on the end of it with a coil of rope in his hand; the pent steam is screaming through the gauge-cocks; the captain lifts his hand, a bell rings, the wheels stop; then they turn back, churning the water to foam, and the steamer is at rest. Then such a scramble as there is to get aboard, and to get ashore, and to take in freight and to discharge freight, all at one and the same time; and such a yelling and cursing as the mates facilitate it all with! Ten minutes later the steamer is under way again, with no flag at the jack-staff and no black smoke issuing from the chimneys. After ten more minutes the town is dead again, and the town drunkard asleep by the skids once more.

My father was a justice of the peace, and I supposed he possessed the power of life and death over all men, and could hang anybody that offended him. This was distinction enough for me as a general thing; but the desire to be a steamboatman kept intruding, nevertheless. I first wanted to be a cabin-boy, so that I could come out with a white apron on and shake a table-cloth over the side, where all my old comrades could see me; later I thought I would rather be the deck-hand who stood on the end of the stage-plank with the coil of rope in his hand, because he was particularly conspicuous. But these were only day-dreams — they were too heavenly to be contemplated as real possibilities. By and by one of our boys went away. He was not heard of for a long time. At last he turned up as apprentice engineer or "striker" on a steamboat. This thing shook the bottom out of all my Sunday-school teachings. That boy had been notoriously worldly, and I just the reverse; yet he was exalted to this eminence, and I left in obscurity and misery. There was nothing generous about this fellow in his greatness. He would always manage to have a rusty bolt to scrub while his boat tarried at our town, and he would sit on the inside guard and scrub it, where we all could see him and envy him and loathe him. And whenever his boat was laid up he would come home and swell around the town in his blackest and greasiest clothes, so that nobody could help remembering that he was a steamboatman; and he used all sorts of steamboat technicalities in his talk, as if he were so used to them that he forgot common people could not understand them. He would speak of the "labbord" side of a horse in an easy, natural way that would make one wish he was dead. And he was always talking about "St. Looy" like an old citizen; he would refer casually to occasions when he was "coming down Fourth Street," or when he was "passing by the Planter's House," or when there was a fire and he took a turn on the brakes of "the old Big Missouri"; and then he would go on and lie about how many towns the size of ours were burned down there that day. Two or three of the boys had long been persons of consideration among us because they had been to St. Louis once and had a vague general knowledge of its wonders, but the day of their glory was over now. They lapsed into a humble silence, and learned to disappear when the ruthless "cub"-engineer approached. This fellow had money, too, and hair-oil. Also an ignorant silver watch and a showy brass watch-chain.

He wore a leather belt and used no suspenders. If ever a youth was cordially admired and hated by his comrades, this one was. No girl could withstand his charms. He "cut out" every boy in the village. When his boat blew up at last, it diffused a tranquil contentment among us such as we had not known for months. But when he came home the next week, alive, renowned, and appeared in church all battered up and bandaged, a shining hero, stared at and wondered over by everybody, it seemed to us that the partiality of Providence for an undeserving reptile had reached a point where it was open to criticism.

This creature's career could produce but one result, and it speedily followed. Boy after boy managed to get on the river. The minister's son became an engineer. The doctor's and the postmaster's sons became " mud clerks "; the wholesale liquor dealer's son became a barkeeper on a boat; four sons of the chief merchant, and two sons of the county judge, became pilots. Pilot was the grandest position of all. The pilot, even in those days of trivial wages, had a princely salary — from a hundred and fifty to two hundred and fifty dollars a month, and no board to pay. Two months of his wages would pay a preacher's salary for a year. Now some of us were left disconsolate. We could not get on the river — at least our parents would not let us.

So, by and by, I ran away. I said I would never come home again till I was a pilot and could come in glory. But somehow I could not manage it. I went meekly aboard a few of the boats that lay packed together like sardines at the long St. Louis wharf, and humbly inquired for the pilots, but got only a cold shoulder and short words from mates and clerks. I had to make the best of this sort of treatment for the time being, but I had comforting day-dreams of a future when I should be a great and honored pilot, with plenty of money, and could kill some of these mates and clerks and pay for them.

II. *A Cub-Pilot's Experience*

I entered upon the small enterprise of "learning" twelve or thirteen hundred miles of the great Mississippi River with the easy confidence of my time of life. If I had really known what I was about to require of my faculties, I should not have had the courage to begin. I supposed that all a pilot had to do was to keep his boat in the river, and I did not consider that that could be much of a trick, since it was so wide.

The boat backed out from New Orleans at four in the afternoon, and it was "our watch" until eight. Mr. Bixby, my chief, "straightened her up," plowed her along past the sterns of the other boats that lay at the Levee, and then said, "Here, take her; shave those steamships as close as you'd peal an apple." I took the wheel, and my heartbeat fluttered up into the hundreds; for it seemed to me that we were about to scrape the side off every ship in the line, we were so close. I held my breath and began to claw the boat away from the danger; and I had my own opinion of the pilot who had known no better than to get us into such peril, but I was too wise to express it. In half a minute I had a wide margin of safety intervening between the *Paul Jones* and the ships; and within ten seconds more I was set aside in disgrace, and Mr. Bixby was going into danger again and flaying me alive with abuse of my cowardice. I was stung, but I was obliged to admire the easy confidence with which my chief loafed from side to side of his wheel, and trimmed the ships so closely that disaster seemed ceaselessly imminent. When he had cooled a little he told me that the easy water was close ashore and the current outside, and therefore we must hug the bank, up-stream, to get the benefit of the former, and stay well out, down-stream, to take advantage of the latter. In my own mind I resolved to be a down-stream pilot and leave the up-streaming to people dead to prudence.

Now and then Mr. Bixby called my attention to certain things. Said he, "This is Six-Mile Point." I assented. It was pleasant enough information, but I could not see the bearing of it. I was not conscious that it was a matter of any interest to me. Another time he said, "This is Nine-Mile Point." Later he said, "This is Twelve-Mile Point." They were all about level with the water's edge; they all looked about alike to me; they were monotonously unpicturesque. I hoped Mr. Bixby would change the subject. But no; he would crowd up around a point, hugging the shore with affection, and then say: "The slack water ends here, abreast this bunch of China trees; now we cross over." So he crossed over. He gave me the wheel once or twice, but I had no luck. I either came near chipping off the edge of a sugar-plantation, or I yawed too far from shore, and so dropped back into disgrace again and got abused.

The watch was ended at last, and we took supper and went to bed. At midnight the glare of a lantern shone in my eyes, and the night watchman said:

"Come, turn out!"

And then he left. I could not understand this extraordinary procedure; so I presently gave up trying to, and dozed off to sleep. Pretty soon the watchman was back again, and this time he was gruff. I was annoyed. I said:

"What do you want to come bothering around here in the middle of the night for? Now, as like as not, I'll not get to sleep again to-night."

The watchman said:

"Well, if this ain't good, I'm blessed."

The "off-watch" was just turning in, and I heard some brutal laughter from them, and such remarks as "Hello, watchman! ain't the new cub turned out yet? He's delicate, likely. Give him some sugar in a rag, and send for the chambermaid to sing 'Rock-a-by Baby,' to him."

About this time Mr. Bixby appeared on the scene. Something like a minute later I was climbing the pilot-house steps with some of my clothes on and the rest in my arms. Mr. Bixby was close behind, commenting. Here was something fresh — this thing of getting up in the middle of the night to go to work. It was a detail in piloting that had never occurred to me at all. I knew that boats ran all night, but somehow I had never happened to reflect that somebody had to get up out of a warm bed to run them. I began to fear that piloting was not quite so romantic as I had imagined it was; there was something very real and worklike about this new phase of it.

It was a rather dingy night, although a fair number of stars were out. The big mate was at the wheel, and he had the old tub pointed at a star and was holding her straight up the middle of the river. The shores on either hand were not much more than half a mile apart, but they seemed wonderfully far away and ever so vague and indistinct. The mate said:

"We've got to land at Jones's plantation, sir."

The vengeful spirit in me exulted. I said to myself, "I wish you joy of your job, Mr. Bixby; you'll have a good time finding Mr. Jones's plantation such a night as this; and I hope you never *will* find it as long as you live."

Mr. Bixby said to the mate:

"Upper end of the plantation, or the lower?"

"Upper."

"I can't do it. The stumps there are out of water at this stage. It's no great distance to the lower, and you'll have to get along with that."

"All right, sir. If Jones don't like it, he'll have to lump it, I reckon."

And then the mate left. My exultation began to cool and my wonder to come up. Here was a man who not only proposed to find this plantation on such a night, but to find either end of it you preferred. I dreadfully wanted to ask a question, but I was carrying about as many short answers as my cargo-room would admit of, so I held my peace. All I desired to ask Mr. Bixby was the simple question whether he was ass enough to really imagine he was going to find that plantation on a night when all plantations were exactly alike and all of the same color. But I held in. I used to have fine inspirations of prudence in those days.

Mr. Bixby made for the shore and soon was scraping it, just the same as if it had been daylight. And not only that, but singing:

"Father in heaven, the day is declining," etc.

It seemed to me that I had put my life in the keeping of a peculiarly reckless outcast. Presently he turned on me and said:

"What's the name of the first point above New Orleans?"

I was gratified to be able to answer promptly, and I did. I said I didn't know.

"Don't *know?*"

This manner jolted me. I was down at the foot again, in a moment. But I had to say just what I had said before.

"Well, you're a smart one!" said Mr. Bixby. "What's the name of the next point?"

Once more I didn't know.

"Well, this beats anything. Tell me the name of *any* point or place I told you."

I studied awhile and decided that I couldn't.

"Look here! What do you start out from, above Twelve-Mile Point, to cross over?"

"I — I — don't know."

"You — you — don't know?" mimicking my drawling manner of speech. "What *do* you know?"

"I — I — nothing, for certain."

"By the great Cæsar's ghost, I believe you! You're the stupidest dunderhead I ever saw or ever heard of, so help me Moses! The idea of *you* being a pilot — *you!* Why, you don't know enough to pilot a cow down a lane."

Oh, but his wrath was up! He was a nervous man, and he shuffled from one side of his wheel to the other as if the floor was hot. He would boil awhile to himself, and then overflow and scald me again.

"Look here! What do you suppose I told you the names of those points for?"

I tremblingly considered a moment, and then the devil of temptation provoked me to say:

"Well to — to — be entertaining, I thought."

This was a red rag to the bull. He raged and stormed so (he was crossing the river at the time) that I judged it made him blind, because he ran over the steering-oar of a trading-scow. Of course the traders sent up a volley of red-hot profanity. Never was a man so grateful as Mr. Bixby was; because he was brimful, and here were subjects who could *talk back*. He threw open a window, thrust his head out, and such an irruption followed as I never had heard before. The fainter and farther away the scowmen's curses drifted, the higher Mr. Bixby lifted his voice and the weightier his adjectives grew. When he closed the window he was empty. You could have drawn a seine through his system and not caught curses enough to disturb your mother with. Presently he said to me in the gentlest way:

"My boy, you must get a little memorandum-book; and every time I tell you a thing, put it down right away. There's only one way to be a pilot, and that is to get this entire river by heart. You have to know it just like A B C."

That was a dismal revelation to me; for my memory was never loaded with anything but blank cartridges. However, I did not feel discouraged long. I judged that it was best to make some allowance, for doubtless Mr. Bixby was "stretching." Presently he pulled a rope and struck a few strokes on the big bell. The stars were all gone now, and the night was as black as ink. I could hear the wheels churn along the bank, but I was not entirely certain that I could see the shore. The voice of the invisible watchman called up from the hurricane-deck:

"What's this, sir?"

"Jones's plantation."

I said to myself, "I wish I might venture to offer a small bet that it isn't." But I did not chirp. I only waited to see. Mr. Bixby handled the engine-bells, and in due time the boat's nose came to the land, a torch glowed from the forecastle, a man skipped ashore, a darky's voice on the bank said: "Gimme de k'yarpet-bag, Mass' Jones," and the next moment we were standing up the river again, all serene. I reflected deeply awhile, and then said — but not aloud — "Well, the finding of that plantation was the luckiest accident that ever happened; but it couldn't happen again in a hundred years." And I fully believed it *was* an accident, too.

By the time we had gone seven or eight hundred miles up the river, I had learned to be a tolerably plucky up-stream steersman, in daylight; and before we reached St. Louis I had made a trifle of progress in night work, but only a trifle. I had a note-book that fairly bristled with the names of towns, "points," bars, islands, bends, reaches, etc.; but the information was to be found only in the note-book — none of it was in my head. It made my heart ache to think I had only got half of the river set down; for as our watch was four hours off and four hours on, day and night, there was a long four-hour gap in my book for every time I had slept since the voyage began.

My chief was presently hired to go on a big New Orleans boat, and I packed my satchel and went with him. She was a grand affair. When I stood in her pilot-house I was so far above the water that I seemed perched on a mountain; and her decks stretched so far away, fore and aft, below me, that I wondered how I could ever have considered the little *Paul Jones* a large craft. There were other differences, too. The *Paul Jones's* pilot-house was a cheap, dingy, battered rattletrap, cramped for room; but here was a sumptuous glass temple; room enough to have a dance in; showy red and gold window-curtains; an imposing sofa; leather cushions and a back to the high bench where visiting pilots sit, to spin yarns and "look at the river"; bright, fanciful "cuspidores," instead of a broad wooden box filled with sawdust; nice new oilcloth on the floor; a hospitable big stove for winter; a wheel as high as my head, costly with inlaid work; a wire tiller-rope; bright brass knobs for the bells; and a tidy, white-aproned, black "texas-tender," to bring up tarts and ices and coffee during mid-watch, day and night. Now this was "something like"; and so I began to take heart once more to believe that piloting was a romantic sort of occupation after all. The moment we were under way I began to prowl about the great steamer and fill myself with joy. She was as clean and as dainty as a drawing-room; when I looked down her long, gilded saloon, it was like gazing through a splendid tunnel; she had an oil-picture, by some gifted sign-painter, on every stateroom door; she glittered with no end of prism-fringed chandeliers; the clerk's office was elegant, the bar was marvelous, and the barkeeper had been barbered and upholstered at incredible cost. The boiler-deck (*i.e.*, the second story of the boat, so to speak) was as spacious as a church, it seemed to me; so with the forecastle; and there was no pitiful handful of deck-hands, firemen, and roustabouts down there, but a whole battalion of men. The fires were fiercely glaring from a long row of furnaces, and over them were eight huge boilers! This was unutterable pomp. The mighty engines — but enough of this. I had never felt so fine before. And when I found that the regiment of natty servants respectfully "sir'd" me, my satisfaction was complete.

III. *Perplexing Lessons*

At the end of what seemed a tedious while, I had managed to pack my head full of islands, towns, bars, "points," and bends; and a curiously inanimate mass of lumber it was, too. However, inasmuch as I could shut my eyes and reel off a good long string of these names without leaving out more than ten miles of river in every fifty, I began to feel that I could take a boat down to New Orleans if I could make her skip those little gaps. But of course my complacency could hardly get start enough to lift my nose a trifle into the air, before Mr. Bixby would think of something to fetch it down again. One day he turned on me suddenly with this settler:

"What is the shape of Walnut Bend?"

He might as well have asked me my grandmother's opinion of protoplasm. I reflected respectfully, and then said I didn't know it had any particular shape. My gun-powdery chief went off with a bang, of course, and then went on loading and firing until he was out of adjectives.

I had learned long ago that he only carried just so many rounds of ammunition, and was sure to subside into a very placable and even remorseful old smooth-bore as soon as they were all gone. That word "old" is merely affectionate; he was not more than thirty-four. I waited. By and by he said:

"My boy, you've got to know the *shape* of the river perfectly. It is all there is left to steer by on a very dark night. Everything else is blotted out and gone. But mind you, it hasn't the same shape in the night that it has in the day-time.

"How on earth am I ever going to learn it, then?"

"How do you follow a hall at home in the dark? Because you know the shape of it. You can't see it."

"Do you mean to say that I've got to know all the million trifling variations of shape in the banks of this interminable river as well as I know the shape of the front hall at home?"

"On my honor, you've got to know them *better* than any man ever did know the shapes of the halls in his own house."

"I wish I was dead!"

"Now I don't want to discourage you, but—"

"Well, pile it on me; I might as well have it now as another time."

"You see, this has got to be learned; there isn't any getting around it. A clear starlight night throws such heavy shadows that, if you didn't know the shape of a shore perfectly, you would claw away from every bunch of timber, because you would take the black shadow of it for a solid cape; and you see you would be getting scared to death every fifteen minutes by the watch. You would be fifty yards from shore all the time when you ought to be within fifty feet of it. You can't see a snag in one of those shadows, but you know exactly where it is, and the shape of the river tells you when you are coming to it. Then there's your pitch-dark night; the river is a very different shape on a pitch-dark night from what it is on a starlight night. All shores seem to be straight lines, then, and mighty dim ones, too; and you'd *run* them for straight lines, only you know better. You boldly drive your boat right into what seems to be a solid, straight wall (you knowing very well that in reality there is a curve there), and that wall falls back and makes way for you. Then there's your gray mist. You take a night when there's one of these grisly, drizzly, gray mists, and then there isn't *any* particular shape to a shore. A gray mist would tangle the head of the oldest man that ever lived. Well, then, different kinds of *moonlight* change the shape of the river in different ways. You see — "

"Oh, don't say any more, please! Have I got to learn the shape of the river according to all these five hundred thousand different ways? If I tried to carry all that cargo in my head it would make me stoop-shouldered."

"*No!* you only learn *the* shape of the river; and you learn it with such absolute certainty that you can always steer by the shape that's *in your head,* and never mind the one that's before your eyes."

"Very well, I'll try it; but, after I have learned it, can I depend on it? Will it keep the same form and not go fooling around?"

Before Mr. Bixby could answer, Mr. W. came in to take the watch, and he said:

"Bixby, you'll have to look out for President's Island, and all that country clear away up above the Old Hen and Chickens. The banks are caving and the shape of the shore's changing like everything. Why, you wouldn't know the point above 40. You can go up inside the old sycamore snag, now."

So that question was answered. Here were leagues of shore changing shape. My spirits were down in the mud again. Two things seemed pretty apparent to me. One was, that in order to be a pilot a man had got to learn more than any one man ought to be allowed to know; and the other was, that he must learn it all over again in a different way every twenty-four hours.

That night we had the watch until twelve. Now it was an ancient river custom for the two pilots to chat a bit when the watch changed. While the relieving pilot put on his gloves and lit his cigar, his partner, the retiring pilot, would say something like this:

"I judge the upper bar is making down a little at Hale's Point; had quarter twain with the lower lead and mark twain with the other."

"Yes, I thought it was making down a little, last trip. Meet any boats?"

"Met one abreast the head of 21, but she was away over hugging the bar, and I couldn't make her out entirely. I took her for the *Sunny South* — hadn't any skylights forward of the chimneys."

And so on. And as the relieving pilot took the wheel his partner would mention that we were in such-and-such a bend, and say we were abreast of such-and-such a man's woodyard or plantation. This was courtesy; I supposed it was *necessity*. But Mr. W. came on watch full twelve minutes late on this particular night — a tremendous breach of etiquette; in fact, it is the unpardonable sin among pilots. So Mr. Bixby gave him no greeting whatever, but simply surrendered the wheel and marched out of the pilot-house without a word. I was appalled; it was a villainous night for blackness, we were in a particularly wide and blind part of the river, where there was no shape or substance to anything, and it seemed incredible that Mr. Bixby should have left that poor fellow to kill the boat, trying to find out where

he was. But I resolved that I would stand by him anyway.
He should find that he was not wholly friendless. So I stood
around, and waited to be asked where we were. But Mr. W.
plunged on serenely through the solid firmament of black
cats that stood for an atmosphere, and never opened his mouth.
"Here is a proud devil!" thought I; "here is a limb of
Satan that would rather send us all to destruction than put
himself under obligations to me, because I am not yet one
of the salt of the earth and privileged to snub captains and
lord it over everything dead and alive in a steamboat." I
presently climbed up on the bench; I did not think it was
safe to go to sleep while this lunatic was on watch.

However, I must have gone to sleep in the course of time,
because the next thing I was aware of was the fact that day
was breaking, Mr. W. gone, and Mr. Bixby at the wheel
again. So it was four o'clock and all well — but me; I felt
like a skinful of dry bones, and all of them trying to ache at
once.

Mr. Bixby asked me what I had stayed up there for. I
confessed that it was to do Mr. W. a benevolence — tell him
where he was. It took five minutes for the entire prepos-
terousness of the thing to filter into Mr. Bixby's system, and
then I judge it filled him nearly up to the chin; because he
paid me a compliment — and not much of a one either. He
said:

"Well, taking you by and large, you do seem to be more
different kinds of an ass than any creature I ever saw before.
What did you suppose he wanted to know for?"

I said I thought it might be a convenience to him.

"Convenience! D——nation! Didn't I tell you that a
man's got to know the river in the night the same as he'd
know his own front hall?"

"Well, I can follow the front hall in the dark if I know it
is the front hall; but suppose you set me down in the middle
of it in the dark and not tell me which hall it is; how am *I*
to know?"

"Well, you've *got* to, on the river!"

"All right. Then I'm glad I never said anything to Mr. W."

"I should say so! Why, he'd have slammed you through the window and utterly ruined a hundred dollars' worth of window-sash and stuff."

I was glad this damage had been saved, for it would have made me unpopular with the owners. They always hated anybody who had the name of being careless and injuring things.

I went to work now to learn the shape of the river; and of all the eluding and ungraspable objects that ever I tried to get mind or hands on, that was the chief. I would fasten my eyes upon a sharp, wooded point that projected far into the river some miles ahead of me, and go to laboriously photographing its shape upon my brain; and just as I was beginning to succeed to my satisfaction, we would draw up toward it and the exasperating thing would begin to melt away and fold back into the bank! If there had been a conspicuous dead tree standing upon the very point of the cape, I would find that tree inconspicuously merged into the general forest, and occupying the middle of a straight shore, when I got abreast of it! No prominent hill would stick to its shape long enough for me to make up my mind what its form really was, but it was as dissolving and changeful as if it had been a mountain of butter in the hottest corner of the tropics. Nothing ever had the same shape when I was coming down-stream that it had borne when I went up. I mentioned these little difficulties to Mr. Bixby. He said:

"That's the very main virtue of the thing. If the shapes didn't change every three seconds they wouldn't be of any use. Take this place where we are now, for instance. As long as that hill over yonder is only one hill, I can boom right along the way I'm going; but the moment it splits at the top and forms a V, I know I've got to scratch to starboard in a hurry, or I'll bang this boat's brains out against a rock; and then the moment one of the prongs of the V swings behind the other, I've got to waltz to larboard again, or I'll have a misunderstanding with a snag that would snatch the keelson out of this steamboat as neatly as if it were a sliver in your hand. If that hill didn't change its shape on bad nights there would be an awful steamboat graveyard around here inside of a year."

It was plain that I had got to learn the shape of the river in all the different ways that could be thought of — upside down, wrong end first, inside out, fore-and-aft, and "thort-ships" — and then know what to do on gray nights when it hadn't any shape at all. So I set about it. In the course of time I began to get the best of this knotty lesson, and my self-complacency moved to the front once more. Mr. Bixby was all fixed, and ready to start it to the rear again. He opened on me after this fashion:

"How much water did we have in the middle crossing at Hole-in-the-Wall, trip before last?"

I considered this an outrage. I said:

"Every trip, down and up, the leadsmen are singing through that tangled place for three-quarters of an hour on a stretch. How do you reckon I can remember such a mess as that?"

"My boy, you've got to remember it. You've got to re-member the exact spot and the exact marks the boat lay in when we had the shoalest water, in every one of the five hundred shoal places between St. Louis and New Orleans; and you mustn't get the shoal soundings and marks of one trip mixed up with the shoal soundings and marks of an-other, either, for they're not often twice alike. You must keep them separate."

When I came to myself again, I said:

"When I get so that I can do that, I'll be able to raise the dead, and then I won't have to pilot a steamboat to make a living. I want to retire from this business. I want a slush-bucket and a brush; I'm only fit for a roustabout. I haven't got brains enough to be a pilot; and if I had I wouldn't have strength enough to carry them around, unless I went on crutches."

"Now drop that! When I say I'll learn a man the river, I mean it. And you can depend on it, I'll learn him or kill him."

JOHN MUIR

1838–1914

49   *The Water-Ouzel*

THE water-falls of the Sierra Nevada are frequented by only one bird, the ouzel or water-thrush (*Cinclus Mexicanus*, Sw.). He is a singularly joyous and lovable little fellow, about the size of a robin, clad in a plain water-proof suit of a blackish, bluish gray, with a tinge of chocolate on the head and shoulders. In form he is about as smoothly plump and compact as a pot-hole pebble; the flowing contour of his body being interrupted only by his strong feet and bill, and the crisp wing-tips, and up-slanted wrenish tail.

Among all the countless water-falls I have met in the course of eight years' explorations in the Sierra, whether in the icy Alps, or warm foot-hills, or in the profound Yosemite cañons of the middle region, not one was found without its ouzel. No cañon is too cold for him, none too lonely, provided it be rich in white falling water. Find a fall, or cascade, or rushing rapid, anywhere upon a clear crystalline stream, and there you will surely find its complementary ouzel, flitting about in the spray, diving in foaming eddies, whirling like a leaf among beaten foam-bells; ever vigorous and enthusiastic, yet self-contained, and neither seeking nor shunning your company.

If disturbed while dipping about in the margin shallows, he either sets off with a rapid whir to some other feeding-ground up or down the stream, or alights on some half-submerged rock or snag out in the foaming current, and immediately begins to nod and courtesy like a wren, turning his head from side to side and performing many other odd dainty manners as if he had been trained at some bird dancing-school.

He is the mountain streams' own darling, — the humming-bird of blooming waters, loving rocky ripple-slopes and sheets of foam, as a bee loves flowers, — as a lark loves sunshine and meadows. Among all the mountain birds, none has cheered me so much in my lonely wanderings, — none so un-failing. For winter and summer he sings, independent alike of sunshine and love; requiring no other inspiration than the stream on which he dwells. While water sings, so must he; in heat or cold, calm or storm, ever attuning his voice in sure accord; low in the drought of summer and drought of winter, but never silent.

During the golden days of Indian summer the mountain streams are feeble, — a succession of silent pools, linked to-gether with strips of silvery lace-work; then the song of the ouzel is at its lowest ebb. But as soon as the winter clouds have bloomed, and the mountain treasuries are once more replenished with snow, the voices of the streams and ouzels begin to increase in strength and richness until the flood season of early summer. Then the glad torrents chant their noblest anthems, and then too is the flood-time of our song-ster's melody. But as to the influence of the weather, dark days and sun days are the same to him. The voices of most song-birds, however joyous, suffer a long winter eclipse; but the ouzel sings on around all the seasons, and through every kind of storm. Indeed no storm can be more violent than those of the water-falls in the midst of which he delights to dwell. At least, from whatever cause, while the weather is darkest and most boisterous, snowing, blowing, cloudy or clear, all the same he sings, and never a note of sadness. No need of spring sunshine to thaw *his* song, for it never freezes. Never shall you hear anything wintry from *his* warm breast; no pinched cheeping, no wavering notes between sadness and joy; his mellow, fluty voice is ever tuned to downright glad-ness, as free from every trace of dejection as cock-crowing.

It is pitiful to see wee frost-pinched sparrows, on cold mornings, shaking the snow from their feathers, and hop-ping about as if anxious to be cheery, then hastening back to their hidings out of the wind, puffing out their breast feathers, and subsiding among the leaves, cold and breakfastless, while the snow continues to fall, and no sign of clearing. But the ouzel never calls forth a single touch of pity; not because he is strong to endure, but rather because he seems to live a charmed life beyond the reach of every influence that makes endurance necessary.

One wild winter morning, when Yosemite Valley was swept from west to east by a cordial snow-storm, I sallied forth to see what I might learn and enjoy. A sort of gray, gloaming-like darkness was kept up by the storm, and the loudest booming of the falls was at times buried beneath its sublime roar. The snow was already over five feet deep on the meadows, making very extended walks impossible without the aid of snowshoes. I found no great difficulty, however, in making my way to a certain riffle on the river where one of my ouzels lived. He was at home as usual, gleaning his breakfast among the pebbles of a shallow portion of the margin, and apparently altogether unconscious of anything extraordinary in the weather. Presently he flew out to a stone against which the icy current was beating, and turning his back to the wind, sang delightfully as a lark in spring-time.

After spending an hour or two with my favorite, I went plodding through the drifts, to learn as definitely as possible how the other birds were spending their time. The Yosemite birds are easily found during the winter, because all excepting the ouzel are restricted to the sunny north side of the valley, the south side being constantly eclipsed by the great frosty shadow of the wall. And because the Indian Cañon groves from their peculiar exposure are the warmest, all the birds congregate there, more especially in severe weather.

I found most of the robins cowering on the lee side of the larger branches where the snow could not fall upon them, while two or three of the most enterprising were making desperate efforts to reach the mistletoe berries by clinging nervously to the under side of the snow-crowned masses, back downward, like woodpeckers. Every now and then they would dislodge some of the loose fringes of the snow-crown which would come sifting down upon their heads and send them screaming back to camp, where they would subside among their companions with a shiver, muttering in low, querulous chatters like hungry children.

Some of the sparrows were busy at the foot of the larger trees gleaning seeds and benumbed insects, joined now and then by a robin weary of his unsuccessful attempts upon the snow-covered berries. The brave woodpeckers were clinging to the snowless sides of the larger boles and overarching branches of the camp trees, making short flights from side to side of the grove, pecking and chattering aimlessly as if unable to keep still, yet evidently putting in the time in a very dull way, like storm-bound travelers at a country tavern. The hardy nut-hatches were threading the open furrows of the bark in their usual industrious manner, and uttering their quaint notes, evidently much less discomposed than their neighbors. The Steller's jays were of course making more noisy stir than all the other birds combined; ever coming and going with loud bluster, screaming as if each had a lump of melting sludge in his throat, and taking very good care to improve the favorable opportunity afforded by the storm to steal from the acorn stores of the woodpeckers. I also noticed one solitary gray eagle braving the storm on the top of a tall pine stump just outside the main grove. He was standing bolt upright with his back to the wind, and with a tuft of snow piled on his square shoulders, the very type of passive endurance. Thus every snowbound bird seemed more or less uncomfortable if not in positive distress. The storm was reflected in every gesture, and not one cheerful note, not to say song, came from a single bill; their cowering, joyless endurance offering a most striking contrast to the spontaneous, irrepressible gladness of the ouzel, who could no more help exhaling sweet song, than a rose sweet fragrance. He *must* sing if the heavens fall. I remember noticing the distress of a pair of robins during the violent earthquake of the year 1872, when the pines of the valley, with strange movements, flapped and waved their branches, and beetling rock-brows came thundering to the meadows in fiery avalanches. It did not occur to me in the midst of the excitement of other observations to look for the ouzels, but I doubt not they were singing straight on through it all, regarding its terrible thunders as fearlessly as they do the booming of the water-falls.

What may be regarded as the separate songs of the ouzel are exceedingly difficult of description, because they are so variable and at the same time so confluent. I have been acquainted with my favorite for eight years, and though during most of this time I have heard him sing nearly every day, I still detect notes and strains that are quite new to me. Nearly all of his music is very sweet and tender, lapsing from his round breast like water over the smooth lip of a pool, then breaking farther on into a rich sparkling foam of melodious notes, which glow with subdued enthusiasm, yet without expressing much of the strong, gushing ecstasy of the bobolink or sky-lark.

The more striking strains are perfect arabesques of melody, composed of a few full, round, mellow notes, embroidered with a great variety of delicate trills which fade in long slender cadences like the silken fringes of summer clouds melting in the azure. But as a whole, his music is that of the stream itself, infinitely organized, spiritualized. The deep booming notes of the falls are in it, the trills of rapids, the swirling and gurgling of pot-holes, low hushes of levels, the rapturous bounce and dance of rocky cascades, and the sweet tinkle of separate drops oozing from the ends of mosses and falling into tranquil pools.

The ouzel never sings in chorus with other birds, nor with his kind, but only with the streams. And like flowers that bloom beneath the surface of the ground, some of our favorite's best song-blossoms never rise above the surface of the heavier music of the water. I have oftentimes observed him singing in the midst of beaten spray, his music completely buried beneath the water's roar; yet I knew he was surely singing by the movements of his bill.

His food consists of all kinds of water insects, which in summer are chiefly procured along shallow margins. Here he wades about ducking his head under water, and deftly turning over pebbles and fallen leaves with his bill, seldom choosing to go into deep water where he has to use his wings in diving.

He seems to be especially fond of the larvæ of mosquitoes, found in great quantities attached to the bottom of smooth rock channels where the current is swift and shallow. When feeding in such places he wades up-stream, and oftentimes while his head is under water the swift current is deflected upward along the glossy curves of his neck and shoulders, in the form of a clear, crystalline shell, which fairly incloses him like a bell-glass, the shell being constantly broken and reformed as he lifts and dips his head; while ever and anon he sidles out to where the too powerful current carries him off his feet, and sweeps him rapidly down-stream; then he dexterously rises on the wing and goes gleaning again in shallower places.

But during the winter, when the stream-banks are all deeply embossed in snow, and the streams themselves are chilled nearly to the freezing point, so that the snow falling into them in stormy weather is not wholly dissolved, but forms a thin blue sludge, thus rendering the current opaque — then he seeks the deeper portions of the main rivers, where he may dive to clear portions of the channel beneath the sludge. Or he repairs to some open lake or millpond, at the bottom of which he feeds in perfect safety.

When thus compelled to betake himself to a lake, he does not plunge into it at once like a duck, but always alights in the first place upon some rock or fallen pine along the shore, then flying out thirty or forty yards, more or less, according to the character of the bottom, he alights with a dainty glint on the surface, swims about, looks down, finally makes up his mind and disappears with a sharp stroke of his wings. After feeding for two or three minutes he suddenly reappears, showers the water from his wings with one vigorous shake, and rises abruptly into the air as if pushed up from beneath, comes back to his perch, sings a few minutes and goes out to dive again; thus coming and going, singing and diving at the same places for hours.

I once observed three thus spending a winter morning in company, upon a small glacier lake, on the Upper Merced, about 7,500 feet above the level of the sea.

A storm had occurred during the night, but the morning sun shone unclouded, and the shadowy lake, gleaming darkly in its setting of fresh snow, lay smooth and motionless as a mirror.

My camp chanced to be within a few feet of the water's edge, opposite a fallen pine, some of the branches of which leaned out over the lake. Here my three dearly welcome visitors took up their station, and at once began to embroider the frosty air with their delicious melody, doubly delightful to me that particular morning, as I had been somewhat apprehensive of danger in breaking my way down to the lowlands.

The portion of the lake bottom selected for a feeding-ground lies at a depth of fifteen or twenty feet below the surface, and is covered with a short growth of algæ and other aquatic plants, — facts I chanced to be able to determine by having previously floated over it on a raft and made soundings.

After alighting on the glassy surface, the birds would occasionally indulge in a little play, chasing each other round about in small circles; then all three would suddenly dive together, and come ashore and sing. They are usually found singly, however, rarely in pairs excepting during the breeding season, and *very* rarely in threes or fours.

They seldom swim more than a few yards on the surface, for, not being web-footed, they make rather slow progress, but by means of their strong, crisp wings they swim, or rather fly, with great celerity under the surface, often to considerable distances.

But it is in withstanding the force of rushing torrents that their strength of wing in this respect is most strikingly manifested. The following may be regarded as a fair illustration of their easy, unconscious powers of sub-aquatic flight. One winter morning, when the Merced River was blue and green with unmelted snow, I observed one of my ouzels perched on a snag out in the midst of a swift rushing rapid. He sang cheerily, as if everything was just to his mind, and while I stood on the bank admiring him, he suddenly plunged into the sludgy current, leaving his song broken abruptly off. After feeding a minute or two at the bottom, and when one would suppose he must inevitably be swept far downstream, he emerged just where he went down, alighted on the same snag, showered the water beads from his feathers, and at once continued his unfinished song, splicing it together as if it had suffered no interruption.

The ouzel alone of all birds dares to enter a white torrent. And though strictly terrestrial in structure, no other is so inseparably related to water, not even the duck, or bold ocean albatross, or storm-petrel. Ducks go ashore when they have done feeding in undisturbed places, and frequently make long overland flights from lake to lake or from field to field. The same is true of most other aquatic birds. But our ouzel, born on the very brink of a stream, seldom leaves it for a single moment. For, notwithstanding he is often on the wing, he never flies overland, but whirs with rapid, quail-like beat above the stream, tracing all its winding modulations with great minuteness. Even when the stream is quite small, say from five to ten feet wide, he will not try to shorten his flight by crossing a bend, however abrupt it may be; and even when disturbed by meeting someone on the bank, he prefers to fly over one's head, to dodging out over the ground. When therefore his flight along a crooked stream is viewed endwise, it appears most strikingly wavered — an interpretation of every curve inscribed with lightning-like rapidity on the air.

The vertical curves and angles of the most precipitous Alpine torrents he traces with the same rigid fidelity. Swooping adown the inclines of cascades, dropping sheer over dizzy falls amid the spray, and ascending with the same fearlessness and ease, seldom seeking to lessen the steepness of the acclivity by beginning to ascend before reaching the base of the fall. No matter how high it may be, he holds straight on as if about to dash headlong into the throng of booming rockets, then darts abruptly upward, and, after alighting at the top of the precipice to rest a moment, proceeds to feed and sing. His flight is solid and impetuous without any intermission of wing-beats, — one homogeneous buzz like that of a laden bee on its way home. And while thus buzzing freely from fall to fall, he is frequently heard giving utterance to a long out-drawn train of unmodulated notes, in no way connected with his song, but corresponding closely with his flight, both in sustained vigor and homogeneity of substance.

Were the flights of every individual ouzel in the Sierra traced on a chart, they would indicate the direction of the flow of the entire system of ancient glaciers, from about the period of the breaking up of the ice-sheet until near the close of the glacial winter; because the streams which the ouzels so rigidly follow, are, with the unimportant exceptions of a few side tributaries, all flowing in channels eroded for them out of the solid flank of the range by the vanished glaciers, — the streams tracing the glaciers, the ouzels tracing the streams. Nor do we find so complete compliance to glacial conditions in the life of any other mountain bird, or animal of any kind. Bears frequently accept the path-ways laid down by glaciers as the easiest to travel; but then, they often leave them and cross over from cañon to cañon. So also, most birds found in rocky cañons at all usually fly across at right angles to the courses of the vanished glaciers, because the main forests of these regions to which they come and go are growing upon the lateral moraines which always stretch along the tops of the cañon walls.

The ouzel's nest is one of the most extraordinary pieces of bird architecture I ever beheld; so odd and novel in design, and so perfectly fresh and beautiful, and in every way so fully worthy of the genius of the little builder. It is about a foot in diameter, round and bossy in outline, with a neatly arched opening near the bottom, somewhat like an old-fashioned brick oven, or Hottentot's hut. It is built almost exclusively of green and yellow mosses, chiefly the beautiful fronded hypnum that covers the rocks and old drift-logs in the vicinity of water-falls. These are deftly interwoven, and felted together into a charming little hut; and so situated that many of the outer mosses continue to flourish as if they had not been plucked. A few fine silky-stemmed grasses are occasionally found interwoven with the mosses, but, with the exception of a thin layer lining the floor, their presence seems accidental, as they are of a species found growing with the mosses and are probably plucked with them. The site chosen for this curious mansion is usually some little rock-shelf within reach of the spray of a water-fall, so that its walls are kept green and growing, at least during the time of high water.

No harsh lines are presented by any portion of the nest as seen *in situ*, but when removed from its shelf, the back and bottom, and sometimes a portion of the top, is found quite sharply angular because it is made to conform to the surface of the rock, upon which and against which it is built; the little architect always taking advantage of slight crevices and protuberances that may chance to offer, to render his structure stable by means of a kind of gripping and dovetailing.

In choosing a building spot, concealment does not seem to be taken into consideration at all; yet notwithstanding the nest is so large, and so guilelessly exposed to view, it is far from being easily detected, chiefly because it swells forward like any other bulging moss-cushion growing naturally in such situations. This is more especially the case where the nest is kept fresh by being well sprinkled. Sometimes these romantic little huts have their beauty enhanced by tasteful decorations of rock-ferns and grasses, that spring up around the walls or in front of the doorsill, all dripping with crystal beads.

Furthermore, at certain hours of the day when the sunshine is poured down at the required angle, the whole mass of the spray enveloping the fairy establishment is brilliantly irised; and it is through so glorious a rainbow atmosphere as this that some of our blessed ouzels obtain their first peep at the world.

Ouzels seem so completely part and parcel of the streams they inhabit, they scarce suggest any other origin than the streams themselves; and one might almost be pardoned in fancying they come direct from the living waters like flowers from the ground,—a kind of winged water-lily. At least, from whatever cause, it never occurred to me to look for their nests until more than a year after I had made the acquaintance of the birds themselves, although I found one the very day on which I began the search. In making my way from Yosemite to the glaciers of the adjacent Alps, I camped in a particularly wild and romantic portion of the Nevada cañon where in previous excursions I had never once failed to enjoy the delightful company of my favorites, who were attracted here, no doubt, by the extraordinary abundance of white water. The river, for miles above and below, consists of a succession of small falls from ten to sixty feet in height, connected by flat, plume-like cascades that go flashing from fall to fall, free and channelless, over waving folds of glacier-polished granite.

On the south side of one of the falls, that portion of the precipice which is bathed by the spray presents a series of little shelves and tablets caused by the development of planes of cleavage in the granite, and the consequent fall of masses through the action of the water. "Now *here,*" said I, "of all places, is the most charming spot for an ouzel's nest."

Then carefully scanning the fretted face of the precipice through the spray, I at length noticed a large, yellowish moss-cushion, growing on the edge of a level tablet within five or six feet of the outer folds of the fall. But apart from the fact of its being situated exactly where one acquainted with the lives of ouzels would fancy an ouzel's nest ought to be, there was nothing in its appearance visible at first sight, to distinguish it from other bosses or rock-moss, similarly situated with reference to perennial spray; and it was not until I had scrutinized it again and again, and had removed my shoes and stockings and crept along the face of the rock within eight or ten feet of it, that I could decide certainly whether it was the nest I was so eagerly seeking or a natural growth.

In these moss huts are laid three or four eggs, — white, like foam bubbles; and well may the little ouzels hatched from them sing water songs, for they hear them all their lives, and even before they are born.

I have oftentimes observed the young just out of the nest making their odd gestures, and seeming in every way as much at home as their experienced parents, — like young bees in their first excursions to the flower fields. No amount of familiarity with people and their ways seems to change them in the least. To all appearance their behavior is just the same on seeing a man for the first time, as when seeing him every day.

On the lower reaches of the rivers where mills are built, they sing on through the din of the machinery, and all the concomitant confusion of dogs, cattle, and workmen. On one occasion, while a wood-chopper was at work on the river-bank, I observed one cheerily singing within reach of the flying chips. Nor does any kind of unwonted disturbance put him in bad humor, or frighten him out of calm self-possession. In passing through a narrow gorge, I drove one ahead of me from rapid to rapid, disturbing him four times in quick succession, where he could not very well fly past me on account of the narrowness of the channel. Most birds under similar circumstances fancy themselves pursued, and become suspiciously uneasy; but, instead of growing nervous about it, he made his usual dippings, and sang one of his most tranquil strains. When observed within a few yards their eyes are seen to express remarkable gentleness and intelligence; but they seldom allow a sufficiently near approach. On one occasion, while rambling along the shore of a mountain lake, where the birds, at least those born that season, had never seen a man, I sat down to rest upon a large stone close to the water's edge, upon which it seemed the ouzels and sandpipers were in the habit of alighting when they came to feed on that part of the shore, and some of the other birds also, when they came down to wash or drink. After I had sat a few minutes, along came a whirring ouzel and alighted on the stone beside me, within reach of my hand. Then observing me, all at once he stooped nervously as if about to fly on the instant, but as I remained motionless as the stone, he gained confidence, and looked me steadily in the face for about a minute, then flew quietly to the outlet and began to sing. A sandpiper came next and gazed at me with much the same guileless expression of eye as the ouzel's. Lastly, down with a swoop came a Steller's jay out of a fir-tree, probably with the intention of moistening his noisy throat. But instead of sitting confidingly as my other visitors had done, he rushed off at once, nearly tumbling heels over head into the lake in his suspicious confusion, and with loud screams roused the neighborhood.

Love for song-birds, with their sweet human voices, appears to be far more universal and unfailing than love for flowers. Everyone loves flowers, to some extent at least in life's fresh morning, attracted by them as instinctively as humming-birds and bees. Even the young Digger Indians have sufficient love for the brightest of those found growing on the mountains to gather them and braid them as decorations for the hair. And I was glad to discover, through the few Indians that could be induced to talk on the subject, that they have names for the wild rose and the lily, and other conspicuous flowers, whether available as food or otherwise. Most men, however, whether savage or civilized, become apathetic toward all plants that have no other apparent use than the use of beauty. But fortunately one's first instinctive love of song-birds is never wholly obliterated, no matter what the influences upon our lives may be. I have often been delighted to see a pure, spiritual glow come into the countenances of hard business men, and dissipated old miners, when a song-bird chanced to alight near them. Nevertheless, the little mouthful of meat that swells out the breasts of some song-birds is too often the cause of their death. Larks and robins in particular are brought to market in hundreds. But fortunately the ouzel has no enemy so eager for his little body as to follow him into the mountain solitudes. I never even knew him to be chased by hawks.

An acquaintance of mine, a sort of foot-hill mountaineer, had a pet cat, a great, dozy, overgrown creature, about as broad-shouldered as a lynx. During the winter while the snow lay deep, the mountaineer sat in his lonely cabin among the pines, smoking his pipe, and wearing the dull time away. Tom was his sole companion, sharing his bed, and sitting beside him on a stool, with much the same drowsy expression of eye as his master.

The good-natured bachelor was content with his hard fare of soda bread and bacon, but Tom, the only creature in the world acknowledging dependence on him, must needs be provided with fresh meat. Accordingly, he bestirred himself to contrive squirrel traps, and waded the snowy woods with his gun, making sad havoc among the few winter birds, sparing neither robin, sparrow, nor tiny nut-hatch, and the pleasure of seeing Tom eat them was his great reward.

One cold afternoon, while hunting along the river-bank he noticed a plain-feathered little bird skipping about in the shallows, and immediately raised his gun. But just then the confiding little songster began to sing, and after listening to his rare summery melody, he turned away, saying, "Bless your little heart, I can't shoot *you*, not even for Tom."

The species is distributed all along the mountain ranges of the Pacific coast from Alaska to Mexico, and east to the Rocky Mountains. Nevertheless, it is as yet but little known, even among naturalists. Audubon and Wilson did not meet it at all. Swainson was, I believe, the first to describe a specimen from Mexico. Specimens were shortly afterward procured by Drummond near the sources of the Athabasca River, between the fifty-fourth and fifty-sixth parallels; and it has been collected by nearly all of the numerous exploring expeditions undertaken of late through our western states and territories; for it never fails to engage the attention of naturalists in a very particular manner.

Such, then, is the life of our little cinclus, beloved of everyone who is so happy as to know him. Tracing on strong wing every curve of the most precipitous torrent, from one extremity of the Californian Alps to the other; not fearing to follow them through their darkest gorges, and coldest snow-tunnels; acquainted with every water-fall, echoing their divine music; and throughout the whole of their beautiful lives interpreting all that we in our unbelief call terrible in the utterances of torrents, as only varied expressions of God's eternal love.

HENRY ADAMS

1838–1918

50 *American Character*

UNTIL 1815 nothing in the future of the American Union was regarded as settled. As late as January, 1815, division into several nationalities was still thought to be possible. Such a destiny, repeating the usual experience of history, was not necessarily more unfortunate than the career of a single nationality wholly American; for if the effects of divided nationality were certain to be unhappy, those of a single society with equal certainty defied experience or sound speculation. One uniform and harmonious system appealed to the imagination as a triumph of human progress, offering prospects of peace and ease, contentment and philanthropy, such as the world had not seen; but it invited dangers, formidable because unusual or altogether unknown. The corruption of such a system might prove to be proportionate with its dimensions, and uniformity might lead to evils as serious as were commonly ascribed to diversity.

The laws of human progress were matter not for dogmatic faith, but for study; and although society instinctively regarded small States, with their clashing interests and incessant wars, as the chief obstacle to improvement, such progress as the world knew had been coupled with those drawbacks. The few examples offered by history of great political societies, relieved from external competition or rivalry, were not commonly thought encouraging. War had been the severest test of political and social character, laying bare whatever was feeble, and calling out whatever was strong; and the effect of removing such a test was an untried problem.

In 1815 for the first time Americans ceased to doubt the path they were to follow. Not only was the unity of their nation established, but its probable divergence from older societies was also well defined. Already in 1817 the difference between Europe and America was decided. In politics the distinction was more evident than in social, religious, literary, or scientific directions; and the result was singular. For a time the aggressions of England and France forced the United States into a path that seemed to lead toward European methods of government; but the popular resistance, or inertia, was so great that the most popular party leaders failed to overcome it, and no sooner did foreign dangers disappear than the system began to revert to American practices; the national government tried to lay aside its assumed powers. When Madison vetoed the bill for internal improvements he could have had no other motive than that of restoring to the government, as far as possible, its original American character.

The result was not easy to understand in theory or to

make efficient in practice; but while the drift of public opinion, and still more of practical necessity, drew the government slowly toward the European standard of true political sovereignty, nothing showed that the compromise, which must probably serve the public purpose, was to be European in form or feeling. As far as politics supplied a test, the national character had already diverged from any foreign type. Opinions might differ whether the political movement was progressive or retrograde, but in any case the American, in his political character, was a new variety of man.

The social movement was also decided. The war gave a severe shock to the Anglican sympathies of society, and peace seemed to widen the breach between European and American tastes. Interest in Europe languished after Napoleon's overthrow. France ceased to affect American opinion. England became an object of less alarm. Peace produced in the United States a social and economical revolution which greatly curtailed the influence of New England, and with it the social authority of Great Britain. The invention of the steamboat counterbalanced ocean commerce. The South and West gave to society a character more aggressively American than had been known before. That Europe, within certain limits, might tend toward American ideas was possible, but that America should under any circumstances follow the experiences of European development might thenceforward be reckoned as improbable. American character was formed, if not fixed.

The scientific interest of American history centered in national character, and in the workings of a society destined to become vast, in which individuals were important chiefly as types. Although this kind of interest was different from that of European history, it was at least as important to the world. Should history ever become a true science, it must expect to establish its laws, not from the complicated story of rival European nationalities, but from the economical evolution of a great democracy. North America was the most favorable field on the globe for the spread of a society so large, uniform, and isolated as to answer the purposes of science. There a single homogeneous society could easily attain proportions of three or four hundred million persons, under conditions of undisturbed growth.

In Europe or Asia, except perhaps in China, undisturbed social evolution had been unknown. Without disturbance, evolution seemed to cease. Wherever disturbance occurred, permanence was impossible. Every people in turn adapted itself to the law of necessity. Such a system as that of the United States could hardly have existed for half a century in Europe except under the protection of another power. In the fierce struggle characteristic of European society, systems were permanent in nothing except in the general law, that, whatever other character they might possess they must always be chiefly military.

The want of permanence was not the only or the most confusing obstacle to the treatment of European history as a science. The intensity of the struggle gave prominence to the individual, until the hero seemed all, society nothing; and what was worse for science, the men were far more interesting than the societies. In the dramatic view of history, the hero deserved more to be studied than the community to which he belonged; in truth, he was the society, which existed only to produce him and to perish with him. Against such a view historians were among the last to protest, and protested but faintly when they did so at all. They felt as strongly as their audiences that the highest achievements were alone worth remembering either in history or in art, and that a reiteration of commonplaces was commonplace. With all the advantages of European movement and color, few historians succeeded in enlivening or dignifying the lack of motive, intelligence, and morality, the helplessness characteristic of many long periods in the face of crushing problems, and the futility of human efforts to escape from difficulties religious, political, and social. In a period extending over four or five thousand years, more or less capable of historical treatment, historians were content to illustrate here and there the most dramatic moments of the most sriking communities. The hero was their favorite. War was the chief field of heroic action, and even the history of England was chiefly the story of war.

The history of the United States promised to be free from such disturbances. War counted for little, the hero for less; on the people alone the eye could permanently rest. The steady growth of a vast population without the social distinctions that confused other histories, — without kings, nobles, or armies; without church, traditions, and prejudices, — seemed a subject for the man of science rather than for dramatists or poets. To scientific treatment only one great obstacle existed. Americans, like Europeans, were not disposed to make of their history a mechanical evolution. They felt that they even more than other nations needed the heroic element, because they breathed an atmosphere of peace and industry where heroism could seldom be displayed; and in unconscious protest against their own social conditions they adorned with imaginary qualities scores of supposed leaders, whose only merit was their faculty of reflecting a popular trait. Instinctively they clung to ancient history as though conscious that of all misfortunes that could befall the national character, the greatest would be the loss of the established ideals which alone ennobled human weakness. Without heroes, the national character of the United States had few charms of imagination even to Americans.

Historians and readers maintained Old-World standards. No historian cared to hasten the coming of an epoch when man should study his own history in the same spirit and by the same methods with which he studied the formation of a crystal. Yet history had its scientific as well as its human side, and in American history the scientific interest was greater than the human. Elsewhere the student could study under better conditions the evolution of the individual, but nowhere could he study so well the evolution of a race. The interest of such a subject exceeded that of any other branch of science, for it brought mankind within sight of its own end.

Travelers in Switzerland who stepped across the Rhine where it flowed from its glacier could follow its course among mediæval towns and feudal ruins, until it became a highway for modern industry, and at last arrived at a permanent equilibrium in the ocean. American history followed the same course. With prehistoric glaciers and mediæval feudalism the story had little to do; but from the moment it came within sight of the ocean it acquired interest almost painful. A child could find his way in a river-valley, and a hoy could float on the waters of Holland; but science alone could sound the depths of the ocean, measure its currents, foretell its storms, or fix its relations to the system of Nature. In a democratic ocean science could see something ultimate. Man could go no further. The atom might move, but the general equilibrium could not change.

Whether the scientific or the heroic view were taken, in either case the starting-point was the same, and the chief object of interest was to define national character. Whether the figures of history were treated as heroes or as types, they must be taken to represent the people. American types were especially worth study if they were to represent the greatest democratic evolution the world could know. Readers might judge for themselves what share the individual possessed in creating or shaping the nation; but whether it was small or great, the nation could be understood only by studying the individual. For that reason, in the story of Jefferson and Madison individuals retained their old interest as types of character, if not as sources of power.

In the American character antipathy to war ranked first among political traits. The majority of Americans regarded war in a peculiar light, the consequence of comparative security. No European nation could have conducted a war, as the people of America conducted the War of 1812. The possibility of doing so without destruction explained the existence of the national trait, and assured its continuance. In politics, the divergence of America from Europe perpetuated itself in the popular instinct for peaceable methods. The

Union took shape originally on the general lines that divided the civil from the military elements of the British constitution. The party of Jefferson and Gallatin was founded on dislike of every function of government necessary in a military system. Although Jefferson carried his pacific theories to an extreme, and brought about a military reaction, the reactionary movement was neither universal, violent, nor lasting; and society showed no sign of changing its convictions. With greater strength the country might acquire greater familiarity with warlike methods, but in the same degree was less likely to suffer any general change of habits. Nothing but prolonged intestine contests could convert the population of an entire continent into a race of warriors.

A people whose chief trait was antipathy to war, and to any system organized with military energy, could scarcely develop great results in national administration; yet the Americans prided themselves chiefly on their political capacity. Even the war did not undeceive them, although the incapacity brought into evidence by the war was undisputed, and was most remarkable among the communities which believed themselves to be most gifted with political sagacity. Virginia and Massachusetts by turns admitted failure in dealing with issues so simple that the newest societies, like Tennessee and Ohio, understood them by instinct. That incapacity in national politics should appear as a leading trait in American character was unexpected by Americans, but might naturally result from their conditions. The better test of American character was not political but social, and was to be found not in the government but in the people.

The sixteen years of Jefferson's and Madison's rule furnished international tests of popular intelligence upon which Americans could depend. The ocean was the only open field for competition among nations. Americans enjoyed there no natural or artificial advantages over Englishmen, Frenchmen, or Spaniards; indeed, all these countries possessed navies, resources, and experience greater than were to be found in the United States. Yet the Americans developed, in the course of twenty years, a surprising degree of skill in naval affairs. The evidence of their success was to be found nowhere so complete as in the avowals of Englishmen who knew best the history of naval progress. The American invention of the fast-sailing schooner or clipper was the more remarkable because, of all American inventions, this alone sprang from direct competition with Europe. During ten centuries of struggle the nations of Europe had labored to obtain superiority over each other in ship-construction, yet Americans instantly made improvements which gave them superiority, and which Europeans were unable immediately to imitate even after seeing them. Not only were American vessels better in model, faster in sailing, easier and quicker in handling, and more economical in working than the European, but they were also better equipped. The English complained as a grievance that the Americans adopted new and unwarranted devices in naval warfare; that their vessels were heavier and better constructed, and their missiles of unusual shape and improper use. The Americans resorted to expedients that had not been tried before, and excited a mixture of irritation and respect in the English service, until Yankee smartness became a national misdemeanor.

The English admitted themselves to be slow to change their habits, but the French were both quick and scientific; yet Americans did on the ocean what the French, under stronger inducements, failed to do. The French privateer preyed upon British commerce for twenty years without seriously injuring it; but no sooner did the American privateer sail from French ports, than the rates of insurance doubled in London, and an outcry for protection arose among English shippers which the Admiralty could not calm. The British newspapers were filled with assertions that the American cruiser was the superior of any vessel of its class, and threatened to overthrow England's supremacy on the ocean.

Another test of relative intelligence was furnished by the

battles at sea. Instantly after the loss of the "Guerriere" the English discovered and complained that American gunnery was superior to their own. They explained their inferiority by the length of time that had elapsed since their navy had found on the ocean an enemy to fight. Every vestige of hostile fleets had been swept away, until, after the battle of Trafalgar, British frigates ceased practice with their guns. Doubtless the British navy had become somewhat careless in the absence of a dangerous enemy, but Englishmen were themselves aware that some other cause must have affected their losses. Nothing showed that Nelson's line-of-battle ships, frigates, or sloops were as a rule better fought than the "Macedonian" and "Java," the "Avon" and "Reindeer." Sir Howard Douglas, the chief authority on the subject, attempted in vain to explain British reverses by the deterioration of British gunnery. His analysis showed only that American gunnery was extraordinarily good. Of all vessels, the sloop-of-war, — on account of its smallness, its quick motion, and its more accurate armament of thirty-two-pound carronades, — offered the best test of relative gunnery, and Sir Howard Douglas in commenting upon the destruction of the "Peacock" and "Avon" could only say, —

"In these two actions it is clear that the fire of the British vessels was thrown too high, and that the ordnance of their opponents were expressly and carefully aimed at and took effect chiefly in the hull."

The battle of the "Hornet" and "Penguin" as well as those of the "Reindeer" and "Avon," showed that the excellence of American gunnery continued till the close of the war. Whether at point-blank range or at long-distance practice, the Americans used guns as they had never been used at sea before.

None of the reports of former British victories showed that the British fire had been more destructive at any previous time than in 1812, and no report of any commander since the British navy existed showed so much damage inflicted on an opponent in so short a time as was proved to have been inflicted on themselves by the reports of British commanders in the American war. The strongest proof of American superiority was given by the best British officers, like Broke, who strained every nerve to maintain an equality with American gunnery. So instantaneous and energetic was the effort that, according to the British historian of the war, "a British forty-six-gun frigate of 1813 was half as effective again as a British forty-six-gun frigate of 1812;" and, as he justly said, "the slaughtered crews and the shattered hulks" of the captured British ships proved that no want of their old fighting qualities accounted for their repeated and almost habitual mortifications.

Unwilling as the English were to admit the superior skill of Americans on the ocean, they did not hesitate to admit it, in certain respects, on land. The American rifle in American hands was affirmed to have no equal in the world. This admission could scarcely be withheld after the lists of killed and wounded which followed almost every battle; but the admission served to check a wider inquiry. In truth, the rifle played but a small part in the war. Winchester's men at the river Raisin may have owed their over-confidence, as the British Forty-first owed its losses, to that weapon, and at New Orleans five or six hundred of Coffee's men, who were out of range, were armed with the rifle; but the surprising losses of the British were commonly due to artillery and musketry fire. At New Orleans the artillery was chiefly engaged. The artillery battle of January 1, according to British accounts, amply proved the superiority of American gunnery on that occasion, which was probably the fairest test during the war. The battle of January 8 was also chiefly an artillery battle; the main British column never arrived within fair musket range; Pakenham was killed by a grape-shot, and the main column of his troops halted more than one hundred yards from the parapet.

The best test of British and American military qualities, both for men and weapons, was Scott's battle of Chippawa.

Nothing intervened to throw a doubt over the fairness of the trial. Two parallel lines of regular soldiers, practically equal in numbers, armed with similar weapons, moved in close order toward each other, across a wide open plain, without cover or advantage of position, stopping at intervals to load and fire, until one line broke and retired. At the same time two three-gun batteries, the British being the heavier, maintained a steady fire from positions opposite each other. According to the reports, the two infantry lines in the center never came nearer than eighty yards. Major-General Riall reported that then, owing to severe losses, his troops broke and could not be rallied. Comparison of the official reports showed that the British lost in killed and wounded four hundred and sixty-nine men; the Americans, two hundred and ninety-six. Some doubts always affect the returns of wounded, because the severity of the wound cannot be known; but dead men tell their own tale. Riall reported one hundred and forty-eight killed; Scott reported sixty-one. The severity of the losses showed that the battle was sharply contested, and proved the personal bravery of both armies. Marksmanship decided the result, and the returns proved that the American fire was superior to that of the British in the proportion of more than fifty per cent if estimated by the entire loss, and of two hundred and forty-two to one hundred if estimated by the deaths alone.

The conclusion seemed incredible, but it was supported by the results of the naval battles. The Americans showed superiority amounting in some cases to twice the efficiency of their enemies in the use of weapons. The best French critic of the naval war, Jurien de la Gravière, said: "An enormous superiority in the rapidity and precision of their fire can alone explain the difference in the losses sustained by the combatants." So far from denying this conclusion the British press constantly alleged it, and the British officers complained of it. The discovery caused great surprise, and in both British services much attention was at once directed to improvement in artillery and musketry. Nothing could

exceed the frankness with which Englishmen avowed their
inferiority. According to Sir Francis Head, "gunnery was
in naval warfare in the extraordinary state of ignorance we
have just described, when our lean children, the American
people, taught us, rod in hand, our first lesson in the art."
The English textbook on Naval Gunnery, written by Major-
General Sir Howard Douglas immediately after the peace,
devoted more attention to the short American war than to
all the battles of Napoleon, and began by admitting that
Great Britain had "entered with too great confidence on war
with a marine much more expert than that of any of our
European enemies." The admission appeared "objection-
able" even to the author; but he did not add, what was
equally true, that it applied as well to the land as to the
sea service.

No one questioned the bravery of the British forces, or
the ease with which they often routed larger bodies of
militia; but the losses they inflicted were rarely as great as
those they suffered. Even at Bladensburg, where they met
little resistance, their loss was several times greater than
that of the Americans. At Plattsburg, where the intelligence
and quickness of Macdonough and his men alone won the
victory, his ships were in effect stationary batteries, and enjoyed the same superiority in gunnery. "The 'Saratoga,'"
said his official report, "had fifty-five round-shot in her hull;
the 'Confiance,' one hundred and five. The enemy's shot
passed principally just over our heads, as there were not
twenty whole hammocks in the nettings at the close of the
action."

The greater skill of the Americans was not due to special
training, for the British service was better trained in gunnery,
as in everything else, than the motley armies and fleets that
fought at New Orleans and on the Lakes. Critics constantly
said that every American had learned from his childhood the
use of the rifle, but he certainly had not learned to use cannon
in shooting birds or hunting deer, and he knew less than the
Englishman about the handling of artillery and muskets.

As if to add unnecessary evidence, the battle of Chrystler's Farm proved only too well that this American efficiency was not confined to citizens of the United States.

Another significant result of the war was the sudden development of scientific engineering in the United States. This branch of the military service owed its efficiency and almost its existence to the military school at West Point, established in 1802. The school was at first much neglected by the government. The number of graduates before the year 1812 was very small; but at the outbreak of the war the corps of engineers was already efficient. Its chief was Colonel Joseph Gardner Swift, of Massachusetts, the first graduate of the academy: Colonel Swift planned the defenses of New York harbor. The lieutenant-colonel in 1812 was Walker Keith Armistead, of Virginia, — the third graduate, who planned the defenses of Norfolk. Major William McRee, of North Carolina, became chief engineer to General Brown, and constructed the fortifications at Fort Erie, which cost the British General Gordon Drummond the loss of half his army, besides the mortification of defeat. Captain Eleazer Derby Wood, of New York, constructed Fort Meigs, which enabled Harrison to defeat the attack of Proctor in May, 1813. Captain Joseph Gilbert Totten, of New York, was chief engineer to General Izard at Plattsburg, where he directed the fortifications that stopped the advance of Prevost's great army. None of the works constructed by a graduate of West Point was captured by the enemy; and had an engineer been employed at Washington by Armstrong and Winder, the city would have been easily saved.

Perhaps without exaggeration the West Point Academy might be said to have decided, next to the navy, the result of the war. The works at New Orleans were simple in character, and as far as they were due to engineering skill were directed by Major Latour, a Frenchman; but the war was already ended when the battle of New Orleans was fought. During the critical campaign of 1814, the West Point engineers doubled the capacity of the little American army for resistance, and introduced a new and scientific character into American life.

In the application of science the steamboat was the most striking success; but Fulton's invention, however useful, was neither the most original nor the most ingenious of American efforts, nor did it offer the best example of popular characteristics. Perhaps Fulton's torpedo and Stevens's screw-propeller showed more originality than was proved by the "Clermont." The fast-sailing schooner with its pivot-gun — an invention that grew out of the common stock of nautical intelligence — best illustrated the character of the people.

That the individual should rise to a higher order either of intelligence or morality than had existed in former ages was not to be expected, for the United States offered less field for the development of individuality than had been offered by older and smaller societies. The chief function of the American Union was to raise the average standard of popular intelligence and well-being, and at the close of the War of 1812 the superior average intelligence of Americans was so far admitted that Yankee acuteness, or smartness, became a national reproach; but much doubt remained whether the intelligence belonged to a high order, or proved a high morality. From the earliest ages, shrewdness was associated with unscrupulousness; and Americans were freely charged with wanting honesty. The charge could neither be proved nor disproved. American morality was such as suited a people so endowed, and was high when compared with the morality of many older societies; but, like American intelligence, it discouraged excess. Probably the political morality shown by the government and by public men during the first sixteen years of the century offered a fair gauge of social morality. Like the character of the popular inventions, the character of the morals corresponded to the wants of a growing democratic society; but time alone could decide whether it would result in a high or a low national ideal.

Finer analysis showed other signs of divergence from ordinary standards. If Englishmen took pride in one trait more than in another, it was in the steady uniformity of their progress. The innovating and revolutionary quality of the French mind irritated them. America showed an un-English rapidity in movement. In politics, the American people between 1787 and 1817 accepted greater changes than had been known in England since 1688. In religion, the Unitarian movement of Boston and Harvard College would never have been possible in England, where the defection of Oxford or Cambridge, and the best educated society in the United Kingdom, would have shaken Church and State to their foundations. In literature the American school was chiefly remarkable for the rapidity with which it matured. The first book of Irving was a successful burlesque of his own ancestral history; the first poem of Bryant sang of the earth only as a universal tomb; the first preaching of Channing assumed to overthrow the Trinity; and the first paintings of Allston aspired to recover the ideal perfection of Raphael and Titian. In all these directions the American mind showed tendencies that surprised Englishmen more than they struck Americans. Allston defended himself from the criticism of friends who made complaint of his return to America. He found there, as he maintained, not only a growing taste for art, but "a quicker appreciation" of artistic effort than in any European land. If the highest intelligence of American society were to move with such rapidity, the time could not be far distant when it would pass into regions which England never liked to contemplate.

Another intellectual trait, as has been already noticed, was the disposition to relax severity. Between the theology of Jonathan Edwards and that of William Ellery Channing was an enormous gap, not only in doctrines but also in methods. Whatever might be thought of the conclusions reached by Edwards and Hopkins, the force of their reasoning commanded respect. Not often had a more strenuous effort than theirs been made to ascertain God's will, and to follow it without regard to weaknesses of the flesh. The idea that the nature of God's attributes was to be preached only as subordinate to the improvement of man, agreed little with the spirit of their religion. The Unitarian and Universalist movements marked the beginning of an epoch when ethical and humanitarian ideas took the place of metaphysics, and even New England turned from contemplating the omnipotence of the Deity in order to praise the perfections of his creatures.

The spread of great popular sects like the Universalists and Campbellites, founded on assumptions such as no Orthodox theology could tolerate, showed a growing tendency to relaxation of thought in that direction. The struggle for existence was already mitigated, and the first effect of the change was seen in the increasing cheerfulness of religion. Only when men found their actual world almost a heaven, could they lose overpowering anxiety about the world to come. Life had taken a softer aspect, and as a consequence God was no longer terrible. Even the wicked became less mischievous in an atmosphere where virtue was easier than vice. Punishments seemed mild in a society where every offender could cast off his past, and create a new career. For the first time in history, great bodies of men turned away from their old religion, giving no better reason than that it required them to believe in a cruel Deity, and rejected necessary conclusions of theology because they were inconsistent with human self-esteem.

The same optimism marked the political movement. Society was weary of strife, and settled gladly into a political system which left every disputed point undetermined. The public seemed obstinate only in believing that all was for the best, as far as the United States were concerned, in the affairs of mankind. The contrast was great between this temper of mind and that in which the Constitution had been framed; but it was no greater than the contrast in the religious opinions of the two periods, while the same reaction against severity marked the new literature. The rapid accumulation of wealth and increase in physical comfort told the same story from the standpoint of economy. On every side society showed that ease was for a time to take the place of severity, and enjoyment was to have its full share in the future national existence.

The traits of intelligence, rapidity, and mildness seemed fixed in the national character as early as 1817, and were likely to become more marked as time should pass. A vast amount of conservatism still lingered among the people; but the future spirit of society could hardly fail to be intelligent, rapid in movement, and mild in method. Only in the distant future could serious change occur, and even then no return to European characteristics seemed likely. The American continent was happier in its conditions and easier in its resources than the regions of Europe and Asia, where Nature reveled in diversity and conflict. If at any time American character should change, it might as probably become sluggish as revert to the violence and extravagances of Old-World development. The inertia of several hundred million people, all formed in a similar social mold, was as likely to stifle energy as to stimulate evolution.

With the establishment of these conclusions, a new episode in American history began in 1815. New subjects demanded new treatment, no longer dramatic but steadily tending to become scientific. The traits of American character were fixed; the rate of physical and economical growth was established; and history, certain that at a given distance of time the Union would contain so many millions of people, with wealth valued at so many millions of dollars, became thenceforward chiefly concerned to know what kind of people these millions were to be. They were intelligent, but what paths would their intelligence select? They were quick, but what solution of insoluble problems would quickness hurry? They were scientific, and what control would their science exercise over their destiny? They were mild, but what corruptions would their relaxations bring? They were peaceful, but by what machinery were their corruptions to be purged? What interests were to vivify a society so vast and uniform? What ideals were to ennoble it? What object, besides physical content, must a democratic continent aspire to attain? For the treatment of such questions, history required another century of experience.

HENRY JAMES

1843–1916

51 *Charleston*

CHARLESTON early in the morning, on my driving from the station, was, it had to be admitted, no very finished picture, but at least, already, it was different — ever so different in aspect and "feeling," and above all for intimation and suggestion, from any passage of the American scene as yet deciphered; and such became on the spot one's appetite for local color that one was fairly grateful to a friend who, by having promised to arrive from the interior of the State the night before, gave one a pretext for seeking him up and down. My quest, for the moment, proved vain; but the intimations and suggestions, while I proceeded from door to door in the sweet blank freshness of the day, of the climate, of the streets, began to swarm at such a rate that I had the sense of gathering my harvest with almost too eager a thrift. It was like standing steeped at the bookstall itself in the volume picked up and opened — though I may add that when I had presently retreated upon the hotel, to which I should in the first instance have addressed myself, it was quite, for a turning of pages, as if I had gone on with the "set." Thus, before breakfast, I entered upon my brief residence with the right vibrations already determined and unable really to say which of a couple of contacts just enjoyed would have most ministered to them. I had roused, guilelessly, through an easy misunderstanding, two more or less sleeping households; but if I had still missed my clew to my friend I had yet put myself into possession of much of whatever else I had wanted. What had I most wanted, I could easily ask myself, but some small inkling (a mere specimen-scrap would do) of the sense, as I have to keep forever calling my wanton synthesis, of "the South before the War"? — an air-bubble only to be blown, in any case, through some odd fragment of a pipe. My pair of early Charleston impressions were thus a pair of thin prismatic bubbles — which could have floated before me moreover but for a few seconds, collapsing even while I stood there.

Prismatically, none the less, they had shown me the "old" South; in one case by the mere tragic of the manner in which a small, scared, starved person of color, of very light color, an elderly mulattress in an improvised wrapper, just barely held open for me a door through which I felt I might have looked straight and far back into the past. The past, that of the vanished order, was hanging on there behind her — as much of it as the scant place would accommodate; and she knew this, and that I had so quickly guessed it; which led her, in fine, before I could see more, and that I might not sound the secret of shy misfortune, of faded pretension, to shut the door in my face. So, it seemed to me, had I been confronted, in Italy, under quite such a morning air and light, quite the same touch of a tepid, odorous medium, with the ancient sallow crones who guard the locked portals and the fallen pride of provincial *palazzini*. That was all, in the one instance; there had been no more of it than of the little flare of a struck match — which lasted long enough, however, to light the sedative cigarette, smoked and thrown away, that renews itself forever between the picture-seeker's lips. The small historic whiff I had momentarily inhaled required the correction, I should add, of the sweeter breath of my commentary. Fresh altogether was the air behind the garden wall that next gave way to my pursuit; there being a thrill, for that matter, in the fact that here at last again, if nowhere else over the land, rose the real walls that alone make real gardens and that admit to the same by real doors. Close such a door behind you, and you are at once *within* — a local relation, a possibility of retreat, in favor of which the custom of the North has so completely ceased to discriminate. One sacrificed the North, with its mere hard conceit of virtuously meeting exhibition — much as if a house were just a metallic machine, number so-and-so in a catalogue — one sacrificed it on the spot to this finer feeling for the enclosure.

That had really sufficed, no doubt, for my second initiation; since I remember withdrawing, after my fruitless question, as one after the completion of a mystic process. Initiation into *what* I perhaps couldn't have said; only, at the most, into the knowledge that what such Southern walls generally shut in proves exactly what one would have wished. I was to see this loose quantity afterwards in greater profusion; but for the moment the effect was as right as that of privacy for the habit of the siesta. The details escape me, or rather I tenderly withhold them. For the siesta there — what would it have been most like but some deep doze, or call it frankly some final sleep, of the idea of "success"? And how could one better have described the privacy, with the mild street shut off and with the deep gallery, where resignation might sit in the shade or swing without motion in a hammock, shut in, than as some dim dream that things were still as they had been — still pleasant behind garden walls — before the great folly? I was to find myself liking, in the South and in the most monstrous fashion, it appeared, those aspects in which the consequences of the great folly were, for extent and gravity, still traceable; I was cold-bloodedly to prefer them, that is, to the aspects, occasionally to be met, from which the traces had been removed. And this, I need hardly say, from a point of view having so little in common with the vindictive as to be quite directly opposed to it. For what in the world was one candidly to do? It is the manner of the purged and renovated, the disconnected element, anywhere, after great trials, to express itself in forms comparatively vulgar; whereas those parts of the organism that, having been through the fire, still have kept the scorches and scars, resemble for tone, for color and value, the products of the potter's oven;

when the potter, I mean, or when, in other words, history, has been the right great artist. They at least are not cheerful rawnesses — they have been baked beautiful and hard.

I even tried, I fear, when once installed there, to look at my hotel in that light; availing myself, to this end, of its appearance of "dating," with its fine old neo-classic front and a certain romantic grandeur of scale, the scale positively of "Latin" construction, in my vast saloon-like apartment, which opened to a high colonnade. The great canopied and curtained bed was really in the grand manner, and the ghost of a rococo tradition, the tradition of the transatlantic South, memory of other lands, glimmered generally in the decoration. When once I had — though almost exclusively under the charm of these particular faded graces, I admit — again privately protested that the place might have been a "palace," my peace was made with Charleston: I was ripe for the last platitude of appreciation. Let me say indeed that this consciousness had from the first to struggle with another — the immediate sense of the degree in which the American scene is lighted, on occasion, to the critical eye, by the testimony of the hotel. As had been the case for me already at Richmond, so here again the note of that truth was sounded; the visitor interested in manners was too clearly not to escape it, and I scarce know under what slightly sinister warning he braced himself to the fact. He had not, as yet, for repatriation, been thrown much upon the hotel; but this was the high sense of looking further and seeing more, this present promise of that adventure. One is thrown upon it, in America, as straight upon the general painted scene over which the foot-lights of publicity play with their large crudity, and against the freely-brushed texture and grain of which you thus rub your nose more directly, and with less of ceremony, than elsewhere. There are endless things in "Europe," to your vision, behind and beyond the hotel, a multitudinous complicated life; in the States, on the other hand, you see the hotel as itself that life, as constituting for vast numbers of people the richest form of existence. You have to go no distance for this to come over you — twenty appearances so vividly speak of it. It is not so much, no doubt, that "every one" lives at hotels, according to the witless belief of "Europe," but that you so quickly seem to measure the very limited extent to which those who people them, the populations they appeal to in general, may be conceived as "living" out of them. I remember how often, in moving about, the observation that most remained with me appeared to be this note of the hotel, and of the hotel-like chain of Pullman cars, as the supreme social expression. For the Pullmans too, in their way, were eloquent; they affected me ever, by the end of twenty-four hours, as carrying, if not Cæsar and his fortune, at least almost *all* the facts of American life. There were some of course that didn't fit into them, but so many others did, and these fitted somehow so perfectly and with such a congruity.

What it comes back to is that in such conditions the elements of the situation show with all possible, though quite unnoted, intensity; they tell you all about it (about the situation) in a few remarkably plain and distinct words; they make you feel in short how its significance is written upon it. It is as if the figures before you and all round you, less different from each other, less different too, I think, from the objects about them, whatever these in any case may be, than any equal mass of appearances under the sun — it is as if everyone and everything said to you straight: "Yes, this is how we are; this is what it is to enjoy our advantages; this moreover is all there is of us; we give it all out. Make what you can of it!" The restless analyst would have had indeed an unusual fit of languor if he had not begun from the first to make of it what he could, divided even though he was between his sense of this largely-written significance and his wonderment, none the less, as to its value and bearing; which constituted, after all, a shade of perplexity as to its meaning. "Yes, I see how you are, God knows" he was ready with his reply; "for nothing in the world is easier to see, even in all the particulars. But what does it *mean* to be as you are? — since I suppose it means something; something more than your mere one universal type, with its small deflections but never a departure; something more than your way of sitting in silence together at table, than your extraordinary, your enormous passivity, than your apparent absence of criticism or judgment of anything that is put before you or that happens to you (beyond occasionally remarking that it's 'fine' !) than, in a word, the fact of what you eat and the fact of how you eat it. You are not final, complacently as you appear so much of the time to assume it — your mere inevitable shaking about in the Margin must more or less take care of that; since you can't be so inordinately passive (everywhere, one infers, but in your particular wary niche of your 'business-block') without being in *some* degree plastic. Distinct as you are, you are not even definite, and it would be terrible not to be able to suppose that you are as yet but an instalment, a current number, like that of the morning paper, a specimen of a type in course of serialization — like the hero of the magazine novel, by the highly successful author, the climax of which is still far off. Thus, as you are perpetually provisional, the hotels and the Pullmans — the Pullmans that are like rushing hotels and the hotels that are like stationary Pullmans — represent the stages and forms of your evolution, and are not a bit, in themselves, more final than you are. The particulars still to be added either to you or to them form an insoluble question; and meanwhile, clearly, your actual stage will not be short." So much as that, I recall, had hummed about my ears at Richmond, where the strong vertical light of a fine domed and glazed cortile, the spacious and agreeable dining-hall of the inn, had rested on the human scene as with an effect of mechanical pressure. If the scene constituted evidence, the evidence might have been in course of being pressed out, in this shining form, by the application of a weight and the turn of a screw. There it was, accordingly; there was the social, the readable page, with its more or less complete report of the conditions. The report was to be fuller as to some of these at Charleston; but I had at least grasped its general value. And I shall come back to the Charleston report.

It would have been a sorry business here, however, if this had been mainly the source of my impressions — which was so far from the case that I had but to go forth, after breakfast, to find insidious charm, the appeal of the outer, the larger aspect, await me at every turn. The day announced itself as warm and radiant, and, keeping its promise to the end, squared itself there as the golden frame of an interesting picture — interesting above all from the moment one desired with any intensity to find it so. The vision persists, with its charming, touching features; yet when I look back and ask myself what can have made my impression, all round, so positive, I am at a loss for elements to refer to it. Elements there were, certainly; in especial the fact that during these first bland hours, charged with the splendor of spring, I caught the wide-eyed smile of the South, that expression of a temperamental felicity in which shades of character, questions of real feature, other marks and meanings, tend always to lose themselves. But a deficiency was clear, which was neither more nor less than the deficiency of life; without life, all gracefully, the picture managed to compose itself. Even while one felt it do so one missed the precious presence; so that there at least was food for wonderment, for admiration of the art at play. To what, all the while, as one went, could one compare the mystification? — to what if not to the image of some handsome pale person, a beauty (to call her so) of other days, who, besides confessing to the inanimate state from closed eyes and motionless lips, from the arrest of respiration and gesture, was to leave one, by the day's end, with the sense of a figure prepared for romantic interment, stretched in a fair winding-sheet, covered with admirable flowers, surrounded with shining tapers. *That,* one reasoned, would be something to have seen; and yet one's interest was not so limited. Ruins, to be interesting, have to be massive; and poor bitter-sweet Charleston suffered, for the observer, by the merciless law of the thinness, making too much for transparency, for the effect of paucity, still inherent in American groupings; a law under which the attempt to subject them to portraiture, to see them as "composing," resembles the attempt to play whist with an imperfect pack of cards. If one had already, at the North, divined the general complexion as probably thin, in this sense, everywhere — thin, that is, for all note-taking but the statistical, under which it might of course show as portentously thick — it wouldn't turn dense or rich of a sudden, even in an air that could so drench it with benignity. Therefore, if the scene, as one might say, was but the historic Desert without the historic Mausoleum, how was one's impression to give out, as it clearly would, the after-taste of experience?

To let this small problem worry me no longer than it might, I sought an answer, and quickly found one, in the fortunate fact of my not having failed, after all, of the admirably suggestive society of my distinguished and competent friend. He *had* arrived over-night, according to my hope, and had only happened to lodge himself momentarily out of my ken; so that as soon as I had his company to profit by I felt the "analytic" burden of my own blessedly lifted. I took over his analysis, infinitely better adjusted to the case and which clearly would suffice for everything — if only it should itself escape disintegration. Let me say at once that it quite averted — whether consciously or unconsciously, whether as too formidably bristling or as too perfectly pacific — that menace; which success was to provide for us both, I think, a rounded felicity. My companion, a Northerner of Southern descent (as well as still more immediately, on another side, of English), knew his South in general and his Carolina of that ilk in particular, with an intimacy that was like a grab-bag into which, for illustration, he might always dip his hand (a movement that, had the grab-bag been "European," I should describe rather as a plunge of his arm: so that it comes back again to the shallowness of the American grab-bag, as yet, for illustrations other than the statistical). He held up for me his bright critical candle, which even in the intrinsic Charleston vividness made its gay flicker, and it was under this aid that, to my extreme convenience, I was able to "feel" the place. My fortune had indeed an odd sequel — which I mention for its appreciatory value; the mishaps and accidents of appreciation being ever, in their way, I think, as contributive to judgment as the felicities. I was to challenge, too recklessly, the chances of a second day; having by the end of the first, and by the taking of example, quite learned to treat the scene as a grab-bag for my own hand. I went over it again, in an evil hour — whereupon I met afresh the admonition, already repeatedly received, that where, in the States, the interest, where the pleasure of contemplation is concerned, discretion is the better part of valor and insistence too often a betrayal. It is not so much that the hostile fact crops up as that the friendly fact breaks down. If you have luckily *seen,* you have seen; carry off your prize, in this case, instantly and at any risk. Try it again and you don't, you won't, see; for there is in all contemplation, there is even in any clear appreciation, an element of the cruel. These things demand that your exposed object shall, first of all, exist; and to exist for exposure is to be at the best impaled on the naturalist's pin. It takes superpositions, at any rate, to defy sufficiently this sort of attention; it takes either the stoutnesses of history or the rarest rarities of nature to resist fatal penetration. That was to come home to me presently in Florida — through the touched sense of the truth that Florida, ever so amiably, is weak. You may live there serenely, no doubt — as in a void furnished at the most with velvet air; you may in fact live there with an idea, if you are content that your idea shall consist of grapefruit and oranges. Oranges, grapefruit and velvet air constitute, in a manner, I admit, a feast; but press upon the board with any greater weight and it quite gives way — its three or four props treacherously forsake it. That is what I mean by the impression, in the great empty peninsula, of weakness; which I was to feel still clearer about on being able to compare it afterwards with the impression of

California. California was to have — if I may decently be premature about it — her own treachery; but she was to wind one up much higher before she let one down. I was to find her, especially at the first flush, unlike sweet frustrated Florida, ever so amiably strong: which came from the art with which she makes the stoutnesses, as I have called them, of natural beauty stand you in temporary stead of the leannesses of everything else (everything that might be of an order equally interesting). This she is on a short acquaintance quite insolently able to do, thanks to her belonging so completely to the " handsome " side of the continent, of which she is the finest expression. The aspect of natural objects, up and down the Pacific coast, is as " aristocratic " as the comprehensive American condition permits anything to be: it indeed appears to the ingenious mind to represent an instinct on the part of Nature, a sort of shuddering, bristling need, to brace herself in advance against the assault of a society so much less marked with distinction than herself. If I was to conceive therefore under these later lights, that her spirit had put forth nowhere on the sub-tropical Atlantic shore anything to approach this conscious pride, so, doubtless, the Carolinian effect, even at its sweetest, was to strike me as related to it very much as a tinkle is related to a boom.

To stray but for an instant into such an out-of-the-way corner of one's notes, however, is to give the lie to the tenderness that asserted itself so promptly as the very medium of one's perception. There was literally no single object that, from morn to nightfall, it was not more possible to consider with tenderness, a rich consistency of tenderness, than to consider without it: *such* was the subtle trick that Charleston could still play. There echoed for me as I looked out from the Battery the recent speech of a friend which had had at the time a depressing weight; the Battery of the long, curved sea-front, of the waterside public garden furnished with sad old historic guns, with live-oaks draped in trailing moss, with palmettos that, as if still mindful of their State symbolism, seem to try everywhere, though with a melancholy skeptical droop, to repeat the old escutcheon; with its large, thrilling view in particular — thrilling to a Northerner who stands there for the first time. "Filled as I am, in general, while there," my friend had said, "with the sadness and sorrow of the South, I never, at Charleston, look out to the old betrayed Forts without feeling my heart harden again to steel." One remembered that, on the spot, and one waited a little — to see what was happening to one's heart. I found this to take time indeed; everything differed, somehow, from one's old conceived image — or if I had anciently grasped the remoteness of Fort Sumter, near the mouth of the Bay, and of its companion, at the point of the shore forming the other side of the passage, this lucidity had so left me, in the course of the years, that the faraway dimness of the consecrated objects was almost a shock. It was a blow even to one's faded vision of Charleston viciously firing on the Flag; the Flag would have been, from the Battery, such a mere speck in space that the vice of the act lost somehow, with the distance, to say nothing of the forty years, a part of its grossness. The smitten face, however flushed and scarred, was out of sight, though the intention of smiting and the force of the insult were of course still the same. This reflection one made, but the old fancied perspective and proportions were altered; and then the whole picture, at that hour, exhaled an innocence. It was as blank as the face of a child under mention of his naughtiness and his punishment of week before last. The Forts, faintly blue on the twinkling sea, looked like vague marine flowers; innocence, pleasantness ruled the prospect: it was as if the compromised slate, sponged clean of all the wicked words and hung up on the wall for better use, dangled there so vacantly as almost to look foolish. Ah, there again was the word: the air still just tasted of the antique folly; so that in presence of a lesson so sharp and so prolonged, of the general *sterilized* state, of the brightly-lighted, delicate dreariness recording the folly, harshness was conjured away. There was that in the impression which affected me after a

little as one of those refinements of irony that wait on deep
expiations: one could scarce conceive at this time of day
that such a place had ever been dangerously moved. It was
the *bled* condition, and mostly the depleted cerebral condition, that was thus attested — as I had recognized it at
Richmond; and I asked myself, on the Battery, what more
one's sternest justice could have desired. If my heart wasn't
to harden to steel, in short, access to it by the right influence
had found perhaps too many other forms of sensibility in
ambush.

To justify hardness, moreover, one would have had to
meet something hard; and if my peregrination, after this,
had been a search for such an element, I should have to
describe it as made all in vain. Up and down and in and
out, with my companion, I strolled from hour to hour; but
more and more under the impression of the consistency of
softness. One could have expressed the softness in a word,
and the picture so offered would be infinitely touching. It
was a city of gardens and absolutely of no men — or of so
few that, save for the general sweetness, the War might
still have been raging and all the manhood at the front.
The gardens were matter for the women; though even of the
women there were few, and that small company — rare,
discreet, flitting figures that brushed the garden walls with
noiseless skirts in the little melancholy streets of interspaced,
over-tangled abodes — were clad in a rigor of mourning that
was like the garb of a conspiracy. The effect was superficially prim, but so far as it savored of malice prepense, of
the Southern, the sentimental *parti-pris,* it was delightful.
What was it all most like, the incoherent jumble of suggestions? — the suggestion of a social shrinkage and an economic blight unrepaired, irreparable; the suggestion of byways of some old far East infected with triumphant women's
rights, some perspective of builded, plastered lanes over the
enclosures of which the flowering almond drops its petals
into sharp deep bands of shade or of sun. It is not the
muffled ladies who walk about predominantly in the East;

but that is a detail. The likeness was perhaps greater to some little old-world quarter of quiet convents where only priests and nuns steal forth — the priests mistakable at a distance, say, for the nuns. It was indeed thoroughly mystifying, the whole picture — since I was to get, in the freshness of that morning, from the very background of the scene, my quite triumphant little impression of the "old South." I remember feeling with intensity at two or three points in particular that I should never get a better one, that even this was precarious — might melt at any moment, by a wrong touch or a false note, in my grasp — and that I must therefore make the most of it. The rest of my time, I may profess, was spent in so doing. I made the most of it in several successive spots: under the south wall of St. Michael's Church, the sweetest corner of Charleston, and of which there is more to say; out in the old Cemetery on the edge of the lagoon, where the distillation of the past was perhaps clearest and the bribe to tenderness most effective; and even not a little on ground thereunto almost adjacent, that of a kindly Country-Club installed in a fine old semi-sinister mansion, and holding an afternoon revel at which I was privileged briefly to assist. The wrong touch and the false note were doubtless just sensible in this last connection, where the question, probed a little, would apparently have been of some new South that has not yet quite found the effective way romantically, or at least insidiously, to appeal. The South that is cultivating country-clubs is a South presumably, in many connections, quite in the right; whereas the one we were invidiously "after" was the one that had been so utterly in the wrong. Even there, none the less, in presence of more than a single marked sign of the rude Northern contagion, I disengaged, socially speaking, a faint residuum which I mention for proof of the intensity of my quest and of my appreciation.

There were two other places, I may add, where one could but work the impression for all it was, in the modern phrase, "worth," and where I had, I may venture to say, the sense of making as much of it as was likely ever to be made again. Meanings without end were to be read, under tuition, into one of these, which was neither more nor less than a slightly shy, yet after all quite serene place of refection, a luncheon-room or tea-house, denominated for quaint reasons as "Exchange" — *the* very Exchange in fact lately commemorated in a penetrating study, already much known to fame, of the little that is left of the local society. My tuition, at the hands of my ingenious comrade, was the very best it was possible to have. Nothing, usually, is more wonderful than the quantity of significant character that, with such an example set, the imagination may recognize in the scantest group of features, objects, persons. I fantastically feasted here, at my luncheon-table, not only, as the genius of the place demanded, on hot chocolate, sandwiches and "Lady Baltimore" cake (this last a most delectable compound), but on the exact *nuance* of oddity, of bravery, of reduced gentility, of irreducible superiority, to which the opening of such an establishment, without derogation, by the proud daughters of war-wasted families, could exquisitely testify. They hovered, the proud impoverished daughters, singly or in couples, behind the counter — a counter, again, delectably charged; they waited, inscrutably, irreproachably, yet with all that peculiarly chaste *bonhomie* of the Southern tone, on the customers' wants, even coming to ascertain these at the little thrifty tables; and if the drama and its adjusted theater really contained all the elements of history, tragedy, comedy, irony, that a pair of expert romancers, closely associated for the hour, were eager to evoke, the scene would have been, I can only say, supreme of its kind. That desire of the artist to linger where the breath of a "subject," faintly stirring the air, reaches his vigilant sense, would here stay my steps — as this very influence was in fact, to his great good-fortune, to stay those of my companion. The charm I speak of, the charm to cherish, however, was most exhaled for me in other conditions — conditions that scarce permit of any direct reference to their full suggestiveness. If I

alluded above to the vivid Charleston background, where
its "mystification" most scenically persists, the image is all
rounded and complete, for memory, in this connection at
which — as the case is of an admirably mature and preserved interior — I can only glance as I pass. The puzzle-
ment elsewhere is in the sense that though the elements of
earth and air, the color, the tone, the light, the sweetness
in fine, linger on, the "old South" could have had no such
unmitigated mildness, could never have seen itself as subject to such strange feminization. The feminization is there
just to promote for us some eloquent antithesis; just to
make us say that whereas the ancient order was masculine,
fierce and moustachioed, the present is at the most a sort
of sick lioness who has so visibly parted with her teeth and
claws that we may patronizingly walk all round her.

This image really gives us the best word for the general
effect of Charleston — that of the practically vacant cage
which used in the other time to emit sounds, even to those
of the portentous shaking of bars, audible as far away as in
the listening North. It is the vacancy that is a thing by
itself, a thing that makes us endlessly wonder. How, in an
at all complex, a "great political," society, can *everything*
so have gone? — assuming indeed that, under this ægis,
very much ever had come. How can everything so have
gone that the only "Southern" book of any distinction
published for many a year is *The Souls of Black Folk,* by
that most accomplished of members of the negro race, Mr.
W. E. B. Du Bois? Had the *only* focus of life then been
Slavery? — from the point onward that Slavery had reached
a quarter of a century before the War, so that with the
extinction of that interest none other of any sort was left.
To say "yes" seems the only way to account for the degree
of the vacancy, and yet even as I form that word I meet
as a reproach the face of the beautiful old house I just mentioned, whose ample spaces had so unmistakably echoed to
the higher amenities that one seemed to feel the accumulated
traces and tokens gradually come out of their corners like

blest objects taken one by one from a reliquary worn with much handling. The note of such haunted chambers as these — haunted structurally, above all, quite as by the ghost of the grand style — was not, certainly, a thinness of reverberation; so that I had to take refuge here in the fact that everything appeared thoroughly to *antedate*, to refer itself to the larger, the less vitiated past that had closed a quarter of a century or so before the War, before the fatal time when the South, monomaniacal at the parting of the ways, "elected" for extension and conquest. The admirable old house of the stately hall and staircase, of the charming coved and vaulted drawing-room, of the precious mahogany doors, the tall unsophisticated portraits, the delicate dignity of welcome, owed nothing of its noble identity, nothing at all appreciable, to the monomania. However that might be, moreover, I kept finding the mere melancholy charm reassert itself where it could — the charm, I mean, of the flower-crowned waste that was, by my measure, what the monomania had most prepared itself to bequeath. In the old Cemetery by the lagoon, to which I have already alluded, this influence distils an irresistible poetry — as one has courage to say even in remembering how disproportionately, almost anywhere on the American scene, the general place of interment is apt to be invited to testify for the presence of charm. The golden afternoon, the low, silvery, seaward horizon, as of wide, sleepy, game-haunted inlets and reed-smothered banks, possible site of some Venice that had never mustered, the luxury, in the mild air, of shrub and plant and blossom that the pale North can but distantly envy; something that I scarce know how to express but as the proud humility of the whole idle, easy loveliness, made even the restless analyst, for the hour, among the pious inscriptions that scarce ever belie the magniloquent clime or the inimitable tradition, feel himself really capable of the highest Carolinian pitch.

To what height did he rise, on the other hand, on being introduced another day, at no great distance from this point, and where the silvery seaward outlook still prevails, to the lapsed and readministered residence, also already named, that was to give him his one glimpse of any local modernism? This was the nearest approach for him to any reanimation of the flower-crowned waste, and he has still in memory, for symbol of the modernism, a vision of the great living, blazing fire of logs round which, as the afternoon had turned wet and chill, this contribution to his view of a possible new society, a possible youthful tone, a possible Southern future in short, had disposed itself. There were men here, in the picture — a few — and young ones: that odd other sense as of a becraped, feminized world was accordingly for the moment in abeyance. For the moment, I say advisedly — for the moment only; since what aspect of the social scene anywhere in the States strikes any second glance as exempt from that condition? It is overwhelmingly feminized or it *is* not — that is the formula with which its claim to existence pierces the ear. Lest, however, the recognition again of this truth should lead me too far, I content myself with noting a matter perhaps more relevant just here — one's inevitable consciousness, in presence of the "new" manifestations, that the South is in the predicament of having to be tragic, as it were, in order to beguile. It was very hard, I said to myself, and very cruel and very perverse, and above all very strange; but what "use" had the restless analyst here for a lively and oblivious type? Was there not something in the lively and oblivious that, given the materials employed for it and the effect produced by it, threw one back with renewed relish on the unforgetting and the devoted, on the resentful and even, if need might be, the vindictive? These things would represent certainly a bad *état d'âme* — and was one thus cold-bloodedly, critically, to wish such a condition perpetuated? The answer to that seemed to be, monstrously enough, "Well, yes — for these people; since it appears the only way by which they can be interesting. See when they try other ways! Their sadness and sorrow, as my friend called it, has at least for it that it has been expensively produced. Everything else, on the other hand, anything that may pretend to be better — oh, so cheaply!"

One had already, in moving about, winced often enough at sight of where one was, intellectually, to "land," under these last consistencies of observation and reflection; so I may put it here that I *didn't,* after all, land, but recoiled rather and forbore, making my skiff fast to no conclusion whatever, only pushing out again and letting it, for a supreme impression and to prepare in the aftertime the best remembrance, drift where it would. So, accordingly, the aftertime having a little arrived, it touches now once more of its own motion, carries me back and puts me ashore on the one spot where the impression had been perfectly felicitous. I have already named the place — under the mild, the bright south wall of St. Michael's Church, where the whole precinct offered the full-blown Southern spring, that morning, the finest of all canvases to embroider. The canvas here, yes, was of the best; not only did Charleston show me none other so good, but I was doubtless to have met, South or North, none of an equal happy grain and form. The high, complicated, inflated spire of the church has the sincerity, approved of time, that is so rare, over the land, in the work of man's hands, laden though these be with the millions he offers as a vain bribe to it; and in the sweet old church-yard ancient authority seemed to me, on the occasion of my visit, to sit, among the sun-warmed tombs and the interrelated slabs and extravagant flowers, as on the sole cushion the general American bareness in such connections had left it. There was more still of association and impression; I found, under this charm, I confess, character in every feature. Even in the much-maintained interior revolutions and renovations have respected its sturdy, rather somber essence: the place feels itself, in the fine old dusky archaic way, the constituted temple of a faith — archives, in a word, the air of reality that one had seen in every other such case, from town to town and from village to village, missed with an unconsciousness that had to do duty for success.

WILLIAM CRARY BROWNELL

1851–1928

The Art of Prose

EXCLUDING prose from the realm preëmpted by formal poetry — where it is inevitably at a disadvantage and where by definition it has no business, having its own character, which it compromises in leaving its own province — by no means involves its exclusion from the far larger domain of art, where if it have style it belongs. Without style it becomes what, in 1868, Scherer complained the prose of the Second Empire was becoming. Under the imperial régime, which he admitted might be the effect rather than the cause of the enervation of France that he deemed universal, but which in any case typified it, he maintained that "prose which is an art, prose which has literary pretensions, is being supplanted by prose absolutely naked which is mere writing." This state of things he would not have been surprised to learn that our own democracy, which he was pessimistically inclined to misconceive, was later — itself now more or less "imperialized" — to illustrate and even to idealize. The French however have a reliable passion for prose, as indirectly M. France attests in declaring that they do not object to poetry unless it be poetic. As to prose we are less fortunate, especially at the present day, when prose, plus the feeling that should give it style and make it art, is often popularly, though I believe less now than recently, diverted into what is called free verse; and when, following the example of a race in its childhood and civilization in its dawn, our multitude of writers so frequently begin, even in college, with poetry, and if, like Wordsworth, deserted later by the Muse, unlike him, fail to cultivate in their subsequent writing any æsthetic spirit whatever. In fine, we are to ask ourselves if prose is an art or not. If it is and is composed only of clarity and simplicity, however difficult of attainment these qualities may be, it is reasonably clear that it is a reasonably simple one. We may be sure the masters of prose found the matter more complicated, more ambitious as well as more rewarding, imposing, in fact, success in the capture of Beauty, and her imprisonment in an appropriately golden cage.

In the plastic arts there is plenty of appropriate prose which is nevertheless in its degree beautiful. Henry James happily speaks of Magdalen Tower as "that pearl of prose Gothic"; a great deal of beautiful sculpture is prose though not prosaic; similarly with painting. Indeed in painting there is only one of its various departments where poetry is obligatory, though in this one I think it should be so deemed under some effective penalty: the landscape-painter should certainly never forget that "the poetry of earth is never dead." The wisdom of protecting both poetry and prose from "prose poetry" is justified in the manifest interest of each; as a hybrid it is inevitably caricature. But poetic prose on the other hand, or for that matter poetic anything, is no more poetry than, say, a sunset is a poet. Sentiment in itself is poetic and carries its perfume with it everywhere, into prose as well as into verse. And any plea for a richer prose than that which now, as it were, scudding along under bare poles, scurries to the haven of its conclusions, one may legitimately base on the universality of sentiment — on the unity of the æsthetic element and its claims to a more extended penetration of the domain of literature.

Of recent years the striking phenomenon of the expansion of journalism has tended to obstruct this penetration, journalism not only having little weakness for the æsthetic but acting more or less on the principle expressed by French irony in the saying, *Ote-toi de là que je m'y mette*. In fact its own invasion of the domain of literature has been in such force and at so many points that one is rather driven to hope it may, like other invaders, content itself with material conquest and ultimately be assimilated by the higher civilization of the conquered. In political writing the standard of effectiveness perhaps automatically excludes the graces of expression; so far as these are in any degree excursions they must properly be suspect. So far as they may be classified under the head of fitness, however, they have obvious point, and style, being at least not an external embellishment but an inner order, appears with relevance — in, for instance, the successful simplification and calculated precision of the late Frank Cobb's daily application to current events of a pondered political philosophy. But such instances are none too frequent in the political or other fields, and as a rule the invading hosts of journalism, establishing themselves in all the border provinces of literature — notably in the much harried march of criticism — not unnaturally treat with contempt such laws and traditions of the country as hamper their rather exclusively temperamental equipment and expression. In daily journalism, the time factor is remorseless and itself trims a writer's style of superfluities, and the inescapable "Go to it" of necessity is a command carrying with it so radical an inhibition, and so strict a construction, of irrelevance as to produce in the newspaper world, in spite of salient exceptions, a general stylistic result of conspicuous bleakness. In truth, what areas of excellent writing of all kinds, since the days illumined by the sun of eloquence, have stretched their "nude and sere" expanse beneath a leaden sky and shivered in the pale diffused twilight of a wan explicitness, exhibiting with chill detachment a prospect devoid of charm! There have been, as I say, notable exceptions even in the newspaper world, but it has undeniably felt the general frost.

This widespread refrigeration set in long ago more or less coincidently, perhaps, with the rise of the Manchester school, and was very likely in some degree responsible for the dejected view Carlyle took of what he called the Dismal Science. The plantigrade tread of its resolutely inductive process might quite conceivably "get on" nerves as exposed as his. When his Reminiscences appeared — *consule Planco!* — I remember calling the acid but graphic characterization of his friend Mill's talk as "rather wintry" to the attention of the late E. L. Godkin — a Benthamite indeed in whom there was no other guile — and enjoying the latter's amused and unusual accord with the Sage of Chelsea, who (he did not believe much in sages) mostly provoked his impatience. There was nothing "wintry" about Mr. Godkin's writing any more than about his talk or himself. Arthur Sedgwick, his own style distinguished in much the same way, wrote of him: "Mr. Godkin's is what the best English has always been, pointed, strong, and simple. For lucidity and directness it is unequaled among contemporary writers in this country or in England." And he continues, as we should expect him to: "The Essays are contributions to political and economic literature of the most solid sort." However, solid political and economic literature is rarely literature so far as literature is an art, save — may one say? — in inadvertence; usually, at least, it lacks æsthetic claims and to imply that the best English has always been merely pointed, strong, simple, lucid, and direct is to imply that the English of the masters of English prose is not the best. To assert this is not to assert that their English is pointless, weak, complicated, obscure, and circuitous; only that it does something more than avoid these vices and illustrate their antithetical virtues.

This something is to illustrate the æsthetic element of style — style itself as distinct from statement, even from that rare and exemplary order of statement characterized by all the aforesaid virtues. Indeed this element also might have been pointed out in Mr. Godkin's writing. It followed rather rigidly the counsel of concealment of art by art; and its felicities are of course all the greater for being so distinctly not frippery but integral; though he certainly eschewed eloquence and his sustained pressure of order and movement followed closely the contour of the subject. His distinction lay in conceiving his subject in relation to its governing principle and threading the detail which his erudition and experience amply provided in close company with this guide.

WILLIAM CRARY BROWNELL

This unified his essay, or article, and made the net impression it left as definite as its title. But if as a writer he divided with Curtis the primacy among our journalists, instead of holding it unchallenged, it was, I think, because he embodied so exclusively the Emersonian ideal, "See that you hold yourself fast by the intellect." His writing avoided emotional content or color, the writer evidently considering that "all that sort of thing" so far as it could be deemed pertinent at all should go without saying, not to say be reserved for private usage — a preserve of whose inviolability to poaching he was perhaps exorbitantly jealous; which is a little curious considering his fellowship with Burke. Undoubtedly he admired Burke less for his style than for his having, as Arnold says, "saturated politics with thought." Had Godkin not in general so pointedly ignored the æsthetic element, his prose must have been more persuasive, whereas, which was surely regrettable, it was pointedly not persuasive at all. His attitude was a little that of President Seelye on beginning psychology with a new class: "I shall not ask you to believe, but defy you to deny." With maturer readers this was less effective than with undergraduates, and though Godkin's belief was undoubtedly that American newspaper readers, as well as writers, particularly lacked maturity, he hardly allowed for the fact that as to this they distinctly disagreed with him.

Since his day the press has seen great changes. Mr. Talcott Williams in his jewel of a book, "The Newspaper Man," records them impressively as well as vividly. Perhaps in segregating its juvenilia in its other columns it has given its maturity the opportunity to expand editorially as, in many admirable instances, has markedly occurred, though there were certainly giants in those days; any old newspaper man would be recreant to forget it. And development in style has scarcely kept pace with this evolution. The familiar phenomenon in old days of a beautiful piece of writing has grown notably rare, and such a figure as Mr. Kingsbury wears in consequence an air of comparative isolation and survival. With more reason than elsewhere no doubt, but still even here not a justifying amount, in journalism as well as in literature of more permanent purpose, not merely the poetic but the æsthetic element entire has often been excluded from our prose in frigid disregard of its own æsthetic tradition.

Moments when the "craze" of "æstheticism" flourished naturally did this tradition no good, and perhaps it was because, like Pre-Raphaelitism earlier, it became spent with its own extravagances, that the movement subsided, languidly resigning its torch to reactionary hands. In the sense that a man may be said to personify a movement, it may be said that Oscar Wilde extinguished the flame that Pater had lighted. Mr. Yeats says that Wilde "believed himself to value nothing but words in their emotional associations and he had turned his style to a parade as though it were his show and he Lord Mayor." As in the Restoration reaction which succeeded the Puritan orgy of asceticism, according to Arnold, people said: "This type at any rate is amiss; we are not going to be all like *that*," sunflowers or not, and followed after the prophets of a new dispensation, the prophets of the present day, Samuel Butler and Shaw. I must quote what Mr. Yeats says of them, too: "He [Shaw] was right to claim Samuel Butler for his master, for Butler was the first Englishman to make the discovery that it is possible to write with great effect without music, without style either good or bad, to eliminate from the mind all emotional implication and to prefer plain water to every vintage. . . . Presently [after attending a series of Shaw representations] I had a nightmare that I was haunted by a sewing-machine that clicked and shone, but the incredible thing was that the machine smiled, smiled perpetually." One understands Wilde's remark about Shaw, also reported by Mr. Yeats, to the effect that "he had no enemies but was much disliked by his many friends."

Clicking and glitter do vary the current clarity and simplicity on occasion but do not modify them emotionally.

WILLIAM CRARY BROWNELL

For such modification, once admitting the element of feeling to the realm of prose, once agreeing that prose need not always be prosaic, the most fruitful source both of inspiration and of guidance — aside from special study and attentive reading — I think myself would be fellowship with the other arts, the arts concerned with beauty as poetry is and as in the same degree and for the most part no doubt prose is not. Our ideas are perhaps not very clear on this point. Very likely it is more or less vaguely held that beauty is an abstraction which, like style, no one can adequately define; that in the prose explicitly devoted to it — as in much of the poetry and in fact a good deal of the plastic arts, up to their latest phase, at any rate — it oftenest appears as inanity; that, the masters apart, as heretofore understood and incarnated it is apt to be allied with conventionality; and that clarity and simplicity inherently possess a superior order of it after all. On the other hand our prose, at all events, sometimes possesses more than is recognized. "Main Street," for example, so far as quality is concerned, seems to me hardly less remarkable — more so, alas, than its successor — for traces of beauty in landscape and atmosphere and other pictoriality, intimately observed and vividly recorded, than for being Main Street. Yet I do not remember hearing or seeing any notice of its containing any beauty whatever. One could hardly have a better example, if I am right about the fact, of the general insensitiveness to the æsthetic element as shown by a general failure to recognize it unprepared.

The truth is that familiarity with the æsthetic field is not as yet a part of our general culture, and until it is, prose will be the last phase of our cultivated expression to realize its potentialities of beauty and therefore of style. Phases of painting at present equally laggard are likely to be less lasting, being not so much dull to beauty as radically divorced from it and therefore promising a readier reaction. I do not mean that the fine arts have not received conspicuous attention from English and American writers of distinction in

444

this especial field. Quite the contrary is the fact. Our museums too are multiplying, as is well known, and there are striking instances by the score of the progressive dissemination among us of the plastic arts (including, of course, architecture in the term as susceptible of "modeling" in a high degree) and eminently of music. There is, however, a tremendous numerical disproportion between our writers and, I will not say our fine-art practitioners, alone, but even our connoisseurs and professionals put together. Everyone who knows how to read and write is a partially — even though sometimes quite partially — equipped writer, whereas a difficult technic must at the outset be met and mastered in any other art. But the matter is essentially not one of numbers. Essentially it resides in the fact that the cultivated writer, as such, does not in the least feel a knowledge of æsthetic principles, data, and phenomena to be incumbent on him. With this exception *nihil humani,* so far as it comes in his way, escapes his interest or at least pointedly disengages his responsibility. But the exception has only to be pondered to appear extravagant.

Naturally, there are reasons for it. Prominent among them no doubt is the belief that the fine arts constitute an esoteric field from which the profane are warned off by the professional. This belief has been decidedly, and I should say disastrously, fostered by such artists as take their cue from Whistler's dictum that their work should be received by the public in silence — like mathematics, as Whistler said, or perhaps like medicine, a view unfavorable to its widespread absorption and rather more in accord with the initial reception of Whistler's own work by the expert "remnant" composed of his fellow-artists. His work owed the beginnings of its subsequent vogue mainly, perhaps, to the critics and connoisseurs, unless we except Whistler's own talk about it — for which everyone now can see that we ought all to be grateful. However, the professional view also seems supported by the *a priori* consideration that those who handle the tools should be the best judges of the result.

The retort that to judge of an egg it is not necessary to be a hen is hardly convincing refutation, though perhaps on a level with some of the discussion. If this had not been proved interminable, the *amour propre* of each side being enlisted, one might still further suggest the well-known difficulty of judging the forest when among its trees, and the likelihood of an equally serious, not to say far more extended, lay study of results matching a superior professional concentration on process. The result of the Squeers system of learning its spelling by washing the window was the misspelling of "window," and half the expert world in the sphere of fine art can at almost any time be set against the other half on any burning question of *expertise,* the question itself only to be decided later by a general consensus including judges of greater detachment. Even if ever decided, one may add, since the courts of last resort will always be temperamentally divided.

The point mainly pertinent here is that this close corporation view operates infallibly, if insensibly, to accentuate the apathy of the generally cultivated regarding a field which the workers in it guard so jealously from trespass. The public, debarred from entering, remains cold to invitations to look over the fence — even at last, it may be, for the mere "once over" glance. The sincere belief of executants, in a neccessarily narrow and "intensive" practice, that nobody else does or can know anything about it seems, moreover, as I say, logically plausible enough to persuade the public that it is sound. The public forgets that it is open to the critic to know at least all that the artist — many artists — can tell him, besides having resources of his own, and that unless silence is to be rigidly prescribed all around he is as a commentator something of an executant himself. At any rate the result of provincially forcing the esoteric note is not to quiet the critics but to estrange the public. It may be quite negligible as it affects the executant hierarchy, though one might have at least the same doubt about that as the innovating executant in his turn has about the academic. But its obvious effect on the general cultivated public is far-reaching.

And the prose writer as such, belonging essentially quite as much to the general cultivated public as to the profession of letters, so far as any technical classification distinguishes them and, as regards the fine arts, being altogether to be classed with this public, remains — in very much the proportion in which æsthetics is a sealed book to him — uninspired by the element of beauty, or, say, by a third of the ideal universe. Here and there a poet may arise destitute of acquaintance with the monumental and grandiose *corpus* of æsthetic expression that mankind began in the dawn of time and has been adding to ever since, and with its philosophy; nature may inspire as well as produce him. But the prose writer is likely to have to forego the element of beauty in some definite proportion to his ignorance of art. As regards the element of style in general (the æsthetic element in his own style so far as his workmanship is conscious art), he must be at a palpable disadvantage if his equipment is defective and his inspiration limited by the absence of that intimacy with ordered and rhythmic beauty in which all art must live in order to be living art — major or minor, great or small, poetry or prose. In any case, minus art, prose will cease to have the style which is its æsthetic element. So far as prose is concerned Mr. Middleton Murry will be quite right in saying "there are styles but no style" — a logical result of his (not very consistent) exclamation elsewhere: "As if the effort to be unmistakable were not the very secret of style!" A secret, then, one may remark, possibly possessed but certainly not disclosed by linguistic pedants — such as, for a shining example, Fitzedward Hall — in whom this effort is most unmistakable. "The true writer," Mr. Murry proceeds, "insists that the reader shall feel exactly what he intends him to feel." If the writer's effort to be unmistakable is successful the reader may have a perception the more, but how is this perception to be converted into feeling? To feel exactly what the writer intends him to feel merely because the writer makes his meaning clear would often, even if possible, be decidedly risky. He might not like the feeling. The notion is exorbitant. As a mere means of securing cogency, sufficient style to engage the emotions has its value. The most elementary rhetoric prescribes the principles of persuasion as well as those of exposition.

However, the current theory of prose style as consisting of clarity and simplicity is more modest and does not involve illusions about persuasion through anything but substance. What it does involve is, as I began by saying, a confusion of what conditions style with what constitutes it. No one would deny the claims of clarity and simplicity as conditioning elements of style. Even if its burden is rococo its own structure should be simple enough to make definite and coherent the etravagance it is designed to exhibit. But neither clarity nor simplicity is properly to be called an æsthetic element unless it be made to count as one. Neither has anything intrinsically in common with order and movement, harmony and rhythm. In literary composition, in fact, they are not so much qualities of style as of diction and phraseology. Substance once simplified, diction that is not simple lacks taste. There is no excuse for elaborating mere communication; modern euphuism anywhere is absurd. And phraseology that is not clear merely calls for clarification. But it is misleading to regard either clarity or simplicity as an æsthetic factor unless it be vivified into activity and become itself a sensuous element instead of a mere conductor, unless clarity be felt as clearness sensible, and simplicity be accented as such. To reduce style to clarity and simplicity and then reduce clarity and simplicity to imperceptibility in the interest of removing all "barriers" between writer and reader as sometimes advocated (and recently rather naïvely praised in Hudson, for instance) is, as regards style, to effect a reduction to absurdity. Style is interpretative not obstructive, but it is no more a mere vehicle than it is a barrier, and if qualities like clearness and simplicity are to replace or even to color it, they must acquire its character — its character as an element, and an æsthetic element, of expression instead of as altogether a conduit of thought. Lucidity will elucidate not less nor more but better if it is made to count as envelope and atmosphere, thus increasing the sense of the whole in the substance to be communicated — made stylistic, in a word. Clarity in a landscape-painter's technic, for example, is a lens rather than a vacuum. Its aim is not to aid the observer to scrutinize nature, but to enhance her — not being a scientific instrument but an æsthetic value; and in the same sense as that in which Arnold declares: "Truth of science does not become truth of religion till it is made religious," we may say that clarity does not become an æsthetic element until it is made æsthetic.

As to simplicity, it may very well illustrate taste without achieving style. There is more style as style, though style misplaced, in affectation than in artlessness, more — to make the French distinction that Arnold domesticated — in *simplesse* than in *simplicité*. The simplicity of Quaker costume has the effect of style only by contrasting in its rarity with the general apparel. A whole community in this tasteful garb might have order in the sense of orderliness, but its order would be inorganic and would lack movement — contrasting but tamely with, for example, the Spanish black that, even when excessive, unifies the rainbow of brilliant accentuation with which it is besprinkled, everywhere intimating the sense for style existent in Spanish carriage and character, and emergent, condensed and vivid, in Calderon and Velasquez. The Japanese practice of confining domestic decoration to one kakemono at a time in a room, though by giving relief to the picture it achieves a certain play of emphasis, should in the long run be felt as rather meager in style. When an admirer of the Washington Monument alleged its simplicity in justification of his admiration, he evoked the suggestion that no monument would be still simpler. The Greek "nothing too much" is a

counsel of taste, and as applied to style should be supple-
mented by a caution against nothing at all. Leopold Eidlitz,
to whom the Victorian architecture of New York owed so
much, offered, when the Brooklyn Bridge was building, to
make the towers architectural. At the time, public opinion
would have sustained the official declination he met with,
and the bridge remains the strictly engineering monument
it was then considered and considered preferable to have
it. Eidlitz was a native of Prague and would perhaps have
given New York something comparable to the Karlsbrücke
towers, not as appropriate as the Pont Alexandre III is to
Paris, nor as splendid, but in any case a monument of style
which it is still exasperating to remember we have lost. As
it is, we have the simplicity of masonry as masonry to
console us. Subversive as the fact may be of Ruskin's
theory of art, the cave as a place of worship, even if in given
instances it have more beauty, has undoubtedly less style
though more simplicity than the cathedral. The simplicity
of the nude in art should surely have style, but I imagine
that the nude in life is apt to lack it. Perhaps devotees of
simplicity at all hazards are so sweeping because in all
deliberate art they scent affectation. But such timidity is
in this category of circumstances too preponderantly moral.
There is, plainly, simplicity and simplicity. That which is
the result of simplification is quite different from either
monotony or the miscellaneity that is practically undifferen-
tiated — a principle scrupulously observed by the modern
"window-dresser" in whose art style, too often rejected of
other builders, finds a welcome refuge. The academic
haberdasher whose "correct apparel" is instinct with style
that is standard, is his congenial ally. New York, accordingly, particularly Fifth Avenue, owes to both a debt larger
than is generally recognized.

As an achievement — during which it acquires its style —
simplicity has quite other sanctions than the originally
meager. Exiguity of expression may give substance a
salience of contrast equivalent to that of the emphasis of

energy, but no more than this converse excess is blankness properly to be called style. Saint-Gaudens's statue in the Washington cemetery which has fully as much style as the more complicated work more instinctive with him when he was not, as it were, working in unison with artists of the strain of LaFarge and Henry Adams — and they newly returned from the Land of Nirvana — gets its style from its simplification. There is nothing simple in its conception any more than artless in its inspiration. Simplicity and the mystic or even the mysterious are mutually antithetical. The celebrated pentameter,

> " A Mr. Wilkinson, a clergyman."

in parody of Wordsworth's simplicity, attributed to Fitzgerald, has a certain effect of style because it is, contrariwise, *simplesse* — Tennysonian simplicity, one may say, remembering Arnold's citation of " Dora " as an example of the quality. What it parodies, indeed, is less the poet's poetry than his simplicity in deeming poetry that which but for his theory he would have seen as prose. Thus even subtleties as well as broader relevancies substantiate the quite radical distinction between simple simplicity and style. And just as clarity is only to be made æsthetic by density sufficient to render it perceptible, æsthetic simplicity must be the result of simplification in the treatment, given complexity in the theme.

One can, in fancy, see miscellaneity acquire style in the actual process of being simplified. One can, in fact, see in "modern art" the process itself apparently arrested for inspection often on the hither side of any result — other than the half-way effect of simplification proceeding, instead of either style achieved or simplicity attained. The notablest effects of the kind are reached in sculpture, perhaps, and by a reversal of the Beaux-Arts technic of proceeding from the general to the particular. That of Elie Nadelmann has sometimes more than a theoretic interest — though plainly less for others than for the enthusiastic artist himself. Of course simplification may be carried so far as out of mere momentum to o'erleap style, as it were, and alight, a little dazed, in featureless simplicity. On the other hand a theme may be too simple to simplify. People speak of simplicity as if in itself it were an æsthetic value, like size. Size includes its corollary, scale, and though even without scale it is often extremely impressive — its impressiveness as a compositional effect is due less to the artist than to our creating a relation by unconsciously assuming our own scale as an element of contrast, and any relation is a rudiment of style. I remember someone speaking of the impressiveness of the old Mullet post-office at Broadway and Park Row to Eidlitz, who replied that a pile of barrels of the same dimensions would have more — conveying, as unminimized by senseless modeling, a more unmixed sense of the superiority of size. Thus, possibly, the Pyramids — mountains, certainly — "lord it o'er us," as Sterling says is the Dædalian way.

However, featureless simplicity — either implicit in the theme or the result of exaggerated simplification — clearly can't be helped out in this way. Like clarity, simplicity must itself actively contribute to that sense of the whole which it is also the function of style to accentuate in the parts. Converted into active values, both perform a stylistic as well as a rhetorical service in illuminating and vivifying those intrinsic constituents of style in the abstract, order and movement, harmony and rhythm. But surely neither their utility as rhetorical fundamentals, nor their stylistic value, once transformed from conditions into constituents of style, is impeached by denying their entire and exclusive sufficiency for a prose ideal that need in nowise exclude them in including the element of beauty as well. In fine, if prose is an art and not merely a craft, one of the essentials of prose style is beauty. Conversely, certainly, any prose of which the burden is, even remotely, related to *belles-lettres* is irrefutably irrelevant in so far as it is not art, and unless it be science. But I think one may go farther and maintain that all prose in so far as it is *literature* is entitled to some measure of beauty and bound to the requirements of art — in which blend of privilege and obligation it is best sustained by the inspiration, and best forwarded by the guidance, of the genius of style.

EDGAR WATSON HOWE

1853–

53 *Aphorisms*

AFTER a woman has looked at a man three or four times, she notices something about him that should be changed; and, after an acquaintance of a few weeks, she will suggest that the change be made.

Women are forever saying they Expected So Much of their husbands, and that their disillusion was therefore Cruel. As a matter of fact, women say that as a means of Influencing Their Husbands for Good. Every bride has a father, and she has lived around him long enough to know a good deal about him. She *hopes* her husband will be different, but she has heard other women talk enough to cause her to suspect that he won't be. Girls are not as afraid of men and mice as they pretend. We know as much about marrying as we know about life; there is no excuse to be disappointed about either.

From the dawn of language, women have grandly said to men: "I should think you would be ashamed of yourselves!" And the men have been ashamed, although they are more useful than women, and more reliable in the real essentials. Men are always better liked than women as customers at stores, as guests at hotels; in all the practical affairs of life. They are easier regulated, because they have been whipped more. And when it comes to usefulness, men lead by a big majority, in spite of the talk about them, most of it true. Men not only lead in producing the necessities of life; they lead as cooks, milliners, dressmakers, although if women have studied anything, they have studied these things. Women give more attention to music than men, ten times over, yet the best fiddlers, song writers and piano players are men. Women have more sentiment than men, yet the most successful romances and plays are written by men, as are the best books of philosophy. Women are nearly all religious, while men are mainly skeptics, yet there is almost no such thing as a woman preacher. Women believe more in medicine than men, and use more of it, yet the men are the doctors. A woman runs every home. Who builds and supports it? A man who is ashamed of himself; a man who regrets that he is not as good as a woman.

The world cannot be ruled by Love. Love is so generous it makes promises it cannot fulfill: it gives worlds when it is as poor as a church.

Love is usually regarded as a divine thing everyone should toy with, but it is a devilish little affair that should be closely watched. Rum and cigarettes, arch fiends though they are, have never bothered me; but love has been whipping me vigorously ever since I was twelve years old.

I have read many times of a certain modern man who gave his life for the benefit of mankind. The story commonly told is that he was young, happily married, successful in his profession, and in good health. Yet he gave up his life that other men might *know* one fact — one fact about one disease. No such man ever lived. Every martyr believed he would be able to escape martyrdom. There never was, and there never will be, a man who knowingly accepts pain and death for the good of mankind. All such stories are told by men who are making a pretense of doing more for the world than they really are.

If a man succeeds in life, he must do it in spite of the efforts of others to pull him down. There is nothing in the idea that people are willing to help those who are willing to help themselves. People are willing to help the man who *can't* help himself, but as soon as a man is able to help himself, and does it, they join in "talking" about him, and making his life as uncomfortable as possible.

Financial sense is knowing that many men will promise to do a certain thing, and fail to do it.

Man is still a savage to the extent that he has little respect for anything that cannot hurt him.

Nearly every man likes to think he is such a devil that it is proper for quiet, inoffensive people to pray for him; indeed, he thinks it not beyond reason for some good person to *die* for him. Still, he does not imagine he is altogether a bad fellow: he thinks his instincts are good; that he has a good heart; that on occasion he would do a great deal for others — he even has visions of becoming a reformer, and saving others.

Every man who says he is not selfish is a liar; all are selfish. The man who says to the world that he desires only its good, is a liar; a greater liar than I am. And I am a liar; all men are. But I have conquered untruthfulness to an extent; to an extent greater than many of those who pretend much more. I tell the truth nine times out of ten; and am ashamed of the tenth slip. I habitually and cheerfully give freely to those less fortunate; more so than many who announce that they are without sin. I will not lie about myself: others do it habitually, and call their lying virtue. No man's talk about doing good is greater than his accomplishment in doing good. I know what men are; I know two different machines cannot be made in the same mold. I know what has happened when a child is born; what will happen as he lives and when he dies. You liars do not fool as many as you think: I know what is said about you behind your backs, and it is usually the truth.

Every man is better for being watched. Put your affairs unreservedly into any hands, and your agent will exact the best of it, when he might have been fair if watched and frequently checked up.

A writing man is something of a black sheep, like the village fiddler; occasionally the fiddler becomes a violinist, and is a credit to his family, but as a rule he would have done better had his tendency been toward saving, industry, and what we call business. A fiddler's notions about practical things are notoriously bad; the notions of a writer or orator are apt to be. When you go to hear a fiddler play, you do not seek him later, and ask his advice about matters of real moment; you know he is notably weak in such things: for advice about your affairs of importance you call on a banker, merchant, manufacturer, farmer, mechanic, or other expert. So it doesn't make much difference what the literary men say in their writing; their idea is to entertain: to make you laugh, or cry, or indignant. For instruction, go to the professors in the University of Fact: indeed, you needn't go to them: they'll look you up.

There is a great library of books; every man of reasonable intelligence will look into it, to see what it contains that may be of value to him. And its value is not anywhere near as great as has been intimated; probably seven-tenths of it is rubbish, although much rubbish is curious and interesting. Select the wisest and best man in your community, and he knows more than Adam Smith; with his years he will have acquired a practical philosophy better fitted to your needs than the philosophy of Marcus Aurelius. There are a number of things you do not know. Who knows it better? Those who have lived longer, had more experience, and have greater and clearer brain power. And there are plenty of such men in your community willing to talk, if you will listen, and get rid of the disposition to tell what *you* think.

EDGAR WATSON HOWE

No man may write interestingly and keep within the bounds of your beliefs. He must occasionally go so far as to pleasantly shock you, and cause the uncomfortable feeling that a good man cannot follow him all the way. The author who aims to write nothing offensive to anyone presently writes only hymns and leaflets explaining the Sunday school lesson; and then only children read him; and they read him because they fear they will be scolded if they do not. Only interesting writers are actually read. But an interesting writer with wrong opinions is not necessarily mischievous. If I come across a book really worth while, it does not change my beliefs; if the author attacks an opinion I hold, he confirms it, and I have the added pleasure of thinking: "Here is a smart man, and a good writer; but how blind he is in the presence of Truth!" A mere book or newspaper article does not change your opinions. The blood you inherited has much to do with them; your experiences in life gradually form them, and you cannot change in an hour or a moment to oblige a good writer or talker. So I beg that you do not neglect good writers because you have heard they have false notions.

How we love the word Liberty! Yet how many men, women and children have been saved by lack of it! In every house a signboard might be erected reading: "No liberty in this house!" At the entrance to every town, a signboard containing these words might be erected: "No liberty in this town!" And you will find a policeman at every corner to carry out the orders on the signboard. In New York harbor, a huge signboard might truthfully read: "No liberty in this country!" Why have we judges, jails, police officers? To punish those who think they are free to do as they please. Why is there a switch in every home? To punish children who think they are free. We are not free; it was never intended we should be. A book of rules is placed in our cradles, and we never get rid of it until we reach our graves. *Then* we are free, and only then.

The fact that good conduct is of first importance is never actually in question. No one doubts it; thieves do not. All parents teach it; it is taught in all schools, and in every shop and business place. Learning is not necessary in acquiring the simple lessons of life, although learning emphasizes them. We teach our animal servants every lesson we teach ourselves. Horses, and cows, and dogs, are taught manners, and, beyond their power to learn, we control them with fences and halters. If an animal becomes a menace to life, and is dangerous, we confine it, or put it to death, as we do dangerous men. There are many confusing teachers, but as to the simple facts, no one need go astray: we know them as we know we live.

The first excuse of every professional teacher of morality is that the people do not know the importance of good conduct, and that he is a noble man in imparting the information. The people do know; the dullest domestic animal knows, and hurries out of the way of a blow when found in a place it does not belong.

The thief pretends to practise the habits of respectable men; fallen women, when in public, try to behave as decent women do. Virtue must be valuable, if men and women of all degrees pretend to have it.

Anyone who bets on his judgment against the judgment of the world, will be punished for folly. In everything in which man is interested, the world knows what is best for him. It has learned from experience, best of all teachers. Millions of men have lived millions of years, and tried everything.

GEORGE SANTAYANA

1863–

54 *Love*

TRUE love, it used to be said, is love at first sight. Manners have much to do with such incidents, and the race which happens to set at a given time the fashion in literature makes its temperament public and exercises a sort of contagion over all men's fancies. If women are rarely seen and ordinarily not to be spoken to; if all imagination has to build upon is a furtive glance or casual motion, people fall in love at first sight. For they must fall in love somehow, and any stimulus is enough if none more powerful is forthcoming. When society, on the contrary, allows constant and easy intercourse between the sexes, a first impression, if not reinforced, will soon be hidden and obliterated by others. Acquaintance becomes necessary for love when it is necessary for memory. But what makes true love is not the information conveyed by acquaintance, nor any circumstantial charms that may be therein discovered: it is still a deep and dumb instinctive affinity, an inexplicable emotion seizing the heart, an influence organizing the world, like a luminous crystal, about one magic point. So that although love seldom springs up suddenly in these days into anything like a full-blown passion, it is sight, it is presence, that makes in time a conquest over the heart; for all virtues, sympathies, confidences will fail to move a man to tenderness and to worship unless a poignant effluence from the object envelops him, so that he begins to walk, as it were, in a dream.

Not to believe in love is a great sign of dullness. There are some people so indirect and lumbering that they think all real affection must rest on circumstantial evidence. But a finely constituted being is sensitive to its deepest affinities. This is precisely what refinement consists in, that we may feel in things immediate and infinitesimal a sure premonition of things ultimate and important. Fine senses vibrate at once to harmonies which it may take long to verify; so sight is finer than touch, and thought than sensation. Well-bred instinct meets reason half-way, and is prepared for the consonances that may follow. Beautiful things, when taste is formed, are obviously and unaccountably beautiful. The grounds we may bring ourselves to assign for our preferences are discovered by analyzing those preferences, and articulate judgments follow upon emotions which they ought to express, but which they sometimes sophisticate. So too the reasons we give for love either express what it feels or else are insincere, attempting to justify at the bar of reason and convention something which is far more primitive than they and underlies them both.

True instinct can dispense with such excuses. It appeals to the event and is justified by the response which nature makes to it. It is of course far from infallible; it cannot dominate circumstances, and has no discursive knowledge; but it is presumably true, and what it foreknows is always essentially possible. Unrealizable it may indeed be in the jumbled context of this world, where the Fates, like an absent-minded printer, seldom allow a single line to stand perfect and unmarred.

The profoundest affinities are those most readily felt, and they remain a background and standard for all happiness. If we trace them out we succeed. If we put them by, although in other respects we may call ourselves happy, we inwardly know that we have dismissed the ideal, and all that was essentially possible has not been realized. Love in that case still owns a hidden and potential object, and we sanctify, perhaps, whatever kindnesses or partialities we indulge in by a secret loyalty to something impersonal and unseen. Such reserve, such religion, would not have been necessary had things responded to our first expectations. We might then have identified the ideal with the object that happened to call it forth. The life of reason might have been led instinctively, and we might have been guided by nature herself into the ways of peace.

GEORGE SANTAYANA

As it is, circumstances, false steps, or the mere lapse of time, force us to shuffle our affections and take them as they come, or as we are suffered to indulge them. A mother is followed by a boyish friend, a friend by a girl, a girl by a wife, a wife by a child, a child by an idea. A divinity passes through these various temples; they may all remain standing, and we may continue our cult in them without outward change, long after the god has fled from the last into his native heaven. We may try to convince ourselves that we have lost nothing when we have lost all. We may take comfort in praising the mixed and perfunctory attachments which cling to us by force of habit and duty, repeating the empty names of creatures that have long ceased to be what we once could love, and assuring ourselves that we have remained constant, without admitting that the world, which is in irreparable flux, has from the first been betraying us.

Ashamed of being so deeply deceived, we may try to smile cynically at the glory that once shone upon us, and call it a dream. But cynicism is wasted on the ideal. There is indeed no idol ever identified with the ideal which honest experience, even without cynicism, will not some day unmask and discredit. Every real object must cease to be what it seemed, and none could ever be what the whole soul desired. Yet what the soul desires is nothing arbitrary. Life is no objectless dream. Everything that satisfies at all, even if partially and for an instant, justifies aspiration and rewards it. Existence, however, cannot be arrested; and only the transmissible forms of things can endure, to match the transmissible faculties which living beings hand down to one another. The ideal is accordingly significant, perpetual, and as constant as the nature it expresses; but it can never itself exist, nor can its particular embodiments endure.

Love is accordingly only half an illusion; the lover, but not his love, is deceived. His madness, as Plato taught, is divine; for though it be folly to identify the idol with the god, faith in the god is inwardly justified. That egregious idolatry may therefore be interpreted ideally and given a symbolic scope worthy of its natural causes and of the mystery it comes to celebrate. The lover knows much more about absolute good and universal beauty than any logician or theologian, unless the latter, too, be lovers in disguise. Logical universals are terms in discourse, without vital ideality, while traditional gods are at best natural existences, more or less indifferent facts. What the lover comes upon, on the contrary, is truly persuasive, and witnesses to itself, so that he worships from the heart and beholds what he worships. That the true object is no natural being but an ideal form essentially eternal and capable of endless embodiments, is far from abolishing its worth; on the contrary, this fact makes love ideally relevant to generation, by which the human soul and body may be forever renewed, and at the same time makes it a thing for large thoughts to be focused upon, a thing representing all rational aims.

Whenever this ideality is absent and a lover sees nothing in his mistress but what everyone else may find in her, loving her honestly in her unvarnished and accidental person, there is a friendly and humorous affection, admirable in itself, but no passion or bewitchment of love; she is a member of his group, not a spirit in his pantheon. Such an affection may be altogether what it should be; it may bring a happiness all the more stable because the heart is quite whole, and no divine shaft has pierced it. It is hard to stanch wounds inflicted by a god. The glance of an ideal love is terrible and glorious, foreboding death and immortality together. Love could not be called divine without platitude if it regarded nothing but its nominal object; to be divine it must not envisage an accidental good but the principle of goodness, that which gives other goods their ultimate meaning.

Love is a true natural religion; it has a visible cult, it is kindled by natural beauties and bows to the best symbol it may find for its hope; it sanctifies a natural mystery; and, finally, when understood, it recognizes that what it worshiped under a figure was truly the principle of all good.

GEORGE SANTAYANA

The loftiest edifices need the deepest foundations. Love would never take so high a flight unless it sprung from something profound and elementary. It is accordingly most truly love when it is irresistible and fatal. The substance of all passion, if we could gather it together, would be the basis of all ideals, to which all goods would have to refer. Lovers are vividly aware of this fact: their ideal, apparently so inarticulate, seems to them to include everything. It shares the mystical quality of all primitive life. Sophisticated people can hardly understand how vague experience is at bottom, and how truly that vagueness supports whatever clearness is afterward attained. They cling to the notion that nothing can have a spiritual scope that does not spring from reflection. But in that case life itself, which brings reflection about, would never support spiritual interests, and all that is moral would be unnatural and consequently self-destructive. In truth, all spiritual interests are supported by animal life; in this the generative function is fundamental; and it is therefore no paradox, but something altogether fitting, that if that function realized all it comprises, nothing human would remain outside. Such an ultimate fulfillment would differ of course from a first satisfaction, just as all that reproduction reproduces differs from the reproductive function itself, and vastly exceeds it. All organs and activities which are inherited, in a sense grow out of the reproductive process and serve to clothe it; so that when the generative energy is awakened all that can ever be is virtually called up and, so to speak, made consciously potential; and love yearns for the universe of values.

This secret is gradually revealed to those who are inwardly attentive and allow love to teach them something. A man who has truly loved, though he may come to recognize the thousand incidental illusions into which love may have led him, will not recant its essential faith. He will keep his sense for the ideal and his power to worship. As a harp, made to vibrate to the fingers, gives some music to every wind, so the nature of man, necessarily susceptible to woman, becomes simultaneously sensitive to other influences, and capable of tenderness toward every object. A philosopher, a soldier, and a courtesan will express the same religion in different ways. In fortunate cases love may glide imperceptibly into settled domestic affections, giving them henceforth a touch of ideality; for when love dies in the odor of sanctity people venerate his relics. In other cases allegiance to the ideal may appear more sullenly, breaking out in whims, or in little sentimental practices which might seem half-conventional. Again, it may inspire a religious conversion, charitable works, or even artistic labors. Nature also is often a second mistress that consoles us for the loss of a first.

In all these ways people attempt more or less seriously to lead the life of reason, expressing outwardly allegiance to whatever in their minds has come to stand for the ideal. The machinery which serves reproduction thus finds kindred but higher uses, as every organ does in a liberal life; and what Plato called a desire for birth in beauty may be sublimated even more, until it yearns for an ideal immortality in a transfigured world, a world made worthy of that love which its children have so often lavished on it in their dreams.

PAUL ELMER MORE

1864–

55   *A Hermit's Notes on Thoreau*

NEAR the secluded village of Shelburne that lies along the peaceful valley of the Androscoggin, I took upon myself to live two years as a hermit after a mild Epicurean fashion of my own. Three maiden aunts wagged their heads ominously; my nearest friend inquired cautiously whether there was any taint of insanity in the family; an old gray-haired lady, a veritable saint who had not been soured by her many deeds of charity, admonished me on the utter selfishness and godlessness of such a proceeding. But I clung heroically to my resolution. Summer tourists in that pleasant valley may still see the little red house among the pines, — empty now, I believe; and I dare say gaudy coaches still draw up at the door, as they used to do, when the gaudier bonnets and hats exchanged wondering remarks on the cabalistic inscription over the lintel, or spoke condescendingly to the great dog lying on the steps. As for the hermit within, having found it impossible to educe any meaning from the tangled habits of mankind while he himself was whirled about in the imbroglio, he had determined to try the efficacy of undisturbed meditation at a distance. So deficient had been his education that he was actually better acquainted with the aspirations and emotions of the old dwellers on the Ganges than with those of the modern toilers by the Hudson or the Potomac. He had been deafened by the "indistinguishable roar" of the streets, and could make no sense of the noisy jargon of the market place. But — shall it be confessed? — although he discovered many things during his contemplative sojourn in the wilderness, and learned that the attempt to criticize and not to create literature was to be his labor in this world, nevertheless he returned to civilization as ignorant, alas, of its meaning as when he left it.

However, it is not my intention to justify the saintly old lady's charge of egotism by telling the story of my exodus to the desert; that, perhaps, may come later and at a more suitable time. I wish now only to record the memories of one perfect day in June, when woods and mountains were as yet a new delight.

The fresh odors of morning were still swaying in the air when I set out on this particular day; and my steps turned instinctively to the great pine forest, called the Cathedral Woods, that filled the valley and climbed the hill slopes behind my house. There, many long roads that are laid down in no map wind hither and thither among the trees, whose leafless trunks tower into the sky and then meet in evergreen arches overhead. There,

The tumult of the times disconsolate

never enters, and no noise of the world is heard save now and then, in winter, the ringing strokes of the woodchopper at his cruel task. How many times I have walked those quiet cathedral aisles, while my great dog paced faithfully on before! Underfoot the dry, purple-hued moss was stretched like a royal carpet; and at intervals a glimpse of the deep sky, caught through an aperture in the groined roof, reminded me of the other world, and carried my thoughts still farther from the desolating memories of this life. Nothing but pure odors were there, sweeter than cloistral incense; and murmurous voices of the pines, more harmonious than the chanting of trained choristers; and in the heart of the wanderer nothing but tranquillity and passionless peace.

Often now the recollection of those scenes comes floating back upon his senses when, in the wakeful seasons of a summer night, he hears the wind at work among the trees; even in barren city streets some sound or spectacle can act upon him as a spell, banishing for a moment the hideous contention of commerce, and placing him beneath the restful shadows of the pines. May his understanding cease its function, and his heart forget to feel, when the memory of those days has utterly left him and he walks in the world without this consolation of remembered peace.

Nor can I recollect that my mind, in these walks, was much called away from contemplation by the petty curiosities of the herbalist or birdlorist, for I am not one zealously addicted to scrutinizing into the minuter secrets of Nature. It never seemed to me that a flower was made sweeter by knowing the construction of its ovaries, or assumed a new importance when I learned its trivial or scientific name. The wood thrush and the veery sing as melodiously to the uninformed as to the subtly curious. Indeed, I sometimes think a little ignorance is wholesome in our communion with Nature, until we are ready to part with her altogether. She is feminine in this as in other respects, and loves to shroud herself in illusions, as the Hindus taught in their books. For they called her Máyâ, the very person and power of deception, whose sway over the beholder must end as soon as her mystery is penetrated.

Dear as the sound of the wood thrush's note still is to my ears, something of charm and allurement has gone from it since I have become intimate with the name and habits of the bird. As a child born and reared in the city, that wild, ringing call was perfectly new and strange to me when, one early dawn, I first heard it during a visit to the Delaware Water Gap. To me whose ears had grown familiar only with the rumble of paved streets, the sound was like a reiterated unearthly summons inviting me from my narrow prison existence out into a wide and unexplored world of impulse and adventure. Long afterwards I learned the name of the songster whose note had made so strong an impression on my childish senses, but still I associate the song with the grandiose scenery, with the sheer forests and streams and the rapid river of the Water Gap. I was indeed almost a man — though the confession may sound incredible in these days — before I again heard the wood thrush's note, and my second adventure impressed me almost as profoundly as the first. In the outer suburbs of the city where my home had always been, I was walking one day with a brother, when suddenly out of a grove of laurel oaks sounded, clear and triumphant, the note which I remembered so well, but which had come to have to my imagination the unreality and mystery of a dream of long ago. Instantly my heart leapt within me. " It is the fateful summons once more! " I cried; and, with my companion who was equally ignorant of bird-lore, I ran into the grove to discover the wild trumpeter. That was a strange chase in the fading twilight, while the unknown songster led us from tree to tree, ever deeper into the woods. Many times we saw him on one of the lower boughs, but could not for a long while bring ourselves to believe that so wondrous a melody should proceed from so plain a minstrel. And at last, when we had satisfied our-selves of his identity, and the night had fallen, we came out into the road with a strange solemnity hanging over us. Our

ears had been opened to the unceasing harmonies of creation, and our eyes had been made aware of the endless
drama of natural life. We had been initiated into the lesser
mysteries; and if the sacred pageantry was not then, and
never was to be, perfectly clear to our understanding, the
imagination was nevertheless awed and purified.

If the knowledge and experience of years have made me
a little more callous to these deeper influences, at least I
have not deliberately closed the door to them by incautious
prying. Perhaps a long course of wayward reading has
taught me to look upon the world with eyes quite different
from those of the modern exquisite searchers into Nature. I
remember the story of Prometheus, and think his punishment is typical of the penalty that falls upon those who grasp
at powers and knowledge not intended for mankind, — some
nemesis of a more material loneliness and a more barren
pride torturing them because they have turned from human
knowledge to an alien and forbidden sphere. Like Prometheus, they shall in the end cry out in vain: —

> O air divine, and O swift-wingëd winds!
> Ye river fountains, and thou myriad-twinkling
> Laughter of ocean waves! O mother earth!
> And thou, O all-discerning orb o' the sun! —
> To you, I cry to you; behold what I,
> A god, endure of evil from the gods.

Nor is the tale of Prometheus alone in teaching this lesson
of prudence, nor was Greece the only land of antiquity
where reverence was deemed more salutary than curiosity.
The myth of the veiled Isis passed in those days from people
to people, and was everywhere received as a symbol of the
veil of illusion about Nature, which no man might lift with
impunity. And the same idea was, if anything, intensified in
the Middle Ages. The common people, and the Church as
well, looked with horror on such scholars as Pope Gerbert,
who was thought, for his knowledge of Nature, to have sold
himself to the devil; and on such discoverers as Roger
Bacon, whose wicked searching into forbidden things cost

him fourteen years in prison. And even in modern times did not the poet Blake say: "I fear Wordsworth loves nature, and nature is the work of the Devil. The Devil is in us as far as we are nature"? It has remained for an age of skepticism to substitute investigation for awe. After all, can any course of study or open-air pedagogics bring us into real communion with the world about us? I fear much of the talk about companionship with Nature that pervades our summer life is little better than cant and self-deception, and he best understands the veiled goddess who most frankly admits her impenetrable secrecy. The peace that comes to us from contemplating the vast panorama spread out before us is due rather to the sense of a great passionless power entirely out of our domain than to any real intimacy with the hidden deity. It was John Woolman, the famous New Jersey Quaker, who wrote, during a journey through the wilderness of Pennsylvania: "In my traveling on the road, I often felt a cry rise from the center of my mind, thus, 'O Lord, I am a stranger on the earth, hide not thy face from me.'"

But I forget that I am myself traveling on the road; and all this long disquisition is only a chapter of reminiscences, due to the multitudinous singing of the thrushes on this side and that, as we — I and my great dog — trod the high cathedral aisles. After a while the sound of running water came to us above the deeper diapason of the pines, and, turning aside, we clambered down to a brook which we had already learned to make the terminus of our walks. Along this stream we had discovered a dozen secret nooks where man and dog might lie or sit at ease, and to-day I stretched myself on a cool, hollow rock, with my eyes looking up the long, leafy chasm of the brook. Just above my couch the current was dammed by a row of mossy boulders, over which the waters poured with a continual murmur and plash. My head was only a little higher than the pool beyond the boulders, and, lying motionless, I watched the flies weaving a pattern over the surface of the quiet water, and now and then was rewarded by seeing a greedy trout leap into the sunlight to capture one of the winged weavers. Surely, if there is any such thing as real intimacy with Nature, it is in just such secluded spots as this; for the grander scenes require of us a moral enthusiasm which can come to the soul only at rare intervals and for brief moments. From these chosen mountain retreats, one might send to a scientist, busy with his books and instruments and curious to pry into the secret powers of Nature, some such an appeal as this: —

> Brother, awhile your impious engines leave;
>   Nor always seek with flame-compelling wires
> Out of the palsied hand of Zeus to reave
>   His dear celestial fires.
>
> What though he drowse upon a tottering bench,
>   Forgetful how his random bolts are hurled!
> Are you to blame? or is it yours to quench
>   The thunders of the world?
>
> Come learn with me through folly to be wise:
>   Think you by cunning laws of optic lore
> To lend the enamelled fields or burning skies
>   One splendour lacked before?
>
> A wizard footrule to the waves of sound
>   You lay, — hath measure in the song of bird
> Or ever in the voice of waters found
>   One melody erst unheard?
>
> Ah, for a season close your magic books,
>   Your rods and crystals in the closet hide;
> I know in covert ways a hundred nooks,
>   High on the mountain side,
>
> Where through the golden hours that follow noon,
>   Under the greenwood shadows you and I
> May talk of happy lives, until too soon
>   Night's shadows fold the sky.
>
> And while like incense blown among the leaves
>   Our fragrant smoke ascends from carven bowl,
> We'll con the lesser wisdom that deceives
>   The Questioner in the soul,

PAUL ELMER MORE

> And laugh to hoodwink where we cannot rout:——
> Did Bruno of the stubborn heart outbrave,
> Or could the mind of Galileo flout
> The folly of the Grave?

So it seemed to me that the lesser wisdom of quiet content before the face of Nature's mysteries might be studied in the untrained garden of my hermitage. But I have been dreaming and moralizing on the little life about me and the greater life of the world too long. So lying near the level of the still pool I began to read. The volume chosen was the most appropriate to the time and place that could be imagined, — Thoreau's *Walden;* and having entered upon an experiment not altogether unlike his, I now set myself to reading the record of his two years of solitude. I learned many things from that morning's perusal. Several times I had read the *Odyssey* within sight of the sea; and the murmur of the waves on the beach, beating through the rhythm of the poem, had taught me how vital a thing a book might be, and how it could acquire a peculiar validity from harmonious surroundings; but now the reading of Thoreau in that charmed and lonely spot emphasized this commonplace truth in a special manner. *Walden* studied in the closet, and *Walden* mused over under the trees, by running water, are two quite different books. And then, from Thoreau, the greatest by far of our writers on Nature, and the creator of a new sentiment in literature, my mind turned to the long list of Americans who have left, or are still composing, a worthy record of their love and appreciation of the natural world. Our land of multiform activities has produced so little that is really creative in literature or art! Hawthorne and Poe, and possibly one or two others, were masters in their own field; yet even they chose not quite the highest realm for their genius to work in. But in one subject our writers have led the way and are still preëminent: Thoreau was the creator of a new manner of writing about Nature. In its deeper essence his work is inimitable, as it is the voice of a unique personality; but in its superficial aspects it has been taken up by a host of living writers, who have caught something of his method, even if they lack his genius and singleness of heart. From these it was an easy transition to compare Thoreau's attitude of mind with that of Wordsworth and the other great poets of his century who went to Nature for their inspiration, and made Nature-writing the characteristic note of modern verse. What is it in Thoreau that is not to be found in Byron and Shelley and Wordsworth, not to mention old Izaak Walton, Gilbert White of Selborne, and a host of others? It was a rare treat, as I lay in that leafy covert, to go over in memory the famous descriptive passages from these authors, and to contrast their spirit with that of the book in my hand.

As I considered these matters, it seemed to me that Thoreau's work was distinguished from that of his American predecessors and imitators by just these qualities of awe and wonder which we, in our communings with Nature, so often cast away. Mere description, though it may at times have a scientific value, is after all a very cheap form of literature; and, as I have already intimated, too much curiosity of detail is likely to exert a deadening influence on the philosophic and poetic contemplation of Nature. Such an influence is, as I believe, specially noticeable at the present time, and even Thoreau was not entirely free from its baneful effect. Much of his writing, perhaps the greater part, is the mere record of observation and classification, and has not the slightest claim on our remembrance, — unless, indeed, it possesses some scientific value, which I doubt. Certainly the parts of his work having permanent interest are just those chapters where he is less the minute observer, and more the contemplative philosopher. Despite the width and exactness of his information, he was far from having the truly scientific spirit; the acquisition of knowledge, with him, was in the end quite subordinate to his interest in the moral significance of Nature, and the words he read in her obscure scroll were a language of strange mysteries, oftentimes of awe. It is a constant reproach to the prying, self-satisfied habits of small minds to see the reverence of this great-hearted observer before the supreme goddess he so loved and studied.

Much of this contemplative spirit of Thoreau is due to the soul of the man himself, to that personal force which no analysis of character can explain. But, besides this, it has always seemed to me that, more than in any other descriptive writer of the land, his mind is the natural outgrowth, and his essays the natural expression, of a feeling deep-rooted in the historical beginnings of New England; and this foundation in the past gives a strength and convincing force to his words that lesser writers utterly lack. Consider the new life of the Puritan colonists in the strange surroundings of their desert home. Consider the case of the adventurous Pilgrims sailing from the comfortable city of Leyden to the unknown wilderness over the sea. As Governor Bradford wrote, "the place they had thoughts on was some of those vast & unpeopled countries of America, which are frutfull & fitt for habitation, being devoyd of all civill inhabitants, wher ther are only salvage and brutish men, which range up and downe, little otherwise than ye wild beasts of the same." In these vast and unpeopled countries, where beast and bird were strange to the eye, and where "salvage" men abounded, — men who did not always make the land so "fitt" for new inhabitants as Bradford might have desired, — it was inevitable that the mind should be turned to explore and report on natural phenomena and on savage life. It is a fact that some of the descriptions of sea and land made by wanderers to Virginia and Massachusetts have a directness and graphic power, touched occasionally with an element of wildness, that render them even to-day agreeable reading.

This was before the time of Rousseau, and before Gray had discovered the beauty of wild mountain scenery; inevitably the early American writers were chiefly interested in Nature as the home of future colonists, and their books are for the most part semi-scientific accounts of what they studied from a utilitarian point of view. But the dryness of detailed description in the New World was from the first modified and lighted up by the wondering awe of men set down in the midst of the strange and often threatening forces of an untried wilderness; and this sense of awful aloofness, which to a certain extent lay dormant in the earlier writers, did nevertheless sink deep into the heart of New England, and when, in the lapse of time, the country entered into its intellectual renaissance, and the genius came who was destined to give full expression to the thoughts of his people before the face of Nature, it was inevitable that his works should be dominated by just this sense of poetic mystery.

It is this New World inheritance, moreover, — joined, of course, with his own inexplicable personality, which must not be left out of account, — that makes Thoreau's attitude toward Nature something quite distinct from that of the great poets who just preceded him. There was in him none of the fiery spirit of the revolution which caused Byron to mingle hatred of men with enthusiasm for the Alpine solitudes. There was none of the passion for beauty and the voluptuous self-abandonment of Keats; these were not in the atmosphere he breathed at Concord. He was not touched with Shelley's unearthly mysticism, nor had he ever fed

> on the aërial kisses
> Of shapes that haunt thought's wildernesses;

his moral sinews were too stark and strong for that form of mental dissipation. Least of all did he, after the manner of Wordsworth, hear in the voice of Nature any compassionate plea for the weakness and sorrow of the downtrodden. Philanthropy and humanitarian sympathies were to him a desolation and a woe. "Philanthropy is almost the only virtue which is sufficiently appreciated by mankind. Nay, it is greatly overrated; and it is our selfishness which overrates it," he writes. And again: "The philanthropist too often surrounds mankind with the remembrance of his own cast-off griefs as an atmosphere, and calls it sympathy."

Similarly his reliance on the human will was too sturdy to be much perturbed by the inequalities and sufferings of mankind, and his faith in the individual was too unshaken to be led into humanitarian interest in the masses. "Alas! this is the crying sin of the age," he declares, "this want of faith in the prevalence of a man."

But the deepest and most essential difference is the lack of pantheistic reverie in Thoreau. It is this brooding over the universal spirit embodied in the material world which almost always marks the return of sympathy with Nature, and which is particularly noticeable in the writers of the past century. So Lord Byron, wracked and broken by his social catastrophes, turns for relief to the fair scenes of Lake Leman, and finds in the high mountains and placid waters a consoling spirit akin to his own.

> Are not the mountains, waves, and skies, a part
> Of me and of my soul, as I of them?

he asks; and in the bitterness of his human disappointment he would "be alone, and love Earth only for its earthly sake." Shelley, too, "mixed awful talk" with the "great parent," and heard in her voice an answer to all his vague dreams of the soul of universal love. No one, so far as I know, has yet studied the relation between Wordsworth's pantheism and his humanitarian sympathies, but we need only glance at his lines on Tintern Abbey to see how closely the two feelings were interknit in his mind. It was because he felt this

> sense sublime
> Of something far more deeply interfused,
> Whose dwelling is the light of setting suns,
> And the round ocean, and the living air,
> And the blue sky, and in the mind of man;

it was because the distinctions of the human will and the consequent perception of individual responsibility were largely absorbed in this dream of the universal spirit, that he heard in Nature "the still, sad music of humanity," and reproduced

it so sympathetically in his own song. Of all this pantheism, whether attended with revolt from responsibility or
languid reverie or humanitarian dreams, there is hardly a
trace in Thoreau. The memory of man's struggle with the
primeval woods and fields was not so lost in antiquity that
the world had grown into an indistinguishable part of human
life. If Nature smiled upon· Thoreau at times, she was
still an alien creature who succumbed only to his force and
tenderness, as she had before given her bounty, though
reluctantly, to the Pilgrim Fathers. A certain companionship he had with the plants and wild beasts of the field, a
certain intimacy with the dumb earth; but he did not seek
to merge his personality in their impersonal life, or look to
them for a response to his own inner moods; he associated
with them as the soul associates with the body.

More characteristic is his sense of awe, even of dread,
toward the great unsubdued forces of the world. The loneliness of the mountains such as they appeared to the early
adventurers in a strange, unexplored country; the repellent
loneliness of the barren heights frowning down inhospitably
upon the pioneer who scratched the soil at their base; the
loneliness and terror of the dark, untrodden forests, where
the wanderer might stray away and be lost forever, where
savage men were more feared than the wild animals, and
where superstition saw the haunt of the Black Man and of
all uncleanness, — all this tradition of somber solitude
made Nature to Thoreau something very different from the
hills and valleys of Old England. "We have not seen pure
Nature," he says, "unless we have seen her thus vast and
drear and inhuman. . . . Man was not to be associated with
it. It was matter, vast, terrific, — not his Mother Earth
that we have heard of, not for him to tread on, or be buried
in, — no, it were being too familiar even to let his bones lie
there, — the home, this, of Necessity and Fate." After reading Byron's invocation to the Alps as the palaces of Nature;
or the ethereal mountain scenes in Shelley's *Alastor*, where
all the sternness of the everlasting hills is dissolved into rain-

bow hues of shifting light as dainty as the poet's own soul;
or Wordsworth's familiar musings in the vale of Grasmere,
—if, after these, we turn to Thoreau's account of the ascent
of Mount Katahdin, we seem at once to be in the home of
another tradition. I am tempted to quote a few sentences
of that account to emphasize the point. On the mountain
heights, he says of the beholder:

> He is more lone than you can imagine. There is less of substantial
> thought and fair understanding in him than in the plains where men
> inhabit. His reason is dispersed and shadowy, more thin and subtile,
> like the air. Vast, Titanic, inhuman Nature has got him at disad-
> vantage, caught him alone, and pilfers him of some of his divine
> faculty. She does not smile on him as in the plains. She seems to say
> sternly, Why came ye here before your time? This ground is not pre-
> pared for you. Is it not enough that I smile in the valleys? I have
> never made this soil for thy feet, this air for thy breathing, these rocks
> for thy neighbours. I cannot pity nor fondle thee here, but forever
> relentlessly drive thee hence to where I *am* kind.

I do not mean to present the work of Thoreau as equal
in value to the achievement of the great poets with whom
I have compared him, but wish merely in this way to bring
out more definitely his characteristic traits. Yet if his
creative genius is less than theirs, I cannot but think his
attitude toward Nature is in many respects truer and more
wholesome. Pantheism, whether on the banks of the Ganges
or of the Thames, seems to bring with it a spreading taint
of effeminacy; and from this the mental attitude of our
Concord naturalist was eminently free. There is something
tonic and bracing in his intercourse with the rude forces
of the forest; he went to Walden Pond because he had "private business to transact," not for relaxation and mystical
reverie. "To be a philosopher," he said, "is not merely to
have subtle thoughts, nor even to found a school, but so to
love wisdom as to live according to its dictates, a life of
simplicity, independence, magnanimity, and trust"; and by
recurring to the solitudes of Nature he thought he could
best develop in himself just these manly virtues. Nature
was to him a discipline of the will as much as a stimulant to

the imagination. He would, if it were possible, "combine the hardiness of the savages with the intellectualness of the civilized man"; and in this method of working out the philosophical life we see again the influence of long and deep-rooted tradition. To the first settlers, the red man was as much an object of curiosity and demanded as much study as the earth they came to cultivate; their books are full of graphic pictures of savage life, and it should seem as if now in Thoreau this inherited interest had received at last its ripest expression. When he traveled in the wilderness of Maine, he was as much absorbed in learning the habits of his Indian guides as in exploring the woods. He had some innate sympathy or perception which taught him to find relics of old Indian life where others would pass them by, and there is a well-known story of his answer to one who asked him where such relics could be discovered: he merely stooped down and picked an arrowhead from the ground.

And withal his stoic virtues never dulled his sense of awe, and his long years of observation never lessened his feeling of strangeness in the presence of solitary Nature. If at times his writing descends into the cataloging style of the ordinary naturalist, yet the old tradition of wonder was too strong in him to be more than temporarily obscured. Unfortunately, his occasional faults have become in some of his recent imitators the staple of their talent; but Thoreau was preëminently the poet and philosopher of his school, and I cannot do better than close these desultory notes with the quotation of a passage which seems to me to convey most vividly his sensitiveness to the solemn mystery of the deep forest:

We heard [he writes in his *Chesuncook*], come faintly echoing, or creeping from afar, through the moss-clad aisles, a dull, dry, rushing sound, with a solid core to it, yet as if half smothered under the grasp of the luxuriant and fungus-like forest, like the shutting of a door in some distant entry of the damp and shaggy wilderness. If we had not been there, no mortal had heard it. When we asked Joe [the Indian guide] in a whisper what it was, he answered, — "Tree fall."

FRANK MOORE COLBY

1865–1925

56   *A Potted Flower*

OUR most anxious social class is that known by courtesy as the intellectuals. Indeed public anxiety is often the only mark by which you can tell that a person belongs to it; and in many of our higher intellectual circles the fear of a peril to civilization from at least one quarter is a necessary qualification for membership.

Recklessness in the face of contemporary perils is almost unknown among our intellectuals, as is shown in the history of our serious magazines. No serious magazine is ever founded except in the fear of something, and none ever maintains its reputation for seriousness except by the constant expression of anxiety over perils the most diverse. Forty-five separate contemporary perils, any one of which is of itself sufficient to destroy human society, is not an unusual annual average for a serious magazine. Indeed, the most highly esteemed contributions to the weightiest of our magazines at any time in twenty years have all been constructed on this simple formula: *Unless measures are taken at once to avert a certain contemporary peril, civilization will either collapse rapidly or will slowly disappear.* There is the greatest diversity in the perils and in the measures to be taken, but the formula is always the same and the degree of anxiety is constant. A serious contributor will often allow himself a change in the objects of his apprehension, but never in its quantity. Human society is from his point of view the tenderest of little potted flowers, watered by weekly or monthly tears, surviving by a miracle during the intervals of magazine publication. No serious writer is much regarded nowadays unless he is battling to keep it alive.

CIVILIZATION in this country, and perhaps everywhere, was drawing to its close in many a serious magazine article, some years ago. I made rather a conscientious survey of the matter at that time, and I recall to this day some of the shocking particulars. Down goes the dike, said one; and it seems to have been the only dike that could have prevented " our civilization from being engulfed in an overwhelming flood of riches, and from sinking in an orgy of brutality." Now that religion has gone, said another, "the old-fashioned principles of right and wrong have also largely disappeared." Turning a few pages, I found the "ulcer in our new morality " : a few more, and I saw the "canker at the root of education." Then I learned how low this nation was rated by a connoisseur of all the nations of the globe. "Of all the countries I have ever met," said he, as his mind reverted along the parallels of latitude to the thirty-seven populations he had intimately known, "this country, to speak candidly, is the least desirable " ; and so he cast off the country as one who throws away a bad cigar.

I could not deny that civilization was then in danger, but it did seem to me that in any serious magazine it always must be in danger. And it so happened at that time that every writer was spared all anxiety about any actual danger. The one thing not noticed on any of the quaking pages I have mentioned was the shadow of the great war, which was then approaching.

The contributor of a peril to a magazine is not, as a rule, an unhappy person. On the contrary, he is often a large, calm man, with a good appetite, and more cheerful in his mind than we. If one could feel toward any menace to humanity as one used to feel toward tales of Jack the Giant Killer, just believing enough for a little goose-flesh, there would be more fun in it. Any man who is about half convinced that he and a few others are the sole remaining friends of civilization finds some dramatic zest in life. It is a mistake to assume that men who earn their living by anxiety are at all anxious in their private lives.

And it is the same way with all great political despairs in private conversation. The most depressing talkers you ever meet are not themselves personally at all depressed. On the contrary, they are, at bottom, rather gay persons. The hopelessness of the situation really adds, for the purpose of conversation, to its charm, by absolving from the need of any personal effort other than the presumably agreeable one of talking. In middle-aged conversation there is always a certain cosiness in political despair.

58 _Some of the Difficulties of Frolicking_

FROLICKING at midnight, a week or so ago, under the rooftree of the New Amsterdam Theatre, I suddenly realized that I was missing some of the gaiety of the occasion.

Midnight frolicking, I may say in passing, is a technical term, and means simply that, for the most part, I sat perfectly still at a small table, looking from time to time at some young ladies in opera-length tights who stood on a glass platform above me; and that twice I skimmed a little wooden mallet over the floor, and hit the feet of a sleeping youth across the room, and that once I touched a lighted cigarette to a toy balloon — sewn on the parti-colored skirt of a chorus girl — and burst it.

I tried to give to both of these gestures an air of easy abandon, but I think I failed. Several others who were manifestly aiming at abandon seemed to me also to fail. They say it is achieved sometimes — not only here but at several other roof theaters and cabarets — but if so, it does not proceed from any of the habitués; it probably bubbles up from some justice of the Supreme Court who is there, incognito, or from the Governor of a Western state.

The crowd that night had the air of having been there, or

in similar places, very often, and (like most "gay" and expensive New York crowds, amid the vivacities and audacities of the white-light region, the glitter, the movement, the dash, dazzle, and all the rest of it) this crowd was exceedingly dull.

Not that it was inappreciative. It showed the usual "gay" crowd's willingness, and likewise its incapacity, for pleasure. Individually its members had the "gay" crowd's usual look. I do not know that I can describe that expression exactly, but in general I should say it was about what a man's face would naturally come to after watching trained dogs ten nights in succession.

Or, take an ardent, hopeful, sensitive stockbroker and place him every evening where he can see eight young women in tights lying on their backs with bells on their toes which sound an octave, and by which, as they alternately wiggle their feet in the air, they play what is almost a tune. In a week he will have the "gay" expression, or what is known, more technically, as the "Broadway pleasure-face." There is nothing pained or peevish about it. It is merely the face of one who has forgotten his day's work and not yet replaced it with any other human interest. You see it often at the theater when the play is just powerful enough to drive away your own thoughts, but unable to put any others in their place. . . .

Some say these places are like Sodom and Gomorrah. But one knew very well that had there been, the other night, some sudden Babylonian extinguishment, it would have taken off many of the simplest, purest, most primitive folk imaginable — hundreds of people almost ascetic for lack of any external inducement to be otherwise.

What excited us most the other night, for example?

Not the dancing, or the waving of bell-ringing legs, or the tight-rope, or the *demi-monde*. Our one real burst of enthusiasm was when we sang, in unison, "Little Brown Jug" and followed it up with "My Old Kentucky Home," along with two banjoists and the rest of the audience. At that moment we let ourselves go quite wildly. Scratch a New Yorker and you get an up-state deacon, probably of unblemished moral character, but at any rate a perfectly pure deacon in taste. Most desperate New York roués are deacons in their bones.

Lulled by these mild reflections I think I may have drowsed off, and it was then that, pulling myself together, I suddenly realized, as I said before, that I was missing some of the gaiety of the occasion. I hope I was not noticeably asleep, for a little incident soon showed with what suspicion sleep was regarded. One of the men exclaimed, suddenly, "Look at the funny drunks," and threw a mallet across the room at two college youths asleep at their little table.

Other mallets followed, and the crowd seemed determined to wake them up, but fortunately their aim was bad, and the mallets didn't disturb them. To be sure, the boys may possibly have been drinking, but even so, in sleeping they were doing only what was natural, reasonable, and appropriate. They were sensible-looking young men, and their sleep was entirely decorous; no sprawling or snoring or drooping of jaws. Possessed of strong, natural intelligence, and richly sensuous artistic natures — but cut off by the hazards of New York social life from any appropriate outlet — they may have wandered in here merely because they had been almost everywhere else, and perhaps they were responding to the occasion in the manner which, after serious reflection, they had concluded was what such occasions deserved.

Habit and Repetition, those twin divinities, protect the chastity of New York's roof and cabaret celibates. Multitude, and miscellany, and iteration save a man from many an entanglement. One could become enamored of a single cabaret nymph or perhaps of three of them, but no manly amorous bosom could hold, at the same time, forty. Women singly do a good deal of harm. Women in bulk are chastening. Great droves of the most enticing beings in the world do not entice. A single pair of graceful legs — if I may speak coarsely — are appealing. Perhaps two pairs, also. But legs conceived merely as railway ties, stretching over the roofs of twenty theaters and hotels, legs regarded as strings of sausages, reaching almost to the Borough of the Bronx, take on a homely and familiar significance.

And passing rapidly from one gay place to another often has a strangely sobering effect. Too many legs together sometimes look like the monuments in Woodlawn Cemetery, as you rush past it in the train.

It is the same way with backs. The first eight or ten backs do, naturally, engage the attention, but the eye that has roamed over four or five acres of backs is as safely at home with them as in a cow-pasture.

Hence the air of fatigue, almost of domesticity, on the faces of the habitually gay. When temptations march monotonously in regiments, one waits for them to pass by.

GEORGE ADE

1866—

59 The Fable of the Misdirected Sympathy and the Come-Back of the Proud Steam-Fitter

ONE Day a lowly Steam-Fitter who received only Seventy Cents an Hour for filling his Pipe was sent to do a Job of Repairing in the Palatial Residence of a Syndicate Mogul.

While he was hammering merrily at his Task, trying to fill out an eight-hour Day, the Lady of the House came and watched him. Her Heart was touched with great Pity for any Man who still had his Appendix and whose Picture had never appeared in the Sunday Papers. So she had the Butler bring some Charlotte Russe for the humble Toiler. After which he borrowed one of her gold-tip Cigarettes and gave her a few Minutes of his Time, in spite of the Fact that she did not belong to the Union.

"This is a Swell Joint you've got here, Lady," said the Steam-Fitter. "The only thing that makes me Sore is to think that all of this Hot Dog you're throwin' on comes out of the Pockets of poor, hard-workin' Guys, such as me."

"You wrong us," said the Great Lady, in a Tone of Gentle Sadness. "My Husband never flimflams the poor Laborer. All that he has he made by shifting the Cut on the small Stockholders. We are much interested in the Working Classes and wish to establish a free Lecture Course, so that the Poor may learn all about Anthropology. Very often I go and sing Solos at Mission Entertainments, but in spite of this my poor Husband is pictured as a hungry Octopus who has taken a death-grip on the Consumer."

"I'd hate to be a Corporation Director," said the Steam-Fitter. "The Mug that controls a Million Bucks ain't got a Friend on Earth except the People who happen to be with him at the time. All the Congressmen throw Bricks at him and the Editorial-Writers toast him to a Crisp. The Rainbow Weeklies put him in Cartoons as having four Chins and a Waist Measurement of fifty-two, whereas all the Money-Getters I ever spotted were as thin as Rails and looked as if they had to live on Tea and Toast. But the Working-Man! He's the Boy that gets all the Violets. When they put me into a Cartoon they make me out to be a handsome Charley with my Sleeves rolled up and a set of Muscles that would make Jeffries ashamed of himself. I always wear a dinky Paper Cap and a full growth of Presbyterian Whiskers. Every time I see a Picture of the American Working-Man in three Colors, I'm glad that I'm not a low-down Capitalist. I may not handle as much Coin as some of the Shell-Workers that hang out in Wall Street, but any time that I feel discouraged all I have to do is to dig up my Thirty Cents and go to a Variety Show, and then I find out that I am the only true-hearted and honest American, except the gallant Volunteer. The very best Friend that Union Labor has in this Country is the Vawdyville Artist who works twenty-eight Minutes a Day for $175 a Week."

"Still, with your restricted Income, you cannot seek the elevating Influences of our kind of Society," said the Lady

of the House. "That must grind you a good deal, especially
if you have Children growing up. I can imagine that it
would be hard lines to know that your Offspring have no Social Careers awaiting them."

"Me and my Wife lay awake Nights and cry about it,"
said the Steam-Fitter. "We thought for a while we might
save up and buy Jimmy an Auto, but when we looked in the
Catalogue we found that the Price was $4000. So we de-
cided if he wanted to practice Homicide it would be cheaper
to get him on the Police Force. Being too poor to send him
to a University, we let him take Lessons at a Boxing Academy, and now, when anyone starts Rough House, he is almost as handy as a regular Student. He can smoke Egyptian Cigarettes and blow the Smoke through his Nose, and
he gives me the Laugh when I call him down, and so I feel
that we have accomplished by Home Training what might
have been expected from a College Course. As for Vivian,
our bright-eyed little Daughter, she is the zippiest High-
Flyer that speeds the Boulevard. When it comes to French
Heels and the long Straight Front and all kinds of Blouse
hanging in front of her, she can make the average Society
Bud look like a wax Imitation. She has one of these wig-
wag Walks — the kind that makes People jump off of the
Sidewalk. Of course, she is only the Daughter of an obscure
Steam-Fitter, but let me give you a Pointer. You can't tell
by lookin' at one of these Fairies nowadays what kind of
Clothes her Father wears. When it comes to Lugs, I can't
see that the Heiress has any Bulge on the simple Working-
Girl. As for butting into the Social Swim, she has a Scheme
all framed up, by which she expects to become acquainted
with all of the gold-plated Johnnies who infest the Munici-
pality. She is going on the Stage to be a Show Girl. She
says that the Débutante seldom has more than one on her
Staff, while the Show Girl can take her Pick of a large Bunch.
So you see that in these Days of Public Schools and cheap
Reading Matter and custom-made Imitations, even the most
Humble can occasionally make a Bluff at being the Real

Thing. So long as my Children hoot at my Suggestions and tell me every Day where to get off or how to back over the Dump, Papa will not be altogether discouraged in regard to their Social Careers. In fact, the only thing that worries me is the Fear that I won't be able to keep up with them."

"I am glad to find you so Philosophical," said the Million-airess. "After reading several Books written by College Professors who disguised themselves as Laborers and went and lived among the down-trodden Masses, I had supposed that a Steam-Fitter was a rather gloomy Proposition."

"Why should I be gloomy? The formal Dinner Party is the Champion Gloom-Factory, and I never have to go near one of them. I don't have to wear my Intellect to a Frazzle keeping up with the Popular Novels. When a Foreign Musician or a Lady with a new System of Culturitis bobs up on the Horizon, I don't have to go chasing around, letting on that I am interested. You never see me at one of these punk Amateur Performances, applauding the Bank Accounts. Nobody expects me to make any Calls, and I never drink Tea except when I want it. The Scandal Sheets never show up my Family History, and as far as I can learn, my Wife never hired a Detective to watch me. It is true that some-times I find nothing on the Menu except Corned Beef and what goes with it, but I tear into it with an Appetite that would be worth $8,000,000 to Rockefeller at this Minute. And now, Lady, according to the Rules of the Union, I must knock off for to-day, as it is five o'clock."

"Your story has interested me," said the Lady of the House. "I should like to visit your Family and write a Paper on the Home Life of the Toilers."

"I'm sorry we can't have you," was the Reply. "You Society Ducks don't care who you invite, but I'm an Officer in the Union and I'll queer myself if I begin to associate with the disreputable Rich. You'll have to put up with your own Kind."

MORAL: The Wealthy have nothing left except Money.

60 *The Fable of the Old Fox and the Young Fox*

AFTER he had lived in Town for many Years and had come to know the Animals and their Ways, even to the occasional Running Amuck of the Bulls and Bears, the Old Fox had gathered to himself a few Hard Lessons which he set down for the Instruction and Betterment of Fox, Jr. One Day he took his Young One into the Private Office for a Session of Fatherly Advice.

"I have a few Nuggets of Truth," said the Old Fox, showing some loose Scraps of Paper on which he had written. "I hesitate to offer them, for, if I remember correctly, the Member of our Family who was best Posted on Business Epigrams went under as far back as 1873. Still, some of these may help you. The Work of turning them out has been a pleasurable Respite from my ordinary Routine. Proverbs are easily Manufactured, my Son. They are Self-Evident Truths, blooming in the Garden of Inexperience. Those which happen to be the right Length to fit into Copy-Books are most likely to Endure. Forty Years Ago I was competent to turn out Dozens of Maxims and Proverbs, each glistering with Truth. You are in the Fluff of Youth, while I am marked with Gray, yet doubtless you could give me Cards and Spades in the Making of Precepts for the Guidance of the Immature. The dear little Girls in the Grammar-Schools write Essays in which Mighty Conclusions are linked together end to end, Emerson Fashion. With one Reading of Poor Richard and some timely Inspiration from Rochefoucauld and Hazlitt, any Upstart may set down our Common Weaknesses and catalogue a full Set of Danger Signals. The Letter of Advice has been the easiest Form of Composition from the time of Chesterfield. However, in preparing you to go out and be of the City Tribe, and come Home each Night with your Brush unbedraggled and your cool, smooth Nose unmarked by Scratches, I flatter myself that I have omitted the usual Rigamarole of Weighty Instructions, my

Experience having convinced me that the machine-made Proverb is seldom brought out except to be Misapplied."

"Thank you, Father," said the Young Fox. "I am glad that you have saved yourself the Trouble of formulating the Generalities for which the Rising Generation is always prepared. I have fixed up for my own Use a Set of Rules which, doubtless, is more Comprehensive and Beautiful than anything you could put together at your Time of Life."

Saying which, the Young Fox showed a pretty Morocco-Leather Booklet, made to fit the Waistcoat Pocket, in which he had written many meaty Paragraphs, the Substance of the same having been deduced from what he had read of the Struggle for Existence.

"Read a few Selections," said the Old Fox, with a Tolerant Smile. "I love to hear the resounding Conclusions of an Oracle."

"But I am not an Oracle," said the Young Fox, modestly. "I am not even an Authority. I am only a bright Juvenile who has sorted out the Essentials for Success and set them down neatly with my Fountain-Pen."

"Do not flatter yourself that I credit you with the Authorship of any of the Matter contained in your little Book," said the Old Fox. "We do not intend to Plagiarize, but all of us absorb our pet Proverbs from the Text-Books, the learned Monthlies, and the Editorial Page. We paraphrase Benjamin Franklin, and put Two and Two together to make Four, and change a Preposition, and presto! the Old Saw seems to be a new Truth evolved without Help or Suggestion. No doubt you have written in your little Guide to Life that a Youthful Frugality insures Comfort throughout the Declining Years, and a Good Name is better than Riches, and to be sure you are Right before you go Ahead."

"Not in those Words, I assure you," said the Young Fox, somewhat testily. "It is true, however, that I have composed certain General Directions in favor of Honesty, Temperance, Economy, Punctuality, Candor, Politeness, and Business Caution."

"All Men declare for these Admirable Traits in their Pocket Note-Books," said the Old Fox. "And no sooner is the Ink dry than they are led astray by the Caprice of Small Happenings. The Trouble with a world-wide Maxim or a great bulky Truth is that it does not dovetail nicely into the Exigencies of a Petty Case. Here at the beginning of the Twentieth Century, my Son, when all Endeavor is being sub-divided and specialized, a Technical Instruction under a Sub-Head has more Practical Value than a huge Proverb that has come bumping down the Ages. The Health Officer who tells you in a terse Bulletin to boil your Drinking-Water does you an Actual Service and the Results are immediate, as the Bacilli can testify. But you might have to hunt around all Day without finding an Opportunity to make use of Mr. Emerson's tremendous Suggestion, 'Hitch your Wagon to a Star.' I am not poking Fun at the Large Rules for Conduct, but I beg to remark that very often you will find that they are Shelf Ornaments instead of Working-Tools kept bright by Use. Like the other Classics of our Literature, they are profoundly respected and seldom Utilized. What you need now, my Son," continued the Old Fox, "is a Set of Proverbs, Precepts, and Maxims brought up to Date and peculiarly adapted to an Era of Horseless Carriages, Limited Trains, Colonial Extension, Corners in Grain, the Booming of New Authors, Combinations of Capital, the Mushroom Growth of an Aristocracy of Wealth, and the Reign of Tailor-Made Clothes. A Majority of the Points to which I shall call your Attention may seem to be Frivolous and hardly worth while, but, as I have already intimated, it is the small Rule, made to fit the Individual Instance, that proves most valuable in the Long Run. Years ago I made a silly little Rule, as follows: 'Never extend Credit to any-one who wears a Blue Necktie.' Childish, say you? Perhaps, but it has saved me Thousands of Dollars. If you will give sincere Heed to what I have inscribed here, you may be able to duplicate my magnificent Career."

Fox, Jr., took the Slips of Paper and read as follows:

GEORGE ADE

1. Get acquainted with the Heads of Departments and permit the Subordinates to become acquainted with you.

2. Always be easily Familiar with those who are termed Great in the Public Prints. They are so accustomed to Deference and Humility, it is a positive Relief to meet a jaunty Equal.

3. As soon as you get an Office of your own, put in a Private Exit, marked, "Escape in Case of a Dear Friend with an Invitation to Dinner."

4. The first Sign of Extravagance is to buy Trousers that one does not need. Every Young Man on a Salary should beware of the Trousers Habit.

5. If you were Cut Out to be a homely American, with a preference for Turnips and Tea Biscuit, do not attempt to Live It Down. The most pathetic Object this year is the Man who wants to be a Degenerate and can't quite make it.

6. A Bird in the Hand may be worth Two in the Bush, but remember also that a Bird in the Hand is a positive Embarrassment to one not in the Poultry Business.

7. Do not give Alms promiscuously. Select the Unworthy Poor and make them Happy. To give to the Deserving is a Duty, but to help the Improvident, Drinking Class is clear Generosity, so that the Donor has a Right to be warmed by a Selfish Pride and count on a most flattering Obituary.

8. There is Everything in a Name. A Rose by any other Name would Smell as Sweet, but would not cost half as much during the Winter Months. This means that you should get a Trade-Mark and keep it displayed on the Bulletin Boards.

9. Never try to get into Society, so-called. Those who Try seldom get in, and if they do edge through the Portals they always feel Clammy and Unworthy when under the Scrutiny of the Elect. Sit outside and appear Indifferent, and after a while they may Send for you. If not, it will be Money in your Pocket.

10. All the Apostles of Repose and the Mental Scientists tell the Business Slave to avoid Worry, but an old Trader's

Advice is to Worry until you have had enough of it and then do something Desperate.

11. Never write when you can Telegraph, and in Wiring always use more than Ten Words. This is the Short-Cut to being regarded as a Napoleon. The Extra Words cost only a few Cents, but they make a Profound Impression upon the Recipient and give the Sender a Standing which could not be obtained by an Expenditure of Four Dollars for a Birthday Gift. A Man never feels more Important than when he receives a Telegram containing more than Ten Words.

12. Remember that the latest Outline for a Business Career is to Rush and Bustle and Strain to accumulate enough Money to pay your Expenses to Carlsbad or Southern California after you have dropped from Overwork. The only Failure is the one who Breaks Down without having got together his Recuperation Fund.

13. An Ounce of Prevention is worth a Pound of Cure and costs more. Don't attempt to prevent Trouble or you will lose your Eyesight watching so many Corners at the same time. Wait until Trouble comes and then consult a Specialist.

14. When a Man is in a New Town his Prospects are determined (1) by the class of Hotel at which he is registered, (2) by his Wardrobe, (3) by the Style of his Business Card, and (4) by the Manner of his Address.

15. A Rolling Stone gathers no Moss and therefore will not be derided as a Moss-Back. Roll as much as possible.

16. If you must Economize, dispense with some of the Necessities. You can bear up under the Realization that the Gas Company knows of your keeping the Jets turned low, but if you go out of a Café followed by the Reproachful Gaze of a Waiter who regards you as Stingy, you will feel Small and Unhappy for Hours afterward and your Work will suffer.

17. It has been accepted as a Law that there can be no absolute Waste of Energy, but you will be putting the Law to a Severe Test if you permit yourself to be drawn into a po-

litical Controversy on a Sleeping-Car with a Stranger who wears a wide Slouch-Hat.

18. The Shorter the Hours, the Larger the Income. Don't get into the Habit of putting in Long Hours or you may be set down into a permanent Subordinate Position.

19. When you believe that you love a Young Woman so earnestly that you will have to Marry her, take a Long Ride on the Cars to find out if the Affection endures while you are Traveling. The Beauty of this Test is that if you really Love her, you never will start on the Trip by yourself.

20. If you expect to be a popular After-Dinner Speaker, don't attempt to work at anything else. That is a sufficiently large Contract for one brief Existence.

21. If you take care to Pronounce correctly the Words usually Mispronounced, you may have the Self-Love of the Purist, but you will not sell any Goods.

22. Never accuse a Man of being Lazy. There is no such thing as Laziness. If a Man does not go about his work with Enthusiasm, it means that he has not yet found the Work that he likes. Every Mortal is a Busy Bee when he comes to the Task that Destiny has set aside for him.

23. Early to Bed and Early to Rise is a Bad Rule for any-one who wishes to become acquainted with our most Prominent and Influential People.

24. Always interline a Contract before signing it, merely to impress the Party of the First Part. The one who puts his Signature to Articles of Agreement drawn up by the Other Fellow is establishing a Dangerous Precedent.

25. Never pretend to have Money except when you are in Straits. The Poor Man who pretends to have a Bank Account betters his Credit and takes no Risk. But the Prosperous Individual who counts his Money in the Street, forthwith will be invited to attend a Charity Bazar.

"Is that all?" asked the Young Fox, when he had con-cluded the reading.

"I thought that would be enough for one Dose," replied the Old Fox.

"But you have not put in anything about depositing a certain Sum in the Bank every Week," said Fox, Jr. "I had always supposed that was the inevitable No. 1 of Parental Suggestions."

"I omitted that time-honored Instruction because I hope you will keep your Money out of the Bank," said the Old Fox. "It is so easy to sign Checks. If you find a Surplus accumulating, go in for Life Insurance, and then you may reasonably hope for the allotted Threescore and Ten Years."

And the Young Fox took the Truth Tablets out to have them Framed.

MORAL: Even the Elders can give a number of Helpful Hints.

STEPHEN CRANE

1871–1900

61   *The Flight*

THE youth cringed as if discovered in a crime. By heavens, they had won after all! The imbecile line had remained and become victors. He could hear cheering.

He lifted himself upon his toes and looked in the direction of the fight. A yellow fog lay wallowing on the treetops. From beneath it came the clatter of musketry. Hoarse cries told of an advance.

He turned away amazed and angry. He felt that he had been wronged.

He had fled, he told himself, because annihilation approached. He had done a good part in saving himself, who was a little piece of the army. He had considered the time, he said, to be one in which it was the duty of every little piece to rescue itself if possible. Later the officers could fit the little pieces together again, and make a battle front. If none of the little pieces were wise enough to save themselves from the flurry of death at such a time, why, then, where would be the army? It was all plain that he had proceeded according to very correct and commendable rules. His actions had been sagacious things. They had been full of strategy. They were the work of a master's legs.

Thoughts of his comrades came to him. The brittle blue line had withstood the blows and won. He grew bitter over it. It seemed that the blind ignorance and stupidity of those little pieces had betrayed him. He had been overturned and crushed by their lack of sense in holding the position, when intelligent deliberation would have convinced them that it was impossible. He, the enlightened man who looks afar in the dark, had fled because of his superior perceptions and knowledge. He felt a great anger against his comrades. He knew it could be proved that they had been fools.

He wondered what they would remark when later he appeared in camp. His mind heard howls of derision. Their density would not enable them to understand his sharper point of view.

He began to pity himself acutely. He was ill used. He was trodden beneath the feet of an iron injustice. He had proceeded with wisdom and from the most righteous motives under heaven's blue only to be frustrated by hateful circumstances.

A dull, animal-like rebellion against his fellows, war in the abstract, and fate grew within him. He shambled along with bowed head, his brain in a tumult of agony and despair. When he looked loweringly up, quivering at each sound, his eyes had the expression of those of a criminal who thinks his guilt and his punishment great, and knows that he can find no words.

He went from the fields into a thick wood, as if resolved to bury himself. He wished to get out of hearing of the cracking shots which were to him like voices.

The ground was cluttered with vines and bushes, and the trees grew close and spread out like bouquets. He was obliged to force his way with much noise. The creepers, catching against his legs, cried out harshly as their sprays were torn from the barks of trees. The swishing saplings tried to make known his presence to the world. He could not conciliate the forest. As he made his way, it was always calling out protestations. When he separated embraces of trees and vines the disturbed foliages waved their arms and turned their face leaves toward him. He dreaded lest these noisy motions and cries should bring men to look at him. So he went far, seeking dark and intricate places.

After a time the sound of musketry grew faint and the cannon boomed in the distance. The sun, suddenly apparent, blazed among the trees. The insects were making rhythmical noises. They seemed to be grinding their teeth in unison. A woodpecker stuck his impudent head around the side of a tree. A bird flew on lighthearted wing.

Off was the rumble of death. It seemed now that Nature had no ears.

This landscape gave him assurance. A fair field holding life. It was the religion of peace. It would die if its timid eyes were compelled to see blood. He conceived Nature to be a woman with a deep aversion to tragedy.

He threw a pine cone at a jovial squirrel, and he ran with chattering fear. High in a treetop he stopped, and, poking his head cautiously from behind a branch, looked down with an air of trepidation.

The youth felt triumphant at this exhibition. There was the law, he said. Nature had given him a sign. The squirrel, immediately upon recognizing danger, had taken to his legs without ado. He did not stand stolidly baring his furry belly to the missile, and die with an upward glance at the sympathetic heavens. On the contrary, he had fled as fast as his legs could carry him; and he was but an ordinary squirrel, too — doubtless no philosopher of his race. The youth wended, feeling that Nature was of his mind. She reënforced his argument with proofs that lived where the sun shone.

Once he found himself almost into a swamp. He was obliged to walk upon bog tufts and watch his feet to keep from the oily mire. Pausing at one time to look about him he saw, out at some black water, a small animal pounce in and emerge directly with a gleaming fish.

The youth went again into the deep thickets. The brushed branches made a noise that drowned the sounds of cannon. He walked on, going from obscurity into promises of a greater obscurity.

At length he reached a place where the high, arching boughs made a chapel. He softly pushed the green doors aside and entered. Pine needles were a gentle brown carpet. There was a religious half light.

Near the threshold he stopped, horror-stricken at the sight of a thing.

He was being looked at by a dead man who was seated with his back against a columnlike tree. The corpse was dressed in a uniform that once had been blue, but was now faded to a melancholy shade of green. The eyes, staring at the youth, had changed to the dull hue to be seen on the side of a dead fish. The mouth was open. Its red had changed to an appalling yellow. Over the gray skin of the face ran little ants. One was trundling some sort of a bundle along the upper lip.

The youth gave a shriek as he confronted the thing. He was for moments turned to stone before it. He remained staring into the liquid-looking eyes. The dead man and the living man exchanged a long look. Then the youth cautiously put one hand behind him and brought it against a tree. Leaning upon this he retreated, step by step, with his face still toward the thing. He feared that if he turned his back the body might spring up and stealthily pursue him.

The branches, pushing against him, threatened to throw him over upon it. His unguided feet, too, caught aggravatingly in brambles; and with it all he received a subtle suggestion to touch the corpse. As he thought of his hand upon it he shuddered profoundly.

At last he burst the bonds which had fastened him to the spot and fled, unheeding the underbrush. He was pursued by a sight of the black ants swarming greedily upon the gray face and venturing horribly near to the eyes.

After a time he paused, and, breathless and panting, listened. He imagined some strange voice would come from the dead throat and squawk after him in horrible menaces.

The trees about the portal of the chapel moved soughingly in a soft wind. A sad silence was upon the little guarding edifice.

The trees began softly to sing a hymn of twilight. The sun sank until slanted bronze rays struck the forest. There was a lull in the noises of insects as if they had bowed their beaks and were making a devotional pause. There was silence save for the chanted chorus of the trees.

Then, upon this stillness, there suddenly broke a tremendous clangor of sounds. A crimson roar came from the distance.

The youth stopped. He was transfixed by this terrific medley of all noises. It was as if worlds were being rended. There was the ripping sound of musketry and the breaking crash of the artillery.

His mind flew in all directions. He conceived the two armies to be at each other panther fashion. He listened for a time. Then he began to run in the direction of the battle. He saw that it was an ironical thing for him to be running thus toward that which he had been at such pains to avoid. But he said, in substance, to himself that if the earth and the moon were about to clash, many persons would doubtless plan to get upon the roofs to witness the collision.

As he ran, he became aware that the forest had stopped its music, as if at last becoming capable of hearing the foreign sounds. The trees hushed and stood motionless. Everything seemed to be listening to the crackle and clatter and ear-shaking thunder. The chorus pealed over the still earth.

It suddenly occurred to the youth that the fight in which he had been was, after all, but perfunctory popping. In the hearing of this present din he was doubtful if he had seen real battle scenes. This uproar explained a celestial battle; it was tumbling hordes a-struggle in the air.

Reflecting, he saw a sort of a humor in the point of view of himself and his fellows during the late encounter. They had taken themselves and the enemy very seriously and had imagined that they were deciding the war. Individuals must have supposed that they were cutting the letters of their names deep into everlasting tablets of brass, or enshrining their reputations forever in the hearts of their countrymen, while, as to fact, the affair would appear in printed reports under a meek and immaterial title. But he saw that it was good, else, he said, in battle everyone would surely run save forlorn hopes and their ilk.

He went rapidly on. He wished to come to the edge of the forest that he might peer out.

As he hastened, there passed through his mind pictures of stupendous conflicts. His accumulated thought upon such subjects was used to form scenes. The noise was as the voice of an eloquent being, describing.

Sometimes the brambles formed chains and tried to hold him back. Trees, confronting him, stretched out their arms and forbade him to pass. After its previous hostility this new resistance of the forest filled him with a fine bitterness. It seemed that Nature could not be quite ready to kill him.

But he obstinately took roundabout ways, and presently he was where he could see long gray walls of vapor where lay battle lines. The voices of cannon shook him. The musketry sounded in long irregular surges that played havoc with his ears. He stood regardant for a moment. His eyes had an awestruck expression. He gawked in the direction of the fight.

Presently he proceeded again on his forward way. The battle was like the grinding of an immense and terrible machine to him. Its complexities and powers, its grim processes, fascinated him. He must go close and see it produce corpses.

He came to a fence and clambered over it. On the far side, the ground was littered with clothes and guns. A newspaper, folded up, lay in the dirt. A dead soldier was stretched with his face hidden in his arm. Farther off there was a group of four or five corpses keeping mournful company. A hot sun had blazed upon the spot.

In this place the youth felt that he was an invader. This forgotten part of the battle ground was owned by the dead men, and he hurried, in the vague apprehension that one of the swollen forms would rise and tell him to begone.

He came finally to a road from which he could see in the distance dark and agitated bodies of troops, smoke-fringed. In the lane was a blood-stained crowd streaming to the rear. The wounded men were cursing, groaning, and wailing. In the air, always, was a mighty swell of sound that it seemed could sway the earth. With the courageous words of the artillery and the spiteful sentences of the musketry mingled red cheers. And from this region of noises came the steady current of the maimed.

One of the wounded men had a shoeful of blood. He hopped like a schoolboy in a game. He was laughing hysterically.

One was swearing that he had been shot in the arm through the commanding general's mismanagement of the army. One was marching with an air imitative of some sublime drum major. Upon his features was an unholy mixture of merriment and agony. As he marched he sang a bit of doggerel in a high and quavering voice:

> " Sing a song 'a vic'try,
> A pocketful 'a bullets,
> Five an' twenty dead men
> Baked in a — pie."

Parts of the procession limped and staggered to this tune.

Another had the gray seal of death already upon his face. His lips were curled in hard lines and his teeth were clinched. His hands were bloody from where he had pressed them upon his wound. He seemed to be awaiting the moment when he should pitch headlong. He stalked like the specter of a soldier, his eyes burning with the power of a stare into the unknown.

There were some who proceeded sullenly, full of anger at their wounds, and ready to turn upon anything as an obscure cause.

An officer was carried along by two privates. He was peevish. "Don't joggle so, Johnson, yeh fool," he cried. "Think m' leg is made of iron? If yeh can't carry me decent, put me down an' let someone else do it."

He bellowed at the tottering crowd who blocked the quick march of his bearers. "Say, make way there, can't yeh? Make way, dickens take it all."

They sulkily parted and went to the roadsides. As he was carried past they made pert remarks to him. When he raged in reply and threatened them, they told him to be damned.

The shoulder of one of the tramping bearers knocked heavily against the spectral soldier who was staring into the unknown.

The youth joined this crowd and marched along with it. The torn bodies expressed the awful machinery in which the men had been entangled.

Orderlies and couriers occasionally broke through the throng in the roadway, scattering wounded men right and left, galloping on followed by howls. The melancholy march was continually disturbed by the messengers, and sometimes by bustling batteries that came swinging and thumping down upon them, the officers shouting orders to clear the way.

There was a tattered man, fouled with dust, blood and powder stain from hair to shoes, who trudged quietly at the youth's side. He was listening with eagerness and much humility to the lurid descriptions of a bearded sergeant. His lean features wore an expression of awe and admiration. He was like a listener in a country store to wondrous tales told among the sugar barrels. He eyed the story-teller with unspeakable wonder. His mouth was agape in yokel fashion.

The sergeant, taking note of this, gave pause to his elaborate history while he administered a sardonic comment. "Be keerful, honey, you 'll be a-ketchin' flies," he said.

The tattered man shrank back abashed.

After a time he began to sidle near to the youth, and in a different way try to make him a friend. His voice was gentle as a girl's voice and his eyes were pleading. The youth saw with surprise that the soldier had two wounds, one in the head, bound with a blood-soaked rag, and the other in the arm, making that member dangle like a broken bough.

After they had walked together for some time the tattered man mustered sufficient courage to speak. "Was pretty good fight, wa'n't it?" he timidly said. The youth, deep in thought, glanced up at the bloody and grim figure with its lamblike eyes. "What?"

"Was pretty good fight, wa'n't it?"

"Yes," said the youth shortly. He quickened his pace.

But the other hobbled industriously after him. There was an air of apology in his manner, but he evidently thought that he needed only to talk for a time, and the youth would perceive that he was a good fellow.

"Was pretty good fight, wa'n't it?" he began in a small voice, and then he achieved the fortitude to continue. "Dern me if I ever see fellers fight so. Laws, how they did fight! I knowed th' boys 'd like when they onct got square at it. Th' boys ain't had no fair chanct up t' now, but this time they showed what they was. I knowed it 'd turn out this way. Yeh can't lick them boys. No, sir! They're fighters, they be."

He breathed a deep breath of humble admiration. He had looked at the youth for encouragement several times. He received none, but gradually he seemed to get absorbed in his subject.

"I was talkin' 'cross pickets with a boy from Georgie, onct, an' that boy, he ses, 'Your fellers 'll all run like hell when they onct hearn a gun,' he ses. 'Mebbe they will,' I ses, 'but I don't b'lieve none of it,' I ses; 'an' b'jiminey,' I ses back t' 'um, 'mebbe your fellers 'll all run like hell when they onct hearn a gun,' I ses. He larfed. Well, they didn't run t' day, did they, hey? No, sir! They fit, an' fit, an' fit."

His homely face was suffused with a light of love for the army which was to him all things beautiful and powerful.

After a time he turned to the youth. "Where yeh hit, ol' boy?" he asked in a brotherly tone.

The youth felt instant panic at this question, although at first its full import was not borne in upon him.

"What?" he asked.

"Where yeh hit?" repeated the tattered man.

"Why," began the youth, "I — I — that is — why — I ——"

He turned away suddenly and slid through the crowd. His brow was heavily flushed, and his fingers were picking nervously at one of his buttons. He bent his head and fastened his eyes studiously upon the button as if it were a little problem.

The tattered man looked after him in astonishment.

The youth fell back in the procession until the tattered soldier was not in sight. Then he started to walk on with the others.

But he was amid wounds. The mob of men was bleeding. Because of the tattered soldier's question he now felt that his shame could be viewed. He was continually casting sidelong glances to see if the men were contemplating the letters of guilt he felt burned into his brow.

At times he regarded the wounded soldiers in an envious way. He conceived persons with torn bodies to be peculiarly happy. He wished that he, too, had a wound, a red badge of courage.

The spectral soldier was at his side like a stalking reproach. The man's eyes were still fixed in a stare into the unknown. His gray, appalling face had attracted attention in the crowd, and men, slowing to his dreary pace, were walking with him. They were discussing his plight, questioning him and giving him advice. In a dogged way he repelled them, signing to them to go on and leave him alone. The shadows of his face were deepening and his tight lips seemed holding in check the moan of great despair. There could be seen a certain stiffness in the movements of his body, as if he were taking infinite care not to arouse the passion of his wounds. As he went on, he seemed always looking for a place, like one who goes to choose a grave.

Something in the gesture of the man as he waved the bloody and pitying soldiers away made the youth start as if bitten. He yelled in horror. Tottering forward he laid a quivering hand upon the man's arm. As the latter slowly turned his waxlike features toward him, the youth screamed:

"Gawd! Jim Conklin!"

The tall soldier made a little commonplace smile. "Hello, Henry," he said.

The youth swayed on his legs and glared strangely. He stuttered and stammered. "Oh, Jim — oh, Jim — oh, Jim ——"

The tall soldier held out his gory hand. There was a curious red and black combination of new blood and old blood upon it. "Where yeh been, Henry?" he asked. He continued in a monotonous voice, "I thought mebbe yeh got keeled over. There's been thunder t' pay t'-day. I was worryin' about it a good deal."

The youth still lamented. "Oh, Jim — oh, Jim — oh, Jim ——"

"Yeh know," said the tall soldier, "I was out there." He made a careful gesture. "An', Lord, what a circus! An', b'jiminey, I got shot — I got shot. Yes, b'jiminey, I got shot." He reiterated this fact in a bewildered way, as if he did not know how it came about.

The youth put forth anxious arms to assist him, but the tall soldier went firmly on as if propelled. Since the youth's arrival as a guardian for his friend, the other wounded men had ceased to display much interest. They occupied themselves again in dragging their own tragedies toward the rear.

Suddenly, as the two friends marched on, the tall soldier

seemed to be overcome by a terror. His face turned to a semblance of gray paste. He clutched the youth's arm and looked all about him, as if dreading to be overheard. Then he began to speak in a shaking whisper:.

"I tell yeh what I'm 'fraid of, Henry — I'll tell yeh what I'm 'fraid of. I'm 'fraid I'll fall down — an' then yeh know — them damned artillery wagons — they like as not'll run over me. That's what I'm 'fraid of——"

The youth cried out to him hysterically: "I'll take care of yeh, Jim! I'll take care of yeh! I swear t' Gawd I will!"

"Sure — will yeh, Henry?" the tall soldier beseeched.

"Yes — yes — I tell yeh — I'll take care of yeh, Jim!" protested the youth. He could not speak accurately because of the gulpings in his throat.

But the tall soldier continued to beg in a lowly way. He now hung babelike to the youth's arm. His eyes rolled in the wildness of his terror. "I was allus a good friend t' yeh, wa'n't I, Henry? I've allus been a pretty good feller, ain't I? An' it ain't much t' ask, is it? Jest t' pull me along outer th' road? I'd do it fer you, wouldn't I, Henry?"

He paused in piteous anxiety to await his friend's reply.

The youth had reached an anguish where the sobs scorched him. He strove to express his loyalty, but he could only make fantastic gestures.

However, the tall soldier seemed suddenly to forget all those fears. He became again the grim, stalking specter of a soldier. He went stonily forward. The youth wished his friend to lean upon him, but the other always shook his head and strangely protested. "No — no — no — leave me be — leave me be——"

His look was fixed again upon the unknown. He moved with mysterious purpose, and all of the youth's offers he brushed aside. "No — no — leave me be — leave me be——"

The youth had to follow.

Presently the latter heard a voice talking softly near his shoulders. Turning he saw that it belonged to the tattered soldier. "Ye'd better take 'im outa th' road, pardner. There's a batt'ry comin' helitywhoop down th' road an' he'll git runned over. He's a goner anyhow in about five minutes — yeh kin see that. Ye'd better take 'im outa th' road. Where th' blazes does he git his stren'th from?"

"Lord knows!" cried the youth. He was shaking his hands helplessly.

He ran forward presently and grasped the tall soldier by the arm. "Jim! Jim!" he coaxed, "come with me."

The tall soldier weakly tried to wrench himself free. "Huh," he said vacantly. He stared at the youth for a moment. At last he spoke as if dimly comprehending. "Oh! Inteh th' fields? Oh!"

He started blindly through the grass.

The youth turned once to look at the lashing riders and jouncing guns of the battery. He was startled from this view by a shrill outcry from the tattered man.

"Gawd! He's runnin'!"

Turning his head swiftly, the youth saw his friend running in a staggering and stumbling way toward a little clump of bushes. His heart seemed to wrench itself almost free from his body at this sight. He made a noise of pain. He and the tattered man began a pursuit. There was a singular race.

When he overtook the tall soldier he began to plead with all the words he could find. "Jim — Jim — what are you doing — what makes you do this way — you'll hurt yerself."

The same purpose was in the tall soldier's face. He protested in a dulled way, keeping his eyes fastened on the mystic place of his intentions. "No — no — don't tech me — leave me be — leave me be ——"

The youth, aghast and filled with wonder at the tall soldier, began quaveringly to question him. "Where yeh goin', Jim? What you thinking about? Where you going? Tell me, won't you, Jim?"

The tall soldier faced about as upon relentless pursuers. In his eyes there was a great appeal. "Leave me be, can't yeh? Leave me be fer a minnit."

The youth recoiled. "Why, Jim," he said, in a dazed way, "what's the matter with you?"

The tall soldier turned and, lurching dangerously, went on. The youth and the tattered soldier followed, sneaking as if whipped, feeling unable to face the stricken man if he should again confront them. They began to have thoughts of a solemn ceremony. There was something rite-like in these movements of the doomed soldier. And there was a resemblance in him to a devotee of a mad religion, blood-sucking, muscle-wrenching, bone-crushing. They were awed and afraid. They hung back lest he have at command a dreadful weapon.

At last, they saw him stop and stand motionless. Hastening up, they perceived that his face wore an expression telling that he had at last found the place for which he had struggled. His spare figure was erect; his bloody hands were quietly at his side. He was waiting with patience for something that he had come to meet. He was at the rendezvous. They paused and stood, expectant.

There was a silence.

Finally, the chest of the doomed soldier began to heave with a strained motion. It increased in violence until it was as if an animal was within and was kicking and tumbling furiously to be free.

This spectacle of gradual strangulation made the youth writhe, and once as his friend rolled his eyes, he saw something in them that made him sink wailing to the ground. He raised his voice in a last supreme call.

"Jim — Jim — Jim —— "

The tall soldier opened his lips and spoke. He made a gesture. "Leave me be — don't tech me — leave me be —— "

There was another silence while he waited.

Suddenly, his form stiffened and straightened. Then it was shaken by a prolonged ague. He stared into space. To the two watchers there was a curious and profound dignity in the firm lines of his awful face.

He was invaded by a creeping strangeness that slowly enveloped him. For a moment the tremor of his legs caused him to dance a sort of hideous hornpipe. His arms beat wildly about his head in expression of implike enthusiasm.

His tall figure stretched itself to its full height. There was a slight rending sound. Then it began to swing forward, slow and straight, in the manner of a falling tree. A swift muscular contortion made the left shoulder strike the ground first.

The body seemed to bounce a little way from the earth. "God!" said the tattered soldier.

The youth had watched, spellbound, this ceremony at the place of meeting. His face had been twisted into an expression of every agony he had imagined for his friend.

He now sprang to his feet, and, going closer, gazed upon the pastelike face. The mouth was opened and the teeth showed in a laugh.

As the flap of the blue jacket fell away from the body, he could see that the side looked as if it had been chewed by wolves.

The youth turned, with sudden, livid rage, toward the battlefield. He shook his fist. He seemed about to deliver a philippic.

"Hell —— "

The red sun was pasted in the sky like a wafer.

SHERWOOD ANDERSON

1876–

62   *The Story-Teller*

WHAT a fellow, wanting to be loved, was my father! And now he is in the farmhouse sitting room and it is late evening and the towheaded children have gone regretfully to bed. There is something in the air of the room, a kind of suspense, a feeling that something is about to happen. Father has so carefully worked that up. He would do it by silences, by sudden breakings out into suppressed laughter, and then by quickly looking sad. I have seen him do the thing, oh, many times. "My dear people — you wait! There is something inside me that is wonderful, and if you will only be patient you will presently see or hear it come forth," he seemed to be saying.

He is by the fire with his legs spread out and his hands are in his trousers pockets. He stares at the floor. He is smoking a cigar. In some ways he always managed to keep himself supplied with the little comforts of life.

And he has so placed his chair that he can look at Tilly, who has retired into her corner, without anyone else in the room seeing the look. Now she is sitting in deep shadows, far away from the kerosene lamp with which the room is lighted and as she sits there, half lost in the darkness, there is suddenly something — a haunting kind of beauty hangs over her.

She is a little excited by something father has managed in some indescribable way to do to the very air of the room. Tilly also was once young and must at some time have had her grand moment in life. Her moment was not very prolonged. Once, when she was a young woman, she went to a country dance and a man, who dealt in horses, took a fancy to her and carried her home after the dance in his buggy. He was a tall man with a heavy mustache and she — it was a moonlight night in October — she grew sad and wistful. The horse dealer half intended — well, he had been buying horses for a trucking company at Toledo, Ohio, had secured all he wanted and was leaving the neighborhood on the next day — the thing he felt during that evening later quite went out of his mind.

As for father he is at the moment perhaps thinking of mother, when she was young and lovely and was a bound girl in just such another farmhouse, and surely he wanted something lovely for mother then as he does for Tilly now. I have no doubt at all that father always wanted lovely things for people — to happen to people — and that he had also an absurd and never-dying faith in himself — that he was, in some inscrutable way, appointed to be the bearer of lovely things to obscure people.

However, there is something else in his mind also. Is he not the fellow who, by his personal charm, is to earn for himself, Aldrich and the horse, board, a bed, a welcome — without pay — until the show is pulled off at the schoolhouse? That is his business now and this is his hour.

In fancy I can hear the tale he would now begin telling. There was that one about his escape from the guards when he was a Union soldier in the Civil War and was being marched off to a Southern prison camp. He would no doubt use that. It was a bull'seye story and always hit the mark! Oh, how often and under what varying circumstances has not my father escaped from prisons! Benvenuto Cellini or the count of Monte Cristo had nothing on him.

Yes, the story he would now tell would be that once when it rained and the Union prisoners, father among them — some forty men in all — were being marched off along a road in the deep mud —

That was indeed a night of adventure! It was a tale he loved telling, and what realistic touches he could put into it: the rain that wet the prisoners to the skin — the cold — the chattering teeth — the groans of weary men — the closeness of the dark forest on either hand — the steady weary chug-chug of the feet of the prisoners in the mud — the line of guards at either side of the road, with the guns over their shoulders — the curses of the Rebel guards when they stumbled in the darkness.

What a night of weary anguish on the part of the prisoners! When they stopped to rest the guards went into a house and left the prisoners to stand outside in the rain, or lie on the bare ground, guarded by part of the company. If any died of exposure — well, there would be that many less men to feed when they were got into the Southern prison camp.

And now, after many days and nights, marching thus, the souls of the prisoners were sick with weariness. A dreary desolated look would come upon father's face as he spoke of it.

They marched steadily along in the deep mud and the rain. How cold the rain was! Now and then, in the darkness, a dog barked, far away somewhere. There was a break in the solid line of timber along the road and the men marched across the crest of a low hill. There are lights to be seen now, in distant farmhouses, far away across a valley — a few lights like stars shining.

The story-teller has got his audience leaning forward in their chairs. Outside the farmhouse in which they sit a wind begins to blow and a broken branch from a near-by tree is blown against the side of the house. The farmer, a heavy, stolid-looking man, starts a little and his wife shivers as with cold and Tilly is absorbed — she does not want to miss a word of the tale.

And now father is describing the darkness of the valley below the hill and the lights seen, far off. Will any of the little company of prisoners ever see their own homes again, their wives, their children, their sweethearts? The lights of the farmhouses in the valley are like stars in the sky of a world turned upside down.

The Rebel commander of the guard has issued a warning and a command: "It's pretty dark here, and if any of the Yanks make a stir to move out of the center of the road fire straight into the mass of them. Kill them like dogs."

A feeling creeps over father. He is, you see, a southern man himself, a man of the Georgia hills and plains. There is no law that shall prevent his having been born in Georgia, although to-morrow night it may be North Carolina or Kentucky. But to-night his birthplace shall be Georgia. He is a man who lives by his fancy and to-night it shall suit his fancy and the drift of his tale to be a Georgian.

And so he, a prisoner of the Rebels, is being marched over the low hill, with the lights from distant farmhouses shining like stars in the darkness below, and suddenly a feeling comes to him, a feeling such as one sometimes has when one is alone in one's own house at night. You have had the feeling. You are alone in the house and there are no lights and it is cold and dark. Everything you touch — feel with your hands in the darkness — is strange and at the same time familiar. You know how it is.

The farmer is nodding his head and his wife has her hands gripped, lying in her lap. Even Aldrich is awake now. The devil! Father has given this particular tale a new turn since he told it last. "This is something like." Aldrich leans forward to listen.

And there is the woman Tilly, in the half darkness. See, she is quite lovely now, quite as she was on that evening when she rode with the horse dealer in the buggy! Something has happened to soften the long, harsh lines of her face and she might be a princess sitting there now in the half-light.

Father would have thought of that. It would be something worth while now to be a tale-teller to a princess. He stops talking to consider for a moment the possibilities of the notion, and then with a sigh gives it up.

It is a sweet notion but it won't do. Tale-teller to a princess, eh! Evenings in a castle and the prince has come in from hunting in a forest. The tale-teller is dressed in flashy clothes and with a crowd of courtiers, ladies in waiting — whatever hangers-on a princess has — is sitting by an open fire. There are great, magnificent dogs lying about too.

Father is considering whether or not it is worth trying some time — the telling of a tale of himself in just that rôle. An idea crosses his mind. The princess has a lover who creeps one night into the castle and the prince has become aware of his presence, is told of his presence by a trusty varlet. Taking his sword in hand the prince creeps through the dark hallways to kill his rival, but father has warned the lovers and they have fled. It afterward comes to the ears of the prince that father has protected the lovers and he — that is to say, father — is compelled to flee for his life. He comes to America and lives the life of an exile, far from the splendor to which he has been accustomed.

Father is thinking whether it would be worth trying — the telling of such a fable of his former existence,
some evening at some farmhouse where he and Aldrich
are staying; and for a moment a sort of George Barr Mc-
Cutcheon light comes into his eyes, but with a sigh he gives
it up.

It wouldn't go over — not in a farmhouse in northern Ohio,
he concludes.

He returns to the table, that so evidently is going over;
but, before he resumes, casts another glance at Tilly. "Oh,
Tilly, thou dear lovely one," he sighs inwardly.

The farmhouse is in the North and he has set himself forth
as a southerner enlisted in the northern army. An explanation is in order, and he makes it, with a flourish.

Born a southerner, the son of a proud southern family,
he was sent to school, to a college in the North. In college
he had a roommate, a dear fellow from the state of Illinois.
The "roommate's father was owner and editor of the *Chicago
Tribune*," he explains.

And during one summer, a few years before the breaking
out of the war, he went on a visit to the home of his Illinois
friend, and while he was there he, with his friend, went to
hear the famous Lincoln-Douglas debates. It was odd, but
the facts were that the young fellow from Illinois became enamored of the brilliant Douglas while he — well, to tell the
truth, his own heart was wrung by the simplicity and nobility
of the rail-splitter, Lincoln. "Never shall I forget the nobility of that countenance," he says in speaking of it. He
appears about to cry and does in fact take a handkerchief from his pocket and wipe his eyes. "Oh, the noble,
the indescribable effect upon my boyhood heart of the stirring words of that man. There he stood like a mighty oak
of the forest breasting the storms. 'A nation cannot exist
half slave and half free. A house divided against itself cannot stand,' he said, and his words thrilled me to the very
marrow of my being."

And then father would have described his homecoming

after that terrific experience. War was coming on and all the South was aflame.

One day at table in his southern home, with his brothers, his father and mother and his beautiful and innocent young sister sitting with him, he dared to say something in defense of Lincoln.

What a storm was then raised! The father getting up from his place at table pointed a trembling finger at his son. All eyes, except only those of his younger sister, were turned on him in wrath and disapproval. "Mention that hated name again in this house and I will shoot you like a dog, though you are my son," his father said, and the son got up from the table and went away, filled with the sense of filial duty that would not let a born southerner answer his own father, but nevertheless determined to stick to the fate aroused in him by the words of the noble Lincoln.

And so he had ridden away from his southern home in the night and had finally joined the Union forces.

What a night — riding away from his father's house in the darkness, leaving his mother behind, leaving all tradition behind, condemning himself to be an outlaw in the hearts of those he had always loved — for the sake of duty!

One can imagine Aldrich blinking a little and rubbing his hands together. "Teddy is laying it on rather thick," he no doubt says to himself; but he must nevertheless have been filled with admiration.

However, let us, who are together revisiting the scene of my father's triumph on that evening in the farmhouse long ago, be not too much in fear for the heart of the woman Tilly. At any rate her physical self, if not her heart, was safe.

Although there can be little doubt that the presence of the virgin Tilly, sitting in the half darkness, and the kindliness of the shadows that had temporarily enhanced her failing beauty, may have had a good deal to do with father's talent on that evening, I am sure nothing else ever came of it. Father, in his own way, was devoted to mother.

And he had his own way of treasuring her. Did he not treasure always the lovelier moments of her?

He had found her in a farmhouse when he was by way of being something of a young swell himself and she was a bound girl; and she was then beautiful — beautiful without the aid of shadows cast by a kerosene lamp.

In reality she was the aristocrat of the two, as the beautiful one is always the aristocrat; and oh, how little beauty in woman is understood! The popular magazine covers and the moving-picture actresses have raised the very devil with our American conception of womanly beauty.

But father had delicacy, of a sort, of that you may be quite sure; and do you not suppose that Tilly, in the Ohio farmhouse, sensed something of his attitude toward what fragment of beauty was left in her, and that she loved him for that attitude — as I am sure my own mother also did?

> My fruit shall not be my fruit until it drops from my arms, into the arms of the others, over the top of the wall.

And now the weary prisoners with their escort have come down off the hillside to a valley and are approaching a large old southern mansion, standing back from the road they have been traveling, and the officers in charge of the prisoners — there were two of them — command the guards to turn in at a gate that leads to the house.

There is an open space before the house where the prisoners are gathered and the ground — covered with firm turf during most of the year — has, under the continuous rains, become soft and yielding. Where each prisoner stands a puddle gathers about his feet.

The house is dark, but for a single light at the back, and one of the officers begins shouting. A large pack of hunting dogs have come from a shed, hidden away in the darkness somewhere, and are gathered growling and barking in a half circle about the prisoners.

One of the dogs rushes through the mass of prisoners and

with a glad cry leaps upon father, and all the others follow so the guards are compelled to drive the dogs off, kicking them and using the butts of their guns. Lights are lit inside the house. The people are astir.

You will understand what a moment this was for father. By one of those strange streaks of fate — which he is very careful to explain to his audience happen much more frequently in life than one imagines — he had been led, as a prisoner on his way to a southern prison pen, right to the door of his own father's house.

What a moment indeed! Being a prisoner he has of course no idea how long he will be kept there. Thank God, he has grown a thick, bushy beard since he left home.

As to his fate — if the prisoners are kept in the yard until daylight comes — well, he knows his own mother.

His own father, old man though he is, has gone off to the war and all his brothers have gone; and his mother has come from a proud old southern family, one of the oldest and proudest. Had she known he was there among the prisoners she would have seen him hanged without a protest and would herself have lent a hand at pulling the rope.

Ah, what had not my father given for his country! Where will his equal be found, even among the whole world's heroes? In the eyes of his own mother and father, in his brother's eyes, in the eyes of all the branches and ramifications of his southern family, in the eyes of all — except only one unsophisticated and innocent girl — he had brought everlasting disgrace on one of the proudest names of the South.

Indeed it was just because he, the son, had gone off to fight with the northern army that his father, a proud old man of sixty, had insisted on being taken into the southern army. "I have a strong old frame and I insist," he had said. "I must make good the loss to my Southland for my own son, who has proven himself a dog and a renegade."

And so the old man had marched off with a gun on his shoulder, insisting on being taken as a common soldier and put where he could face constant and terrible danger, and the seeds of an undying hatred against the son had been planted deep in the hearts of the whole family.

The dullest mind surely will comprehend now what a position father was in when, in answer to the shouts of the officer, lights began to appear all through the house. Was it not a situation to wring tears from the heart of a man of stone! As for a woman's heart — one can scarcely speak of the matter.

And in the house, before father's eyes, there was one — a pure and innocent southern girl of rare beauty — a pearl of womanhood in fact — rarest example of the famed spotless womanhood of the Southland — his younger sister — the only woman child of the family.

You see, as father would so carefully have explained that evening in the farmhouse, he did not care so much for his own life. That had already been given to his country, he would have said proudly.

But, as you will understand quickly enough, had his presence among the prisoners been discovered, his proud mother — eager to wipe out the only stain on the family escutcheon — would at once have insisted that he be hanged to the doorpost of the very house in which he was born, her own hand pulling the rope that was to jerk him up, into the arms of death — to make white again the family escutcheon, you understand.

Could a proud southern woman do less?

And in the event of such an outcome to the adventures of the night, see how that younger sister — the love of his life at that time — see how she would have suffered.

There she was, the pure and innocent girl, the one who understood nothing, to be sure, of the import of his decision to stick to the old flag and fight for the land of Washington and Lincoln, and who, in her innocent way, just loved him. On that day at his father's table, when he — so deeply affected by the Lincoln-Douglas debates — had dared say a word for the cause of the North, it had been her eyes and her eyes alone that had looked at him with love, when all the other eyes of his family had looked at him with hatred and loathing.

And she would just be bursting into womanhood now. The aroma of awakening womanhood would be lying over her as perfume over the opening rosebud.

Think of it! There she, the pure and innocent one, would have to stand and see him hanged. A blight would be brought down upon her young life and her head would, ever after that night, be bowed in lonely and silent sorrow. That brave pure and just girl made old before her time. Ah; well might it be that in one night the mass of golden locks, that now covered her head like a cloud just kissed by the evening sun — that very golden hair might be turned as white as snow!

I can, in fancy, hear my father saying the words I have set down here and coming very near to crying himself as he said them. At the moment he would have believed without question the story he himself was telling.

And now the front door to the old southern mansion is thrown open and there, in the doorway facing the prisoners in the rain, stands a gigantic young negro — my father's own body servant before he left home. (Father stops the flow of his talk long enough to explain how he and the negro boy, as lads together, had fought, wrestled, hunted, fished and lived together like two brothers. I will not go into that, however. Any professional southerner will tell you all about it, if you care to hear. It would have been the most trite part of father's evening effort.)

Anyway, there the gigantic young negro stands in the doorway and he is holding in his hand a candle. Back of him stands my grandmother and back of her the young and innocent sister.

The figure of father's mother is erect. She is old but she is yet tall and strong. One of the officers explains to her that he and his men have been on an all-night march, taking the crowd of Yankee prisoners to a prison camp, and asks for the hospitality of the house. Being a southerner himself he knows that southern hospitality can never fail, even at midnight. "A bite to eat and a cup of hot coffee in the name of our Southland." he asks.

It is granted, of course. The proud woman beckons him and his brother officer into the house and herself steps out into the cold, drizzling rain.

She has ordered the young negro to stand on the porch, holding the candle aloof, and now, marching across the wet lawn, approaches the prisoners. The southern guards have stepped aside, bowing low before southern womanhood, and she goes near the prisoners and looks at them, as well as one may in the uncertain light. "I have a curiosity to see some of the unmannerly dogs of Yanks," she says, leaning forward and staring at them. She is very near her own son now but he has turned his face away and is looking at the ground. Something however causes him to raise his head just as she, to express more fully her contempt, spits at the men.

A little speck of her white spittle lands upon father's thick, tawny beard.

And now his mother has gone back into the house and it is again dark on the lawn in front. The Rebel guards are relieved — two at a time — to go to the kitchen door, where they are given hot coffee and sandwiches. And once his young sister, she of the tender heart, tries to creep to where the prisoners stand in the darkness. She is accompanied by an old negro woman and has planned to give food aid and comfort to the weary men but is prevented. Her mother has missed her inside the house and coming to the door calls to her. "I know your tender heart," she says, "but it shall not be. The teeth of no Yankee dog shall ever bite into food raised on the land of your father. It shall not happen, at least while your mother is alive to prevent. . . ."

As it turned out on that night, when it rained and when he in his young manhood stood just outside the door of that southern mansion house of his childhood, and when his mother, that proud woman of the Southland, spat at him and his companions in misery, so that a white speck of her spittle landed on his beard — where, as he said, it lay like a thing of fire burning into his soul — on that night, I say, he did, by a stroke of fortune, escape the fate that seemed to have him in its clutches.

Dawn was just beginning to break when the two Confederate officers came out at the door of the house and marched their prisoners away.

"We went off into the gray dawn, up out of the valley and over the hills, and then I turned to look back," father explained. Gray and weary and half dead with starvation, he turned to look. If he dropped dead from starvation and weariness on his way to the prison pen, what did it matter now? The light of his life had gone out. He was never again to see any of his own people, that he knew.

But even as he looked he did see something. The company had stopped to rest for a moment and stood where a sharp wind blew over them, just at the crest of a hill. Down in the valley the dawn was just breaking and, as father looked, he could see the gray of the old house and against the gray of it, on the front veranda, just a fleck of white.

That would be his young and innocent sister, come out of the house, you will understand, to look along the road taken by the prisoners, whose evident misery had touched her young heart.

For father it would be, as he would so elaborately explain, a very high spot in his life, perhaps the highest spot he was to reach in all his weary march to the grave.

He stood there on the hillside, quite cold and miserable — in just that utterly miserable and weary state when one is sometimes most alive — the senses, that is to say, are most alive. At the moment he felt, as any man must feel sometimes in life, that an invisible cord does extend from the innermost parts of himself to the innermost parts of some other person. Love comes. For once in a lifetime a state of feeling becomes as definite a thing as a stone wall touched with the hand.

And father had that feeling, at that moment on the hill; and that the person for whom he had it was a woman and his own sister, made it even more an assured thing. He might have expressed the feeling by saying that, as by a miracle, the hill dropped away and he stood on dry level ground in the very presence of his younger sister, so close to her in fact that he might very easily have put out his hand and touched her. So strong was the feeling that he lost for the moment all sense of his presence among the prisoners, all sense of the cold hunger and weariness of the hour and — exactly as the thing might be done, quite ridiculously, by a second-rate actor in the movies — he did in fact step out from among the ranks of prisoners and, with his hands extended before him and his eyes shining, took several steps down the hillside, only to be stopped by an oath from one of the guards.

In the farmhouse, as he told of that moment he would get out of his chair and actually take several steps. He would at bottom be always a good deal of an actor as well as a story-teller, as every story-teller worth his salt inevitably is.

And then came the oath from the guard and an upraised gun, the heavy butt of a gun, ready to swing down upon his head, and back he goes into the ranks of prisoners. He mutters some excuse: "I just wanted to have a look" — and is thus jerked down from the high place, to which his imagination had suddenly lifted him, and back into the weariness of his apparently hopeless journey. Gone, he thought at the moment, was the sister he loved, his boyhood with its memories, all his past life, but it wasn't quite true.

Father did make an escape. How many escapes he, in fancy, made from the hands of the enemy during that Civil War! He lived, you will understand, in a rather dull farming community and loved at least some air of probability hanging over his tales.

And so the Civil War became for him the canvas, the tubes of paint, the brushes with which he painted his pictures. Perhaps one might better say his own imagination was the brush and the Civil War his paint pot. And he did have a fancy for escapes, as I myself have always had. My own tales, told and untold, are full of escapes — by water in the dark and in a leaky boat, escapes from situations, escapes from dullness, from pretense, from the heavy-handed seriousness of the half artists. What writer of tales does not dote upon escapes? They are the very breath in our nostrils.

It is just possible that upon that occasion, father would have put it to his audience that the sight, or the imagined sight, of his sister that morning had given him new hope. She was a virgin and there was something catholic about father.

Very well, then, off he goes down the road with his head held high, thinking of the possible schemes for escape and of his sister. He had been given something, a new flair for life. A ray of new hope had come into the black night of his situation. He walked more stoutly.

> Stout Cortes —
> Silent upon a peak in Darien.

It was just that stout way in which he now walked that gave him his opportunity for escape — that time. All that day the other prisoners went with hanging heads, tramping through the deep mud of the southern roads in winter, but father walked with his head up.

Another night came and they were again in a forest, on a dark and lonely road, with the guards walking at the side and sometimes quite lost in the shadows cast by the trees — the prisoners a dark mass in the very center of the road.

Father stumbled over a stick, the heavy branch of a tree, quite dead and broken off by the wind, and, stooping down, picked it up. Something, perhaps just the impulse of a soldier, led him to sling the stick lightly over his shoulder and carry it like a gun.

There he was, stepping proudly among those who were not proud — that is to say, the other prisoners — and not having any plan in mind — just thinking of his virginal sister back there, I dare say; and one of the two officers of the guard spoke to him kindly.

"Don't walk in there so close to the Yanks, in the deep mud, John," the officer said; "it's better going out here. There is a path here at the side. Get in here back of me."

By his very pride, lifted up out of the ranks of the prisoners, father's mind acted quickly and with a muttered thanks he stepped to the side of the road and became as one of the guards. The men came out on the crest of another low hill and again, in the valley below, there was the faint light of a farmhouse. "Halt!" one of the officers gave command; and then — the younger of the two officers having been told by his superior to send a man down into the valley to the farmhouse to see if there was a chance for the guard and prisoners to rest for a few hours and to get food — he sent father. The officer touched him on the arm. "Go on you," he said. "You go down and find out."

So off father went, down a lane, holding the stick very correctly, like a gun, until he was safely out of sight of the others, and then he threw the stick away and ran.

The devil! He knew every inch of the ground on which he now stood. What an opportunity for escape! One of his boyhood friends had lived in the very house toward which he was supposed to be going, and often, in his young manhood and when he had come home for vacation from the northern school, he had ridden and hunted along the very path his feet now touched. Why, the very dogs and " niggers " on the place knew him as they might have known their master.

And so, if he ran madly now, he ran knowing the ground under his feet. Ah, he would be sure! When his escape was discovered dogs might be set on his trail.

He plunged downward, getting clear of the trees, running across a field — the soft mud clinging to his feet — and so skirted the house and got to where there was a small creek down which he went for a mile in the darkness, walking in the cold water that often came up to his waist. That was to throw dogs off his trail, as any schoolboy should know.

By making a great circle he got back into the road, by which he and the other prisoners had been marched from his own father's house. They had come some twelve miles during the day and early evening, but the night was still young and, after he had gone three or four miles, he knew a short cut through the woods by which several miles could be cut off.

And so, you see, father went back again to his old home after all and once again saw the sister he loved. The dawn was just breaking when he arrived, but the dogs knew him and the negroes knew him. The very negro who had held the light while his mother spat at the prisoners hid him away in the loft of a barn and brought him food.

Not only food was brought, but also a suit of his own clothes that had been left in the house.

And so he stayed hidden in the loft for three days, and then another night came when it rained and was dark.

Then he crept out, with food for the needs of his journey, and knowing that, when he had walked for a mile along the road that led back toward the distant Union camp, a negro would be standing in a little grove with a good horse saddled and bridled for him. The negro, in the late afternoon, had gone off to a distant town, ostensibly for mail and was to be bound to a tree where he would be discovered later by a party of other negroes sent in search of him. Oh, all was arranged — everything elaborately planned to ward off, from his helpers, the wrath of the mother.

There was the night and the rain, and father, with a dark cloak now about his shoulders, creeping from the stables and toward the house. By the window of one of the rooms downstairs his young sister sat playing an organ, and so he crept to the window and stood for a time looking. Ah, there was moving-picture stuff for your soul! Why, oh why, did not father live in another generation? In what affluence might we not all have flourished! The old homestead, a fire burning in the grate, the stern and relentless parent, and outside in the cold and wet father, the outcast son, the disowned, the homeless one, about to ride off into the night in the service of his country — never to return.

On the organ his sister would have been playing "The Last Link is Broken," and there stands father with the great tears rolling down his cheeks.

Then to ride away into the night, to fight again for the flag he loved, and that to him meant more than home, more than family — ah! more than the love of the woman who was long afterward to come into his life, and to console him somewhat for the fair sister he had lost.

For he did love her, quite completely. Is it not odd, when one considers the matter, that the fair sister — who would have been my aunt, and who never perhaps existed except in father's fancy, but concerning whom I have heard him tell so many touching tales — is it not odd that I have never succeeded in inventing a satisfactory name for her? Father never — if I remember correctly — gave her a name and I have never succeeded in doing so.

How often have I tried and without success! Ophelia, Cornelia, Emily, Violet, Eunice. You see the difficulty? It must have a quaint and southern sound and must suggest — what must it not suggest?

But father's tale must have its proper dénouement. One could trust the tale-teller for that. Even had he lived in the days of the movies and had the dénouement quite killed his story — for movie purposes, at least in the northern towns, which would have been the best market — even in the face of all of such difficulties which he fortunately did not have to meet, one could be quite sure of the dénouement.

And he made it splashy. It was at the dreadful battle of Gettysburg, late in the war and on the third of July too. The Confederates had such a dreadful way of getting off on just the wrong foot on the very eve of our national holiday. Vicksburg and Gettysburg for Fourth of July celebrations.

Surely it was, what, during the World War, would have been called "bad war psychology."

There can be no doubt that father had been a soldier of some sort during the Civil War and so, as was natural, he would give his tale a soldier's dénouement, sacrificing even the beloved and innocent younger sister to his purpose (to be brought back to life — oh, many, many times later, and made to serve in many future tales).

It was the second day of that great, that terrible battle of Gettysburg, father had picked upon to serve as the setting for the end of his yarn.

That was a moment! All over the North the people stood waiting; farmers stopped working in the fields and drove into northern towns, waiting for the click of the little telegraph instruments; country doctors let the sick lie unattended and stood with all the others in the streets of towns, where was no running in and out of stores. The whole North stood waiting, listening. No time for talk now.

Ah! that Confederate General Lee — the neat quiet Sunday-school superintendent among generals! One could never tell what he would do next. Was it not all planned that the war should be fought out on southern soil? — and here he had brought a great army of his finest troops far into the North.

Everyone waited and listened. No doubt the South waited and listened too.

No Lincoln and Douglas debates now. "A nation cannot exist half slave and half free."

Now there is the rattle of the box, and the dice that shall decide the fate of a nation are being thrown. In an obscure farmhouse, far in the North, long after the battle of those two terrible days was fought and half forgotten, father also has got his hands on the dice box. He is rattling words in it now. We poor tellers of tales have our moments too, it seems. Like great generals sitting upon horses upon the tops of hills and throwing troops into the arena, we throw the little soldier words into our battles. No uniforms for us, no riders springing away into the gray smoke-mist of battle to carry out orders. We must sit in lonely farmhouses or in cheap rooms in city lodging houses before our typewriters; but if we do not look like generals, we at least feel like that at moments anyway.

Father dropping his little rattling words into the hearts of the farmer, the farmer's wife, Tilly's heart too. At Gettysburg a nation in the death grapple. The innocent sister, fair virgin of the South, cast in too.

Look at the eyes of that stoic Aldrich. They are shining now, eh? Ah! he has been a soldier too. In his youth he also stood firmly amid shot and shell, but ever after, poor dear, he had to be satisfied with mere blank dumbness about it all. At the best he could but turn the crank of a magic-lantern machine or join the G. A. R. and march with other men through the streets of an Ohio town on Decoration days, when the real question in the minds of all the onlookers was as to whether Clyde or Tiffin, Ohio, would win the ball game to be played at Ame's field that afternoon.

A poor sort Aldrich, being able to do nothing but fight. On Decoration days he marched dumbly through the dust to a graveyard and listened to an address made by a candidate for Congress, who had made his money in the wholesale poultry business. At best Aldrich could but speak in low tones to another comrade, as the file of men marched along. "I was with Grant at the Wilderness and before that at Shiloh. Where were you? Oh, you were with Sherman, one of Sherman's bummers, eh?"

That and no more for Aldrich—but for father, ah!

The second day at Gettysburg and Pickett's men ready for their charge. Was that not a moment? What men—those fellows of Pickett's—the very flower of the Southland—young bearded giants, tough like athletes, trained to the minute.

It is growing late on that second day of the fight and Pickett's men are to decide it all. The sun will soon be going down behind the hills of that low flat valley—the valley in which, but a few short days ago, farmers were preparing to gather the grain crops. On the slope of one of the hills a body of men lies waiting. It is the flower of the Union army too. Father is among them, lying there.

They wait.

They are not trembling, but back of them in a thousand towns men and women are both waiting and trembling. Freedom itself waits and trembles — liberty is trembling — "You can't fool all of the people all of the time" is trembling like a broken reed. How many grand passages, words, Decoration day addresses, messages to Congress, Fourth of July addresses of the next two hundred years, not worth eight cents on the dollar at the moment!

And now they come — Pickett's men — down through the valley, in and out of groves of trees and up the little slope. There is a place, known to history as "the bloody angle." There the men of the South rush straight into a storm of iron. A hailstorm of iron swept also in among the men of the North waiting for them.

That wild Rebel yell that broke from the lips of Pickett's men is dying now. The lips of Pickett's men are turning white.

The voice of Meade has spoken and down through the valley go the Union men in their turn — father among them.

It was then that a bullet in the leg dropped him in his tracks, and in memory of that moment he stops the telling of his tale in the farmhouse long enough to pull up his pants leg and show the scar of his wound. Father was a true naturalist, liked to pin his tales down to earth, put a spike of truth in them — at moments.

He pitched forward and fell and the men of his company rolled on to a victory in which he could have no part. He had fallen in what was now, suddenly, a little, quiet place among trees in an old orchard, and there close beside him was a confederate boy, mortally wounded. The two men roll uneasily in their pain and look directly into each other's eyes. It is a long, long look the two men give each other, for one of them the last look into the eyes of a fellow before he goes on, over the river.

The man lying there, and now dying, is just that young man who, as a boy, was father's best friend and comrade, the lad to whose place — some twelve miles from his own father's plantation — he used to ride for days of sport. What rides they had taken together through the forests, a pack of dogs at their heels, and what talks they then had!

You will understand that the young man now dying lived in that very house, far back from the road, toward which father went that night when he escaped the Rebel guard. He had marched off with the stick over his shoulder, you will remember, and had then cut off across fields to his own home where he was concealed by the negroes until the night of his final escape.

And he had gone away from his own home on that dark night, dreaming of a return, some time when the cruel war was over and the wounds it had made were healed; but now he could never return. He was condemned to remain alone, a wanderer always on the face of this earth.

For the lad now dying beside him on the field of Gettysburg was, in his death hour, telling a fearful and tragic story.

Father's family had been entirely wiped out. His father had been killed in battle as had also his brothers.

And now, from the lips of his old comrade, he was to hear the most fearful tale of all.

A party of northern foragers had come to the southern plantation house on just such another dark, rainy night as the one on which he was taken there as a prisoner. They marched as the confederate troops had marched, along the driveway to the front of the house, and stood on the lawn. A northern officer's voice called as the southern officer had called on that other night, and again the tall young negro came to the door with a light, followed by that fiery woman of the Southland.

The negro held the light above his head so that, even in

the darkness, the blue coats of the hated northern troops could be seen.

The old southern woman came to stand at the edge of the porch. She understood for what purpose the northern men had come, and she had sworn that not a bite of food, raised on that plantation, should ever pass the lips of a Yank.

Now she held a shotgun in her hand and, without a word or without any sort of warning, raised it and fired into the mass of the men.

There was a cry of rage, and then many guns were raised to shoulders. A sudden roar of the guns and a hundred leaden bullets cut through the front of the house. It wiped out all of father's family — except just himself — and deprived his sons, too, of a proud southern ancestry; for, just in the moment, before the shower of bullets came, father's young and innocent sister — realizing with that sure instinct that, everyone understands, all women inevitably possess — realizing, I say, that death was about to call her mother — the young girl had rushed panic-stricken out of the door and had thrown her arms about her mother's body, just in time to meet death with her. And so all that was left of the family — except just father — fell there in a heap. The captain of the northern troops — a German brewer's son from Milwaukee, Wisconsin, cried when later he looked down into the white silent face of the young girl, and all his life afterward carried in his heart the remembrance of the dead, pleading young eyes; but, as father so philosophically remarked, what was done was done.

And with that fall there was father — a man left to wander forever stricken and forlorn through life. Later he had, to be sure, married and he had children whom he loved and treasured, but was that the same thing? To the heart of a southerner, as every American understands, ancestry means everything.

The purity of a southern woman is unlike any other purity ever known to mankind. It is something special. The man who has been under the influence of it can never afterward quite escape. Father didn't expect to. He declared always, after he had told the above story, that he did not ever expect to be gay or happy again.

What he expected was that he would go on for the rest of his days doing just what he was doing at the time. Well, he would try to bring a little joy into the hearts of others — he would sing songs, dance a little dance — he would join an old comrade in arms, one whose heart he knew was as true as steel, and give a magic-lantern show. Others, for an hour anyway, would be made to forget that element of sadness and tragedy in life that he, of course, could never quite forget.

On that very night, lying half dead on the field of Gettysburg beside the dead comrade of his youth, he had made up his mind to spend the remaining days of his life bringing what sweetness and joy he could into the lacerated hearts of a nation torn by civil strife. It had been two o'clock in the morning before he was picked up by a squad of men sent out to gather in the wounded, and already the news of the great victory and the triumph of the cause of freedom was sweeping over the northern land. And he had lain looking at the stars and had made his resolution. Others might seek for the applause of the world, but, as for himself, he would go into the dusty highways and byways of life and bring to the lowly and forgotten the joy of a little fun at the schoolhouse.

WILLA SIBERT CATHER
1876–

63   *The Ancient People*

THEA'S life at the Ottenburg ranch was simple and full of light, like the days themselves. She awoke every morning when the first fierce shafts of sunlight darted through the curtainless windows of her room at the ranch house. After breakfast she took her lunch-basket and went down to the canyon. Usually she did not return until sunset.

Panther Canyon was like a thousand others — one of those abrupt fissures with which the earth in the Southwest is riddled; so abrupt that you might walk over the edge of any one of them on a dark night and never know what had happened to you. This canyon headed on the Ottenburg ranch, about a mile from the ranch house, and it was accessible only at its head. The canyon walls, for the first two hundred feet below the surface, were perpendicular cliffs, striped with even-running strata of rock. From there on to the bottom the sides were less abrupt, were shelving, and lightly fringed with *piñons* and dwarf cedars. The effect was that of a gentler canyon within a wilder one. The dead city lay at the point where the perpendicular outer wall ceased and the V-shaped inner gorge began. There a stratum of rock, softer than those above, had been hollowed out by the action of time until it was like a deep groove running along the sides of the canyon. In this hollow (like a great fold in the rock) the Ancient People had built their houses of yellowish stone and mortar. The overhanging cliff above made a roof two hundred feet thick. The hard stratum below was an everlasting floor. The houses stood along in a row, like the buildings in a city block, or like a barracks.

In both walls of the canyon the same streak of soft rock had been washed out, and the long horizontal groove had been built up with houses. The dead city had thus two streets, one set in either cliff, facing each other across the ravine, with a river of blue air between them.

The canyon twisted and wound like a snake, and these two streets went on for four miles or more, interrupted by the abrupt turnings of the gorge, but beginning again within each turn. The canyon had a dozen of these false endings near its head. Beyond, the windings were larger and less perceptible, and it went on for a hundred miles, too narrow, precipitous, and terrible for man to follow it.

The Cliff Dwellers liked wide canyons, where the great
cliffs caught the sun. Panther Canyon had been deserted
for hundreds of years when the first Spanish missionaries
came into Arizona, but the masonry of the houses was
still wonderfully firm; had crumbled only where a land-
slide or a rolling boulder had torn it.

All the houses in the canyon were clean with the clean-
ness of sun-baked, wind-swept places, and they all smelled
of the tough little cedars that twisted themselves into the
very doorways. One of these rock-rooms Thea took for her
own. Fred had told her how to make it comfortable. The
day after she came old Henry brought over on one of the
pack-ponies a roll of Navajo blankets that belonged to
Fred, and Thea lined her cave with them. The room was
not more than eight by ten feet, and she could touch the
stone roof with her finger-tips. This was her old idea: a
nest in a high cliff, full of sun. All morning long the sun
beat upon her cliff, while the ruins on the opposite side of
the canyon were in shadow. In the afternoon, when she
had the shade of two hundred feet of rock wall, the ruins
on the other side of the gulf stood out in the blazing sunlight. Before her door ran the narrow, winding path that
had been the street of the Ancient People. The yucca and
niggerhead cactus grew everywhere. From her doorstep
she looked out on the ocher-colored slope that ran down
several hundred feet to the stream, and this hot rock was
sparsely grown with dwarf trees. Their colors were so pale
that the shadows of the little trees on the rock stood out
sharper than the trees themselves. When Thea first came,
the chokecherry bushes were in blossom, and the scent of
them was almost sickeningly sweet after a shower. At the
very bottom of the canyon, along the stream, there was a
thread of bright, flickering, golden-green, — cottonwood
seedlings. They made a living, chattering screen behind
which she took her bath every morning.

Thea went down to the stream by the Indian water
trail. She had found a bathing-pool with a sand bottom,

where the creek was dammed by fallen trees. The climb back was long and steep, and when she reached her little house in the cliff she always felt fresh delight in its comfort and inaccessibility. By the time she got there, the woolly red-and-gray blankets were saturated with sunlight, and she sometimes fell asleep as soon as she stretched her body on their warm surfaces. She used to wonder at her own inactivity. She could lie there hour after hour in the sun and listen to the strident whir of the big locusts, and to the light, ironical laughter of the quaking asps. All her life she had been hurrying and sputtering, as if she had been born behind time and had been trying to catch up. Now, she reflected, as she drew herself out long upon the rugs, it was as if she were waiting for something to catch up with her. She had got to a place where she was out of the stream of meaningless activity and undirected effort.

Here she could lie for half a day undistracted, holding pleasant and incomplete conceptions in her mind — almost in her hands. They were scarcely clear enough to be called ideas. They had something to do with fragrance and color and sound, but almost nothing to do with words. She was singing very little now, but a song would go through her head all morning, as a spring keeps welling up, and it was like a pleasant sensation indefinitely prolonged. It was much more like a sensation than like an idea, or an act of remembering. Music had never come to her in that sensuous form before. It had always been a thing to be struggled with, had always brought anxiety and exaltation and chagrin — never content and indolence. Thea began to wonder whether people could not utterly lose the power to work, as they can lose their voice or their memory. She had always been a little drudge, hurrying from one task to another — as if it mattered! And now her power to think seemed converted into a power of sustained sensation. She could become a mere receptacle for heat, or become a color, like the bright lizards that darted about on the hot stones outside her door; or she could become a continuous repetition of sound, like the cicadas.

The faculty of observation was never highly developed in Thea Kronborg. A great deal escaped her eye as she passed through the world. But the things which were for her, she saw; she experienced them physically and remembered them as if they had once been a part of herself. The roses she used to see in the florists' shops in Chicago were merely roses. But when she thought of the moon-flowers that grew over Mrs. Tellamantez's door, it was as if she had been that vine and had opened up in white flowers every night. There were memories of light on the sand hills, of masses of prickly-pear blossoms she had found in the desert in early childhood, of the late afternoon sun pouring through the grape leaves and the mint bed in Mrs. Kohler's garden, which she would never lose. These recollections were a part of her mind and personality. In Chicago she had got almost nothing that went into her subconscious self and took root there. But here, in Panther Canyon, there were again things which seemed destined for her.

Panther Canyon was the home of innumerable swallows. They built nests in the wall far above the hollow groove in which Thea's own rock chamber lay. They seldom ventured above the rim of the canyon, to the flat, wind-swept tableland. Their world was the blue air-river between the canyon walls. In that blue gulf the arrow-shaped birds swam all day long, with only an occasional movement of the wings. The only sad thing about them was their timidity; the way in which they lived their lives between the echoing cliffs and never dared to rise out of the shadow of the canyon walls. As they swam past her door, Thea often felt how easy it would be to dream one's life out in some cleft in the world.

From the ancient dwelling there came always a dignified, unobtrusive sadness; now stronger, now fainter,—like the aromatic smell which the dwarf cedars gave out in the sun, — but always present, a part of the air one breathed. At night, when Thea dreamed about the canyon, — or in the early morning when she hurried toward it, anticipating it, — her conception of it was of yellow rocks baking in sunlight, the swallows, the cedar smell, and that peculiar sadness — a voice out of the past, not very loud, that went on saying a few simple things to the solitude eternally.

Standing up in her lodge, Thea could with her thumb nail dislodge flakes of carbon from the rock roof — the cooking-smoke of the Ancient People. They were that near! A timid, nest-building folk, like the swallows. How often Thea remembered Ray Kennedy's moralizing about the cliff cities. He used to say that he never felt the hardness of the human struggle or the sadness of history as he felt it among those ruins. He used to say, too, that it made one feel an obligation to do one's best. On the first day that Thea climbed the water trail she began to have intuitions about the women who had worn the path, and who had spent so great a part of their lives going up and down it. She found herself trying to walk as they must have walked, with a feeling in her feet and knees and loins which she had never known before, — which must have come up to her out of the accustomed dust of that rocky trail. She could feel the weight of an Indian baby hanging to her back as she climbed.

The empty houses, among which she wandered in the afternoon, the blanketed one in which she lay all morning, were haunted by certain fears and desires; feelings about warmth and cold and water and physical strength. It seemed to Thea that a certain understanding of those old people came up to her out of the rock shelf on which she lay; that certain feelings were transmitted to her, suggestions that were simple, insistent, and monotonous, like the beating of Indian drums. They were not expressible in words, but seemed rather to translate themselves into attitudes of body, into degrees of muscular tension or relaxation; the naked strength of youth, sharp as the sun-shafts; the crouching timorousness of age, the sullenness of women who waited for their captors. At the first turning of the canyon there was a half-ruined tower of yellow masonry, a watch-tower upon which the young men used to entice eagles and snare them with nets. Sometimes for a whole morning Thea could see the coppery breast and shoulders of an Indian youth there against the sky; see him throw the net, and watch the struggle with the eagle.

Old Henry Biltmer, at the ranch, had been a great deal among the Pueblo Indians who are the descendants of the Cliff-Dwellers. After supper he used to sit and smoke his pipe by the kitchen stove and talk to Thea about them. He had never found any one before who was interested in his ruins. Every Sunday the old man prowled about in the canyon, and he had come to know a good deal more about it than he could account for. He had gathered up a whole chestful of Cliff-Dweller relics which he meant to take back to Germany with him some day. He taught Thea how to find things among the ruins: grinding-stones, and drills and needles made of turkey-bones. There were fragments of pottery everywhere. Old Henry explained to her that the Ancient People had developed masonry and pottery far beyond any other crafts. After they had made houses for themselves, the next thing was to house the precious water. He explained to her how all their customs and ceremonies and their religion went back to water. The men provided the food, but water was the care of the women. The stupid women carried water for most of their lives; the cleverer ones made the vessels to hold it. Their pottery was their most direct appeal to water, the envelope and sheath of the precious element itself. The strongest Indian need was expressed in those graceful jars, fashioned slowly by hand, without the aid of a wheel.

When Thea took her bath at the bottom of the canyon, in the sunny pool behind the screen of cottonwoods, she sometimes felt as if the water must have sovereign quali-

ties, from having been the object of so much service and
desire. That stream was the only living thing left of the
drama that had been played out in the canyon centuries
ago. In the rapid, restless heart of it, flowing swifter than
the rest, there was a continuity of life that reached back
into the old time. The glittering thread of current had a
kind of lightly worn, loosely knit personality, graceful and
laughing. Thea's bath came to have a ceremonial gravity.
The atmosphere of the canyon was ritualistic.

One morning, as she was standing upright in the pool,
splashing water between her shoulder-blades with a big
sponge, something flashed through her mind that made her
draw herself up and stand still until the water had quite
dried upon her flushed skin. The stream and the broken
pottery: what was any art but an effort to make a sheath,
a mold in which to imprison for a moment the shining,
elusive element which is life itself — life hurrying past
us and running away, too strong to stop, too sweet to
lose? The Indian women had held it in their jars. In the
sculpture she had seen in the Art Institute, it had been
caught in a flash of arrested motion. In singing, one made
a vessel of one's throat and nostrils and held it on one's
breath, caught the stream in a scale of natural intervals.

Thea had a superstitious feeling about the potsherds,
and liked better to have them in the dwellings where
she found them. If she took a few bits back to her own
lodge and hid them under the blankets, she did it guiltily,
as if she were being watched. She was a guest in these
houses, and ought to behave as such. Nearly every afternoon she went to the chambers which contained the most
interesting fragments of pottery, sat and looked at them
for a while. Some of them were beautifully decorated.
This care, expended upon vessels that could not hold food
or water any better for the additional labor put upon
them, made her heart go out to those ancient potters. They
had not only expressed their desire, but they had expressed

it as beautifully as they could. Food, fire, water, and something else — even here, in this crack in the world, so far back in the night of the past! Down here at the beginning that painful thing was already stirring; the seed of sorrow, and of so much delight.

There were jars done in a delicate overlay, like pine cones; and there were many patterns in a low relief, like basket-work. Some of the pottery was decorated in color, red and brown, black and white, in graceful geometrical patterns. One day, on a fragment of a shallow bowl, she found a crested serpent's head, painted in red on terra-cotta. Again she found half a bowl with a broad band of white cliff-houses painted on a black ground. They were scarcely conventionalized at all; there they were in the black border, just as they stood in the rock before her. It brought her centuries nearer to these people to find that they saw their houses exactly as she saw them.

Yes, Ray Kennedy was right. All these things made one feel that one ought to do one's best, and help to fulfill some desire of the dust that slept there. A dream had been dreamed there long ago, in the night of ages, and the wind had whispered some promise to the sadness of the savage. In their own way, those people had felt the beginnings of what was to come. Those potsherds were like fetters that bound one to a long chain of human endeavor.

Not only did the world seem older and richer to Thea now, but she herself seemed older. She had never been alone for so long before, or thought so much. Nothing had ever engrossed her so deeply as the daily contemplation of that line of pale-yellow houses tucked into the wrinkle of the cliff. Moonstone and Chicago had become vague. Here everything was simple and definite, as things had been in childhood. Her mind was like a ragbag into which she had been frantically thrusting whatever she could grab. And here she must throw this lumber away. The things that were really hers separated themselves from the rest. Her ideas were simplified, became sharper and clearer. She felt united and strong.

When Thea had been at the Ottenburg ranch for two months, she got a letter from Fred announcing that he "might be along at almost any time now." The letter came at night, and the next morning she took it down into the canyon with her. She was delighted that he was coming soon. She had never felt so grateful to anyone and she wanted to tell him everything that had happened to her since she had been there — more than had happened in all her life before. Certainly she liked Fred better than anyone else in the world. There was Harsanyi, of course — but Harsanyi was always tired. Just now, and here, she wanted someone who had never been tired, who could catch an idea and run with it.

She was ashamed to think what an apprehensive drudge she must always have seemed to Fred, and she wondered why he had concerned himself about her at all. Perhaps she would never be so happy or so good-looking again, and she would like Fred to see her, for once, at her best. She had not been singing much, but she knew that her voice was more interesting than it had ever been before. She had begun to understand that — with her, at least — voice was, first of all, vitality; a lightness in the body and a driving power in the blood. If she had that, she could sing. When she felt so keenly alive, lying on that insensible shelf of stone, when her body bounded like a rubber ball away from its hardness, then she could sing. This, too, she could explain to Fred. He would know what she meant.

Another week passed. Thea did the same things as before, felt the same influences, went over the same ideas; but there was a livelier movement in her thoughts, and a freshening of sensation, like the brightness which came over the underbrush after a shower. A persistent affirmation — or denial — was going on in her, like the tapping of the woodpecker in the one tall pine tree across the chasm.

Musical phrases drove each other rapidly through her mind, and the song of the cicada was now too long and too sharp. Everything seemed suddenly to take the form of a desire for action.

It was while she was in this abstracted state, waiting for the clock to strike, that Thea at last made up her mind what she was going to try to do in the world, and that she was going to Germany to study without further loss of time. Only by the merest chance had she ever got to Panther Canyon. There was certainly no kindly Providence that directed one's life; and one's parents did not in the least care what became of one, so long as one did not misbehave and endanger their comfort. One's life was at the mercy of blind chance. She had better take it in her own hands and lose everything than meekly draw the plough under the rod of parental guidance. She had seen it when she was at home last summer, — the hostility of comfortable, self-satisfied people toward any serious effort. Even to her father it seemed indecorous. Whenever she spoke seriously, he looked apologetic. Yet she had clung fast to whatever was left of Moonstone in her mind. No more of that! The Cliff-Dwellers had lengthened her past. She had older and higher obligations.

JAMES BRANCH CABELL

1879–

64   *The Demiurge*

I

OFFHAND (began John Charteris) I would say that books are best insured against oblivion through practice of the auctorial virtues of distinction and clarity, of beauty and symmetry, of tenderness and truth and urbanity. That covers the ground, I think: and so it remains merely to cite supporting instances here and there, by mentioning a few writers who have observed these requirements, and

JAMES BRANCH CABELL

thus to substantiate my formula without unnecessary divagation. . . .

Therefore I shall be very brief. And even so, I imagine, you will not be inclined to listen to much of what I am about to say, if only because, like most of us, you are intimidated by that general attitude toward culture and the humanities which has made of American literature, among foreign penmen, if not precisely an object of despairing envy, at least of feeling comment. In particular, I imagine that my frequent references to the affairs and people of fled years will annoy you, since the American book-purchaser shies from such pedantic, and indeed from any, allusion to the past, with that distrust peculiar to persons with criminal records. In fact, this murderer, too, is often haunted, I dare say, by memories of his victim, in thinking of the time he has killed, whether with the "uplifting" or with the "daring" current novels of yesterday.

But you perceive, I trust, that your personal indifference, and the lazy contempt of America as a whole, toward art matters no more affects the eternal verity and the eternal importance of art than do the religious practices of Abyssinia, say, affect the verity and importance of the New Testament. You perceive, I trust, that you ought to be interested in art matters, whatever is your actual emotion. You understand, in fine — as a mere abstract principle — what your feeling "ought to be." Well, it is precisely that tendency to imagine yourself and your emotions as these things "ought to be" which convicts you, over any verbal disclaimer, of a vital interest in art matters: and it is that tendency about which I propose to speak very briefly. . . .

And yet, so insidious is the influence of general opinion, even when manifested as plain unreason, that I confess I myself, whenever anyone talks of "art" and "æsthetic theories," am inclined to find him vaguely ridiculous, and seem to detect in every word he utters a flavor of affectation. So should you prove quite as susceptible as I to the herd-instinct I shall have no ground for complaint. Meanwhile

542

in theory — without of necessity accompanying my friend Felix Kennaston all the way to his conclusion that the sum of corporeal life represents an essay in romantic fiction, — I can perceive plainly enough that the shape-giving principle of all sentient beings is artistic. That is a mere matter of looking at living creatures and noticing their forms. . . . But the principle goes deeper, in that it shapes too the minds of men, by this universal tendency to imagine — and to think of as in reality existent — all the tenants of earth and all the affairs of earth, not as they are, but "as they ought to be." And so it comes about that romance has invariably been the demiurgic and beneficent force, not merely in letters, but in every matter which concerns mankind; and that "realism," with its teaching that the mile-posts along the road are as worthy of consideration as the goal, has always figured as man's chief enemy. . . .

2

Indeed, that scathing criticism which Sophocles passed, however anciently on a contemporary, remains no less familiar than significant, — "He paints men as they are: I paint them as they ought to be." It is aside from the mark that in imputing such veracity to Euripides the singer of Colonos was talking nonsense: the point is that Sophocles saw clearly what was the one unpardonable sin against art and human welfare.

For the Greeks, who were nurtured among art's masterworks, recognized, with much of that perturbing candor wherewith children everywhere appraise their associates, that gracefully to prevaricate about mankind and human existence was art's signal function. As a by-product of this perception, Hellenic literature restrained its endeavors, quite naturally, to embroidering events that were incontestable because time had erased the evidence for or against their actual occurrence: and poets evoked protagonists worth noble handling from bright mists of antiquity, wherethrough, as far as went existent proofs, men might in reality have moved "as they ought to be." Thus, even Homer, the most ancient of great verbal artists, elected to deal with legends that in his day were venerable: and in Homer when Ajax lifts a stone it is with the strength of ten warriors, and Odysseus, when it at all promotes the progress of the story, becomes invisible. It seems — upon the whole — less probable that Homer drew either of these accomplishments from the actual human life about him, than from simple consciousness that it would be very gratifying if men could do these things. And, indeed, as touches enduring art, to write "with the eye upon the object" appears a relatively modern pretense, perhaps not unconnected with the coetaneous phrase of "all my eye."

Then, when the Attic drama came to flowerage, the actors were masked, so that their features might display unhuman perfection; and were mounted upon cothurni, to lend impressiveness to man's physical mediocrity; and were clothed in draperies which philanthropically eclipsed humanity's frugal graces. In painting or sculpture, where the human body could be idealized with a free hand, the Greek rule was nakedness: in drama, where the artist's material was incorrigible flesh, there was nothing for it save to disguise the uncaptivating groundwork through some discreet employment of fair apparel. Thus only could the audience be hoodwinked into forgetting for a while what men and women really looked like. So in drama Theseus declaimed in imperial vestments, and in sculpture wore at the very most a fig-leaf. It is hardly necessary to point out that the Greeks shared few of our delusions concerning "decency": for, of course, they had no more moral aversion to a man's appearing naked in the street than to a toad's doing so, and objected simply on the ground that both were ugly. So they resolutely wrote about — and carved and painted, for that matter — men "as they ought to be" doing such things as it would be gratifying for men to do if these feats were humanly possible. . . . And in the twilit evening of Greek literature you will find Theocritus clinging with unshaken ardor to unreality, and regaling the townfolk of Alexandria with tales of an improbable Sicily, where the inhabitants are on terms of friendly intimacy with cyclopes, water-nymphs and satyrs.

3

Equally in the Middle Ages did literature avoid deviation into the credible. When carpets of brocade were spread in April meadows it was to the end that barons and ladies might listen with delight to peculiarly unplausible accounts of how Sire Roland held the pass at Roncevaux single-handed against an army, and of Lancelot's education at the bottom of a pond by elfin pedagogues, and of how Virgil builded Naples upon eggshells. When English-speaking tale-tellers began to concoct homespun romances they selected such themes as Bevis of Southampton's addiction to giant-killing, and Guy of Warwick's encounter with a man-eating cow eighteen feet long, and the exploits of Thomas of Reading, who exterminated an infinity of dragons and eloped with Prester John's daughter after jilting the Queen of Fairyland. Chaucer, questionless, was so injudicious as to dabble in that muddy stream of contemporaneous happenings which time alone may clarify: but the parts of Chaucer that endure are a Knight's story of mythological events, a Prioress's unsubstantiated account of a miracle, a Nun's Priest's anticipation of Rostand's barnyard fantasy, and a ream or two of other delightful flimflams. From his contemporaries Chaucer got such matter as the Miller's tale of a clerk's misadventures in osculation.

4

But with the invention of printing, thoughts spread so expeditiously that it became possible to acquire quite serviceable ideas without the trouble of thinking: and very few of us since then have cared to risk impairment of our minds by using them. A consequence was that, with inaction, man's imagination in general grew more sluggish, and demurred, just as mental indolence continues to balk, over the exertion of conceiving an unfamiliar *locale,* in any form of art. The deterioration, of course, was gradual, and for a considerable while theatrical audiences remained receptively illiterate. And it seems at first sight gratifying to note that for a lengthy period Marlowe was the most "popular" of the Elizabethan playwrights: for in Marlowe's superb verse there is really very little to indicate that the writer had ever encountered any human beings, and certainly nothing whatever to show that he had seriously considered this especial division of fauna: whereas all his scenes are laid somewhere a long way west of the Hesperides. Yet Marlowe's popularity, one cannot but suspect, was furthered by unæsthetic aids, in divers "comic" scenes which time has beneficently destroyed. At all events, complaisant dramatists, out of a normal preference for butter with their daily bread, soon began to romance about contemporary life. It is not Shakespeare's least claim to applause that he sedulously avoided doing anything of the sort. To the other side, being human, Shakespeare was not untainted by the augmenting trend toward "realism," and in depicting his fellows was prone to limit himself to exaggeration of their powers of fancy and diction. This, as we now know, is a too sparing employment of untruthfulness: and there is ground for sharp arraignment of the imbecility attributed to Lear, and Othello, and Hamlet, and Macbeth, and Romeo — to cite only a few instances, — by any candid estimate of their actions, when deprived of the transfiguring glow wherewith Shakespeare invests what is being done, by evoking a haze of lovely words. For really, to go mad because a hostess resents your bringing a hundred servants on a visit, or to murder your wife because she has misplaced a handkerchief, is much the sort of conduct which is daily chronicled by the morning-paper; and in charity to man's self-respect should be restricted to the ostentatious impermanence of journalism. But at bottom Shakespeare never displayed any very hearty admiration for humanity as a race, and would seem to have found not many more commendable traits in general exercise among mankind than did the authors of the Bible.

Few of the art-reverencing Elizabethans, however, handled the surrounding English life: when they dealt with the contemporaneous it was with a reassuringly remote Italian background, against which almost anything might be supposed to happen, in the way of picturesque iniquity and poisoned wine: so that they composed with much of that fine irresponsibility wherewith American journalists expose the court-life of Madrid. But the Jacobean drama tended spasmodically toward untruths about its audience's workaday life, with such depressing results as *Hyde Park, The Roaring Girl* and *The New Inn*, by men who in the field of unrestricted imagination had showed themselves to be possessed of genuine ability.

5

Then came the gallant protest of the Restoration, when Wycherley and his successors in drama commenced to write of contemporary life in much the spirit of modern musical comedy, which utilizes a fac-simile of the New York Pennsylvania Railroad Station, or of the Capitol at Washington, as an appropriate setting for a ballet and a comedian's colloquy with the orchestra leader. Thus here the scenes are in St. James's Park, outside Westminster, in the New Exchange, and in other places familiar to the audience; and the characters barter jokes on current events: but the laws of the performers' mimic existence are frankly extra-mundane, and their antics, in Restoration days as now, would have subjected them to immediate arrest upon the auditorial side of footlights. A great deal of queer nonsense has been printed concerning the comedy of Gallantry, upon the startling assumption that its authors copied the life about them. It is true that Wycherley, in this the first of English authors to go astray, began the pernicious practice of depicting men as being not very much better than they actually are: of that I will speak later: but Wycherley had the saving grace to present his men and women as trammeled by the social restrictions of Cloud-Cuckoo-Land alone. And, were there nothing else, it seems improbable that Congreve, say, really believed that every young fellow spoke habitually in terms of philosophic wit and hated his father; and that every old hunks possessed, more or less vicariously, a beautiful second wife; and that people married without licenses, or, indeed, without noticing very particularly whom they were marrying; and that monetary competence and hapiness and all-important documents, as well as a sudden turn for heroic verse, were regularly accorded to everybody toward eleven o'clock in the evening.

6

Thus far the illiterate ages, when as yet so few persons could read that literature, tended generally toward the acted drama. The stage could supply much illusory assistance, in the way of pads and wigs and grease-paints and soft lightings, toward making men appear heroic and women charming: but, after all, the rôles were necessarily performed by human beings, and the charitable deceit was not continuous. The audience was ever and anon being reminded, against its firm-set will, that men were mediocre creatures.

Nor could the poets, however rapidly now multiplied their verse-books, satisfactorily delude their patrons into overlooking this unpleasant fact. For one reason or another, men as a whole have never taken kindlily to printed poetry: most of us are unable to put up with it at all, and even to the exceptional person verse after an hour's reading becomes unaccountably tiresome. Prose — for no very patent cause — is much easier going. So the poets proved ineffectual comforters, who could but rarely be-drug even the few to whom their charms did not seem gibberish.

With the advent of the novel, all this was changed. Not merely were you relieved from metrical fatigue, but there came no commonplace flesh-and-blood to give the lie to the artist's pretensions. It was possible, really for the first time, acceptably to present in literature men "as they ought to be." Richardson could dilate as unrestrainedly as he pleased upon the super-eminence in virtue and sin, respectively, of his Grandison and his Lovelace emboldened by the knowledge that there was nothing to check him off save the dubious touchstone of his reader's common-sense. Fielding was not only able to conduct a broad-shouldered young ruffian to fortune and a lovely wife, but could moreover endow Tom Jones with all sorts of heroic and estimable qualities such as (in mere unimportant fact) rascals do not display in actual life. When the novel succeeded the drama it was no longer necessary for the artist to represent human beings with even partial veracity: and this new style of writing at once became emblematic.

And so it has been ever since. Novelists have severally evolved their pleasing symbols wherewith approximately to suggest human beings and the business of human life, much as remote Egyptians drew serrated lines to convey the idea of water and a circle to indicate eternity. The symbols have often varied: but there has rarely been any ill-advised attempt to depict life as it seems in the living of it, or to crystallize the vague notion and feeble sensations with which human beings, actually, muddle through to an epitaph; if only because all sensible persons, obscurely aware that this routine is far from what it ought to be, have always preferred to deny its existence. And moreover, we have come long ago to be guided in any really decisive speech or action by what we have read somewhere; and so, may fairly claim that literature should select (as it does) such speeches and such actions as typical of our essential lives, rather than the gray interstices, which we perforce fill in extempore, and botch.

As concerns the novelists of the day before yesterday, this evasion of veracity is already more or less conceded: the "platitudinous heroics" of Scott and the "exaggerated sentimentalism" of Dickens are notorious in quite authoritative circles whose *ducdame* is the honest belief that art is a branch of pedagogy. Thackeray, as has been pointed out elsewhere, avoids many a logical outcome of circumstance, when recognition thereof would be inconvenient, by killing off somebody and blinding the reader with a tear-drenched handkerchief. And when we sanely appraise the most cried-up writer of genteel "realism," matters are not conducted much more candidly. Here is a fair sample: — "From the very beginning of my acquaintance with you, your manners, impressing me with the fullest belief of your arrogance, your conceit, and your selfish disdain of the feelings of others, were such as to form that groundwork of disapprobation on which succeeding events have built so immovable a dislike, and I had not known you a month before I felt that you were the last man in the world whom I could ever be prevailed on to marry." It is Miss Austen's most famous, most beloved, and most "natural" character replying — not by means of a stilted letter, but colloquially, under the stress of emotion — to a proposal of marriage by the man she loves. This is a crisis which in human life a normal young woman simply does not meet with any such rhetorical architecture. . . . So there really seems small ground for wonder that Mr. Darcy observed, "You have said quite enough, madam"; and no cause whatever for surprise that he hastily left the room, and was heard to open the front-door and quit the house. . . . Yet, be it forthwith added, Scott and Dickens and Thackeray, and even Miss Austen, were in the right, from one or another æsthetic standpoint, in thus variously editing and revising their contemporaries' unsatisfactory disposition of life. Indeed, upon no plea could they be bound to emulate malfeasance.

Criticism as to the veracity of more recent writers is best dismissed with the well-merited commendation that novelists to-day continue rigorously to respect the Second Commandment. Meanwhile it may, with comparative safety, be pointed out that no interred writer of widely conceded genius has ever displayed in depicting the average of human speech and thought and action, and general endowments, such exactness as would be becoming in an affidavit; but rather, when his art touched on these dangerous topics, has regarded romantic prevarication as a necessity. The truth about ourselves is the one truth, above all others, which we are adamantine not to face. And this determination springs, not wholly from vanity, but from a profound race-sense that by such denial we have little to lose, and a great deal to gain.

7

For, as has been said before, an inveterate Sophocles notes clearly that veracity is the one unpardonable sin, not merely against art, but against human welfare. . . . You will observe that the beginnings of fiction everywhere, among all races, take with curious unanimity the same form. It is always the history of the unlooked-for achievements and the ultimate very public triumph of the ill-used youngest son. From the myth of Zeus, third son of Chronos, to the third prince of the fairy-tale, there is no exception. Everywhere it is to the despised weakling that romance accords the final and very public victory. For in the life-battle for existence it was of course the men of puniest build who first developed mental ability, since hardier compeers, who took with bloodied hands that which they wanted, had no especial need of less reliable makeshifts: and everywhere this weakling, quite naturally, afforded himself in imagination what the force of circumstance denied him in fact. Competent persons, then as now, had neither the time nor ability for literature.

By and by a staggering stroke of genius improved the tale by adding the handicap of sex-weakness: and Cinderella (whom romance begot and deified as Psyche) straightway led captive every dreamer's hitherto unvoiced desire. This is the most beloved story in the world's library, and, barring a tremendous exception to which I shall presently return, will always remain without rival. Any author anywhere can gain men's love by remodeling (not too drastically) the history of Cinderella: thousands of calligraphic persons have, of course, availed themselves of this fortunate circumstance: and the seeming miracle is that the naïve and the most sophisticated continue to thrill, at each re-telling of the hackneyed story, with the instant response of fiddlestrings, to an interpretation of life which one is tempted to describe as fiddlesticks. Yet an inevitable very public triumph of the downtrodden — with all imaginable pomp and fanfare — is of necessity a tenet generally acceptable to a world of ineffectual inhabitants, each one of whom is a monarch of dreams incarcerated in a prison of flesh; and each of whom is hourly fretted, no less by the indifference of nature to his plight, than by the irrelevancy thereto of those social orderings he dazedly ballots into existence. . . . Christianity, with its teaching that the oppressed shall be exalted, and the unhappy made free of eternal bliss, thus came in the nick of occasion, to promise what the run of men were eager to believe. Such a delectable prospect, irrespective of its plausibility, could not in the nature of things fail to become popular: as has been strikingly attested by man's wide acceptance of the rather exigent requirements of Christianity, and his honest endeavors ever since to interpret them as meaning whatever happens to be convenient.

In similar fashion, humanity would seem at an early period to have wrenched comfort from prefiguring man as the hero of the cosmic romance. For it was unpleasantly apparent that man did not excel in physical strength, as set against the other creatures of a planet whereon may be encountered tigers and elephants. His senses were of low development, as compared with the senses of insects: and, indeed, senses possessed by some of these small contemporaries man presently found he did not share, nor very clearly understand. The luxury of wings, and even the common comfort of a caudal appendage, was denied him. He walked painfully, without hoofs, and, created naked as a shelled almond, with difficulty outlived a season of inclement weather. Physically, he displayed in not a solitary trait a product of nature's more ambitious labor. . . . He, thus, surpassed the rest of vital creation in nothing except, as was beginning to be rumored, the power to reason; and even so, was apparently too magnanimous to avail himself of the privilege.

But to acknowledge such disconcerting facts would never do: just as inevitably, therefore, as the peafowl came to listen with condescension to the nightingale, and the tortoise to deplore the slapdash ways of his contemporaries, man probably began very early to regale himself with flattering narratives as to his nature and destiny. Among the countless internecine animals that roamed earth, puissant with claw and fang and sinew, an ape reft of his tail, and grown rusty at climbing, was the most formidable, and in the end would triumph. It was of course considered blasphemous to inquire into the grounds for this belief, in view of its patent desirability, for the race was already human. So the prophetic portrait of man treading among cringing pleosauri to browbeat a frightened dinosaur was duly scratched upon the cave's wall, and art began forthwith to accredit human beings with every trait and destiny which they desiderated. . . .

And so to-day, as always, we delight to hear about invincible men and women of unearthly loveliness — corrected and considerably augmented versions of our family circle, — performing feats illimitably beyond our modest powers. And so to-day no one upon the preferable side of Bedlam wishes to be reminded of what we are in actuality, even were it possible, by any disastrous miracle, ever to dispel the mist which romance has evoked about all human doings; and to the golden twilight of which old usage has so accustomed us that, like nocturnal birds, our vision grows perturbed in a clearer atmosphere. And we have come very firmly to believe in the existence of men everywhere, not as in fact they are, but " as they ought to be."

8

Now art, like all the other noteworthy factors in this remarkable world, serves in the end utilitarian purposes. When a trait is held up as desirable, for a convincingly long while, the average person, out of self-respect, pretends to possess it: with time, he acts letter-perfect as one endowed therewith, and comes unshakably to believe that it has guided him from infancy. For while everyone is notoriously swayed by appearances, this is more especially true of his own appearance: cleanliness is, if not actually next to godliness, so far a promoter of benevolence that no man feels upon quite friendly terms with his fellow-beings when conscious that he needs a shave; and if in grief you resolutely contort your mouth into a smile you somehow do become forthwith aware of a considerable mitigation of misery. . . . So it is that man's vanity and hypocrisy and lack of clear thinking are in a fair way to prove in the outcome his salvation.

All is vanity, quoth the son of David, inverting the truth for popular consumption, as became a wise Preacher who knew that vanity is all. For man alone of animals plays the ape to his dreams. That a dog dreams vehemently is matter of public knowledge: it is perfectly possible that in his more ecstatic visions he usurps the shape of his master, and visits Elysian pantries in human form: with awakening, he observes that in point of fact he is a dog, and as a rational animal, makes the best of canineship. But with man the case is otherwise, in that when logic leads to any humiliating conclusion, the sole effect is to discredit logic.

So has man's indomitable vanity made a harem of his instincts, and walled off a seraglio wherein to beget the virtues and refinements and all ennobling factors in man's long progress from gorillaship. As has been suggested, creative literature would seem to have sprung simply from the instinct of any hurt animal to seek revenge, — and "to get even," as the phrase runs, in the field of imagination when such revenge was not feasible in any other arena. . . . Then, too, it is an instinct common to brute creatures that the breeding or even the potential mother must not be bitten, — upon which modest basis a little by a little mankind builded the fair code of *domnei,* or woman-worship, which yet does yeoman service among legislators toward keeping half our citizens " out of the mire of politics." From the shuddering dread that beasts manifest toward uncomprehended forces, such as wind and thunder and tall waves, man developed religion, and a consoling assurance of divine paternity. And when you come to judge what he made of sexual desire, appraising the deed in view as against the wondrous overture of courtship and that infinity of high achievements which time has seen performed as grace-notes, words fail before his egregious thaumaturgy. For after any such stupendous bit of hocus-pocus, there seems to be no limit fixed to the conjurations of human vanity.

9

And these aspiring notions blended a great while since, into what may be termed the Chivalrous attitude toward life. Thus it is that romance, the real demiurge, the first and loveliest daughter of human vanity, contrives all those dynamic illusions which are used to further the ultimate ends of romance. . . . The cornerstone of Chivalry I take to be the idea of vicarship: for the chivalrous person is, in his own eyes at least, the child of God, and goes about this world as his Father's representative in an alien country. It was very adroitly to human pride, through an assumption of man's personal responsibility in his tiniest action, that Chivalry made its appeal; and exhorted every man to keep faith, not merely with the arbitrary will of a strong god, but with himself. There is no cause for wonder that the appeal was irresistible, when to each man it thus admitted that he himself was the one thing seriously to be considered. . . . So man became a chivalrous animal; and about this flattering notion of divine vicarship builded his elaborate mediæval code, to which, in essentials, a great number of persons adhere even nowadays. Questionless, however, the Chivalrous attitude does not very happily fit in with modern conditions, whereby the self-elected obligations of the knight-errant toward repressing evil are (in theory at all events) more efficaciously discharged by an organized police and a jury system. And perhaps it was never, quite, a " practical " attitude, —

no, *mais quel geste!* as was observed by a preëminently chivalrous person. At worst, it is an attitude which one finds very taking to the fancy as the posture is exemplified by divers mediæval chroniclers, who had sound notions about portraying men "as they ought to be" . . . There is Nicolas de Caen, for instance, who in his *Dizain des Reines* (with which I am familiar, I confess, in the English version alone) presents with some naïveté this notion of divine vicarship, in that he would seem to restrict it to the nobility and gentry. "For royal persons and their immediate associates," Dom Nicolas assumes at outset, "are the responsible stewards of Heaven": and regarding them continuously as such, he selects from the lives of various queens ten crucial moments wherein (as Nicolas phrases it), "Destiny has thrust her scepter into the hands of a human being, and left the weakling free to steer the pregnant outcome. Now prove thyself to be at bottom a god or else a beast, saith Destiny, and now eternally abide that choice." Yet this, and this alone, when you come to think of it, is what Destiny says, not merely to "royal persons and their immediate associates," but to everyone. . . . And in his *Roman de Lusignan* Nicolas deals with that quaint development of the Chivalrous attitude to which I just alluded, that took form, as an allied but individual illusion, in *domnei,* or woman-worship; and found in a man's mistress an ever-present reminder, and sometimes a rival, of God. There is something not unpathetic in the thought that this once world-controlling force is restricted to-day to removing a man's hat in an elevator and occasionally compelling a surrender of his seat in a streetcar. . . . But this *Roman de Lusignan* also has been put into English, with an Afterword by the translator wherein the theories of *domnei* are rather painstakingly set forth: and thereto I shall presently recur, for further consideration of this illusion of *domnei.*

Throughout, of course, the Chivalrous attitude was an intelligent attitude, in which one spun romances and accorded no meticulous attention to mere facts. . . . For thus to spin romances is to bring about, in every sense, man's recreation, since man alone of animals can, actually, acquire a trait by assuming, in defiance of reason, that he already possesses it. To spin romances is, indeed, man's proper and peculiar function in a world wherein he only of created beings can make no profitable use of the truth about himself. For man alone of animals plays the ape to his dreams. So he fares onward chivalrously, led by *ignes fatui* no doubt, yet moving onward. And that the goal remains ambiguous seems but a trivial circumstance to any living creature who knows, he knows not how, that to stay still can be esteemed a virtue only in the dead.

10

Indeed, when I consider the race to which I have the honor to belong, I am filled with respectful wonder. . . . All about us flows and gyrates unceasingly the material universe, — an endless inconceivable jumble of rotatory blazing gas and frozen spheres and detonating comets, wherethrough spins Earth like a frail midge. And to this blown molecule adhere what millions and millions of parasites just such as I am, begetting and dreaming and slaying and abnegating and toiling and making mirth, just as did aforetime those countless generations of our forbears, every one of whom was likewise a creature just such as I am! Were the human beings that have been subjected to confinement in flesh each numbered, as is customary in other penal institutes, with what interminable row of digits might one set forth your number, say, or mine?

Nor is this everything. For my reason, such as it is, perceives this race, in its entirety, in the whole outcome of its achievement, to be beyond all wording petty and ineffectual: and no more than thought can estimate the relative proportion to the material universe of our poor Earth, can thought conceive with what quintillionths to express that fractional part which I, as an individual parasite, add to Earth's negligible fretting by ephemeræ.

And still — behold the miracle! — still I believe life to be a personal transaction between myself and Omnipotence; I believe that what I do is somehow of importance; and I believe that I am on a journey toward some very public triumph not unlike that of the third prince in the fairy-tale. . . . Even to-day I believe in this dynamic illusion. For that creed was the first great inspiration of the demiurge, — man's big romantic idea of Chivalry, of himself as his Father's representative in an alien country; — and it is a notion at which mere fact and reason yelp denial unavailingly. For every one of us is so constituted that he knows the romance to be true, and corporal fact and human reason in this matter, as in divers others, to be the suborned and perjured witnesses of "realism."

HENRY LOUIS MENCKEN
1880–

65   *The Feminine Mind*

I

The Maternal Instinct

T A man's women folk, whatever their outward show of respect for his merit and authority, always regard him secretly as an ass, and with something akin to pity. His most gaudy sayings and doings seldom deceive them; they see the actual man within, and know him for a shallow and pathetic fellow. In this fact, perhaps, lies one of the best proofs of feminine intelligence, or, as the common phrase makes it, feminine intuition. The mark of that so-called intuition is simply a sharp and accurate perception of reality, an habitual immunity to emotional enchantment, a relentless capacity for distinguishing clearly between the appearance and the substance. The appearance, in the normal family circle, is a hero, a magnifico, a demigod. The substance is a poor mountebank.

The proverb that no man is a hero to his valet is obviously

of masculine manufacture. It is both insincere and untrue: insincere because it merely masks the egotistic doctrine that he is potentially a hero to everyone else, and untrue because a valet, being a fourth-rate man himself, is likely to be the last person in the world to penetrate his master's charlatanry. Whoever heard of a valet who didn't envy his master wholeheartedly? who wouldn't willingly change places with his master? who didn't secretly wish that he *was* his master? A man's wife labors under no such naïve folly. She may envy her husband, true enough, certain of his more soothing prerogatives and sentimentalities. She may envy him his masculine liberty of movement and occupation, his impenetrable complacency, his peasant-like delight in petty vices, his capacity for hiding the harsh face of reality behind the cloak of romanticism, his general innocence and childishness. But she never envies him his puerile ego; she never envies him his shoddy and preposterous soul.

This shrewd perception of masculine bombast and make-believe, this acute understanding of man as the eternal tragic comedian, is at the bottom of that compassionate irony which passes under the name of the maternal instinct. A woman wishes to mother a man simply because she sees into his helplessness, his need of an amiable environment, his touching self-delusion. That ironical note is not only daily apparent in real life; it sets the whole tone of feminine fiction. The woman novelist, if she be skilful enough to arise out of mere imitation into genuine self-expression, never takes her heroes quite seriously. From the day of George Sand to the day of Selma Lagerlöf she has always got into her character study a touch of superior aloofness, of ill-concealed derision. I can't recall a single masculine figure created by a woman who is not, at bottom, a booby.

2

Women's Intelligence

That it should still be necessary, at this late stage in the senility of the human race, to argue that women have a fine and fluent intelligence is surely an eloquent proof of the defective observation, incurable prejudice, and general imbecility of their lords and masters. One finds very few professors of the subject, even among admitted feminists, approaching the fact as obvious; practically all of them think it necessary to bring up a vast mass of evidence to establish what should be an axiom. Even the Franco-Englishman, W. L. George, one of the most sharp-witted of the faculty, wastes a whole book upon the demonstration, and then, with a great air of uttering something new, gives it the humorless title of "The Intelligence of Women." The intelligence of women, forsooth! As well devote a laborious time to the sagacity of serpents, pickpockets, or Holy Church!

Women, in truth, are not only intelligent; they have almost a monopoly of certain of the subtler and more utile forms of intelligence. The thing itself, indeed, might be reasonably described as a special feminine character; there is in it, in more than one of its manifestations, a femaleness as palpable as the femaleness of cruelty, masochism or rouge. Men are strong. Men are brave in physical combat. Men have sentiment. Men are romantic, and love what they conceive to be virtue and beauty. Men incline to faith, hope and charity. Men know how to sweat and endure. Men are amiable and fond. But in so far as they show the true fundamentals of intelligence — in so far as they reveal a capacity for discovering the kernel of eternal verity in the husk of delusion and hallucination and a passion for bringing it forth — to that extent, at least, they are feminine, and still nourished by the milk of their mothers. "Human creatures," says George, borrowing from Weininger, "are never entirely male or entirely female; there are no men, there are no women, but only sexual majorities." Find me an obviously intelligent man, a man free from sentimentality and illusion, a man hard to deceive, a man of the first class, and I'll show you a man with a wide streak of woman in him. Bonaparte had it; Goethe had it; Schopenhauer had it; Bismarck and Lincoln had it; in Shakespeare, if the Freudians are to be believed, it amounted to downright homosexuality. The essential traits and qualities of the male, the hallmarks of the unpolluted masculine, are at the same time the hall-marks of the *Schafskopf*. The caveman is all muscles and mush. Without a woman to rule him and think for him, he is a truly lamentable spectacle: a baby with whiskers, a rabbit with the frame of an aurochs, a feeble and preposterous caricature of God.

It would be an easy matter, indeed, to demonstrate that superior talent in man is practically always accompanied by this feminine flavor — that complete masculinity and stupidity are often indistinguishable. Lest I be misunderstood I hasten to add that I do not mean to say that masculinity contributes nothing to the complex of chemico-physiological reactions which produces what we call talent; all I mean to say is that this complex is impossible without the feminine contribution — that it is a product of the interplay of the two elements. In women of genius we see the opposite picture. They are commonly distinctly mannish, and shave as well as shine. Think of George Sand, Catherine the Great, Elizabeth of England, Rosa Bonheur, Teresa Carreño or Cosima Wagner. The truth is that neither sex, without some fertilization by the complementary characters of the other, is capable of the highest reaches of human endeavor. Man, without a saving touch of woman in him, is too doltish, too naïve and romantic, too easily deluded and lulled to sleep by his imagination to be anything above a cavalryman, a theologian or a bank director. And woman, without some trace of that divine innocence which is masculine, is too harshly the realist for those vast projections of the fancy which lie at the heart of what we call genius. Here, as elsewhere in the universe, the best effects are obtained by a mingling of elements. The wholly manly man lacks the wit necessary to give objective form to his soaring and secret dreams, and the wholly womanly woman is apt to be too cynical a creature to dream at all.

3

The Masculine Bag of Tricks

What men, in their egoism, constantly mistake for a deficiency of intelligence in woman is merely an incapacity for mastering that mass of small intellectual tricks, that complex of petty knowledges, that collection of cerebral rubber-stamps, which constitutes the chief mental equipment of the average male. A man thinks that he is more intelligent than his wife because he can add up a column of figures more accurately, and because he understands the imbecile jargon of the stock market, and because he is able to distinguish between the ideas of rival politicians, and because he is privy to the minutiae of some sordid and degrading business or profession, say soap-selling or the law. But these empty talents, of course, are not really signs of a profound intelligence; they are, in fact, merely superficial accomplishments, and their acquirement puts little more strain on the mental powers than a chimpanzee suffers in learning how to catch a penny or scratch a match. The whole bag of tricks of the average business man, or even of the average professional man, is inordinately childish. It takes no more actual sagacity to carry on the everyday hawking and haggling of the world, or to ladle out its normal doses of bad medicine and worse law, than it takes to operate a taxicab or fry a pan of fish. No observant person, indeed, can come into close contact with the general run of business and professional men — I confine myself to those who seem to get on in the world, and exclude the admitted failures — without marveling at their intellectual lethargy, their incurable ingenuousness, their appalling lack of ordinary sense. The late Charles Francis Adams, a grandson of one American President and a great-grandson of another, after a long lifetime in intimate association with some of the chief business "geniuses" of that paradise of traders and usurers, the United States, reported in his old age that he had never heard a single one of them say anything worth hearing. These were vigorous and masculine men, and in a man's world they were successful men, but intellectually they were all blank cartridges.

There is, indeed, fair ground for arguing that, if men of that kidney were genuinely intelligent, they would never succeed at their gross and drivelling concerns — that their very capacity to master and retain such balderdash as constitutes their stock in trade is proof of their inferior mentality. The notion is certainly supported by the familiar incompetency of the first-rate men for what are called practical concerns. One could not think of Aristotle or Beethoven multiplying 3,472,701 by 99,999 without making a mistake, nor could one think of him remembering the range of this or that railway share for two years, or the number of tenpenny nails in a hundredweight, or the freight on lard from Galveston to Rotterdam. And by the same token one could not imagine him expert at billiards, or at grouse-shooting, or at golf, or at any other of the idiotic games at which what are called successful men commonly divert themselves. In his great study of British genius, Havelock Ellis found that an incapacity for such petty expertness was visible in almost all first-rate men. They are bad at tying cravats. They do not understand the fashionable card-games. They are puzzled by book-keeping. They know nothing of party politics. In brief, they are inert and impotent in the very fields of endeavor that see the average men's highest performances, and are easily surpassed by men who, in actual intelligence, are about as far below them as the *Simidae*.

This lack of skill at manual and mental tricks of a trivial character — which must inevitably appear to a barber or a dentist as stupidity, and to a successful haberdasher as downright imbecility — is a character that men of the first class share with women of the first, second and even third classes. There is at the bottom of it, in truth, something unmistakably feminine; its appearance in a man is almost invariably accompanied by the other touch of femaleness that I have described. Nothing, indeed, could be plainer than the fact that women, as a class, are sadly deficient in the small expertness of men as a class. One seldom, if ever, hears of them succeeding in the occupations which bring out such expertness most lavishly — for example, tuning pianos, repairing clocks, practising law, (*i.e.*, matching petty tricks with some other lawyer), painting portraits, keeping books, or managing factories — despite the circumstance that the great majority of such occupations are well within their physical powers, and that few of them offer any very formidable social barriers to female entrance. There is no external reason why women shouldn't succeed as operative surgeons; the way is wide open, the rewards are large, and there is a special demand for them on grounds of modesty. Nevertheless, not many women graduates in medicine undertake surgery and it is rare for one of them to make a success of it. There is, again, no external reason why women should not prosper at the bar, or as editors of newspapers, or as managers of the lesser sort of factories, or in the wholesale trade, or as hotel-keepers. The taboos that stand in the way are of very small force; various adventurous women have defied them with impunity; once the door is entered there remains no special handicap within. But, as every one knows, the number of women actually practising these trades and professions is very small, and few of them have attained to any distinction in competition with men.

4

Why Women Fail

The cause thereof, as I say, is not external, but internal. It lies in the same disconcerting apprehension of the larger realities, the same impatience with the paltry and meretricious, the same disqualification for mechanical routine and empty technic which one finds in the higher varieties of men. Even in the pursuits which, by the custom of Christendom, are especially their own, women seldom show any of that elaborately conventionalized and half automatic proficiency which is the pride and boast of most men. It is a commonplace of observation, indeed, that a housewife who actually

knows how to cook, or who can make her own clothes with
enough skill to conceal the fact from the most casual glance,
or who is competent to instruct her children in the elements
of morals, learning and hygiene — it is a platitude that such
a woman is very rare indeed, and that when she is encountered she is not usually esteemed for her general intelligence.
This is particularly true in the United States, where the position of women is higher than in any other civilized or semi-
civilized country, and the old assumption of their intellectual
inferiority has been most successfully challenged. The
American dinner-table, in truth, becomes a monument to the
defective technic of the American housewife. The guest who
respects his oesophagus, invited to feed upon its discordant
and ill-prepared victuals, evades the experience as long and
as often as he can, and resigns himself to it as he might
resign himself to being shaved by a paralytic. Nowhere else
in the world have women more leisure and freedom to improve their minds, and nowhere else do they show a higher
level of intelligence, or take part more effectively in affairs
of the first importance. But nowhere else is there worse
cooking in the home, or a more inept handling of the whole
domestic economy, or a larger dependence upon the aid of
external substitutes, by men provided, for the skill that is
wanting where it theoretically exists. It is surely no mere
coincidence that the land of the emancipated and enthroned
woman is also the land of canned soup, of canned pork and
beans, of whole meals in cans, and of everything else ready-
made. And nowhere else is there a more striking tendency
to throw the whole business of training the minds of children
upon professional teachers, and the whole business of in-
structing them in morals and religion upon so-called Sunday-
schools, and the whole business of developing and caring for
their bodies upon playground experts, sex hygienists and
other such professionals, most of them mountebanks.

In brief, women rebel — often unconsciously, sometimes
even submitting all the while — against the dull, mechanical
tricks of the trade that the present organization of society

compels them to practise for a living, and that rebellion testifies to their intelligence. If they enjoyed and took pride in those tricks, and showed it by diligence and skill, they would be on all fours with such men as are head waiters, ladies' tailors, schoolmasters or carpet-beaters, and proud of it. The inherent tendency of any woman above the most stupid is to evade the whole obligation, and, if she cannot actually evade it, to reduce its demands to the minimum. And when some accident purges her, either temporarily or permanently, of the inclination to marriage (of which much more anon), and she enters into competition with men in the general business of the world, the sort of career that she commonly carves out offers additional evidence of her mental peculiarity. In whatever calls for no more than an invariable technic and a feeble chicanery she usually fails; in whatever calls for independent thought and resourcefulness she usually succeeds. Thus she is almost always a failure as a lawyer, for the law requires only an armament of hollow phrases and stereotyped formulae, and a mental habit which puts these phantasms above sense, truth and justice; and she is almost always a failure in business, for business, in the main, is so foul a compound of trivialities and rogueries that her sense of intellectual integrity revolts against it. But she is usually a success as a sick-nurse, for that profession requires ingenuity, quick comprehension, courage in the face of novel and disconcerting situations, and above all, a capacity for penetrating and dominating character; and whenever she comes into competition with men in the arts, particularly on those secondary planes where simple nimbleness of mind is unaided by the master strokes of genius, she holds her own invariably. The best and most intellectual — *i.e.*, most original and enterprising — play-actors are not men, but women, and so are the best teachers and blackmailers, and a fair share of the best writers, and public functionaries, and executants of music. In the *demi-monde* one will find enough acumen and daring, and enough resilience in the face of special difficulties, to put the equipment of any exclusively male profession to shame. If the work of the average man required half the mental agility and readiness of resource of the work of the average prostitute, the average man would be constantly on the verge of starvation.

5

The Thing Called Intuition

Men, as every one knows, are disposed to question this superior intelligence of women; their egoism demands the denial, and they are seldom reflective enough to dispose of it by logical and evidential analysis. Moreover, as we shall see a bit later on, there is a certain specious appearance of soundness in their position; they have forced upon women an artificial character which well conceals their real character, and women have found it profitable to encourage the deception. But though every normal man thus cherishes the soothing unction that he is the intellectual superior of all women, and particularly of his wife, he constantly gives the lie to his pretension by consulting and deferring to what he calls her intuition. That is to say, he knows by experience that her judgment in many matters of capital concern is more subtle and searching than his own, and, being disinclined to accredit this greater sagacity to a more competent intelligence, he takes refuge behind the doctrine that it is due to some impenetrable and intangible talent for guessing correctly, some half mystical supersense, some vague (and, in essence, infra-human) instinct.

The true nature of this alleged instinct, however, is revealed by an examination of the situations which inspire a man to call it to his aid. These situations do not arise out of the purely technical problems that are his daily concern, but out of the rarer and more fundamental, and hence enormously more difficult problems which beset him only at long and irregular intervals, and so offer a test, not of his mere capacity for being drilled, but of his capacity for genuine ratiocination. No man, I take it, save one consciously inferior and hen-pecked, would consult his wife about hiring a clerk, or about extending credit to some paltry customer, or about some routine piece of tawdry swindling; but not even the most egoistic man would fail to sound the sentiment of his wife about taking a partner into his business, or about standing for public office, or about combating unfair and ruinous competition, or about marrying off their daughter. Such things are of massive importance; they lie at the foundation of well-being; they call for the best thought that the man confronted by them can muster; the perils hidden in a wrong decision overcome even the clamors of vanity. It is in such situations that the superior mental grasp of women is of obvious utility, and has to be admitted. It is here that they rise above the insignificant sentimentalities, superstitions and formulae of men, and apply to the business their singular talent for separating the appearance from the substance, and so exercise what is called their intuition.

Intuition? With all respect, bosh! Then it was intuition that led Darwin to work out the hypothesis of natural selection. Then it was intuition that fabricated the gigantically complex score of "Die Walküre." Then it was intuition that convinced Columbus of the existence of land to the west of the Azores. All this intuition of which so much transcendental rubbish is merchanted is no more and no less than intelligence — intelligence so keen that it can penetrate to the hidden truth through the most formidable wrappings of false semblance and demeanor, and so little corrupted by sentimental prudery that it is equal to the even more difficult task of hauling that truth out into the light, in all its naked hideousness. Women decide the larger questions of life correctly and quickly, not because they are lucky guessers, not because they are divinely inspired, not because they practice a magic inherited from savagery, but simply and solely because they have sense. They see at a glance what most men could not see with searchlights and telescopes; they are at grips with the essentials of a problem before men have finished debating its mere externals. They are the supreme realists of the race. Apparently illogical, they are the possessors of a rare and subtle super-logic. Apparently whimsical, they hang to the truth with a tenacity which carries them through every phase of its incessant, jelly-like shifting of form. Apparently unobservant and easily deceived, they see with bright and horrible eyes. . . . In men, too, the same merciless perspicacity sometimes shows itself — men recognized to be more aloof and uninflammable than the general — men of special talent for the logical — sardonic men, cynics. Men, too, sometimes have brains. But that is a rare, rare man, I venture, who is as steadily intelligent, as constantly sound in judgment, as little put off by appearances, as the average women of forty-eight.

66 *In Memoriam: W. J. B.*

HAS it been duly marked by historians that the late William Jennings Bryan's last secular act on this globe of sin was to catch flies? A curious detail, and not without its sardonic overtones. He was the most sedulous fly-catcher in American history, and in many ways the most successful. His quarry, of course, was not *Musca domestica* but *Homo neandertalensis*. For forty years he tracked it with coo and bellow, up and down the rustic backways of the Republic. Wherever the flambeaux of Chautauqua smoked and guttered, and the bilge of Idealism ran in the veins, and Baptist pastors dammed the brooks with the sanctified, and men gathered who were weary and heavy laden, and their wives who were full of Peruna and as fecund as the shad (*Alosa sapidissima*) — there the indefatigable Jennings set up his traps and spread his bait. He knew every country town in the South and West, and he could crowd the most remote of them to suffocation by simply winding his horn. The city proletariat, transiently flustered by him in 1896, quickly penetrated his buncombe and would have no more of him; the cockney gallery jeered him at every Democratic national convention for twenty-five years. But out where the grass grows high, and the horned cattle dream away the lazy afternoons, and men still fear the powers and principalities of the air — out there between the corn-rows he held his old puissance to the end. There was no need of beaters to drive in his game. The news that he was coming was enough. For miles the flivver dust would choke the roads. And when he rose at the end of the day to discharge his Message there would be such breathless attention, such a rapt and enchanted ecstasy, such a sweet rustle of amens as the world had not known since Johann fell to Herod's ax.

There was something peculiarly fitting in the fact that his last days were spent in a one-horse Tennessee village, and that death found him there. The man felt at home in such simple and Christian scenes. He liked people who sweated freely, and were not debauched by the refinements of the toilet. Making his progress up and down the Main street of little Dayton, surrounded by gaping primates from the upland valleys of the Cumberland Range, his coat laid aside, his bare arms and hairy chest shining damply, his bald head sprinkled with dust — so accoutered and on display he was obviously happy. He liked getting up early in the morning, to the tune of cocks crowing on the dunghill. He liked the heavy, greasy victuals of the farmhouse kitchen. He liked country lawyers, country pastors, all country people. He liked the country sounds and country smells. I believe that this liking was sincere — perhaps the only sincere thing in the man. His nose showed no uneasiness when a hillman in faded overalls and hickory shirt accosted him on the street, and besought him for light upon some mystery of Holy Writ. The simian gabble of the cross-roads was not gabble to him, but wisdom of an occult and superior sort. In the presence of city folks he was palpably uneasy. Their clothes, I suspect, annoyed him, and he was suspicious of their too delicate manners. He knew all the while that they were laughing at him — if not at his baroque theology, then at least at his alpaca pantaloons. But the yokels never laughed at him. To them he was not the huntsman but the prophet, and toward the end, as he gradually forsook mundane politics for more ghostly concerns, they began to elevate him in their hierarchy. When he died he was the peer of Abraham. His old enemy, Wilson, aspiring to the same white and shining robe, came down with a thump. But Bryan made the grade. His place in Tennessee hagiography is secure. If the village barber saved any of his hair, then it is curing gallstones down there to-day.

But what label will he bear in more urbane regions? One, I fear, of a far less flattering kind. Bryan lived too long, and descended too deeply into the mud, to be taken seriously hereafter by fully literate men, even of the kind who write schoolbooks. There was a scattering of sweet words in his funeral notice, but it was no more than a response to conventional sentimentality. The best verdict the most romantic editorial writer could dredge up, save in the humorless South, was to the general effect that his imbecilities were excused by his earnestness — that under his clowning, as under that of the juggler of Notre Dame, there was the zeal of a steadfast soul. But this was apology, not praise; precisely the same thing might be said of Mary Baker G. Eddy, the late Czar Nicholas, or Czolgosz. The truth is that even Bryan's sincerity will probably yield to what is called, in other fields, definitive criticism. Was he sincere when he opposed imperialism in the Philippines, or when he fed it with deserving Democrats in Santo Domingo? Was he sincere when he tried to shove the Prohibitionists under the table, or when he seized their banner and began to lead them with loud whoops? Was he sincere when he bellowed against war, or when he dreamed of himself as a tin-soldier in uniform, with a grave reserved among the generals? Was he sincere when he denounced the late John W. Davis, or when he swallowed Davis? Was he sincere when he fawned over Champ Clark, or when he betrayed Clark? Was he sincere when he pleaded for tolerance in New York, or when he bawled for the faggot and the stake in Tennessee?

This talk of sincerity, I confess, fatigues me. If the fellow was sincere, then so was P. T. Barnum. The word is disgraced and degraded by such uses. He was, in fact, a charlatan, a mountebank, a zany without shame or dignity. His career brought him into contact with the first men of his time; he preferred the company of rustic ignoramuses. It was hard to believe, watching him at Dayton, that he had traveled, that he had been received in civilized societies, that he had been a high officer of state. He seemed only a poor clod like those around him, deluded by a childish technology, full of an almost pathological hatred of all learning, all human dignity, all beauty, all fine and noble things. He was a peasant come home to the barnyard. Imagine a gentleman, and you have imagined everything that he was not. What animated him from end to end of his grotesque career was simply ambition — the ambition of a common man to get his hand upon the collar of his superiors, or, failing that, to get his thumb into their eyes. He was born with a roaring voice, and it had the trick of inflaming half-wits. His whole career was devoted to raising those half-wits against their betters, that he himself might shine. His last battle will be grossly misunderstood if it is thought of as a mere exercise in fanaticism — that is, if Bryan the Fundamentalist Pope is mistaken for one of the bucolic Fundamentalists. There was much more in it than that, as everyone knows who saw him on the field. What moved him, at bottom, was simply hatred of the city men who had laughed at him so long, and brought him at last to so tatterdemalion an estate. He lusted for revenge upon them. He yearned to lead the anthropoid rabble against them, to punish them for their execution upon him by attacking the very vitals of their civilization. He went far beyond the bounds of any merely religious frenzy, however inordinate. When he began denouncing the notion that man is a mammal even some of the hinds at Dayton were agape. And when, brought upon Darrow's cruel hook, he writhed and tossed in a very fury of malignancy, bawling against the baldest elements of sense and decency like a man frantic — when he came to that tragic climax of his striving there were snickers among the hinds as well as hosannas.

Upon that hook, in truth, Bryan committed suicide, as a legend as well as in the body. He staggered from the rustic court ready to die, and he staggered from it ready to be forgotten, save as a character in a third-rate farce, witless and in poor taste. It was plain to everyone who knew him, when he came to Dayton, that his great days were behind him — that, for all the fury of his hatred, he was now definitely an old man, and headed at last for silence. There was a vague, unpleasant manginess about his appearance; he somehow seemed dirty, though a close glance showed him as carefully shaven as an actor, and clad in immaculate linen. All the hair was gone from the dome of his head, and it had begun to fall out, too, behind his ears, in the obscene manner of the late Samuel Gompers. The resonance had departed from his voice; what was once a bugle blast had become reedy and quavering. Who knows that, like Demosthenes, he had a lisp? In the old days, under the magic of his eloquence, no one noticed it. But when he spoke in Dayton it was always audible.

When I first encountered him, on the sidewalk in front of the office of the rustic lawyers who were his associates in the Scopes case, the trial was yet to begin, and so he was still expansive and amiable. I had printed in the *Nation,* a week or so before, an article arguing that the Tennessee anti-evolution law, whatever its wisdom, was at least constitutional — that the rustics of the State had a clear right to have their progeny taught whatever they chose, and kept secure from whatever knowledge violated their superstitions. The old boy professed to be delighted with the argument, and gave the gaping bystanders to understand that I was a publicist of parts. Not to be outdone, I admired the preposterous country shirt that he wore — sleeveless and with the neck cut very low. We parted in the manner of two ambassadors. But that was the last touch of amiability that I was destined to see in Bryan. The next day the battle joined and his face became hard. By the end of the week he was simply a walking fever. Hour by hour he grew more bitter. What the Christian Scientists call malicious animal magnetism seemed to radiate from him like heat from a stove. From my place in the courtroom, standing upon a table, I looked directly down upon him, sweating horribly and pumping his palm-leaf fan. His eyes fascinated me; I watched them all day long. They were blazing points of hatred. They glittered like occult and sinister gems. Now and then they wandered to me, and I got my share, for my reports of the trial had come back to Dayton, and he had read them. It was like coming under fire.

Thus he fought his last fight, thirsting savagely for blood. All sense departed from him. He bit right and left, like a dog with rabies. He descended to demagogy so dreadful that his very associates at the trial table blushed. His one yearning was to keep his yokels heated up — to lead his forlorn mob of imbeciles against the foe. That foe, alas, refused to be alarmed. It insisted upon seeing the whole battle as a comedy. Even Darrow, who knew better, occasionally yielded to the prevailing spirit. One day he lured poor Bryan into the folly I have mentioned: his astounding argument against the notion that man is a mammal. I am glad I heard it, for otherwise I'd never believe in it. There stood the man who had been thrice a candidate for the Presidency of the Republic — there he stood in the glare of the world, uttering stuff that a boy of eight would laugh at! The artful Darrow led him on: he repeated it, ranted for it, bellowed it in his cracked voice. So he was prepared for the final slaughter. He came into life a hero, a Galahad, in bright and shining armor. He was passing out a poor mountebank.

The chances are that history will put the peak of democracy in America in his time; it has been on the downward curve among us since the campaign of 1896. He will be remembered perhaps, as its supreme impostor, the *reductio ad absurdum* of its pretension. Bryan came very near being President. In 1896, it is possible, he was actually elected.

He lived long enough to make patriots thank the inscrutable gods for Harding, even for Coolidge. Dullness has got into the White House, and the smell of cabbage boiling, but there is at least nothing to compare to the intolerable buffoonery that went on in Tennessee. The President of the United States may be an ass, but he at least doesn't believe that the earth is square, and that witches should be put to death, and that Jonah swallowed the whale. The Golden Text is not painted weekly on the White House wall, and there is no need to keep ambassadors waiting while Pastor Simpson, of Smithville, prays for rain in the Blue Room. We have escaped something — by a narrow margin, but still we have escaped.

That is, so far. The Fundamentalists, once apparently sweeping all before them, now face minorities prepared for battle even in the South — here and there with some assurance of success. But it is too early, it seems to me, to send the firemen home; the fire is still burning on many a far-flung hill, and it may begin to roar again at any moment. The evil that men do lives after them. Bryan, in his malice, started something that it will not be easy to stop. In ten thousand country towns his old heelers, the evangelical pastors, are propagating his gospel, and everywhere the yokels are ready for it. When he disappeared from the big cities, the big cities made the capital error of assuming that he was done for. If they heard of him at all, it was only as a crimp for real-estate speculators — the heroic foe of the unearned increment hauling it in with both hands. He seemed preposterous, and hence harmless. But all the while he was busy among his old lieges, preparing for a *jacquerie* that should floor all his enemies at one blow. He did his job competently. He had vast skill at such enterprises. Heave an egg out of a Pullman window, and you will hit a Fundamentalist almost everywhere in the United States to-day. They swarm in the country towns, inflamed by their *shamans*, and with a saint, now, to venerate. They are thick in the mean streets behind the gas-works. They are everywhere

where learning is too heavy a burden for mortal minds to carry, even the vague, pathetic learning on tap in little red schoolhouses. They march with the Klan, with the Christian Endeavor Society, with the Junior Order of United American Mechanics, with the Epworth League, with all the rococo bands that poor and unhappy folk organize to bring some light of purpose into their lives. They have had a thrill, and they are ready for more.

Such is Bryan's legacy to his country. He couldn't be President, but he could at least help magnificently in the solemn business of shutting off the Presidency from every intelligent and self-respecting man. The storm, perhaps, won't last long, as time goes in history. It may help, indeed, to break up the democratic delusion, now already showing weakness, and so hasten its own end. But while it lasts it will blow off some roofs.

STUART PRATT SHERMAN

1881–1925

67 The Skepticism of Anatole France

JULES LEMAÎTRE, one of the most delicately appreciative of French critics, thus defined for himself the charm of Anatole France: "I feel the saturation of his work with all its antecedents; I find in it the latest state of the human consciousness."

His work thus accomplishes what Mona Lisa, according to Pater, accomplishes in art — "the summing up in itself all modes of thought and life." One escapes in his books from the shallow and savorless modernity of contemporary literature. He is a cosmopolitan not merely of the present year of grace; he was a citizen of the world before the Christian era. A leisurely aristocrat, polished, impertubable, he has strolled with ironic smile among the neglected ruins of antiquity, and has reanimated their fallen splendor. He has walked under the plane trees without the city wall conversing with Socrates and the Sophists on the reality of our ideas. He has discussed Greek philosophy in the Tusculan villa with Cicero, has sauntered over the Aventine chatting with Horace, and has listened with bowed head while Virgil read to the grief-stricken household his divine praise of the young Marcellus. He observed the strange star in the East, heard the stories of Lazarus and Magdalen, and dined with Pilate, Procurator of Judea. In the Egyptian desert he occupied a cell with the Christian cenobites; in Alexandria he tasted the last luxuries of the pagan world. He caught from the catacombs the fervent murmur of prayer and the mysterious hymns of the martyrs. He saw with a regretful smile nymphs and dryads and fauns at twilight scurrying through country woodlands in terror of the cathedral bell. A lover of masquerade, he has crept into the cassock of mediæval monks, and gravely announced the performance of miracles, or discoursed upon the lusts of the flesh and the pride of life, or whiled away long hours on a settle in the cloister splitting theological hairs with the church fathers. Especially, has he haunted the steps of the Brides of Christ, irresistibly drawn by the allurement of their celestial robes, hoping, perhaps, to catch a drop of the spilled milk of Paradise. And all this he has told, not as one passing feverishly through successive stages of intellectual intoxication, but as one sitting at ease and leaning indolently out from a casement in Elysium.

More fascinating than all this selected world-experience is the point of view of the narrator. He keeps us wondering where he is. The detachment of M. France is not that of Flaubert or of Maupassant. The realist withdraws a little from his object to gain the proper focus for his microscope. He is nevertheless savagely absorbed in it. He means to bring it home to us, to make us enter into it and feel it tingling in our five senses. M. France, on the other hand, seeks in general to tranquilize the senses. When I say this, I do not forget the vein of cold salacity which runs through his works. In presenting the simian proclivities of man he maintains an air of smiling aloofness. He contemplates the troubled face of the world through serene leagues of motionless ether. He will report mundane affairs not to the prurient ears of mortals, but to the gods of Epicurus who inhabit the quiet above the clouds and winds, and feel from time to time a mild amusement in the human spectacle. Passing beyond the flaming ramparts of the world, he would enter the celestial hall where the blithe Immortals revel, crying: O Shining Ones, let me, a mortal, share your feast. I have withdrawn my heart and hope from the miserable race of men. For they come out of the darkness and struggle like beasts in the brief light and go into the darkness again. All their achievements are but as the excellencies of worms differing among one another. They are rent with a love more cruel than the grave. They are burnt in the fire of their own flesh. They are terrified by the shadows which they cast upon eternity. But I — I have learned the secret of your immortal calm. I have found that there is peace for those who are content to perceive and not to possess the world. I have learned to look upon the labors of Hercules without an impulse to lift a finger, upon the temptations of St. Anthony with no stirring of the flesh, upon the crucifixion of the martyrs with scarcely a throb of sympathetic pain. To the ego wisely isolated from the contagious fevers of existence all these things are but as the fierce vexation of a dream. Make me, therefore, a place beside you, and I will tell you tales of men, provoking supernal mirth.

If one rereads the works of M. France in the English translation, one unconsciously associates each successive volume with the bland and laureled old Epicurean stamped in gold upon the cover. Even with the translator's note reminding us that the volume entitled *Jocasta and the Famished Cat* was his first venture in fiction, originally published in 1879, it is difficult to think of the author as a young writer, for already he is surveying his contemporaries in their keenest self-absorption with the cool detachment of an old resident in the ivory tower. *Jocasta* appeared in the

heyday of naturalism two years after *L'Assommoir,* and in
its elements it is an ugly piece of bourgeois tragedy with a
sentimental heroine hanging herself in a bathhouse with her
nephew's necktie, loved by a young surgeon who analyzes
his sensations and dissects the nervous system of frogs. In
the hands of almost any other writer of his generation this
material would have taken shape as a depressing "human
document" illustrative of a mechanical theory of life. But
M. France has never grimly adopted the mechanical theory
of life; he has only played with it and amused himself with
the spectacle of those who were in the grip of it. "A delightfully novel basis for composition," he seems to murmur
to himself, "in this notion of scientifically dissecting the
nervous system of frogs and heroines. Let us see what can
be made of it." The air of artifice, of technical experi-
mentation, removes, for my sense, the sting of actuality; so
that the suicide of the modern heroine affects me less than a
knife thrust in an old tale of Boccaccio. It affects me rather
like a demonstration in geometry or the last move in a game
of chess.

Still, if this somber matter has left a bad taste in the
mouth, one has only to turn the page and forget the sordid
sorrows of Philistines in a gorgeous chronicle of the picturesque denizens of the Latin Quarter who foregathered at
the sign of the Famished Cat. "No one who is sane affords
me much amusement," quotes M. France with approval;
and, as he sees it, all Bohemia wears motley. From the
windows of the ivory tower he looks down upon the poetical
enthusiast in his garret no less than upon the scientific enthusiast in his laboratory. Yet though he preserves here his
attitude of aloofness, he portrays his troop of intoxicated
originals with an incomparable zest in their idiosyncrasies
and with a mellowness of mirth that suggest an only half-
extinguished sympathy. Labanne, the sculptor, who thinks
he must read fifteen hundred volumes on the *pigmentum* of
the black races and the geological formation of the Antilles
before he can touch clay for his statue of Black Liberty,

STUART PRATT SHERMAN

must occupy a warm place in his creator's learned heart.
Indeed, the door of Labanne's studio, with its strange conflict of inscriptions carved and chalked by "various people,"
will seem to some readers almost to epitomize M. France's
bewildering "criticism of life." These are some of the
inscriptions:

"Woman is more bitter than death."

"Academicians are all bourgeois, Cabanel is a hair-dresser's assistant."

"Laud we the womanly form, which still, as of old, uplifts
Chants hieratic, in praise of the greatest of beauty's gifts.
— Paul Dion."

"I have brought back the clean linen. Monday I will call for the
dirty at the porter's lodge."

"Athens, ever venerable city, if thou hadst not existed, the world
would not yet know the meaning of beauty."

"Labanne is a rat. I don't care a damn for him.
— Maria."

And there were many others on the door.

The career of Thaïs, a fair Alexandrian courtesan of the
fourth century, offered unusual attractions to the feasting
eye of the philosophic angel. No other writer has realized
so completely— so *deliciously,* as a disciple of Renan would
say — certain artistic possibilities in ecclesiastical history and
the legends of saints and martyrs. With few exceptions,
romances in English concerned with the lives of the early
Christians are to any but juvenile readers extremely insipid.
It must be admitted that an ulterior religious purpose seldom seems entirely favorable to the art of fiction. Cardinal
Newman wrote his pallid and long-forgotten romances in a
religious ascetic's revulsion from paganism and with an eye
to furthering the cause of Rome. Kingsley, with a more
virile art, wrote with a keen detestation of asceticism and
with a special pleasure in barking at Newman. Anatole
France, perhaps knowing as much about certain aspects of
the saints as Newman, and certainly knowing as much about
sinners as Kingsley, aspires to write of both like a philosophical angel, hovering a little above the earth, spectator
of everything, participator in nothing. The belief and the

580

unbelief of Gentile and Jew concern him not at all save as they offer to the æsthetic sense some new note of intensity, some unexploited mingling of strangeness with beauty. It is difficult to say whether he enters with more penetrating and illuminating curiosity into the life of the Alexandrian beauty and her favorites set in the dazzling luxury of the wicked city, or into the gaunt soul and body of the stylite Paphnutius ringed by the tombs and the desert. The picturesque qualities of both engage him, but from both he preserves a complete spiritual detachment. In the end, however, the mask slips a little from the observant angel and reveals the smile of the lurking cynic. It is made perfectly clear that Thaïs turned toward heaven merely from satiety of the flesh, and that Paphnutius turned toward hell merely from satiety of the spirit — a conclusion sufficiently devoid of edification. There is not one breath of genuine holiness in the book. Yet for piquancy of attack, for malicious insight into the psychology of the anchorite, and for sheer brilliancy of representation there is nothing like this in English.

M. France is one of the innumerable champions of intellectual emancipation who have compromised the cause of liberty by their libertinism. He will pay his penalty in the inevitable reaction. Inspired by a quite righteous indignation against his subtle voluptuousness and his moral impotence, various French critics have in recent years attempted to damage or to destroy his reputation as a creative artist. His work, they tell us, is deficient in originality; it is but a superlatively brilliant *pastiche*. A writer whose work is saturated, as M. Lemaître says, with everything that has preceded it lays himself open to that sort of attack; and it must be admitted that many of his volumes are very loosely composed. Some of his books, nevertheless, will last as long as men continue to read Lucian, Boccaccio, Rabelais, Voltaire. *Sylvestre Bonnard* has already established itself as a student's classic. *At the Sign of the Reine Pédauque* will probably never attain that honor — and for "good and

sufficient" reasons; but it is likely to live without that aid.
When you have turned the last page, you will recognize that
the work belongs on the Index, you may think that it should
be supplied with an appendix like Don Juan's classics, you
may pitch it into the fire, chuckling like the delighted mo-
nastic censors in the painting. But you know very well
that you cannot put an end to the abounding life that is in
Monsieur l'Abbé Jérôme Coignard and his reverent pupil
Tournebroche. With all their gross imperfections on their
heads they are marked, like Tom Jones and Falstaff, for
immortality. The English parallels are very inadequate.
Tom Jones is only a spirited young animal. Falstaff resembles the abbé in his girth, his geniality, his drunkenness,
his larceny, his carnality, and his sentimentality; and yet,
after all, Falstaff is but an amiable brutal Englishman
without culture or philosophy other than that which we attribute nowadays to the man in the street. Jérôme Coignard
partakes heartily of the common sinful humanity of Sir
John, but he includes, besides, within his ample sphere,
nearly everything that his creator finds to love, pity, and
deride in the civilization of the ancients, the Latin Christianity filtered through the Middle Ages, and the rationalism
of the early eighteenth century. He is one of the richly
endowed rogues of whom one says, "Of course he is an
unspeakable rascal, yet you can't resist him."

Ex-priest, ex-professor of eloquence in the college of
Beauvais, ex-librarian to the bishop of Séez, author of a
translation of Zozimus the Panopolitan, this wine-drinking,
wenching, mellow-hearted debauchee is, like M. France himself, a follower at the same time of Epicurus and Saint Francis
of Assisi. A child of the "enlightenment" before the En-
cyclopædists and a disciple of Descartes, he keeps his religion
and his philosophy in water-tight compartments: "Jacques
Tournebroche, my son, be mindful never to put faith in
absurdities, but to bring everything to the test of reason save
in the matter of our holy religion." A student of theology,
he is deeply read in the Fathers, and when he is in the vein,

can be unctuous, devout, and seriously concerned for the salvation of his soul. He is also a classical scholar versed in the most recondite Grecian and Roman authors, and his rich table-talk is redolent of a charming erudition; but, when he is buried in a library and weary of labor and devotion, he does not hesitate to indulge his powerful sensuality in fare fitter for Trimalchio's feast than for the provender of a man of God. Escaping with stolen diamonds and some bottles of white wine from a drunken brawl in which he has stabbed a man, the good abbé is delayed on the Lyons road by the wrecking of his coach, overtaken by his pursuers at nightfall, and mortally wounded. Yet he lives long enough to make a beautiful repentance, obtaining salvation in the moment of death, and he expires in a pleasant odor of sanctity, not a little consoled by the fact that, as he had been struck down by a Jew, he "perished a victim to a descendant of the executioners of Christ."

M. France has given us his personal commentary on the abbé in a pleasant study of thirty-five pages prefixed to the companion volume, *Les Opinions de M. Jérôme Coignard,* published in the same year, 1893, with the *Reine Pédauque.* In 1909 he returned to the theme with *Les Contes de Jacques Tournebroche.* I mention these facts because, in the two or three pages of general appreciation with which Mr. W. J. Locke introduces the English translation, he does not mention them. After due reflection I cannot guess why Mr. Locke was asked to write this preface, unless it was because he is the author of a popular book called *The Beloved Vagabond.* If my conjecture is correct, he has neglected a very pretty opportunity to acknowledge a debt and to discourse on the differences between the spirit of English and French fiction. The relation between *At the Sign of the Reine Pédauque* and *The Beloved Vagabond* is interesting. That Mr. Locke has borrowed in some fashion the happy invention of Coignard and Tournebroche — *cela saute aux yeux.* He sets out, just as M. France does, with the adoption of a clever boy, engaged in a menial occupation, by a very learned, very

dirty, very benevolent vagabond of philosophical habit; and
the boy in each case writes the memoirs of the alliance. But
the two authors walk only a short way together. Mr. Locke's
tale is conceived in English sentiment; his philosopher conceals beneath his soiled shirt a deathless romantic passion.
M. France's tale is conceived in philosophical irony and
Gallic cynicism; beneath all his classical and Christian culture, M. Jérôme Coignard is a sensualist, pure and simple —
or, more strictly speaking, impure and complex. Mr. Locke
would persuade us that man is a flower that at heart smells
sweet though it blossoms in the dust. M. France, on the
contrary, would have us believe that man is an " obscene and
evil fly " remarkably imprisoned in the amber of his ideals.

When M. France, after forty years of philosophical ro-
mancing in the garden of Epicurus, published his *Vie de
Jeanne d'Arc,* the professional historians were shocked and
the Epicureans were perplexed. It did not seem quite
respectful to the Muse of History, for the author of *Le Lys
Rouge* to present her with the life of the virgin of Domrémy.
On the other hand, it appeared out of character for the author
of M. Jérôme Coignard to take the scholarly ideal so seriously. To most of his followers his perilous charm had been
that he always seemed to say — Mr. George Santayana has
said it, too, in three lines of a seductive sonnet:

> The crown of olive let another wear;
> It is my crown to mock the runner's heat
> With gentle wonder and with laughter sweet.

Nor was it clear what garland a novice of over threescore
could hope to win in the trite and well-gleaned field of history
where he made his début. To be sure, some critics tried to
show that this work did not really represent a new departure
in M. France's development; for, they said, even in his
romances he had been an historian, as even in his history he
had been a romancer. Both views are partly right; the
history of Jeanne d'Arc was, in a sense, only the latest in a
long series of naturalistic and iconoclastic saints' lives. But

there was a difference. How explain the lengthy preface discussing predecessors, theories of history, original documents? M. France had sent his fine Ariel often enough among ancient libraries, but had never allowed him to appear in the sunlight with dust on his wings. What conviction, slowly formulating, had brought this volant, elusive spirit, this mocking beguiler of an empty day into step with his sober contemporaries? Let us not attempt to discover, said M. Achille Luchaire, reviewing the first volume of the work, *ne cherchons pas à pénétrer le mystère de cette évolution.*

M. France has something of Prosper Mérimée's repugnance to being divined. On the heels of Jeanne d'Arc, as if anxious to complicate the chart of his evolution, he sends a satirical afterpiece, *L'Ile des Pingouins,* which dissipates in peals of derisive laughter any notion that its author has joined the modern historians. This, too, is a history prefaced by a critical account of sources; but, though shorter, it is much more comprehensive than its forerunner. It is an abridgment of all history that has been or shall be, under the form of a veiled comic history of France. "In spite of the apparent diversity of the amusements which seem to attract me," begins the preface in the old ironical vein, "my life has only one object. It is wholly bent toward the accomplishment of one great design. I am writing the history of the Penguins." In the search for the buried monuments of this people, continues the author, "I have excavated by the seashore an unviolated tumulus; I found in it, *according to custom,* stone axes, swords of bronze, Roman coins, and a twenty-sous piece with the head of Louis-Philippe I, King of the French."

Embarrassed by difficulties attendant on the interpretation of conflicting evidence, the historian called in counsel several eminent archæologists and palæographers: — "They looked at me with a smile of pity which seemed to say: 'Do we write history? Do we attempt to extract from a text, from a document the least scrap of life or truth? We publish texts pure and simple. We stick to the letter. The letter alone is appreciable and definite. The spirit is not; ideas are crotchets. One must be very presumptuous to write history; one must have imagination.'" A surviving historian of the old school was more encouraging — "Why take the trouble to compose a history when you have only to copy the standard works, as everyone does. . . . One word more. If you wish your book to be welcomed, neglect no opportunity to extol the virtues upon which societies are based: devotion to riches, pious sentiments, and especially the resignation of the poor, which is the foundation of order. Assert, sir, that the origins of property, nobility, and gendarmery will be treated in your history with all the respect which these institutions merit. Have it understood that you admit the supernatural when it appears. On that condition you will succeed in good company." — "I have meditated these judicious observations," says M. France demurely, "and have paid good heed to them."

The narrative accordingly begins with the apostolic calling of Saint Maël, and his wonderful conversions, his wide wanderings, and finally his voyage in a miraculous stone trough over the turbulent Northern Sea to an undiscovered island. After a detour of the place, the holy man, somewhat advanced in age and understanding, comes upon a circle of penguins. Mistaking them for a primitive heathen people, Saint Maël explains to them successively Adoption, Rebirth, Regeneration, and Illumination, and then in three days and three nights baptizes them all. "When the baptism of the penguins was known in Heaven," proceeds the historian with the suave gravity which heightens the effect of his daring, "it caused there neither joy nor sorrow, but extreme surprise. The Lord himself was embarrassed. He called an assembly of scholars and theologians and asked them if they considered the baptism valid." As a result of a long, hot debate, participated in by St. Patrick and Saint Catherine, Saint Augustine and Saint Antony, Tertullian, Orosius, and Saint Gregory of Nazianzen, with interposed questions and objections by the Lord, it was decided that the penguins must be changed into men. And it was done.

STUART PRATT SHERMAN

Thus does M. France admit the supernatural, when it appears! Since Lucian set the infernal gods to quarreling over the ferry hire in Hades, dramatized the loves of the Olympians, and represented Zeus, when Timon began to rail, as inquiring casually of Hermes what dirty fellow was bawling from Attica beside Hymettus, no one, perhaps, has dealt so unabashedly with the reigning dynasty of the Heavenly Ones. A late unpersecuted Voltaire — tolerance has made a long march since the eighteenth century — he would gently laugh Jehovah out of Paradise. *Rien ne'st plus lâche,* says Pascal, *que de faire le brave contre Dieu.* True, one can fancy Anatole France replying, but see: The walls of chrysoprase, the solemn temples of the twelve-gated city are fast dissolving like an insubstantial pageant of the air. Is it not better to smile than to weep?

With similar fidelity to the instructions of his adviser against disparaging sacred institutions, M. France describes the origins of "property, nobility, and gendarmery." Shortly after the baptism and transformation of the penguins, they begin to clothe themselves, inclose land, and fight. One brains his neighbor with a club; another furious fellow fixes his teeth in the nose of his prostrate adversary; a third brays the head of a woman under an enormous stone. Saint Maël is horrified, but he is assured by a religious brother of wider experience that the penguins are accomplishing the most august of functions — "they are creating law; they are founding property; they are establishing the principles of civilization." All this reminds one of the *Social Contract* and the famous *Discourses* of Rousseau, but it is to be remembered that in the state of nature the penguins are feathered bipeds. No golden age glimmers for Anatole France behind the age of blood. Indeed, in *Jérôme Coignard* he has subjected the revolutionary illusions to the most penetrating criticism: "If one is going to take a hand in governing men," he declares, "one must not forget that they are bad monkeys." The history of the penguin nation is the history of half-intelligent beasts — the history of Yahoos and Houyhnhnms. At this point, I cannot forbear quoting the brief, mordant sketch of " Draco the Great," a hero of the Middle Ages:

> He carried fire indifferently over the territory of the enemy and his own domain. And he was wont to say, to explain his conduct: " War without burning is like tripe without mustard; it is insipid." His justice was rigorous. When the peasants whom he had taken prisoners could not pay their ransom, he had them hanged on a tree, and if any unfortunate woman came to beg mercy on her penniless husband, he dragged her by the hair at the tail of his horse. He lived like a soldier, free from all effeminacy (*Il vécut en soldat, sans mollesse*). It is a pleasure to acknowledge that his morals were pure.

Something in that reminds one at the same time of Swift and of Tacitus. If the style is indeed the man himself, there is a tincture of iron in the blood of this Epicure.

There is much piquancy in the contemptuous account of *Les Temps Modernes,* but one feels the author's point most sharply in the exultant pessimism of his vision of the future. The notion that there is a grim limit set to the evolution of life on our planet has long been dear to the heart of M. France. Long ago he prophetically buried the last desperate relic of our race in the frozen rind of the sunless world. But here he has worked out more fully the stages by which the human tragedy is to decline to the ultimate catastrophe. Before the somewhat remote Last Day there are to be a number of false or temporary endings precipitated by forces at work within the social organism. M. France seems now to have turned his back upon the socialistic hope which he courted a few years ago. To the centralizing tendency of wealth no effective check can be imposed; in the long run, it is as irresistible as gravitation, the rising of sap in forests, the swing of planets in their orbits. But at certain periods when the remorseless oppression of capitalists brings the lower orders to the verge of extinction, they will gain for themselves a dreary breathing space with dynamite. They will level all populous cities to the dust and incinerate the painfully acquired material and intellectual riches of civilization. For a little while the exhausted survivors will rest, and gasping in dismal anarchy recover their animal strength. Then the old blind urge of life will begin anew; step by step poor posterity will fight its way up the long ascent again; once more the many-storied cities will hum, and lean anæmic millionaires, Pharaohs half-mummified, lord it over the Egyptian millions laying the bricks for their mausoleums. And so the old wheel of life will turn round and round in concentric circles, ever shortening its diameter, till, at last it vanishes in a point, and the barren globe freed of its feverish animalcules journeys on through the void!

"It is the duty of every thinker who has formed an idea of the world," said M. France in one of his essays on contemporary literature, " to express that idea, whatever it may be." If the last chapters of *L'Ile des Pingouins* were a faithful transcript of his sense of the facts of life crowding in upon the sensitive consciousness, we should have deeply to commiserate the author. But the pessimism of M. France is partly polemical. "The spiritualist," Emerson tells us, "finds himself driven to express his faith in a series of skepticisms." M. France began life as a devout humanist, forming his taste and his style on the noblest literature of Greece and Rome. In early manhood, however, he felt powerfully the new hope and enthusiasm of the early followers of Darwin. To the young men of his generation, it was a fresh, firmly-founded revolutionary gospel. But as the century wore on, the scientific millennium receded into the infinitely remote future. To believe in it demanded as pure an exercise of faith as to believe in the New Jerusalem. M. France's faith was unequal to the task. What faith remained in him reverted to his early humanism. Meantime the unreflecting mass of humanity had caught the fanatic fervor of the scientific dream, and had left humanism far in the rear. When M. France returned to the temples of his gods he found them empty of worshipers. And so, like most humanists to-day, he is a disheartened humanist. He would, perhaps, have spoken seriously of his faith if he could have found serious listeners. It is rather dreary to praise Pallas Athene in perfect solitude. It is more diverting to steal into the camp of the victors, and mock their cause and insinuate horrible doubt into every heart. Yet by a happy law of the universe only the potential philanthropist can be misanthropic. The Olympian detachment of M. France is illusory. Without a place to stand on, a man can no more despise his fellows than Archimedes could lift the world. So long as M. France despises us, we need not despair; the earth beneath his scornful feet is a part of the common heritage.

I find a still more serious flaw in the would-be seamless garment of M. France's skepticism. He has often assured us that the skeptic is a good citizen, because, uncertain of all things, he is the least radical of men. But the salt of the right skeptic is the love of truth. Whatever enters his head he reports freely, as one holding a commission to act as the disinterested intelligence of mankind, surveying the past and present and spying out the future. That salt was in the virile fiber of Montaigne sitting in his tower in Perigord, cupboarding the choice viands of the ancients and portraying with unflinching hand the manners and mind of the man he knew best. But Anatole France — does he candidly attempt to represent the world as it appears? Does he love the truth and search for the truth above all else? As it seems to me he loves above all else the luxury of philosophic despair. He is a kind of refined, philosophical sentimentalist. With the assiduity of the Graveyard Poets, he cultivates and cherishes those truths, or seeming truths, which make for melancholy. We hear every day: This is the truth; we must face it. The fact is we may usually turn our backs upon it, and it is often the part of wisdom to do so. There may be a more wholesome truth at the opposite point of the compass. It is true that when a good man dies he rots like a rascal. It is also true that he lives a fragrant life in the memory of his friends. To embrace the latter truth strengthens the heart; but a certain kind of sentimentalist always embraces the worm that inherits the shroud. It is the truth; we must face it. But no man can face all truth. We judge a man's wisdom by his power of making intimates of those truths which give channel and speed to the languid, diffusive drift of his days. M. France has sought through all the world for the truths inducing in the perceiver a pensive and helpless sadness. M. France is too much concerned about the misery of the last man. If the good die young, as there is some warrant for believing, the last man will deserve hanging.

The skepticism of M. France is largely a literary pose. It is his justification for making capital of unspeakable things. It is his justification for unlimited intellectual self-indulgence. For a good skeptic he knows altogether too much about the future. When a man's philosophy has carried him to the point where several million years of civilization are as tomorrow, are as nothing, to him, it is a pity that it should not go a step further to the point where space vanishes and time expires and the illusive ages evaporate into the eternity of the everlasting Now. For a good skeptic he is altogether too sure that the world has exhausted its possibilities. He holds, indeed, that we live in a bright-flowing mist of days and nights, of sleeping and waking dreams. But he does not hold this belief with strength enough to be dumb and astonished at thought of the germs of new orders of ideas now forming in society or slumbering as yet unstirred in the unused mind of the world. He does not recognize as frankly as a skeptic should how plastic is the eternal flux under the creative energy of the desire of man, who had only to say, "Let the flux be peopled with demons and with seraphim," and it was. Only the new-born babe enjoys, however, that purity of uncertainty to which M. France pretends. And as soon as the babe first sniffs the vital air, it is a judge as well as an observer. It discovers at once that for the present at least some things are good and beautiful, and others terrible and necessary.

I

THE Suevia, scheduled to reach New York on the ninth day, did not arrive until the fifteenth. Not a fleck of sunshine all those days; a sky almost black, a piping wind, a turbulent sea dashing up in huge steel-gray waves with bottle-green under-curves and fierce, white, fang-like edges. A primeval, chaotic, brutal sea. The great ship quivered and creaked and wheezed; the water slapped against the port-holes and ran down the round, dim panes; almost hourly the propeller was punched clear above sea-level and whirred with a naked, metallic grind. . . . My mother was hopelessly sea-sick the whole time; my father and I led a dim, nebulous existence, when possible on deck, when not, in the red-carpeted saloon. But the sea got hold of the innermost core of my mind; it became part of my life, and in inland places I have often caught myself tense with desire after its tang and roar.

Our land-fall was still gray but quiet. Afar off lay a dim, hook-like shore. The voyage had liberated my father's mind from terror and madness. He was so strengthened and cheered that even my mother smiled. To come to land at all seemed, after our tremendous experience, almost like coming home. But the pier at Hoboken was rough and wild, a place of hoarse cries and brute haste and infernal confusion. A kindly German-American fellow-passenger helped us; saw to it that our luggage was not unduly searched and put us in a rumbling hack on our way to an hotel. It was Meyer's Hotel, a comfortable, unpretentious place. We were worn out and rested well during our first night on American soil under the strange mosquito-bars.

The place where my uncle lived and whither we were

bound lay far away in the South Atlantic States. But my father and mother thought that we ought to rest for a day or two and see a city so great and famous as New York. A curious timidity kept us, however, from venturing far through the grime and rattle. We crossed the Brooklyn Bridge, I know, and saw the gilt dome of the World Building, then the tallest structure on this hemisphere, and the elevated railroad. But we did not go up town nor into the financial section, drifted somehow into a lake of mud shaken by trucks and drays on Canal Street and retreated to Hoboken.

Being ill-advised we took ship again and spent nearly fifty hours on a coast-wise voyage South. We could eat no food. Negro stewards served it and over it was the strange flavor of bananas and Concord grapes. There was no storm or gloom now. But the brilliantly radiant sea was rough and choppy and the steamer small. The weather grew milder and milder and when we steamed into Queenshaven harbor the day was like spring.

The bay is one of the most beautiful in the world. In its fold lies the old city with its gardens and verandas and its few slender spires. Golden-green islands extend its curves. The coloring of sea and sky, in whatever mood, is of so infinite and delicate a variety as though the glow and splendor of all the jewels in the world had been melted there. And over city and bay lies a rich quietude that steals upon the heart through the liquid softness of that untroubled air. I heard my father and mother speak of the beauty of the scene; my own sense of it must have been vague. But I cannot dissociate that early vision from an hundred later ones. For that city and bay came to mean my boyhood and youth, high passion and aspiration, and later a grief that darkened my life. I close my eyes: I can see every stone of the old city, every wave of the bay. But my mind sees both garbed in a cruel and unearthly sweetness. My bodily eyes could endure to see neither of them any more. . . . Friends of my uncle who were commissioned to meet us missed the boat. My father summoned his scraps of English, hired a four-wheeler and took us to the Queenshaven Hotel. There these people found us, astonished that my parents had not yet acquired the habits of poverty but had gone boldly to the best hotel in the city. They took us to their house where the children astonished me by speaking English. It did not seem to me nearly so curious in grown persons. I stared at the tattered Negroes in the yard, almost too tired to be impressed by any strangeness. In the afternoon our friends took us to our train, shoved us into a day-coach and hurried off.

I recall vividly the long, shabby, crowded car and its peculiar reeks of peanuts, stale whiskey and chewing-tobacco. Half of the passengers were burly Negroes who gabbled and laughed weirdly. The white men wore broad-rimmed wool-hats, whittled and spat and talked in drawling tones. I very distinctly shared my parents' sense of the wildness, savagery and roughness of the scene, their horrified perception of its contrast to anything they had ever known or seen. Soon the dark fell and at the wayside stations queer, panlike lamps flared up in reddish ribbands of fire. At one station a group of men entered carrying tall cudgels. They opened jack-knives and proceeded to peel and devour these cudgels. My mother grew almost hysterical; my father racked his mind and discovered some half-forgotten information on the subject of sugar-cane. . . . At ten o'clock we reached Saint Mark's and trudged out of the car. A man with heavy moustaches and clad in a red sweater lifted me from the platform. From my previous experience of life I judged him to be a porter or a cabby. To my disgust and amazement he called me by name and kissed me on the mouth. It was my uncle.

II

In 1890 the village of St. Mark's in South Carolina was raw; it had more than a touch of wildness and through its life there ran a strain of violence. It consisted of two principal streets running diagonally to each other and of half a dozen lesser streets that trailed off into cotton-fields and pine-forests. There was a cotton-seed oil mill, a saw mill and twenty to thirty general merchandise stores. Three or four of these were housed in one-story buildings of red brick. For the rest the village was built of wood and many of the houses were unpainted, showing the browned and weather-beaten boards. There was a Methodist Church and a Baptist Church, each with a grave-yard behind it. North of the village straggled a Negro grave-yard, its graves decorated with colored pebbles, bits of iridescent glass and the broken shards of cheap vases. Here and there, behind houses or in chance lanes were small, black, one-rounded huts inhabited by Negro women. These women were in domestic service in the village and, as I learned later, plied, in addition and quite openly, an equally ancient but less honest trade. Despite eight or ten bar-rooms the streets were quiet except on Saturday. Then the village flared into life. Many hundreds of Negroes came in from the sparsely settled country; they rode in on horses or mules or oxen or drove rough carts and primitive wagons, and were themselves generally clad in garments of which the original homespun had disappeared in a mass of gaudy patches. They traded and drank and, child-like, spent their money on foolish things — perfumes and handsome whips and sweets. Toward dusk they reeled in a hot tur-moil and filled the air with that characteristic odor of pea-nuts and stale whiskey and chewing tobacco.

I watched the village life with a deep sense of its strange-ness but almost without astonishment. Soon I was merged into it and felt quite at home. No, not quite. During at least a year, at lengthening intervals of course, I felt a sharp nostalgia for the land of my birth and its life. Suddenly, at the edge of the forest, a sense of grief would overcome me. Somewhere beyond those dark trees, beyond leagues of coun-try, beyond the ocean, lay our home. . . . And I would weep bitterly. And still, in my maturer years the edge of a forest or else a few solitary trees at a great distance bring back to me that old sense of wistfulness and yearning — no longer for

definite scenes or associations, but for the mystery of delight
I have not known, beauty I have not seen, peace I have
sought in vain. . . .

The Southern country-side awakened in me, child that I
was, a rich, and almost massive joy in nature. About a mile
beyond the lonely little railroad station with its bales of cotton and acrid-smelling sacks of yellow guano lay the "red
hills." These hills were not very high; I could climb them
easily; they were covered with very tall, very straight pine-
trees that seemed to me shaft-like and sky-piercing.
Through a fold of the hills ran a rapid, very shallow little
brook over a bed of clean, bright pebbles. In spring the dog-
wood showed its white blossoms there; in the mild Southern
autumn a child could lie on the deep layers of brownish pine-
needles and play with the aromatic cones and gaze up at
the brilliant blue of the sky.

The summer stirred me deeply. I had been used to the
cool, chaste, frugal summers of the North. Here the heat
smote; the vegetation sprang into rank and hot luxuriance
—noisome weeds with white ooze in their stems and bell-
like pink flowers invaded the paths and streets. I felt a
strange throbbing, followed by sickish languor and a dumb
terror at the frequent, fierce thunderstorms. Both my intelligence and my instincts ripened with morbid rapidity
and I attribute many abnormalities of temper and taste that
are mine to that sudden transplantation into a semi-tropical
world. . . .

I was a thorough child nevertheless and delighted in certain acquisitions which the new world brought me — a per-
cussion cap pistol, a mouth organ, a Jew's harp. Nor did I
give up my old life. My books had been saved and, one
day, my father discovered that he had forgotten a small
balance in the Deutsche Bank. For this money he ordered
books from Germany, and I came into possession of a set
of very red volumes: the marvelous chap-books of the Reformation age — Griseldis, Genoveva, Robert the Devil, Dr.
Faustus — naive and knightly or magical and grim; and of

two slimmer volumes called Beckers Erzählungen aus der Alten Welt, which contained the Iliad and the Odyssey in simple, lucid German prose. In the reading of these, especially of the Odyssey, culminated the imaginative joys of my childhood. I do not know Greek; I cannot read Homer in the original. Yet I am sure that I know what Homer is. In a plain room behind the store in which apples and cloth and furniture and plough-shares and rice and tinned fish were sold to chattering Negroes, I sat with my book and clearly heard

" The surge and thunder of the Odyssey "

and saw Nausikaa and her maidens, white limbed and fair, on the shore of the wine-dark sea, and dwelt with Odysseus on the island of Callypso and returned home with him to Ithaca — not without tears — and listened to the twanging bow-string that sped the avenging arrows. The wood-cut that was the frontispiece of the little volume showed Hermes on his mission of command to Circe. Above floats the god with his staff and his winged cap and sandals. Below him stretches the immeasurable stream of ocean. In the background, small and far but very clear, lies an island with a tiny fane of Doric columns. I gazed at the picture for hours and knew the freshness, the grace and the clarity of that morning of the world.

III

My uncle and aunt received us into their queer little house which was huddled, as though for protection, against the shop. The walls of the house were of the rudest; the wind blew through knot-holes in the timber. My father and mother were bitterly disappointed. My uncle had sent the St. Mark's Herald to Berlin and my father, who did not understand the art and vocabulary of town-booming nor the society items of an American village newspaper, assumed that St. Mark's was a town of some importance and my uncle a prominent citizen. And here he had come to a squalid village, the guest of a man well-enough liked by his fellow-citizens but wretchedly poor. My aunt, moreover, though a woman of some kindly qualities, was a Jewess of the Eastern tradition, narrow-minded, given over to the clattering ritual of pots and pans — "meaty" and "milky" — and very ignorant. On the very evening of our arrival, having at last withdrawn to the one spare bed-room, my father and mother looked blankly at each other. A chill wind blew in thin, keen streams through chinks in the bare, wooden wall, the geese squawked loudly in the muddy yard, my aunt was heard scolding her little girls in a mixture of Yiddish and English, a little, unshaded kerosene lamp made the grim room look all the gloomier. My mother sat down on the springless bed, a picture of desolation. The sudden plunge unnerved her. All through the voyage we had lived on our accustomed plane of civilized comfort. Only here did the descent begin.

She had one consolation that apparently justified the whole adventure. My father was a changed man. From now on and for many years he was full of energy and buoyancy, splendidly patient and brave, always ready to cheer her in her fits of loneliness and depression. He had shaken off his morbid inhibitions and immediately started out into the village to see what he could do.

The people of the village, storekeepers, a few retired farmers, three physicians, three or four lawyers, came of various stocks — English, Scotch-Irish, German, even French and Dutch. But they were all descended from early nineteenth century settlers and had become thorough Americans. Everybody belonged to either the Baptist or the Methodist church. The Methodists were, upon the whole, more refined, had better manners than the Baptists and were less illiterate. Among all the villagers there was a moderate amount of hard drinking and a good deal of sexual irregularity, especially with Mulatto women. I have since wondered that there was not more. The life was sterile and monotonous enough. They were all kindly, even the rougher ones, not very avaricious, no drivers of hard bargains, given to talking about shooting but doing very little of it. (During the two years of our residence two men were shot and in each case upon extreme provocation.) Also, so far as their light went, they were liberal. This was well illustrated by the position of the Jews in the village. Of these there were about ten families, all recent immigrants, and so aliens in speech and race and faith. Most of them, moreover, were quite prosperous. Yet between them and these Southern villagers the relations were hearty and pleasant and consolidated by mutual kindness and tolerance. Only one Jew, and that was my father, was looked upon with some suspicion by the severer among his Gentile neighbors. The reason was curious and significant; he did not perform the external rites of the Jewish faith and, upon entering a fraternal life insurance order, he smiled and hesitated when asked to affirm categorically his belief in a personal God.

He soon saw that there was nothing to be done in St. Mark's except add another to the existing shops. But since nearly every one seemed to have prospered and since the quiet and the easy, democratic atmosphere of the place appealed to him, he hesitated but little. Help and good advice were offered alike by Jew and Gentile and, at the end of a few months, we were installed in some pleasant rooms beside one of the few brick stores on Main Street. There was the usual heterogeneous stock of food and implements, furniture and dry-goods. My mother went to Queenshaven and bought adequate furniture for our little home.

Although she yearned very bitterly for her native land, her friends and kin, for music and for all the subtle supports of the civilization in which she was so deeply rooted, life opened fairly enough. Domestic service cost next to nothing, food was plentiful and cheap. Even friends were not wanting. Our landlord and his family, prominent members of the Methodist church, saw soon enough that my father and mother were of a different mental type and of different antecedents from the other Jews in St. Mark's. There followed an exchange of visits. Mrs. C. gave my mother much good advice, explained to her many American ways and manners that seemed very strange, and tried to console her in regard to her most burning and immediate problem — that of my education. This friendship led to others. And so when summer came, we who had no vegetable garden — and would have been just as helpless had we had one — received daily attentions from our Gentile friends: baskets of tomatoes or okra or sweet-corn or bell-pepper. And one friend, a very aged physician who liked and admired my mother and had a dim but steady perception of her profound spiritual isolation, sent her weekly a great basketful of roses. My father, at the same time, found a congenial companion in a young lawyer. The two played chess together and from him my father borrowed Shakespeare and Byron, Dickens and Thackeray and Scott with whose works he was, like all educated Germans, thoroughly familiar and whom he now read with avidity in their own language. We saw a good deal of my uncle and his family and their friends. But culturally we really felt closer to the better sort of Americans in the community, and so there began in those early days that alienation from my own race which has been the source to me of some good but of more evil.

CARL VAN DOREN

1885–

69   *Conjured Spirit*

"LIFE is a tragedy," Swift said, "wherein we sit as spectators awhile, and then act our own part in it." But Swift had never waited for tragedy to come to him. He had always run to meet it. He had, dramatic and perverse, insisted upon playing the most tragic parts. He had, whether quite consciously or not, identified himself with that "conjured spirit" which a "person of great honor in Ireland" had seen in him when he was young.

Suppose some such spirit had been conjured up by an

experiment of nature, by a hoax of nature, and had been let loose among men. The spirit's course would have been like Swift's. The spirit would have brought with it enough angelic light, enough diabolic pride, to make it restless in its human flesh. It would expect to command the inferior beings it outwardly resembled. It would fret when it saw that its flesh condemned it to be mistaken for a creature that was merely flesh. Learning that most men knew nothing beyond mankind, the spirit would regard them as a wilderness of fools. Learning that the few who ruled the many were not much less foolish, the spirit would regard the few as knaves. Both fools and knaves would be repulsive to it.

But the spirit itself, with its burden and disguise of flesh, must be more or less a man in whatever it did. Too much a spirit to become easy among men, it would be too much a man to resist some human beings: men to be friends with, women to love or be loved by. Too much a spirit to be willing to take its contented stand with the fools ruled by the knaves, or with the knaves, it would be too much a man to stand altogether aside and ridicule the world lumbering or raving by. The spirit would, as Swift did, try to make its way by something which was neither the authority of a spirit nor the arts of a man. Divided within itself, it could not trust its instincts to know just what force, what craft was needed at what times. The spirit could be hoodwinked through the man. The man could be deluded through the spirit. Even if the spirit rose to power, it could get only a man's reward, and only the reward of a man handicapped by what the spirit had done to alienate other men.

That reward would never satisfy the spirit. Sent to govern a province, the spirit would still think of the empire. The respect, the love, the veneration of the province might reward the man. The spirit would despise them. To accept them and be satisfied would be to agree too well with the flesh which the spirit had been conjured to put on. It would not agree. It could not. It must, helplessly a spirit, endure its burden and disguise till they were worn out. It could hardly wear out its flesh. It would have tainted its mortal body with a dark immortality. It would outlive the men and women whose love had made it less wretched than it might have been. In the end it would escape only with fearful convulsions of its heavy carcass.

Swift's lifelong metaphor of the conjured spirit was mythological, but only a metaphor could give reality to a man whose spirit so rode his flesh.

An extraordinary man, with a boundless appetite for power, must master or please ordinary men, or else go hungry. Swift was born without the rank and fortune which are such a man's natural advantages. Worse, Swift was born without the hide of brass and bowels of iron which would have been nearly as good for him as rank and fortune. He could not climb without caring what he set his feet on. He was clumsy with scruples. He could not take snubs and kicks and stabs as incidental, hardly personal to him, and unimportant so long as he could survive them. He was sensitive to every scratch and had quick, ungovernable impulses to strike back. He could not center his energies without mercy even for himself. No man is so extraordinary that he can, starting below many of his fellows, scramble past them all without a stubborn, insolent devotion to the main path. Swift was not single-minded enough to master his world.

Nor would Swift rise, as some men do, by pleasing. He would have had to be more supple than he was to wriggle far. Even in an age when it was still barely a disgrace to court a lord, Swift could not court one long. He was more ready to bully than to flatter. And with his equals and inferiors he could or would not assure them that their shortcomings were virtues, their prejudices wisdom. He used a winter speech in the most comfortable summers. Above all, he had no zeal to please, and felt small delight in his small successes. He was half ashamed when he pleased, as if he were a tragedian who had raised a laugh. This was not his part. This was for mountebanks.

Nothing about Swift was more extraordinary than his blindness to the part which he played so well while he was failing in the one on which he had fixed his desire. Still in his twenties, or just out of them, he raged at Moor Park because he had no chance to command. Yet in those same years he flung off a prose satire such as no Englishman had ever written before and such as no Englishman but Swift ever wrote again. In London, scheming to rule among the Whigs or Tories, half winning, and then disappointed after his spell of power, Swift, almost without effort or concern, ruled the wits. In Ireland, where he thought of himself as a despairing exile, he wrote pamphlets that are monuments, poems that added to poetry what was almost a new species. He wrote his travels in a vain fury of revenge, and entertained the world. On the other side of every failure was a triumph.

On the other side of all his hatreds were loves. Swift was a misanthropist, but he is famous for his friendships. He shrank from women, but he made two women famous. He detested Ireland, but he has the eternal affection of the Irish. He loathed the human race, but he has been a delight to it for two centuries. It was his extraordinary fortune to draw an interest of love from a principal of hate.

No doubt Swift should have measured his gifts more exactly and should have put himself into more fitting rôles, like any ordinary man of talent. Swift was outside the shrewd discipline of talent. He could not sit down and write prose and verse as if they were sufficient ends. Prose and verse were the weapons he found in his fists, scarcely realizing how they came there. He used them in his tragic rôle, in the war of his ambition, not because he valued them but because they were the only weapons he had. After he had lost his war, and had — singularly like Temple — given it up as hopeless when he was only forty-five, Swift would never again allow himself to be consoled. He would not see that he had been winning, and still was winning, a great war while he was losing a small one. His pride blinded him.

A few years reverse many verdicts. While Swift was still alive, king of Ireland but pretending to be king of triflers, he had good reasons for foreseeing the true verdict upon him. In the long run, he might have guessed, he would be remembered for what he had written at Moor Park, before he had even tried the world, or for what he had written and done in Ireland, after he had bitterly renounced his expectations. What he had thought his glorious episode, the years with Oxford and Bolingbroke, would look a little shabby. In time Swift would seem to have been most splendid when he had been most himself, and not the satellite of politicians.

Still, Swift might also have understood, if he had been without his blindness, that simple formulas would not explain him. To do what he had done he had needed the blind obsession of his will. As a lover who does nothing but love is seldom the best lover, so the writer who desires only to write is seldom the best writer. What had raised Swift, scattered and random as most of his writing was, to the first rank among writers, had been the high reach of his pride, the magnificence of his scorn. He had won the war in which he hardly noticed that he was fighting because he had fought with so much passion in a war which was not worth it. It was his passion that had mattered, and not his long illusion. Nature, when it demands prose and verse of its creatures, cares no more whether they are begotten in illusion than it cares whether children are begotten in moods of unreason.

If there had been in Dublin some subtle expert able to pry into Swift's mind and point out how he could resolve his conflicts, how he could make his will submit and take what it could get in place of what it wanted, it might have made Swift happier. Happier and duller. As it was, he went on in his own way of life to his own way of death.

In April 1740 he wrote his cousin that he had been " these two days in so miserable a way, and so cruelly tortured, that it can hardly be conceived. The whole of last night I was equally struck as if I had been in Phalaris's

brazen bull, and roared as loud for eight or nine hours."
After three months he wrote her again. "I have been very
miserable all night, and today extremely deaf and full of
pain. I am so stupid and confounded that I cannot express
the mortification I am under both in body and mind. All I
can say is that I am not in torture but I daily and hourly
expect it. Pray let me know how your health is and your
family. I hardly understand one word I write. I am sure
my days will be very few; few and miserable they must
be. . . . If I do not blunder, it is Saturday, July 26, 1740."

He had still five years, two of torture and three of a dreadful peace, in which to keep on outliving his friends. He
made his will. Accustomed to giving a third of his income
to charity, he now became more avaricious than ever, to have
more money to give. He shut out the world. His house was
his dungeon. His deafness was almost complete, his giddi-
ness almost unceasing.

Blood seeped through the membranes which his sly fate
had made too thin, into the labyrinth of his ear. A drop
there was enough to overpower him with the din of water-
mills, with the thunder of oceans. What was all his pride,
what was all his intellect, against this everlasting tumult?
It had been beating upon his nerves for half a century. It
now beat louder and louder, with fewer intervals in which
he might recover his patience. He had never had any
patience. What he had had was lost in floods of irritation.
His reason was clear, when he could rest from the insensate
drums that sounded in his head, but his memory was dull and
thick. He could not remember the words which he had
started to say. In torment and the fear of torment, he could
not even tell what was hurting him. He could not bear to
see the few friends that remained. They might pity him.
They could not help him. His old habits drove him to a
furious activity, wearing out his strength. He was all agony
and all rebellion. Once he was found threatening his reflection in a mirror. His misanthropy had given up the last exception. He hated himself.

Yet out of this murk could come an occasional glare that was still Swift. As late as January 1742 he wrote an exhortation to his Chapter. "Whereas my infirmities of age and ill health have prevented me to preside in the chapters held for the good order and government of my Cathedral Church of St. Patrick's, Dublin," he began. He had heard that various members of the choir had assisted at public musical performances. He would not have it. "And whereas it hath been reported that I gave a licence to certain vicars to assist at a club of fiddlers in Fishamble Street, I hereby declare that I remember no such licence to have been ever signed or sealed by me; and that if ever such pretended licence should be produced, I do hereby annul and vacate the said licence: entreating my said Sub-Dean and Chapter to punish such vicars as shall ever appear there, as songsters, fiddlers, pipers, trumpeters, drummers, drum-majors, or in any sonal quality, according to the flagitious aggravations of their respective disobedience, rebellion, perfidy, and ingratitude. I require my said Sub-Dean to proceed to the extremity of expulsion if the said vicars should be found ungovernable, impenitent, or self-sufficient. . . . My resolution is to preserve the dignity of my station and the honour of my Chapter; and, gentlemen, it is incumbent upon you to aid me, and to show who and what the Dean and Chapter of St. Patrick's are."

These are the last words, except in the Cathedral accounts, which Swift is known to have written. The Chapter could have no doubt who the Dean of St. Patrick's was, though he was as old and desolate as Lear. In February, when Walpole lost his office, Swift, who had vowed to buy a coach if ever that should happen, bought a coach. He might have little time left in which to use it, but he would ride through the streets of Dublin exulting over Walpole's followers. All Dublin should know who the Dean of St. Patrick's was.

He fell like a tower, first a rush of warning stones, then a vast collapse. In March guardians were assigned to him by the Court of Chancery. In August a commission inquired into his sanity and found that he was "of unsound mind and memory, and not capable of taking care of his person or fortune, and that he hath been so since the twentieth day of May last past." From being irritable he became violent. He raged if anybody, besides his servants, looked at him. "He walked ten hours a day," his cousin said, "would not eat or drink if his servant stayed in the room. His meat was served up ready cut, and sometimes it would lie an hour on the table before he would touch it, and then eat it walking."

In September and October his torment reached its horrible peak, beyond what even he had imagined in his ruthless account of the struldbrugs. A sudden tumor forced his left eye almost out of its socket. He had as many boils as Job. "The torture he was in," his cousin said, "is not to be described. Five persons could scarce hold him, for a week, from tearing out his own eyes, and for near a month he did not sleep two hours in twenty-four." He had a quiet day or two. When his pain left him his understanding came back, as if his madness had been only agony. Nothing less than a cataclysm could subdue that burning mind. A cataclysm or a stroke of paralysis.

Paralysis brought him the relief of apathy. Swift had submitted. It took him three years to die, but he lived without rebellion. He no longer paced his cage. He would hardly leave his chair. His body got back its flesh. His face lost its wrinkles. His expression was now benign or childlike. He recognized the few persons whom he saw, but he seldom spoke. When he tried to speak, he could not always find words. What he said seemed to come by chance to his tongue, though it was never nonsense. Once, when his housekeeper took a knife out of his reach, "he shrugged his shoulders and, rocking himself, said 'I am what I am, I am what I am,' and about six minutes afterwards repeated the same words two or three times over."

Hundreds of stories were invented during those three years about the great mad Dean. One story, not true, was that he sat all day cursing in his chair. Another, probably not true, was that his servants exhibited him for money — "And Swift expires a driveller and a show." The stories, however, are proof enough of the vigor of the legend which had gathered around Swift and which still lives in Ireland. The Irish would not believe that he had hated them as he claimed. His abuse had been affectionate scolding, no rougher than they could enjoy. He had stood between them and England. He was a patriot, a man of learning, very near a saint. There must be magic in him. When he died, 19 October 1745, the people crowded to the deanery to see his body. They came in reverence. One of them, when nobody was looking, cut off some of his hair, which "was like flax on the pillow."

He was buried in the Cathedral beside Stella, as his will directed, "as privately as possible, and at twelve o'clock at night." His will was published as a sixpenny pamphlet almost as soon as he was dead. The people would be curious, he had said in his poem on his death, about his will. He left his fortune, about eleven thousand pounds, to build a hospital for idiots and lunatics. —

> " He left the little wealth he had
> To build a house for fools and mad;
> And showed by one satiric touch
> No nation wanted it so much." —

He left the tithes of the parish of Effernock to the vicars of Laracor "for the time being, that is to say, so long as the present Episcopal religion shall continue to be the national established faith and profession of this kingdom." After that, the tithes should go, "while Christianity under any shape shall be tolerated among us," to the poor of Laracor, "still excepting professed Jews, atheists, and infidels."

To various friends and relatives he left legacies, some of which were his final jests. To Robert Grattan: "my strong box, on condition of his giving the sole use of the said box to his brother Dr. James Grattan, who hath more occasion for it, and the second best beaver hat I shall die possessed of." To John Grattan: "my silver box in which the freedom of the

city of Cork was presented to me; in which I desire the said
John to keep the tobacco he usually cheweth, called pigtail."
To John Jackson: "my third best beaver hat." To John
Worrall: "my best beaver hat."

In the same document with these dry bequests he left to
the world his aching epitaph. It was to say to any traveler
who came to see it that the body of Jonathan Swift, Dean of
this Cathedral, was buried here in a place where his furious
indignation could no longer lacerate his heart. It was to tell
the traveler to go and imitate, if he could, this strenuous defender of manly liberty. The inscription was to be on black
marble, "in large letters, deeply cut and strongly gilded,"
and in the stately language of the Church and of the ancient
Romans.

HIC DEPOSITUM EST CORPUS

JONATHAN SWIFT S.T.P.

HUJUS ECCLESIAE CATHEDRALIS

DECANI

UBI SAEVA INDIGNATIO

ULTERIUS COR LACERARE NEQUIT

ABI VIATOR

ET IMITARE SI POTERIS

STRENUUM PRO VIRILI LIBERTATIS VINDICEM

RING LARDNER

1885–

70 *I Can't Breathe*

July 12

I AM staying here at the Inn for two weeks with my Uncle
Nat and Aunt Jule and I think I will keep a kind of a
diary while I am here to help pass the time and so I can have
a record of things that happen though goodness knows there
isn't lightly to anything happen, that is anything exciting
with Uncle Nat and Aunt Jule making the plans as they are
both at least 35 years old and maybe older.

Dad and mother are abroad to be gone a month and me

coming here is supposed to be a recompense for them not taking me with them. A fine recompense to be left with old people that come to a place like this to rest. Still it would be a heavenly place under different conditions, for instance if Walter were here, too. It would be heavenly if he were here, the very thought of it makes my heart stop.

I can't stand it. I won't think about it.

This is our first separation since we have been engaged, nearly 17 days. It will be 17 days to-morrow. And the hotel orchestra at dinner this evening played that old thing " Oh how I miss you to-night " and it seemed as if they must be playing it for my benefit though of course the person in that song is talking about how they miss their mother though of course I miss mother too, but a person gets used to missing their mother and it isn't like Walter or the person you are engaged to.

But there won't be any more separations much longer, we are going to be married in December even if mother does laugh when I talk to her about it because she says I am crazy to even think of getting married at 18.

She got married herself when she was 18, but of course that was "different," she wasn't crazy like I am, she knew whom she was marrying. As if Walter were a policeman or a foreigner or something. And she says she was only engaged once while I have been engaged at least five times a year since I was 14, of course it really isn't as bad as that and I have really only been really what I call engaged six times altogether, but is getting engaged my fault when they keep insisting and hammering at you and if you didn't say yes they would never go home.

But it is different with Walter. I honestly believe if he had not asked me I would have asked him. Of course I wouldn't have, but I would have died. And this is the first time I have ever been engaged to be really married. The other times when they talked about when should we get married I just laughed at them, but I hadn't been engaged to Walter ten minutes when he brought up the subject of marriage and I didn't laugh. I wouldn't be engaged to him unless it was to be married. I couldn't stand it.

Anyway mother may as well get used to the idea because it is "No Foolin'" this time and we have got our plans all made and I am going to be married at home and go out to California and Hollywood on our honeymoon. December, five months away. I can't stand it. I can't wait.

There were a couple of awfully nice looking boys sitting together alone in the dining room tonight. One of them wasn't so much, but the other was cute. And he——

There's the dance orchestra playing "Always," what they played at the Biltmore the day I met Walter. "Not for just an hour not for just a day." I can't live. I can't breathe.

July 13

This has been a much more exciting day than I expected under the circumstances. In the first place I got two long night letters, one from Walter and one from Gordon Flint. I don't see how Walter ever had the nerve to send his, there was everything in it and it must have been horribly embarrassing for him while the telegraph operator was reading it over and counting the words to say nothing of embarrassing for the operator.

But the one from Gordon was a kind of a shock. He just got back from a trip around the world, left last December to go on it and got back yesterday and called up our house and Helga gave him my address, and his telegram, well it was nearly as bad as Walter's. The trouble is that Gordon and I were engaged when he went away, or at least he thought so and he wrote to me right along all the time he was away and sent cables and things and for a while I answered his letters, but then I lost track of his itinery and couldn't write to him any more and when I got really engaged to Walter I couldn't let Gordon know because I had no idea where he was besides not wanting to spoil his trip.

And now he still thinks we are engaged and he is going to call me up to-morrow from Chicago and how in the world can I explain things and get him to understand because he is really serious and I like him ever and ever so much and in lots of ways he is nicer than Walter, not really nicer but better looking and there is no comparison between their dancing. Walter simply can't learn to dance, that is really dance. He says it is because he is flat footed, he says that as a joke, but it is true and I wish to heavens it wasn't.

All forenoon I thought and thought and thought about what to say to Gordon when he calls up and finally I couldn't stand thinking about it any more and just made up my mind I wouldn't think about it any more. But I will tell the truth though it will kill me to hurt him.

I went down to lunch with Uncle Nat and Aunt Jule and they were going out to play golf this afternoon and were insisting that I go with them, but I told them I had a headache and then I had a terrible time getting them to go without me. I didn't have a headache at all and just wanted to be alone to think about Walter and besides when you play with Uncle Nat he is always correcting your stance or your swing or something and always puts his hands on my arms or shoulders to show me the right way and I can't stand it to have old men touch me, even if they are your uncle.

I finally got rid of them and I was sitting watching the tennis when that boy that I saw last night, the cute one, came and sat right next to me and of course I didn't look at him and I was going to smoke a cigarette and found I had left my lighter upstairs and I started to get up and go after it when all of a sudden he was offering me his lighter and I couldn't very well refuse it without being rude. So we got to talking and he is even cuter than he looks, the most original and wittiest person I believe I ever met and I haven't laughed so much in I don't know how long.

For one thing he asked me if I had heard Rockefeller's

song and I said no and he began singing "Oil alone." Then he asked me if I knew the orange juice song and I told him no again and he said it was "Orange juice sorry you made me cry." I was in hysterics before we had been together ten minutes.

His name is Frank Caswell and he has been out of Dartmouth a year and is 24 years old. That isn't so terribly old, only two years older than Walter and three years older than Gordon. I hate the name Frank, but Caswell is all right and he is so cute.

He was out in California last winter and visited Hollywood and met everybody in the world and it is fascinating to listen to him. He met Norma Shearer and he said he thought she was the prettiest thing he had ever seen. What he said was "I did think she was the prettiest girl in the world, till to-day." I was going to pretend I didn't get it, but I finally told him to be sensible or I would never be able to believe anything he said.

Well, he wanted me to dance with him to-night after dinner and the next question was how to explain how we had met each other to Uncle Nat and Aunt Jule. Frank said he would fix that all right and sure enough he got himself introduced to Uncle Nat when Uncle Nat came in from golf and after dinner Uncle Nat introduced him to me and Aunt Jule too and we danced together all evening, that is not Aunt Jule. They went to bed, thank heavens.

He is a heavenly dancer, as good as Gordon. One dance we were dancing and for one of the encores the orchestra played "In a cottage small by a waterfall" and I simply couldn't dance to it. I just stopped still and said "Listen, I can't bear it, I can't breathe" and poor Frank thought I was sick or something and I had to explain that that was the tune the orchestra played the night I sat at the next table to Jack Barrymore at Barney Gallant's.

I made him sit out that encore and wouldn't let him talk till they got through playing it. Then they played something else and I was all right again and Frank told me about meeting Jack Barrymore. Imagine meeting him. I couldn't live.

I promised Aunt Jule I would go to bed at eleven and it is way past that now, but I am all ready for bed and have just been writing this. To-morrow Gordon is going to call up and what will I say to him? I just won't think about it.

July 14

Gordon called up this morning from Chicago and it was wonderful to hear his voice again though the connection was terrible. He asked me if I still loved him and I tried to tell him no, but I knew that would mean an explanation and the connection was so bad that I never could make him understand so I said yes, but I almost whispered it purposely, thinking he wouldn't hear me, but he heard me all right and said that made everything all right with the world. He said he thought I had stopped loving him because I had stopped writing.

I wish the connection had been decent and I could have told him how things were, but now it is terrible because he is planning to get to New York the day I get there and heaven knows what I will do because Walter will be there, too. I just won't think about it.

Aunt Jule came in my room just after I was through talking to Gordon, thank heavens. The room was full of flowers. Walter had sent me some and so had Frank. I got another long night letter from Walter, just as silly as the first one. I wish he would say those things in letters instead of night letters so everybody in the world wouldn't see them. Aunt Jule wanted me to read it aloud to her. I would have died.

While she was still in the room, Frank called up and asked me to play golf with him and I said all right and Aunt Jule said she was glad my headache was gone. She was trying to be funny.

I played golf with Frank this afternoon. He is a beautiful golfer and it is thrilling to watch him drive, his swing is so much more graceful than Walter's. I asked him to watch me swing and tell me what was the matter with me, but he said he couldn't look at anything but my face and there wasn't anything the matter with that.

He told me the boy who was here with him had been called home and he was glad of it because I might have liked him, the other boy, better than himself. I told him that couldn't be possible and he asked me if I really meant that and I said of course, but I smiled when I said it so he wouldn't take it too seriously.

We danced again to-night and Uncle Nat and Aunt Jule sat with us a while and danced a couple of dances themselves, but they were really there to get better acquainted with Frank and see if he was all right for me to be with. I know they certainly couldn't have enjoyed their own dancing, no old people really can enjoy it because they can't really *do* anything.

They were favorably impressed with Frank I think, at least Aunt Jule didn't say I must be in bed at eleven, but just not to stay up too late. I guess it is a big surprise to a girl's parents and aunts and uncles to find out that the boys you go around with are all right, they always seem to think that if I seem to like somebody and the person pays a little attention to me, why he must be a convict or a policeman or a drunkard or something queer.

Frank had some more songs for me to-night. He asked me if I knew the asthma song and I said I didn't and he said "Oh, you must know that. It goes, yes, sir, asthma baby." Then he told me about the underwear song, "I underwear my baby is to-night." He keeps you in hysterics and yet he has his serious side, in fact he was awfully serious when he said good night to me and his eyes simply shown. I wish Walter were more like him in some ways, but I mustn't think about that.

July 15

I simply can't live and I know I'll never sleep to-night. I am in a terrible predicament or rather I won't know whether

I really am or not till to-morrow and that is what makes it so terrible.

After we had danced two or three dances, Frank asked me to go for a ride with him and we went for a ride in his car and he had had some cocktails and during the ride he had some drinks out of a flask and finally he told me he loved me and I said not to be silly, but he said he was perfectly serious and he certainly acted that way. He asked me if I loved anybody else and I said yes and he asked if I didn't love him more than anybody else and I said yes, but only because I thought he had probably had too much to drink and wouldn't remember it anyway and the best thing to do was humor him under the circumstances.

Then all of a sudden he asked me when I could marry him and I said, just as a joke, that I couldn't possibly marry him before December. He said that was a long time to wait, but I was certainly worth waiting for and he said a lot of other things and maybe I humored him a little too much, but that is just the trouble, I don't know.

I was absolutely sure he was tight and would forget the whole thing, but that was early in the evening, and when we said good night he was a whole lot more sober than he had been and now I am not sure how it stands. If he doesn't remember anything about it, of course I am all right. But if he does remember and if he took me seriously, I will simply have to tell him about Walter and maybe about Gordon, too. And it isn't going to be easy. The suspense is what is maddening and I know I'll never live through this night.

July 16

I can't stand it, I can't breathe, life is impossible. Frank remembered everything about last night and firmly believes we are engaged and going to be married in December. His people live in New York and he says he is going back when I do and have them meet me.

Of course it can't go on and to-morrow I will tell him

about Walter or Gordon or both of them. I know it is going to hurt him terribly, perhaps spoil his life and I would give anything in the world not to have had it happen. I hate so to hurt him because he is so nice besides being so cute and attractive.

He sent me the loveliest flowers this morning and called up at ten and wanted to know how soon he could see me and I hope the girl wasn't listening in because the things he said were, well, like Walter's night letters.

And that is another terrible thing, to-day I didn't get a night letter from Walter, but there was a regular letter instead and I carried it around in my purse all this afternoon and evening and never remembered to read it till ten minutes ago when I came up in the room. Walter is worried because I have only sent him two telegrams and written him one letter since I have been here, he would be a lot more worried if he knew what has happened now, though of course it can't make any difference because he is the one I am really engaged to be married to and the one I told mother I was going to marry in December and I wouldn't dare tell her it was somebody else.

I met Frank for lunch and we went for a ride this afternoon and he was so much in love and so lovely to me that I simply did not have the heart to tell him the truth, I am surely going to tell him to-morrow and telling him to-day would have just meant one more day of unhappiness for both of us.

He said his people had plenty of money and his father had offered to take him into partnership and he might accept, but he thinks his true vocation is journalism with a view to eventually writing novels and if I was willing to undergo a few hardships just at first we would probably both be happier later on if he was doing something he really liked. I didn't know what to say, but finally I said I wanted him to suit himself and money wasn't everything.

He asked me where I would like to go on my honeymoon and I suppose I ought to have told him my honeymoon was all planned, that I was going to California, with Walter, but all I said was that I had always wanted to go to California and he was enthusiastic and said that is where we would surely go and he would take me to Hollywood and introduce me to all those wonderful people he met there last winter. It nearly takes my breath away to think of it, going there with someone who really knows people and has the entrée.

We danced again to-night, just two or three dances, and then went out and sat in the tennis-court, but I came upstairs early because Aunt Jule had acted kind of funny at dinner. And I wanted to be alone, too, and think, but the more I think the worse it gets.

Sometimes I wish I were dead, maybe that is the only solution and it would be best for everyone concerned. I *will* die if things keep on the way they have been. But of course to-morrow it will be all over, with Frank I mean, for I must tell him the truth no matter how much it hurts us both. Though I don't care how much it hurts me. The thought of hurting him is what is driving me mad. I can't bear it.

July 18

I have skipped a day. I was busy every minute of yesterday and so exhausted when I came upstairs that I was tempted to fall into bed with all my clothes on. First Gordon called me up from Chicago to remind me that he would be in New York the day I got there and that when he comes he wants me all to himself all the time and we can make plans for our wedding. The connection was bad again and I just couldn't explain to him about Walter.

I had an engagement with Frank for lunch and just as we were going in another long distance call came, from Walter this time. He wanted to know why I haven't written more letters and sent him more telegrams and asked me if I still loved him and of course I told him yes because I really do. Then he asked if I had met any men here and I told him

I had met one, a friend of Uncle Nat's. After all it was Uncle Nat who introduced me to Frank. He reminded me that he would be in New York on the 25th which is the day I expect to get home, and said he would have theater tickets for that night and we would go somewhere afterwards and dance.

Frank insisted on knowing who had kept me talking so long and I told him it was a boy I had known a long while, a very dear friend of mine and a friend of my family's. Frank was jealous and kept asking questions till I thought I would go mad. He was so serious and kind of cross and gruff that I gave up the plan of telling him the truth till some time when he is in better spirits.

I played golf with Frank in the afternoon and we took a ride last night and I wanted to get in early because I had promised both Walter and Gordon that I would write them long letters, but Frank wouldn't bring me back to the Inn till I had named a definite date in December. I finally told him the 10th and he said all right if I was sure that wasn't a Sunday. I said I would have to look it up, but as a matter of fact I know the 10th falls on a Friday because the date Walter and I have agreed on for our wedding is Saturday the 11th.

To-day has just been the same thing over again, two more night letters, a long distance call from Chicago, golf and a ride with Frank, and the room full of flowers. But to-morrow I am going to tell Frank and I am going to write Gordon a long letter and tell him, too, because this simply can't go on any longer. I can't breathe. I can't live.

July 21

I wrote to Gordon yesterday, but I didn't say anything about Walter because I don't think it is a thing a person ought to do by letter. I can tell him when he gets to New York and then I will be sure that he doesn't take it too hard and I can promise him that I will be friends with him always and make him promise not to do anything silly, while if I told it to him in a letter there is no telling what he would do, there all alone.

And I haven't told Frank because he hasn't been feeling well, he is terribly sunburned and it hurts him terribly so he can hardly play golf or dance, and I want him to be feeling his best when I do tell him, but whether he is all right or not I simply must tell him to-morrow because he is actually planning to leave here on the same train with us Saturday night and I can't let him do that.

Life is so hopeless and it could be so wonderful. For instance how heavenly it would be if I could marry Frank first and stay married to him five years and he would be the one who would take me to Hollywood and maybe we could go on parties with Norman Kerry and Jack Barrymore and Buster Collier and Marion Davies and Lois Moran.

And at the end of five years Frank could go into journalism and write novels and I would only be 23 and I could marry Gordon and he would be ready for another trip around the world and he could show me things better than someone who had never seen them before.

Gordon and I would separate at the end of five years and I would be 28 and I know of lots of women that never even got married the first time till they were 28 though I don't suppose that was their fault, but I would marry Walter then, for after all he is the one I really love and want to spend most of my life with and I wouldn't care whether he could dance or not when I was that old. Before long we would be as old as Uncle Nat and Aunt Jule and I certainly wouldn't want to dance at their age when all you can do is just hobble around the floor. But Walter is so wonderful as a companion and we would enjoy the same things and be pals and maybe we would begin to have children.

But that is all impossible though it wouldn't be if older people just had sense and would look at things the right way.

It is only half past ten, the earliest I have gone to bed in weeks, but I am worn out and Frank went to bed early so he could put cold cream on his sunburn.

Listen, diary, the orchestra is playing " Limehouse Blues." The first tune I danced to with Merle Oliver, two years ago. I can't stand it. And how funny that they should play that old tune to-night of all nights, when I have been thinking of Merle off and on all day, and I hadn't thought of him before in weeks and weeks. I wonder where he is, I wonder if it is just an accident or if it means I am going to see him again. I simply mustn't think about it or I'll die.

July 22

I knew it wasn't an accident. I knew it must mean something, and it did.

Merle is coming here to-day, here to this Inn, and just to see me. And there can only be one reason. And only one answer. I knew that when I heard his voice calling from Boston. How could I ever have thought I loved anyone else? How could he ever have thought I meant it when I told him I was engaged to George Morse?

A whole year and he still cares and I still care. That shows we were always intended for each other and for no one else. I won't make *him* wait till December. I doubt if we even wait till dad and mother get home. And as for a honeymoon I will go with him to Long Beach or the Bronx Zoo, wherever he wants to take me.

After all this is the best way out of it, the only way. I won't have to say anything to Frank, he will guess when he sees me with Merle. And when I get home Sunday and Walter and Gordon call me up, I will invite them both to dinner and Merle can tell them himself, with two of them there it will only hurt each one half as much as if they were alone.

The train is due at 2:40, almost three hours from now. I can't wait. And what if it should be late? I can't stand it.

71   *"Highbrow" and "Lowbrow"*

I

AT the time when he was trying to release humanity from the cross of gold on which, as he said, it was crucified, the Apostle of Free Silver — in this matter, at least, representing the old American frame of mind — announced that the opinion of all the professors in the United States would not affect his opinions in the least. Now this, plainly, was a very formidable dilemma. For on the one hand stood a body of supposed experts in economic theory, on the other a man whose profession it was to change and reform economic practice, — the one knowing, the other doing; and not only was there no compatibility between them but an openly avowed and cynical contempt of theory on the part of practice was a principal element in the popularity of a popular hero. Was Mr. Bryan, however, to blame for it? To know anything of the economic theory which is taught in American universities — in many cases compulsorily taught — is to confess that blame is not the right word. For this economic theory is at the least equally cynical. It revolves round and round in its tree-top dream of the economic man; and no matter how much the wind blows political economy never comes down. Incompatibility, mutual contempt between theory and practice, is in the very nature of things.

One might extend the illustration to literature, merely substituting one professor for another and putting any typical best-selling novelist in the place of Mr. Bryan. It is a peculiar twist in the academic mind to suppose that a writer belongs to literature only when he is dead; living he is, vaguely, something else; and an habitual remoteness from the creative mood has made American professors quite peculiarly academic. "Literature," as distinguished from excellent writing, is, in the American universities, a thing felt to have been done, and while for all one knows it may continue to be done the quality in it which makes it literature only comes out, like the quality in wines, with age.

Now I suppose that most of the American novelists in our day are university men; they have learned to regard literature as an august compound of Browning, Ben Jonson, and Hesiod; and consequently when they themselves begin to write it is in a spirit of real humility that they set themselves to the composition of richly rewarded trash. I am sure of this: it is modesty that lies behind the "best-seller"; and there is an aspect in which the spectacle of writers regarding themselves as humble tradesfolk has a certain charm. But the conception of literature as something, so to speak, high and dry, gives to the craft of authorship in America a latitude like that of morality in Catholic countries: so long as the heavenly virtues are upheld mundane virtues may shift as they will. In a word, writers are relieved of responsibility, and while their ethical conscience remains quite sound they absolve themselves from any artistic conscience whatsoever. And the worst of it is that precisely these writers of immitigable trash are often the bright, vigorous, intuitive souls who *could* make literature out of American life. Has it ever been considered how great a knowledge of men, what psychological gifts of the first order their incomparable achievement of popularity implies?

These two attitudes of mind have been phrased once for all in our vernacular as "Highbrow" and "Lowbrow." I have proposed these terms to a Russian, an Englishman, and a German, asking each in turn whether in his country there was anything to correspond with the conceptions implied in them. In each case they have been returned to me as quite American, authentically our very own, and, I should add, highly suggestive.

What side of American life is not touched by this antithesis? What explanation of American life is more central or more illuminating? In everything one finds this frank acceptance of twin values which are not expected to have anything in common: on the one hand a quite unclouded, quite unhypocritical assumption of transcendent theory ("high ideals"); on the other a simultaneous acceptance of catchpenny realities. Between university ethics and business ethics, between American culture and American humor, between Good Government and Tammany, between academic pedantry and pavement slang, there is no community, no genial middle ground.

The very accent of the words "Highbrow" and "Lowbrow" implies an instinctive perception that this is a very unsatisfactory state of affairs. For both are used in a derogatory sense. The "Highbrow" is the superior person whose virtue is admitted but felt to be an inept unpalatable virtue; while the "Lowbrow" is a good fellow one readily takes to, but with a certain scorn for him and all his works. And what is true of them as personal types is true of what they stand for. They are equally undesirable, and they are incompatible; but they divide American life between them.

II

They always have divided American life between them; and to understand them one has to go back to the beginning of things, — for without doubt the Puritan Theocracy is the all-influential fact in the history of the American mind. It was the Puritan conception of the Deity as not alone all-determining but precisely responsible for the practical affairs of the race, as constituting, in fact, the State itself, which precluded in advance any central bond, any responsibility, any common feeling in American affairs and which justified the unlimited centrifugal expediency which has always marked American life. And the same instinct that made against centrality in government made against centrality in thought, against common standards of any kind. The imminent eternal issues the Puritans felt so keenly, the equally imminent practical issues they experienced so monotonously threw almost no light on one another; there was no middle ground between to mitigate, combine, or harmonize them.

So it is that from the beginning we find two main currents in the American mind running side by side but rarely mingling — a current of overtones and a current of undertones — and both equally unsocial: on the one hand, the current of Transcendentalism, originating in the piety of the Puritans, becoming a philosophy in Jonathan Edwards, passing through Emerson, producing the fastidious refinement and aloofness of the chief American writers, and, as the coherent ideals and beliefs of Transcendentalism gradually faded out, resulting in the final unreality of most contemporary American culture; and on the other hand the current of catchpenny opportunism, originating in the practical shifts of Puritan life, becoming a philosophy in Franklin, passing through the American humorists, and resulting in the atmosphere of contemporary business life.

Thus the literature of the seventeenth century in America is composed in equal parts, one may fairly say, of piety and advertisement; and the revered chronicles of New England had the double effect of proving how many pilgrim souls had been elected to salvation and of populating with hopeful immigrants a land where heaven had proved so indulgent.

For three generations the prevailing American character was compact in one type, the man of action who was also the man of God. Not until the eighteenth century did the rift appear and with it the essential distinction between "Highbrow" and "Lowbrow." It appeared in the two philosophers, Jonathan Edwards and Benjamin Franklin, who share the eighteenth century between them. In their amazing purity of type and in the apparent incompatibility of their aims they determined the American character as a racial fact, and after them the Revolution became inevitable. Channing, Lincoln, Emerson, Whitman, Grant, Webster, Garrison, Edison, Mr. Rockefeller, Mrs. Eddy are all, in one way or another, permutations and combinations of these two grand progenitors of the American character.

Strange that at the very outset two men should have arisen so aptly side by side and fixed the poles of our national life! For no one has ever more fully and typically than Jonathan Edwards displayed the infinite inflexibility of the upper levels of the American mind, nor any one more typically than Franklin the intimate flexibility of its lower levels.

The intellect of Jonathan Edwards was like the Matterhorn, steep, icy, and pinnacled. At its base were green slopes and singing valleys filled with all sorts of little tender wild-flowers — for he was the most lovable of men; but as soon as the ground began to rise in good earnest all this verdurous life came to an abrupt end: not one green or living thing could subsist in that frozen soil, on those pale heights. It was the solitude of logic that led him to see in destiny only a wrathful tyrant and a viper's trail in the mischievous ways of little boys and girls.

I confess to an old-time and so to speak aboriginal affection for this man, so gently solicitous to make up in his daily walk and conversation for the ferocious impulses of that brain of his. He was even the most romantic of men, as I thought once, and I well remember that immense old musty book of his theology, covered with mildew, with its desert of tiny print, which I carried out with me into the fields and read, in the intervals of birdnesting, under the hedgerows and along the borders of the wood: the sun fell for the first time on those clammy old pages and the pallid thoughts that lay in them, and the field-sparrows all about were twittering in a language which, to tell the truth, was no more unintelligible to me. But everything that springs from solitude shines by a light of its own, and Manfred among the Alps was not more lonely than this rapt scholar in his parsonage among the Indians.

There are, however, solitudes and solitudes. Great poets and fruitful thinkers live apart themselves, perhaps, but they have society and the ways of men in their blood. They recollect in tranquillity, as it were, gestate, live again, and reveal the last significance of active generations rich in human stuff, in experience, in emotion, in common reason. Nothing like this existed in the background of Jonathan Edwards, no profound and complex race-life. Intellect in him, isolated and not responsible to the other faculties, went on its way unchecked; and he was able to spin those inept sublimities of his by subtracting from his mind every trace of experience, every touch of human nature as it really was among his innocent country-folk.

Notoriously, of course, our great Dr. Franklin simplified existence in precisely the opposite way; for the opposite of unmitigated theory is unmitigated practice. Who can deny that in *Poor Richard* the "Lowbrow" point of view for the first time took definite shape, stayed itself with axioms, and found a sanction in the idea of "policy"? It emerges there full-fledged, in its classical form, a two-dimensional wisdom, a wisdom shorn of overtones, the most accommodating wisdom in the world.

Were ever two views of life more incompatible than these? What indeed could Poor Richard have in common with an Angry God?

And what can Mr. Bryan have in common with political economy?

III

"Our people," said Emerson, "have their intellectual culture from one country and their duties from another." In how many spheres that phrase can be applied! Desiccated culture at one end and stark utility at the other have created a deadlock in the American mind, and all our life drifts chaotically between the two extremes. Consider, for example, our use of the English language. Literary English in England is naturally a living speech, which occupies the middle of the field and expresses the flesh and blood of an evolving race. Literary English with us is a tradition, just as Anglo-Saxon law with us is a tradition. They persist not as the normal expressions of a race, the essential fibre of which is permanently Anglo-Saxon, but through prestige and precedent and the will and habit of a dominating class largely out of touch with a national fabric unconsciously taking form " out of school." No wonder that our literary style is "pure," that our literary tradition, our tradition especially in oratory and political prose, retains the spirit of the eighteenth century. But at what a cost! At the cost of expressing a popular life which bubbles with energy and spreads and grows and slips away ever more and more from the control of tested ideas, a popular life "with the lid off," which demands an intellectual outlet and finds one in slang, journalism, and unmannerly fiction.

After seventy years Carlyle's well-known appeal to Emerson still applies to the spirit of American culture: " For the rest, I have to object still (what you will call objecting against the Law of Nature) that we find you a speaker indeed, but as it were a *Soliloquizer* on the eternal mountaintops only, in vast solitudes where men and their affairs lie all hushed in a very dim remoteness; and only *the man* and the stars and the earth are visible — whom, so fine a fellow seems he, we could perpetually punch into, and say, 'Why won't you come and help us then? We have terrible need of one man like you down among us! It is cold and vacant up there; nothing paintable but rainbows and emotions; come down and you shall do life-pictures, passions, facts. . . .'"

And what a comment on the same utterance that at this very moment an amiable New Englander should have been painting in Parson Wilbur and Hosea Biglow, respectively, unconscious of any tragic symbolism of things to come, the unbridgeable chasm between literate and illiterate America! Morally, no doubt, in Jaalam, they understood one another and got along very well, as Yankees will. But in Chicago?

IV

To pass now from the social to the personal question, since the question is at bottom a personal one, let us figure to ourselves how this divergence comes about and how it is that our educational system, instead of creating what President Eliot calls a "serviceable fellowship" between theory and practice, tends to set them apart and to confirm us all either in the one extreme or in the other.

Let us figure to ourselves a typical American who has grown up, as an American typically does grow up, in a sort of orgy of lofty examples, moralized poems, national anthems, and baccalaureate sermons; until he is charged with all manner of ideal purities, ideal honorabilities, ideal femininities, flag-wavings and skyscrapings of every sort; — until he comes to feel in himself the hovering presence of all manner of fine potentialities, remote, vaporous, and evanescent as a rainbow. All this time, it can fairly be said, he has not been taught to associate himself personally with ends even much lower than these, he has not been taught that life is a legitimate progress toward spiritual or intellectual ends at all, his instincts of acquisition, pleasure, enterprise, and desire have in no way been linked and connected with disinterested ends; he has had it very firmly embedded in his mind that the getting of a living is not a necessity incidental to some higher and more disinterested end, but that it is the prime and central end in things, and as a corollary to this he has been encouraged to assume that the world is a stamping-ground for every untrained, greedy, and aggressive impulse in him, that, in short, society is fair prey for what he can get out of it.

Let us imagine that, having grown up in this way, he is sent to college. And here, in order to keep the case a typical one, we shall have to exercise a little discrimination in the choice of a university.

It will not be Harvard, because the ideal of Harvard, as I shall point out, is not a typically modern American ideal.

Nor will it be one of the modern utilitarian universities, which have no ideal at all. It will be any one of the others; and when I say this I mean that each of the others is in one way or another a development of the old American country college; its ideal, its experience, its tradition spring out of and lead one back to that. Now among these old colleges Harvard might have been figured as an ever-developing, ever-liberalizing catholicism, of which they were all sectarian off-shoots, established on a principle of progressive theological fragmentation, each one defending an orthodoxy its predecessors had outworn or violently setting up in defense of some private orthodoxy of its own. They founded themselves each on a remote dogma or system of dogma as their central and sufficient basis, and all their wheels turned in relation to the central theological dynamo. In a sense of course this was true also of Harvard, but with a marked difference. For the theologians who founded Harvard were men of action as well; in the seventeenth century a New England minister was also a politician, and the education of ministers for which Harvard was mainly established implied an education for public affairs as well, an education for society, so far as the word society can be used in connection with the early Puritans at all. Thus at the outset the founders of Harvard drove in the wedge of secularism: Harvard had from the beginning a sort of national basis, at least among New Englanders, and its dogmatic structure consequently reflected and shifted with and accommodated itself to the currents of national thought. Remaining in touch with society, it educated to a certain extent, relatively to an extraordinary extent, the social function of its students; and it is thus no accident that so large a proportion of the political, the literary, and the scientific life of America has sprung from it. But in the eighteenth century the conditions under which Harvard was established had ceased to be true. The minister was no longer a man of affairs, — he was a stark theologian, and usually of a type which the majority of his flock had outgrown. Yale, Princeton, and virtually all the other typically American colleges were founded by men of this type. Jonathan Edwards may figure for them all; the motive which led him to become the president of Princeton being precisely that his flock in Connecticut could no longer see the anger of God eye to eye with him. Already in his time the fathers and mothers of young America had submitted to the charms of *Poor Richard's Almanac* — they had themselves for the most part become inveterately "Lowbrow"; but they seem to have believed that an Angry God might still be a good influence over young America himself.

To return now to the typical case with whom we began, let us imagine that he makes a typical choice and goes to a typical university. Having arrived there will he be confronted with an Angry God, or any sort of direct theological dogma? By no means. But there will have remained in the air a certain fragrance and vibration, as if an ideal had passed that way and not stayed, there will be intangible whispers and seductions, there will be a certain faint, rarefied, remote, but curiously pervasive and insistent influence — like the sound of an Æolian harp or the recollection of Plato in some uncouth slum; there will be memories and portraits of many an old metaphysician, white, unearthly, fragile. It will all seem very much as if, the significance of these remote dogmas having evaporated, only the remoteness, in a way, had remained.

One would have to be very insensitive not to feel the quite unbalancing charm of this quality — so different from its comparatively robust Oxford parallel — in the old New England colleges, as in Princeton, Yale, and the other universities which have developed out of them; but one cannot help feeling also, I think, something vaguely Circean in it. And in fact, given the preliminary method of bringing up which I have sketched, what will be its effect in the case we are considering? Suddenly confronted during four years with just this remote influence of ideals, out of which the intellectual structure has evaporated and which never possessed a social structure, will he not find them too vague, too intangible, too unprepared for to be incorporated into his nature? Certainly ideals of this kind, in this way presented, in this way prepared for, cannot enrich life, because they are wanting in all the elements of personal contact. Wholly dreamlike and vaporous, they end by breeding nothing but cynicism and chagrin; and in becoming permanently catalogued in the mind as impracticable they lead to a belief in the essential unreality of ideas as well.

Indeed there is nothing so tragic and so ominous as the familiar saying that college is the happiest time of one's life. Yet perhaps a majority of college men think of their college life in this way. They deliberately put their Golden Age behind them — and, as things are, they know it is behind them. But consider what a comment this is on the American university itself, — a place, one can fairly say, where ideals are cherished precisely because they are ineffectual, because they are ineptly and mournfully beautiful, because they make one cynical, because they make life progressively uninteresting, because, practically and in effect, they are illusions and frauds and infinitely charming lies. There surely is the last and the most impenetrable stronghold of Puritanism, refined to the last degree of intangibility, which persists in making the world a world inevitably sordid, basely practical, and whose very definition of the ideal consequently is, that which has no connection with the world!

Thus far then for our typical university graduate. He has been consistently educated in twin values which are incompatible. The theoretical atmosphere in which he has lived is one that bears no relation to society, the practical atmosphere in which he has lived bears no relation to ideals. Theory has become for him permanently a world in itself, a kind of *ding an sich;* practice has become simply a world of dollars.

Now supposing he has already become interested in the study, let us say, of economics, three paths are open to him: either he can give himself once for all to economics, or he can go the way of all flesh, *i.e.,* into business, or he can hesitate between the two, becoming an economist for the time being and eventually going into business.

It is just here, at the moment of choice, that the want of ballast in his education becomes manifest. There is nothing for him but to lurch violently to the one extreme or the other; and this, according as there is in his nature a crude preponderance either of intellect or of the sense of action, he does. If he is preponderantly intellectual he adopts the first course; that is to say, he dedicates himself to the service of a type of economic theory that bears no relation to this wicked world at all, leaving all the good people who are managing the economic practice of society (and, for the want of him, chiefly muddling it) — leaving all these good people to talk nonsense in the wilderness. If he is preponderantly a man of action, he adopts the second course; that is to say, he dedicates himself to the service of a private end which knows nothing of theory, which is most cynically contemptuous of ideals, flatulent or other, and which is precisely as indifferent to the economic life of society as the professor of economics himself.

Well, good riddance to both of them, one might be inclined to say, except that on second thought the professor and the business man between them hold in their hands so great a part of human destiny. It is the third case that is really interesting and really tragic. For just so far as our typical student is a normal man, just so far as he shares the twin elements of intellect and action in equal parts, just so far will he be on the fence. The probability is that in this case he will become a professor for as long as he can stand it and then burst into business and become a first-rate millionaire as quickly as possible. The sense of action in him will rebel against the sense of theory and finding in theory no basis for action, no relation to action, will press him into a fresh life where the theoretical side of his nature will at least be of some slight use in furthering his own aggrandizement, and that alone.

V

Naturally the question of economics is only typical. Any branch of human activity which is represented by professors at all — and which is not? — would serve as well. Human nature itself in America exists on two irreconcilable planes, the plane of stark theory and the plane of stark business; and in the back of its mind is heaven knows what world of poetry, hidden away, too inaccessible, too intangible, too unreal in fact ever to be brought into the open, or to serve, as the poetry of life rightly should serve, in harnessing thought and action together, turning life into a disinterested adventure.

Argue which way you will, from the individual to society or from society to the individual, it is the same. Just as the American attitude toward the State has been the attitude of an oratorical and vague patriotism which has not based itself on a concrete interest in public affairs; just as, in consequence of this, the " invisible government " of business has swept in and taken possession of the field and become the actual government under which we live, overgrowing and supplanting the government we recognize: so also in the case of the individual; the cherishing of ideals that are simply unmapped regions to which nobody has the least intention of building roads, the baccalaureate sermons that are no just, organic comment on the educational system that precedes them — precisely these themselves strengthen the forces from below; the invisible government of self-interest, built up carefully from the beginning by maxim and example, fills the vacuum a disinterested purpose ought to have occupied.

Twenty, even ten years, ago, it would have been universally assumed that the only hope for American society lay in somehow lifting the " Lowbrow " elements in it to the level of the " Highbrow " elements. But that quickening realism which belongs to contemporary thought makes it plain on the one hand that the mere idealism of university ethics, the mere loftiness of what is called culture, the mere purity of so-called Good Government, left to themselves, not only produce a glassy inflexible priggishness on the upper levels which paralyzes life; but that the lower levels have a certain humanity, flexibility, tangibility which are indispensable in any program: that Tammany has quite as much to teach Good Government as Good Government has to teach Tammany, that slang has quite as much in store for so-called culture as culture has for slang — that the universities, while emphatically not becoming more "practical," must base their disinterestedness on human, moral, social, artistic, and personal needs, impulses, and experience.

But society cannot become humane of itself; and it is for this reason that the movements of Reform are so external and so superficial. The will to reform springs from a conviction *ex post facto,* and is strictly analogous to the frame of mind of business men who retire at sixty and collect pictures. Nothing so exemplifies it as the spectacle of Mr. Carnegie spending three quarters of his life in providing steel for battleships and the last quarter of it in trying to abolish war. He himself surely has not been conscious of any inward revolution; plainly with him as with others the will to create disorder and the will to reform it spring from the same inner condition of mind. The impetus of Reform is evidently derived from the hope that a sufficient number of reformers can be trained and brought into the field to match the forces of business — the one group cancelling the other group. The ideal of Reform, in short, is the attainment of zero.

Nothing is more absurd than to attack business as such. But the motives and circumstances of business vary from age to age, and there is a world of difference between industry conceived as a social process and trade conceived as a private end. A familiar distinction between the nineteenth century and the twentieth is that the problem of civilization is no longer the problem of want but the problem of surplus. Roughly speaking, the hereditary American class — the prevailing class, I mean — is faced with the problem not of making money but of spending it; the prevailing American class is in a position of relative, but relatively great, economic freedom, and under these conditions it is plain that in them economic self-assertion ("enterprise") has become to a large extent a vicious anachronism. But force of habit, the sheer impetus and ground-swell of an antiquated pioneering spirit finds them with no means of personal outlet except a continued economic self-assertion on the one hand, and on the other a reckless and essentially impersonal overflow of surplus wealth which takes the form of doing what everybody else does, and doing it as much more so as possible.

Because it was for so long the law of the tribe economic self-assertion still remains to most Americans a sort of moral obligation; while self-fulfillment still looks like a pretty word for selfishness. Yet self-fulfillment through science, or literature, or mechanics, or industry itself — the working out of one's own personality, one's own inventiveness through forms of activity that are directly social, as all these activities *are* directly social, gives a man, through his very sociality, through the feeling he has that as a good workman he is coöperating with all other good workmen, a life-interest apart from his rewards. And just as this principle becomes generally diffused and understood the incentive is withdrawn from economic self-assertion, a relative competence being notoriously satisfying to the man whose prime end is the fulfilling of his own creative instincts; and the wealth of the world is already socialized.

You cannot have personality, you cannot have the expressions of personality so long as the end of society is an impersonal end like the accumulation of money. For the individual whose personal end varies too greatly from the end of the mass of men about him not only suffers acutely and becomes abnormal, he actually cannot accomplish anything healthily fine at all. The best and most disinterested individual can only express the better intuitions and desires of his age and place; — there must be some sympathetic touch between him and some visible or invisible host about him, since the mind is a flower that has an organic connection with the soil it springs from.

The only serious approach to society is the personal approach, and what I have called the quickening realism of contemporary social thought is at bottom simply a restatement for the mass of commercialized men, and in relation to issues which directly concern the mass of men as a whole, of those personal instincts that have been the essence of art, religion, literature — the essence of personality itself — since the beginning of things. It will remain of the least importance to patch up politics, to become infected with social consciousness, or to do any of the other easy popular contemporary things unless, in some way, personality can be made to release itself on a middle plane between vaporous idealism and self-interested practicality; unless, in short, self-fulfillment as an ideal can be substituted for self-assertion as an ideal. On the economic plane that implies socialism; on every other plane it implies something which a majority of Americans in our day certainly do not possess — an object in living.

VI

It is perhaps just as well that Cervantes lived and died in Spain three hundred years ago. Had he been born an American of the twentieth century he might have found the task of satire an all too overwhelming one. Yet his fable, which has its personal bearing in all men always, has in America a social bearing that is perhaps unique. Don Quixote is the eternal " Highbrow " under a polite name, just as Sancho Panza is the eternal " Lowbrow "; and if the adorable Dulcinea is not a vision of the night and a daily goal in the mind of our professors, then there is no money in Wall Street. One admits the charm of both extremes, the one so fantastically above, the other so fantastically below the level of right reason; to have any kind of relish for muddled humanity is necessarily to feel the charm of both extremes. But where is all that is real, where is personality and all its works, if it is not essentially somewhere, somehow, in some not very vague way, between?

THOMAS STEARNS ELIOT

1888–

72   *Tradition and the Individual Talent*

I

IN English writing we seldom speak of tradition, though we occasionally apply its name in deploring its absence. We cannot refer to " the tradition " or to " a tradition "; at most, we employ the adjective in saying that the poetry of So-and-so is " traditional " or even " too traditional." Seldom, perhaps, does the word appear except in a phrase of censure. If otherwise, it is vaguely approbative, with the implication, as to the work approved, of some pleasing archæological reconstruction. You can hardly make the word agreeable to English ears without this comfortable reference to the reassuring science of archæology.

Certainly the word is not likely to appear in our appreciations of living or dead writers. Every nation, every race, has not only its own creative, but its own critical turn of mind; and is even more oblivious of the shortcomings and limitations of its critical habits than of those of its creative genius. We know, or think we know, from the enormous mass of critical writing that has appeared in the French language the critical method or habit of the French; we only conclude (we are such unconscious people) that the French are " more critical " than we, and sometimes even plume ourselves a little with the fact, as if the French were the less spontaneous. Perhaps they are; but we might remind ourselves that criticism is as inevitable as breathing, and that we should be none the worse for articulating what passes in our minds when we read a book and feel an emotion about it, for criticizing our own minds in their work of criticism. One of the facts that might come to light in this process is our tendency to insist, when we praise a poet, upon those aspects of his work in which he least resembles anyone else. In these aspects or parts of his work we pretend to find what is individual, what is the peculiar essence of the man. We dwell with satisfaction upon the poet's difference from his predecessors, especially his immediate predecessors; we endeavor to find something that can be isolated in order to be enjoyed. Whereas if we approach a poet without this prejudice we shall often find that not only the best, but the most individual parts of his work may be those in which the dead poets, his ancestors, assert their immortality most vigorously. And I do not mean the impressionable period of adolescence, but the period of full maturity.

Yet if the only form of tradition, of handing down, consisted in following the ways of the immediate generation before us in a blind or timid adherence to its successes, "tradition" should positively be discouraged. We have seen many such simple currents soon lost in the sand; and novelty is better than repetition. Tradition is a matter of much wider significance. It cannot be inherited, and if you want it you must obtain it by great labor. It involves, in the first place, the historical sense, which we may call nearly indispensable to anyone who would continue to be a poet beyond his twenty-fifth year; and the historical sense involves a perception, not only of the pastness of the past, but of its presence; the historical sense compels a man to write not merely with his own generation in his bones, but with a feeling that the whole of the literature of Europe from Homer and within it the whole of the literature of his own country has a simultaneous existence and composes a simultaneous order. This historical sense, which is a sense of the timeless as well as of the temporal and of the timeless and of the temporal together, is what makes a writer traditional. And it is at the same time what makes a writer most acutely conscious of his place in time, of his contemporaneity.

THOMAS STEARNS ELIOT

No poet, no artist of any art, has his complete meaning alone. His significance, his appreciation is the appreciation of his relation to the dead poets and artists. You cannot value him alone; you must set him, for contrast and comparison, among the dead. I mean this as a principle of æsthetic, not merely historical, criticism. The necessity that he shall conform, that he shall cohere, is not one-sided; what happens when a new work of art is created is something that happens simultaneously to all the works of art which preceded it. The existing monuments form an ideal order among themselves, which is modified by the introduction of the new (the really new) work of art among them. The existing order is complete before the new work arrives; for order to persist after the supervention of novelty, the *whole* existing order must be, if ever so slightly, altered; and so the relations, proportions, values of each work of art toward the whole are readjusted; and this is conformity between the old and the new. Whoever has approved this idea of order, of the form of European, of English literature, will not find it preposterous that the past should be altered by the present as much as the present is directed by the past. And the poet who is aware of this will be aware of great difficulties and responsibilities.

In a peculiar sense he will be aware also that he must inevitably be judged by the standards of the past. I say judged, not amputated, by them; not judged to be as good as, or worse or better than, the dead; and certainly not judged by the canons of dead critics. It is a judgment, a comparison, in which two things are measured by each other. To conform merely would be for the new work not really to conform at all; it would not be new, and would therefore not be a work of art. And we do not quite say that the new is more valuable because it fits in; but its fitting in is a test of its value — a test, it is true, which can only be slowly and cautiously applied, for we are none of us infallible judges of conformity. We say: it appears to conform, and is perhaps individual, or it appears individual, and may conform;

but we are hardly likely to find that it is one and not the other.

To proceed to a more intelligible exposition of the relation of the poet to the past: he can neither take the past as a lump, an indiscriminate bolus, nor can he form himself wholly on one or two private admirations, nor can he form himself wholly upon one preferred period. The first course is inadmissible, the second is an important experience of youth, and the third is a pleasant and highly desirable supplement. The poet must be very conscious of the main current, which does not at all flow invariably through the most distinguished reputations. He must be quite aware of the obvious fact that art never improves, but that the material of art is never quite the same. He must be aware that the mind of Europe — the mind of his own country — a mind which he learns in time to be much more important than his own private mind — is a mind which changes, and that this change is a development which abandons nothing *en route,* which does not superannuate either Shakespeare, or Homer, or the rock drawing of the Magdalenian draughtsmen. That this development, refinement perhaps, complication certainly, is not, from the point of view of the artist, any improvement. Perhaps not even an improvement from the point of view of the psychologist or not to the extent which we imagine; perhaps only in the end based upon a complication in economics and machinery. But the difference between the present and the past is that the conscious present is an awareness of the past in a way and to an extent which the past's awareness of itself cannot show.

Some one said: " The dead writers are remote from us because we *know* so much more than they did." Precisely, and they are that which we know.

I am alive to a usual objection to what is clearly part of my program for the *métier* of poetry. The objection is that the doctrine requires a ridiculous amount of erudition (pedantry), a claim which can be rejected by appeal to the lives of poets in any pantheon. It will even be affirmed that much learning deadens or perverts poetic sensibility. While, however, we persist in believing that a poet ought to know as much as will not encroach upon his necessary receptivity and necessary laziness, it is not desirable to confine knowledge to whatever can be put into a useful shape for examinations, drawing-rooms, or the still more pretentious modes of publicity. Some can absorb knowledge, the more tardy must sweat for it. Shakespeare acquired more essential history from Plutarch than most men could from the whole British Museum. What is to be insisted upon is that the poet must develop or procure the consciousness of the past and that he should continue to develop this consciousness throughout his career.

What happens is a continual surrender of himself as he is at the moment to something which is more valuable. The progress of an artist is a continual self-sacrifice, a continual extinction of personality.

There remains to define this process of depersonalization and its relation to the sense of tradition. It is in this depersonalization that art may be said to approach the condition of science. I shall, therefore, invite you to consider, as a suggestive analogy, the action which takes place when a bit of finely filiated platinum is introduced into a chamber containing oxygen and sulphur dioxide.

II

Honest criticism and sensitive appreciation is directed not upon the poet but upon the poetry. If we attend to the confused cries of the newspaper critics and the susurrus of popular repetition that follows, we shall hear the names of poets in great numbers; if we seek not Blue-book knowledge but the enjoyment of poetry, and ask for a poem, we shall seldom find it. In the last article I tried to point out the importance of the relation of the poem to other poems by other authors, and suggested the conception of poetry as a living whole of all the poetry that has ever been written. The other aspect of this Impersonal theory of poetry is the relation of the poem to its author. And I hinted, by an analogy, that the mind of the mature poet differs from that of the immature one not precisely in any valuation of " personality," not by being necessarily more interesting, or having " more to say," but rather by being a more finely perfected medium in which special, or very varied, feelings are at liberty to enter into new combinations.

The analogy was that of the catalyst. When the two gases previously mentioned are mixed in the presence of a filament of platinum, they form sulphurous acid. This combination takes place only if the platinum is present; nevertheless the newly formed acid contains no trace of platinum, and the platinum itself is apparently unaffected; has remained inert, neutral, and unchanged. The mind of the poet is the shred of platinum. It may partly or exclusively operate upon the experience of the man himself; but, the more perfect the artist, the more completely separate in him will be the man who suffers and the mind which creates; the more perfectly will the mind digest and transmute the passions which are its material.

The experience, you will notice, the elements which enter the presence of the transforming catalyst, are of two kinds: emotions and feelings. The effect of a work of art upon the person who enjoys it is an experience different in kind from any experience not of art. It may be formed out of one emotion, or may be a combination of several; and various feelings, inhering for the writer in particular words or phrases or images, may be added to compose the final result. Or great poetry may be made without the direct use of any emotion whatever: composed out of feelings solely. Canto XV of the *Inferno* (Brunetto Latini) is a working up of the emotion evident in the situation; but the effect, though single as that of any work of art, is obtained by considerable complexity of detail. The last quatrain gives an image, a feeling attaching to an image, which " came," which did not develop simply out of what precedes, but which was probably in suspension in the poet's mind until the proper combination arrived for it to add itself to. The poet's mind is in fact a receptacle for seizing and storing up numberless feelings, phrases, images, which remain there until all the particles which can unite to form a new compound are present together.

If you compare several representative passages of the greatest poetry you see how great is the variety of types of combination, and also how completely any semi-ethical criterion of " sublimity " misses the mark. For it is not the " greatness," the intensity, of the emotions, the components, but the intensity of the artistic process, the pressure, so to speak, under which the fusion takes place, that counts. The episode of Paolo and Francesca employs a definite emotion, but the intensity of the poetry is something quite different from whatever intensity in the supposed experience it may give the impression of. It is no more intense, furthermore, than Canto XXVI, the voyage of Ulysses, which has not the direct dependence upon an emotion. Great variety is possible in the process of transmution of emotion: the murder of Agamemnon, or the agony of Othello, gives an artistic effect apparently closer to a possible original than the scenes from Dante. In the *Agamemnon,* the artistic emotion approximates to the emotion of an actual spectator; in *Othello* to the emotion of the protagonist himself. But the difference between art and the event is always absolute; the combination which is the murder of Agamemnon is probably as complex as that which is the voyage of Ulysses. In either case there has been a fusion of elements. The ode of Keats contains a number of feelings which have nothing particular to do with the nightingale, but which the nightingale, partly, perhaps, because of its attractive name, and partly because of its reputation, served to bring together.

The point of view which I am struggling to attack is perhaps related to the metaphysical theory of the substantial unity of the soul: for my meaning is, that the poet has, not a " personality " to express, but a particular medium, which is only a medium and not a personality, in which impressions and experiences combine in peculiar and unexpected ways. Impressions and experiences which are important for the man may take no place in the poetry, and those which become important in the poetry may play quite a negligible part in the man, the personality.

I will quote a passage which is unfamiliar enough to be regarded with fresh attention in the light — or darkness — of these observations:

> And now methinks I could e'en chide myself
> For doating on her beauty, though her death
> Shall be revenged after no common action.
> Does the silkworm expend her yellow labours
> For thee? For thee does she undo herself?
> Are lordships sold to maintain ladyships
> For the poor benefit of a bewildering minute?
> Why does yon fellow falsify highways,
> And put his life between the judge's lips,
> To refine such a thing — keeps horse and men
> To beat their valours for her? . . .

In this passage (as is evident if it is taken in its context) there is a combination of positive and negative emotions: an intensely strong attraction toward beauty and an equally intense fascination by the ugliness which is contrasted with it and which destroys it. This balance of contrasted emotion is in the dramatic situation to which the speech is pertinent, but that situation alone is inadequate to it. This is, so to speak, the structural emotion, provided by the drama. But the whole effect, the dominant tone, is due to the fact that a number of floating feelings, having an affinity to this emotion by no means superficially evident, have combined with it to give us a new art emotion.

It is not in his personal emotions, the emotions provoked by particular events in his life, that the poet is in any way remarkable or interesting. His particular emotions may be simple, or crude, or flat. The emotion in his poetry will be a very complex thing, but not with the complexity of the emotions of people who have very complex or unusual emotions in life. One error, in fact, of eccentricity in poetry is to seek for new human emotions to express; and in this search for novelty in the wrong place it discovers the perverse. The business of the poet is not to find new emotions, but to use the ordinary ones and, in working them up into poetry, to express feelings which are not in actual emotions at all. And emotions which he has never experienced will serve his turn as well as those familiar to him. Consequently, we must believe that "emotion recollected in tranquillity" is an inexact formula. For it is neither emotion, nor recollection, nor, without distortion of meaning, tranquillity. It is a concentration, and a new thing resulting from the concentration, of a very great number of experiences which to the practical and active person would not seem to be experiences at all; it is a concentration which does not happen consciously or of deliberation. These experiences are not "recollected," and they finally unite in an atmosphere which is "tranquil" only in that it is a passive attending upon the event. Of course this is not quite the whole story. There is a great deal, in the writing of poetry, which must be conscious and deliberate. In fact, the bad poet is usually unconscious where he ought to be conscious, and conscious where he ought to be unconscious. Both errors tend to make him "personal." Poetry is not a turning loose of emotion, but an escape from emotion; it is not the expression of personality, but an escape from personality. But, of course, only those who have personality and emotions know what it means to want to escape from these things.

III

ὁ δὲ νοῦς ἴσως θειότερόν τι καὶ ἀπαθές ἐστιν

This essay proposes to halt at the frontier of metaphysics or mysticism, and confine itself to such practical conclusions as can be applied by the responsible person interested in poetry. To divert interest from the poet to the poetry is a laudable aim: for it would conduce to a juster estimation of actual poetry, good and bad. There are many people who appreciate the expression of sincere emotion in verse, and there is a smaller number of people who can appreciate technical excellence. But very few know when there is expression of *significant* emotion, emotion which has its life in the poem and not in the history of the poet. The emotion of art is impersonal. And the poet cannot reach this impersonality without surrendering himself wholly to the work to be done. And he is not likely to know what is to be done unless he lives in what is not merely the present, but the present moment of the past, unless he is conscious, not of what is dead, but of what is already living.

JOSEPH WOOD KRUTCH

1893–

73   *The Death of Man*

I

IT is not by thought that men live. Life begins in organisms so simple that one may reasonably doubt even their ability to feel, much less think, and animals cling to or fight for it with a determination which we might be inclined to call superhuman if we did not know that a will to live so thoughtless and so unconditional is the attribute of beings rather below than above the human level. All efforts to find a rational justification of life, to declare it worth the living for this reason or that, are, in themselves, a confession of weakness, since life at its strongest never feels the need of any such justification and since the most optimistic philosopher is less optimistic than that man or animal who, his belief that life is good being too immediate to require the interposition of thought, is no philosopher at all.

In view of this fact it is not surprising that the subtlest intellectual contortions of modern metaphysics should fail to establish the existence of satisfactory aims for life when, as a matter of fact, any effort to do so fails as soon as it begins and can only arise as the result of a weakening of that self-justifying vitality which is the source of all life and of all optimism. As soon as thought begins to seek the "ends" or "aims" to which life is subservient it has already confessed its inability to achieve that animal acceptance of life for life's sake which is responsible for the most determined efforts to live and, in one sense, we may say that even the firmest medieval belief in a perfectly concrete salvation after death marks already the beginning of the completest despair, since that belief could not arise before thought had rendered primitive vitality no longer all-sufficient.

The decadent civilizations of the past were not saved by their philosophers but by the influx of simpler peoples who had centuries yet to live before their minds should be ripe for despair. Neither Socrates nor Plato could teach his compatriots any wisdom from which they could draw the strength to compete with the crude energy of their Roman neighbors, and even their thought inevitably declined soon after it had exhausted their vital energy. Nor could these Romans, who flourished longer for the very reason, perhaps, that they had slower and less subtle intellects, live forever; they too were compelled to give way in their time to barbarians innocent alike both of philosophy and of any possible need to call upon it.

The subhuman will to live which is all-sufficient for the animal may be replaced by faith, faith may be replaced by philosophy, and philosophy may attenuate itself until it becomes, like modern metaphysics, a mere game; but each of these developments marks a stage in a progressive enfeeblement of that will to live for the gradual weakening of which it is the function of each to compensate. Vitality calls upon faith for aid, faith turns gradually to philosophy for support, and then philosophy, losing all confidence in its own conclusions, begins to babble of "beneficent fictions" instead of talking about Truth; but each is less confident than what went before and each is, by consequence, less easy to live by. Taken together, they represent the successive and increasingly desperate expedients by means of which man, the ambitious animal, endeavors to postpone the inevitable realization that living is merely a physiological process with only a physiological meaning and that it is most satisfactorily conducted by creatures who never feel the need to attempt to give it any other. But they are at best no more than expedients, and when the last has been exhausted there remains nothing except the possibility that the human species will be revitalized by some race or some class which is capable of beginning all over again.

Under the circumstances it is not strange that decadent civilizations are likely to think that the collapse of their culture is in reality the end of the human story. Perhaps some of the last of the old Roman intelligentsia realized that the future belonged to the barbarians from the north and that it belonged to them for the very reason that they were incapable of assimilating ancient thought, but even among the early Christian theologians there was a widespread belief that the end of Rome could mean nothing except the end of the world, and, for similar reasons, it is difficult for us to believe in the possibility of anything except either the continuation of modern culture or the extinction of human life. But a glance at history should make us hesitate before asserting that either one of these alternative possibilities is likely to become a reality. On the one hand all cultures have ultimately collapsed and human life has, on the other hand, always persisted — not because philosophers have arisen to solve its problems but because naïver creatures, incapable of understanding the problems and hence not feeling the need to solve them, have appeared somewhere upon the face of the globe.

If modern civilization is decadent then perhaps it will be rejuvenated, but not by the philosophers whose subtlest thoughts are only symptoms of the disease which they are endeavoring to combat. If the future belongs to anybody it belongs to those to whom it has always belonged, to those, that is to say, too absorbed in living to feel the need for thought, and they will come, as the barbarians have always come, absorbed in the processes of life for their own sake, eating without asking if it is worth while to eat, begetting children without asking why they should beget them, and conquering without asking for what purpose they conquer.

Doubtless even those among the last of the Romans who had some dim conception of the fact that the centuries immediately to follow would belong to the barbarians were not, for the most part, greatly interested in or cheered by the fact. Thoughtful people come inevitably to feel that if life has any value at all, then that value lies in thought, and to the Roman it probably seemed that it was hardly worth while to save the human animal if he could be saved only by the destruction of all that which his own ancestors had achieved, and by the forgetting of everything which he cared to remember. The annihilation of ancient culture was to him equivalent to the annihilation of humanity, and a modern who has come to think in a similar fashion can have only a languid interest in a possible animal rejuvenation which would inevitably involve a blunting of that delicate sensibility and that exquisite subtlety of intellect upon which he has come to set the very highest value.

But doubtless this ancient Roman speculated idly, and it is impossible for us not to do the same. Whence will the barbarians (and we may use that word, not as a term of contempt, but merely as a way of identifying these people animated by vitally simple thoughts) come? We are not surrounded as the Romans were by childlike savages, and we can hardly imagine the black tribes of Africa pushing in upon us. Have we, within the confines of our own cities, populations quite as little affected by modern thought as the Goths were affected by Greek philosophy, and hence quite capable either of carrying peaceably on as the aristocracy dies quietly off at the top or of arising sometime to overwhelm us? Has China, having died once, lain fallow long enough to have become once more primitive, or are the Russians indeed the new barbarians, even if they are such in a somewhat different sense than that implied in the sensational literature of anti-communist propaganda?

II

These Russians are young in the only sense of the word which can have a meaning when applied to any part of the human family. If all men had a common ancestor, then all races are equally old in years, but those which have never passed through the successive and debilitating stages of culture retain that potentiality for doing so which constitutes them racially young, and the Russians, who have always lived upon the frontiers of Europe, are in this sense a primitive race, since European culture has never been for them more than the exotic diversion of a small class. For the first time in history the mass of the people is in a position to employ its constructive faculties, and it so happens that their domain is one which offers an enormous field for the employment of such faculties.

Young races like young individuals need toys to play with. Before the advent of the machine, the Romans amused themselves with military and social organization, pushing the boundaries of their empire farther and farther back into unknown territory until their energy was exhausted and they were compelled to begin a gradual retraction; today, the processes of industrial development are capable of absorbing much of the vitality which could formerly find an outlet only in conquest; but if modern people amuse themselves by building factories or digging mines they do so for exactly the same reason that the Romans annexed the British Isles — because, that is to say, there is little temptation to ask ultimate questions as long as there are many tangible things to do and plenty of energy to do them with. Russia has both, and for that very reason there is no other place in the world where one will find to-day an optimism so simple and so terrible.

We — particularly we in America — have done all that.

We have dug our mines, piped our oil, built our factories, and, having done so, we have begun to settle down in our comfortable houses to ask what comes next. But the Russians are at least a century away from such a condition. They begin at a point at least as far back as we began a century ago and they are in the happy position of desiring certain things which they have good reason to believe ultimately achievable. Not only do they want to grow rich and to establish a form of society which will provide for an equitable distribution of their riches, but they find on every side some tangible task capable of being accomplished in such a way as to further their ambition. Perhaps when this ambition has been achieved, when all men are as materially comfortable as some few men are to-day, then the comfortable masses will discover what the comfortable few have discovered already, which is, of course, that comfort seems enough only when one happens not to have it. But that day is still long distant. Not only will the complete industrial development of the country occupy many years but the problems of the new society are themselves so complicated that they are not likely to be solved for generations and hence, in all probability, Russia will not grow ripe so rapidly as the United States did.

As a result of these conditions there has already developed in Russia a new philosophy of life which, in spite of the fact that it has taken a form influenced by modern industrial conditions, is easily recognizable as being essentially primitive in its simplicity. Sweeping aside the intellectual and emotional problems of Europe, refusing even in its art to concern itself with the psychology of the individual soul, Communism assumes that nothing is really important except those things upon which the welfare of the race depends, and in assuming that it is assuming exactly what a primitive society always assumes. Its drama and its poetry celebrate the machine exactly as the literature of a primitive people celebrates the process of hunting or of agriculture, and they do so for exactly the same reason, for the reason, that is to say, that agriculture on the one hand and industry on the other are the two fundamental processes by which the life of the people is sustained.

Communistic Utopianism is based upon the assumption that the only maladjustments from which mankind suffers are social in character and hence it is sustained by the belief that in a perfect state all men would be perfectly happy. Fundamentally materialistic, it refuses to remember that physical well-being is no guarantee of felicity and that, as a matter of fact, as soon as the individual finds himself in a perfectly satisfactory physical environment he begins to be aware of those more fundamental maladjustments which subsist, not between man and society, but between the human spirit and the natural universe. And though, for this reason, it must seem to the cultivated European essentially naïve, yet in that very naïveté lies its strength as a social philosophy. Thanks to the fact that the perfect Communist is not aware of the existence of any problems more subtle than those involved in the production and distribution of wealth, he can throw himself into the business of living with a firm faith in the value of what he is doing and he can display an energy in practical affairs not to be equaled by any one incapable of a similar belief in their ultimate importance.

All societies which have passed the first vigor of their youth reveal their loss of faith in life itself by the fact that they no longer consider such fundamental processes as other than means toward an end. Food, clothes, and warmth are considered merely as instruments, and the most eager attention is directed, not toward attaining them, but toward the activities which men are at liberty to pursue when such fundamental things are granted. Productive labor is regarded as an evil, and when anything is said concerning the possibility of improving the condition of the masses, such improvement is always thought of as consisting essentially in so shortening even their hours of labor as to make possible for them also certain hours of freedom. Primitive societies, on the other hand, have no desire to escape from such fundamental processes. They do not hunt in order to live but they live in order to hunt, because for them the value of life lies in the activities necessary to carry it on; and the communist philosophy of labor is based upon a similarly primitive outlook. Factories are considered, not as means toward an end, but as ends in themselves. A full life is to consist, not in one spent in the pursuit of those thoughts or the cultivation of those emotions which are possible only when productive labor has been reduced to a minimum, but in one completely absorbed by such labor.

Hence it is that to the good communist, as to the good tribesman, any question concerning the meaning of life is in itself completely meaningless and he will live the complicated industrial life of to-day exactly as the tribesman lives the simple life of his tribe — not in thought but in action. He has a sort of God, but his God is in reality what anthropologists call a culture-god; merely, that is to say, the spirit which presides over and infuses itself with the germination of the seed, the ripening of the fruit, or the whirring of the machine.

Such a philosophy comes nearer than any other to that unformulated one by which an animal lives. It does not ask any of the questions which a weary people inevitably ask and it is, as a matter of fact, less a system of thought than a translation into simple words of the will to live and thrive. But it is, for all that, only the more impressive as an evidence of the vigorous youth of the Russian mind. The visitor to Moscow who sees how eagerly its inhabitants live under conditions which are still very difficult, how gladly they accept both labor and, when necessary, privation, cannot but realize that they are sustained by a fundamental optimism unknown anywhere else in the world. At the present moment the inhabitants of many European countries *have* much more but they *hope* much less, and they are incapable of any acceptance of life so vital and so complete.

If the Communistic experiment is economically a failure, then these hopes may be soon disappointed; if it becomes economically a success, then they will doubtless still be disappointed in that more distant day when, the perfect state having been achieved, its inhabitants come to realize that the natural universe is as imperfectly adapted as ever to human needs. But man-the-animal lives in Time. A hope is a hope up to the instant when it is dashed, and the Russia of to-day is filled with a confidence hardly less elementary than that of the animal which, under the influence of the vital urge, acts as though the litter which it has just brought into the world were so tremendously worth saving that nothing else which had occurred since the dawn of the first day were of equal importance.

Perhaps, then, Europe has good reason to speak of the "Bolshevik menace," but if so the events which she fears are not quite the ones most likely to occur. If Russia or the Russian spirit conquers Europe it will not be with the bomb of the anarchist but with the vitality of the young barbarian who may destroy many things but who destroys them only that he may begin over again. Such calamities are calamitous only from the point of view of a humanism which values the complexity of its feelings and the subtlety of its intellect far more than Nature does. To her they are merely the reassertion of her right to recapture her own world, merely the process by which she repeoples the earth with creatures simple enough to live joyously there.

III

To us, however, such speculations as these are doubly vain. In the first place the future may belong not to the Russians, but to some class of people not yet thought of in this connection, and in the second place none of these possible futures is one which can have anything to do with us or our traditions. Though the new barbarians may forget we will remember that the paradox of humanism and the tragic fallacy are not to be altered by the establishment of new societies and that the despair which was the fruit of both ancient and modern civilization must inevitably ripen again in the course of the development of any society which enters upon the pursuit of human values.

Some critics of communism have, to be sure, maintained that its tendencies were fundamentally anti-human and that, should it ever become established, it would so arrest the development of the humanistic spirit as to fix mankind in some changelessly efficient routine like that of an ant-hill. But even if this be true it does not alter the fact that its hopes are no hopes in which we can have any part, since we would be even more alien to such a society than to one which promised to recapitulate our own youth. The world may be rejuvenated in one way or another, but we will not. Skepticism has entered too deeply into our souls ever to be replaced by faith, and we can never forget the things which the new barbarians will never need to have known. This world in which an unresolvable discord is the fundamental fact is the world in which we must continue to live, and for us wisdom must consist, not in searching for a means of escape which does not exist, but in making such peace with it as we may.

Nor is there any reason why we should fail to realize the fact that the acceptance of such despair as must inevitably be ours does not, after all, involve a misery so acute as that which many have been compelled to endure. Terror can be blacker than that and so can the extremes of physical want and pain. The most human human being has still more of the animal than of anything else and no love of rhetoric should betray one into seeming to deny that he who has escaped animal pain has escaped much. Despair of the sort which has here been described is a luxury in the sense that it is possible only to those who have much that many people do without, and philosophical pessimism, dry as it may leave the soul, is more easily endured than hunger or cold.

Leaving the future to those who have faith in it, we may survey our world and, if we bear in mind the facts just stated, we may permit ourselves to exclaim, a little rhetorically perhaps,

JOSEPH WOOD KRUTCH

Hail, horrors, hail,
Infernal world! and thou profoundest hell,
Receive thy new possessor.

If Humanism and Nature are fundamentally antithetical, if the human virtues have a definite limit set to their development, and if they may be cultivated only by a process which renders us progressively unfit to fulfill our biological duties, then we may at least permit ourselves a certain defiant satisfaction when we realize that we have made our choice and that we are resolved to abide by the consequences. Some small part of the tragic fallacy may be said indeed to be still valid for us, for if we cannot feel ourselves great as Shakespeare did, if we no longer believe in either our infinite capacities or our importance to the universe, we know at least that we have discovered the trick which has been played upon us and that whatever else we may be we are no longer dupes.

Rejuvenation may be offered to us at a certain price. Nature, issuing her last warning, may bid us embrace some new illusion before it is too late and accord ourselves once more with her. But we prefer rather to fail in our own way than to succeed in hers. Our human world may have no existence outside of our own desires, but those are more imperious than anything else we know, and we will cling to our own lost cause, choosing always rather to know than to be. Doubtless fresh people have still a long way to go with Nature before they are compelled to realize that they too have come to the parting of the ways, but though we may wish them well we do not envy them. If death for us and our kind is the inevitable result of our stubbornness then we can only say, "So be it." Ours is a lost cause and there is no place for us in the natural universe, but we are not, for all that, sorry to be human. We should rather die as men than live as animals.

INDEX OF AUTHORS, TITLES
AND SOURCES

INDEX OF AUTHORS

TITLES AND SOURCES

INDEX OF AUTHORS

Date Due

APR 1 4 1958			
	PRINTED	IN U. S. A.	